WOMEN
IN THE
HEBREW BIBLE

WOMEN
IN THE
HEBREW BIBLE

A READER

EDITED BY
ALICE BACH

ROUTLEDGE
NEW YORK AND LONDON

Published in 1999 by
Routledge
29 West 35th Street
New York, NY 10001

Published in Great Britain by
Routledge
11 New Fetter Lane
London EC4P 4EE

Transliterations of Hebrew follow each author's original style, and thus show great variety.

Printed in the United States of America on acid-free paper.

10 9 8 7 6 5 4 3 2 1

Library of Congress Cataloging-in-Publication Data
Women in the Hebrew Bible : a reader / edited by Alice Bach.
    p. cm.
   Includes bibliographical references.
   ISBN 0-415-91560-0 (hardcover : alk. paper).—ISBN 0-415-91561-9
(pbk. : alk. paper)
   1. Women in the Bible. 2. Bible. O.T.—Criticism,
interpretation, etc. 3. Bible. O.T.—Feminist criticism.
I. Bach, Alice.
BS1199.W7W65   1999
221.8'3054—dc21   98-3774
                                            CIP

For Mary Callaway and Jennifer Glancy,
Women of the Book

Contents

Goddesses and Women of Magic

Rereading Women in the Bible

Sexual Politics in the Hebrew Bible

Feminist Identities in Biblical Interpretation

A Case History: Numbers 5:11–31

Editor's Note

In putting together this Reader I sought the advice of a number of colleagues, who were thoughtful and helpful in suggesting articles. Mieke Bal, Athalya Brenner, Cheryl Exum, Ed Greenstein, and David Gunn were particularly generous with their time. As with any Reader, the main difficulty is having about three times as much important scholarly material as one can fit into the publisher's requirements for the project. It is a joy to announce that there are many more stimulating articles and books devoted to questions about the status of women in the ancient Near Eastern world, feminist readings of biblical and extrabiblical texts from the ancient Mediterranean world, and a growing dialogue of sophisticated concerns by scholars adapting literary, sociologic, anthropologic, and cultural methodologies to the biblical corpus. To ease my own frustration with selection I have included a very full bibliography of articles and books where many of these items can be found. Engaging the articles in this Reader is the beginning of a process, of climbing deep into the roots, to the places where women and the Bible intersect.

Introduction
Man's World, Women's Place
Sexual Politics in the Hebrew Bible

ALICE BACH

For many women the most difficult part of reading the Bible today is remembering how we read the Bible in school, in church or synagogue, and what we were told about the good women and the bad women. As a test of this premise, think of what the names Eve, Jezebel, Delilah evoke. In a 1938 film, Bette Davis played a flirtatious girl with too-easy morals. Her name and the name of the film: Jezebel. Could you trust a woman named Delilah with a pair of scissors? Would you eat food offered by a curious Eve? These stock interpretations of female biblical characters are part of the cultural baggage we lug around. For most women the baggage weighs a bit heavier than it does for men.

The major objective of this Reader is to examine attitudes toward women and their status in the ancient Near Eastern societies, focusing on the Israelite society as portrayed in the Hebrew Bible. What has been traditionally studied as "history" is really the history written by the winners, the dominant societies; the record of the male-dominant, authoritarian, and war-centered societies. Thus, a central challenge is to explore ways in which we can reach the stories of women in a world shaped by male interests. As modern readers who have experienced abrupt changes in social attitudes, especially in respect to issues of gender, sexuality, and marriage, we shall read these ancient texts conscious that our modern attitudes challenge traditional values. Thus, we shall have to read with bifocal lenses: aware of our modern attitudes while simultaneously understanding the religious and cultural traditions and practices that shaped ancient texts.

Even though we will be concentrating upon literary texts about women, the texts that we shall read were not written by women. A major difficulty in coming to conclusions about the lives of women in the ancient world is that almost all the texts about women have been written by men. We have no direct evidence about what women thought, said, or felt (except for some fragments of the classical Greek poet Sappho's lyrics and some funerary inscriptions). We have only male blueprints for female behavior.

The stories are men's imaginings about women: the good wives who support men's dreams and the seducers who lead men astray. Of course, these writers chronicled women's lives more subtly than the designations of wives and witches, bad girls and sad girls, might indicate. There are women whose courage saves the community; there are goddesses whose ferocity as warriors is matched by their passionate love-making. One of the most confounding questions for gendered readings of these texts is why there was such an enormous gap between the powerful goddesses and the dramatic female literary heroes, and the low status of real women?

Several questions will run through our investigation of women in the ancient world. The most central question concerns whether men's descriptions of women's roles reflect actual societal behavior or whether they are fantasies that run counter to the familiar. Is the detailed delineation of *the perfect wife* in Proverbs 31 a reflection of a real woman or merely a man's dreamy construction? Another question that confronts the modern reader concerns the ways in which these religious and literary texts function to preserve patriarchal society. Must the texts be read as supportive of traditional social values?

Some feminist historians and archeologists, especially Maria Gimbutas and Riane Eisler, argue against the standard view that the beginning of European civilization is marked by the emergence in ancient Greece of the Indo-Europeans. Instead, these scholars consider the arrival of the Indo-Europeans as the truncation of European civilization. Gimbutas calls this period the civilization of Old Europe. Theirs was a pastoral, peaceful agrarian society—and, most important, both matrifocal and matrilineal. It was the incursions of barbarians who brought "the angry gods of thunder and war," writes Eisler, "and everywhere left destruction and devastation in their wake." This view has not been accepted by mainstream scholars, and I do not include it here to convince the reader that once upon a time was really once upon an ideal women-centered time. Rather, I include this view to illustrate two things, which I believe are connected. One is the desire on the part of feminist scholars to prove that a matriarchal world would be one of peace and serenity; the other is the difficulty that feminist scholars have in getting their work taken seriously by the mainstream.

It is tempting to imagine a society where domination and destruction did not exist, and that the creation and maintenance of such a world should be credited to women, but I would caution the reader against replacing a view of male domination with that of female domination. A second caution involves giving too much weight to societies that worshiped female gods as well as male ones or instead of male gods. There is no proof that such a society would be matriarchal. Imagine concluding that a society in which women were idealized was matriarchal. Several images come to mind: the outpouring of grief and the mounds of flowers, candles, and notes left at Kensington Palace following the death of Princess Diana. Clearly one could not conclude that the British people were a goddess-centered society worshiping the spirits of nature. Or think of female American film stars who become icons, but not in a world dominated by the power of women.

To call women spiritual and peace-loving and to describe men as violent and destructive is to continue polarization of gender. Through readings of the female characters in the Hebrew Bible, one finds warrior women like Judith and Jael, and men calling for peace and justice, like the prophets Amos, Hosea, and Isaiah. One finds Abigail, a woman who can manage a large estate with equanimity, and Saul, a king whose fearsome visions leave him a helpless victim. Thus, a responsible feminist reading is not one that dreams of matriarchy and imagines a world in which women are in control as a spiritual realm that enhances life. The key word is power, for any hierarchized power structure is going to award power to some and deny it to others. For me, a successful feminist interpretation of a biblical narrative text will not be biased in favor of women or put the blame for humanity's ills only at the feet of men.

In the Wilderness

Another central task of exchanging Man's World for Women's Place involves reading these ancient texts for clues about the beginning of gender bias in Western culture. Our literary and cultural heritage is so heavily textured with these patterns that we think they are natural. From the time of Homer and the Bible we have been taught this is the way it should be, the way society is supposed to function. Part of our work in this Reader, then, will be to peel away the ideology from the story. The following sections of this Introduction will raise some issues that will jump-start the peeling process.

What, then, are some theoretical problems occurring within the early feminist literary studies (1980s) found in the edited collections of Collins, Russell (1985), and Tolbert (*Semeia* 28)? Since the figures of women are usually fragmented in the Bible, feminists in this formative period wishing to offer literary studies generally followed one of two roads: (1) they exposed through close readings the patriarchal portrait of an individual woman, which has led to a gallery of biblical female victims; (2) they focused upon scraps of linguistic, rhetorical, and narratologic evidence to highlight feminine aspects of the deity and feminine echoes or ghosts in the text, popularly known as "recovering submerged female voices." Both these feminist strategies have, in my opinion, a limited future. The time for gleaning is bound by the time for reaping. Feminist critics need not, however, discard the model of Ruth, playing the patriarchal game to get her needs fulfilled. Rather, like Ruth they need to join their male colleagues on the threshing floor, where who leads and who follows is not determined by the text. There is finite ground to be worked so long as gleaning fragmented portraits of women is the goal of feminist readings. As more feminist scholars enter the field as gleaners, the number of female figures left to pump up as heroes or to deflate as victims of male authorship is dwindling. Thus, our readings need to be more nuanced, not a case of good woman, bad woman—that slaps a judgment on any woman who questions authority. Through transdisciplinary readings of biblical figures and other literary figures, one can develop a three-dimensional interpretation.

It must be said emphatically that scores of valuable insights have been offered in these first-wave analyses of female literary figures; many interesting readings of isolated narrative units within the biblical corpus have been offered by feminist scholars. But like the texts they have read, the insights have been fragmented and have not resulted in advances in feminist biblical literary theory. So following one path, that of creating a "portrait" of a biblical female figure, results in her continued isolation. Comparing the characters in the Bible with other literary figures is another strategy that can be used to avoid static portraits of these characters. It might be helpful to think of future readings as films rather than paintings, more kinetic than static. We need examples of female figures within the continuous movement of text, frame upon frame.

Some feminist scholars, such as Claudia V. Camp, J. Cheryl Exum, and Carol A.

Newsom have begun to explore the social and cultural causes of the pain so carefully delineated in Phyllis Trible's *Texts of Terror*. Employing a rhetoric of rupture and rebellion, in order to provide contemporary relevance to ancient Western literary texts, they have analyzed biblical texts without a theological lens. Camp's work has provided us with exciting new models of metaphorical analysis, in her sophisticated investigation of the gendered images of woman wisdom. Accepting the phallogocentric nature of biblical texts in which female characters have been silenced by their male creators, Exum is no longer satisfied with an examination of the formalist patterns and conventions discovered through surface readings. Her most recent work reflects her concern for looking at the way the Bible has been appropriated by visual artists in various time periods. Similarly, Newsom has recognized that traditional readings of literary texts not only represent ideology, but also in circular fashion support it as well. Another important scholar of both ancient and modern Jewish texts, Esther Fuchs, has continually adopted the stance of a marginal reader, questioning the ideology of whatever biblical text she is analyzing. She reads with a clear-eyed regard for gender as a social product, an institution, yet remaining within the biblical canon as a closed universe presented problems too.

Feminist Theologies

To seek a coherent pattern in biblical portraits of women is bound to marginalize women unless one lays bare the social, cultural, and gender codes reflected in the texts. Feminist biblical critic Mary Ann Tolbert admits that her own feminist analysis reveals "bias in favor of the Bible. I frankly want to claim that text as a continuing resource for living in the modern age." While it is salutary to find a critic who self-consciously acknowledges her own theological biases, a problem with the faithful perspective is that the furthest it can extend is to observe the positions in the male landscape where women are hidden or drawn poorly, lacking perspective and depth. After a nod to diversity among feminist theologies, Elizabeth Achtemeier concludes that "if God is addressed in female terms, however, his holy otherness is lost sight of" (55), learned through and perpetuated by culture.

Judith Plaskow rereads traditional Jewish interpretation, trying to reclaim a place for women at Sinai (1990). I also recommend Plaskow's challenge (1978) to Christian feminists about inherent anti-Semitic attitudes on the part of Christian scholars who portray ancient Judaism as a patriarchal tradition in contrast with the liberating elements of Christianity. Another important Jewish feminist theologian is Susannah Heschel. What is vital to both Plaskow and Heschel is their new wave of doing theology. Not only do they challenge male domination, but they also point up the Christocentric assumptions and perspectives of many feminist theologians.

While the focus of this Reader is not feminist theologies, a field in which much bold work is being done, I would like to call the reader's attention to the voices of Katie Cannon, Cheryl Gilkes, Jacqueline Grant, and Renita Weems as womanist (African-American) scholars, Ada-Maria Isasi-Diaz, a *mujerista* (Latina) theologian, and Hyun Chung, who uses Eastern sources to enrich and extend Western Christian models. Each of these scholars examines racial and sexist biases within interpretive scholarship of traditional male theologians, creating syncretistic theologies, rich in story-telling of women's struggles to reshape the male traditions that had been imposed upon them. Other important collections of third-world feminist hermeneutics are edited by Tamez; Fabella and Lee; Fabella and Mercy Amba Oduyoye. These collections offer strategies for removing the racist and colonialist blinders of women theologians within the discipline (See the bibliography of recent works in both feminist and womanist theology, p. 533).

Analyzing and Recovering the Social World of Ancient Israel

Another avenue that seems to offer particular promise is the reading of the social codes within a literary work. Here the work of several feminist scholars is notable: Phyllis Bird, Carol Meyers, and Tikva Frymer-Kensky. These scholars attempt to read biblical narratives against the context of the dominant traditions and cultural milieu of the ancient world. When we place the text within the legal and social structures in which ancient authors and readers found themselves, the net of patriarchy emerges not as a villainous trap for women but rather as the canvas on which the whole world, male and female, was painted. The early work of Carol Meyers and Phyllis Bird in the area of social perspectives has paralleled the first wave of literary critics: an attempt to preserve and applaud biblical stories within the traditions in which women found themselves. Instead of presenting portraits of particular literary figures, Meyers and Bird have sliced the text according to socially relevant figures, e.g., the prostitute and the Iron Age Israelite woman. While this work has produced important insights into the status of women, the problem is again one of isolation, the subject of women not integrated into the society or compared cross-culturally with the position of women in similarly constructed societies.

As Bird herself has noted in an elegant response to her own earlier work, "Religion defined in male terms or according to male models has difficulty placing women and assessing their piety, whether it imitates men's, in which case it rarely achieves parity, or assumes distinctive female forms, which may either go unacknowledged or be identified with foreign or heterodox cults." The shift in Bird's perception, asking of herself new questions about women's religion in ancient Israel, quite probably involving a syncretistic form of religious expression within the Yahwistic cult, heralds an exciting advance in studying gender-differentiated systems of ancient religion. Bird's perspective suggests to me a profitable strategy for feminist scholars whose methods are undergoing change. Acknowledging the movement in one's own perceptions from an earlier position is a feminist move that allows the critic to subject her work to self-analysis and to trace its development. The influence of the discipline of anthropology is clear within Bird's work. Deconstructive literary theory has pointed to the importance of analyzing the ideology of a literary work to Cheryl Exum and thus suggests to her a rereading of an earlier work on the function of the women in Exodus 1–2 (*A Feminist Companion to Exodus–Deuteronomy* 1994). This article from Exum points up the vital understanding that even feminist readings are not absolute, permanent, immutable.

Goddesses and Popular Religion

What do we do about the goddesses, those elusive female figures, stronger than human males, more dangerous than male deities, who represent not real women but the dreams of real men? Frymer-Kensky argues that the descent of the goddess from power to powerless is simple and linear. Each reader can make up her own mind, after reading the selections from the Mesopotamian and Canaanite religious epics. My reading of the Sumerian and Canaanite corpus reveals that *the* goddess does not exist; rather, there are diverse goddesses, who are dominant/triumphant in some texts and duped/victimized in others. Their loss of power is often regained in later texts, refuting the concept of linear descent. The images of the goddesses also changed according to the fortunes of the city for which she was a tutelary deity, or the social context in which each found herself, e.g., the powerful first-century cult of the syncretistic Isis, whose ancestors were to be found in the cultures where Frymer-Kensky situates their demise. Neither Frymer-Kensky nor I have a lock on the interpretations of these texts. Make up your minds. It is the power that each reader possesses.

Certainly the work of those trying to unearth the popular religion of ancient Israel including goddess worship will add important dimensions to our understanding of the ancient patriarchal theological agenda. One of Carole Fontaine's major concerns has been an exploration of whether patriarchal texts can speak the reality of women's lives. She searches for a model to evaluate the status of ancient women and the relationship of that status to the presence of goddesses and their worship. Similar concerns drive Peggy Day's interest in popular religion, which has lead to engaging work on the Canaanite goddess Anat.

Feminist Studies of the Mediterranean World

Moving among ancient narratives that remain outside the canon is another strategy that opens the gate to move outside the literary zone of narratives of character. Bernadette Brooten has demonstrated that women served as leaders in a number of synagogues during the Roman and Byzantine periods. Amy Jill Levine's work offers literary readings that remain within a historical framework and seek out social context. Not remaining within either biblical canon, Levine has applied sophisticated feminist cultural criticism to both Hellenistic Jewish and early Christian texts. Ross S. Kraemer's studies in ancient Greco-Roman and Jewish texts have allowed the beginnings of cross-cultural work. These extracanonical scholars have helped to grasp a moment in time: When did gender become hierarchized and when did literary texts first reflect this hierarchy? While there is clearly no grasping this ephemeral instant, I have argued elsewhere that reading classical, biblical, and Hellenistic texts together provides some examples of what happens to female literary figures framed within the entrenchment of the wife/wicked woman dichotomy. The frame-up has simultaneously supported and reflected the "gender-conditioning" that has deprived us of female literary heroes.

Literary Theories

The work of literary scholars whose academic credentials are not within the discipline of biblical studies has sometimes been treated with suspicion by some members of the biblical guild. Recently, literary scholars such as Regina Schwartz, Nelly Furman, and Susan Lanser have gained limited notice for dealing with biblical narratives. Schwartz approaches the text as a literary scholar, and Furman as a feminist critic; both are engaged in critical rereadings of the established canon. Lanser spans both categories. Their work has not, however, changed the direction of biblical studies or the focus of scholars within the biblical guild. That primary challenge was taken up by another literary scholar, now awarded acclaim by the usually hermetic biblical guild: Mieke Bal, a literary and cultural theorist who has challenged and enlivened the scope of biblical investigations with feminist postmodern readings. Bal's sustained effort of several years' focus upon the Bible has resulted in three major works of literary theory, related to feminism not only through the analysis of literary texts but also as a cultural and political force that needs to be acknowledged throughout the society.

Not surprisingly, Bal is relentless in delineating the implicit codes—the moral, religious, and aesthetic codes—that too often go unnoticed in a text, "smuggled in like contraband," she says. These are the voices that are so familiar we tune them out. But they are also the cultural conventions that attempt to control meaning, to preserve the status quo. To affirm the connections between texts and the actualities of human life, politics and events, one must unmask the implicit codes, make them explicit. By using a method of examining codes from various academic disciplines, as well as the thematic and gender codes that cross disciplinary lines, she demonstrated in *Murder and Difference* that the codes lead the reader "far into the understanding of the text and its cultural background, but at the same time they reveal to what degree their bias imposes, stimulates, or permits a practice of censorship that stems from the restriction and the institutionalization of codes" (9).

Privileging one code, allowing it the voice of authority, does not reflect social realities. Codes, like the communities that construct them, coexist as a panoply of voices. To silence any one is to risk domination by another. Understanding the necessity for the reader to oscillate between codes, Bal has presented a challenge to biblical interpreters to deconstruct traditional interpretations of texts as well as the texts themselves to demonstrate the ways in which ancient biases entwine modern readers, especially women.

If Phyllis Trible cracked open the geode of biblical narratives in the 1970s, then Mieke Bal is the scholar who proclaimed a decade later that the crystals were not all from the same geode. One must recognize, of course, the limits to any one scholar's theorizing, given the vantage point of her or his interests, training, and situation. In discussing the development of feminist biblical scholarship, it is tempting to identify winners and even greater winners. But the search for a Perfect 10 is surely antithetical to feminist theories of support and inclusion. While biblical literary scholars have begun to hail Bal's work as plotting a new direction in biblical studies, one needs to acknowledge the threat inherent in trying to build a comprehensive theoretical context for the practice of feminist theory. Interestingly enough, it is interpreters of Bal's work rather than the critic herself who has made such extravagant claims. Rather than continuing to explore the discourse between the biblical text and its subsequent interpreters, her most recent work is focused upon eliminating another set of traditional disciplinary borders, those between visual and literary works. Bal's *Reading "Rembrandt"* (1991) explores problems pertaining to the interpretation of verbal and visual art. The method that Bal employs in juxtaposing iconography with narratology tempts other interpreters into deeper and more complex incursions into interdisciplinarity.

Bal's importance to scholars of the Bible, therefore, is not that she has resolved the differences between feminist readers and traditional scholars, or that she has concluded the search for methods of feminist investigation, but rather that she has created a most fertile ground for conscientious debate. One element of Bal's strategy that has not yet been sufficiently examined is the homogeneous, biased position of traditional interpreters. Even though one can uncover the ideological bias inherent in these interpretive texts, too often the blinders of race, class, and even of theology have stayed in place. Thus, reading the canonical unit and its traditional interpretive accompaniment have not escaped the well-defended borders of class, ethnicity, and race that are common to both ancient and modern biblical scholars. As more scholars pursue the continuing discourse we have with past interpreters, we will need to cut through partisan antagonisms as well as the adversarial roles that may be more easily defined. Clarifying issues is not enough; they need to be debated, refusing to grant either authors and editors or traditional commentators of biblical texts the authority they seek to control interpretation.

Reading about Reading the Bible

In the land of biblical thought, I hear the old warnings echoing from the ancient authors. When female figures such as Ruth, Hannah, and Tamar long to preserve the Covenant by having sons, they are rewarded, not only with the desired male heir but also with narratorial praise. What the paradigmatic story leaves out is that women could not own property. Without a son to protect her, a widow had to depend on the generosity of her husband's brothers. Or worse, she had to return to her own brothers, who had families of their own to care for. Another silent element is that one in four women in the ancient Near East died in childbirth. To pray to become pregnant was a life-threatening wish.

When women become curious, like the woman in the Garden for a taste of that mysterious fruit, or Lot's wife for a last glimpse of home, they are cast out. Women are not encouraged to reach out for the fruit of knowledge, no matter how tempting. When women try to form communities, they do not fare well either. Dinah goes out to visit the women of the land (Genesis 34) and gets raped by Shechem. After wandering the hills with her female companions, the daughter of Jephthah returns home to be sacrificed, a result of her father's foolish vow (Judges 11). Leah and Rachel gnaw at each other, more eager to possess Jacob than to share female commonality. And I tire from the always steep climb up the rocky face of patriarchy.

Rules of the Game

It is important to note the sly nature of categories. We hear of the good women in the Bible and the bad ones. Think carefully before following those assignments. When learning the rules of the game (according to the patriarchal rulers), keep in mind that the values of good women (wives) and bad (sexual temptresses) found in the book of Proverbs are not exclusively the rules of the Hebrew tribes. Compare the portraits of women and the warnings about women found in the Greek writer Hesiod, whose *Theogony* and *Works and Days* are contemporaneous with Homer and close in time to the world that produced the book of Proverbs. The Bad Girls may well be considered Good Girls in another time or by another culture: the Warrior Women are good only if the reader or the reading community shares their victories.

Whose Game Is it, Anyway?

When you are reading the story of the Woman in the Garden (Genesis 2–3), it may be helpful to compare it with a fragmented text from the Nag Hammadi Library, "The Hypostases of the Archons," a text that parallels the Genesis text, but one that values the actions of the woman, that prefers the desire for knowledge over obedience. Elaine Pagels's introduction to *The Gnostic Gospels* presents an excellent overview of the subject of suppressed theological texts in the Bible. Karen King's edited volume, *Images of the Feminine in Gnosticism: Studies in Antiquity and Christianity* (1988), provides insightful scholarly articles on various gnostic texts, laying out the problems these texts raise as well as making suggestions about the female deities who are their subject.

Understanding ancient beliefs about the physical bodies of men and women and ancient views of sexuality in the Mediterranean world, is also important for filling out a critical portrait of the male authors who wrote about women. You will find valuable source material in Aristotle's *Generation of Animals* as well as in the medical texts of Hippocrates and Galen.

Feminists Changing the Rules of the Game

As you will see from the lists of stories about women—Good and Bad, Warrior and Victim—many of the characters are both good and bad, both warrior and victim. There is no one slot into which the characters fit. (Note: The Table of Contents of this Reader reflects the difficulty of assigning topics to a group of articles.) A central task of the feminist Reader is to present interpretations in which the female characters are nuanced, not merely categorized. Thus, Delilah is a wicked woman if you are a reader loyal to Samson. But if you are a Philistine, then Delilah is a warrior hero, like Deborah or Judith or Jael. Speaking of Jael, she would hardly be a hero in the eyes of the mother of Sisera. Would Rebekah be a "good mother" to Esau, or Sarah to Ishmael? Judith is a hero to the Israelites she saved, but let's not forget that she beheaded a man, as surely as Jael drove a tent-peg through Sisera's skull. Good or bad, venerable or vixen?

Wives

Sarah (Hagar) and Abraham	Genesis 16, 20
Rebekah & Isaac	Genesis 26
Leah (& Rachel) & Jacob	Genesis 28–33
Hannah (& Pennina) & Elkhanah	1 Samuel 1–2
Michal & David	1 Samuel 17

Good Girls

Tamar	Genesis 38
Shiprah and Puah	Exodus 1–2
Acsah	Judges 1
Abigail	1 Samuel 25
Rizpah	2 Samuel 21
Bathsheba	2 Samuel 11–12; 1 Kings 1–2
Ruth	The Book of Ruth
Esther	The Book of Esther

Ordinary Women

Are there ordinary women in these narratives? Is Sarah, who gives birth at the biblical age of ninety, an ordinary woman? Are Shiprah and Puah, who go against the Pharonic law of the land in Exodus 2, ordinary? Are the Sad Girls ordinary? Are rape and death and losing your life to male vows and/or male anger ordinary? Is Miriam, the prophet and sister of Moses and Aaron, ordinary? Compare her with a nameless woman in the back of the long line of people leaving Egypt in the Exodus narrative. A nameless woman who has never met Moses, does not understand why they are going on this terrible, hard journey, and gets no answers from anyone around her. It is part of the task of a feminist reader to keep an eye on the nameless women and men at the back of the line, at the edge of the battle, far away from King David's court.

Angels in the House: Female Deities in Israel

While the focus of this Reader has been the narratives of women in the Hebrew Bible, there is the question of gender and the divine that must not be overlooked. While the mainstream theologians who produced the final authoritative version of the Hebrew narratives maintained that there was one God, YHWH, male, celibate, lacking in history and family, there are certainly shadows of goddess worship that appear in the Bible. In this Reader are important articles on goddess worship by Ackerman and Fontaine. I would recommend further reading among contemporary scholars on this central subject of the reception and repression of Anat and Asherah, and goddess worship in ancient Israel. Among the most illuminating, in my opinion, are Umberto Cassuto, *The Goddess Anath; Canaanite Epics of the Patriarchal Age* (Eng. trans. 1971); the very quirky but stimulating *Violent Goddess: Anat in the Ras Shamra Texts* (1969) by Arvin Kapelrud; and Tikva Frymer-Kensky, *In the Wake of the Goddess* (1993). Also important are Saul Olyan, *Asherah and the Cult of Yahweh in Israel;* and articles by William Dever, "Asherah, Consort Of Yahweh?: New Evidence from Kuntillet ʿAjrud," and Umberto Cassutto, "The Epic Of Baal." On the subject of Anat, see Neal Walls, *The Goddess Anat in Ugaritic Myth.* A fine translation of the Baal/Anat cycle of texts from Ugarit is edited by Mark S. Smith: *The Ugaritic Baal Cycle* (1994). Not surprisingly, not all of these works are written from a feminist perspective. At this writing, the most complete scholarship on real women and goddesses in the Mediterranean world are Sarah Pomeroy's *Goddesses, Whores, Wives, and Slaves: Women in Classical Antiquity* and Ross Kraemer's *Maenads, Martyrs, Matrons, Monastics : A Sourcebook on Women's Religions in the Greco-Roman World.*

A Subversive Companion for Reading Ancient Texts

I have included questions to jump-start your reading of the articles in the Reader. Also ask yourself these feminist questions while you are reading the ancient texts, searching for the scent of a woman. How does the identity of a woman reader/interpreter influence the reading of male texts? Can women positively appropriate androcentric texts as authoritative texts for their religious experience? How can a man read like a woman?

1. What sort of text am I reading?

Is this a narrative, legal text, allegory, medical/scientific text, ritual text? Was this text originally a spoken text or a written text? Keep in mind that the biblical stories were written down after centuries of oral transmission. Where is the woman, then, in this process of male generation of texts? Undoubtedly, women had their own dreams, personal desires, and secrets. Can we find them embedded in these male-authored texts?

2. What does this text tell me about the ancient social world?

These ancient biblical texts were written by men. Thus, we are reading texts about women written by men. What conclusions do the texts lead us to draw about good women and bad ones? How do you react as a reader to the male image of the ideal wife? Keep in mind that women also support the social order that envisions a sexual hierarchy: men in the outside world and women inside; the hunter and the keeper of the hearth. For background on the ancient Mediterranean world, see Kraemer, *Her Share of the Blessings: Women's Religions among Pagans, Jews, and Christians in the Greco-Roman World* (1992); and Pomeroy, *Women's History and Ancient History* (1991) and *Families in Classical and Hellenistic Greece: Representations and Realities* (1996). For views on Jewish women in early rabbinic times, see Brooten, *Women Leaders in the Ancient Synagogue: Inscriptional Evidence and Background Issues (1982).*

Look at the list of qualities of the good woman in Proverbs 31: Would you want to live the life of such a woman? Would you want to be married to such a woman? Hmmm.

3. How does the text reflect and support the patriarchal structure of Western society? Can I as a reader stand outside this structure and cast off the underpinnings of misogyny?

The first part of this question assumes that there is a patriarchal structure to Western society. The challenge of our communal endeavor is to read against the grain of the text, to come up with readings that acknowledge the roots of authority that have shaped these texts but to resist becoming imprisoned in the conventional reading that concludes "that's the way it's supposed to be." In her book, *Plotted, Shot, and Painted* (1996), J. Cheryl Exum illustrates a variety of ways in which feminist readings can break free of the patriarchal text.

4. What images of female goodness does this text present? How do I feel about the angel in the house?

It seems that the ideal woman that male authors dream of (and create in their narratives) is an angel. Virginia Woolf has observed that the "angel in the house" is the most pernicious image male authors have ever imposed upon literary women. Is this image more pernicious than that of the wicked women, the female fiends who use their femaleness to entrap and destroy men?

5. Do the good woman, the angel in the house, and her sister, the serpentine siren, have stories of their own? Can you uproot her story from inside his story?

You will add to this list of questions as you struggle against the familiarity in these biblical texts. The questions are at the core of our work as feminists: they are the currency we pay when we attempt to define ourselves in unacceptable ways.

Recipes for Reading: Who's Reading the Text

Reading is seen traditionally as a transparent activity, like breathing, which we either do not think about or, if we do, believe we understand quite well. A readerly concern, by contrast, problematizes reading—which is to say, wonders what it is that is going on, and how whatever it is actually works. It is only recently that scholars have begun to analyze what happens when one reads, that is, how the reader makes meaning from the words of a text. Texts do not have meanings that readers proceed to discover. In some way or other, the creation of meaning arises at the intersection between text and reader. Thus, scholars have learned to focus upon the reader rather than upon the author or the text itself to understand how meaning happens.

The combination of the reader's own interests, values, and commitments is what makes her or him a person with identity and integrity. Each reader of texts, including biblical texts, brings her or his own prejudices, biases, and presuppositions to the task of reading. Each person has and should become conscious of her or his own agenda for interpretation, that is, the mutual transaction between text and reader. Of course, a feminist concentrates not only on the female characters in a narrative, but also upon the social context of power and authority in the society in which the narrative takes place. And never to be overlooked in a literature as old as the Bible is how one's own agenda has influenced the hundreds of years of interpretation that overlay our own readings. Thus, a feminist reading of a biblical text will take into account the agenda of the interpreter—be it a rabbi or church father with theological issues on his mind, or a poor landless outsider, who wonders whatever happened to the Canaanites, and who spoke for them.

1. *What does the text say or fail to say about the reader's own set of issues?*
As biblical scholar David Clines once advised,

> If you are a pacifist vegetarian feminist and do not immediately see these issues developed in biblical texts, do not discard the text and do not allow the text or earlier interpreters to set the agenda and change your focus. Look for clues that touch your issues. Stewardship of the earth and its creatures bears on your agenda, even if it is not specifically headlined pacifist, vegetarian, or feminist. This is an example, not everyone is expected to share the agenda of our fictional feminist pacifist vegan.

2. *Do not allow the text to set the agenda.*
In learning to identify the process of reading, one needs to learn how writers write. The strategies that writers use involve plotting, delineation of character, use of dialogue, and silence contrasted with speech. In reading biblical narratives, it is critically important to distinguish between the author and the narrator, the early audience or ideal reader and the contemporary reader. Try to separate the voice of the narrator from the voices of the characters he (we are probably dealing with male narrators in these male-authored texts, although the narrator is anonymous) describes as either male and female. Keep in mind that the male narrator is "gazing" at the scene he describes (the narratorial term for this is "focalization").

3. *Learning to read all over again . . .*
In trying to unravel and expose the strategies of the author, ask of the narrative the three big questions:

WHO SPEAKS   WHO SEES   WHO ACTS

Follow the thread through the narrative labyrinth and ask yourself
whose story is told fully (or more fully) than the other characters'
whose agenda is fulfilled in the story
which characters are approved of and disapproved of by the narrator
whose agenda supports the social order

4. *Try to read a text with alternative interpretations.*
The sheer possibility of a different reading shows that the reader can cast off the dominance of the established "acceptable" reading. The possibility of dominance, that attractiveness of coherence and authority in culture, is the source rather than the consequence of sexism. A major point of literary analysis is to realize that there is no one universal truth, and where the truth is absent, women and ethnic minorities can creep in and rewrite themselves back into the history of ideology. Once you have identified the dominant agenda—that is, the one that supports the social order—turn the text on its head to find a reading too long suppressed.

5. *Reading as women (not just for women only).*

Turning the text on its head is what feminists do. Any time any reader reads against the grain of the text, reads with a suspicious eye toward how the narrator wants you to read, you are performing a feminist reading. Focusing on the presence or absence of women in the text makes the reading a gendered one, not the eyes of a woman reading the text. Of course, one can also focus on the characterizations of the men in the story to do a "masculinist" reading, also a gendered reading. Traditional interpreters of texts used to refer to masculinist readings as "the truth." Both women and men need to examine male roles in the biblical texts. Are all the male characters in the text equally privileged? Are the marginalized males in a better position than the female figures who are married to the powerful males? Finally, do remember in your reading and interpreting of texts that qualities such as compassion, tenderness, gentleness, as well as violence, cruelty, anger are not inherently gender based. That is, do not fall into the interpretive trap of stereotyping either male or female characters.

The Social World of Women
in Ancient Israel

The Place of Women
in the Israelite Cultus

PHYLLIS BIRD

Despite the timeliness of the question posed in the title of this essay, it is not a new one in the history of Old Testament scholarship.[1] It occasioned lively debate at the turn of the century, in terms remarkably similar to arguments heard today. A key figure in that early debate was J. Wellhausen, whose analysis of Israelite religion emphasized its masculine, martial, and aristocratic nature, positing an original coincidence of military, politicolegal, and religious assemblies, in which males alone had full rights and duties of membership.[2] Others argued that women were disqualified from cultic service by reference to an original ancestral cult of the dead which could be maintained only by a male heir.[3] A further argument associated women's disability or disinterest in the Yahweh cult with a special attraction to foreign cults or pre-Yahwistic beliefs and practices involving local numina.[4]

Underlying these arguments and assumptions concerning the marginal or subordinate status of women in the Israelite cultus was a common understanding of early Israel as a kinship-structured society of nomadic origin, whose basic social and religious unit was the patrilineal and patriarchal family.[5] Though it was the agricultural village with its assembly of free landowners that Wellhausen had in mind when he correlated political and religious status, the principle he articulated had broader applicability: "Wer politisch nicht vollberechtigt war, war es auch religiös nicht."[6] Women, who were disenfranchised in the political realm, were disenfranchised in the religious realm as well.

Stated in such terms of disability—or disinterest and disaffection—the widely held view of women's inferior status in the Israelite cultus, exhibited in the critical historiography of the period, elicited vigorous rebuttal in a series of studies aimed at clarifying, and defending, women's position in ancient Israelite religion and society.[7] While the arguments and conclusions of these studies differed, the general outcome was to demonstrate that women's participation in the religious life of ancient Israel was in fact broader and more significant than commonly depicted.[8]

Today many of the same arguments and much of the same evidence put forward in the earlier discussion are being employed once more in a renewed debate over the andro-centric and patriarchal character of Israelite religion.[9] This time, however, the discussion appearing in scholarly publications, or in works by biblical scholars, is fueled by a debate arising outside the academy and borne by a literature that is primarily lay-oriented and largely lay-authored, a literature marked by the anger and urgency of profound existen-tial and institutional conflict.[10] Modern feminist critique of the Bible as male-centered and male-dominated has elicited widely differing historiographical and hermeneutical responses, ranging from denial of the fact or intent of female subordination to rejection of the authority of the Scriptures as fundamentally and irredeemably sexist.

In the current debate, with its heavy charge of personal and theological interest, the biblical historian has a limited but essential contribution to make by isolating and clarifying the historical question. The task of Old Testament historiography must be to determine as accurately as possible the actual roles and activities of women in Israelite religion throughout the Old Testament period and the meaning of those roles and activ-ities in their ancient socioreligious contexts. The question for the historian today is the same as that addressed to earlier scholars, but it must be answered in a new way—because of new data, new methods of analysis, and a new understanding of history. The following is an attempt to set forth a rationale and a plan for that new answer.

The question about the place of women in the Israelite cultus exposes a defect in traditional historiography—beginning already in Israelite times. It is a question about a forgotten or neglected element in traditional conceptions and presentations of Israelite religion, which typically focus on the activities and offices of males. Where women appear at all in the standard works, it is in incidental references, as exceptional figures, or in limited discussions of practices or customs relating especially to women. This skewed presentation may be explained by the limits of the available sources and may even be understood as an accurate representation of the Israelite cultus as a male-constituted or male-dominated institution. But it can no longer be viewed as an adequate portrait of Israelite religion. The religion of Israel was the religion of men and women, whose dis-tinctive roles and experience require critical attention, as well as their common activities and obligations. To comprehend Israelite religion as the religion of a people, rather than the religion of males, women's roles, activities, and experience must be fully represented and fully integrated into the discussion. What is needed is a new reconstruction of the history of Israelite religion, not a new chapter on women. Until that is done, the place of women in the Israelite cultus will remain incomprehensible and inconsequential in its isolation, and our understanding of Israelite religion will remain partial, distorted, and finally unintelligible.

A first step toward this integrated reconstruction must be an attempt to recover the hidden history of women and to view the religion through their eyes, so that women's viewpoint as well as their presence is represented in the final account.[11] The obstacles to that effort are immense, but, I shall argue, not insurmountable. They do, however, require that critical attention be given to methodology before any reconstruction can proceed. That being the case, this chapter can offer no more than a highly provisional sketch of the assigned subject, prefaced by a summary of the methodological study that forms the essential introduction.

Preliminary Methodological Considerations

1. Two fundamental shifts in focus or perspective are necessary to the reconstruction I have proposed: (*a*) The cultus must be understood in relation to the total religious life in all of its various forms and expressions, "private" as well as public; heterodox, sectarian, and "foreign" as well as officially sanctioned;[12] and (*b*) religious institutions and activities must be viewed in relation to other social institutions, such as the family, and in the context of the total social, economic, and political life. While both of these shifts are essential to an understanding of Israelite religion as a total complex, they have particular consequence for the understanding of women's place and roles.

2. The information needed to give a fully adequate account of the place of women in Israelite religion, including the cultus, is in large measure unavailable—and unrecoverable—from either biblical or extrabiblical sources. We have at best isolated fragments of evidence, often without clues to context. As a consequence, any reconstruction must be tentative and qualified. The same, however, is true, though in less extreme degree, of our knowledge of men's roles, and demands similar caution and qualification. Our fullest and best information is partial and skewed.

3. A comprehensive and coherent account of Israelite religion and of women's place in it requires the use of an interpretive model, not only to comprehend the available evidence but also to locate, identify, and interpret missing information—which is often the most important.[13] The blanks in the construct are as essential to the final portrait as the areas described by known data. They must be held open (as the boxes in an organizational chart)—or imaginatively filled—if the structure is not to collapse or the picture is not to be rendered inaccurate or unintelligible. The primary means of filling the blanks is imaginative reconstruction informed by analogy.

4. The closest analogies may be found in other ancient Near Eastern societies. They are limited, however, by dependence on written documents, most of which come from the spheres of men's activities and reflect male perspectives.

5. Modern ethnographic studies of individual societies and institutions and cross-cultural studies of women's roles in contemporary non-Western societies can aid the Old Testament historian in formulating questions and constructing models.[14] Such studies are especially valuable for their attempts to view societies as total systems as well as for their attention to features that native historians and lay members of the society may overlook or deem unimportant. Because they do not depend on written records but are based on observation and interview of participants, they give us access to women's roles and experience that is otherwise unavailable.

6. Androcentric bias is a pervasive feature of the ancient sources, their subjects, and their interpreters. It has also characterized most anthropological research and writing until recently.[15]

Summary of Findings of Cross-Cultural Studies

The most important finding of cross-cultural studies for a reconstruction of women's religious roles in ancient Israel is the universal phenomenon of sexual division of labor, which is particularly pronounced in pre-industrial agricultural societies.[16] Basic to this division of labor is an understanding of women's primary work as reproductive work, including care of children and associated household tasks, with a consequent identification of the domestic sphere as the female sphere, to which women's activities may be restricted in varying degrees.[17] This fundamental sexual division of labor has far-reaching consequences for the status and roles of women in the society as a whole as well as their patterns of activity and participation in the major social institutions. In all of the primary institutions of the public sphere, which is the male sphere, women have limited or marginal roles, if any. Thus leadership roles in the official cultus are rarely women's roles or occupied by women.[18]

Conversely, however, women's religious activities—and needs—tend to center in the domestic realm and relate to women's sexually determined work. As a consequence, those institutions and activities which appear from public records or male perspective as central may be viewed quite differently by women, who may see them as inaccessible, restricting, irrelevant, or censuring. Local shrines, saints and spirits, home rituals in the company of other women (often with women ritual leaders), the making and paying of vows (often by holding feasts), life-cycle rites, especially those related to birth and death—these widely attested elements of women's religious practice appear better suited to women's spiritual and emotional needs and the patterns of their lives than the rituals of the central sanctuary, the great pilgrimages and assemblies, and the liturgical calendar of the agricultural year.[19] But the public sphere with its male-oriented and male-controlled institutions dominates and governs the domestic sphere, with the result that women's activities and beliefs are often viewed by "official" opinion as frivolous, superstitious, subversive, or foreign.[20]

Women in Israelite Religion and Cultus: Observations and Hypotheses

We have argued that an adequate understanding of the place of women in the Israelite cultus requires attention both to the place of the cultus in the total religious and social life of the society and to the place of women in the society—including consideration of the society's understanding of male and female nature, capacities, and inclinations and its organization and assignment of male and female roles, activities, rights, and duties. Despite the efforts of the Israelite cultus to exert a controlling influence over the total life of the society and despite its significant stamp on the culture, the cultus must still be seen as one institution among others, influenced by general social and cultural norms, especially as they define appropriate male and female roles and activities. Consequently, we should expect significant correspondence between women's roles and status in the cultus and in the society as a whole. Three prominent elements of that general understanding of women's nature and duty have direct bearing on women's place in the cultus: (1) the periodic impurity of women during their reproductive years;[21] (2) the legal subordination of women within the family, which places a woman under the male authority of father, husband, or brother, together with a corresponding subordination in the public sphere in which the community is represented by its male members; and (3) an understanding of women's primary work and social duty as family-centered reproductive work in the role of wife-mother.

The effect of each of these determinants is to restrict the sphere of women's activities—spatially, temporally, and functionally. Only roles that were compatible with women's primary domestic-reproductive role and could be exercised in periods or situations free from ritual taboo, or from the requirement of ritual purity, were open to women. While restrictions also existed on men's ability to participate in particular cultic roles and activities (e.g., economic constraints on offering vows and sacrifices and restriction of priestly office to members of priestly families), these did not affect all males as a class. A significant distinction between male and female relationships to the cultus may be seen in the fact that for women, but not for men, conflict between social and cultic obligation is a recurring phenomenon—which is resolved by giving priority to social demands. Examples may be seen in the annulment of a woman's vows by her father or husband (Num 30:1–15)[22] and in the "exemption" of women from the requirement of the annual pilgrim feasts (Exod 23:17; 34:23; Deut 16:16). In both of these cases one may argue that responsibility to the family is the underlying principle and that it is understood as a religious, not merely a social, obligation; but a contrast remains between the understanding of a male and a female religious obligation.[23]

This explanation assumes a conflict of duty or interest (defined socially, not individually) as grounds for women's limited role in the Israelite cultus, but the limitation might also be explained by an understanding of the cultus as an originally, or essentially, male institution or association. The evidence suggests that there is truth in both views.

Wellhausen was surely right in recognizing behind the generic language of many texts and translations a cultus conceived and operated as a male association to which women were related, if at all, in a marginal and mediated way. Evidence for an understanding of the cultic community as fundamentally a body of males is substantial. While the best examples relate to the early period, they are not confined to it: for example, the prescription for the pilgrim feasts ("Three times in the year shall all your males appear before the Lord God," Exod 23:17; cf. Deut 16:16); the instructions to the "people" at the mountain of God ("Be ready by the third day; do not go near a woman," Exod 19:15); the tenth commandment ("You shall not covet your neighbor's wife," Exod 20:17); and other injunctions, exhortations, blessings, and so forth, that address the cultic community as male ("Blessed is everyone who fears the Lord. . . . Your wife will be like a fruitful vine," Ps 128:1–3; "Jeremiah said to all the people and all the women," Jer 44:24).

Further evidence may be seen in the Hebrew onomasticon, where theophoric names describing the individual as a worshiper or votary of the deity (names compounded with *ʿebed/ʿōbēd*, i.e., "servant of") are reserved to males and have no female counterpart—in contrast to Akkadian and Phoenician practice.[24]

Objections to Wellhausen's view that seek to show broad participation of women in religious and cultic activities fail to challenge his basic argument, which is not that women were prohibited from participation, but rather that their participation was not essential and that it played a less central or less important role in women's lives than in men's. Wellhausen's insight was also sound in positing an "original" coincidence or congruence of military, legal, and cultic assemblies; the three represent the primary institutions of the public sphere, which is everywhere the sphere of male activity. His understanding of the correspondence of rights and duties in these overlapping realms can also be substantially affirmed, though areas of divergence require greater attention together with cases of status incongruity. A further modification is required by the extension of both the cultic and the legal spheres beyond the circle of males to encompass the broader community.[25] As a consequence, women, who were excluded from the governing or representative institutions of both (namely, the priesthood and the cultic assembly, and the council of elders and the assembly of landholders), were nevertheless brought within their spheres of interest and authority.[26] Thus women possessed dual status in the legal and cultic realm, being members of the outer circle governed by the community's norms but restricted in varying degree from the inner circle where the norms were formulated, inculcated, and rationalized.

In the cultic realm, differentiation of roles is associated with a hierarchy of offices and prerogatives ordered according to a concept of graduated degrees of holiness (represented spatially, e.g., in the plan of the Temple and its courts). At the center, which is also the apex of authority, stands the priest or high priest, surrounded by other members of the priesthood and/or other orders of cultic personnel (the local shrine represents the simplest form of cultic leadership, invested in a resident priest—and his family—while the Temple cultus occupies the other end of the spectrum, with its elaborate, graded system of special orders and offices). Beyond the priesthood stand members of the community (more specifically, the free citizens), bound by duty of pilgrimage, addressed directly by the cultic proclamation and having limited rights of sacrifice (varying according to period). The outer circle is represented by women, dependents, and resident aliens. They are also addressed by the cultic proclamation, but usually indirectly; both their hearing and their response is commonly mediated by a male guardian.

While this scheme gives a general picture of the relationship of women to the Israelite cultus, it must be qualified in a number of ways, especially with regard to changes or variations in internal and external relationships over the Old Testament period, some of which appear to have significant consequence for the nature and extent of women's participation. Factors requiring consideration include the number of cultic centers, the types of activities associated with them, and the relationships among them; the status and affiliation of the cultic personnel, the degree of centralization, and the extent of professionalization or specialization of cultic maintenance roles; and the relationship of the central cultus to other institutions and spheres of life.

While this chapter does not permit detailed study of the complex assortment of data embedded in the Old Testament text, a summary review of the more prominent features of the major periods may help to provide a context for a series of concluding hypotheses concerning patterns of participation and changes in women's relationship to the cultus.

The fullest and richest evidence for women's religious activity is found in literature pertaining to the premonarchic period, which also provides the richest portrait of women in leadership roles. We see Miriam leading the Israelites in a song of victory at the sea (Exod 15:20–21), punished for claiming equality with Moses as one through whom the Lord had also spoken (Num 12:2), and ranked with Aaron and Moses as leaders of the people (Num 12:2–8; Mic 6:4);[27] women "ministering" at the tent of meeting (Exod 38:8; 1 Sam 2:22); Deborah honored as a "mother in Israel" (Judg 5:7), as a judge and a prophet summoning the forces of Israel to holy war at Yahweh's command and accompanying them into battle (Judg 4:4–10; 5:7, 12–15), and as a singer of Israel's victory through Yahweh (Judg 5:1); Jephthah's virgin daughter "initiating" an annual ritual of mourning by the daughters of Israel (Judg 11: 34–40);[28] Micah's mother commissioning an image for the family shrine established by her son (Judg 17:1–13, esp. v 4); women dancing at the yearly feast at Shiloh (Judg 21:19–21); Hannah and Peninnah accompanying their husband on his annual pilgrimage to Shiloh and sharing the portions of the sacrifice (1 Sam 1:1–4); and Hannah, weeping, praying, vowing at the sanctuary, and finally paying her vow with the dedication of the child (1 Sam 1:9–28). In these images we see most of the roles attested in the later period.

Sources pertaining to the period of the monarchy and to the postexilic period expand the references to heterodox practices and sharpen the distinction between legitimate and illegitimate roles and activities. Two female prophets, Huldah (2 Kgs 22: 14–20) and the unnamed *něbîʾâ* of Isa 8:3, are the only women portrayed in approved cultic roles.[29] The rest are viewed as illegitimate. These include references to *qědēšôt* (Hos 4:14; Deut 23:18);[30] to queens and queen mothers who introduced foreign cults and cult objects (Maacah—1 Kgs 15:13; Jezebel—1 Kgs 18:19 [cf. 16:31–32]; Athaliah—2 Kgs 11:18; cf. Solomon—1 Kgs 11:1–8); to women weaving vestments for Asherah (2 Kgs 23:7); and to women baking cakes/burning incense for the Queen of Heaven (Jer 7:17–18; 44:15–25), weeping for Tammuz (Ezek 8:14), and engaging in sorcery ("prophesying"—Ezek 13:17–23). Postexilic literature yields only a prophet opponent of Nehemiah (Noadiah—Neh 6:14), showing a continuation of women in the class of prophets.[31] The number and nature of references to women's religious roles and activities during the monarchy appear to reflect the consequences of the centralization of the cultus under royal control and a tendency, culminating in the Deuteronomic reform, to brand all worship at the local sanctuaries idolatrous/promiscuous.[32]

Evidence from the patriarchal traditions depicts a family-centered or clan type of cultus in which the patriarchs perform all of the roles of sacrifice and blessing and are portrayed as founders of various local shrines or cults (Gen 22:9–14; 26:23–25; 28:18–19; 35:6–7, 14–15).[33] Rachel's stealing of the teraphim (as cultic objects belonging to her father) is further witness to clan-based religious practice, but it tells us nothing about women's religious roles. Her audacious and amusing act of theft and coverup in which she "protects" the sacred objects by professing defilement does not describe the institutionalization of an action. Rachel remains a dependent as she cleverly assists her husband in robbing her father.

Summary Generalizations

The following is an attempt to summarize the evidence in a series of preliminary generalizations.

Women in Cultic Service

1. Leadership of the cultus appears at all times to have been in the hands of males (though with differing patterns and sources of recruitment into the leadership group). Women, however, were not excluded absolutely from cultic service or sacred space, though increasing restriction is suggested, correlated with increasing centralization, specialization, and power (at least in Judah) under a royally sanctioned Zadokite priesthood. Persistence of women in cultic roles in the later period is identified in the canonical texts with heterodox practice.

2. The attested roles of men and women in the service of the cultus appear to exhibit a sexual division of labor corresponding closely to that discernible in the society as a whole.

a. Males occupy the positions of greatest authority, sanctity, and honor and perform tasks requiring technical skill and training. They preside over the presentation of sacrifices and offerings,[34] have charge of the sacred lots, interpret the sacred law and instruct the congregation, pronounce blessing and curse, declare absolution and pardon, and guard the purity of the sanctuary and the worshipers; that is, they perform the priestly service in both sacrificial and oracular functions. Priestly office in Israel, as in the rest of the ancient Near East, was reserved to males. Contrary to popular opinion, Israelite Yahwism was not distinguished from the surrounding religions by its rejection of women in priestly office, but conformed to common practice.[35] The Israelite cultus in its basic institutional forms appears to have shared the essential features of the cultus known in surrounding cultures.

b. Women's cultic service seems to have been confined largely to maintenance and support roles, essential to the operation of the cultus but not requiring clergy status—or prescription in texts concerned with the proper performance of the required rituals. Since these roles are poorly documented in the biblical sources, we can only speculate based on chance clues, parallels in domestic life, and the suggestions afforded by comparative studies of cultic organization and maintenance elsewhere in the ancient Near East. The following tasks appear likely (further suggestions must await a fuller study of comparative materials): the weaving and sewing of vestments, hangings, and other textiles for cultic use;[36] the preparation of cultic meals or foods used in the ritual;[37] and the cleaning of cultic vessels, furniture, and quarters.[38]

c. Some references to women associated with the cultus point to more public and representative or symbolic roles, suggesting a need to include within the cultus activities or attributes specifically identified with women, for example, as singers and dancers[39] or as attendants in the sanctuary. Both the *ṣōbĕʾôt* (Exod 38:8; 1 Sam 2:22)[40] and the *qĕdēsôt* (Gen 38:21–22; Deut 23:17; Hos 4:14)[41] are associated with the service of the sanctuary, though the exact nature and form of their respective service remains unclear. Both represent classes rejected or superseded by the normative cultus that preserved the record of their existence, suggesting that they played a larger role (for a longer period of time) than the meager references would at first intimate. The identifying symbol or implement of the former group (a mirror) and the innuendo in references to the latter suggest that in both cases female sexuality was a significant aspect of the role.

d. If we posit any specialized service of women within the cultus, we must also consider the social organization that would enable permanent or continuous (short-term or long-term) cultic activity. Since women's place in society is determined by their place within the family, women are not normally free to operate for extended periods outside this sphere. The well-known exceptions are the widow, the prostitute, and the hierodule. Two possible arrangements may be suggested to account for women's service in the Israelite cultus. One would see the women as members of priestly families, hence resident at or near the sanctuary and sharing in some degree the special sanctity of the priest, which would give them access to the sacred space. The other would assume that they are women without families (whether widows, virgins, or women separated from their families by a vow). In the latter case we may expect, as in the case of the various classes of

Babylonian hierodules, that the cultus will assume the authority and control of father or husband and that restrictions, comparable to those applying within the family, will be placed on the woman's sexual activity for the duration of her service (whether as a prohibition of sexual activity or of having or keeping children).

e. Women might also on occasion play a role in the royal cultus through their roles in the ruling house. A queen, in the absence of a male ruler (or in the presence of a weak one), might assume the role of titular head and patron of the state cult. Since our best Old Testament example is provided by a foreign queen (Jezebel), presiding over a foreign cult, the cultic role of the king's wife or mother may not have been as fully developed in Israel as elsewhere—or it may have been rejected. This specialized cultic role is in any case dependent upon a secular role and the particular politicoreligious relationship of the royal cultus.

3. The most important and best-documented religious office occupied by women in ancient Israel, that of prophet, stands in an ambiguous relationship to the cultus. Whatever the role of the prophet within the cultus, it was clearly not a priestly office. Since recruitment was by divine designation (charismatic gift) and not dependent upon family or status, it was the one religious office with broad power that was not mediated or directly controlled by the cultic or civil hierarchy and the one religious office open to women. Because recruitment to and exercise of the role did not depend on socially or sexually defined status but on personal attributes, it was also the one role shared by men and women, a pattern attested in Mesopotamia and in cross-cultural studies.

The lack of formal restrictions to women's assumption of the office does not mean, however, that women were equally free to exercise it. Here, as in the case of other extrafamilial roles, women were confronted with a dual vocation, which was normally— and perhaps always—resolved in favor of the domestic obligation. Women prophets probably exercised their charismatic vocation alongside their family responsibilities or after their child-rearing duties were past. As a consequence of this complementary or sequential pattern of women's prophetic activity—and as a consequence of the normal patterns of social organization, which placed women as dependents in family-centered units—one would not expect to find women organized in prophetic guilds (the professional guild is a male form of organization). Nor would one expect to find women prophets as heads of schools or having the freedom of action and access to political and cultic power that is apparent in the case of their most prominent male counterparts. It is therefore not unexpected that no prophetic books carry the names of women, and it requires no explanation of prejudice or conspiratorial silence—but rather conflict of duty, which made every woman a mother before she would exercise another vocation.

4. Some forms of cultic service by women associated with the central Yahwistic cultus were judged heterodox or foreign by the canonical sources. In addition to these references the Old Testament contains frequent references to local cults of alien gods and to foreign cults brought into the central cultus. These references, which are always polemical and usually formulated in very general terms, do not supply us with adequate information about the related cultic personnel, but presumably some of these were women (e.g., *qĕdēšîm* in 1 Kgs 15:12; 2 Kgs 23:7 may be understood as an inclusive use of the generic plural). It is impossible on the basis of our sources, however, to determine whether women played a larger role in the service of non-Yahwistic cults. Evidence for a female deity or female aspect of deity as a persistent and at times, perhaps, legitimate

element of the Yahwistic cultus requires reassessment of the terms "foreign" and "syncretistic" as descriptions of discredited worship as well as a reassessment of the ritual and personnel of such cults. The sources suggest that disavowal, rather than discontinuance, of the practices and beliefs is what is indicated in the increasing and increasingly polemical attention to "foreign" cults and cultic practices in late sources.

Women as Worshipers

1. Since women rarely emerge in the text from behind the facade of generic male terminology, it is impossible to determine with certainty the extent of their participation in prescribed or reported activities. Isolated clues suggest, however, that women attended the major communal feasts and rituals, insofar as personal and domestic circumstances permitted, and presumably contributed to the preparation of meals and of food (especially grain) offerings. Animal slaughter and sacrifice, as an action of the worshiper, was reserved to males—as elsewhere generally—but this appears to have been the sole specific exclusion or reservation. In the major pilgrim feasts and other festivals at local shrines, as well as in family-based ritual meals, the woman participates as a member of a family unit. But she may also exercise her role in "the great congregation" and as "a daughter of Israel" bound by covenant law in individual acts of devotion and duty: in songs of praise (1 Sam 2:1–10) and prayers of petition (1 Sam 1:10–16), in the making and performing of vows (1 Sam 1:11, 24–28; Num 30:3–15), in seeking oracles (2 Kgs 4:22–23; cf. 1 Kgs 14:2–5), in bringing offerings, and in performing the rituals prescribed for ritual cleansing, absolution, and so forth (Lev 12:1–8; 13:29–39; 15:19–29). The locus of these activities might be the central shrine (on occasions of pilgrimage) but was surely most commonly a local shrine or holy place or simply the place of daily activity. That women's communion with the deity was common and that women were recipients of divine communications is indicated by a number of theophany traditions—though where the response to the appearing deity takes cultic form, as in the case of Manoah's wife, the action shifts to the male (Manoah presents the offering and questions the angel, cf. Judg 13:2–7 and 8–20).

2. Of family-centered ritual we know even less, except in the case of the Passover. We may expect in this and in other cases that the normal male and female roles in the family will be reflected in the ritual, with food preparation belonging to the women and the presiding role, reading and recitation, assumed by males. The alternative practice of segregated dining and ritual, common in Islamic custom, was more likely the rule in cultic meals of larger groups or societies formed for such purposes.

3. Peculiarly or predominantly female forms of ritual and worship are suggested in the canonical sources only in reference to heterodox cults, the clearest examples of which are the women weeping for Tammuz (Ezek 8:14) and making offerings to the Queen of Heaven (Jer 7:17–18; 44:19). Though the whole population is explicitly implicated in the latter case, the women seem to have a special role. Prophetic use of the metaphor of the promiscuous bride to describe Israel's apostasy may reflect a special proclivity of Israelite women for "foreign" cults, but the sin that is condemned is the sin of the people, and this usage alone is insufficient to demonstrate a pattern. Of possible greater significance for an understanding of women's religious participation and the total religious life of the community is the hidden realm of women's rituals and devotions that take place entirely within the domestic sphere and/or in the company of other women.

Cross-cultural studies show that these often constitute the emotional center of women's religious life as well as the bulk of their religious activity, especially where their participation in the central cultus is limited. For such practices, however, we have little or no direct testimony, as this order of religious practice is generally seen as unworthy of note unless it challenges or undermines the central cultus. (Women's rites may even be unknown to men, who have no part in them.) Ceremonies and practices that belong to this category might include birth and mourning rites and other rituals of the life cycle performed in the home or the village, especially with a woman as ritual specialist; prayers; vows and their performance in such actions as holding a feast, endowing a shrine, or dedicating some prized possession; making pilgrimages; consulting mediums and seers; and participation in spirit-possession cults or rituals. The line between religion and magic or orthodox and heterodox is more difficult to draw in this realm of practice and belief since the controls of the central cultus, its priesthood and theology, are largely absent. Like folk religion everywhere, it is typically seen as debased or corrupted and often as syncretistic.

The freedom to engage in such actions may vary considerably, relating in part to the degree to which they may be seen as convergent with or contrary to cultically prescribed duties. For example, ritual prescriptions governing the state of impurity associated with childbirth draw the otherwise private birth event into the sphere of the central cultus in its attempt to maintain the purity of the people as a cultically defined community. But the satisfaction of the cultic requirement does not exhaust the ritual need associated with the birth, which may be supplied by a naming ceremony, circumcision feast, and/or special rituals to assist the mother in the birth—rituals in which a female specialist such as a midwife may play a role closely analogous to the role of a priest in other situations of crisis. Women's private rituals or actions favored by women may also be opposed by male authorities as frivolous, superstitious, costly, and unnecessary. But opposition does not always mean compliance. Women may take vows that are costly and undertake forbidden pilgrimages as actions of rebellion or flight from oppressive household responsibilities and restrictions. As religiously sanctioned actions they may offer limited relief to women whose options for action were often severely circumscribed.

4. On the boundary of the sacred sphere that is organized by the central cultus or claimed by rival cults, a sphere extended in the name of the principal deity, or deities, to the rituals of daily life, there exists a quasi-religious sphere of spirits, demons, and various malevolent or amoral forces that trouble people and over which they attempt to gain control by special knowledge and defensive action. Those skilled in discerning and controlling these forces, by sorcery, witchcraft, necromancy, medicine, or other means, may be acknowledged by the cultus as practitioners of valuable practical arts or proscribed as challenging the fundamental claims of the deity to embody or control all forms of superhuman power. While some religions might incorporate such beliefs and practices into their belief systems, Israelite Yahwism, from the time of Saul, proscribed the practices and banned the practitioners (1 Sam 23:3, 8). It has often been suggested that women had a special attraction to these quasi-religious practices, both as clients and as practitioners, and it makes sense that women should prefer to seek help for their problems from a local specialist than from a general practitioner or ritual specialist serving a remote God. That women should also constitute a significant proportion of the mediums and other specialists in spirit manipulation is also understandable. However, the Old

Testament evidence is insufficient to confirm such a pattern of preference and contains more references to male than to female classes of occult practitioners.

Conclusion

During the period reflected in the Old Testament sources there appear to have been a number of changes within the cultus and in its relationship to the population as a whole that had significance for women's participation. The progressive movement from multiple cultic centers to a central site that finally claimed sole legitimacy and control over certain ritual events necessarily restricted the participation of women in pilgrim feasts and limited opportunities for women to seek guidance, release, and consolation at local shrines, which were declared illegitimate or demolished. At the same time, increased specialization and hierarchal ordering of priestly/levitical ranks within the royal/national cultus deprived males in general (as well as Levites) of earlier priestly prerogatives, increasing the distance or sharpening the boundary between the professional guardians of the cultus and the larger circle of male Israelites who comprised the religious assembly. Reorganization of the cultus under the monarchy and again in the postexilic period appears to have limited or eliminated roles earlier assigned to women. On the other hand, there appears to have been a move (most clearly evident in the Deuteronomic legislation) to bring women more fully and directly into the religious assembly, so that the congregation is redefined as a body of lay men and women. As the priesthood becomes more powerful and specialized, the primary cultic distinction or boundary within the community becomes that between priest and laity rather than between male and female.

NOTES

1. This chapter is a preliminary and highly abbreviated form of the introduction to a book-length work (in preparation) on women in Israelite religion.

2. J. Wellhausen, *Israelitische und jüdische Geschichte* (3d ed.; Berlin: Georg Reimer, 1897) 89–90.

3. I. Benzinger, *Hebräische Archäologie* (Freiburg im Breisgau and Leipzig: J.C.B. Mohr, 1894) 140, and W. Nowack, *Lehrbuch der hebräischen Archäologie* (Frieburg im Breisgau and Leipzig: J.C.B. Mohr, 1894) 154, 348.

4. See, e.g., B. Stade, *Biblische Theologie des Alten Testaments* (Tübingen: J.C.B. Mohr, 1905) 1. 40. Cf. E. König, *Geschichte der alttestamentlichen Religion* (Gütersloh: Bertelsmann, 1912) 216 n. 1.

5. See, e.g., Benzinger, *Archäologie* (1907) 102; Nowack, Lehrbuch, 153–54.

6. Wellhausen, *Geschichte*, 94.

7. The earliest (1898) and most positive in its assessment was that of I. Peritz, "Women in the Ancient Hebrew Cult," *JBL* 17 (1898) 111–48. Other major studies include the following: M. Lohr, *Die Stellung des Weibes zur Jahwe-Religion und -Kult* (Leipzig: Hinrichs, 1908); G. Beer, *Die soziale und religiöse Stellung der Frau im israelitischen Altertum* (Tübingen: J.C.B. Mohr [Paul Siebeck], 1919); and E.M. McDonald, *The Position of Women as Reflected in Semitic Codes of Law* (Toronto: University of Toronto Press, 1931).

8. For an excellent review and assessment of the history of scholarship on women in Israelite religion, see chap. 1 of U. Winter's *Frau und Göttin. Exegetische und ikonographische Stu-*

dien zum weiblichen Gottesbild im alten Israel und in dessen Umwelt (Freiburg and Göttingen: Universitäts-/Vandenhoeck & Ruprecht, 1983). Winter's work, which became available to me only after the completion of my initial draft, exhibits substantial parallels to my own approach and significant accord with my analysis.

9. See, e.g., C.J. Vos, *Woman in Old Testament Worship* (Delft: Judels & Brinkman, 1968); J. Otwell, *And Sarah Laughed: The Status of Women in the Old Testament* (Philadelphia: Westminster Press, 1977); and Winter, *Frau und Göttin.*

10. By "lay" I mean nonbiblical specialist. This literature, which is a product of, or response to, the modern women's movement, is largely, though by no means exclusively, written by women and is characterized by a high degree of existential involvement and political intention (protest and advocacy). In the decades since the appearance of Simone de Beauvoir's *The Second Sex* (New York: Alfred A. Knopf, 1953; French orig., 1949), it has swelled to a flood, establishing itself as a major new category in both religious and secular publishing—and affecting the entire field of publishing in its attention to gendered language and images. While this literature treats a broad range of social, psychological, and historical issues, a recurring theme, in secular as well as religious writings, is the legacy of biblical tradition in Western understanding of the nature and status of women. Recent scholarly attention to women in the biblical world has arisen, in part at least, as an effort to correct and inform the "popular" discussion (cf. Winter, *Frau und Göttin,* 17).

11. Cf. E. Schüssler Fiorenza's groundbreaking work for the New Testament, *In Memory of Her: A Feminist Theological Reconstruction of Christian Origins* (New York: Crossroad Publishing Co., 1983).

12. By cultus I understand the organized, usually public, aspects of religious life centered in a temple, shrine, or other sacred site, maintained by a priesthood and/or other specialized offices and roles, and finding expression in sacrifices, offerings, teaching and oracular pronouncement, feasts, fasts, and other ceremonies and ritual actions. Since our knowledge of Israelite religion is limited almost entirely to the "national" cultus and its several schools of theology or streams of tradition, it is easy to slip from analysis of the cultus to generalizations about the religion. This tendency has been qualified to some extent by the recognition that we have no direct evidence for North Israelite theology and practice and by attempts to recover and reconstruct it from elements surviving within Judean compositions. It is also being qualified by new attention to local or folk traditions of Israelite Yahwism evidenced in extrabiblical texts. The question about women in the cultus, I shall argue, raises the question about the role of the cultus in the total religious life of Israel in an even broader and more radical way.

13. The need for consciously articulated interpretive models has been convincingly argued in recent decades and needs no further defense. It does need reiteration, however, as paucity of evidence intensifies the need. For example, if we assume that the Israelite congregation was composed of all adults, we will picture women as a silent constituent even where no reference is made to their presence. But if we construe the congregation as a body of males, we must give a different account of the missing women—and of the role of the cultus in the society.

14. This is an exceedingly rich and suggestive literature combining descriptive and theoretical interests. It is also expanding so rapidly that it is impossible to list even the most important works. The following is a sample of works I have found useful: M.K. Whyte, *The Status of Women in Preindustrial Societies* (Princeton: Princeton University Press, 1978); M.K. Martin and B. Voorhies, *Female of the Species* (New York: Columbia University Press, 1975); M. Rosaldo and L. Lamphere, eds., *Woman, Culture, and Society* (Stanford: Stanford University Press, 1974); N.A. Falk and R.M. Gross, eds., *Unspoken Worlds: Women's Religious Lives in Non-Western Cultures* (San Francisco: Harper & Row, 1980); E.W. Fernea, *Guests of the Sheik: An Ethnography of an Iraqi Village* (Garden City, N.Y.: Doubleday & Co., 1969); E. Bourguignon et al., *A World of Women: Anthropological Studies of Women in the Societies of the World* (New York: Praeger Publishers,

1980); and S.W. Tiffany, ed., *Women and Society: An Anthropological Reader* (Montreal: Eden Press Women's Publications, 1979).

15. For efforts to identify and counter this bias and an introduction to the study of gender as a major new field of anthropological theory, see especially J. Shapiro, "Anthropology and the Study of Gender," *A Feminist Perspective in the Academy: The Difference It Makes* (ed. E. Langland and W. Gove; Chicago: University of Chicago Press, 1981) 110–29; N. Quinn, "Anthropological Studies on Women's Status" (*Annual Review of Anthropology* 6 [1977] 182–222); and S. Ortner and H. Whitehead, eds., *Sexual Meanings* (Cambridge: Cambridge University Press, 1981).

16. M. Rosaldo, "Woman, Culture, and Society: A Theoretical Overview," Rosaldo and Lamphere, *Women,* 18, and J.K. Brown, "A Note on the Division of Labor by Sex," *American Anthropologist* 72 (1970) 1074–78. Cf. Martin and Voorhies, *Female of the Species,* 276–332, and Whyte, *Status of Women,* esp. 156–73.

17. Rosaldo, "Woman, Culture, and Society," 26–27. See further H. Papanek and G. Minault, eds., *Separate Worlds: Studies of Purdah in South Asia* (Delhi: Chanakya Publications, 1982) esp. 3–53 and 54–78; Fernea, *Guests;* and Martin and Voorhies, *Female of the Species,* 290–95. Women's activities are never completely confined to the home, but sexual division is the rule in both work and play wherever mixed groups are found. See Brown, "A Note"; P.R. Sanday, "Female Status in the Public Domain," Rosaldo and Lamphere, *Woman,* 189–206; and E. Friedl, *Women and Men: An Anthropologist's View* (New York: Holt, Rinehart & Winston, 1975) 8. For Old Testament examples, cf. the young women (*nĕʿārôt*) as distinct from the young men (*nĕʿārîm*) working in Boaz's field (Ruth 2:8, 9; cf. 2:22, 23). Note the sexual division of labor described in 1 Sam 8:11–13. Cf. also Old Testament references to women drawing water (Gen 24:11; 1 Sam 9:11), grinding grain (Job 31:10; cf. Matt 24:41), cooking and baking (1 Sam 8:13; Lev 26:26), and dancing and singing (Exod 15:20; 1 Sam 18:6–7).

18. Rosaldo, "Woman, Culture, and Society," 17, 19–21. Cf. Ortner and Whitehead, *Sexual Meanings,* 4 and passim; P.R. Sanday, *Female Power and Male Dominance* (Cambridge: Cambridge University Press, 1981); and Shapiro, "Anthropology," 118–22.

19. These generalizations summarize an extensive review of descriptive literature and case studies, which cannot be documented here. For a fuller analysis with examples and references, see my forthcoming work.

20. Cf. I.M. Lewis, *Ecstatic Religion* (New York: Penguin Books, 1971) 86–88, 96–97, 101.

21. While the menstrual taboo is cultically defined and regulated, it is so universal a factor of human culture that it may be viewed as a general social concept apart from its specific interpretation and institutionalization in the Israelite cultus.

22. The divorced woman and the widow alone are free of overriding male authority.

23. The consequences and implications of this conflict in ordering, or contrast in defining, the religious priorities for women are far-reaching. In a society in which cultic service is accorded highest value, women are disadvantaged when they are excepted from that obligation. The various attempts within the Old Testament to extend to women obligations and options that were originally formulated with males in mind leave unaddressed the tension between the requirement and the ability to fulfill it.

24. Old Babylonian *amat*-DN names, i.e., "handmaid of [divine name]," exceed *warad*- ("servant-") names proportionally, even when the names of *nadītu* women are excluded as cloister names. The data for these comparisons together with a full analysis of sexual distinction in naming are found in my unpublished study, "Sexual Distinction in Israelite Personal Names: A Socio-Religious Investigation."

25. The cultic assembly is not, I believe, to be understood as a male sect or society (though the early cultus has many of the features of a men's religious organization) but rather as a male-

constituted and directed institution at the center of Israelite society, representing the community as a whole and directing and controlling its life. The way in which it related to the larger community and the understanding of its own constitution seem to have changed over time in the direction of greater openness and inclusiveness, in respect not only to women but also to slaves, dependents, and resident aliens (cf. Deut 16:10– 11, 13–14). See Conclusion.

26. Thus women shared many of the same rights and duties as men, made use of the same aid provided or mediated by the institutions, and, as men, were held accountable by them. Women, in common with men, prayed, consulted oracles, attended festivals and sought justice in the courts, received theophanies and divine commissions, sought oracular judgments and legal redress for wrongs suffered and received punishment for wrongs committed. It appears that they were not as a rule prohibited from general religious practices but rather were hindered from fuller participation by competing interest or duty (see below) or attracted by their own particular circumstances to make use of some means of religious expression more than others.

27. Miriam's historical role is impossible to reconstruct, but her ranking alongside Moses and Aaron suggests a position of considerable importance—and a cultic role. She is not identified by a husband but by her "brothers," the priest and the prophet. The roles of cultic singer and prophet are suggested.

28. The mythic and aetiological character of the narrative does not limit its value as evidence for a women's ritual.

29. The meaning of *nĕbî'â* in the latter case is disputed. It is clear, however, that the term in Isa 8:3 is used as a role designation ("*the* prophetess," not "my wife") whether or not it designates Isaiah's wife, and that it designates one who is to assist in the symbolic act that will complete Isaiah's sign.

30. The term used in Gen 38:21–22 is intended to describe a Canaanite practitioner in a Canaanite (and pre-Israelite) setting. Cf. n. 41, below.

31. Here opponents of Nehemiah. The Greek and Syriac apparently understood the name as masculine.

32. The narrowing of acceptable roles for women is correlated with a general narrowing of options in religious practice. The greater variety of roles and the fuller or more candid descriptions of practice in the premonarchic period in comparison with the later period raises the question whether the earlier practices disappeared or were simply reinterpreted (as heterodox) and/or suppressed. What is allowed to stand in the tradition of the earlier period was interpreted, in part at least, as evidence of the low moral state of the time—a judgment made explicit in the final editing of the Book of Judges (19:1, 30; etc.).

33. Use of the patriarchal traditions as sources for social reconstruction requires particular caution; they depict individuals or families with little attention to social context and treat them as representative or symbolic figures.

34. The one religious activity from which women appear to have been excluded by principle rather than circumstances was the offering of sacrifices, which eventually became the sole prerogative of the priest. The exclusion may ultimately be connected with the menstrual taboo, but it is not confined to periods of menstrual impurity. It appears, rather, to have been common practice elevated to a principle (cf. Winter, *Frau und Göttin*, 38–40) or to have been understood more in symbolic than in practical terms. Efforts to show that women offered sacrifices fail, I believe, in the case of biblical evidence. Presenting a sacrificial offering to the priest is not itself a sacrificial action (contra Peritz, "Women," 126–27) but an act of offering to which all are bound. In the case of the offering required for a woman's purification (Lev 12:6–7), a clear distinction is made between the woman's presentation of the animal to the priest ("she shall bring a lamb . . . to the priest," v 6) and the offering made *by* the priest *for* the woman ("and he shall offer it . . . and make atonement for her," v 7) (cf. Lev. 15:19–33). Nor is the sharing of a sacrificial meal an act of sacrifice, though

it is an important form of cultic participation, as Peritz insists ("Women in the Ancient Hebrew Cult," 123–25). Manoah prepares and offers the sacrifice on behalf of his nameless wife to whom the angel has appeared (Judg 13:19), and Elkanah sacrifices (*wayyizbah*) at the shrine of Shiloh, distributing portions to his wives and children (1 Sam 1:4).

35. J. Renger's study of the Old Babylonian "priesthood" based on the *lú* = *amēlu* list shows only one among the nineteen classes identified as *Kultpriester* in which men and women are identified by a common term, namely, the *en*, the highest ranked and earliest attested office in the list ("Untersuchungen zum Priestertum in der altbabylonischen Zeit" [*ZA* NF 24 (1967) 110–88] 113). The sex of the *en* appears to have been complementary to that of the deity, suggesting that the *en* was understood to represent the divine spouse. The rest of the classes are distinguished by gender and nomenclature and grouped (with the exception of the *entum*, the later Akkadian designation of the female *en*) in the typical hierarchical order of male-female, strongly suggesting sexual division of labor within the cultus rather than shared roles. Despite Renger's use of the term *Priesterinnen* to describe the female classes, they do not appear to have performed activities that would properly be described as "priestly." Use of the term "priestess" to describe such women is misleading, since it suggests comparable, if not identical, roles and equal status with priests.

The third group in the *lú* = *amēlu* list, exorcists, consists of five classes, all male—as we might expect, since these represent offices requiring technical skills and mastery of a body of esoteric knowledge, like the *baru* diviners in the second group. It is only in the second group, comprising the oracular speakers, that we find professional classes with both male and female members, namely, the *šāʾiltum*/ (*šāʿilum*), *maḫḫum, maḫḫūtum,* and *āpilum/āpiltum*. The pattern presented in the Old Babylonian sources corresponds exactly to that which the more meager, and less specialized, Old Testament data suggest: priestly roles involving technical expertise and leadership in the sacrificial cult or other cultic ritual were male, as well as other roles demanding specialized knowledge, while the more charismatic forms of divination open to lay as well as professional practitioners involved women as well as men, just as their Old Testament prophetic counterpart. Cf. R. Harris: "Except for the religious functions of royal women and dream interpretation and divination, women played a minor role in cultic life. Only in the lower echelons of the 'clergy' did female singers, dancers, and musicians participate in the cult" ("Woman in the Ancient Near East," *IDBSup*, 960–63 62).

Syrian and Canaanite sources are too meager to confirm a pattern. The Ugaritic texts contain no reference to any class of female cultic personnel as a recognizable group. Phoenician and Punic sources contain the only known ancient feminine form of *khn* ("priest"). In the Eshmunazar sarcophagus inscription (*KAI,* 14:15) it is applied to the queen of Sidon as royal patron, and hence chief official, of the city god Ashtart. I would interpret this as evidence of a royal cultus in which the king/queen, qua ruler, assumed the title and role of priest/presider in the official cultus, not as evidence for a class of female priests. The status and function of the women bearing this title in several Punic inscriptions (*KAI,* 70:1; 93:1; 145:45[?]; 140:2) cannot be determined. See now J.A. Hackett, *The Balaam Text from Deir ʿAllā* (Chico: Scholars Press, 1984) 25.

36. While the women weavers expelled from the Temple by Josiah were associated with the service of a "foreign" deity or cult object, the Yahweh cultus also had need of such service. According to Exod 34:25–26, the material for the tabernacle hangings was spun by women. The weaving of the hangings, however, was supervised by the master craftsman Bezalel or his male assistant (Exod 34:35), an example of the male professionalization of female crafts observed in cross-cultural studies of gender roles. It is not certain who actually did the work; the *kol ḥăkam-leb bĕʿōśeh hammĕlāʾkāh* ("everyone able to do the work") with its masculine plural verb could be a generic use of the masculine to describe a group of workers of mixed gender.

37. This is suggested on the analogy of work in the domestic sphere, though cultic specialization might well make cooking and baking male activities. Nevertheless it is worth speculating

who prepared the sacrificial victims for the communion meals eaten at the sanctuary and who baked the shewbread. In the report of the "priests' custom with the people" in 1 Sam 2:13–17, it is clear that neither the priest nor the priest's servant is involved in boiling the meat, since the priest's servant takes or demands the portion desired by the priest. The man sacrificing is addressed in 1 Sam 2:15, but did he cook as well as slaughter the animal? Might not his accompanying wife have performed her usual work for the family feast? Or when the sacrifice later became a priestly prerogative, might not women of priestly families have performed this service?

Ezekiel's provisions for the restored Temple include designation of areas for cooking and baking within the Temple complex, carefully separating the place where the priests were to boil the *ᵓāšām* and the *ḥaṭṭāᵓt* offerings and bake the *minḥâ*—which was to be within the inner court (Ezek 46:20)—and the "kitchens" (*bē hammĕbaššĕlîm*) where "those who minister at the Temple" (*mĕšārĕtê habbayit*) were to boil the "sacrifices of the people" (*zebaḥ hā ᶜam*)—which were located in the outer court (Ezek 46:21–24). This late scheme clearly assigns all actions related to the sanctuary to priests, guarding this sphere from that in which the preparation of meals for the people took place. Hearths are provided for the latter purpose and the activity was supervised by a lower class of Temple personnel (not priests). This stage of prescription for the cultus has professionalized actions earlier performed by the worshiper, including the slaughter of the sacrificial victims, which is now assigned to the Levites (Ezek 44:12; cf. Lev 2:4–7 and 3:1–17).

The mention of women as cooks and bakers in the palace service (1 Sam 8:13) may also provide a clue, at least for the earlier period, since the administration of the Temple was similar in many ways to the administration of the palace. A third type of female work mentioned in 1 Sam 8:13, that of "perfumers," has a counterpart in the cultus in the preparation of the holy anointing oil, a special skill described by the use of the same verb (*raqqāḥôt; rōqĕaḥ*, Exod 30:25). However, the distinction in the use of the aromatic oils produced for the cultus may make this a male specialty in the cultic setting.

38. The suggestion is again by analogy to the almost universal assignment of housecleaning to women—or slaves. In large public buildings, palaces, etc., such work is usually done by slaves or low-caste groups, with tasks divided by sex, and that may have been the case in the Temple too. But at local shrines presided over by a single priest, the housekeeping chores of the deity's house might well have fallen to the female members of the priest's family.

39. Women are widely identified with singing and dancing as well as instrumental music-making in both biblical and extrabiblical texts and in pictorial representations (see, e.g., *ANEP*, 63–66, 111, 346; I. Seibert, *Woman in Ancient Near East* [Leipzig: Fortschritt Erfuhrt, 1974], pls. 10, 34, 99; O. Keel, *The Symbolism of the Biblical World* [New York: Seabury/Crossroad, 1978] 336–39). None of these activities was restricted to women (cf. *ANEP*, 63–66, David's reputation as a singer, and his dance before the Ark, 2 Sam 6:14, 16), though some types of instruments and performance may have been regarded as peculiarly or typically female. The "timbrel," (*top*), e.g., appears to have been a preferred instrument of women (cf. Winter, *Frau und Göttin*, 33 n. 164; E. Werner, "Musical Instruments" [*IDB* 3. 469–76] 474); women musicians and dancers are widely attested as professional entertainers of men (cf. the Arabic *shayka*, the Japanese geisha, and the Old Testament image of the prostitute as a troubadour, singing to the tune of her harp [Isa 23:14–15]); and women typically formed a welcoming chorus line to greet warriors returning from battle (Exod 15:20; 1 Sam 18:6). The disputed question is whether women participated as musicians or dancers in cultic celebrations and whether they belonged to the personnel of the sanctuary.

The question is too complex for adequate treatment here. It may be that references to cultic dancing should be eliminated altogether, or at least those described by *māḥôl/mĕḥôlâ* and verbal forms of *ḥwl*, which appear always to designate actions of the congregation or groups of lay women, not a professional activity, and may refer to antiphonal singing rather than dance (see J.M.

Sasson, "The Worship of the Golden Calf," *Orient and Occident: Essays Presented to Cyrus H. Gordon*, AOAT 22 [1973] 151–59 157; cf. Winter, *Frau und Göttin*, 32–33). The function of the three daughters of Heman, mentioned in a parenthetical note in 1 Chron 25:5, is unclear, though the sons constituted a major Levitical guild of musicians in the Second Temple. The *mĕšōrĕrîm ûmĕšōrĕrôt* of Ezra 2:65 clearly represent a different class from the Temple singers described by the same term (masculine plural) in Ezra 2:41; Neh 7:44. Their place in the list following male and female servants and preceding the horses suggests a menial class of entertainers.

It seems likely that the public, professional roles of musicians in the Temple service were assigned to males, at least in the later period of the monarchy and the Second Temple period, while women's specialized musical activity was limited to secular entertainment and funeral dirges (a "home" ritual). The earlier period, however, suggests a different picture in the attribution of two important songs of praise to women, both called prophets (Exod 15:20–21; Judg 4:4; 5:1; cf. 1 Chron 25:1, which describes the function of the Temple musicians as "prophesying" with lyres, harps, and cymbals). While the narrative contexts point to a traditional secular role of women in greeting returning warriors (cf. Winter, *Frau und Göttin*, 33), both texts may also be understood to describe cultic actions, whose setting is the celebration of Yahweh's victories, not simply as one-time historical acts, but as repeated cultic actions recalling the great victories (or does the shift in attribution of the Song at the Sea from Miriam to Moses reflect a cultic institutionalization of the victory song in which the secular/lay role of the woman leader is transformed into a cultic/professional male role?). Psalm 68:26 suggests that in the Temple period at least women formed a recognized group among the Temple musicians *ʿălāmôt tôpēpôt*, mentioned between *šārîm* and *nōgĕnîm* in the procession to the sanctuary; cf. Winter, *Frau und Göttin*, 34–35).

40. The many questions about these women cannot be explored adequately here, much less resolved. For the most recent discussion and review of literature, see Winter, *Frau und Göttin*, 58–65. Both the Samuel and the Exodus passages suggest the persistence of the office or institution after the initiation of the Yahwistic cultus and its tent shrine in the desert. Winter has seen rightly, I believe, that the significant information in the archaic Exodus tradition is the reference to the mirrors (*Frau und Göttin*, 60). For a critique of his interpretation, which views the mirror as the symbol of a female deity associated with fertility and the women as *Hofdamen* visiting the sanctuary, rather than cultic personnel, see my forthcoming work. Cf. J. Morgenstern, "The Ark, the Ephod, and the Tent," *HUCA* 17 (1942–43) 153–265, *HUCA* 18 (1943–44) 1–52, for an interpretation of the women as shrine attendants based on pre-Islamic Arabic parallels.

41. This is not the place to review the evidence and arguments concerning the *qĕdēšâ*. The literature is far larger than that on the women at the entrance to the tent of meeting and the presence of cognates and of presumed parallel institutions in other ancient Near Eastern cultures requires a more thorough investigation and report than this piece permits. Of the three Old Testament references, two suggest a foreign origin or, at least, a non-Yahwistic institution (Deut 23:17 and Gen 38:21–22), while all three parallel the term with *zônâ* ("prostitute"). The cultic nature of the office or role is clear from the etymology and from the one text that describes an activity (Hos 4:14): "[The men] sacrifice with *qĕdēšôt*." Since the term is paired in Deut 23:17 with the masculine *qādēš*—in the reverse of the normal male-female order—any judgment about the *qĕdēšâ* must involve consideration of the whole class of cognate terms. In overview, it appears that the Old Testament usage is so generalized and polemical that it may serve more as a cover term for proscribed cultic roles rather than as the precise designation of a particular office or function. Since all of the masculine references (all apparently collective, except Deut 23:17, and therefore conceivably inclusive) are in Deuteronomic contexts, the possibility must be considered that the term was used in Deuteronomistic circles to describe roles or offices, such as that of the *ṣōbĕʾôt* of the Tent of Meeting, that were at one time considered a legitimate part of the Israelite cultus.

"And the Women Knead Dough"
The Worship of the Queen of Heaven in Sixth-Century Judah

Susan Ackerman

The typical historian of ancient Israelite religion, especially the historian of the first-millennium cult, relies heavily, if not exclusively, on the Bible. This is unavoidable, since the Bible is in essence the only written source (and indeed the only significant source of any kind) that describes the religion of first-millennium Israel and Judah. Yet it has become increasingly obvious to historians of Israelite religion that the Bible's descriptions of the first-millennium cult are highly selective. The biblical materials, which come predominantly from the hands of priests and prophets, present priestly and prophetic religion as normative and orthodox in ancient Israel. Nonpriestly and nonprophetic religious beliefs and practices are condemned as heterodox and deviant. A more nuanced reconstruction of the religion of ancient Israel, however, would suggest that despite the biblical witness neither the priestly nor prophetic cult was normative in the religion of the first millennium. Rather, a diversity of beliefs and practices thrived and were accepted by the ancients as legitimate forms of religious expression.

Uncovering this diverse character of ancient Israelite religion requires a special methodology. First, we must train ourselves to supplement continually the biblical picture of Israelite religion by referring to other sources. Archaeological remains from Israel, especially iconographic and epigraphic materials, are crucial, as is comparative data from the ancient Near East and from elsewhere in the Mediterranean world. This evidence, however, often is sparse and not easily interpreted. Thus, more important methodologically is that we learn to treat our major source, the Bible, differently. We must examine the biblical presentations of the orthodox with an eye to the heterodox, seeking, for example, to look without prejudice at those cultic practices that the biblical writers so harshly condemn. Only when we acknowledge the polemical nature of many biblical texts can we see underlying their words evidence of the multifaceted nature of ancient Israelite religion.

It is this second methodological point in particular that helps illuminate an often overlooked aspect of ancient Israelite religion: women's religion. The all-male biblical writers treat this issue with silence or hostility; still, a careful reading of the biblical texts suggests that the women of Judah and Israel had a rich religious tradition.[1] The women of early sixth-century Judah, for example, devoted themselves to the worship of a goddess called the Queen of Heaven (Jer. 7:16–20; 44:15–19, 25). Indeed, although the prophet Jeremiah makes the women of Judah and Jerusalem the object of his special scorn due to their devotion to the Queen of Heaven (Jer. 44:25), the women are steadfast in their worship of the goddess: baking cakes "in her image" as offerings (Jer. 7:18; 44:19) and pouring out libations and burning incense to her (Jer. 44:15, 19). This devotion in the face of persecution indicates that the worship of the Queen of Heaven was an important part of women's religious expression in the sixth century. Here, by establishing the identity of the goddess called in the Bible the Queen of Heaven,[2] I propose to explore why the women of Judah found this goddess's cult so appealing.

Scholars, unfortunately, have reached no consensus on the identity of the Queen of Heaven. The great east Semitic goddess Ištar,[3] Ištar's west Semitic counterpart, Astarte,[4] the west Semitic goddess Anat,[5] and even the Canaanite goddess Šapšu[6] have been suggested. Other scholars maintain that it is impossible, given the available data, to determine to which of the Semitic goddesses the Queen of Heaven corresponds.[7] Finally, there are some who believe that the Queen of Heaven is not one deity, but rather a syncretistic goddess who combines the characteristics of east Semitic Ištar and west Semitic Astarte.[8]

My own sympathies lie with this latter position, which sees in the Queen of Heaven characteristics of both west Semitic Astarte and east Semitic Ištar. The Queen of Heaven as described in the Bible certainly shares with Astarte many features, first, the title of Queen or some related epithet. In texts from the Egyptian New Kingdom (1570–1085 B.C.E.) Astarte is called "Lady of Heaven."[9] More notably, in the first millennium Astarte bears the title Queen. On the obverse face of the Kition tariff inscription, which lists the monthly expenditures for the temple of Astarte at Kition, Astarte is referred to as "the holy Queen" and "the Queen."[10] The Phoenician hierophant Sakkunyaton also refers to Astarte's queenly role in first-millennium religion. He describes her as the co-regent of King Zeus Demarous (Canaanite Baʿl Haddu) and remarks that she wears on her head a bull's head as an emblem of "kingship" (basileias).[11]

The biblical Queen of Heaven also shares with Astarte an association with the heavens. Astarte's astral features, already indicated in the second millennium by the Egyptian title "Lady of Heaven," are numerous in first-millennium religion. In both the Eshmunazor and the Bodashtart inscriptions from Phoenicia Astarte's sacred precinct in Sidon is called "the highest heavens."[12] Elsewhere in the Mediterranean world Astarte's association with the heavens is suggested by her identification with Greek Aphrodite, the goddess of Venus, the Morning and Evening Star. This identification of Astarte with Aphrodite is made clear by Sakkunyaton, who writes, "the Phoenicians say that Astarte is Aphrodite,"[13] and also by a fourth-century Greek/Phoenician bilingual that translates the Phoenician name "Abdʿaštart the Ashkelonite" as "Aphrodisios the Ashkelonite."[14] Notably, moreover, the Astarte or Aphrodite worshiped by Abdʿaštart and other Ashkelonites was Aphrodite of the Heavens (Aphroditē ourania); Herodotus (1.105)[15] and Pausanius (1.14.7) remark on the cult of Aphrodite of the Heavens in Ashkelon. This correspondence of Astarte with Greek Aphrodite of the Heavens is confirmed by a second-century inscription from Delos dedicated to "Palestinian Astarte, that is, Aphrodite of the Heavens."[16]

Another datum showing Astarte's association with the heavens comes from Pyrgi, a site on the west coast of Italy about thirty miles west-northwest of Rome. The bilingual inscription found at Pyrgi is dedicated in its Phoenician version to Astarte and in its Etruscan form to the goddess Uni. J. Fitzmyer notes that Etruscan Uni is Roman Juno, and, significantly, that Uni is "closely associated" with "Juno of the Heavens" (*Juno caelestis*) in Roman Africa.[17] More evidence, later in date, comes from Herodian, who reports that the Phoenicians call Aphrodite of the Heavens (= Astarte) "Queen of the Stars" (*astroarchē*).[18] Moreover, Apuleius calls Caelestis Venus of Paphos "Queen of Heaven" (*regina caeli*).[19] Latin *Caelestis Venus* is a simple translation of Greek *Aphroditē ourania*, Aphrodite of the Heavens, whom we have identified with Palestinian Astarte.

In addition to the fact that Astarte in her epithets can be associated with the heavens, it is important to note that Astarte has other astral aspects.[20] In her iconography Astarte is symbolized by a star. Like Greek Aphrodite and Ištar, her Mesopotamian counterpart, Astarte is identified with Venus, the Morning and Evening Star. Sakkunyaton also remarks on Astarte's astral features: "When traveling around the world, she [Astarte] discovered a star which had fallen from the sky. She took it and consecrated it in Tyre, the holy island."[21]

A third characteristic Astarte shares with the biblical Queen of Heaven is her close association with fertility. The fertility aspects of the Queen of Heaven are made clear in Jer. 44:17, where the people of Judah claim that when they worshiped the Queen of Heaven, "we had plenty of food and we prospered." Conversely, "since we stopped worshiping the Queen of Heaven and stopped pouring out libations to her, we have lacked everything and been consumed . . . by famine" (44:18). At the same time, the Queen of Heaven seems to have a secondary association with war: according to her followers as quoted in Jeremiah, her proper worship guaranteed that the people "saw no evil" (44:17), but when her cult was abandoned, "we were consumed by the sword" (44:18). Astarte, too, has in addition to attributes of fertility associations with war.

The most striking evidence for Astarte's role as a guarantor of fertility is found in the Hebrew Bible, where the noun *ʿaštārôt*, a form of the divine name Astarte (*ʿaštart*), means "increase, progeny." Astarte's association with fertility is also demonstrated by her characterization as a goddess of sexual love at Ugarit, the thriving Levantine metropolis of the late second millennium. There Astarte plays the role of divine courtesan. This is particularly clear in one text, where El, the high god of the Ugaritic pantheon, sits enthroned at a royal banquet, flanked by Astarte, his lover, and Baʿl Haddu, his regent.[22] This depiction of Astarte as a goddess of sexual love continues into the mid- to late first millennium, as her identification with Greek Aphrodite, the Greek goddess of love, indicates. It is also known from Egypt, where Astarte, along with the goddess Anat, is called one of "the great goddesses who conceive but do not bear."[23]

Astarte's associations with war are in general not as well known as her character as a fertility goddess. An Egyptian New Kingdom stele of Merneptah from Memphis depicts the goddess with shield and spear,[24] and other Egyptian representations of Astarte show her on horseback carrying weapons of war.[25] Pharaoh Thutmose IV (Eighteenth Dynasty) is described as being mighty in the chariot like Astarte.[26] Along with Anat, Astarte is called a shield to Pharaoh Ramesses III[27] and a part of a thirteenth-century king's war chariot.[28] In the second millennium she carries the epithet "Lady of Combat";[29] similarly an Egyptian text from the Ptolemaic period (late first millennium) describes her as "Astarte, Mistress of Horses, Lady of the Chariot."[30] In the Canaanite realm Astarte acts as a war goddess in concert with Horon in Ugaritic mythology.[31] In biblical tradition the armor of the dead Saul is taken by the Philistines to the temple of Astarte (1 Sam. 31:10), which may also indicate the goddess's associations with war.

A fourth reason for identifying Astarte with the biblical Queen of Heaven is that the cult of Astarte has as a crucial element the offering of cakes, a ritual that also plays an important role in the worship of the Queen of Heaven (Jer. 7:18; 44:19). The Kition Tariff inscription mentioned above is again noteworthy, for line 10 of that inscription mentions "the two bakers who baked the basket of cakes for the Queen";[32] the Queen, I have argued, must be Astarte.[33] In addition, W. Culican has drawn attention to a Hellenistic votive model found off the Phoenician coast.[34] The model shows six figures positioned around a domed object. Culican identifies four identical seated females as votaresses. Another female figure stands and is pregnant; Culican believes her to be the fertility goddess, Astarte. This identification cannot be certain, but Astarte's well-attested popularity in the Phoenician and Punic realm in the late first millennium (see below), coupled with her known fertility attributes, make Culican's hypothesis attractive. Culican identifies the sixth figure on the model, a male, as a priest of the goddess. The domed object around which the six figures cluster is interpreted as a beehive oven. Culican proposes the scene is a cake-baking ritual in honor of Astarte. This is a speculative, but, in light of the Kition Tariff inscription and Jer. 7:18 and 44:19, an appealing suggestion.

A fifth and final factor that suggests that the biblical Queen of Heaven is Astarte is the popularity of the goddess Astarte in the west Semitic cult of the first millennium. Hundreds of Phoenician and Punic personal names incorporate the divine element ʿštrt, Astarte.[35] The goddess's name also appears in many Phoenician and Punic inscriptions, both from the Phoenician mainland and from the Mediterranean world and North Africa. The inscription of Paalaštart from Memphis (KAI 48), in addition to other first-millennium Egyptian material cited above, attests to the popularity of Astarte in Egypt. In Israel the Deuteronomistic historians accuse the people of worshiping Astarte in Judg. 2:13; 10:6; 1 Sam. 7:4; 12:10; 1 Kgs. 11:5, 33; and 2 Kgs. 23:13.[36] Also in Sakkunyaton Astarte is an important goddess, a wife of Kronos[37] and, as we have noted, a co-regent with Zeus Demarous/Baʿl Haddu.[38] Astarte is thus a worthy candidate for the Queen of Heaven.

But certain elements of the worship of the Queen of Heaven remain unexplained if we interpret the cult of the Queen of Heaven only as a cult of west Semitic Astarte. For example, the word used in Jer. 7:18 and 44:19 for the cakes baked for the Queen, *kawwānîm*, is used nowhere in the extrabiblical materials that pertain to Astarte. Similarly, the biblical reference to baking cakes "in her image" (Jer. 44:19) cannot be understood by reference to the worship of west Semitic Astarte. Third, west Semitic evidence attests to no special role for women in the cult of Astarte. However, as we will see, these elements in the cult of the Queen of Heaven can be explained if we examine the cult of the east Semitic goddess, Ištar.

Certainly Ištar is a goddess who appropriately bears the title "Queen of Heaven." Indeed, the ancient Sumerian name of Ištar, Inanna, was thought by the subsequent inhabitants of Mesopotamia, the Akkadians, to mean "Queen of Heaven" (reading [*N*]*IN.AN.NA*[*K*]), and thus the name Inanna is routinely rendered in Akkadian texts as "Queen of Heaven" (*šarrat šamē*) or "Lady of Heaven" (*bēlet šamê*).[39] Ištar is also called by related epithets: "Queen of Heaven and the Stars," "Queen of Heaven and Earth," "Lady of Heaven and Earth," "Sovereign of Heaven and Earth," and "Ruler of Heaven and Earth."[40] In the West, too, Ištar is known as "Lady of Heaven." In an Egyptian New Kingdom inscription from Memphis Ištar of Nineveh (called by the ancient scribe Hurrian Astarte[41]) is given this title.[42] Ištar has other astral features in addition to her epithets.[43] In Mesopotamia, for example, Ištar is equated with Sumerian *DIL.BAT*, the Sumerian name of the planet Venus.

Also Ištar is a fertility goddess, as the Mesopotamian stories of Dumuzi/Tammuz and Inanna/Ištar show. These stories tell of the young fertility god, Tammuz, a symbol of prosperity and yield, and his courting and wooing of the maiden Ištar, who represents the communal storehouse in which harvested foodstuffs were kept. Tammuz is successful in his courtship, and the young fertility god and goddess marry. With their sexual union they guarantee fruitfulness in the land and bounty in the storehouse. This is symbolized in the myth by the fact that Tammuz, as his wedding gift to Ištar, brings to Ištar produce to be placed in her storehouse.[44] The identification of Ištar with the grain storehouse in these myths and elsewhere demonstrates her role in guaranteeing continual prosperity and preventing famine, an attribute associated with the Queen of Heaven in Jer. 44:17–18.

Ištar also has associations with war. In the Epilogue to the Code of Hammurapi, Hammurapi calls Ištar "the lady of the battle and of the fight" (Col. 50 [Rs. 27], 92–93). Her powers on the battlefield are clearly indicated by the curse she is to inflict on Hammurapi's enemy (Col. 51 [Rs. 28], 2–23):

> May she shatter his weapon at the battle site. May she establish for him confusion (and) rioting. May she cause his warriors to fail. May she give the earth their blood to drink. May she pile up everywhere on the plain heaps of corpses from his army. May she not take pity. As for him, may she give him into the hands of his enemies. May she lead him, bound, to the land of his enemies!

The myth of Inanna and Ebeh, in which Inanna/Ištar assaults the mountain Ebeh, also attests to Ištar's warring nature.[45]

Lexicographers generally agree that *kawwānim*, the word used for the cakes baked for the Queen of Heaven in Jer. 7:18 and 44:19, is a loan word from Akkadian *kamānu*, "cake."[46] In Akkadian texts *kamānu* cakes are often associated with the cult of Ištar. A hymn to Ištar reads as follows:

> O Ištar, merciful goddess, I have come to visit you,
> I have prepared for you an offering, pure milk, a pure cake baked in ashes
>   (*kamān tumri*),
> I stood up for you a vessel for libations, hear me and act favorably toward me![47]

Another text describes a healing ritual associated with the Ištar cult, in which a cake baked in ashes (*kamān tumri*) is prepared in honor of the goddess.[48] Finally in the Gilgamesh epic, Gilgamesh describes how Tammuz brought ash cakes (*tumru*) to his lover Ištar (Gilg. 6.58–60). Although *kamānu* cakes are not specifically mentioned in the Gilgamesh passage, most commentators assume that the reference to *tumru* is a shorthand expression for the *kamān tumri*, "cake baked in ashes," the cake associated with the Ištar cult in our first two examples.[49]

Scholars who have commented on the biblical cult of the Queen of Heaven are generally puzzled by the phrase "cakes in her image" (*lĕhaʿăṣībāh*).[50] Those holding that the Queen of Heaven is Ištar often explain what "in her image" means by pointing to several clay molds found at Mari, a site in northwest Mesopotamia. These molds portray a nude female figure who holds her hands cupped under her breasts. Her hips are large and prominent.[51] It has been suggested that the molds represent Ištar, and that they were used to shape cakes baked in the image of the goddess. These cakes were then offered to Ištar as part of her sacrificial cult.[52] Although there are problems with this suggestion,[53] the proposal to relate the Mari molds to biblical *lĕhaʿăṣībāh* is intriguing.

Finally, we observe that women seem to have a special place in the Ištar cult. In Mesopotamian mythology, as we have noted, the largest complex of stories about Ištar deals with her courtship and marriage to the young fertility god Tammuz. Tammuz symbolizes in the myths the spring season of prosperity and yield, a season when dates and grain were harvested, calves and lambs were born, and milk ran during the spring milking season. But when the spring harvest season ended, the mythology perceived that the god Tammuz had died.[54] The death of Tammuz was an occasion of sorrow for his young bride, Ištar, and Akkadian mythology preserves many of her laments over her dead lover.[55] And as a woman, Ištar, laments the death of her lover in myth, it is women, devotees of Ištar, who lament Tammuz's passing in the rituals of the Mesopotamian Tammuz cult.[56] The place of women in the Mesopotamian Tammuz cult is vividly illustrated by Ezek. 8:14, where it is women who are specifically identified as those who sit at the gate of the Jerusalem temple's inner court mourning the death of the fertility god. I suggest that it is this special place of women in the cult of Tammuz that is reflected in the biblical materials about the Queen of Heaven.

At first glance, it may seem a long jump from the role of women in the mourning rites of the Tammuz cult to the role of women in baking cakes for the Queen of Heaven. But, in fact, the two are closely related. The *kamānu* cakes associated with the Ištar cult (the *kawwānîm* baked as offerings to the Queen of Heaven) are a staple food of Mesopotamian shepherds.[57] Tammuz is the prototypical and patron shepherd of Mesopotamia. Moreover, as we noted above, in the Gilgamesh epic Gilgamesh describes Tammuz as the one who heaps up ash cakes for his lover Ištar (Gilg. 6.58–60). The cult of Tammuz the shepherd is closely tied to the Ištar cult that involves the baking of offering cakes. The cultic participants who mourn the death of Tammuz are thus the worshipers who bake cakes for Ištar, the Queen of Heaven. And, as women play a crucial role in the ritual mourning over Tammuz, they also play an important role in the cult involving the baking of *kamānu* cakes.

I submit that the Queen of Heaven is a syncretistic deity whose character incorporates aspects of west Semitic Astarte and east Semitic Ištar. This syncretism probably occurred early in Canaanite religious history, well before the sixth century. Certainly the people of Judah, in Jer. 44:17, and Jeremiah himself, in Jer. 44:21, describe the cult as one practiced by past generations. Moreover, we know that the cult of Ištar of Nineveh is attested in Egypt during the New Kingdom[58] and as far west as Spain by the eighth century B.C.E.[59] This would suggest that the cults of Astarte and Ištar were exposed to each other and began intermingling sometime during the last centuries of the second millennium. This syncretism then continued throughout the Iron Age. Indeed, the cult of the Queen of Heaven in the Iron Age prospered, attracting in particular the women of sixth-century Judah and Jerusalem.

But surprisingly, this women's cult did not prosper only in those spheres such as the home and the family where we might expect to find women's religion. To be sure, there is a strong domestic component to the cult, seen especially in Jer. 7:18, where "the children gather wood, the fathers kindle fire, and the women knead dough to make cakes for the Queen of Heaven." But if Jer. 44:17 and 21 are to be taken at all seriously, then the "kings and princes" of Judah are also among those who worshiped the Queen. And, if the worship of the Queen of Heaven was a part of the religion of the monarchy, the Queen's cult may also have been at home in what was essentially the monarch's private chapel, the temple. This is certainly suggested by Ezek. 8:14, where the women who participate in the related cult of wailing over the Queen's deceased lover, Tammuz, sit at the north gates of the temple's inner court. The presence of a temple dedicated to the Queen of Heaven in fifth-century Egypt, a century after Jeremiah, in Jeremiah 44, berates the Judahites who have fled to Egypt for worshiping the Queen of Heaven, is also suggestive.

J.A. Hackett has argued that women in ancient Israelite society had a higher status and more opportunities to hold public and powerful positions in times of social dysfunction.[60] Certainly the calamitous years of the late seventh and early sixth centuries, which witnessed the senseless death of King Josiah, the David *revividus,* in 609, the Babylonian exiles of 597 and 587, the final destruction of the temple by the Babylonians in 587, and the simultaneous end of Judahite political independence, qualify as a period of severe dysfunction. There is, admittedly, little evidence from this period for women wielding political power. But the biblical data about the Queen of Heaven do suggest that the women of late seventh- and early sixth-century Judah and Jerusalem exercised religious power.[61] They worshiped a goddess whose cult they found particularly appealing and went so far as to introduce the cult of that goddess into the temple compound itself.

Since it is winners who write history, the importance of this women's cult in the history of the religion of Israel has been obscured by our sources. The ultimate "winners" in the religion of early sixth-century Judah, the Deuteronomistic historians, the priest-prophet Ezekiel, and the prophet Jeremiah, were men. The biblical texts these men wrote malign non-Deuteronomistic, non-priestly, and non-prophetic religion, and in the case of the cult of the Queen of Heaven they malign the religion of women. But fortunately for us, the sources have not completely ignored some women's cults. The losers have not been totally lost. If historians of Israelite religion continue to push beyond biblical polemic, we should hear more and more the voices of the women of Israel witnessing to their religious convictions.

NOTES

1. See P. Bird's recent article ("The Place of Women in the Israelite Cultus," in *Ancient Israelite Religion: Essays in Honor of Frank Moore Cross*, eds., P.D. Miller Jr., P.D. Hanson, S.D. McBride [Philadelphia: Fortress, 1987], 397–419) for a good introduction to this subject.

2. The consonantal Hebrew text reads *lmlkt*, "to the Queen of" (Jer. 7:18; 44:17,18, 19,25). But the MT vocalizes *limleket*, as if the word were *lmlʾkt*, "to the work of [heaven]," i.e., "to the heavenly host." Indeed, many Hebrew manuscripts read *lmlʾkt* (with an *ʾalep*), which is supported by the Targum and Peshitta and, apparently, by the G in Jer. 7:18 (*tē stratia*). But as is commonly recognized, the Masoretic pointing is an apologetic attempt to remove any hint that the people of Judah worshiped the Queen of Heaven. See R.P. Gordon, "Aleph Apologeticum," *JQR* 69 (1978–79): 112. The correct reading is *lĕmalkat*, "to the Queen of," supported by Symmachus, Theodotian, Aquila, the Vg, and the G of Jer. 44:17,18,19,25.

3. J. Bright, *Jeremiah*, AB 21 (Garden City, N.Y.: Doubleday, 1965), 56; M. Held, "Studies in Biblical Lexicography in the Light of Akkadian," *Eretz Israel* 16 (1982): 76–77 (Hebrew); M.H. Pope, *Song of Songs*, AB 7c (Garden City, N.Y.: Doubleday, 1977), 149 (but see n. 4); W.E. Rast, "Cakes for the Queen of Heaven," in *Scripture in History and Theology: Studies in Honor of J. Coert Rylaarsdam*, eds., A.L. Merrill and T.W. Overholt, PTMS 17 (Pittsburgh: Pickwick, 1977), 167–80; W. Rudolph, *Jeremia*, 3d ed. (Tübingen: J.C.B. Mohr, 1968), 55; M. Weinfeld, "The Worship of Molech and the Queen of Heaven and its Background," *UF* 4 (1972): 148–54; A. Weiser, *Das Buch des Propheten Jeremia*, ATD 20, 21 (Göttingen: Vandenhoeck und Ruprecht, 1952), 70.

4. E. Bresciani and M. Kamil, *Le lettere aramaiche di Hermopoli*, Atti della Accademia Nazionale dei Lincei 8/12 (Roma: Accademia Nazionale dei Lincei, 1966), 400; R. du Mesnil du Buisson, *Etudes sur les dieux phéniciens hérités par l'Empire Romain* (Leiden: Brill, 1970), 126–27; W. Culican, "A Votive Model from the Sea," *PEQ* 108 (1976): 121–22; J. Fitzmyer, "The Phoenician Inscription from Pyrgi," *JAOS* 86 (1966): 287–88; W. Herrmann, "Aštart," *Mitteilungen des Instituts für Orientforschung* 15 (1969): 29, n. 67; W.L. Holladay, *Jeremiah 1*, Hermeneia (Philadelphia: Fortress, 1986), 254–55; M.H. Pope, "ʿAttart, ʿAštart, Astarte," in M.H. Pope and W. Röllig, "Syrien. Die Mythologie der Ugariter und Phonizier," *Wörterbuch der Mythologie*, vol. 1: *Götter und Mythen im vorderen Orient* (ed. H.W. Haussig; Stuttgart: Ernst Klett, 1965), 251 (but see n. 3); M.H. Silverman, *Religious Values in the Jewish Proper Names at Elephantine*, AOAT 217 (Kevelaer: Butzon & Bercker; Neukirchen-Vluyn: Neukirchener Verlag, 1985), 225, n. 6. In a newly published article, which appeared after I had completed my essay, S.M. Olyan also identifies the Queen as Astarte ("Some Observations Concerning the Identity of the Queen of Heaven," *UF* 19 [1987]: 161–74).

5. W.F. Albright, *Yahweh and the Gods of Canaan; A Historical Analysis of Two Contrasting Faiths* (Winona Lake, Ind.: Eisenbrauns, 1968), 130; M. Cogan, *Imperialism and Religion: Assyria, Judah and Israel in the Eighth and Seventh Centuries B.C.E.*, SBLMS 19 (Missoula, Mont.: Scholars, 1974), 85; A.S. Kapelrud, *The Violent Goddess; Anat in the Ras Shamra Texts* (Oslo: Universitetsforlaget, 1969), 13, 16; J. McKay, *Religion in Judah under the Assyrians, 739–609 B.C*, SBT (Second Series) 26 (Naperville, Ill.: A.R. Allenson, 1973), 110–11, n. 19; B. Porten, *Archives from Elephantine; The Life of an Ancient Jewish Military Colony* (Berkeley and Los Angeles: University of California, 1968), 165, 177; A. Vincent, *La religion des Judéo-Araméens d'Elephantine* (Paris: Geuthner, 1937), 635, 649–51.

6. M. Dahood, "La Regina del Cielo in Geremia," *RivB* 8 (1960): 166–68.

7. For example, J. Gray, "Queen of Heaven," *IDB* 3, 975a, b.

8. Note the comments of Fitzmyer, "Pyrgi," *JAOS* 86 (1966): 287, of Rast, "Cakes for the Queen of Heaven," *Scripture in History and Theology*, 170; and cf. Bright, *Jeremiah*, 56. M.H.

Pope may also indirectly indicate his support of such a thesis, since he identifies the Queen of Heaven as Astarte in *Wörterbuch der Mythologie,* 251 (n. 4), but as Ištar in Song, 149 (n. 3).

9. Egyptian *nbt pt.* D.B. Redford ("New Light on the Asiatic Campaigning of Horemheb," *BASOR* 211 [1973]: 37) finds this epithet on a stone bowl of the Eighteenth Dynasty; the bowl is also discussed by M. Delcor ("La culte de la 'Reine du Ciel' selon Jer. 7, 18; 44, 17–19, 25 et ses survivances," *Von Kanaan bis Kerala,* AOAT 211 [Kevelaer: Butzon & Bercker; Neukirchen-Vluyn: Neukirchener Verlag, 1982], 114). For Nineteenth Dynasty inscriptions, see W.M.F. Petrie, *Memphis* 1 (London: School of Archaeology in Egypt and Bernard Quaritch, 1909), 19, and M.G. Maspero, "Notes de Voyage," *Annales du service des antiquités de l'Egypte* 10 (1909): 131–32; Also Delcor, "La culte de la 'Reine du Ciel,'" *Von Kanaan bis Kerala,* 114; W. Helck, *Die Beziehungen Aegyptens zu Vorderasien im 3. und 2. Jahrtausend v. Chr.,* Ägyptologische Abhandlungen 5, 2d ed. (Wiesbaden: Otto Harrassowitz, 1971), 457–58; J. Leclant, "Astarté à cheval d'après les représentations égyptiennes," *Syria* 37 (1960): 10–13, and Fig. 1; R. Stadelmann, *Syrisch-Palästinensische Gottheiten in Ägypten,* Probleme der Ägyptologie 5 (Leiden: Brill, 1967), 104, 106.

10. See *CIS* 86 A; *KAI* 37 A, *mlkt qdšt* (line 7) and *mlkt* (line 10). (I am following the line numbers of *KAI* and most commentators; see further J.B. Peckham, "Notes on a Fifth-Century Phoenician Inscription from Kition, Cyprus (*CIS* 86)," *Or* 37 [1968]: 304, n. 2.) Note that although Astarte is not mentioned by name in lines 7 and 10, the title "queen" in an inscription concerned with the cult and temple of Astarte can refer to no other. This is acknowledged by almost all commentators. See as representative J.C.L. Gibson, *Textbook of Syrian Semitic Inscriptions* 3 (Oxford: Clarendon, 1982), 128, J.P. Healey, "The Kition Tariffs and the Phoenician Cursive Series," *BASOR* 216 (1974): 55; O. Masson and M. Sznycer, *Recherches sur les phéniciens à Chypre,* Hautes Etudes Orientales 2/3 (Genève et Paris: Librairie Droz, 1972), 44; Peckham, "Kition," *Or* 37 (1968): 312–13. The suggestion of H. Donner and W. Röllig (*KAI* 2, 55) that *mlkt* is a mistake for *mlˀkt,* "service," in line 7 (they do not comment on line 10) is surely not correct, as the scribe demonstrates in line 13 that he knows the proper spelling of *mlˀkt,* that is, with an *ˀalep* (see Masson and Sznycer, *Recherches,* 44).

11. Eusebius, *Praeparatio evangelica* 1.10.31. Also in connection with Astarte's royalty note the Tyrian "Throne of Astarte" (*KAI* 17) and the uninscribed "thrones" like it. See J.T. Milik, "Les papyrus araméens d'Hermoupolis et les cultes syro-phéniciens en Egypte perse," *Bib* 48 (1967): 572, and the bibliography listed there.

12. *šmm ˀdrm* in *KAI* 14 (Eshmunazor), 16 and 17; *šmm rmm* in *KAI* 15 (Bodashtart). On *KAI* 14 see further Gibson, *Syrian Semitic Inscriptions* 3, 112; Milik, "Les papyrus araméens," *Bib* 48 (1967): 561 and n. 2 on that page; J. Teixidor, *The Pagan God; Popular Religion in the Greco-Roman Near East* (Princeton: Princeton University, 1977), 39. On *KAI* 15 see F.M. Cross, *Canaanite Myth and Hebrew Epic; Essays in the History of the Religion of Israel* (Cambridge, Mass.: Harvard University, 1973), 142; Gibson, *Syrian Semitic Inscriptions* 3, 112; Milik, "Les papyrus araméens," *Bib* 48 (1967): 597–98; and, especially, O. Eissfeldt, "Schamemrumim 'Hoher Himmel,' ein Stadtteil von Gross-Sidon," *Ras Schamra und Sanchunjaton* (Halle: Max Niemeyer, 1939), 62–67 (No. 14).

13. Eusebius, *Praeparatio evangelica* 1.10.32; translation, H.W. Attridge and R.A. Oden, *Philo of Byblos, The Phoenician History; Introduction, Critical Text, Translation, and Notes,* CBQMS 9 (Washington, D.C.: Catholic Biblical Association of America, 1981), 55.

14. *KAI* 54. Phoenician *ˁbdˁštrt ˀšqlny;* Greek *Aphrodisiou Askalōnitēs.*

15. Note also 1.131 and 3.8.

16. *Astartē palaistinē, Aphroditē ouranią.* See P. Roussel and M. Launey, *Inscriptions de Délos* (Paris: Honoré Champion, 1937), #2305 (*editio princeps:* M. Clermont-Ganneau, "Une dédicace à 'Aštarte Palestinienne,' découverte à Délos," *CRAIBL* [1909]: 307–17). Also see

Delos inscription #1719 in Roussel and Launey (*editio princeps:* A. Plassart, *Délos* 11 [Paris: E. de Boccard, 1928], 287), and the discussions of Delcor, "La culte de la 'Reine du Ciel,'" *Von Kanaan bis Kerala,* 117; R.A.S. Macalister, *The Philistines, their History and Civilization* (London: Oxford University, 1914), 94; McKay, *Religion in Judah,* 51.

17. Fitzmyer, "Pyrgi," *JAOS* 86 (1966): 288. The identification of Astarte with Juno, rather than with Etruscan *Turan,* Roman Venus, the usual equivalent of Greek Aphrodite, need not give pause, given the tremendous fluidity of the great Canaanite goddesses in the first millennium.

18. 5.6.4; pointed out by Delcor, "La culte de la 'Reine du Ciel,'" *Von Kanaan bis Kerala,* 115.

19. *Metamorphoses* 11.2; pointed out by Teixidor, *The Pagan God,* 36. *RES* 921, which reads [ʿš]trt pp[s], confirms that the cult of Palestinian Astarte was known at Paphos. See A. Dupont-Sommer, "Les Phéniciens à Chypre," *Report of the Department of Antiquities, Cyprus, 1974* (Nicosia: Department of Antiquities, Cyprus, and Zavallis Press, 1974), 93–94.

20. In addition to the data cited below, see J.J.M. Roberts, *The Earliest Semitic Pantheon* (Baltimore and London: Johns Hopkins University, 1972) 101, n. 285.

21. Eusebius, *Praeparatio evangelica* 1.10.31, trans., Attridge and Oden, *Philo of Byblos,* 55.

22. *Ugaritica* 5.2 (RS 24.252); see also *CTA* 14.3.146.

23. From the Papyrus Harris; see W.F. Albright, "The North Canaanite Epic of ʾAlʾeyân Baʿal and Môt," *JPOS* 12 (1932): 193, W.F. Albright, *Archaeology and the Religion of Israel* (Baltimore: Johns Hopkins University, 1942), 75; Helck *Beziehungen,* 462; Leclant, "Astarté à cheval," *Syria* 37 (1960): 7; J.B. Pritchard, *Palestinian Figurines in Relation to Certain Goddesses Known throughout Literature,* AOS 24 (New Haven: American Oriental Society, 1943), 79. Also from Egypt, note the plaque of the composite goddess, Qudšu-Astarte-Anat, where the goddess holds a lotus and serpent, symbols of fertility (I.E.S. Edwards, "A Relief of Qudshu-Astarte-Anath in the Winchester College Collection," *JNES* 14 [1955]: 49–51).

24. Petrie, *Memphis* 1, 8, and Pl. 15, No. 37. See also Leclant, "Astarté à cheval," *Syria* 37 (1960): 10–13, and Fig. 1.

25. Leclant, "Astarté à cheval," *Syria* 37 (1960), *passim.* See also the "Lady Godiva" plaque found in D. Ussishkin's excavations at Lachish, which shows a goddess, Astarte, I would argue, standing astride a horse. See. D. Ussishkin, "Excavations at Tel Lachish—1973–1977. Preliminary Report," *Tel Aviv* 5 (1978): 21, and Pl. 8.

26. H. Carter and P.E. Newberry, *The Tomb of Thoutmosis IV,* Catalogue général des antiquités égyptiennes du Musée du Caire 15 (Westminster: Archibald Constable and Co., 1904), 27 and Pl. 10; also *ANET,* 250a and n. 16.

27. W.F. Edgerton and J.A. Wilson, *Historical Records of Ramesses III,* Studies in Ancient Oriental Civilization 12 (Chicago: University of Chicago, 1936), 75, also *ANET,* 250a and n. 18.

28. W.R. Dawson and T.E. Peet, "The So-Called Poem on the King's Chariot," *JEA* 19 (1933): 169 (verso, lines 12–14); also *ANET,* 250a and n. 17.

29. Leclant, "Astarté à cheval," *Syria* 37 (1960): 25.

30. Leclant, "Astarté à cheval," *Syria* 37 (1960): 54–58, especially p. 57, and Pl. 4 (opposite p. 49); *ANET,* 250a, n. 16.

31. *CTA* 2.1.7–8; 16.6.54–57. W. Herrmann has pointed out that the obverse of *PRU* 5.1 (19.39) also describes Astarte as a war goddess (Herrmann, "Aštart," *Mitteilungen des Instituts für Orientforschung* 15 [1969]: 7–16).

32. For the reading (lʾpm ‖ ʾšʾpyt tnʾ hlt) and translation adopted here, see Peckham, "Kition," *Or* 37 (1968): 305–6. Peckham is followed by Gibson, *Syrian Semitic Inscriptions* 3, 124–25, and by Masson and Sznycer, *Recherches,* 26–27, 28–29. Healey ("Kition," *BASOR* 216 [1974]: 54) offers an alternative reconstruction, lʾpm ‖ ʾšʾp mntspʾ hlt lmlkt, "For the two bakers, who baked choice food, loaves for the Queen."

33. Among those who associate the reference in the Kition inscription with the worship of the Queen of Heaven, see Culican, "A Votive Model," *PEQ* 108 (1976): 122; Delcor, "La culte de la 'Reine du Ciel,'" *Von Kanaan bis Kerala*, 110–12; Peckham, "Kition," *Or* 37 (1968): 314–15, and n. 2 on p. 315.

34. Culican, "A Votive Model," *PEQ* 108 (1976), *passim*.

35. Cf. J. Tigay, *Ye Shall Have No Other Gods: Israelite Religion in the Light of Hebrew Inscriptions*, Harvard Semitic Studies 31 (Atlanta: Scholars, 1986); idem, "Israelite Religion: The Onomastic and Epigraphic Evidence," *Ancient Israelite Religion*, 157–94.

36. The G, in addition, reads *Astartē* for MT *ʾăšērâ* in 2 Chr. 15:16 and *Astartais* for MT *ʾăšērîm* in 2 Chr. 24:18. In 2 Chr. 15:16, which describes how Maʾacah, the queen mother, made an abominable image for the goddess, the MT is clearly primitive.

37. Eusebius, *Praeparatio evangelica* 1.10.22, 24.

38. Eusebius, *Praeparatio evangelica* 1.10.31.

39. O. Edzard, "Inanna, Ištar," in "Mesopotamien. Die Mythologie der Sumerer und Akkader," *Wörterbuch der Mythologie*, 81; A. Falkenstein, *Die Inschriften Gudeas von Lagas* 1, *Einleitung*, AnOr 30 (Roma: Pontificium Institutum Biblicum, 1966), 78–79; W. Helck, *Betrachtungen zur grossen Göttin und den ihr verbundenen Gottheiten*, Religion und Kultur der alten Mittelmeerwelt in Parallelforschungen 2 (Munchen und Wien: R. Oldenbourg, 1971), 73; Held, "Biblical Lexicography," *Eretz Israel* 16 (1982): 80, n. 24; S.N. Kramer, *The Sumerians: Their History, Culture, and Character* (Chicago: University of Chicago, 1963), 153.

40. *šarrat šamê u kakkābani, šarrat šamê u erṣeti, bēlet šamê (u) erṣeti, etellet šamê (u) erṣetim, malkat šamāmī u qaqqari*. See K. Tallqvist, *Akkadische Gotterepitheta*, StudOr 7 (Helsinki: Societas Orientalis Fennica, 1938), 39, 64, 129, 239–40; cf. 333–34.

41. Albright, *Yahweh and the Gods of Canaan*, 143, n. 88; F.M. Cross, "The Old Phoenician Inscription from Spain Dedicated to Hurrian Astarte," *HTR* 64 (1971): 192; Helck, *Beziehungen*, 459–60; idem, *Betrachtungen*, 213–16; Stadelmann, *Gottheiten*, 107.

42. For this inscription, see E. von Bergmann, "Inschriftliche Denkmäler der Sammlung ägyptischer Alterthümer des österr. Kaiserhauses," *Receuil de travaux* 7 (1886): 196; also the comments of Culican, "A Votive Model," *PEQ* 108 (1976): 122; H. Ranke, "Ištar als Heilgottin in Agypten," *Studies Presented to E Ll. Griffith* (London: Oxford University, 1932), 412–18; Stadelmann, *Gottheiten*, 107; John A. Wilson, "The Egyptians and the Gods of Asia," *ANET*, 250, n. 19. Also note a second Memphis inscription in which Hurrian Astarte (Ištar of Nineveh) is called Lady of Heaven. See H. Madsen, "Zwei Inschriften in Kopenhagen," *Zeitschrift für Ägyptische Sprache und Altertumskunde* 41 (1904): 114, and the comments of Culican, "A Votive Model," *PEQ* 108 (1976): 122.

43. See Edzard, "Inanna, Ištar," *Wörterbuch der Mythologie*, 85–86.

44. See T. Jacobsen, "Fourth Millennium Metaphors. The Gods as Providers: Dying Gods of Fertility," *The Treasures of Darkness* (New Haven and London: Yale University, 1976), 23–73.

45. See S.N. Kramer, *Sumerian Mythology* (Philadelphia: American Philosophical Society, 1944), 83.

46. See as representative *AHW*, 430a, s. v. *kamānu; HALAT* 2, 444a, b, s. v. *kawwān;* KB, 428a, s. v. *kawwān*. See also A. Jeremias, *Das Alte Testament im Lichte des Alten Orients*, 3d ed. (Leipzig: J.C. Hinrichs, 1916), 611–12; H. Zimmern, *Akkadische Fremdwörter* (Leipzig: J.C. Hinrichs, 1916), 38; Held, "Biblical Lexicography," *Eretz Israel* 16 (1982): 76–77.

47. The text can be found in J.A. Craig, *Assyrian and Babylonian Religious Texts* 1 (Leipzig: J.C. Hinrichs, 1885), 15:20–22. For transcription, translation, and notes, see E. Ebeling, "Quellen zur Kenntnis der babylonischen Religion, II," MVAAG 23/2 (1918), 4, lines 20–22, and 12.

48. The text can be found in E. Ebeling, *Keilschrifttexte aus Assur religiösen Inhalts* 1 (Osnabrück: Otto Zeller, 1972), 42:25. For transcription, translation, and some notes, see Ebeling, "Quellen, II" MVAAG 23/2 (1918), 22, line 25, and 27.

49. So, for example, *AHW,* 1370b, s. v. *tumru*(*m*); A.L. Oppenheim, "Mesopotamian Mythology II," *Or* 17 (1948): 36, n. 6; H.W.F. Saggs, *The Greatness that was Babylon* (New York: Hawthorn, 1962), 395; A. Schott and W. von Soden, *Das Gilgamesch-Epos* (Stuttgart: Reclam, 1977), 52; E.A. Speiser, "The Epic of Gilgamesh," *ANET,* 84b. But cf. A. Heidel, *The Gilgamesh Epic and Old Testament Parallels* (Chicago: University of Chicago, 1946, 1949), 51, who translates "charcoals." Against Heidel's translation, see B. Landsberger, *Der Kultische Kalender der Babylonier und Assyrer,* Leipziger Semitistische Studien 6/1–2 (Leipzig: J.C. Hinrichs, 1915), 121, n. 1.

50. Reading *lĕha ʿăṣībāh* for MT *lĕha ʿăṣībâ*. On suffixal *hē* without *mappiq,* see GKC, 56g and cf. 91e.

51. The molds were first published by A. Parrot, *Mission archéologique de Mari* 2. *Le palais-documents et monuments* (Paris: Geuthner, 1959), 37–38, and Pl. 19. For a readily accessible photograph of the largest and best-preserved mold, see A. Malamat, "Mari," *BA* 34 (1971), Fig. 9 (p. 21), or Pope, *Song,* Pl. 1 (opposite p. 360).

52. This is proposed by Rast, "Cakes for the Queen of Heaven," *Scripture in History and Theology,* 171–74, and by Pope, *Song,* 379. See also Holladay, *Jeremiah* 1, 254.

53. A. Parrot writes (*Le palais,* 37), "L'identification nous échappe: simple mortelle, femme de haut rang, divinité?"

54. Although seasonal interpretations of ancient Near Eastern myths are often unwarranted, the myths of Tammuz do seem best understood as having agricultural concerns as their main (but not exclusive) focus.

55. See, for example, the laments collected in Jacobsen, *Treasures of Darkness,* 49–50, 53–54.

56. Although facile equations of myth and ritual must be avoided (see, most recently, R.S. Hendel, *The Epic of the Patriarch: The Jacob Cycle and the Narrative Traditions of Canaan and Israel,* HSM 42 [Atlanta: Scholars, 1987], 69–71; in addition to Hendel's references, note W. Burkert, *Homo Necans: The Anthropology of Ancient Greek Sacrificial Ritual and Myth* [Berkeley, Los Angeles, London: University of California, 1983], 29–34), it is acknowledged by all commentators that the Mesopotamian myth of Tammuz is to some degree reflective of and at the same time reflected in Mesopotamian ritual and cult.

57. See CAD K (vol. 8), 111a, s. v. *kamānu:* "Baked in ashes, the *k.*-cake seems to have been a dish of the shepherd"; also note the references listed there.

58. See above; also Helck, *Beziehungen,* 458–60; idem, *Betrachtungen,* 213–16.

59. See Cross, "Hurrian Astarte," *HTR* 64 (1971): 189–95.

60. J.A. Hackett, "In the Days of Jael: Reclaiming the History of Women in Ancient Israel," in *Immaculate and Powerful: The Female in Sacred Image and Social Reality,* eds. C.W. Atkinson, C.H. Buchanan, M.R. Miles (Boston: Beacon, 1985), 15–38.

61. It is perhaps not coincidental that Huldah, the first prophetess reported by the biblical writers since the period of the League, is active at approximately the same time, the last quarter of the seventh century (2 Kgs. 23:14–20).

Women and the Domestic Economy of Early Israel

Carol Meyers

Introduction

The investigation of women's history no longer needs justification. Years of research have made the recovery of the female past a field of its own, or a sub-discipline within the various fields of historical research.[1] The energies and resourcefulness of the current generation of scholars are meeting the difficulties of a remote subject matter and of a relative paucity of sources.

When it comes to investigating women in the biblical past, a particular problem emerges that is not present, or at least is not felt so strongly in other areas of historical inquiry. Modern Western culture has been shaped by biblical[2] images and ideas. Yet these images and ideas typically do not exert their influence in their original context or with their Iron Age meanings, but rather as they have been transmitted and interpreted by post-biblical Christian and Jewish traditions. This is particularly true with biblical materials that relate to women. Many of the traditional interpretations of biblical texts dealing with gender implicitly or explicitly involve ideas of female inferiority or submissiveness as they emerged in late biblical or post-biblical settings. A case in point is the Eden story. Our familiarity with that narrative and our sense of what it means are colored more by the New Testament (especially I Timothy 2:11–15) and by Milton's *Paradise Lost* than by an analysis of the original Hebrew text.[3] Similar readings or misreadings of biblical texts on the ideological level, and to the detriment of women, are present in all sorts of contemporary secular as well as religious contexts. Consequently, recovering the position of women in the Israelite world means not only searching for clues in the texts of ancient Israel and in the material remains of the Israelite world, but also breaking through the incredibly strong web of post-biblical interpretations.

The focus in this paper is not on women in the Bible or on biblical women but rather on women in ancient Israel. As the methodological discussion will make clear, these two groups are not necessarily the same. Even though there is a general assumption that the Bible is an accurate reflection of at least some aspects of Israelite society, and although this assumption may be valid at many levels, when it comes to gender it must be carefully examined. Theologians and feminists alike need to be cautious in drawing conclusions about Israelite women from biblical texts[4] not only because an overlay of interpretation may occlude the texts but also because the texts themselves may not have a one-to-one correspondence with reality.

Methodological Considerations and Analytical Perspectives

1. Perhaps the most difficult problem confronting the researcher's attempt to discover the role and status of women in Israelite society is the procurement of data. To be sure, the Bible is an unparalleled source of information about ancient Israel. Without it, even with all that archaeology and other Near Eastern materials have provided, we would be quite in the dark about Israelite life and history. Yet the Bible as an informant about gender relations is a biased source of information; and those biases must be recognized.

Just what are its biases? First and foremost, from the perspective of feminist inquiry, is the fact that the Bible was written almost entirely by males. The Pentateuch, complicated and ancient as its components may be, is in its final redaction a product of priestly activity (and only men were priests). Most of the historical books stem from the royal court in Jerusalem and its bureaucrats, that is, from a king and his male courtiers. Occasionally women's voices can be heard. Some early poems are attributed to women; and one biblical book, the Song of Songs, may be a woman's composition. But the bulk of biblical writings must be attributed to male authorship. The social distance of females from the shapers of sacred tradition has its effect in the androcentric orientation of biblical writings. This androcentric aspect of the Bible has several implications for attempts to understand women's lives: 1) Relatively little attention or mention is given in the Bible to women's lives or concerns, except insofar as they are part of "all Israel," which is the overriding focus of the biblical authors. 2) The perspective on issues which do impinge on women's lives is a male one and cannot be expected to represent situations as they might be seen from a female perspective.

Second, the Hebrew Bible by its very nature is largely concerned with public and/or national life. For most (but not all; see below) of Israelite history, public life was almost exclusively male life. Leadership positions, with several notable exceptions, were held by men. Israel's very existence, in the much fought-over territory of Iron Age (1200–587 BCE) Palestine, was contingent upon military and political manipulation. The army was a male institution, as were the political and government bodies. With the public sector being almost exclusively male, the chief public document (the Bible) was inevitably the result of male literary and chronistic activity.

Third, the Bible is in large measure a product of urban life, and mostly the life of one atypical city, Jerusalem, the seat of the political and religious institutional life of Israel for the greater part of its existence. Because of this, the Bible does not properly deal with rural and/or non-Jerusalem life. But Jerusalem was an exceptional city in the ancient Levant.[5] Thus the biblical orientation to Jerusalem is at the expense of a perspective on rural life and even on life in other cities. Even though there were a number of other urban centers in Israel, they were not cities like Jerusalem and certainly not like cities in our post-industrial world. Ancient Palestinian cities were tied to the agricultural hinterland.[6] Israel was an agrarian society; and the urban segment of such societies was never larger than ten percent and was more likely to have been below five percent.[7] The large majority of the population were peasant farmers living in small, relatively isolated villages.

A fourth point, not itself a bias but nonetheless a problem deriving from the nature of the biblical materials, is a chronological one. The Bible spans almost a thousand years in its compositional history and even longer in the history of its subject matter. Hebraic society underwent radical changes during that span. Hence biblical materials concerning gender cannot necessarily be lumped together for an overview of biblical women let alone of Israelite women; the chronological place of individual texts must be taken into account, and this is sometimes impossible.

For all these reasons, and others that our next few points will touch on, the Bible is a biased informant and must be used very cautiously as a source for women's history.

2. Our next methodological consideration concerns the relationship between formal gender arrangements and social reality. Ethnographic research has revealed that there is normally a disjunction between societal ideas or ideology (as expressed in laws, for example, or in normative narratives) and social behavior. Sir Edmund Leach's warning to anthropologists is relevant to investigators of Israelite antiquity: "The observer must distinguish between what people do and what people say they do; that is between normal custom as individually interpreted on the one hand and normative rule on the other . . . [The researcher] must distinguish behavior from ideology."[8] Insofar as we are interested in behavior, ideology-bearing sources must be treated circumspectly. For ancient Israel as for any society, ideology cannot be simply equated with daily reality, which can diverge from the normative expression contained in the sacred texts.

Related to the above point is the difficulty in evaluating the existence of the signs of patriarchal structures, such as the patrilineal transferral of property across generations and the patrilineal organization of social units, in terms of the effective power of such structures in the dynamics of gender relationships in daily life. The apparent hierarchical control of men over women may have been functionally far less powerful than might be expected. Again, anthropologists have pointed out that formal rights may favor males but that daily informal interaction may exhibit a "balance of gender power" or even some signs or areas of female dominance.[9] This is particularly true in certain social and economic circumstances, such as those obtaining in early Israel (see below). While agrarian societies exhibit clear gender distinctions that have great functional value and that are often "elaborated in cultural ideologies,"[10] such distinctions do not necessarily signify actual differentials of power.

3. Our contemporary assumptions that male prerogatives and privileges are innately more valued than those of females[11] should not be automatically superimposed upon an ancient society. Such assumptions have been shaped by the course of events in the industrialized West and may not be appropriate for the assessment of a pre-modern, oriental culture. For this reason, the very use of the term "patriarchal," which has implicit connotations of hierarchical arrangements that devalue females, cannot be easily applied to Israelite society. The term itself is controversial. Not only are there a variety of definitions attached to it, but also the origins and functions of patriarchal systems are much debated.[12] Some researchers would prefer not to use it.[13] For ancient Israel, especially for the pre-state period to which we shall soon turn our attention, the idea of patriarchy and its assumptions of male superiority should be avoided. Contemporary Western

measures of status, role, value, etc. cannot be simply transposed to a radically different setting.[14]

4. Related to the above point about assumptions of gender value in contemporary versus ancient societies is the very problem of the legitimacy of evaluating the role of an individual person living in an ancient agrarian society. As for most agrarian or peasant societies, the Hebraic concept of the individual was not developed in ways in which it is in the modern world.[15] Although it is normal for us to think of persons as autonomous human beings and to differentiate ourselves as individuals from social relationships and family ties, it would have been rare for the ancient Israelite to have done so in quite the same way. People experienced themselves relationally rather than through individuation and separation. Thus, while males and females had sharply defined roles, such roles were seen as integrally related, as parts of a whole piece that contributed to the survival and welfare of the group. This communal orientation means that one cannot really consider the exploitation of individuals in the same way that we do in the modern world. Individual existence is subsumed into a corporate structure in a way essential for group survival. Thus the possibility of dehumanizing or abusive behavior toward categories of individuals that were integral to the basic units of social organization may have been virtually nonexistent.

The probable lack of a separate concept of individual identity does not mean that highly differentiated roles for individuals did not exist. On the contrary, defined roles—positions in society filled by individuals in response to recurring needs—were of critical importance.[16] But the very fact that specific roles along age and gender lines were of crucial importance meant that the social group depended on the individuals fulfilling those roles and that those individuals operated to meet group needs, not individual needs.

5. Finally, as the above considerations have indicated, biblical texts alone are not sufficient nor reliable for the reconstruction of gender roles in early Israel. The potential for reaching the Israelite woman lies in the use of extra-biblical materials provided by archaeology as well as in the examination of biblical texts; and it also involves the application of social scientific analytical perspectives. The task of investigating the lives of Israelite women must begin with the Iron I Period, ancient Israel's formative period. Patterns of gender relationships, as of many aspects of Israelite life, were established in the early centuries of Israelite existence. Despite the often radical shifts in political and social organization that subsequently occurred, residuals of the pattern established early in Israelite history would have been sustained well into the Iron II Period, the era of monarchic rule.

Thus our focus is on the reconstruction of the social fabric of Israelite life in the pre-monarchic age. Archaeological work in the past two decades, as influenced by the goals and methods of the "new archaeology,"[17] has made significant strides in investigating the small, isolated, highland villages that all too often had been ignored by earlier generations of archaeologists, who were interested in political history and monumental remains. The work on those villages of the hill country that most investigators are willing to call "Israelite" enables us to establish, first, what the environmental conditions were for emergent Israel, and then what the economic, social, and political responses were to those conditions. This kind of analysis draws heavily upon social scientific methodologies for understanding the structure of the society represented by the inhabitants of these villages.

As helpful as archaeology is in establishing the setting in which Israelite women lived, it has frustratingly little to tell us about their lives. Like the Bible, archaeology cannot easily or directly be used to reconstruct the place of women. While archaeology is extremely helpful in its attention to the physical context of the ancients, direct correlation between artifacts or structures and gender is rarely possible. Archaeological remains, however we wish it were otherwise, are rarely "gender noisy." Yet the information now available about early Israelite villages lends itself to the application of further social scientific models. Using analogies from the study of societies with similar economic and domestic patterns, we can begin to visualize what roles women played in Israelite life in a way that would not be possible were we to use only the biblical text or only the artifactual remains.

Women in Early Israelite Society

1. Establishing the place of women in Israelite society depends, first, on examining the nature of early Israel's environment and technology as they would have impinged upon gender roles. Much recent research material[18] deals directly with Israel's environment and with the technological and social adaptation of early Israel to that environment. The conclusions of this historical, material-cultural research as it relates to gender roles can be briefly summarized, especially as it reveals aspects of the labor requirements in the highland villages of the early Iron Age.

First, early Israel was a pioneer society. The numerous highland sites assumed to be Israelite were situated in underdeveloped areas of the central hill country, areas that were rocky, forested, and under-watered. The demands of such an environment involved substantial commitments of labor, largely by men, for clearing the overgrowth, digging cisterns to create a year-round water supply, and constructing terraces to help retain water and to provide flat land for horticultural development and also for field crops where the intermontane valleys were few and small. All of these activities required large outputs of labor.[19] The construction of terraces, for example, while a great boon to the Israelite settlers and perhaps the *sina qua non* of dry farming in the highlands, required not only substantial initial efforts but also an ongoing, relatively large investment of labor, particularly during the rainy season and often at times when the agricultural calendar imposed other heavy labor demands.[20] That is, the agrarian economy of the highland villages involved labor-intensive periods.

Second, Israel came into existence at a time in which the population of the eastern Mediterranean world in general was in decline, in which famine, disease, and warfare in the preceding Late Bronze Age had reduced the already short life expectancy of the ancients.[21] Excavation of tombs and paleopathological analysis indicate lowered lifespans for both males and females, with female life expectancies being up to ten years less than those of males.

These factors—the demographic decline of that era, along with the existence of a labor-intensive economy and the extra labor needs of the pioneer period—would have had several important implications for women's lives. First, the labor requirements of Israelite families, as of all farm families, meant an emphasis on large families. The domestic use of child labor was critical for the maintenance of food supply, which is the overriding priority of agrarian peoples.[22] The maternal imperative was thus especially strong for

early Israel. Biblical passages emphasizing female fertility and the overcoming of barrenness must be understood in this context: they give ideological sanction to the adaptive
strategy of increasing birthrate. As in many agrarian societies, beliefs and practices promoting fertility are "fundamental to the adaptive strategies by which agrarian parents"
obtain their immediate survival and also secure their long-term security.[23] Second, high
labor demands meant the active participation of women in agrarian work. The intensifi-
cation of woman's productive as well as reproductive tasks is typical of agrarian societies
with an agricultural calendar involving labor intensive periods. Especially when there
exist pioneer tasks that typically fall to males and when there are sporadic military
encounters drawing males away from the family lands, females participate in more of the
"everyday" agricultural jobs than might otherwise be the case.[24]

The two female roles—the productive and the reproductive—should not be seen
as competing or incompatible, as they are in the modern Western world. Bearing and
caring for children are subsumed into the daily routine in agrarian settings, and the
labors of childbirth do not radically disrupt female subsistence labors.[25] Having children
was normally not viewed as a discrete role that precluded or interfered with other social
and economic roles.

2. This general picture of the highland setting and its labor and reproductive
imperatives for women can be supplemented by delineating the specific social setting—
the actual structures—in which the villagers lived. In looking at living arrangements,
both the physical and social configurations of daily life are significant.

The archaeological recovery of highland village sites has revealed a number of
salient features. First, the relative absence of imported wares or other indications of a
market economy suggests that the villages were relatively self-sufficient. Second, the fact
that the living units are mostly the same size points to a relatively egalitarian social structure. Third, the existence of individual installations, within each household area, for
commodity processing and storage, and the concomitant absence of public works as
would indicate centralizing governmental structures, shows the household units to be
relatively autonomous. These general features of highland villages and their component
units have been supplemented by further sociological analysis, most notably by Stager's
work on the "Archaeology of the Family."[26] His study of the village plans and of the configuration of structures has produced an understanding of the dwelling units themselves
and also a sense of how they relate to levels of social organization.

The highland villages in the early Iron Age consisted not of nuclear family dwellings but rather of dwelling clusters or residential compounds, with two or three small
dwellings structurally linked and sharing facilities for food production, processing, and
storage. Such units, which can be related, though imperfectly, to the biblical term *beth
ʾav*, were occupied by compound family groupings. Social scientific study of the history
of the family[27]—in this case better designated "family household" to accommodate the
way in which the household involved related persons and also the residential quarters,
outbuildings, tools and equipment, livestock, and even fields and orchards[28]—indicates
that such groupings were atypical. Compound families, whether extended vertically or
horizontally, are difficult to manage and often involve complex and tense interpersonal
relations.[29] They apparently emerge in response to particularly difficult problems of subsistence, when the pooling of labor and of resources increases chances of survival.

Therefore, in a setting in which women have a large economic role, by supplying labor through their children and on their own, we see households that are larger and more complex than the norm. This datum must then be set against the fact that in tribal Israel, with its relative lack of social, political, and economic hierarchies, the locus of power was at the bottom of the social structure,[30] viz., with the family household. (Thereafter, with the rise of the monarchy and centralized structures, the base of power shifted to the top.)

3. The role of women within such autonomous and complex household groups can be theoretically reconstructed. The economic role of the female was, as we have already suggested, crucial. Women were undoubtedly involved in all aspects of economic life: in producing, transforming, and allocating resources. Much of what they did required considerable technological skill. While we cannot be sure exactly which tasks they performed, we can be fairly certain that the differentiation of tasks by gender (and age) meant female expertise in and control of a range of indispensable activities. The economic roles of women included not only tasks performed but also, with respect to senior females in a multiple family compound, the management of the activities of others: other females to be sure, and probably also younger males. Fulfillment of distinct economic roles by both females and males in agrarian societies creates efficiency in carrying out tasks essential for food production and thus for survival. It also functions socially, stimulating cooperation and interdependence and thereby strengthening group life.[31]

Female participation in societal roles, of course, was not limited to the crucial economic tasks.[32] Parenting—the socialization and education of the young—was inextricably linked to maternity and was interwoven with the technological specialties of the females. Transmission of many aspects of culture was thus part of the female's role; children of both genders absorbed modes of behavior, cultural forms, and social values from the direct or indirect instructions of the mother. One particular aspect of this culture transmission function, which another paper in this collection describes,[33] is the place of women in the formal and informal religious or ritual activities that took place within the household and in local village settings. Clearly women played active, diverse, and vital roles in the complex households of early Israel.

Although the existence of complex families is believed, in many traditional social scientific arguments, to be related to hierarchical structures in which males dominate, this predicted relationship is *not* borne out for pre-state societies. On the contrary, the power accruing to women by virtue of their technical contributions to family subsistence is augmented when there are more family members involved.[34] Thus, in their managerial roles, senior females gained authority—the recognized right to control—by virtue of having more people with whom to interact. As expressed for ancient Israel by the fifth command of the Decalogue and by the seemingly harsh case laws related to that commandment,[35] filial obedience to mother as well as father was imperative for maintaining order and accomplishing subsistence activities, and was no doubt sanctioned in customary and then in Pentateuchal law.

We can thus re-vision the place of women in pre-monarchic village households and suggest that the vital productive and reproductive roles of women, along with their essential social and socializing roles, created a situation of gender complementarity that is consonant with the date supplied by cross-cultural studies.[36]

4. The implications of this reconstruction of female roles in early Israel, in which a situation of near parity of female and male contributions existed and in which females exerted control over significant tasks and over numbers of persons, become clear when the context we have delineated is set against the analytical opposition of domestic and public realms found in much of the social scientific discussion of female roles and status.[37] Thus far we have refrained from using the term "domestic" in reference to the arena of female activity in early Israel because, in the pre-monarchic period, there was a marked lack of formal supra-household structures or professions that would be labeled "public." Thus, to use the term "domestic" for household would be to suggest an alternate "public" realm, which hardly existed at all during the tribal period. With the family household being the dominant level of social organization, the role of the female therein constituted a general, one might even say a "public," role. As long as the society was based on a household production system, and as long as there was a relative absence of the public hierarchies that usually favor males, females would have had great social impact, beyond the household. Female control of certain aspects of household life was not a trivial matter in a context in which the family household was the primary economic and social unit and in which determinative social forms lay at the bottom rather than at the top.

5. This discussion can come full circle now by suggesting that there are, in fact, biblical texts that reflect the social situation we have described and that have survived the growing androcentrism of Israelite society as it moved into its long centuries of monarchic existence. I have treated some of these texts elsewhere at considerable length; some have been discussed by others; and still others remain to be examined. All such texts deserve more extensive analysis than can be provided here. But nonetheless several examples can be mentioned briefly.

First, consider the exceptional nature of the Book of Judges. With respect to women it deals specifically with the pre-state period, and it is marked by an unusual number of stories involving females. Perhaps women are not so marginalized in these narratives as they are elsewhere in Hebrew scripture because the pre-state social milieu of the Judges stories is one in which women were central figures.[38]

Second, consider the Song of Songs, with its largely non-public setting and its concomitant favoring of female figures and modes over male ones, despite the basic mutuality of the relationship of the woman and the man in the poems. Note also that the figurative language of Canticles contains power imagery—military forms and fierce animals—exclusively in relationship to the female.[39]

Third, consider the function of the Eden story in Genesis 2–3 as a wisdom tale, to enhance the acceptance by both females and males of the often harsh realities of highland life and to provide ideological sanction for large families and for intense physical toil in subsistence activities.[40]

Fourth, consider, as C. Camp has done,[41] the images of female wisdom against the backdrop of female creativity, female instruction in household contexts, and possibly superior female skills in interpersonal relationships (females being less able to resort to force and therefore more adept at finding alternative, indirect ways to resolve conflict).

Fifth, consider that many of the legal materials that seem to favor males over females are related to property transmission and may be a response to informal female controls interfering with the expected male domination in a patrilineal system.[42] Furthermore, it is not appropriate to generalize authoritative or dominant behavior from one category of interaction to all categories or even to assume that the concept of dominance always existed and meant the same as it does in our urban industrial world.[43]

Looking at such passages, and others too, suggests that despite the increasing hierarchization of Israelite society along gender lines (and other lines as well) during the monarchy, some materials from a time of socially significant female power have survived in the canonical literature.

NOTES

1. For a perceptive discussion of the emergence of feminist scholarship and its impact on several of the major disciplines, including history, in the academy, see E.C. DuBois, G.P. Kelly, E.L. Kennedy, C. Korsmyer, and L.S. Robinson, *Feminist Scholarship: Kindling in the Groves of Academe* (Urbana, 1985).

2. In this paper, references to the "Bible" are references to Hebrew Scripture, which is called the Old Testament by Christians.

3. Some of the consequent misunderstandings of Genesis 2–3 are listed in my paper "Recovering Eve: Biblical Woman without Post-biblical Dogma," *Women and a New Academy: Gender and Cultural Contexts,* ed. J.F. O'Barr (Madison, Wisconsin: 1989). See also P. Trible, *God and the Rhetoric of Sexuality* (Philadelphia: 1978), 72–74, and J. Higgins, "The Myth of Eve the Temptress," *JAAR* 44 (1976): 439–47.

4. One of the most blatant examples of a prominent feminist theologian erroneously presuming that biblical texts portray Israelite reality is R.R. Ruether's pronouncement about the "enslavement of persons [women and slaves] within the Hebrew family." See Ruether's "Feminist Interpretation: A Method of Correlation," *Feminist Interpretation of the Bible,* ed. Letty M. Russell (Philadelphia, 1985), 119.

5. Most of the sacred Priestly and Deuteronomic traditions were shaped in Jerusalem after the eighth century, when urban expansion made the capital of Judah at least ten times larger than other contemporary Palestinian cities; cf., Y. Shiloh, "Archaeology and the History of Jerusalem," graduate seminar at Duke University, 1986.

6. F.S. Frick, *The City in Ancient Israel* (S.B.L. Dissertation Series, 36: Missoula, Montana, 1977), 6–8, 91–97.

7. G.E. Lenski, *Power and Privilege: A Theory of Social Stratification,* 2nd ed. (Chapel Hill, 1984), 199–200.

8. E. Leach, *Social Anthropology* (Glasgow, 1982), 130.

9. The research of several anthropologists has demonstrated this. See S.C. Rogers, "Female Forms of Power and the Myth of Male Dominance: A Model of Female/Male Interaction in Peasant Society," *American Ethnologist* 2 (1975): 727–56; C. Cronin, "Illusion and Reality in Sicily," *Sexual Stratification: A Cross-Cultural View,* ed. A. Schlegel (New York, 1977), 67–93; and E. Friedl, "The Position of Women: Appearance and Reality," *Anthropological Quarterly* 40 (1967): 47–108.

10. S. LeVine and R.J. LeVine, "Age, Gender, and the Demographic Transition: The Life Course in Agrarian Societies," *Gender and the Life Course,* ed. A.S. Rossi (New York, 1985), 30. LeVine and LeVine review characteristic features of agrarian societies, with respect to age and gender, that are helpful in reconstructing early Israelite village society.

11. For a classical statement of this assumption see M.Z. Rosaldo's pioneering essay, "Women, Culture, and Society: A Theoretical Overview," *Women, Culture and Society,* ed. M.Z. Rosaldo and L. Lamphere (Stanford, 1974), 18–21. Rosaldo's claims have been subjected to considerable discussion, and she defends them in "The Use and Abuse of Anthropology: Reflections

on Feminism and Cross-cultural Understanding," *SIGNS* 5 (1980): 393–96. See also M. Gould, "Review Essay: The New Sociology," *SIGNS* 5 (1980): 464.

12. See e.g., S. Rowbotham, "The Trouble with Patriarchy," *The New Statesman* (21/28 December, 1979): 970–71. See my chapter on "The Problem of Patriarchy," in *Discovering Eve: Ancient Israelite Women in Context* (New York, 1988) for a discussion of patriarchy, its use in feminist research, and its relationship to patrilineality and to power structures.

13. P. Bird, "Images of Women in the Old Testament," *Religion and Sexism*, ed. R.R. Ruether (New York, 1974), 77, n. 1, explains her judicious avoidance of the term in her discussion of biblical passages dealing with women.

14. As demonstrated by the research of M.K. Whyte, *The Status of Women in Preindustrial Societies* (Princeton, 1978).

15. LeVine and LeVine, 31; cf. J. Pedersen, *Israel: Its Life and Culture* (2 vols.; London, 1926), 1, 259, 263.

16. G.E. Lenski and J. Lenski, *Human Societies*, 5th ed. (New York, 1987), 75.

17. A useful description of the new archaeology as developed by W.W. Taylor, L.R. Binford, and others, can be found in D.H. Thomas, *Archaeology* (New York, 1979): 44–60. The influence of the new archaeology on "biblical" archaeology is discussed by W.G. Dever, "The Impact of the 'New Archaeology' on Syro-Palestinian Archaeology," *BASOR* 242 (1981): 15–29.

18. E.g. F.S. Frick, *The Formation of the State in Ancient Israel* (The Social World of Biblical Antiquity Series, 4; Sheffield, England, 1985), and D.C. Hopkins, *The Highlands of Canaan* (The Social World of Biblical Antiquity Series, 3; Sheffield, England, 1985). Cf. N.K. Gottwald, *The Tribes of Yahweh* (New York, 1979), 650–66.

19. In horticultural societies, and presumably also agrarian ones, those pioneer tasks are close to constituting a male monopoly, so E. Friedl, *Women and Men: An Anthropologist's View* (New York, 1975), 53–54.

20. Hopkins, 173–86, 213–35.

21. See the data presented in my article "The Roots of Restriction: Women in Early Israel," *BA* 41 (1978): 95–99.

22. LeVine and LeVine, 31.

23. *Ibid.*, 30. Note that the familiar biblical charge, "Be fruitful and multiply," uses plural verbs in the Hebrew. God's command to increase population is addressed to society as a whole and thus indicates that the female maternal role is embedded in community goals, the securing of highland territories, as well as in family labor needs.

24. The social scientific and biblical evidence for this situation existing in early Israel is presented in my article "Procreation, Production, and Protection: Male-Female Balance in Early Israel," *JAAR* 51 (1983): 569–93.

25. L. Tilly, "The Social Sciences and the Study of Women: A Review Article," *Comparative Studies in Society and History* 20 (1978): 167.

26. L.A. Stager, "The Archaeology of the Family in Ancient Israel," *BASOR* 260 (1985): 1–36.

27. E.g. by R. McC. Netting, R.R. Wilk, and E.J. Arnould (eds.), *Household: Comparative and Historical Studies of the Domestic Group* (Berkeley, 1984); see especially the editors' "Introduction," xiii–xxxviii. Cf. S.J. Yanagisako, "Family and Household: The Analysis of Domestic Groups," *Annual Review of Anthropology* 8 (1979): 161–205.

28. This inclusive aspect of the ancient Near Eastern household has been pointed out by, among others, I.J. Gelb, "Approaches to the Study of Ancient Society," *JAOS* 87 (1967): 5.

29. B. Pasternak, C.R. Ember, and M. Ember, "On the Conditions Favoring Extended Family Households," *Journal of Anthropological Research* 32 (1976): 109–23.

30. A.D.H. Mayes, *Judges*, Old Testament Guides (Sheffield, England, 1985), 46–51.

31. Lenski and Lenski, 44–45.

32. My chapter on "Household Function and Female Roles," in *Discovering Eve,* explains in considerable detail the reconstruction of economic and of other female roles in pre-monarchic Israel.

33. P. Bird, "Women's Religion in Ancient Israel," in ed. B. Lesko (Atlanta, Georgia, 1989); cf. Bird's paper on "The Place of Women in the Israelite Cultus," *Ancient Israelite Religion,* ed. P.D. Miller, Jr., P.D. Hanson, and J.D. McBride (Philadelphia, 1987), 397–420.

34. Whyte, 135.

35. Exod 20:12 and Deut 5:16; Exod 21:15; Lev 20:9; Deut 21:18–21; Deut 27:16.

36. See the works cited above in n. 9.

37. For a critique of this dichotomizing distance between public and private realms, see DuBois et al., 113–25; S.C. Rogers, "Woman's Place: A Critical Review of Anthropological Theory," *Comparative Studies in Society and History* 20 (1978): 147–53; and Rosaldo, "Uses and Abuses," 396–401.

38. Another possibility is that women are prominent in Judges because the book as a whole deals with marginalization; see M.P. O'Connor, "The Women in the Book of Judges," *Hebrew Annual Review* 10 (1986): 277–93.

39. Analyzed in my "Gender Imagery in the Song of Songs," *Hebrew Annual Review* 10 (1986): 209–23

40. See my "Gender Roles and Genesis 3:16 Revisited," *The Word of the Lord Shall Go Forth,* ed. C. Meyers and M.P. O'Connor (Philadelphia, 1983), 337–54.

41. *Wisdom and the Feminine in the Book of Proverbs* (Bible and Literature series, 11; Sheffield, England, 1985), and "The Wise Women of 2 Samuel: A Role Model for Women in Early Israel," *CBQ* 43 (1981): 14–29.

42. Meyers, *Discovering Eve,* 38–40, 155, 183–87.

43. R.R. Reiter, "Introduction," *Towards an Anthropology of Women,* ed. R.R. Reiter (New York, 1975), 15.

Structure and Patriarchal Functions in the Biblical Betrothal Type-Scene
Some Preliminary Notes

ESTHER FUCHS

Three times in the Hebrew Bible, a prospective wife and husband (or the husband's representative) meet at a well (Gen. 24:1–58; Gen. 29:1–20; Ex. 2:16–21). Despite considerable variation in the characterization of the participants and the literary construction of the particular scenes, the three stories contain identical motifs and are based on an identical progression of events. All three encounters lead to the betrothal of the girl and the groom. The two meet by the well; the prospective bride draws water from the well, and then hurries to tell her family about the stranger. This leads to the stranger's being invited to a meal by the girl's family, and then to a betrothal agreement.

The threefold repetition of what came to be known as the betrothal type-scene was explained by Robert C. Culley as the result of the oral transmission of the stories.[1] A more detailed analysis of the betrothal type-scene is offered by Robert Alter, who suggests that each scene signals the groom's "emergence from the immediate family circle . . . to discover a mate in the world outside," while the well symbolizes fertility or even femininity itself.[2] According to Alter, the variations in the betrothal type-scenes are determined by their foreshadowing functions. Each scene alludes to the specific nature and structure of the bridegroom's future career. Focusing on the bride's function in the betrothal type-scene, James G. Williams agrees that it is rather limited in comparison with the groom's active role: "The only active role of the arche-mother in the betrothal scenes is to hurry home to report the appearance of the male protagonist at the well, although Rebecca's [sic] small share in the dialogue is dramatically significant."[3]

In what follows, I will argue that not only is it impossible to generalize about the literary status of the bride, but that at the differences between the various bride figures are helpful hermeneutic keys to one of the structuring ideologies of the betrothal type-scenes.[4] The following comparison of the various scenes and especially of the power relations between bride and groom in each of them reveals a gradual diminishment in the literary status of the bride and an increasing emphasis on the role of the groom. As I have suggested elsewhere, in biblical annunciation type-scenes this progression constitutes a strategy that serves the Bible's patriarchal ideology, or the interlocking values and principles validating male political supremacy.[5] By "progression" I do not refer to the historical development of events allegedly reflected by the scenes, or to the dates of their composition, but rather to the order underlying their sequential appearance in the *final version and shape of the text*.[6] Does this mean that the redactor(s) responsible for the final shape of the biblical text arranged the present sequence of betrothal type-scenes so as to promote patriarchal ideology? The interdependence of ideology and literature is best understood as position rather than intention. To argue that the text has a patriarchal position is to speak of its ideology. To speak of the alleged intentions of biblical writers and redactors is to psychologize the text's ideological positions. This is not to say that the biblical text is inspired only by a patriarchal ideology. It is to say that its patriarchal ideology is the focus of the present discussion of the literary structure and order of biblical betrothal scenes in the Hebrew Bible.

The first betrothal type-scene is the longest and most elaborate. Taking up most of Genesis 24, it relates in great detail the circumstances surrounding the betrothal of Isaac and Rebekah. The pace of plot development is slowed down by the repetition of phrases, the detailed description of action, and frequent dialogue. For example, Rebekah's act of offering water to Abraham's servant and watering his camels is repeated four times: it first appears as a projected act in the servant's prayer to Yahweh (Gen. 24:14), and next as a real action (vss. 18–20). The third time, it appears in the servant's dialogue with Rebekah's family (vss. 43–44) as a reported projected act, and finally it appears as a reported real action in the same dialogue (vss. 45–56).

One function of this fourfold repetition is to emphasize that the encounter with Rebekah and the consequent betrothal are divinely sanctioned. It also stresses Rebekah's generosity and kindness by juxtaposing the servant's hopes and Rebekah's actual response. For instance, although he planned to ask her just to "tilt" or "lower" her jar, and then proceeded to request only "a little water" to sip, "she hastened to let down her jar upon her hand, and let him drink" (Gen. 24:18). Rebekah is quick to respond to the stranger as "my lord." She spares no effort; instead of merely tilting her jar to let him sip "a little water," she takes it down to him, and instead of just handing over the jar, she holds it in her hand and allows him to drink until satiated. In addition, she not only offers water for the servant's camels but "hastens" to draw water for them until they, too, have drunk their fill.

Rebekah's attributes are also seen in a favorable light when contrasted with those of her brother Laban. Whereas Rebekah provides water to one whom she perceives is a stranger, and expects no reward, Laban reacts only upon learning that the man in question is wealthy and therefore worthy of his attention: "When he saw the ring, and the bracelet on his sister's arms . . . he said: 'Come in, blessed of the Lord; why do you stand outside? For I have cleared the house, and made room for the camels'" (vss. 30–31). The temporal clause preceding Laban's rather sententious welcome establishes an unmistakable causal link between his show of hospitality and his ulterior motives. Furthermore, whereas Rebekah assures the servant that he will not be imposing, as they have "straw and provender enough and room to lodge in" (vs. 25), Laban stresses that room had to be made for the guest and his retinue, thus hinting that his efforts should not go unrewarded.

It should not elude us, however, that Rebekah's actions imply receptivity, acquiescence, and obedience. She not only consents to water the servant's camels, but accepts her family's judgment—or, more specifically, that of her father and brother—and agrees to follow the servant to another country to meet her future husband. In this respect Rebekah behaves as a typical biblical heroine.[7] It should also be noted that all three speech acts attributed to Rebekah amount to positive responses to the servant's questions and requests. As speech acts they entail consent, obedience, a readiness to comply with a male speaker's wishes.

Neither should it elude us that despite Isaac's peripheral role in the scene, it is he who dominates its ending, as he meets Rebekah, brings her into his mother's tent, and takes her as his wife. In the represented interaction of bride and bridegroom, the former becomes a prized object received and managed by the latter. Syntactically, Isaac is the subject of three consecutive transitive verbs (brought, took, loved), while Rebekah serves as their direct object (vs. 67). The ending also omits any reference to the bride's emotional attitude toward her groom, focusing instead on her role within the framework of his life. Rebekah is allowed to outshine Abraham's servant and her brother, but her autonomy and activity diminish considerably in her interaction with her future husband. Nevertheless, Rebekah remains the most active, assertive, and talkative female in the betrothal type-scene. In many ways, her active role in the betrothal type-scene foreshadows her important role in securing for her preferred son, Jacob, his father's blessing.

The second betrothal type-scene, involving Jacob and Rachel, contains most of the conventional motifs mentioned in the first one, but is also markedly different. It is much more limited in its narrative span, taking up a mere seventeen verses in Genesis 29, compared to the fifty-seven verses of the previous scene. In addition, the second scene is dominated throughout by Jacob's point of view, and emphasizes his qualities rather than those of his bride.

Just as Rebekah makes her appearance as soon as the servant has completed his prayer to Yahweh, so Rachel appears only after Jacob has questioned the shepherds about Laban. Instead of introducing the bride, as the first type-scene does, the text continues to focus on Jacob's actions and feelings—on the warm welcome he extends to Rachel and on his mighty act of rolling a heavy stone off the well. The information the scene offers about Rachel is limited to her kinship to Laban and Jacob and to her appearance: "Rachel was of beautiful form and beautiful to look at" (Gen. 29:17). The reference to Rachel's beauty occurs in the context of Jacob's request for her hand in marriage, and serves to explain his preference for her over her sister, rather than to introduce her as an autonomous character. In contrast to her dynamic predecessor, who draws water for herself and for others, Rachel allows Jacob to draw water for her sheep. Her passivity and weakness act as a foil for Jacob's resourcefulness and physical strength. The text stresses that it usually requires the collaboration of several shepherds to remove the heavy stone (Gen. 29:2–3; 8). It is possible that Rachel's appearance inspires Jacob to remove the stone single-handedly, but she herself does not undertake any action, or express any thought or emotion of her own.

Jacob dominates the scene; Rachel is not allowed to control even a single verse, and is tucked away, as it were, as the subject of subordinate clauses (Gen. 29:6, 9, 12, 16, 17), or else functions as a direct object (vss. 10–12; 18–19). The three intransitive verbs she controls as subject, "come," "run," and "tell," evoke the role of a messenger. And indeed Rachel serves as little more than a hyphen between Jacob and Laban. As soon as Laban appears on the scene, Rachel disappears; the narrative focus shifts from Jacob and the shepherds to Jacob and Laban.

The second betrothal type-scene provides another example of the bride's decrease in status: the bride's father and her prospective husband conclude a betrothal agreement without so much as informing the bride. While it is true that, in the first scene, Rebekah does not participate in the betrothal treaty concluded between Abraham's servant and her family, she is at least summoned and consulted when the servant insists he must leave with the bride immediately (Gen. 24:56). In the second pact, Rachel is a prize to be exchanged for the groom's services. When she does not appear as the object of Jacob's attention, she is presented in conjunction with her sister Leah, and this portrayal of Rachel as half of a unit of two daughters foreshadows her marital status as only part of a polygynous unit. She may be the beloved bride, and later the preferred co-wife, but she will never be the exclusive wife, a fact that later will deeply affect her status and power relations with her husband.

The third betrothal type-scene involves Moses and Zipporah, and reflects a further reduction in the status of the bride, as well as in the status of the betrothal scene in general. The third scene is shorter and more compact than the previous one, taking up a mere five verses (Ex. 2:16–21), and is compressed within the story of Israel's oppression by Pharaoh and of Moses's preparation for national leadership. The limited narrative span the scene occupies in the Moses cycle reflects the peripheral role of both wife and marriage in the leader's life.

Like the previous type-scene, this one manipulates the conventional motifs for two major purposes: to reveal Yahweh's continued interest in the hero, and to justify this interest by presenting the heroic features of the divinely designated man. The conduct of Moses by the well suggests that he is divinely empowered. Alone, he faces a group of hostile shepherds who are keeping Reuel's daughters from watering their father's flock (Ex. 2:17). Moses's intervention on behalf of the helpless girls is consistent with his intervention, described in the preceding episode (Ex. 2:11–14), on behalf of the Hebrew underdogs. It also foreshadows his successful confrontation with Pharaoh. The text brings out Moses's heroic characteristics by detailing the different stages and aspects of his actions; Moses is said to "stand up," "rescue" the girls, and "water" Reuel's flock. This is repeated for emphasis in the girls' report to their father about their wondrous rescuer.

The scene's relentless focus on the character of the bridegroom visibly diminishes the role of the bride. Although Moses is presented at this point as a vagabond and an empty-handed foreigner, he is far more powerful than the daughters of the respectable native priest, Reuel. The girls are shown to be not only physically powerless, but even lacking the resourcefulness of their predecessor, Rachel. Unlike Rebekah and Rachel, who hurry to report the encounter with the stranger at the well to their respective families, Reuel's daughters neither thank the stranger nor volunteer any information once they are home. The scene all but ignores the relationship between bride and bridegroom, focusing instead on the relationship between the bridegroom and his future father-in-law: "And Moses was content to dwell with the man, and he gave Moses Zipporah his daughter" (Ex. 2:21). Unlike the previous scene, in which Jacob's desire for Rachel is listed as the primary motivation for their marriage, here the betrothal is more a product of the men's mutual trust and friendship. Zipporah's feelings and thoughts, her appearance, even the feelings she might have evoked in Moses are unknown. The scene does not distinguish her from her sisters by noting her conduct or looks; neither does it explain why Reuel chooses her over her sisters as Moses's bride.

The diminishing role of the bride on the representational level indicates a steady development in the biblical narrative toward de-emphasizing the status and the significance of the bride vis-à-vis her future husband, the biblical hero. The increasing brevity of the betrothal scene and, more significantly, its absence from contexts that would seem to require it (i.e., the betrothals of judges, kings, and prophets), imply that not only the bride, but the act of betrothal itself is less and less significant for the divinely appointed heroes of Israel, as well as for the biblical text. The acquisition of a bride becomes an act increasingly taken for granted, and one whose importance is eclipsed by other events.

A closer look at the betrothal scenes themselves reveals an important discrepancy in the way they function for the bride and for the groom. For the groom, the betrothal scene signals his initiation into adult independence and autonomy. Preceding scenes have presented him as a dependent or undependable youth, or both. Isaac, Abraham's son, is dependent for his very life on his father's will (Gen. 22); Rebekah's son Jacob is shown obeying her advice and following his father's order (Gen. 28:1–5); and Moses, a rather brash lad, acting on impulse, risks his life in his confrontation with the Egyptian task-master and the Hebrew slave (Ex. 2:11–15).

The betrothal type-scene, from the bride's perspective, is merely her transfer from her father's custody to her husband's custody. Although the dramatic scenes do not clarify the legal terms of the engagement, they still reflect the basic legal reality empowering the father to dispose of his daughter as he sees fit. Even in the first betrothal scene, with its exceptional description of the bride's personality, it is after all Rebekah's father and brother who make the decision to transfer her to Isaac: "Then Laban and Bethuel answered . . . 'Behold, Rebekah is before you, *take* her and go, and let her be the wife of your master's son, as the Lord has spoken'" (Gen. 24:50–51, emphasis added). While the bridegroom's representative here "takes" (*lqh*) (Gen. 24:37, 38, 51), her father (and brother) "give" (*ntn*) (Gen. 24:41) the bride to him. These terms recur in all the betrothal narratives, reflecting the bride's subservient status vis-à-vis her father and future husband; she is, clearly, the object of the transaction.

The bride is not merely shown as a transferable object; she is often characterized as a *prized* object whose acquisition exacts a price from the bridegroom. The value of the biblical bride is determined in purely androcentric terms, for instance, according to her virginity and good looks (Gen. 24:16 and 29:17). While the betrothal type-scene makes no reference to the groom's looks or virginity, these qualities are ascribed to the bride as signifiers of her special value.

Although the financial component in the first betrothal type-scene is underplayed in comparison with the element of divine intervention, its role is unmistakable. Abraham's servant gives Rebekah the expensive jewels as a spontaneous token of gratitude for her generosity; nevertheless one can speculate that their impact on her family does not entirely escape him. And indeed, the text registers the effect on Rebekah's brother (Gen. 24:30). Later, as the servant describes Abraham's great wealth, he alludes to the monetary aspect of the proposal he offers the Nahor clan: "The Lord has greatly blessed my master, and he has become great. He has given him flocks and herds, silver and gold, servants and maids and camels and donkeys" (Gen. 24:30).

The second type-scene presents the financial aspect not as incidental to the agreement, but as its underlying reason. Jacob states clearly that he prefers to receive Rachel in return for his labor instead of wages: "I will serve you seven years for your younger daughter, Rachel" (Gen. 29:18). The betrothal agreement becomes exploitative when Laban gives him Leah, and requires seven additional years of labor in return for Rachel (Gen. 29:27). What the text implicitly censures, however, is Laban's deceptive treatment of Jacob, and not the fact that he bargains over his own daughters. The scene does not question the fundamentally economic nature of the agreement, nor the fact that brides are treated as chattel.

Though few would argue with the proposition that the biblical narrative is inspired by a patriarchal ideology, few studies have undertaken to analyze its literary manifestations. The burgeoning field of biblical poetics has tended to ignore the manifestations and implications of the Bible's patriarchalism, while feminist literary analyses have tended to focus on what has come to be known as the Bible's antipatriarchal counterculture, or a "positive" evaluation of the biblical text.[8] A systematic analysis of the relationship between the literary presentation of female characters and the ideological moorings of these presentations is long overdue. In these pages I began to suggest how the structure and order of type-scenes—repetition, omission, informational gaps, the presentation of dialogue, and the orchestration of familiar motifs—can be decoded as patriarchal strategies. Much more needs to be done, however, before we learn how to recognize the subtle and complex strategies that passed for so long as transparent "reflections" of historical reality, or as the merely aesthetic structures of innocent tales.

NOTES

1. *Studies in the Structure of Hebrew Narrative* (Philadelphia and Missoula: Fortress and Scholars, 1976), pp. 41–43.

2. *The Art of Biblical Narrative* (New York: Basic Books, 1981), p. 52. On the concept and structure of the biblical type-scene, see pp. 47–62.

3. *Women Recounted: Narrative Thinking and the God of Israel* (Sheffield: Almond, 1982), p. 46.

4. For a discussion of the interrelations of ideology and biblical poetics see Meir Sternberg, *The Poetics of Biblical Narrative: Ideological Literature and the Drama of Reading* (Bloomington: Indiana University Press, 1985), pp. 84–128. Sternberg does not discuss, however, the Bible's patriarchal ideology.

5. See Esther Fuchs, "The Literary Characterization of Mothers and Sexual Politics in the Hebrew Bible," in *Feminist Perspectives on Biblical Scholarship*, ed. Adela Yarbro Collins (Chico, Calif.: Scholars, 1985), pp. 117–136.

6. The concern with the final shape of the text is a fundamental principle of literary criticism as opposed to source criticism. Many studies have been written in an effort to explain the conceptual differences between literary and traditional criticism of the Bible. Good introductions are

included in Alter, pp. 3–22; Sternberg, pp. 1–57. See also Adele Berlin, *Poetics and Interpretation of Biblical Narrative* (Sheffield: Almond, 1983), pp. 13–22.

7. See Esther Fuchs, "Status and Role of Female Heroines in the Biblical Narrative," *Mankind Quarterly* 23, no. 2 (1982): 149–160.

8. See for example Phyllis Trible, *God and the Rhetoric of Sexuality* (Philadelphia: Fortress, 1978); Mary Ann Tolbert, "Defining the Problem: The Bible and Feminist Hermeneutics," *Semeia* 28 (1983): 113–126; J. Cheryl Exum, "'Mother in Israel': A Familiar Story Reconsidered," in *Feminist Interpretations of the Bible*, ed. Letty M. Russell (Philadelphia: Westminster, 1985), pp. 73–85.

The Problem of the Body for the People of the Book

HOWARD EILBERG-SCHWARTZ

> *Perhaps all social systems are built on contradiction, in some sense at war with themselves.*
>
> DOUGLAS 1966, 140

While many cultures are preoccupied with the body, there are specific, local reasons why the body emerges as problematic in any given cultural formation.[1] This chapter explores factors indigenous to ancient Judaism that turned the human body into a problem. To anticipate, I shall argue that the human body was the object around which conflicting cultural representations met and clashed. Like other religious cultures, ancient Judaism was not a tidy entity. Tidiness is a characteristic of philosophic systems, not cultures. Each culture has its own set of conflicting impulses that struggle against one another for hegemony. In the case of ancient Judaism, at least in one of its formations, it was the human body that was caught between contradictory impulses. To cite two of the more important examples: 1) humans are understood as created in the image of God, yet God has "no-body"—neither others with whom to interact nor a fully conceptualized body with which to do it, and 2) procreation is enjoined as a mandate from God, yet semen is considered polluting, even when discharged during intercourse. These contradictions, which first surface in one form of Israelite religion, are inherited by the rabbis (200–600 C.E.), who continue to find the body a source of conflict.

In relying on the idea of cultural contradictions, I depart from the general tendency to think of Judaism as "a system" or series of systems, a metaphor that implicitly and often explicitly guides research on Judaism. This metaphor induces interpreters to produce a coherence that does not always exist; the result is that one impulse of the culture is selected as exemplary at the expense of others. The idea of cultural contradictions allows interpreters to explore the full "dispersion" of cultural assertions (Foucault 1972).

The idea of cultural contradictions has intrigued many theorists of society and

53

culture, including Marx, Freud, Lévi-Strauss, Gluckman, Spiro, B. Turner, V. Turner, Girard, and others. Contradictions operate at various levels and in various ways. For Marx, they are part of a complex social process such as capitalism that produces a conflict between the technological level and social condition of technological progress (Kolakowski 1978, 299). Contradictions are also a phenomenon of culture. The *Mythologies* of Lévi-Strauss (1969, 1975, 1978) show how myths are generated by and attempt to solve or hide logical contradictions that trouble the mind. Other theorists have examined how individuals are caught between competing demands emanating from various sources. Freud and his followers are particularly interested in the ways in which conflicts between physiological drives and cultural demands are handled. Spiro (1987, 59–60), for example, notes the intolerable contradiction in which pubescent boys and girls were placed in the early years of the Israeli kibbutz movement. In their attempt to create a sexual equality, in which sexual differences would assume little more importance than other anatomical differences, the kibbutz pioneers established a practice in which boys and girls would be routinely exposed to each other's bodies in lavatories, showers, and sleeping quarters. But at the age of puberty, the kibbutz severely prohibited any sexual contact between the sexes. "Here," writes Spiro (1987, 80–81), "is a classic example of incompatible demands. Such a contradiction can only result in intolerable conflict and unbearable frustration." In this case, Spiro argues, the contradiction seems to be generated by an attempt of culture to override biological impulses. Other theorists, such as Max Gluckman (1955), Mary Douglas (1966, 140–158) and Victor Turner (1967, 1–92), have noted how such conflicts may arise from competing social commitments or competing claims of the social system. For example, Ndembu women experience a conflict between patrilocal marriage and matrilineal descent. Women live with their husband's family yet feel the pull of their matrilineal kin. Fathers want their sons to remain with them. But the mother's kin want her and her child to return to them. This culturally produced conflict manifests itself in a variety of physical ailments that are attributed to the attacks of deceased matrilineal ancestors. A similar sort of cultural conflict explains the disorder of anorexia nervosa. Young women afflicted with this disorder experience psychic conflict generated by irreconcilable cultural expectations (B. Turner 1984, 192–197). On this point, I find myself in agreement with Girard (1977, 147), who writes that, "far from being restricted to a limited number of pathological cases . . . the double bind, a contradictory double imperative, or rather a whole network of contradictory imperatives—is an extremely common phenomenon."

Expanding on the ideas of these theorists, I suggest that the idea of cultural conflicts explains why certain objects arrest more attention than others. Vast cultural and symbolic resources are invested in those objects around which conflicting representations revolve. The symbolic elaboration that occurs around such "conflicted objects" is both a consequence of and strategy for dealing with the conflict in question. Objects that are caught between incompatible impulses are evocative, puzzling, and dangerous. The multiplication of rules that often occurs around such objects has the effect both of mastering a threatening object and of glossing the generative conflict. Under the sheer weight of legal minutiae, the original contradiction is lost from view. These conflicted objects make valuable symbolic resources. Caught between conflicting cultural processes, these objects are volatile; their power or energy can be transferred by association to other more stable cultural meanings. Consequently, these charged objects are often used to symbolize and hence empower a variety of cultural messages.[2] In turn, the established cultural messages, now associated with a potential source of conflict, help to control an otherwise unruly object.

In ancient Judaism, cultural conflicts of this sort developed around the human body, generating an intense preoccupation with the body and its processes. Ancient Jews multiplied rules that both regulated the body and turned the body into a symbol of other significant religious concerns. It is to the conflicted Jewish body that our attention now turns.

The Problem of the Body for the People of the Book

To some it may come as a surprise that Judaism is a tradition that is preoccupied with the body. Judaism is often depicted as having a predominantly favorable attitude toward the body. As evidence of this positive tendency, interpreters point out that Jews are enjoined to procreate with the result that sexuality has a positive regard within the tradition (e.g., Feldman 1968, 21–71; P. Brown 1988, 63; Gordis 1978, 98–109; Pagels 1988, 12–13). Consequently, one generally does not find the tendency toward sexual asceticism within Judaism as in other traditions such as Christianity. Nor does the Hebrew Bible or subsequent rabbinic tradition treat sexuality as a consequence of "a fall" (Sapp 1977; Anderson [1991]). Sexuality is regarded as a natural human act that is part of what it means to be human; the sexual asceticism evidenced among the Jews at Qumran is thus regarded as a deviation. In addition, the sharp dualism of body and soul, characteristic of Greek philosophical traditions, is absent in the Hebrew Scriptures and is resisted in classic rabbinic sources (Urbach 1987, 241; Rubin 1988).

While these characterizations are true, they are also misleading.[3] They ignore the way in which the government of the body has always been a central preoccupation within Judaism.[4] Despite any sharp antithesis between body and soul, and despite the importance of procreation, certain bodily processes are regarded as problematic.

The problem of the body in Judaism is already evident in those very writings that made the Jews a "People of the Book." It is in the Hebrew Scriptures, particularly that strand contributed by the Israelite priests, that the body first appears as a central issue of control. This part of Scripture, which is generally designated as "P" (after its priestly origin), includes narratives and laws, which were generally thought to be written sometime in the sixth to fifth centuries.[5] It is in the writings of the priests, especially the book of Leviticus, but also in the writings of the prophet Ezekiel (who was also of priestly descent), that the boundaries and integrity of the body arouse sustained interest.[6] Leviticus pays particular attention to what passes in and out of the orifices, particularly the mouth and the genitals. Certain kinds of food may not be taken into the body (Lev. 11). Various genital emissions, such as menstrual blood, semen, and other irregular discharges, create pollution (Lev. 12; 15). Concern with the body's integrity expresses itself in elaborate rules concerning skin diseases that are contaminating (Lev. 13–14) as well as interest in congenital or accidental disfigurations of the body (Lev. 21:16–23), which disqualify a priest from serving in the Temple. Leviticus also proscribes intentional disfigurations of the body such as shaving the corners of the face or acts of mutilation associated with mourning (Lev. 19:27; 21:5). In addition to these concerns about bodily boundaries and integrity, Leviticus strictly regulates the use to which persons put their bodies in sexual alliances (Lev. 18; 20:10–21).

This government of the body has both prophylactic and moral motivations. Many of the bodily regulations are intended to protect the sacrificial cult from contamination (Milgrom 1976, 390–99). A priest with a disfiguration or with a discharge cannot perform the sacrifices that must be done in a state of purity and wholeness. Furthermore, contamination that occurs among Israelites who are not priests can jeopardize the purity of the cult. "You shall put the Israelites on guard against their uncleanness, lest they die through their uncleanness by defiling My Tabernacle which is among them" (Lev. 15:30).[7]

But the concern with purity is not exclusively a cultic matter. Israel is enjoined to be holy, just as God is holy. Being holy includes observing the regulations governing what goes in and out of the body (Douglas 1966, 51–52; Wenham 1979). "You shall not eat, among all things that swarm upon the earth, anything that crawls on its belly . . . you shall not make yourselves unclean therewith and thus become unclean. For I the Lord am your God: you shall sanctify yourselves and be holy for I am holy" (Lev. 11:42–44). While being impure is not considered a sin, the state of uncleanness does signify an alienation from God. Furthermore, the violation of certain rules governing the body, particularly those related to sexuality, does constitute an offense against God (Lev. 20:10–26).

It is from the priestly writings that the concern with the government of the body first enters Judaism. Subsequent groups of Jews, including those at Qumran (second and first centuries B.C.E.) and the rabbis (200–600 C.E.) take up and elaborate upon the levitical rules governing the body. The Dead Sea Scrolls and the rabbinic writings both reflect a preoccupation with many of the concerns established in Leviticus. To be sure, this is not a passive acquiescence to tradition since these groups transform the rules in sometimes radical ways. I have explored some of these transformations in another context (Eilberg-Schwartz 1990, 195–216). Nonetheless, had it not been for Leviticus, the problem of governing the body would not have had the prominence it does within subsequent forms of Judaism. What follows, then, is an attempt to understand why the government of the body so preoccupied the priestly community.

The Conflicted Body

Mary Douglas has already speculated about why the body so preoccupied ancient Jews. The body, she argues, is frequently a symbol of society and thus the dangers and concerns of the social structure are reproduced on the human body. "The Israelites were always in their history a hard-pressed minority. In their beliefs all the bodily issues were polluting, blood, pus, excreta, semen, etc. The threatened boundaries of their body politics would be well mirrored in their care for the integrity, unity and purity of the physical body" (Douglas 1966, 124). Douglas also suggests that the levitical restrictions on the body stem from a concern with wholeness. Body emissions, skin-disease, and defects are threats to the integrity of the body and like other things that violate notions of wholeness, they are deemed impure (Douglas 1966, 51–52). Douglas's argument has now been canonized in commentaries to Leviticus (e.g. Wenham 1979, 222–23).

But Douglas's arguments are not entirely satisfying. To begin with, Douglas fails to explain why the body became particularly problematic to one specific group of ancient Jews, namely the Israelite priests. If the external pressures on Israel induced a preoccupation with the body, why are the same sorts of concerns not visible in all genres of Israelite literature? Why is this preoccupation located principally in the writings of the priests? Furthermore, Douglas fails to explain why body emissions would be considered a threat to notions of wholeness. Why was wholeness defined in this and not some other way? The answer to these questions emerges when we consider the distinctive religious formation of the Israelite priests.

Within this religious culture, conflicting and to some extent incompatible representations crystallized around the human body. On the one hand, the priests celebrated procreation. They not only believed that God commanded humans to be fruitful and multiply (Gen. 1:27), but regarded reproduction as a central dimension of the covenant between God and Abraham (Gen. 17). But this impulse, which sprung from the social organization and self-understanding of the priestly community, came into conflict with an important religious conception, namely, that humans are made in the image of God (Gen. 1:26–7). There is a fundamental tension between being made in God's image and being obliged to reproduce. The dilemma arises because Israelite religion places certain limitations on the representation of God. To oversimplify for a moment, God has "nobody," neither others with whom to interact nor a body, or at least a fully conceptualized body, with which to do it. Thus the dual expectations of being like God and being obliged to reproduce pulled in opposite directions. There was no escape for the body. Pressed between these conflicting impulses, the body became an object of cultural elaboration. Let me unravel this conflict in more detail.

Be Fruitful and Multiply

Of all the Israelites who contributed to the Hebrew Bible, the priestly community is by far the most concerned with human reproduction. Procreation is regarded as a central human quality and responsibility. In the priestly myth of creation, for example, the command to reproduce immediately follows the creation of man and woman (Gen. 1:28). In fact, "be fruitful and multiply" are the first words that God addresses directly to humanity. According to the priestly writings, God twice reiterates this instruction to the survivors of the flood (Gen. 9:1, 7). The importance of human fertility is underscored by its close and frequent association with divine blessing (Bird 1981, 157; Sapp 1977, 10; Cohen 1989, 13–24). In both the myths of creation and the flood, the command to procreate is immediately preceded by the statement that God conferred a blessing (Gen. 9:1).

It is not surprising then that the priestly writings regard this blessing as central to the covenant that God makes with Abraham and his descendants.

> As for Me, this is My covenant with you: You shall be the father of a multitude of nations. And you shall no longer be called Abram, but your name shall be Abraham, for I make you the father of a multitude of nations. I will make you exceedingly fertile and make nations of you and kings shall come forth from you. (Gen. 17:4–6)

As I have argued elsewhere (Eilberg-Schwartz 1990, 141–177), the priests regard the rite of circumcision as the physical inscription of God's promise of genealogical proliferation on the body of all Abraham's male descendants. In the priestly understanding, circumcision is not an arbitrary sign of the covenant, as many interpreters construe it, but a symbol that alludes directly to the substance of God's promise to Abraham, namely to multiply Abraham's seed. It is no accident that the symbol of the covenant is impressed on the penis. The penis is the male organ through which the genealogy of Israel is perpetuated. The removal of the foreskin has the effect of giving the penis the appearance it has when erect, thus symbolizing great things to come. Furthermore, the priestly writings suggest an analogy between an uncircumcised male organ and an immature fruit tree. They thus associate the circumcision of the male with pruning juvenile fruit trees; like the latter, circumcision symbolically readies the stem for producing fruit.

The priestly writings trace the fate of this blessing. When Isaac gives Jacob his final blessing, he prays that God "bless you, make you fertile and numerous, so that you become an assembly of peoples. May God grant the blessing of Abraham to you and your offspring, that you may possess the land where you are sojourning, which God gave to Abraham" (Gen. 28:3). This wish is subsequently fulfilled upon Jacob's return to Canaan when God blesses him with fertility (Gen. 35:11). As his death approaches, Jacob recalls this blessing when he adopts Joseph's sons, Jacob's grandchildren, into his patrilineage (Gen. 48:3–5). The book of Exodus begins by noting that this blessing has been fulfilled. "The Israelites were fertile and prolific; they multiplied and increased very greatly, so that the land was filled with them" (Exod. 1:6).

As is now evident, the preoccupation with procreation is intimately tied to the issue of descent. The priestly writings are interested in reproduction as the means through which the genealogy of Abraham and then Jacob (Israel) is perpetuated and expanded (Eilberg-Schwartz 1990, 163–176; Sapp, 1977, 12). In particular it is the patriline, that is, the line of male descendants, that evokes interest within the priestly writings. This interest is evident by the fact that the priestly genealogies generally list only male names; the names of wives and daughters are absent (Bird 1981, 134–37; Jay 1985, 283–309, 1988, 52–70; Eilberg-Schwartz 1990, 171–73). The rite of circumcision also serves as a token of this symbolic link between masculinity, genealogy, and reproduction. Impressing a symbol of fertility on the male organ of reproduction establishes a connection between procreation and masculinity and creates a community of men who are linked to one another through a similar mark on their male members. By contrast, the potential connection between women and procreation is symbolically undermined: menstrual blood and blood of birth, which could easily symbolize procreative capacities, are instead associated with death.[8] There is a tension, therefore, between genealogy and reproduction. For the purposes of genealogical reckoning, wives and hence sexual intercourse cannot exist. But the presence of women is always necessary because men cannot reproduce alone.

The preoccupation with these twin themes of procreation and genealogy makes sense given the historical situation and social organization of the priestly community. Israelite priests were an elite community who presided over the sacrificial cult during the Israelite monarchy (tenth to sixth centuries B.C.E.). During this time, they regulated the sacrificial system in the Jerusalem Temple as well as in local sanctuaries outside Jerusalem. In the late seventh century, the cult was centralized in Jerusalem and priests continued to preside over the animal sacrifices in the Jerusalem Temple.

Scholars frequently date the priestly writings to the period during or shortly after the Babylonian exile, when pressures to increase the population may have been particularly acute. But there are other reasons, springing from the self-understanding and organization of priestly community, that would also explain the concern with procreation. The priesthood was inherited patrilineally, from father to son. All priests were purportedly descended from Levi or one of his descendants, such as Aaron. The priesthood, therefore, legitimated itself with a kinship idiom. This idiom shaped the larger interests of the priestly community and accounts for the obsessive interest in detailing genealogies. The "begats" of the Genesis narratives are primarily the work of the priests. The interest in genealogy and reproduction are obviously linked. Since lineages are replenished through the reproduction of its members, societies that define themselves through a kinship idiom frequently focus intense interest on human fecundity and clear lines of descent.[9] To put it another way, without procreation there would be no genealogy and thus no priestly community.

It is for these reasons that the priestly community could not have produced a myth of creation such as Genesis 2 in which the first person is initially created alone (Gen. 2:7).[10] It is true that in this other myth God eventually creates a human partner for Adam, authorizes marriage and apparently sexuality (von Rad 1976, 84–85; Sapp 1977, 12–16). But here God's original intention does not explicitly include sexuality or human companionship. The decision to create a human partner is the result of a process. After creating the first person, God unilaterally decides that it is not good for the first person to be alone and decides to make a fitting partner for the earthling (Gen. 2:18). It is at this point that God creates the animals, as if they might be a fitting partner for the first person. It is only when the animals turn out to be inadequate companions that God fashions a second person from part of the first person. In this myth, then, the first act of reproduction is a kind of fission: a second person is split off from the body of the first. The first act of reproduction thus does not involve sexuality. With the creation of the second person emerges the difference between man and woman, and this provides the basis for the institution of marriage, and presumably sexual intercourse and reproduction. While the authorization of marriage is regarded as the climax of the story by some interpreters (Trible 1978, 102; Sapp 1977, 12–16), another reading is also possible, namely, that sexual intercourse and reproduction are not part of the human essence. After all, God originally created the first person alone; human companionship, intercourse, and reproduction were divine afterthoughts. Thus it is possible to construe this myth as suggesting that the human is most like God when sexual relations are renounced.

It is with these sorts of conclusions, if not this particular myth, that the priestly story of creation takes exception.[11] By synchronizing the creation of man and woman, the priestly myth avoids the otherwise possible conclusion that the sexual division of humanity and hence sexual intercourse and reproduction are not part of God's original intention in creating humanity. By locating authority for procreation not only in the creation account, but at the very moment of human origins, the priestly myth makes reproduction an essential human trait (see Sapp 1977, 10; Otwell 1977, 16).

But the synchronization of man's and woman's creation while solving one problem, generates another in its wake. Specifically, this notion of creation creates a strain with another important conviction of the priestly writer, namely, that God created humanity in the divine image. In what sense can a sexually divided humanity, one that is expected to reproduce, be made in the image of a monotheistic God, who has no partners? It is to this problem that we now turn.

In the Image of God

And God said, "Let us make Man (*adam*) in our image, after our likeness . . . They shall rule the fish of the sea, the birds of the sky, the cattle, the whole earth, and all the creeping things that creep on earth." And God created Man in His image, in the image of God He created him; male and female He created them. God blessed them and God said to them, "Be fertile and increase, fill the earth and master it; and rule the fish of the sea, the birds of the sky, and all the living things that creep on earth." (Gen. 1:26–28)

There are a number of conflicting interpretations of what it means to say God made humanity in the divine image. It is not my intention to decide which of these interpretations is correct, a hopeless task for reasons I shall suggest. Rather, I explore the implications of each interpretation *on the presumption* that it is correct. In other words, assuming that each interpretation is valid, what implications does it have for human embodiment and sexuality? To anticipate, I shall argue that no matter how the priestly community may originally have construed this passage, if indeed there ever was an original meaning, it must have experienced tension around the human body.

The conflict in question springs from certain limitations that Israelite culture imposed on the representation and conceptualization of God. These limitations made it difficult, if not impossible, to reconcile aspects of human embodiment, particularly human sexual relations, with the idea of being made in the divine image. If these religious convictions had gained the upper hand, they might have generated either a renunciation of the body in general or sexuality in particular. But these impulses in Israelite religion came in conflict with the priests' equally strong commitment to the importance of human sexuality as the vehicle for reproduction. I will sometimes refer to these tensions as the "contradictions of monotheism." But it is important to bear in mind that these tensions appear most forcefully in one particular formation of monotheism, that of the Israelite priests. It is when the conviction that humans are made in the image of God appears in the same cultural formation which exalts human reproduction and sexuality that these tensions emerge most powerfully.

Despite the voluminous literature on the "image of God" passage, the interpretations can be categorized into three major groupings. There are a variety of technical historical and linguistic arguments that support or discount each of these interpretations. These do not bear on the present argument, which attempts to show that the body is rendered problematic regardless of which of these interpretations is correct.

A Bodiless God

Certain strands within Israelite literature suggest that God has no form, at least no form that humans can see or imagine:

The Lord spoke to you out of the fire; you heard the sound of words but perceived no shape—nothing but a voice. . . . For your own sake, therefore, be most careful—since you saw no shape when the Lord your God spoke to you at Horeb out of the fire— not to act wickedly and make for yourselves a sculptured image in any likeness whatever: the form of a man or a woman, the form of any beast on the earth. . . . Take care, then, not to forget the covenant that the Lord your God concluded with you and not to make for yourselves a sculptured image in any likeness, against which the Lord your God has enjoined you. For the Lord your God is a consuming fire, an impassioned God. (Deut. 4:12–24)

This passage, dating to the late seventh century B.C.E., asserts that Israelites heard a voice but did not see any divine form during the revelation on Horeb. This is given as the reason for the prohibitions on depicting the deity in plastic art, a prohibition with roots in a much older tradition (Exod. 20:4, 20:23, 34:17; Deut. 5:8, 27:15) (von Rad 1966, 49; Childs 1974, 405–06).[12] What the original motivation for this prohibition is, is debatable.[13] Archaeological evidence confirms that Israelite art did not represent God sitting on the divine throne (Hendel 1988), a proscription that may originally have stemmed from an Israelite ambivalence toward the institution of kingship. The representation of a god on the throne was one means through which ancient Near Eastern cultures legitimated royal authority. The prohibitions of such depictions in Israelite religion may reflect a desire to delegitimize the institution of kingship, a desire that developed during the Israelite tribal league when there were no kings in Israel (Hendel 1988). Below, I will suggest another possible reason for this prohibition. But whatever its prime motivation, the effect of the proscription is clearly to place restrictions on the visualization of God.

Many interpreters reasonably assume that these Israelite impulses to "de-form" God provide the background for the priestly claim that humans are made in the image of God (e.g. Cassuto 1978, 34–35; Barr 1968–69; Bird 1981).[14] In other words, humans resemble God in some qualitative sense only. Being made in God's image implies no resemblance between the human and divine forms. Interpreters disagree as to the particular qualities humans and God share.[15] But generally they include the "spiritual" or "higher" human functions. Nahum Sarna (1970, 15–16) is representative of this trend when he writes "the idea of man 'in the image of God' must inevitably include within the scope of its meaning all those faculties and gifts of character that distinguish man from the beast and that are needed for the fulfillment of his task on earth, namely, intellect, free will, self-awareness, consciousness of the existence of others, conscience, responsibility and self-control." Other interpreters suggest that humans are like God in ruling over creation. Indeed, the idea that humanity is made in the image of God who is king of the universe slides easily into the idea that humans rule the earth: "They shall rule the fish of the sea, the birds of the sky, the cattle, the whole earth, and all the creeping things that creep on earth" (Gen. 1:26). This line of interpretation is supported by ancient Near Eastern parallels in which the King is said to be the image of God (Bird 1981, 140; Cohen 1989, 16; Miller 1972, 289–304; von Rad 1976, 59; Westermann 1984, 150ff).[16] In addition, the priests considered God's activity at creation paradigmatic in establishing an order that Israelites were responsible for maintaining. Israelites were expected to preserve those classifications that God had implanted at creation (Douglas 1966, 29–57; Eilberg-Schwartz 1990, 217–225).

According to these qualitative interpretations, the priests understood humans to be made in the image of a disembodied and sexless God. "The Creator in Genesis is uniquely without any female counterpart and the very association of sex with God is utterly alien to the religion of the Bible" (Sarna 1970, 13). Embodiment and sexuality are thus traits that humans share with animals "*Unlike* God, but *like* the other creatures, *adam* is characterized by sexual differentiation" (Bird 1981, 148).[17] On this reading, the image of God does not parallel the human differentiation into male and female. It is "generic Man" that is the image of God, but not humankind as sexually differentiated. The "image of God refers to neither Adam alone nor to Eve, but only to the two of them together" (Sapp 1977, 10). "Man's procreative ability is not here understood as an emanation or manifestation of his creation in God's image" (von Rad 1976, 60).

We must be careful not to assume that because biblical writers associated reproduction with animals they therefore regarded sexual intercourse as a "beastly" activity. On the contrary, the command to be fruitful and multiply is considered a blessing that humans share with animals (Gen. 1:21–22) (Bird 1981, 157; Sapp 1977, 10). Indeed, Israel is metaphorically identified with the herds and flocks (Eilberg-Schwartz 1990, 115–140) and multiplying like animals is regarded as a positive image. "I will increase Israel with men as a flock of sheep," says God (Ezek. 34:31).

Nonetheless, these interpretations leave the human body caught between contradictory expectations. On the one hand, human embodiment and sexuality are considered good; but they are good because God said so (Gen. 1:31), and because they are products of God's creative activity. Yet at the same time they are the very symbols of human difference from God. That is, it is the nonsexual and nonembodied part of the human person that is made in God's image. For this reason, there is a tension between obeying God and being like God. A person who wishes to obey God should be fruitful and multiply. But in doing so, one engages precisely that dimension of human experience that denies one's similarity to God. In fact, sexual intercourse contaminates a couple, alienating them from the sacred and hence from God. These dilemmas arise on any of the strictly qualitative or spiritual interpretations.

But not all strands of Israelite religion deny that God has a form or body, as many interpreters have observed (Barr 1959; Kaufman 1972, 236–237; von Rad 1976, 58; Westermann 1984, 149ff; Mopsik 1989; Boyarin 1990). Indeed, several sources make it clear that some Israelites imagined that God has or at least assumes a human appearance (e.g. Exod. 24:9–11; 33:17; 1 Kings 22:19; Amos 9:1; Isa. 6:1; Ezek. 1:26–28; Dan. 7:9). "Then Moses and Aaron, Nadab and Abihu, and seventy elders of Israel ascended and they saw the God of Israel: under His feet there was a likeness of a pavement of sapphire, like the very sky of purity. Yet He did not raise His hand against the leaders of the Israelites; they beheld God and they ate and drank" (Exod. 24:9).

> And the Lord said [to Moses], "See, there is a place near Me. Station yourself on the rock and, as My presence passes by, I will put you in a cleft of the rock and shield you with My hand until I have passed by. Then I will take My hand away and you will see My back; but My face must not be seen." (Exod. 33:23)

The most detailed description of God is given in the book of Ezekiel. Ezekiel sees "a semblance of a human form. From what appeared as his loins up, I saw a gleam as of amber . . . and from what appeared as his loins down, I saw what looked like fire. There was a radiance all about him . . . That was the appearance of the semblance of the Presence of the Lord" (Ezek. 1:26–28). Since Ezekiel is a priest, it is possible that Ezekiel's image of God was shared by the priestly author of Gen. 1.

There is, then, an important impulse in Israelite religion that does ascribe a human form to God and assumes that, under certain conditions, the divine form is visible. Given this impulse within Israelite religion, an alternative understanding emerges of what it means to be made in God's image, namely, that the human body resembles the divine form.[18] Support for this view comes from the use of the word "image" (*ṣelem*), which most interpreters construe to mean a physical likeness.[19] Furthermore, in Gen. 5:1–3, the terms "image" and "likeness" are used to describe the resemblance between Adam and his son Seth. The repetition of the same terminology here suggests that humanity resembles God in the same way that Seth resembles Adam, which includes a physical resemblance (Sapp 1977, 8; Mopsik 1989, 52).[20] This latter interpretation of the "image of God" passage is compatible with the qualitative interpretations given above. Humans can be like God both in their appearance and qualities (Westermann 1984, 151ff; von Rad 1976, 58; Sapp 1977, 7).

Advocates of the second interpretation, which "re-forms" God, believe this reading rehabilitates the human body in important ways. And to some extent they are right. Since the human form mirrors the divine appearance, having a body is part of what it means for humans to be made in the image of God. The form of the body ceases to be a sign of human and divine difference. But on further reflection, it becomes clear that even the ascription of a human form to God does not completely solve the problem of human embodiment since having the form of a body does not mean that God is materially embodied. From those sources that depict God's body, it is impossible to determine whether it is substantive. Indeed, one can make the argument that God's materialization takes other forms, such as fire (Exod. 3:2; Deut. 4:11–12). If God's body is immaterial, one that does not die, have emissions, require sexual intercourse, and so forth, then it is only the form of the human body that is legitimated but not the experience of embodiment itself.

Furthermore, Israelite sources are extremely reticent about describing the divine body. Indeed, seeing God is considered dangerous and consequently appears to be the privilege of certain qualified leaders (Barr 1959; Boyarin 1990). According to one passage, God tells Moses you "cannot see My face, for no person may see Me and live" (Exod. 33:17–23). Even those sources that suggest that the full body of God is visible avoid any descriptions. When Moses, Aaron, and the elders reportedly see God, the text only describes what is under God's feet. Even Ezekiel is careful to qualify his description of God in fundamental ways. He sees only "the appearance of the semblance of the Presence of the Lord." This circumspection about God's body—about describing and representing it—is also evident in the way Israelite literature avoids *certain* kinds of anthropomorphisms. While God does a variety of humanlike things, including speaking, walking, and laughing, God does not perform "baser" human functions, such as eating, digesting, urinating, or defecating.[21]

In the official conceptions of Israelite religion, then, God's body is only partially conceptualized. This reticence has the effect and may indeed be partially motivated by the desire to veil the divine sex.[22] Ezekiel's description of God, for example, does not make clear whether God's lower regions are human in form: "from what appeared as his loins down, I saw what looked like fire."[23]

A similar concern may be present in the story in which God only allows Moses to see the divine back. Indeed, this incident (which is from the J source) is reminiscent of another story recounted by the same author (Gen. 9:20–27): when Noah is drunk, his son Ham (which means "hot") sees his father's nakedness. This is purportedly the sin for which Canaan, Ham's son, is subsequently cursed. When Ham tells his brothers, Shem and Japheth, what he has seen, they take a cloth, place it against both their backs and walking backward, cover their father's nakedness; "their faces were turned the other way, so that they did not see their father's nakedness." The similarities between these two accounts are too striking to be passed over. Noah's sons walk backward and divert their gaze so they cannot see their father's nakedness, while God turns away so that Moses can only see the divine behind.[24] It is as if God is being modest about disclosing the divine sex.

Does God have genitals and, if so, of which sex? It is interesting that interpreters have generally avoided this question. This seems a particularly important lacuna for interpreters who understand Gen. 1:26–27 to mean that the human body is made in the image of deity. By avoiding the question of God's sex, they skirt a fundamental question: how can male and female bodies both resemble the divine form? Since God's sex is veiled, however, any conclusions have to be inferred indirectly from statements about God's gender. But however this question is answered poses a problem for human embodiment generally and sexuality in particular. If God is asexual, as many interpreters would have it, then only part of the human body is made in the image of God.

But suppose Israelites did imagine that God had a sex. Given the preponderance of masculine imagery for God (e.g., as man of war, king, father), Israelites would presumably have assumed that God had a penis, if they had bothered to think about it.[25] The story about the sons of God taking wives from daughters of men (Gen. 6:1–4, by the J writer) gives support to the assumption that the divine is considered male. And the parallel between the story of Noah's nakedness and the story of Moses seeing God's back might also suggest that what God is hiding is a phallus.

While the assumption of a divine phallus may legitimate the male body, it nonetheless leaves human sexuality problematic. To put it bluntly, what would a monotheistic God do with a reproductive organ? In official Israelite monotheism, God had no divine partners with whom to consort. Thus, in contrast to other ancient Near Eastern creation myths in which the gods copulate, Israelite creation stories depict God as creating the world alone (Sarna 1970, 12–13; Sapp 1977, 2–3; von Rad 1976, 58–60). And in the priestly story, God creates the world by speaking (Sapp 1977, 1; Scarry 1985, 181–210).[26] Feminists have emphasized the way that an image of a male God creates a problem for being a woman. If God has the physical likeness of a male, the female body is by definition problematic. But what is emphasized much less frequently is how a monotheistic, male God also leaves males in conflict with their own bodies. If males are to be like God, then their penises are only for show; they should not be used for reproduction. The form of reproduction that can most easily be reconciled with a monotheistic God is fission, as in the second story of creation. Thus even on the interpretation that treats the human form as made in the image of God, the body remains a problem in certain fundamental ways. If God has no sex, then the reproductive organs of both males and females are rendered problematic. And if God does have a sex, whether male or female, God's reproductive organs are useless.[27]

These religious convictions, of course, could easily generate a sexual asceticism. But it is important to remember that the priests could not entertain this option. The theme of reproduction was so deeply embedded in their self-understanding and organization as a patrilineally defined community that to reject these themes would have been tantamount to dismantling their community. So even if the priests had imagined an embodied God, the human body would have been left facing fundamental and irresolvable tensions. But these tensions are generally not visible. And they are not visible because the debate about the image of God passage generally revolves around the question of whether that passage implies a similarity between the human body and the divine form. That debate draws attention away from the deepest contradiction of all: namely, the purpose of reproductive organs on the body of a monotheistic God. And it is perhaps this dilemma that contributes to the prohibition on representing God in material form, which is another way of hiding the problem of God's sex.

The Sexuality of God

If the attempt to embody God does so at the expense of God's sexuality (a monotheistic God can have no sexual experience), the obverse is also true: sexuality can only be predicated of God at the cost of divine embodiment. In other words, a monotheistic God cannot have both a body and a sexual experience. This second form of incompatibility is evident in the attempt by some interpreters to reconcile the sexual division of humanity with the image of God. After all, it is reasonable to read Gen. 1:26–28 as suggesting that men and women are both made in the image of God. Phyllis Trible's *God and the Rhetoric of Sexuality* is one of the most articulate expositions of this argument.[28] In Trible's view, the division into male and female is what distinguishes humans from animals. "Procreation is shared by humankind with the animal world . . . sexuality is not" (Trible 1978, 15). That is, although Gen. 1 says that both animals and humans reproduce, the attributes of male and female are exclusively human characteristics, at least in Gen. 1.[29] Animals, by contrast, are divided "according to their kinds," a form of categorization that does not apply to humans. Through a literary analysis, Trible goes on to suggest that "male" and "female" correspond structurally to "the image of God." That is not to say that sexual differentiation can be applied to God (Trible 1978, 21). But sexuality is one of the human experiences that points toward an understanding of Israel's transcendent deity. Trible develops her argument by exploring the metaphors used to depict God. Not only is God metaphorically a father, husband, king, and warrior but also a woman who conceives, gets pregnant, gives birth, nurses, and mothers children.

Trible's interpretation is self-consciously an attempt to recover female imagery and motifs within the Hebrew Scriptures. As suggested by the title of her book, her project includes the attempt to redeem human embodiment and sexuality. Her interpretation thus goes a long way toward reconciling human sexuality with the conviction that humans are made in the image of God.

But in crucial ways this interpretation also leaves the experience of embodiment and sexuality problematic. It is striking that Trible completely ignores the interpretation that ascribes a form or body to God. This omission is interesting in a book that seeks to redeem sexuality. Upon reflection, however, it is clear that this omission is a necessary precondition for any interpretation that seeks a reconciliation between the sexual division of humanity and the image of God. Since there are no other gods, God's act of copulation *can only be metaphoric*. Ezekiel, for example, invokes the metaphor of sexual intercourse to depict the covenant between God and Israel (Ezek. 16:8). While these metaphors do validate human sexuality in important ways, they still leave something to be desired. God cannot have an embodied sexual experience. If God has a penis, it plays no role in the divine relationship with Israel. From this perspective, the metaphor of God having intercourse with Israel actually devalues human copulation in one significant way. If the relation of God to Israel is analogous to that of husband and wife, then what parallels the human act of intercourse is revelation, the insemination of Israel with God's will. Divine intercourse with Israel is mediated through speech. This substitution of speech for sexual intercourse is evident in Ezekiel's depiction of God's intercourse with Israel. Thus God says, "I spread My robe over you and covered your nakedness and I entered into a covenant with you *by oath*" (Ezek. 16:8). Israel is inseminated with the divine will. It is even less clear how the analogy works when God is metaphorically a woman who is impregnated and conceives. Who is Israel's metaphorical father? So when the metaphor of human copulation is projected onto the relationship between God and Israel, it effects only a partial reconciliation between human sexuality and the conviction that humans are made in the divine image. The rehabilitation of human sexuality must take place at the expense of God's body. It is impossible to simultaneously embrace the idea that God has a body with a sex and is a sexual being. As soon as one of these ideas is grasped, the other slides into obscurity. In order for God to have sex, God must not have a body, and to have a body, God can have no sex.

Myth, Contradiction, and Ambiguity

I have consciously avoided favoring any interpretation of the image of God passage in order to show that on any of the interpretations, the priests are left with their bodies caught in a morass of fundamental tensions. It is impossible to affirm both the conviction that human sexuality and reproduction are divinely authorized aspects of human experience and the assertion that humans are made in God's image without at the same time rendering the human body or sexuality problematic in some aspect or another. To push this line of thinking further, it is possible that the image of God passage never had a single meaning. James Barr (1968–69, 13) anticipates me in writing that "there is no reason to believe that this writer had in his mind any definite idea about the content or the location of the image of God." But according to Barr, this hesitation stemmed from a "delicacy and questionability . . . of any idea of analogies to God." But another possible explanation is now obvious. The ambiguity of the image of God passage may attempt to hide the fundamental dilemmas implicit in the religious formation of the priests. If so, then none of the contemporary interpretations of Gen. 1:26–28 can be construed as the original meaning of this passage. Rather, the wide range of interpretations testify to the power of this myth to simultaneously hold together what are radically different possibilities and thus gloss irresolvable tensions in the priestly religious culture. Indeed, it seems that the passage is carefully formulated so as to obscure, as much as is possible, these various problems.

The shift between plural and singular nouns and verb tenses is one means by which this myth negotiates the conflict between a monotheistic God and a humanity that is sexually divided. The plural "Let us create" has always been puzzling to interpreters. Is the plural referring to other divine beings (von Rad 1976, 58; Sawyer 1974, 423–424) or is it a royal "we" (Speiser 1964, 7)? However this question is answered, it is clear that this construction glosses the problematic fact that there is only one God but two sexes of human beings. Phyllis Bird (1981, 148) writes that "'Let us' cannot be a slip . . . it appears also to have been selected by P as a means of breaking the direct identification between *adam* and God suggested by the metaphor of image, a way of blurring or obscuring the referent of *ṣelem*." A similar obfuscation is accomplished by the shift from singular to plural in speaking of humanity (He created *him,* male and female he created *them*). The use of two nouns "image" (*ṣelem*) and "likeness" (*dĕmût*), the former which seems to imply a plastic representation and the later a more abstract, qualitative similarity (Miller 1972, 291), also contributes to the confusion.[30] Furthermore, interpretations of the image of God passages differ depending on which of these terms is taken as primary and which secondary. For example, most interpreters argue that the priestly writer introduced the more abstract term "likeness" to qualify the more graphic term "image" so as to avoid any suggestion that the human appearance resembles the divine form (Sawyer 1974, 420).[31] Miller, by contrast, argues that the term "likeness" (*dĕmût*), which has linguistic affinity with the word for "blood" (*dām*), was original and goes back to Mesopotamian myths that conceive of humans as made from the blood of the gods. The introduction of the term "image" was intended to rule out this sort of interpretation by substituting a word for resemblance that did not have associations to blood.

The second image of God passage only adds to the confusion. This passage employs the term "likeness" to describe the similarity between God and humanity: "This is the record of Adam's line—When God created man, He made him in the likeness of God; male and female He created them." But the passage then goes on to use the terms "likeness" and "image" to describe the similarity of Adam and his son Seth: "When Adam had lived 130 years, he begot a son in his likeness after his image, and he named him Seth" (Gen. 5:1–3). If Gen. 5:1–3 is read by itself, it seems to suggest that the likeness between God and humanity is of a different order than the likeness between a father and son. The resemblance between God and humanity is described by the word "likeness" only. But Adam begets a son who is both in his likeness and image. But if Gen. 5:1–3 is read as a supplement to Gen. 1:26–28, the opposite is the case: the same terms are used to describe the resemblance between Seth and Adam (Gen. 5:3) and between God and humanity (Gen. 1:26–27). The point of these myths, then, may be to hide the basic tensions through a screen of confusion. To be sure, these maneuvers do not entirely hide the problem. But given an impossible task, these myths rise to the occasion.

It is important to realize that the tensions that I am describing were not characteristic of all Israelite writers. As long as humans were understood as different from God, the impulse toward monotheism and the impoverished conceptualization of God's body need not have rendered human embodiment or sexuality problematic. The asexual or formless nature of God would pose less of a problem to the human body on the assumption that humans are made from the dust of the earth (Gen. 2:7). As an earthly substance, humans would be expected to have functions and needs that God does not. Neither the impulse toward monotheism nor toward a disembodied God by themselves necessarily creates a problem for the human body. It is only when these tendencies are coupled with the conviction that humans are created in the likeness and image of God, as the priests suggest (Gen. 1:26–7), that human bodies become problematic.

For these reasons, it is in the priestly writings in particular, and not in Israelite religion as a whole, that the boundaries and integrity of the body become such an intense preoccupation. This cultural obsession, I have suggested, springs from the fact that the human body is caught between contending cultural impulses. This higher order contradiction is reproduced at a lower level in rules governing sexuality. While the priests regard reproduction as one of the most important religious injunctions, semen is contaminating, even if ejaculated during a legitimate act of intercourse (Lev. 15:16–18). One might say that for the priests, therefore, one is "damned if one does and damned if one doesn't." In the very act of carrying out God's will, one alienates oneself from God by becoming contaminated.

These tensions help explain the obsessive interest in the human body in priestly culture. The elaboration of the rules around the body was in part an attempt to control a puzzling object. But these rules did more than control a "foreign body." The absorption in legal regulations also diverted attention from the fundamental conflicts that surrounded the body. Absorbed by the legal particularities surrounding ejaculation, menstruation, and skin disease, those inside and outside the priestly community would have lost sight of the larger dilemmas that inhered in the priests' religious culture. It is for this reason too that the body became one of the richest sources of symbols in the priestly community. As I have shown elsewhere, the circumcised penis is a symbol of the covenant, procreation, and patrilineal descent. In addition, distinctions among body fluids are associated with other symbolic meanings, such as that between life and death, control and lack of control, themes embedded in the larger cultural system of ancient Israel (Eilberg-Schwartz 1990, 141–194). The superimposing of such themes on bodily processes and organs effects a transfer of energy from the conflicted object to the theme symbolized and thus heightens the power of the latter. The human body, then, was the site at which conflicting cultural impulses met and clashed. It was that conflict that made the Jews more than just a People of the Book. They also became a People of the Body.

NOTES

1. I would like to thank Robert Cohn, Ronald Hendel, Martin Jaffee, Louis Newman, and Riv-Ellen Prell who all made helpful suggestions on an earlier draft. I also profited greatly from conversations with Tikvah Frymer-Kensky.

2. This idea has an affinity with Victor Turner's (1967, 54–55) insight that physiological processes are often symbolic of more abstract cultural messages because they lend those messages a power that they otherwise would not have. The present argument differs from Turner's in seeing that power as deriving not from physiological processes, but from contradictions in a cultural formation.

3. See also Biale (forthcoming), who is attempting to correct this overly apologetic presentation of Judaism.

4. I am indebted to B. Turner for the concept and term "government of the body."

5. Some scholars following Yehezkel Kaufman defend a pre-exilic date for P. A review of this issue can be found in G. Wenham 1979, 9–13. See also Richard E. Friedman 1989, 161ff. This debate is not crucial for the present argument, which does not depend on pinpointing the historical context in which the priestly writings were produced.

6. I am not making any claims about any specific *literary* relationship between the Book of Ezekiel and the P source in the Hebrew Bible, a problem that has exercised a great deal of biblical scholarship. Rather, I am suggesting that Ezekiel's priestly origin may have contributed to his concern with the government of the body.

7. All quotations of the Hebrew Bible are taken from the translations of the Jewish Publication Society (1962, 1978, 1982).

8. See my discussion of circumcision, menstruation, and the issues of genealogy (Eilberg-Schwartz 1990, 141–195).

9. See my survey of ethnographic studies of circumcision in Africa, which show a recurring linkage between issues of genealogy, virility, and reproduction (Eilberg-Schwartz 1990, 141–177).

10. Most interpreters regard Adam in this story as male and Eve as being separated from a male body. See, however, Phyllis Trible 1978, 72–105 and Bal 1987, 104–131, who argue that the original Adam is neuter and that sexual differentiation occurs only when a split is introduced. To avoid attributing a sex to the first human creation, I refer to Adam as "the first person."

11. See Frank Cross 1973, 293–325, who argues that the priestly writer did not write a complete narrative paralleling the JE narrative, but rather expanded and supplemented it. If so, then the priestly writer felt compelled to supplement the creation story as told in Gen. 2.

12. See von Rad and Childs for the possible connection between the prohibition on images of God and the Deuteronomic idea that Israel only heard but did not see God at Horeb. The latter idea is very likely a later interpretation of the already existing prohibition.

13. Childs (1974, 407–408) summarizes various attempts to explain this prohibition. Von Rad, for example, argues that images were prohibited because they failed to deal adequately with the nature of God. Similarly, Zimmerli argues that the prohibition reflects the idea that God has chosen to be revealed not in a static image, but in ambiguity of dynamic history. Below, I will suggest an additional reason for the prohibition: the representation of God would require defining the sex of God, which would force to the surface the complex tensions surrounding gender and sexuality that are implicit in Israelite monotheism.

14. James Barr (1959, 31–38) originally suggested that the image of God passage presupposes the resemblance between the human and divine forms. But he (1968–69, 11–26) subsequently retracted that view based on historical and linguistic analysis.

15. Westermann (1984, 147) provides a review of interpreters who hold this position.

16. For a review of the relevant arguments and the ancient Near Eastern evidence, see especially Westermann 1984, 150ff.

17. It is interesting to compare Bird and Trible on this issue. Bird notes that in other contexts the priestly writer treats the categories of "male" and "female" as applicable to animals. Trible, for her part, argues that in Gen. 1 the division into "male" and "female" is unique to humankind since the animals are divided "according to their kinds," a type of categorization that does not apply to humans. According to Trible (1978, 15), "Procreation is shared by humankind with the animal world . . . sexuality is not."

18. Barr (1959) originally suggests this possibility and then changes his mind. For a history of this interpretation see Miller 1972, 292 and Westermann 1984, 149ff.

19. Not all interpreters agree with this interpretation of *ṣelem*. For a different reading, see Barr 1968–69. Furthermore, most interpreters argue that the other term, "likeness" (*dĕmût*), qualifies the term "image" and is intended to rule out the idea that the human and divine forms are similar.

20. This is not the only reading of the relation between Gen. 1:28 and 5:1–3. I discuss an alternative below.

21. Sexual intercourse is one exception that I shall take up below.

22. In a subsequent context, I hope to consider this whole issue from the vantage point of Lacan's argument that the phallus must be veiled (Lacan 1977, 281–291). [See *God's Phallus* (Beacon 1994).]

23. I would like to thank my colleague Tikvah Frymer-Kensky for pointing this out to me.

24. The text suggests that God's modesty is motivated by a desire to hide the divine face "for man may not see my face and live" (Exod. 33:20). In another context, I hope to explore how God's face, or more specifically the divine mouth, is treated as a genital organ because of its generative role in creation.

25. Some feminist writers have assumed that God's sex is male on this basis. For example, in *Beyond God the Father*, Mary Daly, in a section entitled "Castrating 'God,'" writes that "I have already suggested that if God is male, then the male is God. . . . The process of cutting away the Supreme Phallus can hardly be a merely 'rational' affair."

Trible and others have noted the feminine images of God. But none of these writers have argued that Israelites would have imagined God as being female, that is, as having a body with breasts, vagina, and womb. For a possible interesting exception, see Biale (1982). Biale argues that the priests thought of God as a "God of Breasts." This is reflected in the priests use of the term "El Shaddai" to describe God, a term that traditionally has been interpreted as "God Almighty." But the word *shaddai* also refers to "breasts," enabling the expression "El Shaddai" to be read as "God of Breasts." To strengthen his interpretation, Biale shows that this association is explicit in one early biblical passage and that the priestly writings use the term "El Shaddai" precisely in those contexts dealing with promises of fertility.

26. Scarry offers a provocative reading of biblical texts in the context of her larger argument about the relationship of voice, body, and pain. She sees a dialectic set in play by the fact that God is imagined as disembodied, as only a voice, whereas humans are embodied. This distance is frequently transversed by a weapon, which mirrors the relationship between a torturer, who magnifies a regime's voice through torture, and the victim, who loses his or her voice through the magnification of bodily pain. Scarry's reading is illuminating in many ways. But her theory needs to be nuanced since it does not deal with those texts that imagine God in human form, an idea that confounds the sharp dichotomies with which she is working.

27. The only remaining possibility is that God is androgynous, an idea that does develop in late antique religions. On this view, male and female bodies are both partially made in God's image. Moreover, it is in the act of sexual intercourse, in the joining of male and female bodies together, that the human achieves the most complete reflection of the androgynous deity. This interpretation comes the closest to reconciling the division of the sexes with the image of God. But there does not seem to be any biblical evidence to support it. Moreover, a hermaphroditic God is a kind of hybrid, and the priestly writers generally find hybrids and other anomalies abhorrent. Finally, an androgynous deity does not procreate or have a sexual experience, thus still leaving an important difference between humans and the deity.

28. Trible's interpretation has been dismissed by some as a feminist reading that does not pay sufficient attention to the place of Gen. 1 in the larger context of the priestly writings (see, for example, Bird). To a certain extent, this criticism is valid. To read Gen. 1 as an example of incipient egalitarianism ignores the fact that the priestly writings generally privilege the male over the female. As noted previously, the priestly genealogies do not even mention the presence of wives. But Trible's reading cannot be dismissed out of hand. As I have suggested, the simultaneous creation of male and female is motivated by a desire to legitimate procreation. But in order to do so, the priests had to tolerate the seeming implication that both male and female are made in the image of God. To reformulate Trible's question, then, it is interesting to ask how and why the priests managed to tolerate the association of "the female" with the image of God.

29. As noted earlier, Bird points out that the categorization of male and female is used elsewhere in the priestly writings to talk about animals.

30. See, however, Barr (1968–69), who argues that *ṣelem* was the term most apt for avoiding the suggestion of resemblance of the human body and divine form.

31. See Miller 1972, 293 for other references to this argument.

REFERENCES

Bal, Mieke
1987   *Lethal Love: Feminist Literary Readings of Biblical Love Stories.* Bloomington: Indiana University.

Barr, James
1959   "Theophany and Anthropomorphism in the Old Testament." In *Vetus Testamentum, Supplements* 7:31–38.
1968–69   "The Image of God in the Book of Genesis—A Study of Terminology." *Bulletin of the John Rylands Library* 51:11–26.

Biale, David
1982   "The God With Breasts: El Shaddai in the Bible." In *History of Religions* 21:3, 240–256.
1996   *Eros and the Jews.* New York: Basic.

Bird, Phyllis
1981   "'Male and Female He Created Them': Gen 1:27b in the Context of the Priestly Account of Creation." *Harvard Theological Review* 74 (2):129–159.

Boyarin, Daniel
1990   "The Eye in the Torah: Ocular Desire in Midrashic Hermeneutic." *Critical Inquiry* 16 (3): 532–550.

Brown, Peter
1988   *The Body and Society: Sexual Renunciation in Early Christianity.* New York: Columbia University.

Cassuto, U.
1978   *A Commentary on The Book of Genesis* [Heb.]. Pt. 1. Jerusalem: Magnes.

Childs, Brevard S.
1974   *The Book of Exodus.* Philadelphia: Westminster.

Cohen, Jeremy
1989   *Be Fertile and Increase, Fill the Earth and Master It.* Ithaca: Cornell University.

Cross, Frank
1973   *Canaanite Myth and Hebrew Epic.* Cambridge, Mass.: Harvard University.

Daly, Mary
1973   *Beyond God the Father.* Boston: Beacon.

Douglas, Mary
1966   *Purity and Danger.* London: Routledge and Kegan Paul.

Eilberg-Schwartz, Howard
1990   *The Savage in Judaism: An Anthropology of Israelite Religion and Ancient Judaism.* Bloomington: Indiana University.
forthcoming,   "Damned If You Do and Damned If You Don't: Rabbinic Ambivalence Towards Sex and Body." In *Center for Hermeneutical Studies Protocol Series.* Vol. 61. Berkeley.

Feldman, David M.
1968   *Marital Relations, Birth Control and Abortion in Jewish Law.* New York: Schocken.

Friedman, Richard E.
1987   *Who Wrote the Bible?* New York: Harper and Row.

Foucault, Michel
1972   *The Archaeology of Knowledge.* Trans. A.M. Sheridan Smith.

Girard, René
1977   *Violence and the Sacred.* Trans. Patrick Gregory. Baltimore: Johns Hopkins University.

Gluckman, Max
1955   *Custom and Conflict in Africa.* Oxford: Blackwells.

Gordis, Robert
1978   *Love and Sex: A Modern Jewish Perspective.* New York: Hippocrene.

Hendel, Ronald
1988   "The Social Origins of the Aniconic Tradition in Early Israel." *Catholic Biblical Quarterly*
        50 (3):365–382.

Jay, Nancy
1985   "Sacrifice as Remedy for Having Been Born of Woman." In *Immaculate and Powerful.* ed.
        C.W. Atkinson et al., 283–309. Boston: Beacon.
1988   "Sacrifice, Descent, and the Patriarchs." In *Vetus Testamentum* 38 (1):52–70.

Jewish Publication Society
1962   *The Torah.* Philadelphia: The Jewish Publication Society of America.
1978   *The Prophets.* Philadelphia: The Jewish Publication Society of America.
1982   *The Writings.* Philadelphia: The Jewish Publication Society of America.

Kaufman, Yehezkel
1972   *The Religion of Israel.* Trans. and abdg. Moshe Greenberg. New York: Schocken.

Kolakowski, Leszek
1978   *Main Currents of Marxism.* Vol. 1. Oxford: Oxford University.

Lacan, Jacques
1977   "The Signification of the Phallus." *Ecrits.* Trans. by Alan Sheridan. New York: Norton.

Lévi-Strauss, Claude
1969   *The Raw and the Cooked.* Trans. John and Doreen Weightman. New York: Harper and
        Row.
1973   *From Honey to Ashes.* Trans. John and Doreen Weightman. New York: Harper and Row.
1978   *The Origin of Table Manners.* Trans. John and Doreen Weightman. New York: Harper and
        Row.

Milgrom, Jacob
1976   "Israel's Sanctuary: The Priestly Picture of Dorian Gray." *Revue Biblique* 83:390–399.

Miller, J. Maxwell
1972   "In the 'Image' and 'Likeness' of God." *Journal of Biblical Literature* 91:289–304.

Mopsik, Charles
1989   "The Body of Engenderment in the Hebrew Bible, the Rabbinic Tradition and the Kab-
        balah." In *Zone: Fragments for a History of the Human Body.* Pt. 1. Ed. Michael Feher with
        Ramona Naddoff and Nadia Tazi. New York: Ozone.

Otwell, John H.
1977   *And Sarah Laughed: The Status of Woman in the Old Testament*. Philadelphia: Westminster.

Pagels, Elaine
1988   *Adam, Eve and the Serpent*. New York: Random.

Rubin, Nisan
1988   "Body and Soul in Talmudic and Mishnaic Sources." *Koroth* 9:151–164.

Sapp, Stephen
1977   *Sexuality, the Bible and Science*. Fortress: Philadelphia.

Sarna, Nahum
1970   *Understanding Genesis*. New York: Schocken.

Sawyer, John F.A.
1974   "The Meaning of 'In the Image of God' in Genesis I–XI." *Journal of Theological Studies* (ns) 25:418–426.

Scarry, Elaine
1985   *The Body in Pain*. New York: Oxford University.

Speiser, E.A.
1964   *Genesis*. The Anchor Bible. Garden City: Doubleday.

Spiro, Melford
1987   *Culture and Human Nature*. Ed. Benjamin Kilborne and L.L. Langness. Chicago: University of Chicago.

Trible, Phyllis
1978   *God and the Rhetoric of Sexuality*. Philadelphia: Fortress.

Turner, Bryan
1984   *The Body and Society: Explorations in Social Theory*. Oxford: Oxford University.

Turner, Victor
1967   *The Forest of Symbols*. Ithaca: Cornell University.

Urbach, Ephraim E.
1987   *The Sages: Their Concepts and Beliefs*. Cambridge, Mass.: Harvard University.

von Rad, Gerhard
1976   *Genesis*. Trans. John H. Marks. Philadelphia: Westminster.
1966   *Deuteronomy*. Trans. Dorothea Barton. Philadelphia: Westminster.

Wenham, G.J.
1979   *The Book of Leviticus*. The New International Commentary on the Old Testament. Grand Rapids, Mich.: William B. Eerdmans.

Westermann, Claus
1984   *Genesis 1–11*. Trans. John J. Scullion. Minneapolis: Augsburg.

Reading Women into Biblical Narratives

Status and Role of Female Heroines in the Biblical Narrative

ESTHER FUCHS

The books of Ruth and Esther are the only book-length narratives in the Hebrew Bible revolving around female characters. No other female characters in the Hebrew canon dominate the narrative scene for more than one chapter, not even the extraordinary character of Deborah, in the book of Judges. It is for this reason that I would like to explore in the next pages the characters of these heroines and the underlying literary and ideological patterns of both books, the only ones to be entitled with women's names, with a view to detecting what light they may throw on the status and role of females in the Semitic, or more precisely Hebraic, culture of the period in which they and the authors of these books lived.

There are many generic and structural differences between the two books. The book of Ruth is closer to the psychological realism of the book of Genesis. Despite the brief span of four chapters, the characters are plausibly individuated through both action and dialogue. As Robert Alter puts it, the book of Ruth is "a verisimilar historicized fiction" in its treatment of human psychology and actual social institutions" (Alter 1981:34). The book of Esther, on the other hand, is a post-exilic creation which is little more than fairy tale, though it presents itself as a piece of political history affecting the main diaspora community. Its comic art and schematic neatness depart quite blatantly from historical verisimilitude. Yet, both are stories about women, as their titles imply, and it is this which serves as the only methodological justification for the following comparative study, whose major aim is to point out the ideological reasons underlying their inclusion in the canon.

In opposition to the men whose names entitle most biblical books, these women are not military or political leaders, neither are they prophets or thinkers. Their merit was not won by a military struggle on behalf of the nation, by an impassioned effort to understand the mystery of Yahweh, or by preaching Yahweh's words to his people. On the contrary, what distinguishes the books of Ruth and Esther is the protagonists' almost total lack of awareness of Yahweh, and the almost total suppression of explicit references to divine intervention in the story. Clearly the narratives intend to display Yahweh's designs in contrast to human action.[1] The all too many propitious coincidences and happy endings characterizing both plots unquestionably allude to Yahweh's involvement in the action. Nevertheless, in the book of Esther his name is completely suppressed. In the book of Ruth his name appears in Naomi's speech of despair (1:21), in Ruth's formalistic response, and in the congratulatory speech of the women of Bethlehem (4:14–15) at the end of the book. Ruth mentions god as part of an expression of loyalty to Naomi, her mother-in-law (1:16–17). I strongly disagree with Phyllis Trible's comparison between the radical faith of Ruth and that of Abraham (Trible 1978:173).

Abraham responds to a direct call from Yahweh (Gen. 12:1–5). His willingness to forsake Haran and go to Canaan stems only from his faith in Yahweh. His obedience is an act of loyalty to God. There are no other motives whatsoever. Ruth, however, is willing to forsake Moab and go to Canaan out of loyalty to Naomi, as she clearly states: "Entreat me not to leave thee, and to return from following after thee; for whither thou goest, I will go; and where thou lodgest, I will lodge; thy people shall be my people, and thy God my God; where thou diest, will I die, and there will I be buried; the Lord do so to me, and more also, if ought but death part thee and me" (Ruth 1:16–17).

"God" constitutes the subject of one penteme in this synonymous parallelism. "God" is only one aspect in Naomi's identity, which Ruth desires to assimilate. The name of Yahweh is employed in an oath formula by which Ruth underscores her resolution. "God" is employed here for rhetorical purposes; it does not appear as a subject to which Ruth vows allegiance.

As opposed to Abraham, Ruth the Moabite does not follow Naomi the Judaite because of her faith in God, but rather the contrary—she accepts Yahweh because of her love for Naomi.[2] In the case of Abraham, the biblical narrative spares no effort to emphasize that the patriarch acts out of religious consciousness. This is not the case with Ruth. Nowhere in the narrative is she revealed as conscious of God's providence. Even at the end of the narrative, when the patrilineal chain is restored by Ruth's marriage to Boaz, there is nothing to indicate that she is conscious of Yahweh's decisive role in shaping the course of events. Reference to God is made by a chorus of women who collectively congratulate Naomi upon the birth of her grandson: "And the women said unto Naomi: 'Blessed be the Lord, who hath not left thee this day without a near kinsman, and let his name be famous in Israel'" (4:14). The possessive pronoun in the second distich refers to the new-born male who is to continue the patrilineal chain, not to Yahweh.

It is true that Abraham too is an agent of God, a means for spreading Yahweh's dominion in the world, but he is a conscious agent. Ruth, on the other hand, is a means in the process of restoring *man's* name to the world; that of Mahlon, her husband, and of Elimelech, her father-in-law. Her battle is not for monotheism but for the continuity of patriarchy. Unlike Abraham who battles for an idea, she struggles for physical survival and patrilineal continuity. Both functions are closely related. Ruth's search for food leads her into the arms of Boaz, and consequently to the restoration of her husband's name.

This factor should be clearly appreciated by scholars. Ruth does not merely fight for "life" or the "future" as abstract and general values, but for the life and future of her deceased husband and father-in-law. Thus, Ruth is the paradigmatic upholder of patriarchal ideology. She is willing to exchange her own family, country, and god for those of her dead husband. She follows Naomi back to the famine-stricken Bethlehem, not only renouncing her identity but also risking her life and security.

Ruth's loyalty to her dead husband's name and continuity is evocative of Tamar's loyalty to her dead husband's name (Gen. 38). Tamar too is willing to risk her life in order to bear a son who would continue her husband's name, Er. Were it not for her precaution and ruse, she would have been burnt at the stake by Judah, her father-in-law, as a harlot (Gen. 38:24). But Tamar valiantly and shrewdly takes initiative on behalf of her dead husband, showing more loyalty to the name of Judah than Judah himself, who keeps Shela, his son, from marrying his brother's widow as law decrees. Tamar does not act out of concern for her own well-being. She does not insist on marrying Shela, nor does she take initiative because she is lonely or wants to get married. The text in both cases, takes great pains to emphasize that the heroines act selflessly. In the case of Tamar this is even more pronounced because the person she lures to her bed is her father-in-law. Both Ruth and Tamar use tricks and wiles in order to get a man twice their age to bed. Tamar disguises herself as a cult-prostitute (Genesis 38:14), and Ruth sneaks into Boaz's sleeping place at night, uncovers the lower part of his body and lies down by his feet (Ruth 3:7). Neither Tamar nor Ruth takes a direct approach, for though conventional tribal justice is on their side, and despite their loyalty to partiarchal values, women could not always be straightforward in the male-dominated society of the early Israelites. Tamar must resort to wiles and guiles even in her selfless struggles for what is regarded as right and noble. Though decried in other circumstances, female deceptiveness in these narratives is portrayed as positive initiative and good sense. Both women are rewarded by Yahweh for their actions. Tamar conceives male twins, Peretz and Zerah, and Ruth conceives a son, Obed. Peretz, son of Judah, is the ancestor of Oved, father of David—thus the patrilineal chain from Judah to King David is established and secured by the self-abnegation, wisdom, and loyalty of two helpless widows. It is the heroines' exceptional performance as wives and mothers and their relentless allegiance to patriarchy that the text stresses as their most exalted properties.

As noted before our digressive analogy, Ruth's relationship with Yahweh is not the focus of the narrative. It is not her loyalty to Yahweh which distinguishes her as a biblical heroine. Esther is characterized as God-fearing, but she is not inspired or driven by religious faith either. The only reference to her religious stance is dramatized by her decision to fast for three days (Esther 4:16). But, even in this context, no direct reference is made to God. As in Ruth's case, Esther's main concern is to insure survival and continuity, but in her case these moments are enacted on a grand scale, for she helps redeem not only one family, but a whole branch of the Jewish nation. Esther is celebrated as having succeeded in saving the Jews of Persia from genocide. Even in the most desperate circumstance she is not described as appealing directly to Yahweh. Aware of the personal risk she faces through her actions, she asks Mordecai to gather the Jewish community and to fast for three days on her behalf (4:16). The omission of any direct dialogue with Yahweh is congruous with a more comprehensive biblical policy which allows women characters to hold direct discourse with God (or his agent) only in a "procreative" context.

In fact, Esther serves not only as Yahweh's agent but also as the obedient agent of Mordecai, her uncle.[3] The very act of saving the Jewish community from destruction by Haman stems not from Esther's initiative but from Mordecai's orders: "Then Mordecai bade them answer unto Esther: 'Think not with thyself that thou shalt escape in the king's house, more than all the Jews. For if thou altogether holdest thy peace at this time, then will relief and deliverance arise to the Jews from another place, but thou and thy father's house will perish; and who knoweth whether thou art not come to royal estate for such a time as this'" (Esther 4:13–14) The peremptory and threatening tone of Mordecai's message resonates with more vigor and authority in the Hebrew original, which is far more condensed and somewhat choppy. Esther is not credited with being particularly zealous in her desire to save her own people. In point of fact she seems to be unaware of the court's order to destroy the Jews and as the king's favorite wife is in no danger herself. Though the king's edict "to destroy, slay and annihilate" all the Jews "young and old, babies and women in one day" (3:13) was well publicized all over the kingdom, the queen is too busy with her makeup and other skin-deep activities and is unaware of the imminent danger to her people. Esther learns about Haman's plot from Mordecai (via her servant Hatach), and it is Mordecai who urges her to act on behalf of her people. At first Esther is reluctant to act, for fear for her own life (4:14), but following Mordecai's ominous and threatening message she changes her mind. Esther's trepidity at breaking court etiquette and entering the "internal court" is blatantly contrasted with Mordecai's temerity. Whereas she is afraid to approach the king, despite the obvious affection of Ahasuerus towards her, the masculine Mordecai is portrayed as a proud Jew who refuses to bow to Haman at the fate of the palace, in open defiance of the king's orders.

Thus we are given the impression that Esther acts not out of independent initiative or spontaneous concern for her people, but out of filial deference, possibly even fear of her uncle, who had adopted and raised her as his own daughter (2:7). Morphologically speaking, she is an agent rather than a genuine heroine (Propp, 1968).

The obvious incongruity between Esther's apprehensions and the king's response points up the untenability of her gloomy predictions. Esther is not only invited into the internal court but is welcomed and encouraged to express her desire by the king's generous promise to grant all her wishes "even to half the kingdom." Still, Esther procrastinates over her duty until the time of the second banquet she arranges for Ahasuerus and Haman. When her husband, the king, gives her full control over Haman's house and possessions, Esther then proceeds to share this authority with her uncle Mordecai. Thus it is Mordecai and not Esther who in effect now carries the royal seal and the power which his enemy the Persian had exercised prior to Esther's intervention. Though Esther beseeches Ahasuerus to transmute Haman's edict, it is Mordecai who actually performs the transmutation of the edict (8:9); it is Mordecai who is shown as the king's executive, and who is in reality the leader of the Jews. It is Mordecai who orders all the officers in the vast Persian empire to reverse Haman's order, and who authorizes the Jews to take revenge on their persecutors, and to "destroy, slay and annihilate" their enemies (8:11).

The ministers, officers, and king's representatives obey Mordecai's orders and not Esther's. It is "Mordecai's fear that has befallen them" (9:3). "For Mordecai was great in the king's house; and his fame went forth throughout all the provinces; for the *man* Mordecai waxed greater and greater" (9:4).

The narrative even implies that Mordecai gains the king's trust prior to Esther's intervention. On the night preceding Esther's party, due to a felicitous spell of insomnia, the king decides to reward Mordecai for his loyalty. On the next day, the king orders

Mordecai dressed in royal attire, mounted on a horse led by Haman, his foe, throughout the town and proclaimed by him to be the man "whom the king delighteth to honor" (6:11). The reversal of events in favor of Mordecai is portrayed as having begun even before Esther intercedes with the king on behalf of her people.

Mordecai is portrayed always as alert, courageous, resourceful, authoritative, and faithful. Esther is described in terms that imply she is pretty, obedient, silver-tongued, and somewhat manipulative. She constantly flatters the king and never fails to recognize and stress his authority. She waits patiently and obediently till the king's permission is given for an audience; only then she speaks. She is shown to fall on her knees, cry, and implore the king (8:3). Mordecai, on the other hand, stays proud and regal throughout the story. He appears undaunted when persecuted and not overly grateful when extolled. His status is metonymically described by the repeated references to his royal garb (6:11; 8:15). Esther's external features are addressed in relation to her physical beauty (1:8).[4] The external description of Mordecai dramatizes the reward for his upright and courageous actions. In Esther's case, the description of external features appears not as a victorious *effect* but as cause for success. Because of her beauty, Esther is taken to the palace and provided with make-up and other beauty aids to enhance her physical charms (2:9). After the rather detailed description of the cosmetic treatment, the reader is introduced to her spiritual properties: her modesty, humility, and submissiveness. Mordecai inspires respect and awe. Esther "pleases Hegai, keeper of women" (2:9), and "finds favor in the sight of the king" (2:7). Aesthetic grace paves the way for the woman's success, whereas man's power rests on his ethical fiber.

It is true that as queen Esther outwits two rather stupid males. It is true that the final victory of the Jews is due as much to Haman's foolishness in falling into Esther's trap; but it is also true that, as in the book of Ruth, the pivotal moment occurs within the framework of a bedroom scene. Ruth addresses her plea to Boaz in the barn in the middle of the night. Esther reclines on her own bed during the second banquet she offers for Ahasuerus and the king. Seeing Haman "fallen upon the couch whereon Esther was" (7:8) the king jealously mistakes Haman's fear for lechery, and his resultant anger seals the death penalty for the enemy of the Jews. Esther's tactics are quite different, then, from Mordecai's. So is her discourse. In her repeated pleas to the king, Esther uses placatory language and ingratiating formulas: "If it seems good unto the king" (5:4); "If I have found favor in thy sight, O king, and it please the king" (7:3); ". . . then answered Esther, and said: 'thy petition and my request is—if I have found favor in the sight of the king, and if it please the king to grant my petition, and to perform my request—let the king and Haman come to the banquet that I shall prepare for them, and I will do tomorrow as the king hath said" (8:8).

Throughout the narrative, Esther's actions constitute mostly supplicatory speech acts. Mordecai, on the other hand, is represented by a single direct speech which takes up two verses in the entire narrative (4:13–16). The speech is peremptory, authoritative, and concise. The economy of his speech is compensated by energetic activity: he "orders," "takes," "informs," "writes," "sends," "signs," "comes in," and "goes forth." The hero is shown to speak less and act more than the heroine. Yet both are exemplary figures. Their excellence, however, is characterized by remarkably contrasted sex roles.

The character of Esther is contrasted with yet another foil—the recalcitrant first wife of Ahasuerus, Vashti. Vashti refuses to humiliate herself when summoned by the

king to parade her beauty during one of the banquets (1:11–12). She refuses to be
flaunted by her husband as a mere ornament, a dazzling possession. Vashti's rebellious-
ness infuriates the king, who decides, after consultations with his advisers and ministers,
to divorce her, lest all the other women in the kingdom imitate her proud conduct
(1:17). Memuchan convinces the king that Vashti wronged not only the king, but all
"the ministers and all the peoples" (1:16) because as a woman she dared stand up to a
man's order and challenge his authority. Vashti is demoted, and her penalty is well publicized so that "all the wives will give honor to their husbands" (1:20). The willful Persian
wife is replaced by a seemingly meek and selfless Esther. This obedient wife earns the
honor of becoming a biblical heroine; Vashti effectively disappears from the story. The
literary prominence given to Esther, at the expense of Vashti, demonstrates the biblical
stance on sexual politics. Apart from the implied commendation of Esther's loyalty as a
Jewess, the text also implies approbation for her portrayed role as an obedient daughter
and submissive (even though manipulative) wife.

It is true that Ruth shows more character and resolution than Esther. Unlike the
latter, she is not "taken" as a bride but rather uses her feminine charms to manipulate
Boaz into marrying her. Yet as a woman Ruth is portrayed as being just as submissive as
Esther. She not only follows her mother-in-law to Canaan, but she also obeys Naomi's
advice: in response to Naomi's advice to join Boaz in the barn she says: "All that thou
sayest unto me I will do" (3:5). Washed, anointed, and finely dressed (3:3), Ruth goes to
Boaz's barn, uncovers his lower body, and lies down by his feet (*lemargelotav*). The
Hebrew term for "feet" is often used in the Bible as a euphemism for genitals. Thus the
scene implies both a sexual and a master-slave relationship between the woman and the
man. This act reminds us of Esther's strategy. Esther does not confront the king directly.
She procrastinates her request, thus tantalizing the king. The deceptive and circuitous
strategy is characteristic of the conciliatory strategy wise women are forced to use in the
patriarchal world.

Ruth's rhetorical style is similar in its supplicating accents to the way in which
Esther addresses the king. Ruth implores Boaz to grant her protection, referring to herself as his "maid-servant" (3:9). Her gestures, too, like those of Esther's, indicate submissiveness to Boaz: "Then she fell on her face, and bowed down to the ground" (2:10).
Both women move from a master-slave relationship to conjugal bliss. Marriage in both
cases is cause for redemption for them and their kinsmen.

Despite their literary predominance both heroines serve as agents rather than free
actants. They mediate between "senders" and "helpers." Both obey rather than initiate.
The sender and the addressee in both cases are older, authoritative figures.[5] Both heroines succeed in their mission thanks to submission, subtle manipulation, and sexual
appeal.

After their successful intercession with their respective husband-redeemers, both
heroines recede to the background. The redemptive process moves into a male-dominated
scene. In the book of Ruth, both Naomi and Ruth are virtually excluded from the central
action of the final chapter. Ruth is presented as a mere piece of property; along with
Naomi's field she is *purchased* by Boaz from Naomi's closer kin (4:10). In the only two
verses in which she is mentioned, Ruth appears as direct object. In verse 10 she complements the transitive verb "acquire." The blatancy of the original *qaniti* is somewhat
mitigated by the English translation. In verse 13, Ruth complements as direct object the

transitive "take" (*vayyiqqah*). The quick succession of verbs in this verse dramatizes the movement towards the goal. Boaz takes Ruth; she becomes his wife; he comes to her; she conceives and bears a son (4:13). The story concludes with a genealogical list from Peretz to David, all but excluding the women involved. Neither Tamar, mother of Peretz, nor Ruth, mother of Obed, is mentioned. In this final section, Boaz is the one credited as progenitor: "and Boaz begot Obed; and Obed begot Jesse; and Jesse begot David" (4:216–22).

In the penultimate chapter of the book of Esther, the scene is virtually taken over by Mordecai, who orchestrates the reversal of events from tragedy to happy ending. Esther is said to entreat the king one more time (9:12–13) and to cooperate with Mordecai in writing down the great events of the day (9:29).

The final chapter ignores the heroine altogether. The final verse sings the praises only of Mordecai:

> For Mordecai the Jew was next unto the king Ahasuerus, the great among the Jews, and accepted of the multitude of his brethren: seeking the good of his people and speaking peace to all his seed. (10:3)

Both stories start with a temporary destabilization of the patriarchal order. Both Ruth and Esther personify the reinstitution of patriarchal order. Only by reenacting the roles assigned to them by the patriarchal system as wives or mothers can women become national heroines.

The gender-related constraints on these characters become even clearer when juxtaposed with the story of Deborah. In Deborah's case, it is her public actions, and not her relations with her husband, father, or sons that turn her into a heroine. Deborah is the one who initiates the resistance against Yabin, King of Canaan, and his ruthless officer, Sisera. Deborah is not only a political and strategic leader, but she is also a self-conscious feminist. Aware of the status of women in Hebraic patriarchal society, she warns Barak, son of Avinoam, not to brag of his future military victory, "for the Lord will give Sisera over into the hand of a woman" (Judges 4:9). Unlike the other judges, however, she is unable to win the guerrilla war against Sisera by herself. She is assisted by Barak, son of Avinoam and Yael the Kanite. The final victory is shared by three major figures. This pattern is extraordinary in the book of Judges. All the other judges fully control the campaigns against the oppressors. Nevertheless, the story of Deborah does offer a positive portrait of a heroine as a national public figure, independent of traditional patriarchal roles. From a literary point of view, Deborah remains a flat and one-dimensional character. Her literary function is consummated by a single action. From this point of view, she differs little from Ruth or Esther, who disappear from the scene as soon as they perform their role. Ruth brings redemption to her husband's family, and Esther to her people. But despite their importance, they function as performers rather than full-fledged characters. Robert Alter points out that unlike the Homeric epic, the biblical narrative is highly selective and reticent in its method of characterization.

This is especially true in regard to secondary characters. In the case of female characters, even central figures lack the complexity and depth granted to their male counterparts Jacob, Joseph, Moses, Joshua, Samson, Saul, and David. The female protagonists remain flat, static, and essentially functional; they move in a single direction (normally from the custody of one male to another) with no conflict, pain, or regret. Even as central characters, they fail to transcend their circumscribed roles and gender-determined status.

The stories of Ruth and Esther are not only stories told *by* a man's world, but also *for* a man's world. These are not stories of women, but stories of female role models determined and fostered by the strongly developed patriarchal ideology so characteristic of the society in which they lived.

NOTES

1. A similar example is the story of Joseph, Genesis 37 and 39–45, but Joseph is well aware of God's providence as evidenced in his solution for Pharaoh s dream.

2. Orpah, wife of Chilion, Naomi's other son, determines to stay in Moab, though she, too, is at first willing to follow Naomi, the mother-in-law to Judah, her husband's country. In contrast to Orpah, Ruth is not convinced by Naomi's discouragement and insists on joining her husband's mother.

3. This is not the first time in which Esther serves as agent rather than independent actant. Previous to the conflict with Haman, Mordecai exposes a plot to kill Ahasuerus while Esther conveys her uncle's message to Hatach and her husband (Esther 3:2).

4. The biblical narrative refers to a character's external features only when they fulfill a vital role in the progression of the plot (Bar-Efrat 1979:77–78).

5. Esther is Mordecai's adopted daughter. Ruth is Naomi's daughter-in-law, and is referred to by Boaz as "my daughter" (3:11).

REFERENCES

Alter, Robert
1981   *The Art of Biblical Narrative*. Philadelphia: The Jewish Publication Society of America.

Bar-Efrat, Shimeon
1979   *Ha-isuv ha-omanuti shel ha-sipur ba-miqra (The Art of the Biblical Story)*. Tel Aviv: Sifriat Poalim.

Bird, Phyllis
1974   "Images of Women in the Old Testament," *Religion and Sexism*, ed. R.R. Reuther. New York: Simon and Schuster.

Daly, Mary
1973   *Beyond God and Father*. Boston: Beacon Press.

Millet, Kate
1969   *Sexual Politics*. New York: Ballantine Books.

Propp, Vladimir
1955   *The Holy Scriptures*. Philadelphia: The Jewish Publication Society of America.
1968   *The Morphology of the Folktale*. Austin: University of Texas.

Trible, Phyllis
1978   *God and the Rhetoric of Sexuality*. Philadelphia: Fortress Press.

Woman and the Discourse of Patriarchal Wisdom
A Study of Proverbs 1–9

CAROL A. NEWSOM

casual reader asked to describe Proverbs 1–9 might reply that it was the words of a father talking to his son, mostly about women. While that might be a naive reading, its very naiveté brings into focus some of the features of Proverbs 1–9 that have not always been sufficiently attended to in scholarly discussions. First, these chapters are virtually all talk. They are, to use a currently fashionable word, discourse. But even more importantly, discourse, the dialogic, social dimension of language, becomes a central topic of these chapters. Second, the cast of characters is severely limited, and the privileged axis of communication is that from father to son. The reader's locus of self-identification, that is, the subject position established for the reader, is that of the son, the character who never speaks. Third, discourse embodies and generates a symbolic world. Consequently, it is significant that though woman is not the sole topic of the chapters, talk about women and women's speech occupies an astonishing amount of the text—men, preoccupied with speech, talking about women and women's speech. What role, then, does sexual difference play in this symbolic world both in making men's speech possible but at the same time rendering it problematic?

Proverbs 1:2–9

Although it is widely recognized that the father/son address of Proverbs 1–9 is not to be taken literally, very little attention is generally given to the significance of the fictional level established by these terms. It is a rather minimal fiction, but nonetheless important. The father, who speaks, is the "I" of the discourse. The son, addressed in the vocative and with imperative verbs, is the "you." Though other types of speech are occasionally embedded within it, the fiction never moves beyond this repeated moment of address. The linguist Emile Benveniste has drawn attention to the peculiar nature of the pronouns "I" and "you." What is unique to them becomes evident when one asks what they refer to. They don't refer either to a concept (the way that nouns like "tree" do), nor do they refer to unique individuals (the way that proper names do). Instead "I" and "you" are linguistic blanks or empty signs filled only when individual speakers and addressees appropriate them in specific instances of discourse. Their oddity among linguistic signs is related to "the problem they serve to solve, which is none other than that of intersubjective communication."[1] In fact Benveniste claims that it is through language that our subjectivity, our ability to constitute ourselves as subjects, is made possible. "Consciousness of self is only possible if it is experienced by contrast. I use *I* only when I am speaking to someone who will be a *you* in my address. It is this condition of dialogue that is constitutive of person."[2] The striking prominence of the pronouns "I" and "you" and the repeated use of vocative and imperative address in Proverbs 1–9 are clear indicators of what is at stake in these chapters: the formation of the subjectivity of the reader.[3]

Because of the social nature of discourse in which subjectivity is established, it can never be ideologically neutral. There is no Cartesian self that can be established apart from all else, but always a self in relation. The emergence of subjectivity is always in the context of ideology. In a well-known analogy the Marxist theoretician Louis Althusser speaks of the way in which ideology "recruits" subjects, "hails" them as a policeman might: "Hey, you there!" The individual, recognizing himself or herself as the one addressed, turns around in response to the hailing. And with that gesture he or she becomes a subject, takes up a particular subject position in a particular ideology. Althusser uses the term *interpellation* for this process.[4] The actual hailing by ideology is seldom as direct as one finds in the instruction literature of Proverbs 1–9. But here the intent is explicit and self-conscious. The reader of this text is called upon to take up the subject position of son in relation to an authoritative father. Now that would be a rather banal statement if this were a piece of children's literature, used exclusively in a school setting and then outgrown. But clearly it is not. The intended readers identified by the text include not only the naive youth (v. 4) but also the mature sage (v. 5). All readers of this text, whatever their actual identities, are called upon to take up the subject position of son in relation to an authoritative father. Through its imitation of a familiar scene of interpellation the text continually reinterpellates its readers.

The familiar scene, a father advising his son, is important. Proverbs 1–9 takes a moment from the history of the patriarchal family and gives it a privileged status as a continuing social norm.[5] The choice of the patriarchal family as the symbol of the authority structure of wisdom has important implications. Since it is in the family that one's subjectivity is first formed, the malleability called for in the text is made to seem innocent, natural, inevitable. In addition, the symbol of the family causes the discourse to appear to stand outside of specific class interests. This is not a landed aristocrat speaking, not a senior bureaucrat, not a member of the urban middle class or a disenfranchised intellectual, but "your father." Families are not ideologically innocent places, but because everyone has one, they give the appearance of being so.

The specific social dimensions of Proverbs 1–9 are also cloaked by the preference for abstract terms, such as "righteousness, justice, and equity" (1:3). The pragmatic meaning of these terms is seldom clear from the text. And yet it is precisely in the struggle to control the meaning of such terms that one finds evidence of ideological conflict between social groups.[6] Occasionally, one can catch a hint as to the social location of wisdom discourse, but the type of speech used in Proverbs 1–9 largely serves to deflect that inquiry. What is important for Proverbs 1–9 is the issue of interpellation and the need for continual reinterpellation.

Proverbs 1:10–19

The first speech that is addressed to the son is precisely about how to resist interpellation by a rival discourse ("My son, if sinners try to persuade you, do not consent," v. 10). Because the discourse of the "sinners" is presented by the father, their alleged speech is really completely controlled by the father. In fact the sinners' speech is crowded with negative markers: they are made to describe their own victims as "innocent" (v. 12a). Their metaphor for themselves is that of death itself, Sheol swallowing up life (v. 12b). They act gratuitously, "for the hell of it" (Heb. *ḥinnām*, v. 11). Assuming, with many commentators, that verse 16 is a late marginal comment drawn from Isaiah 59:7, the father follows an interesting rhetorical strategy in soliciting the son's agreement to his point of view. He first reiterates his admonition (v. 15) and then poses a challenge: "in vain is the net spread in full view of the bird" (v. 17). The wise son, the reader who can "deconstruct" the discourse of the sinners, won't be trapped in their net of words. Since the self-incriminating elements of the hypothetical speech are hard to miss, the reader enjoys a moment of self-congratulation, a moment that bonds the reader closer to the father. The father then confirms the reader's judgment in verse 18, making explicit the self-destructive quality of the sinners.

But what else is going on here? Who and what is the son really being warned against? It seems scarcely credible that the advice should be taken at face value as career counseling. It is much more likely that this depiction of brigands is a metaphor for something else. Indeed, verse 19 confirms it. The summary statement of the address explains that "such are the ways of all who cut a big profit." Here at least is one clue to the social location of the text, though we still do not know precisely what economic activity is identified by the pejorative phrase. A closer look at the sinners' speech offers a different avenue of approach. The structure of authority embodied there is strikingly different from that of the overall discourse of Proverbs 1–9. The persuaders are not fathers hierarchically related to the son, but peers. Their speech uses the cohortative rather than the direct imperative. Featured pronouns are not the counterposed "I-you" pair but the often repeated "us," "we." The egalitarian subtext is made explicit in verse 14b, "we will all share a common purse." The rival discourse against which the father argues can be made visible in its general outlines: it is one with a horizontal rather than a vertical structure of authority based not on patriarchal family affiliation but on common enterprise, and one that offers young men immediate access to wealth rather than the deferred wealth of inheritance. What lurks under the surface is the generational chasm, the division of power between older and younger men in patriarchal society. The genuine appeal to younger men of the set of values just described is cleverly defused by associating them with what is clearly outside the law.

Proverbs 1:20–33

Here and in chapter 8 the father's discourse is interrupted by speeches of personified wisdom. These speeches serve to buttress what the father has said, however, and belong to the same cultural voice that speaks through the father. Although the pronouns and inflected verb forms identify wisdom as female, the significance of her gender emerges more clearly in the later part of Proverbs 1–9. Here I want to focus on the relative positions of speaker and addressee established in the speech. That *Ḥokmot* (personified wisdom) is an extension of the cultural voice that speaks through the father can be seen in the complementary authoritative position she occupies. Where the father is the authoritative voice in the family, *Ḥokmot* is the corresponding public voice ("in the streets," "in the public squares," v. 20) who occupies the places that are physically symbolic of collective authority and power ("at the entrance of the gates," v. 21). She also has the power to save from disaster (vv. 26–33). Although she addresses a plurality of listeners, the frequent second-person forms identify the reader as directly addressed. Perhaps the most interesting feature of the text is that it posits a past to the relationship between *Ḥokmot* and the reader. Her first words are "How long will you . . ." (v. 22). The reader's subjectivity is furnished not only with a past but with a guilty one. As one who is "naive," "cocky," and "complacent" (v. 22), he has refused advice and correction. The reader discovers himself in the text as always, already at fault. And the fault is recalcitrance before legitimate authority.

The two paired speeches of chapter 1 have attempted to construct a subject who is extremely submissive: perennially a son, willing to forego the attractions of nonhierarchical order, and yet despite it all, somehow never quite submissive enough. But one may sense, lurking behind this nearly supine persona, a shadow figure of significant power. A world made of discourse, a symbolic order, an ideology exists only by consensus. If it cannot recruit new adherents and if those whom it reinterpellates do not recognize themselves in its hailing, it ceases to have reality. *Ḥokmot* may threaten the recalcitrant with destruction, but the inverse is also true: enough recalcitrance and *Ḥokmot* ceases to exist.[7]

Proverbs 2

The problematic aspects of discourse already present in chapter 1 are given a sharper focus in the carefully constructed composition of Proverbs 2. One can summarize the argument as follows: Accept my words and internalize them with the help of God (vv. 1–11), and they will protect you from the man who speaks perversely (vv. 12–15) and from the strange, smooth-talking woman (vv. 16–20). The world is presented as a place of competing and conflicting discourses: the words of the father, the words of the crooked man, the words of the strange woman. One is hailed from many directions, offered subject positions in discourses that construe the world very differently. Far from valuing the plurality of discourses that intersect a culture, Proverbs 1–9 seeks the hegemony of its own discourse. If one has internalized a discourse, one is insulated from, or as the text more polemically puts it, protected from other voices.

But how is this to occur? How is one's subjectivity formed in that definitive way? Verses 1–11 make the astute observation that allegiance precedes understanding, not the other way around. We should not be surprised that these wisdom discourses do not closely define the pragmatic content of wisdom and contrast it with the competing discourses, seeking to convince the hearer of its superiority. Rather, it repeatedly asks first for allegiance ("accept my words," "treasure up my strictures," "incline your ear," "extend your heart," vv. 1–2). Nor is the allegiance passive. It must involve active participation ("call out," "seek," vv. 3–4). Only then does understanding follow ("then you will understand fear of Yahweh," v. 5; "then you will understand righteousness and justice and equity, every good path," v. 9), for at that point habituation to the assumptions, values, and cultural practices of the group will make them seem one's own ("for wisdom will come into your heart and your soul will delight in knowledge," v. 10). As Althusser pungently paraphrases Pascal, "Kneel down, move your lips in prayer, and you will believe."[8]

For this reason it isn't surprising that the metaphors of "way," "path," and "track," which occur throughout Proverbs 1–9, appear in this chapter with particular density (twelve occurrences in vv. 8–20). "Way" or "path" may be a hackneyed metaphor for customary behavior, but its connotations are worth some reflection. A path is a social product, made by many feet over a period of time. But its purely physical record of customary social behavior is often transposed in terms of a teleology and a will ("Where does that path lead?"). A path does not, in fact, exclude movement in any direction. It only makes its own direction the easiest, most natural, most logical way of proceeding. As each individual "freely" chooses to walk the path, that act incises the path more deeply. Finally, a path orders the world in a particular way as it establishes relations between place and place, relations that are not necessarily the shortest distance between two points. It is understandable why, in a chapter that construes the world as a place of conflicting discourses, the metaphor of the path figures so prominently. Customary social behavior, represented by the image of the path, is a type of nonverbal discourse. Manners, dress, food, orientation to time, divisions of labor, and so forth, are all elements of a social group's discourse, alongside its explicit words. Words and ways are related, as the parallelism of verse 12 suggests.

But against whom is the father arguing so strenuously? Who are the man and woman whose speech the son is warned about? Of the man all we learn is that he is associated with inversion of values (he delights in what is bad, v. 14a; his words are all "turned about," v. 12) and with perversion of values ("twisted," "crooked," v. 15), the opposite of the quality of "uprightness" and "perfection" associated with the father's advice (v. 21). His function is definitional. He simply serves to signify whatever stands over against "us," the group of the father's discourse.

It is with the symbol of the strange woman, however, that the text discovers its primary image of otherness. For a patriarchal discourse in which the self is defined as male, woman qua woman is the quintessential other. Much ink has been spilled in attempting to clarify why she is identified as a "strange" or "foreign" woman, whether the terms refer to an ethnic, legal, or social status. But it may not be an either/or question. Whether the terms were originally ambiguous or have only become so after the passage of years, any and all of the possible interpretations underscore the quality of otherness that she already possesses as woman in male discourse. As a foreigner, she would recall the strong Israelite cultural preference for endogamy over exogamy, the choice of same over other. If, as seems to be clearly the case in chapter 7, she is an adulteress, then she may be called strange/foreign because she is legally "off limits."[9] Or, if 2:17 is meant to suggest that she has left her husband ("one who has abandoned the companion of her youth"), then she is strange/foreign because she is an anomaly who no longer has a place in the system of socially regulated sexuality and now belongs on the side of the chaotic. In any case her otherness serves to identify the boundary and what must be repressed or excluded.

Woman is a much more serviceable symbol for this definitionally important "other" than was the man of verses 12–15 because she can be posited as a figure of ambivalence, both frightening and attractive. Her words are described as "smooth," a term that suggests both pleasure and danger (= slippery). Once experienced, the ambivalence has to be tilted in the proper direction, and so she is identified with the ultimate boundary, death. A textual problem in verse 18 provides a clue to the psychological basis for the equation. Judging from the parallelism and the meaning of the verb, one expects the text to read "her path sinks down to death, her tracks are toward the shades." As it stands, it reads "her house sinks down to death. . . ." If the MT is a textual corruption, it is in truth a Freudian slip, for "house" is a common symbolic representation of woman or womb.[10] The ambivalence is the attraction and fear of a return to the womb. The strange woman is the devouring woman, for "none who go in to her will return" (v. 19).

With this text one can begin to see the significance of sexual difference for the existence of patriarchal discourse. Invoking the strange woman as a threat provides a basis for solidarity between father and son. Her difference makes available a shared sameness for father and son that bridges the generational divisions of patriarchy that were visible in Proverbs 1. But more importantly the woman and her discourse exist as a persistent irritant located, to borrow Julia Kristeva's phrase, at the margin.[11] In the following chapters she continues to preoccupy the father's advice. He can never quite be finished with her. The competition she represents is the cause of the father's speech, the incentive for its very existence. The strange woman figures the irreducible difference that prevents any discourse from establishing itself unproblematically. That is to say, she is not simply the speech of actual women, but she is the symbolic figure of a variety of marginal discourses. She is the contradiction, the dissonance that forces a dominant discourse to articulate itself and at the same time threatens to subvert it. Those dissonances can no more be eliminated than can sexual difference itself. And their existence is a source of slow but profound change in symbolic orders.

Proverbs 3

In giving discourse a privileged position and in representing the world as a place of conflicting discourses, Proverbs 1–9 appears to acknowledge the socially constructed nature of reality and the problematic status of truth. Such reflections were part of the broader wisdom tradition, as the saying in Proverbs 18:17 illustrates: "The one who argues his case first seems right, until someone else is brought forward and cross-examines him." The implications are disturbing for the representatives of authority. What can ensure that the content given to the terms "righteousness, justice, and equity" or "wisdom, knowledge, and discernment" can be stabilized according to the values of the tradents of Proverbs 1–9 and not captured by rival discourses? The text has attempted to buttress its authoritative position by claiming the symbol of the patriarchal father and by discrediting other voices as alien and criminal. Thus the signifiers point to the father and to the law. Though powerful, that is not sufficient. What is needed is an anchorage beyond the contestable social world, in short, a transcendental signified to which all terms point and from which they derive their stable meanings.[12] In a provisional way the parallel between the speech of the father and the speech of *Ḥokmot* in chapter 1 provided this anchorage. But that strategy is not fully developed until chapter 8. In chapter 3 we encounter the first sustained effort to provide the transcendental signified that stops the threatening slippage of meaning.

The first indication is in the initial call for hearing: "My son, don't forget my teaching (Heb. *tôrātî*) and let your heart guard my commands" (Heb. *miṣwôtay*). Various paired terms refer to the father's instruction throughout the chapters. But this particular pair has resonances of God's *torah* and *miṣwot* to Israel and so subtly positions the father in association with divine authority. The benefits of long life and peace that are promised (v. 2) also suggest that the father's teaching and commands derive from transcendent power. In verse 4 it is made explicit. The father's advice will be validated both in the social and in the transcendent realms ("before the eyes of God and humankind"). For several further verses the father actually speaks on behalf of God, urging the son to obedience to God and promising rewards. The appeal parallels in structure and motivation the father's call for obedience to himself in vv. 1–4. It comes as no surprise that in the MT the passage concludes in v. 12 with the metaphor of God as a father reproving his son. It is not enough to ground the authority structure of Proverbs 1–9 in the patriarchal father. The authority of the transcendent Father of fathers is needed.

Having claimed access to the transcendent realm through the alignment of the father and God, the chapter next turns to secure the stability of its comprehensive terms of value, "wisdom," and "understanding" (vv. 13–21). A variety of linked images carries the argument. First wisdom is compared with riches. Then it is personified as a woman holding riches and honor in one hand, long life in the other. The tableau may well be an evocation of the Egyptian goddess Maat, but the meaning of the image does not require knowledge of the allusion. A figure who holds life in her hand belongs to the transcendent. References to her pleasant ways and safe paths recall the paths of the strange woman of chapter 2 and establish this figure as her opposite. As death belongs to one, life belongs to the other. The chain of association completes itself with another mythic image, wisdom as the tree of life. Such a phrase sets up an intertextual play with Genesis 2–3. Here the two trees of Genesis are condensed into one—knowledge that gives life. In the Genesis narrative the quest for knowledge was marked as rebellion and resulted in exclusion from the source of life. Here it is submissive obedience that is correlated with wisdom and with life. In Genesis the desire "to be like God" with respect to wisdom ("knowing good and evil") was a mark of hubris. Here the one who finds wisdom (v. 13) is blessed precisely because he is like God, having found that by which God created the world (vv. 19–20). Wisdom is not one discourse among others but the stuff of reality itself. The values of the father are built into the structures of the world.

Proverbs 4

In Proverbs 4:3–4 the father speaks and says "I was a son to my father; a precious only son to my mother. And he taught me and said to me. . . ." In part this is a strengthening of the claim to authority, as fathers quote earlier fathers. But there is another function. I made the point earlier that the subject position of the reader in Proverbs 1–9 is that of the son, established through the fiction of direct address by the father. But the situation is somewhat more complex than that. There is always a measure of identification between father and son, so that a son understands and thinks "when I grow up, that's what I will be." The father-status already exists as potentiality in the son. That identification is, of course, vital in negotiating the intergenerational divide of patriarchal society. For the young male deferral is not endless. So, in Proverbs 1–9, where the reader is continually reinterpellated in the subject position of the son, chapter 4 speaks of the transformation of sons into fathers in the chain of tradition. The male subject is to a certain degree apportioned between father and son. One is always a subordinate son to the collective authority of the symbolic order. But its transcending father-status is what underwrites the father-status of those who occupy positions of authority within it.

Each of the following poetic sections of Proverbs 4 is built up by a playful use of one or more metaphoric conceits that employ various cultural codes. Despite the apparent heterogeneity, the various sections all relate to the familiar issues of subjectivity, discourse, and allegiance. In vv. 5–9 what appears to be an economic code ("acquire wisdom," "with all of your acquisition, acquire understanding") is combined with an erotic code ("don't abandon," "love," "embrace"). What seems to connect the two is the notion of the relationship as a transaction between the son and wisdom, an exchange of value. Verses 10–19 develop a code of movement: way, lead, walk, paths, steps, run, stumble, go, come, road, go straight, avoid, cross over, etc. At least some of the possible connotations have been discussed above in connection with chapter 2.

The most curious of the codes is the rewriting of the self as a series of body parts in verses 20–27: ear, eyes, heart, flesh, mouth, lips, eyes, pupils, feet. Intertwined with this inventory of the body are terms from a code of physical orientation (incline, extend, twist away, turn aside, twistedness, crookedness, make distant, straight, in front, straight before, swerve to right or left). The values associated with straightness and twistedness were made explicit in chapter 2. What is of more interest is the subdivision of the body. There are two other similar poems in 6:12–15 and 6:16–19. In the first of these we are introduced to the man "who goes about with a twisted mouth." What is wrong with his speech is made evident in v. 13. He allows other body parts to act, improperly, as speaking mouths, setting up commentaries or other discourses that invert the words of the mouth. "He winks with his eyes, communicates with his feet, instructs with his fingers." No wonder his speech is duplicitous. In the numerical poem that follows there is a catalog of the crucial body parts and their characteristic misuses: arrogant eyes, a lying tongue, hands shedding innocent blood, a scheming heart, feet that speed to whatever is bad. The self is not presented as a simple entity. Or perhaps it is better to say that various parts of the body can represent the whole by synecdoche. The individual's subjectivity can be seen as invested in each of these parts, any of which has the power to work his ruin. But it seems odd that one part of the body, that part that males traditionally have considered to be the privileged representation of their subjectivity, is not mentioned. Although the phallus is never referred to explicitly, the problems of that important but unruly member are taken up in chapters 5–6.

Proverbs 5–6

If the image of the woman has figured importantly in the first chapters of Proverbs 1–9, it utterly dominates the second half of the text. The most vivid and extensive representations are those of the strange woman. As in chapter 2, her sexuality is repeatedly associated with speech. She has "a smooth tongue" (6:24), "smooth words" (7:5), "smooth lips" (7:21). In the most explicitly erotic description it is said that "her lips drip with honey" and the inside of her mouth is "smoother than oil" (5:3). That she figures as the father's chief rival for the allegiance of the son would be clear simply from the length and intensity of the attack on her, but in 7:21 it is even said that she misleads the naive youth with her "teaching," a term used of the father's instruction as well (4:2). The fear that the father has of her is revealed in one of the images used to describe her deceptiveness. In patriarchal thinking it is woman's lack of the phallus and the privilege that the male associates with its possession that grounds woman's inferiority. In the father's phantasm the danger is that behind that reassuring smoothness, that visible absence of the phallus, there lurks something "sharp as a two edged sword" (5:4). The fantasy is that she not only possesses a hidden super potency but that it is a castrating potency as well. She threatens to reverse the body symbolism on which the father's authority is established.

The simple opposition between male and female is fundamental to the symbolic order of patriarchy, but it does not exhaust the role of woman in the symbolic economy. The triple association of sexuality, speech, and authority needs to be followed a bit further. The association of authority with speech is clear. In Proverbs 1–9 the father speaks, the son is spoken to. The father's control of speech is further indicated in that the speech of the sinners and of the strange woman does not reach the son directly but only as filtered through the father's speech. And in general, the silencing of women in patriarchal society is both symbol and result of the inferior status based on their perceived sexual "lack." On the other hand sexuality is by its nature dialogical, as the term "intercourse" well suggests. Culturally, it is closely associated with speech: courting speech, seductive speech, love songs, whispered sweet nothings. The point at which the horizontal speech of the woman's sexuality comes into conflict with the vertical speech of the father's authority is precisely at the point of generational transition, when the boy becomes a man. In her provocative study of the Samson story Mieke Bal makes reference to the moment of sexual maturity as the point at which "the trinity of the nuclear family is sacrificed to the alienating relationship with the other, the fourth person."[13] The sexual maturation of the son is a critical moment not only in psychoanalytic terms but also a critical moment for the social and symbolic order. It is the moment at which the patriarchal family will be successfully replicated or threatened. The system of approved and disapproved sexual relations forms a language through which men define their relations with one another. Proverbs 5:7–14, 15–20; and 6:20–35 set up three parallel situations: the woman outside the group/the proper wife/the wife of another man inside the group.[14]

It is interesting to see how the benefits and consequences of each are described. Sexual relations with the first woman ("approaching the door to her house," 5:8) are described in terms of depletion: ". . . lest you give to others your wealth and your years to the merciless; lest strangers batten on your strength and your labors in the house of a foreigner. You will be sorry afterwards when your flesh and body are consumed"

(5:9–11).[15] Although there is an obvious element of psychosexual fantasy here, it is overwritten by social references. The others/the merciless/the strangers/the foreigner who are the devourers here are all masculine nouns and imply the community of males to whom the woman belongs. Exogamy is deplorable because it results in the alienation of wealth. The communal context is further indicated by the concluding lament: "I was quickly brought to ruin in the midst of the congregation and the assembly." Going outside deprives a man of standing in his own group as well.

By contrast, appropriate sexual relations have a centripetal direction. In 5:15–20 sexual connections are described under the figure of water contained and dispersed. "Drink water from your own cistern and running water from your own well. [Don't] let your springs overflow outside, streams of water in the public squares. Let them be for yourself alone, not for strangers with you."

Because there is a considerable subjective investment in one's own proper wife ("your cistern, your well, for yourself alone"), the selfhood of individual males and the solidarity of the community is severely threatened by adultery. The "foreign" woman of 6:20–35 is not ethnically foreign but off limits because she is "the wife of one's neighbor." As in the first example, the code of property crops up, here in a comparison between theft and adultery (vv. 30–31). The point of comparison is not between the rights of the male to the woman or property but to the social rather than the merely private dimensions of the offense. The criminal is in each case the object of contempt or scorn, though much more so in the case of the adulterer.[16] Not only will the wronged husband refuse an offered settlement; the entire community is implacable in its judgment of "his reproach which can never be effaced" (v. 33). The code of behavior between men and women is raised up in these passages as an important code of signifying behavior among groups of men. Metaphorically, in the social fabric of patriarchy woman is the essential thread that joins the pieces. But equally she indicates the seams where the fabric is subject to tears.

Although much of the advice offered in Proverbs 5–6 about relations with women appears to be strictly pragmatic, one often has a sense of a curious slippage between the literal and the symbolic. When one understands from Proverbs 5:15–20 that a good marriage will protect a man from foreign women and "thy neighbor's wife," one also remembers the themes of protection associated with personified wisdom in 4:6–9. When the ruined son recollects in Proverbs 5:12–13 how he "hated discipline," "despised criticism," and never listened to his teachers, his regrets seem to refer to more than just the lesson on sex. Is the strange woman not a problem in sexual mores after all, but an allegory of folly? The final pairing in chapter 9 of the allegorical women *Hokmot* and *Kesilut* (Wisdom and Folly) would seem to point in that direction. But it would be a mistake to pose the pragmatic and the allegorical as either/or alternatives. When symbolic thinking is carried forward by means of concrete objects or persons, statements and actions pertaining to these concrete entities can never be merely pragmatic on the one hand or simply metaphorical on the other. All customary praxis involving women is nonverbal symbolic construction. All use of the feminine in symbolic representation implicates behavior. So long as a society's discourse is carried on by males alone, that fact is scarcely noticeable. But as women enter into public discourse as speaking subjects, the habit of patriarchy to think symbolically by means of woman is thrown into confusion. Woman cannot occupy the same symbolic relation to herself that she does to man. With that change the long, slow crisis of the symbolic order is at hand.

Proverbs 7–9

Something of the both/and, pragmatic/symbolic totality of woman in the discourse of Proverbs 1–9 can be seen in the two great paired poems of Proverbs 7 and 8. Although very different in style and content, these poems of the strange woman and of personified wisdom form a diptych. Chapter 8, with its strong mythic overtones, is written largely in the symbolic register; chapter 7 largely in the realistic. But in the framing of chapter 7 there are certain elements that establish its relationship to chapter 8 and disclose its mythic dimensions. In the father's account of the meeting between the vapid youth and the strange woman the words are ominous and negative. The woman is associated with many of the wisdom tradition's bad values, yet appears to be an ordinary, mundane character. The setting is twilight, so that the woman arrives with the onset of "night and darkness" (v. 9). She is associated with concealment and with the appearance of what is illicit (v. 10). Where wisdom tradition values quietness, she is "noisy" (v. 11), and her movement is characterized as restless, vagrant, and flitting. When she is still, she is "lying in wait" (v. 12), a predatory quality that is made explicit in verses 22–23. Her smooth speech "turns" the young man (v. 21). The symbolic register is more explicitly evoked in the introductory and concluding remarks of the father. Calling wisdom "sister" and "kinswoman" (v. 4) introduces explicit personification. Those words also set up a relation of equivalence between wisdom and "the wife of your youth" from chapter 5, instilling actual marriage with the protective values of wisdom. Similarly, the father's concluding words in verses 24–27 expose the monstrous, mythic dimension of the strange woman. She is not just a woman who has seduced a simple-minded young man. She is a predator who has slain multitudes. Indeed, her vagina is the gate of Sheol. Her womb, death itself.

Chapter 8 is radically different in style. Where the strange woman's speech is passed through the father's admonitory speech, wisdom speaks autonomously. Although there are traces of the erotic associated with her ("love" in v. 17, perhaps the reference to "delighting" in vv. 30–31, and the allusion to the man waiting and watching at her gate in v. 34), her speech and self-presentation are thoroughly unlike the strange woman's. Her movement is public, direct, and authoritative. Unlike the smooth, seductive, but deceptive speech of the strange woman, wisdom's is like that of the father: "straight," "right," and "true," not "twisted," or "crooked." Her voice, of course, is the cultural voice that speaks through the father, the voice that grounds the social fathers: the kings, rulers, princes, nobles of verses 15–16. Hers is the voice that mediates between the transcendent father and his earthly sons.

But how can it be, when so much energy has been invested in disclosing the terrifying dangerousness of woman as represented in the strange woman, that Proverbs 1–9 turns to woman also for its ideal representation of the central term of value, wisdom itself? In fact it is not surprising at all. Thinking in terms of sexual difference, of woman as man's other, difference serves to articulate both what is inferior and what is superior. Toril Moi develops Julia Kristeva's understanding of women's position of marginal-

ity in patriarchal thinking in a way that precisely explains the symbolic projection of
Proverbs 7–8:

> If patriarchy sees women as occupying a marginal position within the symbolic order,
> then it can construe them as the limit or borderline of that order. From a phallocentric
> point of view, women will then come to represent the necessary frontier between man
> and chaos; but because of their very marginality they will also always seem to recede
> into and merge with the chaos of the outside. Women seen as the limit of the symbolic
> order will in other words share in the disconcerting properties of all frontiers: they will
> be neither inside nor outside, neither known nor unknown. It is this position that has
> enabled male culture sometimes to vilify women as representing darkness and chaos,
> to view them as Lilith or the Whore of Babylon, and sometimes to elevate them as the
> representatives of a higher and purer nature, to venerate them as Virgins and Mothers
> of God. In the first instance the borderline is seen as part of the chaotic wilderness
> outside, and in the second it is seen as an inherent part of the inside: the part that pro-
> tects and shields the symbolic order from the imaginary chaos.[17]

Wisdom's self-presentation as a divine figure in chapter 8 not only serves to anchor wisdom discourse in the transcendent realm. It also positions her as the counterpart of the
strange woman. One is the gate of Sheol, the other the gate of Heaven. Together they define and secure the boundaries of the symbolic order of patriarchal wisdom. Chapter 9 draws
the conclusion self-consciously with its explicit parallel of personified wisdom and folly.

Conclusion

Analyzing the symbolic structure of Proverbs 1–9 is not merely an antiquarian
exercise. Phallocentric constructions of the world continue to be deeply dependent on
such uses of sexual difference for their articulation. A good illustration of the profound
psychic attachment to this mode of thinking as well as the symbolic dimensions of apparently "realistic" speech is the 1987 film *Fatal Attraction*. Its subtitle could easily have
been "cling to the wife of your youth, and she will save you from the strange woman." In
the film the viewer's subjectivity is rigorously identified with that of the male character,
Dan (Michael Douglas). He is consistently depicted as a good but naive and occasionally
impulsive man, an object of seduction. The "strange woman," Alex (Glenn Close), is
portrayed as belonging to the margin in many ways. Her family background is obscure,
her employment with the company recent. She has no husband or recognized lover. She
stands outside the realm of socially ordered sexuality. Her apartment is located in an
ambiguous commercial/residential neighborhood, where workers ominously carry about
large pieces of butchered animals ("like an ox to the slaughter," 7:22). Like the strange
woman of Proverbs 7 she has a brilliant power of speech, always more than a match
for her male victim. But also like the strange woman of Proverbs, it is only an illusion that
we encounter her and her speech directly. She is not a speaking subject but rather is an
effect of someone else's speech, the paternal speech of the film itself.[18]

When the predatory seduction has been accomplished, the chaotic, monstrous
dimensions of Alex become evident: madness, violence, an uncanny unstoppable will. In
an allusion to the tradition of horror films, Alex is drowned (we see her staring eyes and
parted lips) and yet comes back from the dead. Against the inbreaking of chaos, the male
character proves himself to be finally helpless. It is "the wife of his youth" who must res-

cue him. The wife has been presented, as is the wife of Proverbs 5, as herself a deeply erotic, desirable woman. Equally, she is the center of the domesticity of the patriarchal family. Her symbol is the house, where, more than once, we see the brightly burning kitchen hearth. It is in her climactic appearance, however, that we glimpse her mythic status. In contrast to the frantic, ineffectual, and messy struggle of the husband, her single shot is decisive. But it is her bearing when the camera turns to view her that has such an effect on the viewer. She stands framed in the doorway, quiet, impassive, erect, authoritative. She is a dea ex machina and, for one familiar with Proverbs 1–9, a figure evocative of *Ḥokmot*.

As is well known, the original end of the film was changed by director Adrian Lyne in response to the reaction of the audience in test screenings.[19] He had originally filmed an ending that was a twist on the Madame Butterfly theme, in which Alex's suicide would implicate Dan as her murderer. Preview audiences, however, disliked the ending. They recognized the mythic structure of the film and insisted on its "proper" conclusion. The version of the film as we have it is thus the result of a collective writing. The extraordinary emotional reaction from subsequent audiences, especially among men, confirms how deep is the investment in the patriarchal positioning of women as the inner and outer linings of its symbolic order.

Although the similarity of the symbolic positioning of woman in *Fatal Attraction* and Proverbs 1–9 is unmistakable, it is the difference in their manner of presentation that makes Proverbs 1–9 of particular interest to feminist analysis. Where the film skillfully attempts to naturalize its discourse, to conceal its speaking subject, and mask its interpellation of the viewer, Proverbs 1–9 emphasizes precisely these features. Certainly, Proverbs 1–9 also makes its own claims to universality and transcendent authority, but its explicit self-consciousness about the central role of discourses in competition provides an internal basis for questioning its own claims. Having learned from the father how to resist interpellation by hearing the internal contradictions in discourse, one is prepared to resist the patriarchal interpellation of the father as well. For the reader who does not take up the subject position offered by the text, Proverbs 1–9 ceases to be a simple text of initiation and becomes a text about the problematic nature of discourse itself. Not only the dazzling (and defensive) rhetoric of the father but also the pregnant silence of the son and the dissidence that speaks from the margin in the person of the strange woman become matters of significance. Israel's wisdom tradition never examined its patriarchal assumptions. But its commitment to the centrality of discourse as such and its fascination with the dissident voice in Job and Qohelet made it the locus within Israel for radical challenges to the complacency of the dominant symbolic order.

NOTES

1. E. Benveniste, *Problems in General Linguistics*, Miami linguistics series no. 8 (Coral Gables, Fla.: University of Miami, 1971), 219.

2. Benveniste, *Problems in General Linguistics*, 224–25.

3. Because of the masculine subject position offered to the reader, I will refer to the reader as "he."

4. L. Althusser, *Lenin and Philosophy*, trans. B. Brewster (London: Monthly Review, 1971), 174–75.

5. I say "family" because the mother's authority as well as the father's is invoked (1:8; 4:3; 6:20). In no way is she seen as constituting an independent voice, however, but serves as a confirmer of what is presented as essentially patriarchal authority.

6. Both the Soviet Union and the United States use the term "human rights." Only when the term is precisely defined does one become aware of the assumptions of totalitarian socialism implicit in the use of this term by Soviet speakers and bourgeois liberalism and capitalism by American speakers.

7. J. Crenshaw has drawn attention to the problematic nature of authority in ancient instruction literature. "Sapiential Rhetoric and Its Warrants," *VTSup* 32 (1981): 16.

8. Althusser, *Lenin and Philosophy,* 168.

9. Mieke Bal observes that "there is a verb in Dutch for 'to commit adultery,' which is literally 'to go strange,' to go with a stranger (*vreemd gaan*)." *Lethal Love,* Indiana studies in biblical literature (Bloomington and Indianapolis: Indiana University, 1987), 43.

10. We can be certain that the error is not a meaningless one since the image of the house recurs in chapters 5, 7, and 9. For a discussion of the house/female body symbolism in the Samson story see Mieke Bal, *Lethal Love,* 49–58.

11. See J. Kristeva, "Women's Time" (187–213), and "A New Type of Intellectual: The Dissident" (292–300) in *The Kristeva Reader,* ed. Toril Moi (New York: Columbia University, 1986). Ironically, Roland Barthes entitled an early review of Kristeva's work "L'Etrangere," the strange or foreign woman, referring to her Bulgarian nationality and the unsettling quality of her work. See Toril Moi, *Sexual/Textual Politics: Feminist Literary Theory* (London: Methuen, 1985), 150.

12. The illusory nature of the transcendental signified is argued by Jacques Derrida in *Writing and Difference,* trans. Alan Bass (Chicago: University of Chicago, 1978), 278–80.

13. Bal, *Lethal Love,* 57.

14. Not all commentators understand 5:7–14 to refer to social or ethnic outsiders. Some argue that adultery is at issue. The language is probably intentionally ambiguous and polyvalent. But the contrast between "others, strangers, foreigner" in 5:9–10 and "your neighbor" in 6:29 (where adultery is explicitly at issue) suggests that the connotations of social or ethnic alienness are to the fore in 5:7–14. There is also a sharp contrast in the relation between improper sex and money in 5:9–10 and 6:35, implying different social situations.

15. Reading *wĕniḥamtā* in v. 11. Cf. LXX. The Greek text also suggests that "your wealth" in v. 9 may be an error for "your life," which would fit the parallelism better.

16. I read v. 30 as an implied question.

17. Toril Moi, *Sexual/Textual Politics,* 167.

18. For an excellent discussion of the problem of enunciation and subjectivity in film see chap. 5 of Kaja Silverman, *The Subject of Semiotics* (New York: Oxford University, 1983).

19. Myra Forsberg, "James Dearden: Life After 'Fatal Attraction,'" *New York Times,* 24 July 1988, p. 21.

The Harlot as Heroine
Narrative Art and Social Presupposition in Three Old Testament Texts

PHYLLIS BIRD

A desire for brevity and alliteration in the title has led me to overextend the meaning of the term "heroine." It is intended here as a cover term for three cases in which a harlot (or assumed harlot) plays a major role in a biblical narrative. My aim in this article is to explore the role of social presupposition in narrative construction or story telling, using the case of the harlot, or prostitute,[1] as an example. I am convinced that literary art and social presuppositions are so interrelated in any literary work that adequate interpretation requires the employment of both literary criticism and social analysis. Neither alone suffices. Each makes assumptions about the other, often leaving them unrecognized and uncriticized. Here I want to focus on their interrelationships.

Narrative art, in whatever form and whatever degree of sophistication, depends upon highly selective and purposeful use of language and images. The narratives of the Hebrew Bible, especially those contained within the Pentateuch and Deuteronomistic History, represent a particularly compressed and selective form of story-telling art, in which individual terms or figures must carry far more weight of suggested meaning than in the more expansive and nuanced prose of the modern novel, or even of the novella (ancient or modern). Thus, when a designation such as *zônâ* is attached to a name or a figure, a picture is called up in the reader's or hearer's mind and a range of meanings, attitudes, and associations on which the narrator may draw in constructing or relating the story. The twofold question I want to address in this article is (1) what was the image and understanding of the *zônâ* assumed in each of the narratives? and (2) how was that image or understanding employed by the narrator, or how did it influence the construction or narration of the story?

In my analysis I have set aside the question of historicity, insofar as this was possible without violating the terms of the narrative. That is, I have not made a judgment about the historical claims made by any of the narratives. Each of the narratives I shall examine is presented as the account of a historical event, and historical experience may dictate much of the terms of each narrative. But each is also clearly a literary work that has been shaped in its presentation by social and literary considerations. It is to these that I wish to direct my attention.

In the space alotted to me I can neither give a full literary analysis of each narrative nor a complete portrait of the harlot as she is presented in the biblical texts and other relevant records from the ancient Near East. While I will draw from time to time on a broader study,[2] I will concentrate my attention in this article on the information supplied by the three texts or required for their understanding. My procedure will be to comment on those features of the portrait of the harlot that have significance for the particular text under consideration and thus to compose and develop the picture as I move through the three texts. I will begin, however, with a brief preliminary sketch, summarizing those traits or elements that are essential to the portrait of the prostitute in Israelite society. My treatment of the individual cases will attempt to explain and defend that sketch.

First, definition and terminology. A prostitute, or harlot, is a woman who offers sexual favors for pay (Gagnon:592; cf. Gebhard:75–81).[3] In the Hebrew Bible she is normally designated by the single term *zônâ*, a Qal participle from the root *znh*, used either alone, as a substantive, or attributively.[4] Her social status is that of an outcast, though not an outlaw, a tolerated, but dishonored member of society. She normally has the legal status of a free citizen; where she is a slave, or is otherwise legally dependent, it is not because of her occupation. As a free citizen she may seek the legal protection of the state, and as a woman who is not under the authority of a husband, she may have rights of legal action (e.g., signing contracts) not possessed by other women, except hierodules and widows without male guardians. She is typically contrasted to the "normal" woman, i.e., the married woman, from whom she is separated spatially and symbolically, through distinctive dress[5] and habitat. The places and times of her activity maintain distance between her and the married woman She is a woman of the night, who appears on the streets when honorable women are secluded at home. She approaches strangers and businessmen by the roadside and in the public squares, and she lives in the shadow of the wall, on the outskirts of the city, where the refuse is dumped.[6]

Prostitution is not a universal phenomenon, nor can it properly claim to be the world's oldest profession (Gebhard:76). But it *is* characteristic of urban society, and more specifically of urban patriarchal society. It is a product and sign of the unequal distribution of status and power between the sexes in patriarchal societies, which is exhibited, among other ways, in asymmetry of sexual roles, obligations, and expectations. This may be seen in the harlot's lack of a male counterpart. Female prostitution is an accommodation to the conflicting demands of men for exclusive control of their wives' sexuality and for sexual access to other women. The greater the inaccessibility of women in the society due to restrictions on the wife and the unmarried nubile women, the greater the need for an institutionally legitimized "other" woman. The harlot is that "other" woman, tolerated but stigmatized, desired but ostracized.

A fundamental and universal feature of the institution of prostitution wherever it is found is an attitude of ambivalence. The harlot is both desired and despised, sought after and shunned. Attempts to show changes in attitudes toward prostitutes over time or from one culture to another founder on this point. Despite considerable historical and cultural variation in attitudes, the harlot is never a fully accepted person in any society.[7]

What a man desires for himself may be quite different from what he desires for his daughter or wife. One of the earliest and clearest expressions of that fundamental attitude of ambivalence toward the harlot is found in the Gilgamesh Epic. As Enkidu is about to die, he looks back over his life in the civilized world, recalling its pain, and he curses the harlot who initiated him into that world from his former carefree life among the beasts of the steppe. The curse is an aetiology of the harlot as outcast and despised.[8]

> Come, prostitute,[9] I shall establish (your) status,[10]
> a status that shall not end for all eternity.
>
> . . . .
>
> May [your lovers] discard (you) when sated with your charms,
> [May those whom] you love [despise(?) . . .] your favors(?).
>
> . . . .
>
> [Dark corners] of the street shall be your home,
> The shadow of the city's wall shall be your station.
> [Men shall piss there in front of] your feet,
> The drunken and thirsty shall slap your face.

But Shamash, overhearing Enkidu's curse, chides him, reminding him of the fine clothes and food that he had enjoyed and of his companionship with Gilgamesh. All this was the harlot's gift, for which he should be grateful. Enkidu acknowledges the right of Shamash's argument and counters his curse with a blessing. The blessing is an aetiology of the harlot as desired.

> May [your lover(?)] (always) return(?) (to you) [even from far away places]
> [Kings, prin]ces, and nobles shall love [you].
> No one shall slap his thighs (to insult you)
> [Over you the old man will] shake his beard.
> [. . . the young(?)] will unloose his girdle for you.
> [So that you shall receive from him(?)] lapis and gold.
> [May he be paid] back (who) pissed in front of you,
> [May his home be emptied(?)], his filled storehouse.
> [To the presence of] the gods [the priest] shall let you enter.
> [On your account] a wife will be forsaken, (though) a mother of seven.

I. Genesis 38:1–26

Let us turn now to the biblical narratives. Genesis 38 stands as an independent tradition unit within the Joseph story. It recounts a complex story concerning Judah, with a number of aetiological motives. The centerpiece of the chapter, however, and the bulk of the narrative is a fully developed story in itself with its own internal dynamics in which aetiological elements are lacking or play a minor role (cf. Skinner; von Rad; Speiser; Westermann).

The scene is set in the Judean Shephelah in the period before the Israelite settlement, a time when Israel's ancestors lived side by side with the people of the land and intermarried with them, apparently without censure. "At that time," the narrator informs us, "Judah went down from his brothers" and sojourned with an Adullamite named Hirah, marrying a Canaanite woman, who bore him three sons (vv 1–5). For the eldest, Er, Judah selects a wife named Tamar,[11] a woman of the region. But Er dies at the hand of God as does the second son, Onan, who refuses to fulfill the duty of the levirate toward his brother's widow (v 8). Judah, now fearful of losing his only remaining son, sends Tamar home to her father's house, instructing her to remain a widow until the third son, Shelah, grows up. And as a dutiful daughter-in-law she goes, a widow, yet "betrothed" and therefore not free to remarry. Judah in his anxiety has sealed her fate, for he intends her widowhood to be permanent.

With Tamar's dismissal, attention is turned to Judah. Years pass and his wife dies. And when his mourning is over, he sets out with his friend Hirah to attend to the shearing of his flocks at Timnah in the hill country (v 12). The report of Judah's journey is a signal to Tamar, who has perceived her father-in-law's design and is unwilling to accept the fate he has determined for her. His journey provides an opportunity for Tamar to act. But the meaning of her action and her intention in it is not spelled out by the narrator, who simply reports as an observer and thus elicits the reader's speculation. "She put off her widow's garments," he says, "covered herself with a 'veil' and wrapped herself in it (*wattěkas baṣṣā'ip wattit'allāp*) and sat at the entrance to Enaim, which is on the road to Timnah" (v 14).[12]

The language is deliberately opaque and suggestive. The narrator does not say that Tamar dressed as harlot. That is the inference that Judah makes—and is intended to make—but the narrator leaves it to Judah to draw the conclusion. "When Judah saw her, he thought her to be a harlot because she had covered her face" (*wayyaḥšěbehā lězônâ kî kissětâ pānê(y)hā*) (v 15).[13] His action is presented as following naturally from that inference: "[So] he went over to her by the roadside" and propositioned her. And Tamar, in keeping with her assumed role, asks what her favors are worth to him (v 16). Judah offers her a kid from his flock, but Tamar demands a pledge until he is able to send it, specifying his signet, cord, and staff, which he gives her. With the essential negotiation completed, the critical action begins: "He lay with her and she conceived by him" (v 18b). The scene concludes with the note that she departed, removing her veil and resuming her widow's garments (v 19). How are we to understand this scene of entrapment and why does it succeed? Tamar, the victim of her father-in-law's injustice, has been denied the means of performing her duty toward her deceased husband and for achieving a sense of womanly self-worth in bearing a child. Her bold and dangerous plan aims to accomplish that end by the agency of the man that has wronged her.[14] It satisfies both duty and revenge. It is not a husband she wants, but an heir for Judah, and so she approaches the source. It is intercourse she wants, not marriage. Her plan works because of the role she has chosen to accomplish this end. The features of the story that make it work involve commonly held presuppositions concerning the prostitute, some peculiar to the Israelite/Canaanite setting of this story, others widely shared.

First, Judah is needy and therefore vulnerable. At the point where the critical action begins, he is depicted as recently bereaved and hence in need of sexual gratification or diversion. The notice about his wife's death is certainly meant to provide this motivation. He is also a traveler, away from home, desiring entertainment and free to seek it in a strange place. Prostitution is typically offered (and often organized) as a service to travelers, a tourist attraction. Attention is directed to the activity rather than the actor(s). The act is basically anonymous; anyone can provide the service. In this case, that common aspect of anonymity is reinforced by a custom of concealment of the face—at least in public—and apparently also in the execution of the encounter. (A dimly lit room would have aided concealment, though it is unclear from this account just where the union took place.) The harlot's veil is a specific feature of this story and an essential prerequisite for the construction of the tale, or at least for this plan of action. It cannot be universalized, however.[15] Tamar's position is probably just as telling as her garb. A lone woman sitting by the road without apparent business would probably be enough to suggest the wares she was selling.

The climax of the narrative comes, as the text says, "about three months later" (or, at the end of the first trimester), when it is reported to Judah that his daughter-in-law Tamar has "played the harlot" (*zānĕtâ*) and "moreover . . . is with child by harlotry" (*hārâ lizĕnûnîm*, v 24). Now the English translation which I have quoted from the RSV contains a word play that is absent in the Hebrew, or it sharpens a word play that is not focused in the original. The translation of the verb *zānâ* as "play the harlot" is, I think, mistaken (Bird, 1981), but it points to an important socio-linguistic consideration in the language employed to describe Tamar's disguise and her crime. The English translation acknowledges that Tamar "played the harlot" when, in fact, no one but the reader knows that that is literally true. What the Hebrew means in its use of the verb and the qualifying noun *zĕnûnîm* is that Tamar, who is bound by her situation to chastity, has engaged in illicit intercourse, the evidence of which is her pregnancy. The Hebrew word *zānâ*, like its Arabic cognate, covers, I believe, a wide range of extramarital sexual relations, including both fornication and adultery, although its biblical usage appears focused on the activity of the unmarried woman.[16] In any case, when Judah hears this report of his daughter-in-law's unfaithfulness, his response is an immediate unconditioned sentence: "Bring her out and let her be burned!" (v 24).

If the word play in the English translation is overdrawn, the Hebrew use of the common root *znh* in two critical scenes of the narrative is still worthy of note and explanation. A striking contrast is created through use of the same root to describe two situations which occasion very different reactions from Judah. When he perceives that the woman by the road is a *zônâ*, his response is a proposition; when he hears that his daughter-in-law has *zānâ*-ed, his response is a sentence of death. He embraces the whore, but would put to death the daughter-in-law who "whored." The irony on which the story turns is that the two acts and the two women are one, and the use of etymologically related terms as the situation-defining terms strengthens the irony. The essential difference between the two uses is the socio-legal status of the woman involved. In the first instance, the term *zônâ* describes the woman's position or profession (prostitute) as well as the activity on which it is based. Thus, it serves as a class or status designation. In the second instance, the verb describes the activity of one whose socio-legal status makes it a crime. The activity is the same in both instances, as the common vocabulary indicates, namely, non-marital intercourse by a woman. In one case, however, it appears to be licit, bearing no penalty; in the other it is illicit, bearing the extreme penalty of death.

This anomaly is explained by the differing social positions of the actors. What is outlawed for the one by her status as a "married" woman is allowed to the other by her status as an unmarried but non-virgin woman, but not without penalty. The harlot's act is not penalized, I would argue, because her role or occupation is. The harlot is a kind of legal outlaw, standing outside the normal social order with its approved roles for women, ostracized and marginalized, but needed and therefore accommodated.[17] A stigma is always attached to her role and her person, however desired and tolerated her activity.

But she does not bear the stigma alone, although only she is legally ostracized; she passes a measure of it on to her patrons. The cost to the man is admittedly slight and may be understood in different ways, from contamination to humiliation or intimidation. For the harlot not only demands a price, she controls the transaction, as is so well illustrated in our narrative (is this to be understood as a reversal of the normal sex roles?). There is a degree of opprobrium about the whole affair, and a degree of risk for the man, who may be trapped, duped, or "taken." Thus, ambivalence pervades the whole relationship and is, as I argued earlier, a fundamental feature of the institution.

In my analysis of the narrative plot and of the harlot's role within it I omitted a scene which has heavily influenced most discussions of this chapter and is frequently made the central point. The scene is important to our understanding of the narrative, and of the harlot, but it has been over-interpreted and misinterpreted, I believe, precisely because insufficient attention has been given to narrative art in its analysis.

When Judah sends back the kid by his friend the Adullamite and attempts to reclaim his pledge, the friend cannot find her and so inquires of the men of the place (MT: "her place"): "Where is the *qĕdēšâ* who was Enaim by the wayside?" They reply, "There has been no *qĕdēšâ* here" (v 21). Hirah then returns to Judah, repeating their answer verbatim.

What are we to make of this shift in terms? Have we misread Tamar's action? Did she intend to represent herself as a hierodule, a cultic "prostitute," who might be understood to have some particular association with festivals of the yearly cycle such as sheep-shearing? I think not, though it is conceivable that at some stage in the development of this story such an association might have been made. The substitution of terms in this passage is not accidental, and the interchange must indicate some kind of association between the two figures. But there is no justification for the common collapse of the two nor for assuming that the word hierodule is the determining designation for understanding Judah's action.[18]

The term *qĕdēšâ* is confined to the interchange between Hirah the Adullamite and the men of the place. Two possible factors might affect the usage: first, the designation of the woman as a hierodule[19] might reflect the narrator's view of Canaanite usage, for it occurs only in the conversation of non-Israelites; second, it is language used in public speech. Judah's original action was prompted by a private assessment: "he thought her to be a harlot" and acted accordingly. But the search for the shady lady requires public inquiry. The decisive clue to the substitution of terms is given, I believe, in Judah's response to Hirah's report. "Then let her keep the things as her own," he says, *"lest we be laughed at"* (lit. "lest we become an object of contempt"). But what might be the reason for contempt or ridicule? A sacred act of love-making with the hierodule of a Canaanite cult? Hardly, for the people of the place are understood to be Canaanites and would find no cause for contempt in that. Being outwitted, and more specifically "taken," by a common prostitute? Surely.

Here the issue of opprobrium surfaces. Judah, a man of standing, who has surrendered his insignia to a prostitute in a moment of weakness, does not go back in person to retrieve his goods, but sends a friend, a man of the region, to inquire discreetly of the local inhabitants. Hirah knows how to handle the situation; he uses a euphemism—comparable to our substitution of the term "courtesan" for the cruder expression "whore"—(a substitution of court language in the latter instance, cult language in the former).

Here we have an example, I think, of a common contrast between private, or "plain," speech (which may also be described as coarse) and public, or polite, speech (which may also be described as elevated).[20] Such an interchange of terms does not require that the two have identical meanings, especially since euphemism is a characteristic feature of biblical Hebrew usage in describing sexual acts and organs. A foot or a hand is not a phallus, though both terms are used with that meaning. And a *qĕdēšâ*, I would argue, is not a prostitute, though she may share important characteristics with her sister of the streets and highways, including sexual intercourse with strangers.[21]

II. Joshua 2:1–24

The story of Rahab in Joshua 2, like the story of Tamar in Genesis 38, is a distinct literary unit, with its own tradition, clearly set off from the surrounding material. While the history of the Rahab story, in both its literary and pre-literary stages, is more complex than the Tamar story, and while an attempt has been made to integrate the tale into the now dominant account of the miraculous fall of Jericho, the narrative in Joshua 2 can still be analyzed as a discrete literary unit, and the apparent duplication or displacement in the narrative which has taxed many interpreters does not substantially affect my analysis. Only the Deuteronomistic editing, which is both obvious and limited, constitutes a reinterpretation of the tradition that represents a significant literary variant.[22]

The account opens with the sending of two spies from the Israelite camp at Shittim and closes with their return. The spies are instructed by Joshua in the first verse of the chapter to "see the land"[23] (i.e., the land west of the Jordan), which Israel is poised to attack. In the concluding verse, the returned spies report that "Yahweh has given the whole land into our hands; and moreover all the inhabitants of the land are fainthearted because of us" (RSV; NEB "panic stricken," v 24). That language, augmented by the Deuteronomistic editor in the reference to the peoples' response,[24] presupposes the institution or ideology of holy war, in which an assurance of victory is required from Yahweh before the battle can take place. But the assurance which the spies offer is given without consultation of a priest or other oracle, by spies whose mission has been simply to spy out the land. We might assume then that the assurance of victory is an inference from what they have seen. But what lies between the opening and closing sentences is no account of a secret reconnoitering of the land, as commissioned, but the account of a single encounter in Jericho, the spies' first stopping place across the Jordan, an encounter from which they escape only by the skin of their teeth, or more precisely, by a lie and a cord. The key figure in their escape and in their knowledge of the land and its inhabitants is the harlot Rahab. In the present form of the story, she is both savior and oracle.

Commentators invariably discuss the role and reputation of Rahab. Two questions shape that discussion: (1) was Rahab a hierodule? and (2) why would the Israelites consort with a prostitute, who is portrayed as a heroine, without apparent censure of her profession or role? Some commentators claim to find a cult legend at the root of the tradition, an aetiology of a sanctuary or of a class of sacred prostitutes which persisted in later Israel (*inter alia,* Gressmann, 1922:136; Hölscher:54–57; Mowinckel:13–15). Even those who can find nothing in the present story to support a cultic identification feel constrained to observe that the term *zônâ* may designate either a sacred or a secular prostitute and is thus ambiguous, leaving either interpretation as a possibility (e.g.,

Soggin:36; Boling:144; Miller and Tucker:31). The question of Rahab's profession is prompted in part by wonder at her role in the tradition, in which the stigma normally attached to prostitutes is perceived as lacking. Either, it is argued, she cannot have been a common prostitute, or the status of the prostitute must have been higher in Canaanite society, for she appears in the story as a fully accepted member of the society.

In contrast to these opinions, I shall argue that nothing in the story suggests a hierodule and that, conversely, an understanding of Rahab as a harlot is essential to the story. I shall also argue that her portrayal as a heroine in no way cancels the negative social appraisal attached to her role as a harlot.

The narrator begins the account of the spies' mission with a deliberately suggestive lead sentence. "Go, view the land," the spies are instructed, and the report of their action immediately follows: "and they went and came to Jericho[25] and entered the house of a harlot (*bêt- ʾiššâ zônâ*), whose name was Rahab, and slept there (*wayyiškĕbû šāmmâ*).[26] The place should probably be understood as an inn or public house, but the narrator clearly wishes to focus attention immediately on the connection with Rahab and especially on her occupation. Thus the designation *ʾiššâ zônâ* precedes the name as the determining expression following the noun "house." The language is obviously meant to suggest a brothel, and the following verb, *šākab*, reinforces that suggestion.[27]

The association of prostitutes with taverns or beer houses is well attested in Mesopotamian texts,[28] and it may be surmised that a similar association is assumed in our passage.

> As a prostitute he took her in from the street (and) supported her, as a prostitute he married her but gave her back (as separate property) *her tavern. (Ana ittisu* VIII ii 23–25 [CAD, Ḥ:102a])

> When I sit at the entrance of the tavern I (Ishtar) am a loving prostitute.[29] (SBH 106:51–53 [CAD, Ḥ:101b])

Indirect testimony to this association comes from §110 of the Laws of Hammurabi, which decrees death for the *nadītu* who enters a tavern.[30] Since the *nadītu* belonged to a class of hierodules who were bound by a rule of chastity and normally cloistered, the kind of activity associated with the place is apparent. In our passage, the "house" is identified as Rahab's and is clearly not her family home, since her parents and siblings must be brought into *her* house in order to be saved (v 18).[31] In view of her profession, then, it is reasonable to view the house as her place of business.

The narrator's words about the spies' approach to their task tantalizes the reader and elicits speculation about the spies' motive and plan. How is this action meant to serve their mission? What exactly do they think they will do there? Do they hope to obtain information by sleeping with a loose, and presumably, loose-tongued woman? Do they mean to bargain for intelligence from a business woman who will sell anything for a price? Or do they simply hope to overhear the talk of local citizens and travelers who have gathered there or engage them in unguarded conversation over a pitcher of beer? Whatever their precise plan of action may be, they have chosen a natural place to begin their reconnaissance of the land. For the inn, or public house, or brothel, provides them both access and cover. It is a resting place for travelers and a gathering place for all sorts of persons seeking diversion and contacts; strangers will not be conspicuous here and motives will not be questioned. The proprietor's status also makes the harlot's house a logical point of entry, for, as an outsider in her own community, the harlot might be expected to be more open, perhaps even sympathetic, to other outsiders than would her countrymen.

But if the spies have chosen their point of entry wisely, they have not gone unobserved. The king of Jericho has been informed of their entry and whereabouts and sends immediately to Rahab, requesting that she hand over the men who have entered her house. Instead, she hides the spies and shrewdly diverts the king's men with a false report. Here again the ambiguous language of entry/intercourse is employed, first by the king's messengers who command: "Bring out the men who were going in to you (*habbāʾîm ʾēlayik*), who entered your house" (v 3); and then by Rahab, who acknowledges: "They did indeed come in to me" (*bāʾû ʾelay,* v 4).[32] Thus sexual innuendo is not confined to the opening verses but pervades the whole first scene as an element of narrative intention. Rahab's action, however, contradicts the expectations aroused by the suggestive language, leaving the reader to speculate about her intentions.

At the end of the opening sentence the reader is meant to ask: why did the spies go to a harlot's house and what did they do there? At the end of the first scene the reader is left with the question: why did Rahab do what she did? The story has given us no reason to believe that there was any previous relationship between the two parties. What then can explain her action? The reader must speculate—and is invited to do so by the construction of the narrative. But the modern reader must speculate without the "feel" for the situation possessed by the ancient audience. Multiple motives and factors may be involved, either originally or as the result of editorial reinterpretation. Rahab's response may represent hostility to the king and his cohorts. Perhaps she has been harassed before about her establishment and its clients. If dangerous aliens are found on her premises, she will surely be penalized. Her action may then be interpreted as self-interest, an effort to save her own neck, and/or her business and reputation. Or is a connection to be seen in class affinity or class interest? Are we to understand her act as that of a social outcast among her own people protecting the representatives of an outcast people, an outcast people on the move, that may offer her a new future? I must admit that I find no element in the story to suggest the latter understanding, but I will leave the matter open. In the present form of the narrative, the question of Rahab's motivation is answered in the following scene. In an eloquent speech, enhanced by the Deuteronomist, Rahab reveals to the spies, whom she has concealed on the roof, the meaning and purpose of her action. She has come to strike a bargain, and now she presents her terms; *ḥesed* for *ḥesed,* she requests, my life for yours. By her act of protection, here described as an act of *ḥesed,* she has established a bond of obligation with the spies. Now she seeks their protection when they shall be in a position to give it, an act of *ḥesed* on their part, since they are now morally obligated, though not legally bound (Sakenfeld:64–70). Her speech begins with a confession of Yahweh's mighty acts toward Israel and concludes with a request for an oath of assurance from representatives of Yahweh's people.[33] The scene ends with the spies' oath.

In the final scene, Rahab enables the spies to escape by letting them down through a window in the wall, in which she ties a scarlet cord as a sign to the attacking Israelites, so that they will recognize and spare her house. The outcome of this encounter—viz. the saving of all who were in the harlot's house—is reported in chapter 6, with the aetiological note that Rahab "dwelt in Israel to this day" (6:25).

This account supplies us with further information about the harlot in Israel's understanding and corroborates features noted in other ancient Near Eastern texts and in comparative studies. She lives on the outer periphery of the city, where other outcast and low caste groups or professions are commonly located in the ancient city. Her house in the wall (near to the city gate?) would be readily accessible to travelers and easily located. Was the red cord a permanent sign of an ancient red light district, or only specific to this narrative?[34]

It has been argued on the basis of this story that no censure or stigma was attached to the harlot in early Israel—or in Canaanite society—in contrast to later Israel. But this argument misreads the story. The entire account depends upon Rahab's marginal status, in both Canaanite and Israelite societies. Her descendants, persisting in later Israel, form a distinct group, the strange tolerance of which is "explained" by the aetiology of the harlot's loyalty. And it is only because she is an outcast that the men of Israel have access to her (an "honorable" woman would not meet alone with strange men). The narrator has drawn upon popular understanding of the harlot's profession and reputation in the construction of the story and deliberately elicits that understanding in his opening words which place the whole of the subsequent action in a harlot's house. The associations that operate in this story are many and complex, and may never be fully determined by the modern reader, but understanding requires some attempt at specification.

The prostitute's low social status and low reputation are essential, and related, features. The reader does not expect anything from her, or at least not anything of moral strength, courage, or insight. For she is the lowest of the low, and, as Jeremiah's search illustrates, Israel did not expect much from the lowly (Jer 5:4–5). The harlot is viewed as lacking in wisdom, morals, and religious knowledge. Her low status and despised state must be due either to unfortunate circumstance or personal fault, and neither, I think, would elicit much sympathy or charity from an ancient audience. The harlot may be a victim, but she is commonly viewed as a predator, preying on the weakness of men, a mercenary out for her own gain, an opportunist with no loyalty beyond herself, acknowledging no principle or charity in her actions.

These attributes in an enemy may serve the Israelite spies well, though the game they would play with her is a risky one. The story requires no positive assessment of the harlot, no counter to the common portrait, to explain the initial action of the spies, nor, I have suggested, to explain Rahab's action in saving them. For although the harlot lacks wisdom in the popular view, she lives by her wits. She is a shrewd and calculating operator, and men must beware her tricks. Self-interest (here broadened to include her kindred) still plays an important role in the final form of the story and may have played a larger role in the pre-Deuteronomistic version. But while essential to the construction of the tale, it is not the decisive motive. The present form of the story builds on a reversal of expectations. The negative presuppositions are required precisely for their contribution to that reversal.

Rahab does not act as we expect her to act when she protects the spies. Self-interest alone cannot explain her commitment, for the risk of siding with an unknown force against one's own people is too great to ascribe solely to that motive. Either faith or discernment, or both, is required to explain such unproved loyalty (*ḥesed*), and for that there is no place in the ruling stereotype of the harlot. But if the harlot as heroine involves a conflict of expectations, it is also a recognizable subtype of the harlot in literature (and presumably also in life), a romantic antitype to the dominant image: the whore with the heart of gold, the harlot who saves the city, the courtesan who sacrifices for her patron.[35] Her action, which is praiseworthy in itself, is the more so for being unexpected and unsolicited. In her display of loyalty, courage, and altruism, she acts out of keeping with her assumed character as a harlot and thus reveals her true character as a person. But this does not normally lead to a change in her status, or a change in attitudes toward harlots. The determining negative image of the harlot is not fundamentally challenged by the counterimage, but maintained. For the harlot is never allowed to become a good wife, but only a good harlot, a righteous outcast, a noble-hearted courtesan, the exception that proves the rule—just as Robin Hood does not define the type of the bandit, but only the antitype.

Rahab is a heroine because she protects the Israelite spies and, as a consequence, contributes to Israel's victory. If the LXX preserves an original variant, she may have been credited originally with enabling the Israelites to breach the wall and hence with handing over her city to the invaders, a motif which is closely paralleled in two classical texts pointed out by Hans Windisch (189–198).[36] In the present form and setting of the story, the deliverance of the city to Israel is attributed to Yahweh's miraculous action, and Rahab's role is that of an oracle rather than an instrument of that action (her deliverance of the spies may be taken as a kind of proleptic sign of Israel's victory). The Deuteronomistic redaction of the chapter has made Rahab's speech the center of the story. Rahab is here the pagan confessor the one who discerns what others fail to see, and the one who commits her life to the people of Yahweh. She is wiser than the king of Jericho, and also more clever. Like the lowly Hebrew midwives, she outwits the king. Like them, she is bold in rejecting an unrighteous command. Like them, she is given a house and a name in Israel and a story to perpetuate her memory, while the king she opposed remains nameless and forgotten.

The Israelite author has made of the harlot of Jericho a heroine of faith, and a friend of Israel. I have assumed that the story depends on a reversal of expectations. Others have argued that it could also be explained by unnoted affinities, by positive expectations that might serve to qualify the predominantly negative expectations of the harlot. A parallel might be drawn by the narrator—and an affinity recognized—between the low or outcast estate of the harlot of Jericho and the low and outcast estate of the band of escaped slaves beyond the Jordan. While Israel's petition to the kings in the Transjordan was met only by uncomprehending belligerence, their approach to the harlot of Jericho elicits immediate reception and a pledge of support. Rahab knows what the kings do not know, that the Lord is with this outlaw band and no power can stand against them. And so the wise harlot sides with the outcasts whose day is dawning on the Eastern horizon. I find that construction theologically appealing, but I cannot now find historical or literary evidence that would convince me of its plausibility.

The story of Rahab depicts a figure identified with a Canaanite milieu, and a group identified by her name, persisting, anomalously, in later Israel. I find no suggestion of cultic identification either in the narrative of Joshua 2 or in the aetiological note of Joshua 6. It is a clan legend, not a cult legend, memorializing an individual and her family, not a sanctuary or cultic institution. An Israelite lineage, not a class of hierodules, traces its ancestry to this heroine. The harlot designation of its eponym suggests an outcast status for the group, which requires explanation. The story provides the explanation: it was because of the *ḥesed* of Rahab toward our ancestors that her clan dwells among us today.

III. 1 Kings 3:16–27

If the harlot of Joshua 2 and the supposed harlot of Genesis 38 are depicted in Canaanite settings, the existence of prostitution as a recognized institution in Israel is also well attested.[37] Relative incidence is impossible to judge and so are changes in attitudes. If Israelite religion censured the institution, it was still accompanied by the same attitudes of ambivalence displayed in cultures more open to its acceptance. And the basic stereotypes and presuppositions still hold, as we can see from various biblical witnesses. An instructive example from the period of the monarchy is found in the famous story of Solomon's judgment (1 Kings 3:16–27).[38]

The story concerns a case of rival claims brought by two harlots (*nāšîm zōnôt*, v 16) who are described as living together in one house, probably to be understood as a brothel because of the reference to "strangers" in v 18.[39] Both give birth, according to the story, within three days of each other. The women are alone at the time with no others[40] in the house—an unlikely situation in a normal household, but one essential to the story and the case it presents; for as they are harlots and as they are alone, there are no witnesses to the incident they describe, and no husbands or kinsmen to defend the claims of the women or to arbitrate for them. Thus it is a case of one woman's word against another and, more specifically, one harlot's word against another, that is, the words of women whose word cannot be trusted. For the harlot is characterized in the ruling stereotype as a woman of smooth and self-serving speech. One does not expect truth from such as these. And so the case that is presented to Solomon is a case to test the wisest judge. The harlot plaintiffs assure that.

As the case is laid out before the king, the child of the one dies and she substitutes the child of the other for it. Each now claims the living child as her own, and Solomon must judge whose claim is true. Here Solomon's wisdom is displayed, for he does not attempt to discern the truth through interrogation—a hopeless approach with habitual liers. His wisdom lies in recognizing a condition that will compel the truth. The story—and Solomon's action—appeals to another stereotype of the woman, that of the mother, who is bound by the deepest emotional bonds to the fruit of her womb. That bond will not lie. And so Solomon orders a sword to be brought and the child to be divided between the two claimants. At this the true mother reveals herself by relinquishing her claim in order to spare her child.

Again I would argue that the story does not reveal a generally accepting attitude toward harlots, as some have argued, but depends, rather, on their marginal status and their reputation for lying and self-interest. It is these commonly shared presuppositions about the harlot that make this case an ideal test, one by which extraordinary wisdom might be demonstrated. For the audience is meant to see only two prostitutes, but Solomon in his wisdom sees what is hidden by that stereotype, namely, a mother. In this case two counter-images operate, which are normally distinct but are here combined in a single figure. The case is built on the one and resolved on the other.

What I have tried to do in these three examples is to draw out the picture of the prostitute that was operative in each and show how it functioned in the narrative. The author has reckoned in each case with the attitudes and presuppositions that would be called forth from his audience by the use of the term *zônâ*. These presuppositions are, for the most part, subtle and complex and are commonly missed or misread by modern readers who mistake narrative interest for social status, and role in the story for role in life. The harlot heroine, or protagonist, remains a harlot. She is lifted for a moment, as an individual, into the spotlight by the storyteller, but her place remains in the shadows of Israelite society.

NOTES

1. I use the terms interchangeably, adopting "harlot" because of its use by the RSV (on its misuse, see below). Cf. Setel (89–91) for a usage that distinguishes the terms.

2. I am currently engaged in a book-length study of the harlot and the hierodule in Old Testament and Ancient Near Eastern literature and society. (I use the term hierodule as a provisional class designation for all types of cult-related women, without regard to their particular duties, activities, or status.) While the two figures, or classes of women, are commonly identified and even exchanged in interpretive literature, beginning with the Old Testament's polemical treatment of Canaanite religion and culture, there appears to be little or no evidence of confusion or interchange in the primary ancient texts. In her popular treatment of the origins of prostitution, Gerda Lerner rightly criticizes the confusion of the two classes by most authorities as well as the attempt to derive secular prostitution from sacred sexual service (238–45); but she falls prey to the same confusion in her own treatment of the Mesopotamian *ḫarimtu* ("prostitute") (244–46). This essay does not permit discussion of the important but complex question of the relationship between the harlot and the hierodule or assessment of Lerner's arguments, which are based on secondary sources and misconstrue critical Mesopotamian texts.

3. Male prostitution, which was homosexual, appears to have been a limited phenomenon and is poorly attested in our sources (cf. Gebhard:80). It is not considered in this article.

4. I have discussed the problems of the translation and use of this term and the related verbal forms in an unpublished paper (Bird, 1981). Some of the issues are treated in the discussion of the Tamar story below.

5. See Gebhard (76); cf. also the following texts:

> She is not a wife, she is a *ḫarimtu* [prostitute] (JEN 666:14, Nuzi [CAD Ḫ:101b]).
>
> A *qadištu* [hierodule] whom no husband has married (must go) bareheaded in the street, must not veil herself.
>
> A *ḫarimtu* [prostitute] must not veil herself (KAV 1 v 66, Ass. Code § 40 [CAD Ḫ:101b; cn. G:152b]*).

In the latter case, both the harlot and the unmarried hierodule are prohibited from wearing the veil, which is the distinguishing garb of the married woman. The preceding clause requires the married hierodule to veil herself on the street.
*CAD Ḫ:101b mistakenly connects the two clauses cited, understanding the *qadištu* as a class of *ḫarimtu*. Cf. Meek (183).

6. On the harlot's habitat, note the following:

> If a man's wife has not borne him children but a harlot (from) the public square (Lipit-Ishtar Code §27 [Kramer 1955:160]; cf. §32).
>
> If someone regularly approaches a *ḫarimtu* at a streetcrossing (CT 39 45:30, SB Alu [CAD Ḫ:101b]).

Cf. also Sjoberg (133–37) and Oppenheim (41).

7. Attempts to compare attitudes and incidence of prostitution in Canaanite and Israelite society or in different periods of Israelite history are futile, because the data do not permit statistical comparison and because the different literary genres in which the references are preserved dis-

play quite different pictures of the harlot and attitudes toward her (e.g., Proverbs offers practical advice to men, stressing the pocketbook, while Priestly legislation is concerned with the harlot as ritually unclean and her contacts as defiling).

8. The translation and interpretation of the following texts from the Gilgamesh Epic (VII, iii, 6–22 and iv, 1–10) is based on Oppenheim (40–41) and Speiser (1955:86–87). Cf. Tigay (170–72).

9. The term *šamḫatu*, which is interchanged with *ḫarimtu* ("prostitute") in the texts relating to Enkidu and the harlot, is treated as a proper noun by Tigay (171). Speiser translates "harlot-lass" (1955:74–75) or simply "lass" (86), noting the etymological meaning "pleasure girl" (74 n. 23).

10. Oppenheim's rendering of the phrase *ši-ma-tu lu-šim-ki*, conventionally translated "I will decree (your) fate."

11. Heb. "Palm," a fertility symbol. The symbolism in the text is far richer and the literary art more subtle and complex than my limited analysis is able to convey.

12. The location is uncertain (cf. ancient Versions, and commentaries), but unnecessary for our analysis.

13. The "veil" may have been understood immediately by the hearers as a harlot's apparel, but it is more likely that the term is meant to be more general in its application and more ambiguous in the author's use. By suggesting, but not specifying, a harlot's garb, the narrator makes of her act both an act of concealment and an act of invitation.

14. Tamar is legally helpless; therefore she must move outside the law to accomplish what duty (for her the higher "law") demands of her.

15. It is useless to argue from the Middle Assyrian Laws (cf. n. 5) to practices in Canaan/Israel, since dress is a matter of local or regional custom. Restrictions or prescriptions in dress are generally meant to distinguish the married or betrothed woman from all other classes of women, saying, in effect, "hands off!" That the harlot was not always veiled in Israel is suggested by Jeremiah's reference to the "harlot's brow" (Jer 3:3).

16. According to Wehr, Arabic *zanā* has the meaning "to commit adultery, fornicate, whore." Cf. *zinan:* "adultery, fornication;" *zināʾ:* "adultery, fornication;" *zānin:* "fornicator, adulterer;" *zāniya:* "whore, harlot, adulterous." See Mernissi (24–25). While the activity designated by this root is usually understood as illicit, that description does not give adequate account of the differences in attitudes and sanctions related to the sex and status of the actors. See below.

17. Susan Niditch has explained this anomalous position of the prostitute by using the term "liminal," as employed by Victor Turner: "That which is liminal is that which is betwixt and between nearly (*sic*) defined categories. A harlot falls between the two allowable categories for women. She is neither an unmarried virgin, nor a non-virgin wife" (147 n. 13). As a liminal character, outside the social order, Niditch argues, the harlot "belongs to a special class of women who can 'play the harlot' without being condemned." "In effect," she continues, "one could fall between the proper categories and survive, once that outside betwixt-and-between status was itself institutionalized and categorized" (147).

While Niditch's analysis of women's roles and of the harlot's status in ancient Israelite society corresponds closely in substance to my own (made independently in an unpublished paper [Bird, 1980]), I have retained my original characterization of the harlot as a "legal outlaw," because I want to emphasize the ambivalence or conflict in attitudes toward the prostitute and the fact that she is both freed and constrained by her position.

18. Von Rad's interpretation is, unfortunately, typical of this type of reasoning, which invariably appeals to Herodotus: "Tamar . . . does not pretend to be a harlot as we think of it, but rather a married woman who indulges in this practice [sacrifice of chastity in the service of the goddess of love], and Judah too thought of her in this way" (354–55). Cf. Astour (185–96).

19. There is no justification for RSV's translation of "harlot" here.

20. Speiser (1964:300) is one of the few commentators who has recognized this. See Alter (9).

21. Whatever the reasons for the identification of these two marginal classes of women, it is essential to maintain the linguistic distinctions made in the Hebrew. See n. 2 above.

22. Noth's analysis (1953) remains basic. See also Boling; Soggin; Gray 1967; and Hertzberg. On the question of sources, see further Tucker (13–14) and Mowinckel (33–34).

23. Omitting "and Jericho" with LXX, Noth (1953:24) and NEB, as displaced from the following clause (where LXX reads it) or secondarily introduced to explain the following account, which concerns only Jericho.

24. *wĕgam-nāmōgû kol-yōšĕbê hā'āreṣ mippānênû* (24b) is a Deuteronomistic phrase that picks up the words of Rahab's speech: *wĕkî nāmōgû kol-yōšĕbê hā'āreṣ mippĕnêkem* (9bß), the main piece of Deuteronomistic composition in the chapter (Tucker:70).

25. See n. 23. Cf. LXX, which reads Jericho here, but also has a longer text.

26. There is no justification for RSV's "lodged," which eliminates the double entendre in the Hebrew. It rests, however, on ancient precedent; the Old Greek eliminated the sexual intimation by employing *kataluein:* "lodge" (Liddell-Scott), a verb that normally represents the Hebrew root *lwn/lyn* in LXX and is used only here to translate *škb* (Hatch-Redpath).

27. *Bêt zônâ* may be a technical term for a brothel. Cf. Jer 5:7, "they committed adultery and trooped to the harlot's house (*bêt zônâ*)"; Ezek 16:41, *wĕśārĕpû bāttayik bā'ēš . . . wĕhišbattîk mizzônâ:* "they shall burn your houses . . . ; I will make you stop pleasing the harlot" (the whole section, beginning in v 35, is addressed to Israel as a harlot). If *bêt zônâ* is a technical term, then the insertion here of the word "woman" into the construct may represent a weakening of the term in the direction of an individual's house: it was the house of a woman who was a harlot—or a promiscuous woman. It is difficult to judge the force of *'iššâ zônâ,* which appears as a frequent variant of *zônâ* used alone. But however the compound term is interpreted, its use to identify the house can only be understood as provocative. See vv 3 and 4 and n. 31 below.

The qualifying term *zônâ* is not used again in chapter 2. This is in keeping with the author's style in describing the roles of the main figures when they are first introduced (*'ănāšîm mĕraggĕlîm* and *'iššâ zônâ,* v 1) and thereafter referring to them simply as "the men" and "the woman." The qualifying role designations are employed again in chapter 6, where the characters are reintroduced.

28. See Jacobsen and Kramer 1953:176, 1. 106, and 184 n. 68. Cf. also Bergmann:2–3; Falkenstein:118–19; and CAD A 473 (*aštammu*).

29. *ḫa-ri-im-tum ra'imtum.* A variant, written as a gloss, *šarraqitum;* "a female thief," gives testimony to the low repute of the place and of the classes associated with it.

30. The term here is *É-KURRUN(NA)* = *bit-kurrunim*(?): "tavern, ale-house" (cf. Driver and Miles), which may be distinguished from the *É-EŠDAM* = *aštammu* "inn." Jacobsen and Kramer (1953:184–85 n. 68) argue that the latter should be understood as "Gasthaus mit Herberge" rather than "bordello," even though it was typically frequented by and owned by the *ḫarimtu* ("prostitute"). They see it as "the social center of the state or village . . . a place in which the inhabitants would typically gather for talk and recreation after the end of work" (185 n. 68).

31. I take the references to her *bêt-'āb* in 2:12, 18 as ancient expansions of the basic story, belonging to the aetiological motif that comes to expression now in 6:17, 22–23, 25. A distinction must be made between her house and her "father's house" (= family or lineage). The latter survives, the former does not.

32. The Old Greek lacks the suggestive first clause in v 3. MT may be conflate, but the echoing language of v 4 is assumed by all of the Versions and thus is firmly fixed in the tradition.

33. The oath has been commonly understood in recent literature as a covenant oath (e.g., Boling:147 n. 12). But there is no reference here, or in chapter 6, to a covenant, despite recognizable

similarities between this story and the story of the Gibeonites. The oath here functions as a guarantee that the spies will honor their promise to Rahab to spare her family when they take control of the city.

34. The initial reference to the cord in the phrase, "a strand of *this* scarlet cord" (v 18), suggests that it is already known and associated with the house (though it could also be understood as something brought by the spies). One may surmise that a sign, originally associated with the house in one capacity, has been reinterpreted in the story, giving it a new meaning and function.

35. The motif is widespread. I have been given examples from Chinese as well as European literature. For a parallel from Classical literature, see below.

36. Windisch argued that the Rahab story should be seen as one example of a type in which a city is delivered from its enemies (external or internal) by a prostitute and the memory of her action is perpetuated by aetiological legend. His two Classical parallels include a Roman and a Greek legend, the former concerning a prostitute of Capua who remained loyal to Rome when the city fell to Punic invaders, the latter a hierodule of Abydos (referred to as both *hetaira* and *pornē* in the account) who enabled her countrymen to retake the city from enemy occupation.

Windisch notes a common attitude displayed in the transmission of the two stories that honor a common prostitute. As Christian and Jewish interpretation have traditionally shown embarrassment over Rahab's profession and the absence of censure in the biblical narrative, a similar attitude is evident in the Roman tradition in which wonder was expressed at the Senate's action (granting freedom and restoration of possessions) on behalf of a woman of low repute. In the case of Rahab, tradition elevated her by suppressing knowledge of her occupation or making her a convert, allowing her to be a heroine only as an ex-harlot (Windisch:188–192).

37. The term *zônâ* is used in the following texts relating to the period of the monarchy or later: Lev 21:7, 14; Deut 23:19; 1 Kings 3:16; Isa 1:21; 23:15, 16; Jer 3:3; 5:7; Ezek 16:30, 31, 33, 35, 41; 23:44; Hos 4:14; Joel 4:3; Micah 1:7, 7; Nah 3:4; Prov 6:26; 7:10; 1 Kings 22:38; Prov 23:27; 29:3.

38. This story has long been recognized as having the character of popular tradition or folk tale and constituting a distinct literary unit. See Gressmann; Gray, 1970:114–16, 127–29; Noth, 1969:44–48; and Montgomery:108–10.

39. Presumably prostitutes withdrew from active work during advanced stages of pregnancy. Unfortunately, we know virtually nothing about the working conditions of prostitutes in ancient Israel, means of contraception that may have been employed, or arrangements for raising (or disposing of) children. From the story of Jephthah we learn that although he was the son of a harlot, he was apparently raised in his father's household or was at least recognized by his father as a son and potential heir (Judg 11:1–2). The prohibition of priests from marrying harlots (Lev 21:7, 14) implicitly recognizes the practice by others. One may surmise that a man might marry a harlot who had borne him a child, especially a son.

40. The Hebrew is *zār* (v 18), meaning "stranger," one outside the family. It may be assumed from the fact that they were harlots living together that there would be no husbands present, or other members of a normal family. The use of the word "stranger" here refers, presumably, to clients.

References

Alter, Robert
1981   *The Art of Biblical Narrative.* New York; Basic Books.

ANET =
1955   *Ancient Near Eastern Texts Relating to the Old Testament.* 2nd ed. Ed. James B. Pritchard. Princeton: Princeton University.

Astour, M.C.
1966   "Tamar the Hierodule. An Essay in the Method of Vestigal Motifs." *JBL* 85:185–96.

Bergmann, Eugen
1964   "Untersuchungen zu syllabisch geschriebenen sumerischen Texten." *ZA* 56:1–43.

Bird, Phyllis A.
1980   "Harlot and Hierodule: Images of the Feminine in Old Testament Anthropology and Theology." Unpublished Essay, Bunting Institute Colloquium, Radcliffe College, Cambridge.
1989   " 'To Play the Harlot': An Inquiry into an Old Testament Metaphor." In *Gender and Difference in Ancient Israel*. Ed. Peggy Day. Minneapolis: Fortress.

Boling, Robert G.
1982   *Joshua*. AB 6. Garden City: Doubleday.

CAD =
1956   *The Assyrian Dictionary of the Oriental Institute of The University of Chicago*. Chicago: Oriental Institute, University of Chicago.

Driver, G.R., and John G. Miles
1955   *The Babylonian Laws*. 2 vols. Oxford: Clarendon.

Falkenstein, A.
1964   "Sumerische religiösiche Texte." *ZA* 56:44–129.

Cagnon, John H.
1988   "Prostitution." Pp. 592–98 in *The International Encyclopedia of the Social Sciences*. Vol. 12. Ed. David L. Silk. New York: Macmillan and The Free Press.

Gebhard, Paul Henry
1974   "Prostitution." Pp. 75–81 in *The New Encyclopedia Britannica*. Vol. 15. 15th ed. Chicago: University of Chicago.

Gray, John
1967   *Joshua, Judges and Ruth*. NCB. Greenwood, SC: Attic.
1970   *I and II Kings. A Commentary*. 2d ed. OTL. Philadelphia: Westminster.

Gressmann, Hugo
1907   "Das Salomonische Urteil." *Deutsche Rundschau* 130:212–28.
1922   *Die Schriften des Alten Testaments in Answahl*, I/2. Göttingen: Vandenhoeck & Ruprecht.

Hertzberg, Hans Wilhelm
1953   *Die Bücher Josua, Richter, Ruth*. ATD 9. Göttingen: Vandenhoeck & Ruprecht.

Hölscher, Gustav
1919/20   "Zum Ursprung der Rahabsage." *ZAW* 38:54–57.

Jacobsen, Thorkild, and Samuel N. Kramer
1953   "The Myth of Inanna and Bilulu." *JNES* 12:160–71.

Kramer, S.N.
1955   Trans. "Lipit-Ishtar Law Code." Pp. 159–61. ANET.

Lerner, Gerda
1986   "The Origin of Prostitution in Ancient Mesopotamia." *Signs: Journal of Women in Culture and Society* 11:236–54.

Meek, Theophile J.
1955   Trans. "The Middle Assyrian Laws." Pp. 80–88. ANET.

Mernissi, Fatima
1975   *Beyond the Veil. Male-Female Dynamics in a Modern Muslim Society.* New York: John Wiley
        & Sons; Halstead.

Miller, J. Maxwell, and Gene M. Tucker
1974   *The Book of Joshua.* Cambridge: Cambridge University.

Montgomery, James A.
1957   *The Book of Kings.* ICC. Edinburgh: T. & T. Clark.

Mowinckel, Sigmund
1964   *Tetrateuch-Pentateuch-Hexateuch.* BZAW 90. Berlin: Töpelmann.

Niditch, Susan
1979   "The Wronged Woman Righted: An Analysis of Genesis 38." *HTR* 72:143–49.

Noth, Martin
1953   *Das Buch Josua.* 2d ed. HAT I, 7. Tübingen: J.C.B. Mohr (Paul Siebeck).
1969   *Könige,* 1. BKAT 9, 1. Neukirchen-Vluyn: Neukirchener.

Oppenheim, A. Leo
1948   "Mesopotamian Mythology II." *Orientalia* 17:17–58.

Rad, Gerhard von
1972   *Genesis. A Commentary.* Rev. ed. Trans. John H. Marks. OTL. Philadelphia: Westminster.

Sakenfeld, Katherine Doob
1978   *The Meaning of Hesed in the Hebrew Bible: A New Inquiry.* HSM 17. Missoula: Scholars.

Setel, T. Drorah
1985   "Prophets and Pornography: Female Sexual Imagery in Hosea." Pp. 86–95 in *Feminist
        Interpretation of the Bible.* Ed. Letty M. Russell. Philadelphia: Westminster.

Sjoberg, Gideon
1960   *The Preindustrial City, Past and Present.* New York: The Free Press.

Skinner, John
1910   *A Critical and Exegetical Commentary on Genesis.* 2d ed. ICC. Edinburgh: T. & T. Clark.

Soggin, J. Alberto
1972   *Joshua.* Trans. R.A. Wilson. OTL. Philadelphia: Westminster.

Speiser, Ephraim A.
1955   Trans. and ed. "Akkadian Myths and Epics." Pp. 60–119. ANET.
1964   *Genesis.* AB 1. Garden City: Doubleday.

Tigay, Jeffrey H.
1982   *The Evolution of the Gilgamesh Epic.* Philadelphia: University of Pennsylvania.

Tucker, Gene M.
1972   "The Rahab Saga (Joshua 2): Some Form-Critical and Traditio-Historical Observations."
        Pp. 66–86 in *The Use of the Old Testament in the New and Other Essays. Studies in Honor of
        William Franklin Stinespring.* Ed. James M. Efird. Durham: Duke University.

Wehr, Hans
1961   *A Dictionary of Modern Written Arabic*. Ed. J. Milton Cowan. Ithaca: Cornell University.

Westermann, Claus
1986   *Genesis 37–50. A Commentary*. Trans. John J. Scullion. Minneapolis: Augsburg.

Windisch, Hans
1917/18   "Zur Rahabgeschichte (Zwei Parallelen aus der klassischen Literatur)." *ZAW* 37:188–98.

His Story Versus Her Story
Male Genealogy and Female Strategy in the Jacob Cycle

NELLY FURMAN

A text, according to the definition that French semiotician Roland Barthes (73–81) has given the word, is not a literary work or a portion of it, but its conceptualization, that is to say, a reading. Roland Barthes's concept of textuality is often illustrated by the following two metaphors. In the first, the reader is compared to a musician for whom interpretation is an activity, a personal rendition of an original score. Like the musician, the reader proposes a personal understanding of the meaningful aspects of a literary work. Because it is the perception of the reader which creates the text, its coherence is in the eyes of the reader and not in the intentionality of the author(s), narrator(s), or editor(s). The etymology of the word "text" leads us to the second metaphor used to explain the reading process. The Latin noun *textus* means not only text, passage of scripture, but also texture, tissue, structure, and context; the verb *textere* is translated "to construct," "to compose," "to weave." Thus the text is often described as a fabric, a network, or a web. The reader's interest is focused on the materiality of the literary work, the fabric of its narrativity, in other words the processes by which and through which stories are told and understood. The interlacing of narrative threads, the weaving and wavering of the plot, the matter in which a yarn is spun create a substratum of meaning that structures, supports, or undermines our understanding of the story. Insofar as it examines the systems of signs that allow literary communication to take place, textual criticism belongs to the semiotic enterprise. Understood as a semiotic exercise, textual criticism is a reading process that differs substantially in its practice and presuppositions from classical biblical textual approaches and from traditional notions of formal or textual criticism.

Though any number of narrative, linguistic, or thematic features may be used as heuristic devices for a textual reading, features that describe or refer to interpretation are particularly inviting for the semiotician. Thus, characters that function as interpreters and events that emphasize communicative acts are powerful poles of attraction.[1] In this respect, the seduction scene between Joseph and Potiphar's wife (Genesis 39) beckons the interest of the reader, for it deals with two contrary interpretations of one event, two seemingly antithetical readings. Potiphar's wife gives a willfully misleading explanation, which her husband, nonetheless, believes. They are the first set of narrator-narratee encoded in the text. A differing perception of the same event is suggested by the anonymous biblical narrator and Joseph, both of whom guarantee the existence of another viewpoint.

When Jacob's beloved Joseph was taken to Egypt, he was sold to Potiphar, an Egyptian, an officer of Pharaoh and captain of the guard. Pleased with Joseph, Potiphar makes him overseer of his house. While in Potiphar's employ, Joseph, who, according to the narrator, is handsome, attracts the attention of his master's wife. She tries to seduce him. He rejects her advances and explains his refusal in these terms: "Lo, having me my master has no concern about anything in the house, and he has put everything that he has in my hand; he is not greater in this house than I am; nor has he kept back anything from me except yourself, because you are his wife; how then can I do this great wickedness, and sin against God?" (Gen 39:9–10). However, one day when Joseph is alone in the house, Potiphar's wife grabs him by his coat and again makes overtures. He runs out of the house leaving the garment behind in her hands. She calls in the men of the household and tells them the following: "See, he has brought among us a Hebrew to insult us; he came in to me to lie with me, and I cried out with a loud voice; and when he heard that I lifted up my voice and cried, he left his garment with me, and fled and got out of the house" (Gen 39:15–16). She later repeats the same story to her husband, and Joseph is imprisoned.

One piece of clothing, two stories. His story versus her story. In this episode, Joseph's piece of attire is the mediating object between divergent desires. Here, one garment suggests a male and a female text, two gender-marked readings.

If we were to listen solely to the words of Potiphar's wife, as the servants and her husband do, without the leading comments of the narrator, the abandoned garment would stand for his desire and her refusal. The narrator, however, lets us know that Joseph had on previous occasions rejected her advances and that her story is fictional, a total fabrication. Whereas the garment represents for Joseph his loyalty to his master, for her the garment becomes a means of manipulation, a strategic device for a successful frame-up. The interpretation she proposes for the presence of the garment shows that explanation is a matter of point of view and further suggests that it is neither the truth nor the falsehood of the story that matters, but its plausibility. Her husband believes her story, and Joseph is sent to prison. For Joseph, the abandoned garment represents his rejection of Potiphar's wife, and therefore his loyalty to his master, and ultimately his obedience to God. George W. Coats (89) points out that in the context of Joseph's relation to power, the abandoned garment shows first of all "a kind of human enlightenment, a commitment to a fellow man because he is a fellow who trusts the relationship, commitment to a relationship because only in that relationship does life make sense."

For Joseph, garments do have a special meaning and do suggest a specific bond between men. His father, Jacob, gives him a long robe with sleeves for he "loved Joseph more than any other of his children, because he was the son of his old age" (Gen 37:3). Joseph's brothers become resentful and their jealousy turns to hatred after Joseph reports on them to their father and then recounts his dreams, which, according to them, predict that they will bow to him. When Jacob sends his favorite son to see if the others are doing well in the pastures, Joseph's brothers conspire to kill him. Reuben, the oldest, succeeds in convincing them to spare the boy's life. They strip Joseph of his robe and put him in a pit. Midianite traders passing by rescue the boy from the pit and sell him to Ishmaelites. Upon discovering that Joseph had disappeared from the pit where they had hidden him, the brothers take Joseph's robe, dip it in the blood of a goat, and show it to their father. Joseph's bloodied robe stands in lieu of an explanation, and Jacob understandably concludes that his favorite son has been devoured by a wild beast.

Jacob gave Joseph the robe as a token of his affection for him. Joseph abandons his coat in the hands of Potiphar's wife; his stated reason is his respect for his master. In both cases, a piece of attire represents an emotional link, a trust between men. When the Pharaoh makes Joseph vizier of Egypt, he gives the young Hebrew not only his signet ring but also garments of fine linen and a gold chain (Gen 41:42). Joseph will mark his reconciliation with his brothers by giving them ceremonial garments as well as provisions before they leave Egypt (Gen 45:21). For the men, garments express feelings. When overcome with grief, men tear their clothes. Reuben, upon discovering Joseph's disappearance, "rends" his clothes (Gen 37:29), and so does Jacob upon being shown Joseph's bloodied robe (Gen 37:34). Later on, when they are accused of having stolen the divining cup, Joseph's brothers too "rend" their clothes (Gen 44:13). Whether a token of love and respect or a sign of despair and mourning, for Jacob and his sons, garments are symbolic items.

By giving Joseph a long robe with sleeves, Jacob sets Joseph apart from his brothers. Joseph will emulate his father's partiality, for he will give his full brother Benjamin not just one ceremonial vestment, as he gave his other brothers, but "three hundred shekels of silver and five festal garments" (Gen 45:22). By distinguishing among siblings without regard to the order of birth, Jacob sets up a hierarchical order founded on the father's liking for a child, and garments are the distinguishing markers of this new filial order. Joseph's robe establishes a visible link between father and son, the seal of approval for all to see of Joseph's election as favorite son and legitimate heir. Items of clothing are the textual signifiers which, in the latter part of Genesis, support the theme of sibling rivalry and the resulting victory of the youngest. They implement the new hierarchical order of elective dominance in opposition to the "natural" predetermined rule of sovereignty of the first and oldest.

When Rebekah was pregnant with Esau and Jacob, the Lord told her: "Two nations are in your womb, and two peoples, born of you, shall be divided; the one shall be stronger than the other, the elder shall serve the younger" (Gen 25:23). The story of Jacob actualizes the words of the Lord. Esau, the first-born, "came forth red, all his body like a hairy mantle" (Gen 25:25). Jacob first bought Esau's birthright in exchange for some bread and soup. Then, at the urging of Rebekah, Jacob put on his brother's attire. He covered his hands and neck with the skin of kids fetched so that Rebekah could prepare some savory food for him to bring Isaac. Impersonating his brother, Jacob secured Isaac's blessing meant for Esau.

Robert Alter (10–11) reminds us that the midrashic commentators had already noted that the goat and kid established connecting threads between the Judah and Tamar episode and the Joseph story: "The Holy one Praised be He said to Judah, 'You deceived your father with a kid. By your life, Tamar will deceive you with a kid. . . .'"

The kids prepared by Rebekah also belong to this network, and Esau's garment now in Jacob's possession provides us with yet another connecting thread between the stories of Jacob and those of Joseph and Judah. Judah Goldin (27–44) attributes the presence of the Judah and Tamar episode, which is embedded in the story of Joseph, to the thematics of fraternal rivalry. Garments, as we have seen, form the textual support of this theme, and they play as well a prominent role in the story of Judah and Tamar.

Tamar, the widow of Judah's eldest son Er, has remained childless because Onan, Judah's second son, "spilled the semen on the ground, lest he should give offspring to his brother" (Gen 38:9). We are told that this displeased God, and Onan too was slain. Judah sends Tamar back to her father's house promising to send his last son Shelah to her when the lad is grown up. Time passes. Judah does not honor his promise. Having learned that Judah, now himself a widower, was going to shear his sheep, Tamar takes off her widow's clothes, puts on a veil, and sits by the roadside. Judah mistakes her for a harlot and asks to "come into her" (Gen 38:16). She accepts on the condition that she be given his signet, cord, and staff as a pledge of payment for her favors. This time Judah will be true to his word and send her a kid from his flock, but Tamar, having taken off the harlot's veil and dressed in her widow's garment again, cannot be found by Judah's envoy. Three months later, Judah learns that his daughter-in-law is pregnant by harlotry. He orders that she be burned, but upon being shown the signet, the cord, and staff which he recognizes as his, Judah declares: "she is more righteous than I, inasmuch as I did not give her my son Shelah" (Gen 38:26).

In the first ruse, Tamar simply exchanges two symbolically marked garments: the widow's clothes, which denote the absence of both husband and sexual relations; a harlot's veil, which advertises readiness for intercourse without parental responsibility. As Onan's punishment suggests and Judah's words confirm, the point of the story is not sexuality but fertility to assure the family's line of descent, a significance which the harlot's veil does not imply. Tamar's second stratagem is shrewder. Like Potiphar's wife, Tamar makes pieces of attire serve her own interest and purpose. The signet, cord, and staff were supposed to be the guarantee of payment Tamar was to receive for her favors. Tamar, however, does not use these objects as promissory notes. For her the importance of the signet, cord, and staff resides neither in their value as objects nor as down payment for a pledge; they are desirable only because they function as signatures, as evidence of the identity of the progenitor, as proof in a paternity suit. These objects are not meant simply to reveal her identity; rather their purpose is to establish a link between father and progeny, thereby legitimizing the births of Perez and Zerah. Judah's cord, signet, and staff belong to the same network of signifiers as Joseph's robe or the coat Joseph leaves in the hands of Potiphar's wife. They are the visual markers of a father (or master) and son relationship.

Tamar, like Rebekah, gives birth to twins. While she is in labor, one child puts out a hand to which the midwife attaches a scarlet thread. It is the other child, however, who comes out first. Because the midwife exclaims: "What a breach you made for yourself" (Gen 38:29), the first-born is named Perez, which means "a breach." The second child, the one with the red thread around his wrist, is called Zerah. The birth of Perez and Zerah is emblematic of the Joseph story, for like Zerah, who guides his older brother by widening the birth canal, Joseph as vizier of the Pharaoh directs his older brothers when they come to Egypt to fetch food.

The birth of Perez and Zerah recalls the birth of Esau and Jacob. The two sets of twins form a chiasmus. The "red hairy mantle" which distinguishes Esau, the oldest, becomes the red thread around the youngest's wrist. By wearing Esau's attire, Jacob makes Esau's distinguishing marking—namely, his "red hairy mantle"—his own. Isaac's blessing assures Jacob's superiority over his brother, and the garment becomes the signifier of Jacob's prominence. Similarly, when Jacob gives Joseph a long robe with sleeves, it symbolizes Joseph's superiority; and, when the bloodied robe is returned to Jacob, it signals Joseph's elimination from the line of succession. In Egypt, his brothers may well bow before him, but it is not Joseph's progeny that will assure the might of the people of Israel. That task, as we know, will be assumed by Judah's descendant, for Reuben, Jacob's oldest, had sexual intercourse with Bilhah, his father's concubine (Gen 35:22), thus revealing himself unworthy of his father's trust. It is therefore fitting that in his blessing to his sons, Jacob should distinguish Judah, his chosen heir, by his red garment, thereby bestowing upon him, albeit metaphorically, the symbolic marker of genuine legacy. Judah, Jacob tells us, "washes his garments in wine and his vesture in the blood of grapes" (Gen 49:11). In Genesis, Jacob's line of descent stops with the description of the birth of Perez and Zerah; the fact that it is not Zerah but Perez who is named in the ancestry of David (Matt 1:3) suggests that the sibling rivalries characteristic of the Jacob cycle continued beyond the events recounted in Genesis. However, since the eventual ascendancy of Perez lies outside the content of Genesis, it plays no part in the narrative processes at work in the Jacob cycle. For Michael Fishbane (38), the power of the Jacob cycle is that "it personalizes the tensions and dialectics which are also crystallized on a national level at later points: the struggle for blessing; the threat of discontinuity; the conflicts between and within generations; and the wrestling for birth, name and destiny." In the Jacob cycle, garments form the subtext which upholds these concerns. From Jacob to Joseph to Judah to Zerah, the red thread establishes an order of filiation, a metaphorical umbilical cord that relates directly, without the mediation of women, father to son to grandson.

As the Judah and Tamar episode illustrates, in such a system what matters is not who bears the child but the identity of the father. In this male-marked genealogy, women have no say. Their role is strictly biological. The womb as the relevant place of origin is superseded by the progenitor's authority, and ranking of siblings becomes a father's prerogative. It is therefore not surprising that Jacob favors Joseph not because he is the firstborn of his beloved Rachel but because Joseph is "the son of his old age" (Gen 37:3).

Following the path of Claude Lévi-Strauss, Judah Goldin (44) reminds us that stories function somewhat like myths, for they provide acceptable channels for the expression of discontent:

> The law of God may not be abolished, and besides, for the most part, the society assents to its terms because without these there would be chaos. But the resentments are nonetheless real! How are these to find an outlet? By folktales and folklore. Here no frontal attack is made on the divine law. That is the policy of rebellion. But in stories and fables one turns the order of the world upside down without giving up the establishment that provides protection. This is the revenge of the weak against the strong.

For Judah Goldin, "the revenge of the weak against the strong" refers to the theme of fraternal rivalry and the triumph of the youngest. In order to be counted once again among Jacob's sons, Joseph uses a personal item as a ploy to force recognition. The silver divination cup he has placed in Benjamin's sack of grain (Gen 44:2) serves as an excuse to get his brothers to stand before him so that he can reveal his identity to them. Joseph's stratagem recalls the ploys of Rebekah, Potiphar's wife, and Tamar, who like him use objects as the mediating device for their own personal ends. Sibling rivalry and the ensuing importance of the father and son bond erase the privilege of rank among wives and reduce women's function strictly to their reproductive role. In such a patriarchal system, women are still needed, but they are nonetheless outsiders. When Rebekah, Potiphar's wife, or Tamar use a piece of attire for their own personal ends, they do not create a gratuitous disturbance in the order of things. Although in a world under divine guidance their actions can be said to actualize the Lord's will, these actions can also be seen as the expression of women's resentment and rebellion. When Rebekah suggests that Jacob take his brother's place, or when Potiphar's wife tries to seduce Joseph, or when Tamar calls attention to Judah's progeny, their interference breaks up the exclusive father-son dialogue and forces recognition of their presence. It is therefore not surprising that, in the cycle of Jacob, the women use pieces of attire—which are the symbolic markers of the father-son relationship—to reinscribe themselves in the patriarchal system Their intervention in the sequence of events ruptures the continuum of the narrative and reveals the patterns interwoven in the textual fabric. In the latter part of Genesis, garments have his and her story to tell: as used by men, garments form a communicative channel from which women are excluded; but when used by women, garments function as communicative devices between the sexes. For the men, garments are symbolic markers of filial love and recognition, whereas for the women they serve as a means of self-inscription in a system that neglects them. Christine Garside Allen argues that, in securing for Jacob Isaac's blessing meant for Esau, Rebekah was only carrying out God's wishes. For Allen, it is not Isaac but Rebekah who through her selfless obedience shows herself to be a model of sanctity. "It is tempting," she writes (168–69), "to bring Rebekah into relief by maintaining that Isaac was not a saint. In this way Rebekah would be the necessary link between Abraham and Jacob." Allen's analysis clearly shows that, even if seen as a consecrated deed and interpreted from a psychological viewpoint, Rebekah's deceitful action ultimately disturbs the exclusively male genealogical lineage.

For Isaac, as for Jacob and Judah, garments have a fixed meaning: Esau's tunic and Joseph's robe represent specific individuals, Isaac mistakes the garment for the wearer and thus gives his blessing to Jacob instead of Esau. As for Judah, he is unable to recognize his daughter-in-law behind the prostitute's veil. Whereas for the men garments have a determined, precise meaning, that is to say, a truth value, for the women clothes are nothing but signifiers open to a variety of meanings; they are items whose function and referential meaning can easily be changed. When Tamar exchanges her widow's dress for the prostitute's veil, she simultaneously calls attention to two social functions of garments: first, their use as symbols in the sexual code; and, second, their use as masks and disguises. When Potiphar's wife points to Joseph's coat at her side as the proof of Joseph's attempt to seduce her, her story is believable because she provides a sexual significance to an item which, in the social context, can have a sexual referential meaning. She also uses Joseph's coat to hide her own sexual desire. Because for women, garments do not necessarily refer to a specific individual or convey solely one message, they are the place of juncture for a multiplicity of meanings, the locus for the expression of divergent desires. For Tamar, as for Potiphar's wife or Rebekah, garments are the means by which they impart their desire to play a relevant role in the patriarchal hierarchy. By pluralizing the meaning of a piece of attire, Rebekah, Potiphar's wife, and Tamar explode and thereby subvert the closure of the patriarchal representational system and symbolic code. Thus, in the latter part of Genesis, the function of garments, as understood by the women of the cycle of Jacob, can serve as the very metaphor for textuality and the deconstructive nature of modern reading practices which Barbara Johnson (3) describes as "a careful teasing out of warring forces of signification within the text." The patterns woven in the biblical narrative take their shape from the filling as well as the warp; the two strands may have different functions, but they are equally necessary to the making of the textual fabric.

Because it can be construed as a representation of different critical approaches, the episode between Joseph and Potiphar's wife (Gen 39) provided me with a point of entry into the text. Joseph rejects the advances of his master's wife and runs out of the house leaving his coat behind; Potiphar's wife tells her husband that Joseph tried to seduce her; Potiphar believes her and Joseph is incarcerated. Potiphar accepts his wife's explanation because her story does seem plausible, after all. And besides, since for the men in the Jacob cycle garments are a sign of trust and have a symbolic power that lends them even more verity; in the eyes of Potiphar Joseph's "abandoned" coat gives added credence to his wife's words. However, in accepting his wife's explanation as stated, Potiphar ignores the possibility of personal motivation. He is blind not only to his wife's self-serving reasons, but equally blind to what may be his own reasons for wanting to believe her. Potiphar's attitude is an example of a critical perspective that leaves unquestioned both the subjective needs of the storyteller and the conscious or unconscious investment of the interpreter. Yet for each of the characters in this episode, the coat has a special meaning. For Joseph and the biblical narrator, the coat stands as the proof of Joseph's innocence; for Potiphar's wife, it is the reminder of her frustrated desire; for her husband, the evidence of Joseph's guilt. Joseph's coat is the place of juncture for diverging desires; the textual fabric of a narrative is similarly the locus and the product of the interaction of the narrator's and the reader's subjectivities. Not unlike the story told by Potiphar's wife, my version of the stories in the Jacob cycle may be warped, skewed by my feminist and critical concerns. But on the other hand, the anonymous biblical narrator wages for Joseph's innocence. In siding with Joseph, the narrator embraces the ideological structure which Joseph serves, namely, the male desire for an exclusive bond between men. On the question of family lineage or on the subject of human relationships, the position of the biblical narrator is no more "neutral" than that of the feminist reader.

NOTES

1. For a discussion of the question of reading and its relation to criticism, see Suleiman.

REFERENCES

Allen, Christine Garside
1979   "On Me Be the Curse, My Son!" Pp. 159–72 in *Encounter with the Text: Form and History in the Hebrew Bible*. Ed. Martin J. Buss. Philadelphia: Fortress.

Alter, Robert
1981   *The Art of Biblical Narrative*. New York: Basic Books.

Barthes, Roland
1979   "From Work to Text." Pp. 73–81 in *Textual Strategies: Perspectives in Post-Structuralist Criticism*. Ed. Josué Harari. Ithaca: Cornell University.

Coats, George W.
1976   *From Canaan to Egypt: Structural and Theological Context for the Joseph Story*. CBQMS 4. Washington: Catholic Biblical Association.

Fishbane, Michael
1975   "Composition and Structure in the Jacob Cycle (Gen. 25:19–35:22)." *JJS* 26:15–38.

Goldin, Judah
1977   "The Youngest Son or Where Does Genesis 38 Belong." *JBL* 96:27–44.

Johnson, Barbara
1978   "The Critical Difference." *Diaecritics, A Review of Contemporary Criticism*. 8:2–9.

Suleiman, Susan R.
1980   "Introduction: Varieties of Audience-Oriented Criticism." Pp. 3–45 in *The Reader in the Text: Essays on Audience and Interpretation*. Ed. Susan R. Suleiman and Inge Crosman. Princeton: Princeton University.

The Literary Characterization of Mothers and Sexual Politics in the Hebrew Bible

ESTHER FUCHS

The impact of the Hebrew Bible on the present state of sexual politics has been universally recognized by feminist critics.[1] Nevertheless, few of them have gone beyond the "aetiological" myth of Genesis 2–3 to demonstrate the patriarchal conception of the Bible. While the narrative strategies of androcentric "classics" have been challenged (e.g., de Beauvoir; Millet), while feminist philosophers and theologians have worked out critical analyses of biblical patriarchalism (e.g., Daly), and while feminist historians have begun to document the social status of women in ancient Israel (Bird), not a single consistent analysis of the patriarchal (literary) strategies of the biblical narrative has yet been produced. A possible explanation for this remarkable scholarly gap may lie in the traditional appropriation of the Bible by specialists who defined the Bible as anything but literature. A more reasonable explanation would take into consideration the privileged status of the Bible as the alleged locus of divine revelation. This may illuminate the dominant status of what I might call, for lack of a better word, an appropriative tendency among contemporary feminists, who emphasize what they interpret as antipatriarchal or anticultural currents in the biblical text (e.g., Trible:1–30). In what follows, I would like to exemplify how we might approach the literary strategies of biblical patriarchalism. As a part of a more comprehensive study of the patriarchal determinants of the Bible's presentation of women, the present reading focuses on the mother figure.

Although certain female biblical characters create the impression that "the story belongs" to them and to "chance" as Phyllis Trible puts it (178), I would like to argue that they are the product of the Bible's subtle and effective patriarchal didacticism (178). The "legislative" aspect of female characterization is not unique to the biblical narrative. It pervades apparently nonideological narratives written by men (for men) about women. As feminist studies of androcentric fiction demonstrate, male-authored female characters reveal more about the wishful thinking, fears, aspirations, and prejudices of their male creators than about women's lives/experiences/perceptions. The pragmatic or ideological aspect of the literary work characterizes all literary works (Uspensky). The objective or neutral "reflection" of reality in literature is an illusion (Booth).

The fact is that the ideological aspect prevails in all literary characterization. The ascription of motivation, thought, action, and word to a certain character constitutes an indirect means of authorial judgment which exists even in what appears to be the most neutral and objective tale. This is especially the case in the best ideological literature, like the Bible. Yet, even the scholars who acknowledged the didactic aspect of the biblical narrative have focused almost exclusively on its monotheistic ideology, ignoring completely its patriarchal ideology. Thus, for example, it has been suggested that the motif of the miraculous conception of a barren woman in the Bible implies that YHWH is the sole proprietor and master of human life (Alter, 1981:47–52). This fits well the biblical monotheistic framework. As we shall see, however, this recurrent motif is also motivated by the Bible's patriarchal ideology, which seeks to naturalize and legitimate man's political dominance.

The biblical annunciation type-scene consists of three major thematic components: the initial barrenness of the wife, a divine promise of future conception, and the birth of a son (Alter, 1981:49). While these components function largely as constants, the actual scenes vary in narrative span and complexity. As has already been pointed out, the deflections from the standard structure are not coincidental; they function often as foreshadowing techniques alluding to future events in the life of the future son. For our purpose, the most significant variations pertain to the role of the potential mother in the annunciation type-scene (Alter, 1983); these variations, as we shall see next, constitute a consistently increasing emphasis on the potential mother as the true heroine of the annunciation type-scene.

The first biblical annunciation type-scene is preceded by YHWH's direct address to the potential father, Abraham, regarding the future conception of his barren wife, Sarai, "And God said to Abraham, 'As for Sarai your wife, you shall not call her name Sarai, but Sarah shall be her name. I will bless her, and moreover I will give you a son by her; I will bless her, and she shall be the mother of nations; kings of people shall come from her'" (Gen 17:15–16).[2] Although Sarai's status and thereby her fate are discussed in this dialogue, she is referred to in the third person.

YHWH blesses Sarai in her absence and changes her name through her husband. The act of naming signifies a recognition of identity, an endowment of new essence and being, and it suggests the namer's authority. YHWH changes Abram's name to Abraham (17:5) in his direct dialogue with him, yet the names of his wife and his son, which are also determined by YHWH, are to be given by Abraham who represents God's authority as husband and father. More importantly, the blessings of Sarai and the change in her name are preceded by a restatement of YHWH's covenant with Abraham. The transformation of the barren Sarai into a fertile Sarah is a logical and necessary procedure required by YHWH's commitment to Abraham: "And I will make my covenant between me and you, and you shall be the father of a multitude of nations" (vv 2, 4).

In the annunciation type-scene itself Abraham continues to occupy center stage. The scene opens with an introductory verse which leaves no doubt as to the actual addressee of YHWH: "And the Lord appeared to him by the oaks of Mamre, as he sat in the tent door in the heat of the day" (18:1). When the three messengers arrive at the tent, Abraham the generous and hospitable host invites the guests to rest up and refresh themselves, while instructing Sarah, who is inside the tent, to prepare cakes for the men. Sarah's function in this context is no different from that of Abraham's servant who is enjoined to prepare a calf for the meal. Unlike Abraham, who is implicitly praised for this generosity and eagerness to please his guests, Sarah, who is not privy to what is happening outside the tent, receives no credit for her work, since she functions as her husband's adjunct. Throughout the meal, Sarah shows no interest in the guests. The text repeats the fact that Sarah remains inside the tent in Abraham's response to the messengers' query concerning her whereabouts (v 9). This repetition is not coincidental; it emphasizes Sarah's absence from this fateful scene and by contrast, Abraham's central role in it. Instead of becoming actively involved in the conversation Sarah eavesdrops on her husband and guests "at the tent door behind him" [Abraham] (v 10). Once again, although Sarah is the subject of YHWH's address, she is referred to in the third person while her husband functions as the actual addressee: "YHWH said, 'I shall surely return to you when the season comes round and Sarah your wife shall have a son'" (v 10). Even when Sarah is reprimanded for laughing to herself in disbelief, she is addressed through her husband. Only when she denies having laughed, does YHWH speak directly to her, "saying, 'No, but you did laugh'" (v 15). YHWH's only direct reference to Sarah takes the form of an implicit accusation.

The juxtaposition of the husband and wife in this scene enhances the attributes of the first and the drawbacks of the latter. Abraham's activity outside the tent is contrasted by Sarah's passivity. Seventeen verbs predicate Abraham's dedication to his guests. The verbs "run" and "hasten" are repeated twice. Sarah, on the other hand, is the subject of four verbs, none of which demonstrates a high level of exertion: to hear, laugh, deny, and fear. Although there is reason to believe that Sarah obeyed her husband's instructions and, like a good housewife, baked cakes for the guests, the text does not mention this fact explicitly. Sarah emerges from the scene as confined, passive, cowardly, deceptive, and unfaithful. Sarah's participation in the annunciation type-scene amounts to a troublesome interference. If the text is trying to establish a correlation between YHWH's benevolence and the uprightness of his subjects, it is clear that the manifestation of this benevolence, namely, the annunciation type-scene, is related causally to the man's demeanor and concessively to the woman's. The implication is that YHWH violates nature's rules and gives the barren woman a child because of her husband's magnanimity and despite her pettiness. But the fulfillment of the divine promise does not follow the annunciation in the narrative sequence; instead, it is postponed to chapter 21, which opens with a characteristic formula: "And the Lord remembered Sarah" (21:1). The interpolated narrative material refers to Abraham's intercession on behalf of the citizens of Sodom and Gomorrah, the destruction of the iniquitous cities by YHWH (chap. 19) and the episode in Gerar in which Abraham presents his wife as his sister (chap. 20). Sarah is absent from chapter 19, which dramatizes Abraham's compassion and altruism. In chapter 20, she appears as a passive object of sexual possession, taken by Abimelech, King of Gerar, and narrowly saved from committing adultery by the direct intervention of YHWH.

Although Sarah is given full credit for giving birth to Isaac, in chapter 21, the text continues to stress that she is mostly instrumental, and that the miracle is performed for Abraham. Verse 2 does not simply state the fact that Sarah bore a son but that "she bore

Abraham a son." Verse 3 repeats this idea twice: "Abraham called the name of his son who was born to him, whom Sarah bore him, Isaac." Abraham proceeds to establish his paternal authority over his newborn son by naming and circumcising him (v 4), while Sarah comments again on the risibility of her belated conception (v 6).

As we noted, the first annunciation type-scene starts with YHWH's address to Abraham, without being previously solicited by either Abraham or Sarah. In the second annunciation type-scene, Isaac initiates the first move; he pleads with YHWH on behalf of his barren wife, and YHWH grants his prayer (Gen. 25:21). Once again, the wife's conception is attributed to the good relationship of her husband with YHWH; it is not contingent upon the qualities or actions of the wife. Nevertheless, it is YHWH's response to Rebekah that the text reports and not his response to Isaac. In response to Rebekah's complaint about her painful pregnancy, YHWH explains that she is bearing twins, and that the younger of the two will prevail over the older. Whereas in the first annunciation type-scene, YHWH discusses the future son with the father; here He shares His prescience with the mother. Another indication of Rebekah's greater involvement in the future of her children occurs in their naming. Whereas in the case of Isaac, YHWH endows Abraham with the exclusive right to name his son, here the children are named by both parents: "The first came forth red, all his body like a hairy mantle; so they called his name Esau. Afterward, his brother came forth . . . so his name was called Jacob" (vv 25–26). Unlike Sarah, Rebekah appears at center stage, alongside Isaac. She receives greater recognition from YHWH as potential mother, and there is not so much as an allusion to a moral discrepancy between the man and his wife at this point.

The third annunciation type-scene is preceded by a description of the plight and despair of the barren wife. The text presents Rachel as a jealous co-wife, exasperated by the fertility of her rival, Leah. In her despair, Rachel turns to Jacob with what appears to be an impetuous and immature demand: "Give me children, or I shall die" (Gen 30:1). The reader is expected to sympathize with Jacob's angry response: "Am I in the place of God who has withheld from you the fruit of the womb?" (v 2). Indeed, the previous type-scenes bear Jacob's statement out, for was it not YHWH who gave Sarah and Rebekah children? Jacob chastises Rachel angrily and self-righteously. His response implies that his wife's barrenness is outside his sphere of control; he disclaims all responsibility for his wife's condition. The ensuing list of the sons born to Jacob by other concubines and by Leah intimates that Jacob may not be concerned because his progeny was ensured by other means. Finally, the conventional formula announcing divine intervention appears: "Then God remembered Rachel, and God hearkened to her and opened her womb" (v 22). The formula differs from both previous formulas of divine intervention. The first formula presents YHWH's intervention as a fulfillment of a promise: "The Lord visited Sarah as he had said, and the Lord did to Sarah as he had promised" (21:1). The second formula presents divine intervention as a direct response to the husband's plea: "the Lord granted his prayer" (25:21). The third formula, however, stresses the fact that YHWH intervenes in response to Rachel's plight, by repeating that He "remembered her" (*zkr*) "and hearkened to her" (*šmʿ*). In addition, Rachel, like Leah, reserves the right of naming her sons. Jacob accepts the names given to his sons by his wives with the exception of Benjamin. Jacob changes the name Rachel gives to her second son from *ben-ʾônî* ("the son of sorrow"), to *binyāmîn* ("the son of my right hand") (35:18).

The fourth annunciation type-scene, on the other hand, presents the potential father, Manoah, as somewhat of a schlemiel, whereas his unnamed wife emerges as the clear protagonist of the scene. Manoah is absent when the angel of the Lord appears to his wife and informs her that she is to conceive a son who will be a Nazirite and a national redeemer (Judg 13:3–5). Not only is the woman apprised of the future of her son, but she is given a set of instructions to follow during her pregnancy, implying a close interdependence between the mother's actions and the future son's life. When Manoah hears the news, he entreats the Lord to send his messenger once again. When the angel reappears, it is once again the women who sees him first, while sitting alone in the field. The open field points up metonymically the woman's independence, just as the tent underscored Sarah's confinement. Similarly, the words "and Manoah arose and went after his wife" (v 11) signify the husband's dependence on his wife. This constitutes a reverse analogy to the posture of Sarah inside the tent behind Abraham (Gen 18:10).

In response to Manoah's requests, the angel repeats his instructions to the woman, adding nothing at all to what he had previously said to Manoah's wife and to what she had already reported to her husband. Whereas the woman perceives immediately that the messenger is "a man of God," and compares his appearance to the "countenance of an angel of God, very terrible" (Judg 13:6), Manoah treats the divine messenger as a human being, inviting him for a meal. When the angel declines Manoah's invitation, hinting at his divine identity by suggesting that Manoah should use the meal as a burnt offering for the Lord, Manoah misses the hint and proceeds to inquire about the stranger's name, so that "when your words come true, we may honor you" (v 17). This request contrasts with the woman's conscientious and respectful silence (v 6). Even when the stranger answers enigmatically, pointing out that his name is "wondrous" (or "mysterious"), Manoah remains unaware of the stranger's true identity. Only when he witnesses the miraculous ascent to heaven in the flame of the burnt offering, "*then* Manoah knew that he was the angel of the Lord" (v 21). The emphasis on the temporal adverb at the beginning of the sentence adds an additional dash of irony to the satirical presentation of the obtuse husband. But now, Manoah panics: "We shall surely die, for we have seen God" (v 22). Once again, Manoah's wife demonstrates her superior intelligence by pointing out the futility of showing miracles to people who had been singled out for death. The text vindicates her point of view by following this interchange with the final component of the annunciation type-scene, the fulfillment of the divine promise: "And the woman bore a son and called his name Samson" (v 24). The woman does not bear a son "to" her husband; neither does she consult her husband about their son's name.

The thematic and structural parallels between Judges 13 and Genesis 18 highlight the radical shift in the characterization and respective status of the potential mother and father figures. Whereas the hospitality of Abraham is graciously accepted by the three messengers, Manoah's hospitality is rejected. The first scene uses Araham's hospitality to enhance his uprightness, the latter exposes Manoah's hospitality as maladroitness. In the first scene, YHWH addresses Sarah indirectly and peripherally; in the fourth scene God turns to the woman first, and only repeats for her husband things already known to her. Sarah emerges from the first scene as skeptical and parochial housewife, vastly overshadowed by Abraham's magnanimity. Manoah's wife, on the other hand, is perspicacious, sensitive, and devout, outshining her inept husband. Sarah's unnecessary interference in the course of the first annunciation type-scene parallels to a great extent the dispensable contributions of Manoah.

In the next scene, the potential father is pushed even further away from the focus of the story. Hannah, like Rachel, suffers not only from her barrenness, but also from the provocations of Peninnah, her fertile rival. But unlike Rachel, Hannah does not turn to her husband, Elkanah, for help. She decides to address her plea directly to YHWH. She does not even call on Eli, the priest, who is visibly stationed by the doorposts of the temple, but instead pours out her bitter heart in prayer and directly enlists God's help, by offering to dedicate her future son to His service. This is the first time the barren woman is shown to turn directly to YHWH; Rebekah, it will be remembered, turns to YHWH to complain of her difficult pregnancy, not to ask for children. This is also the first time the type-scene reports in direct speech the barren woman's prayer for children.

Hannah circumvents the authority of both Elkanah and Eli by making a vow to YHWH on her own initiative. The text implies support for her initiative by pointing out that Elkanah fails to understand his wife's misery (1 Sam 1:8) and by satirizing Eli as an obtuse old man, who misinterprets Hannah's chagrin for drunkenness. Sure of his perception, he rebukes the embittered woman with harsh words: "How long will you be drunken? Put away your wine from you" (v 14). But confronted with Hannah's eloquent response, Eli retracts his rash accusation and bids the woman to go in peace, adding: "and the God of Israel grant your petition which you have made to him" (v 17). It is not clear whether Eli is promising YHWH's help, or merely expressing his wishful blessings. Either way, Eli remains unaware of Hannah's specific request, which does not add much to his already suspect stature as divine oracle and representative of YHWH.

Unlike the divine messengers earlier, Eli fails to anticipate the miraculous conception. Whereas the previous messengers anticipate and initiate the annunciation, Eli reacts to Hannah's initiative. Furthermore, Eli fails to understand Hannah's plight and, although reacting favorably to her plea, the text implies that he remains unaware of its specific nature.

Neither does Elkanah, the potential father, understand Hannah's anguish. "And Elkanah, her husband, said to her, 'Hannah, why do you weep? And why do you not eat? And why is your heart sad? Am I not better to you than ten sons?'" (v 8). Elkanah's repeated questions indicate his concern for his wife, but at the same time they imply helplessness and a basic lack of understanding for the childless woman. Elkanah's speech functions as ironic self-betrayal; it dramatizes the husband's exaggerated sense of self-importance and his inability to realize that his love cannot compensate for his wife's barrenness. Elkanah's lack of insight into what the Bible presents as woman's greatest tragedy places him in a marginal role within the framework of this drama. Unlike the previous husbands who came in direct contact with divine emissaries (or, in Jacob's case, spoke on behalf of YHWH), Elkanah is absent from the scene dramatizing the divine element.

In his capacity as YHWH's representative, Eli promises Hannah God's help. Fulfilling his role as husband, Elkanah has intercourse with his wife, but none of these male characters are shown to have any awareness of the special significance of their actions. Both are excluded from the privileged point of view of Hannah, the omniscient narrator and the implied reader. Juxtaposed with these male foils, Hannah emerges as the incontestable heroine of the scene. Whereas in the case of Sarah, the text emphasizes that she bore a son "to Abraham," here the text presents the husband as an auxiliary character: "And Elkanah knew Hannah his wife, and the Lord remembered her, and in due time Hannah conceived and bore a son, and she called his name Samuel, for she said, 'I have asked him of the Lord'" (vv 19–20).

If Elkanah is a secondary character, the potential father in the final annunciation type-scene is barely a peripheral figure (Harvey). Gehazi, Elisha's servant, describes him as an old man (2 Kgs 4:14). The text dramatizes him as uninsightful and passive. His contribution to the annunciation scene proper is marginal. Prior to the son's birth, the potential father is referred to only in the third person. He is practically excluded from the interaction between the man of God, Elisha, and his wife, "the great woman of Shunem" (*gĕdôlâ*, v 8). The Shunammite is the one who goes out of her way to "seize" (*wattaḥăzeq*, v 8) Elisha, offering him meals whenever he passes through town. Discontented with her sporadic hospitality, she convinces her husband to dedicate a room in their house for Elisha. The text records the woman's suggestion in great detail and omits the husband's reply, thereby underscoring the woman's initiative and, by contrast, the husband's passivity and possible indifference.

This annunciation type-scene is the first to present the female protagonist as character before focusing on her as a maternal role model. The actions and speeches of the preceding female characters were mostly motivated by the desire for children or by the prospect of giving birth. These characters were described only in conjunction with the binary theme of barrenness-fertility, or with the fate and identity of their prospective sons. In the case of the great woman of Shunem, her character and her relationship with Elisha seem to deserve attention independently of the theme of childlessness. The text insists that the Shunammite's hospitality and generosity stem from her benevolence, not from an ulterior motive. When urged by Elisha to express her needs, in return for her favors, the Shunammite demurs: "I dwell among my own people" is her proud answer (v 13). Only when Gehazi, Elisha's servant, informs him that the woman "has no son, and her husband is old" (v 14) does the reader realize that the Shunammite is childless. This is the first time in which the annunciation type-scene does not attribute childlessness exclusively to woman. The text does not define the woman as "barren" (*ʿăqārâ*) or closed-wombed; on the contrary, by specifying that her husband is old, the text suggests that the man's age may explain the absence of children this time. When Elisha informs her that "at this season, when the time comes round, you shall embrace a son" (v 16), she is incredulous: "no, my lord, oh man of God; do not lie to your maidservant" (v 16). By introducing the woman's qualities prior to the actual annunciation, the narrative establishes a relationship of cause and effect between the episodes. This type-scene is the first to present YHWH's intervention as reward for woman's upright conduct. Hannah conceives, thanks to her ardent prayer to YHWH; the Shunammite conceives, thanks to her selflessness, benevolence, humility, and loyalty to YHWH's emissary.

The first type-scene establishes a causal link between the husband's uprightness and the wife's miraculous conception. The text makes it clear that the postmenopausal and barren Sarah conceives not because of her own conduct but thanks to YHWH's interest in Abraham. The hospitality, generosity, and humility initially ascribed to the potential father are now ascribed to the potential mother. On the other hand, the reticence, passivity, and indifference displayed by the potential mother toward the divine messengers in the first type-scene are transposed to the potential father in the last. Significantly, the text does not stress that the Shunammite bore a son "to" or even by her husband; omitting the husband from the final phase of the scene, it states: "But the woman conceived and bore a son about that time the following spring, as Elisha said to her" (v 17).

The passivity of the Shunammite's husband is further dramatized in his reaction to his son's disease and subsequent death. When the boy complains of a severe headache, his father orders a servant to "carry him to his mother" (v 19). When the Shunammite hurries to see Elisha, her husband, unaware of the disaster, argues "Why will you go to him today? It is neither new moon nor Sabbath" (v 23). The husband's protestations expose his limited understanding of the events. His criticism of his wife backfires. The husband's unanswered questions function here as irony of self-betrayal. As in Elkanah's case, these questions are potential obstructions rather than accelerating factors in the plot progression toward the happy denouement. Whereas Hannah leaves Elkanah's questions unanswered, the Shunammite responds to her old man's irrelevant arguments with a short "*šālôm*" ("It shall be well" [v 23]).

Yet, the husband is not the only character ridiculed by the narrative. I tend to agree with Robert Alter that the narrator of 2 Kings is rather ambivalent toward the figure of Elisha in general (1981:126). In our particular scene, Elisha is not aware that his bene-factor is childless and acts on her behalf only after Gehazi apprises him of the situation. Furthermore, when the Shunammite comes to see him concerning her dead son, he is unaware of the disaster and instructs his servant to greet her and ask her if it is well with her, her husband, and her son (v 26). Realizing that the woman is in great distress he admits that the "Lord has hidden it from me, and has not told me" (v 27). Elisha remains in the dark until the Shunammite speaks; but instead of hurrying to the dead boy, he dispatches his servant Gehazi, instructing him to put his staff on the boy's face (similar to the husband who sends the sick boy to his mother with a servant), a solution which proves later to be ineffective. Only when the woman insists on his personal involvement does Elisha consent to follow her (v 30). The detailed description of Elisha's technical attempts to revive the dead son presents the process of resuscitation as a medical rather than miraculous ordeal. Despite the woman's impeccable conduct and profound piety, Elisha continues to refer to her as "the Shunammite" and sometimes with the more derisive "that Shunammite" (*haššûnammît hallāz* [v 25]), as if he never condescended to learn her name. But clearly Elisha's attitude is not representative of the narrator's point of view.

The growing recognition of the potential mother figure suggests an ever-increasing emphasis within the biblical framework on the institution of motherhood. As Adrienne Rich points out, the social and legal *institution* of motherhood is distinctly different from the personal and psychological aspect of motherhood; the latter refers to "the *potential relationship* of any woman to her powers of reproduction and to children," whereas the former refers to the mechanism aimed at "ensuring that that potential—and all women—shall remain under male control" (xv). The institution of motherhood is a powerful patriarchal mechanism. Male control of female reproductive powers in con-junction with patrilocal monogamous marriage (for the wife) secures the wife as her hus-band's exclusive property and insures the continuity of his name and family possessions via patrinomial customs and patrilineal inheritance patterns. The institution of mother-hood as defined by the patriarchal system guarantees that both the wife and her children will increase his property during his lifetime and perpetuate his achievements and mem-ory after his death.

The annunciation type-scenes surveyed in this study clearly define motherhood as patriarchal institution, *not* as personal tendency of woman. All the mother figures in these scenes are married wives. There is no instance in the biblical narrative in which an unmarried barren woman is visited by God or divine emissary and miraculously released from her barrenness. This would be unthinkable, since the child born out of wedlock would not be able to carry on his father's lineage, and would be ostracized from the community as a *mamzēr* (Deut 23:3), while his mother would at best be branded as *zônâ* ("whore"). YHWH, in the biblical narrative, restricts his interest in barren women to married women and to situations which leave no doubt as to the identity of the potential father. What seems to be a sentimental narrative about the happy transition from emptiness to fullness and from failure to victory is a carefully constructed story intended among other things to promote the institution of motherhood. All the narrative details are designed and orchestrated in accordance with this ideological perspective, from the selection of thematic materials to the organization of motifs, dialogue, plot structure, and characterization. The growing emphasis on the figure of the potential mother may be misinterpreted as a growing recognition of the importance of woman's reproductive powers. The fact is that the annunciation type-scene, in its many variations, drives home the opposite message: that woman has no control at all over her reproductive potential. YHWH has control, and he is often andromorphized in the biblical narrative. Furthermore, all the divine messengers, dispatched to proclaim the imminent miraculous conception, are male figures. The literary constellation of male characters surrounding and determining the fate of the potential mother dramatizes the idea that woman's reproductive potential should be and can be controlled only by men. It is true that the presence of the potential husband progressively decreases in the annunciation type-scene, but his presence is, nevertheless, essential.

Tamar, Judah's daughter-in-law, would be burnt at the stake and condemned as a harlot had she tried to procure children outside of her deceased husband's family (Gen 38:24). The only thing which saves her life and turns her into a biblical heroine is the fact that the man she sleeps with, Judah, is directly related to Er, her deceased husband, who left her with no children. Ruth, too, is extolled as a heroine, thanks to her faithfulness to her deceased husband's patrilineage. What turns her into a biblical heroine is not the fact that she prefers to follow Naomi to the land of Judah rather than to stay in Moab, but the fact that Naomi is her mother-in-law, the mother of Mahlon, her deceased husband who left her childless. She is not merely extolled for her ability to survive physically in adverse circumstances or for her initiative and energy in general as Phyllis Trible suggests (195–96). For Ruth succeeds in finding and marrying a *direct relative of Elimelech,* her father-in-law, and giving birth to children who would carry on the patrilineage of her deceased husband.

Tamar and Ruth achieve the high status of biblical heroines, thanks to their voluntary and active support of the patriarchal institution of the levirate, which insures the patrilineage of a deceased husband (Fuchs). But the biblical narrative is careful *not* to establish too close a link between the interests of patriarchy and woman's sacrifice. On the contrary, the heroine's motivation is normally shown to be self-seeking. Both Ruth and Tamar are shown to fight for their *own* benefit and security. By projecting onto woman what man desires most, the biblical narrative creates womanhood in its own image.

The motif of motherhood in the biblical narrative seems to be closely associated with the motif of female rivalry. The mother-harlot who steals her roommate's son away and encourages the king to kill him acts on the same motivation that drove Sarah to drive out Hagar and her son Ishmael (Gen 21:9–10). Rachel too seems to be driven to despair by her jealousy of her fertile sister. The motif of female rivalry is intertwined with the motif of motherhood in the story of Hannah and Peninnah. The fertile Peninnah taunts and humiliates Hannah for her barrenness (1 Sam 1:16). It is rare to find a biblical narrative presenting mutually supportive mothers. This may be explained as a clever literary strategy in the service of biblical sexual politics. By perpetuating the theme of women's mutual rivalry, especially in a reproductive context, the narrative implies that sisterhood is a precarious alternative to the patriarchal system.

Both the positive and the negative mother figures are shown to prefer their sons' well-being to their own. The best consolation offered to Hagar, who has been driven out by Sarah, refers not to herself but to her son: ". . . and the angel of God called to Hagar from heaven and said to her, 'What troubles you Hagar? Fear not; for God has heard the voice of the lad where he is. Arise, lift up the lad, and hold him fast with your hand; for I will make him a great nation'" (Gen 21:17–18). This consolation which focuses exclusively on the future son, Ishmael, is presented as the only and the most effective divine response to woman's predicament. Her own physical and emotional anguish is not taken into account. The only problem biblical mothers face concerns their sons' well-being, and the only solution to their problems is the assurance that their sons will survive. Thus the biblical narrative presents as the best palliative for a difficult pregnancy a message concerning the future sons. YHWH's promise to the pregnant Rebekah that she will bear twin sons seems to put an end to her intolerable pangs (Gen 25:22–24). Rachel's fatal delivery is presented as peripheral to the birth of Benjamin (Gen 35:17).

Woman's reluctance to give birth or to assume maternal responsibility for her child are options which are completely excluded from the represented reality of the Bible. These possibilities do not even appear as subjects for criticism as they do in the case of men. Onan, for example, refuses to "raise seed unto 'his brother Er'" and consequently is severely punished by YHWH (Gen 38:10). But woman is not even shown to be capable of *not* desiring sons. The biblical narrative is careful to ascribe the desire for sons to its female figures. Rachel is described as most desperate to give birth: "Give me sons, or I shall die" (Gen 30:1). Ironically, Rachel dies not through barrenness but through fertility.

Mother figures are portrayed not only as desirous of children, but also as protective of their children and relentlessly devoted to them. Whereas conflicts between fathers and children appear as prevalent motifs in the biblical narrative (e.g., Laban versus Rachel and Leah; Jacob versus his sons, especially Simeon and Levi; Saul versus Jonathan and Michal; and David versus Absalom), they almost never appear in the context of mother-child relationship. The closest a mother figure comes to being portrayed at cross-purposes with her child is Rebekah scheming against Esau, her elder son. But, we are told, Rebekah does it out of love for Jacob.

On the other hand, the "maternal instinct" is portrayed as highly selfish and confined inclination, mostly focused on one's own child. Sarah's concern for her son, Isaac, is presented as her primary motivation for driving Hagar and Ishmael out (Gen 21: 9–10). The harlot who lost her son shows no pity for the son of her friend, and prefers to see him dead rather than alive in the arms of her rival (1 Kgs 3:26).

Woman's parenthood in the biblical narrative is largely restricted to reproductive and protective functions. Hagar, Zipporah, the Shunammite, and Rizpah all represent the maternal role at its most rudimentary—and reductive. When a mother appears to interfere on behalf of her son in a more sophisticated way, for example, to promote his rights over his siblings, she must circumvent her husband's authority. Thus, when Rebekah interferes on behalf of Jacob, she does not do so openly, for example, by attempting to convince Isaac that his preference for Esau is not in keeping with YHWH's will. Rather, she resorts to deception, which indicates that only in this circuitous manner will she be able to prevail over her husband. But while Rebekah takes initiative independently, Bathsheba does not dare intercede with David on behalf of Solomon before Nathan encourages her to do so. Here, too, the mother is forced to resort to a bit of histrionics in order to win over the father, the final authority over the fate of her child. The mother may be the decisive factor in giving birth to and preserving the life of her children but she remains subservient to her husband's authority over her and her children.

It is interesting to note that whereas mothers are shown to interfere actively on behalf of their sons, they never interfere on behalf of their daughters. The story of Dinah's rape makes no reference to Leah. The only responsible parties are Dinah's father, Jacob (somewhat lamely), and her brothers. The story of Jephthah's daughter does not mention her mother either. The story of the concubine exploited to death by the Benjaminites refers to her father and her master only. Maacah, the mother of Tamar, is absent from the story about her daughter's rape. Aside from the victim, the story mentions only the aggressor, Amnon, the negligent father, David, and the avenger, Absalom, Tamar's brother. By expatiating on mothers who protect or interfere on behalf of their sons, the biblical narrative creates maternal role models which promote the interests of the male rather than the female child. Thus, all the annunciation type-scenes precede the birth of sons. The biblical mothers are usually desirous of sons. This is blatant in the case of Rachel, who demands from Jacob sons. The children born to previously barren mothers are all male. Similarly, Tamar and Ruth are rewarded with the birth of sons. When the biblical narrative mentions birth it almost exclusively refers to a male baby. The only exception is Dinah, Leah's daughter. But even here the daughter seems to be short-changed, since hers is the only case in which the Bible omits the etymology of the name (Gen 30:21). The motif of mother-daughter relationship is practically non-existent in the biblical narrative. Not only is motherhood defined in relation to a lawful husband-father, but it is also determined by the male gender of the child. Furthermore, it can be asserted that the presence of mother figures in the biblical narrative is often contingent upon the identity and importance of their sons. In other words, the narrative frequently deals with the mother figure due to its interest in her immediate or future offspring rather than in her own character. Some narratives involving a mother figure focus mainly on the circumstances leading to her son's birth. Soon after the birth of the son, the mother figure is quickly whisked off the stage (Leah, Tamar, Samson's mother, Ruth). Other mothers survive in a few details concerning their protection of their sons, e.g., Sarah, Rebekah, the Shunammite, and Bathsheba. Sarah manages to drive Hagar and Ishmael away (Gen 21) shortly before she expires (Gen 23:2). Rebekah disappears from the scene as soon as her protective role is completed, allowing the literary focus to shift from Isaac to Jacob. The Shunammite disappears as soon as her son is resuscitated by Elisha, allowing the focus to shift back to Elisha. And Bathsheba disappears from the text as soon as Solomon's rule is insured, allowing the focus to shift from David to Solomon.

The literary frame is particularly significant in the case of the annunciation type-scene, because of its unusual emphasis on the mother figure. Even in these scenes the dramatic climax involves the birth of a son. Additionally, they all start with reference to the father. Even in the later scenes, featuring especially dominant mother figures, the beginning deals with the father, and the ending with the son. The annunciation scene of Samson opens with an exposition relating first to Manoah and later to his wife: "And there was a certain man of Zorah, of the tribe of the Danites, whose name was Manoah; and his wife was barren and had no children" (Judg 13:2). Although Hannah clearly out-shines her husband Elkanah, the annunciation type-scene opens first with reference to the man, presenting the potential mother as his barren co-wife (1 Sam 1:1–2). The Shu-nammite's story extols the woman's virtues, but still it constitutes only a part of a nar-rative series revolving around Elisha. Although she prevails over her husband in the annunciation type-scene, the narrative as a whole is presented as an additional enterprise of the man of God, another aspect of his divine power. This can be seen in the opening verses of the scene: "One day Elisha went on to Shunem, and there lived a great woman who urged (lit. seized) him to eat bread, and so whenever he passed there he would stop (lit. turn) there to eat bread" (2 Kgs 4:8). The Shunammite is introduced in a combined sentence which functions syntactically as a relative clause that refers to Shunem, the place where Elisha used to visit. This strategy is not restricted to the annunciation type-scene; it appears in the story of Tamar and Judah (Gen 38:1–5) and in the story of Ruth and Boaz (Ruth 1:1–5). Despite the unquestionably central role played by mother figures in annunciation type-scenes and in narratives about significant births, the literary frame of the unit, opening and concluding with information regarding male characters, attests to the patriarchal ideology underlying them.

These constraints on the biblical mother figures explain their literary flatness. None of the biblical mother figures matches the depth and complexity of father figures like Abraham, Jacob, Jephthah, and David. Only father figures are shown to experience con-flict between, for example, parental love and the exigencies of divine authority (Abraham and Jephthah). Only they demonstrate the complexity of a situation in which a parent is called upon to scold his most beloved son, or to hide his love for fear of sibling revenge (Jacob). Only they exemplify the human conflict between love for and fear of one's own child (David). The parental role played by the father figure constitutes only one aspect in the character, one that contributes to the depth and many-sidedness of this character. It does not eclipse his other qualities. This is the difference between a multifaceted, well-developed literary character and a type, or a role model. We must conclude that although the procreative context is the only one which allows for a direct communication between woman and YHWH (or his messenger), and although motherhood is the most exalted female role in the biblical narrative, the biblical mother figures attain neither the human nor the literary complexity of their male counterparts. The patriarchal framework of the biblical story prevents the mother figure from becoming a full-fledged *human* role model, while its androcentric perspective confines her to a limited literary role, largely subordinated to the biblical male protagonists.

NOTES

1. "Sexual Politics" refers to the power-structured relations between men and women and more specifically to the economic, social, and ideological arrangements whereby males have tradi-tionally controlled females. See Millet (31–81). "Biblical Sexual Politics" refers to the ways in

which the Bible promotes the idea of woman's subordination to man. "Patriarchy" refers to a value system which legislates women's political subordination as divinely ordained or natural.

2. This and all the following quotations are based on the *Revised Standard Version* with occasional revisions, unless otherwise stated.

REFERENCES

Alter, Robert
1981   *The Art of Biblical Narrative*. New York: Basic Books.
1983   "How Convention Helps Us Read: The Case of the Bible's Annunciation Type-Scene." *Prooftexts* 3:115–30.

Arpali, Boaz
1970   "Attention: A Biblical Story." *Hasifrut* 2:580–97 (in Hebrew).

Beauvoir, Simone de
1952   *The Second Sex*. Trans. ed. H.M. Parshley. New York: Vintage.

Bird, Phyllis
1974   "Images of Women in the Old Testament." Pp. 41–88 in *Religion and Sexism*. Ed. Rosemary Ruether. New York: Simon and Schuster.

Booth, Wayne C.
1961   *The Rhetoric of Fiction*. Chicago: University of Chicago.

Briffault, Robert
1927   *The Mothers*. Vol. 1. New York: Johnson.

Daly, Mary
1973   *Beyond God the Father*. Boston: Beacon.

Fuchs, Esther
1982   "Status and Role of Female Heroines in the Biblical Narrative." *The Mankind Quarterly* 23:149–60.

Harvey, W.J.
1965   *Character and the Novel*. Ithaca: Cornell University.

Millet, Kate
1969   *Sexual Politics*. New York: Ballantine.

Perry, Menahem and Meir Sternberg
1968   "The King Viewed Ironically: On the Narrator's Devices in the Story of David and Bathsheba." *Hasifrut* 1:263–92 (in Hebrew).

Rich, Adrienne
1976   *Of Woman Born*. New York: Norton.

Sternberg, Meir
1977   "The Structure of Repetition in the Biblical Story." *Hasifrut* 25:110–50 (in Hebrew).

Trible, Phyllis
1978   *God and the Rhetoric of Sexuality*. Philadelphia: Fortress.

Uspensky, Boris
1973   *A Poetics of Composition*. Berkeley and Los Angeles: University of California.

Who's Afraid of "The Endangered Ancestress"?

J. CHERYL EXUM

> *Who's afraid of the big bad wolf, the big*
> *bad wolf, the big bad wolf?*
>
> THE THREE LITTLE PIGS
>
> *Let's take a look: we shall find illumination*
> *in what at first seems to obscure matters . . .*
>
> JACQUES LACAN

A Thrice-Told Tale

Three times in Genesis the patriarch, the eponymous ancestor of Israel, travels to a foreign country, where he passes his beautiful wife off as his sister because he fears the locals will kill him on her account if they know he is her husband. Abraham and Sarah are the ancestral couple in the primal scene (Gen. 12, where their names are Abram and Sarai) and in the first repetition (Gen. 20, by which time their names have been changed to Abraham and Sarah). Sarah is taken to be the wife of the foreign ruler (the pharaoh of Egypt in Gen. 12, and Abimelech of Gerar in Gen. 20) and then returned to Abraham when the ruler learns of the ruse. The third version (Gen. 26) concerns Isaac and Rebekah; the foreign ruler is again Abimelech of Gerar; and the matriarch is *not* taken. In all three cases, the patriarch prospers, the foreign ruler is (understandably) upset, and the matriarch has no voice in the affair.

It is generally agreed that the tales are variants on the same theme. The characters change and details vary, but the fabula remains the same. Within biblical scholarship, this thrice-told tale is often referred to as "the Endangered Ancestress" or "the Ancestress of Israel in Danger."[1] The widespread use of this label raises the question, What kind of danger do scholars think the matriarch is in? If, as is generally accepted, these stories represent in some way a threat to the threefold promise to Abraham of land, descendants, and blessing, then the threat is to the promise, and it follows that the patriarch, not the

141

matriarch, is in danger. The promise, after all, was made to him—not to her or to the two of them (see Gen. 12.1–3)—and without his wife how can he have descendants?

Or is the danger faced by the matriarch the loss of honor? This could be said to be an issue in Genesis 20, where the narrative is at pains to assure us that nothing of a sexual nature took place between Abimelech and Sarah. Here the omniscient narrator tells the audience:

> Now Abimelech had not approached her. (Gen. 20.4)

He then gives the statement divine authority by placing it in the mouth of God, who speaks to Abimelech in a dream:

> Therefore I did not let you touch her. (Gen. 20.6)

Finally, by having Abimelech publicly justify Sarah's reputation, he ensures that all the characters in the story share in this knowledge.

> To Sarah he said, "Look, I have given a thousand pieces of silver to your brother; it is your vindication in the eyes of all who are with you; and before everyone you are righted."[2] (Gen. 20.16)

It is not so clear that nothing of a sexual nature happened in the primal scene, Genesis 12, where we hear that "the woman was taken into the pharaoh's house" (v. 15) and the pharaoh says, "I took her for my wife" (v. 19). Interestingly, what did or did not happen to Sarah in the royal harem receives more attention from scholars than it does from Abraham. Bernhard Anderson, in his annotations to the Revised Standard Version, would apparently have us believe that the story is less explicit and shocking than it actually is, for he explains that Sarah "was *almost* taken into Pharaoh's harem" (italics mine). (Does this mean she got only to the door?) Koch, Polzin, Miscall, and Coats, in contrast, assume that Sarah did have sexual relations with the pharaoh.[3] Koch's judgment, incidentally, is as ethnocentric as it is androcentric: "There is one feature of the story missing which would be natural to us: there is no reluctance to surrender the woman's honour." To support his conclusion that the earliest form of the story did have Sarah committing adultery, Koch appeals to what he believes other women would do: "[I]t seems obvious that the Bedouin women are so devoted to their menfolk that to protect a husband's life they would willingly lose their honour."[4]

What is this honor anyway but a male construct based on the double standard, with its insistence on the exclusive sexual rights to the woman by one man? The scene in Genesis 16, where the situation is reversed, is comparable and illuminating. Genesis 12 and Genesis 16 raise the issue of the matriarch or the patriarch having sexual relations with someone else. In Genesis 12, Abraham tells Sarah to let herself be taken by another man "in order that it will go well with me because of you and I may live on your account" (v. 13). In Genesis 16.2, Sarah tells Abraham to have sexual intercourse with Hagar ("go in to my maid") so that she may obtain a child through Hagar. Neither Abraham nor Sarah is concerned with what this intimate encounter might mean for the other parties involved, but only with what he or she stands to gain. In Genesis 16, we are told specifically that Abraham had sexual intercourse with Hagar ("he went in to Hagar and she conceived," v. 4), but such specific detail is omitted from Genesis 12 (we shall return to this point below). Significantly, no one speaks of Abraham's loss of honor in Genesis 16, nor is there much concern for Hagar's honor—a fact that indicates "honor" is not only a male construct but also a class construct. Abraham, who as a man is not required to be monogamous, cannot be dishonored by having sex with Hagar at Sarah's urging. Neither can Hagar be dishonored, since a slave has no honor to lose.

It is not the woman's honor so much as the husband's property rights that are at stake. Still, we might expect the patriarch to show some concern for his wife's well-being. It is thus curious that in all three cases the patriarch does not consider that the matriarch might be in danger. On the contrary, he thinks *he* is in danger:[5]

> I know that you are a beautiful woman. When the Egyptians see you, they will say, "This is his wife"; and they will kill me and let you live. (Gen. 12.11–12)

> It was because I thought, There is surely no fear of God in this place, and they will kill me because of my wife. (Gen. 20.11)

> When the men of the place asked about his wife, he said, "She is my sister," for he feared to say "my wife," thinking, "lest the men of the place kill me because of Rebekah, for she is beautiful." (Gen. 26.7)

Whether or not the patriarch's fear is justified—whether or not he really is in danger or whether his fear is simply displaced—is a question we shall explore. If the patriarch does not suppose that the matriarch is in danger, neither is there any evidence that the *matriarch* thinks she is in danger. In fact, we do not know what she thinks about *anything*, which is a very good indication that the story is not really about the matriarch at all. She neither acts nor speaks in any of the versions, though in the second version speech is indirectly attributed to her: Abimelech tells God that Sarah told him that Abraham was her brother (Gen. 20.5). If her only speech is one reported by another character in the narrative, the matriarch can hardly be said to become a narrative presence in any real sense. She is merely the object in a story about male relations (and we shall inquire below how the two men respond in relation to the object). What, then, is the danger, and to whom? More important, why do we hear about it three times?

Most studies of Genesis 12, 20, and 26 are concerned with the relationship between the three stories: How are they alike and different, and how are the differences to be accounted for (which often means, how can the repetition be explained away)? Now what happens in Genesis 12, 20, and 26 is very disturbing. A man practically throws his wife into another man's harem in order to save his skin. Yet the questions one most often encounters about this text are generally along the lines of: What is the oldest form of this story.[6] Or, Are the three accounts oral or written variants?[7] Are Genesis 20 and 26 more ethical than Genesis 12?[8] The disturbing issues raised by the story are sometimes deplored[9] but then set aside in favor of disengaged discussion of the growth of the tradition, the relative dates of the versions, and such historical questions as whether or not the stories reflect customs of 2000 to 1500 BCE (the so-called patriarchal period), or whether a man could or should marry his half-sister (the controversial evidence of Nuzi).

A few scholars have inquired into the role of these stories in the context of the larger narrative.[10] A sustained contextual reading of the three stories is offered by David Clines, who concludes that the patriarch is more of a danger to foreigners than they are to him.[11] But reading the three tales in their context also exposes problems. For example, in Genesis 20 Sarah would be over ninety years old, and we might wonder why Abraham thinks other men would take such an interest in her. Moreover, Abraham has now been told by God that Sarah will be the mother of his heir, which makes it even harder to understand why he would let another man take her (it may even be the case that Sarah is already pregnant with Isaac).[12] In Genesis 25, Esau and Jacob are born to Isaac and Rebekah, and by the end of the chapter they are already hunting and stealing birthrights respectively. Thus in Genesis 26, when Isaac says of Rebekah, "She is my sister," we might wonder, what has become of the twins? These are only some of the difficulties a contextual reading must engage. I mention them not because I intend to offer a contextual reading here, but rather to underscore how puzzling and uncanny the tale is both in context and in isolation. We encounter one set of problems when the three versions are read in their larger context and other problems when they are considered in their own right. In fact, one might say that this tale in its three forms calls attention to itself by virtue of the surplus of problems it poses to interpretation. I propose that a different kind of approach to the repeated tale in Genesis 12, 20, and 26 could provide new insights into some recurrent difficulties. Specifically, I want to offer a psychoanalytical alternative to previous, largely form and tradition-historical, approaches.

By proposing a psychoanalytic-literary reading as an alternative, I am not claiming that this approach will "solve" the problems posed by these chapters whereas other approaches do not. On the contrary, I maintain that posing questions and opening up new dimensions of a text are as fruitful an enterprise as the traditional critical approach of seeking answers as if answers were objectively verifiable. Like psychoanalysis, psychoanalytical criticism is neither externally verifiable nor falsifiable. We can only follow it, as Freud says about analysis, to see where it will lead,[13] and, in the process, hope to illuminate a hitherto uncharted textual level, the narrative unconscious. My approach appeals to the multiple levels on which stories function; like dreams, they are overdetermined. As Freud points out in comparing texts to dreams, which, he argues, require over-interpretation in order to be fully understood, "All genuinely creative writings are the product of more than a single motive and more than a single impulse in the poet's mind, and are open to more than a single interpretation."[14]

To anticipate my argument: a psychoanalytic-literary approach takes as its point of departure the assumption that the story in Genesis 12, 20, and 26 encodes unthinkable and unacknowledged sexual fantasies. Because there is something fearful and attractive to the (male) narrator about the idea of the wife being taken by another man, a situation that invites the woman's seizure is repeated three times. The tale would thus appear to illustrate Freud's *Wiederholungszwang,* the repetition compulsion—the impulse to work over an experience in the mind until one becomes the master of it—whose locus, according to Freud, is the unconscious repressed.[15] The text is a symptom of the narrator's intra-psychic conflict. But whereas the repetition compulsion is neurotic and an obstacle to awareness, telling the story of the patriarch's repetitive behavior offers the occasion for a "working out" of the neurosis.

> Repetition is both an obstacle to analysis—since the analysand must eventually be led to renunciation of the attempt to reproduce the past—and the principal dynamic of the cure, since only by way of its symbolic enactment in the present can the history of past desire, its objects and scenarios of fulfillment be made known, become manifest in the present discourse.[16]

Repeating the story, working over the conflict until it is resolved, provides a semiotic cure for the neurosis. By the charmed third time the cure is effected; that is to say, it is believed.

In approaching the text from a psychoanalytic-literary perspective, I am not proposing to psychoanalyze the characters. Rather than treat characters in a story as if they were real people with real neuroses, I want to examine the worldview these literary creations represent. Taking a cue from psychoanalytical theory and building upon the similarities between interpreting dreams and interpreting texts, I shall consider all the characters in the text as split-off parts of the narrator. When a dream is analyzed in psychoanalysis, the analysand is brought to recognize aspects of herself or himself in the various characters of the dream. In our thrice-told tale we will consider the characters in the story as aspects of the narrative consciousness. Thus not just the female characters but the male characters also are expressions of male fantasies, anxieties, etc. When I say, "Abraham fears for his life," I refer to Abraham not as if he were a real human being but rather as a vehicle for the androcentric values and the androcentric worldview of the biblical narrative. It bears pointing out that I am not proposing to psychoanalyze the author either, in the sense that the author, any more than Abraham, is a real person. I assume, with most biblical scholars, that these ancient texts are a communal product, and, further, I assume they received their final redaction at the hands of men. The narrative thus does not reflect an individual's unconscious fantasies, but rather, we might say, it owes its creation to a kind of collective androcentric unconscious, whose spokesperson I shall call simply "the narrator."

Features Obscure and Obscuring

In a recent study of the Abraham traditions, Joel Rosenberg remarks that "the 'wife-sister' motif, considered as an item of history and tradition, is an obscure and suggestive theme whose full meaning will probably continue to elude us."[17] As my epigraph from Lacan indicates, I want to look for illumination in what at first glance seems to obscure matters.[18] The tales exhibit many puzzling features. Why, for example, does the patriarch fear that he will be killed for his wife? Why doesn't he consider the possibility that she might simply be taken from him? He could be overpowered and robbed of his wife, or sent away without her, or an attempt could be made to buy him off. He assumes, however, a moral code according to which the foreign men in question will *not* commit adultery but they *will* commit murder. And when he says, in Genesis 12.13 and 20.11, "*They* will kill me," does he imagine that they would all attack him at once (and if so, who would get the woman)? Or, by assuming many men will want his wife, is he simply accepting in advance that there is nothing he can do to save both his wife and his life? He is not concerned about what might happen to his wife in another man's harem, and clearly not interested in protecting her. In fact, by claiming that the beautiful woman is his (unmarried) sister, the patriarch guarantees that his wife *will* be taken.

Having taken the woman (in Genesis 12 and 20), the foreign ruler, upon learning that she is Abraham's wife, gives her back to her husband. He does not kill Abraham, as Abraham had feared, even though now he has good reason, since Abraham's lie about Sarah's status has both placed him in an unacceptable position and brought trouble upon his land (plagues in Genesis 12 and barrenness in Genesis 20). In Genesis 26, Abimelech is incensed at what *might have happened* and takes measures to ensure that it will not happen in the future. What the patriarch seems to fear, and says explicitly that he fears in Genesis 20.11—lack of morality ("there is surely no fear of God in this place")—is proved by events to be not the case. Moreover, he already attributes a certain morality to the foreign men when he assumes they will kill him rather than commit adultery with a married woman.

The crucial question is, Why does the patriarch—twice in the person of Abraham and once Isaac—repeat his mistakes? Why does he need to set things up so that another man will seize his wife not once, but three times? To answer that the threefold repetition is the result of three different pentateuchal sources or of three variants in the oral tradition behind the text is to beg the question.[19] As recent literary criticism of the Bible recognizes, the final form of the text is not a haphazard product but rather the result of complex and meaningful redactional patterning. If the androcentric tradition keeps repeating this story, we can assume that the story fills some need.

The Repetition Compulsion

We begin with what is apparent. The story is about fear and desire: desire of the beautiful woman and fear of death because of her. In all three versions the patriarch considers his wife desirable to other men, and in the first two, he is right: the woman is desired, as is witnessed by the fact that she is taken as a wife by another man. In all three instances, the matriarch's desirability makes the patriarch afraid for his life, though his fear turns out to be unjustified. In assessing the patriarch's behavior in response to the perceived threat, Clines remarks that "the danger is all in the patriarch's mind to begin with."[20] This being the case, a psychoanalytical approach should prove especially useful. But it is not just what might or might not be going on in the patriarch's mind that will concern us. As I have indicated, all the characters in this repeated story are vehicles for the narrative neurosis.

Each of the stories, the primal scene and its repetitions, is preoccupied with the *same unconscious fantasy:* that the wife have sex with another man. Psychoanalysis tells us that this must be the unconscious desire because this is precisely what the patriarch sets up to happen. It is important to keep in mind that the desire is unconscious; what Freud says about Oedipus's desire is applicable here: in reality it would likely cause him to recoil in horror.[21] What is unconsciously desired is also unconsciously feared; as I hope to show, the story is repeated in an effort to envision and simultaneously to deny the possibility of such a sexual encounter taking place between the wife and another man. Psychoanalysis draws attention to the close relationship between desires and fears. Am I afraid of heights because unconsciously I desire to jump? Is homophobia in reality a fear of one's own repressed sexual urges? Fear in Genesis 12, 20, and 26 is conscious but displaced. The patriarch fears for his life, the assumption being that the foreign man will want the woman all to himself. Abraham is willing to let the other man have her, since the woman must belong to one man or the other but cannot be shared; she cannot belong to both. This is the familiar double standard, according to which men may have sexual relations with more than one woman, but a woman cannot have sexual knowledge of a man other than her husband. The remarkable thing about the patriarch's ruse is that it ensures that his wife *will* gain sexual knowledge of another man. Certainty is better, more controllable, than doubt.

Since we are dealing with a text, and not with an analysand who can contribute actively to the psychoanalytical process, we can only speculate about what lies behind the fear and desire. It could be the need to have the woman's erotic value confirmed by other men, what René Girard describes as the mechanism of triangular desire.[22] Having chosen a particular woman as the object of his desire, the man needs other men's desire to validate his choice, and even to increase his desire. Or, losing the woman to another man is desirable because he will be free of the woman and the responsibility she entails. This is the male fantasy of sex without commitment; he will be free to have other women, unhampered by the domesticity that the wife represents. There may be deeper, more distressing, desires as well. The same object (originally, according to much psychoanalytical theory, the mother's body) evokes both reverence and hostility. Thus the fascination with the notion of the woman being taken by another man may mask a fear and hatred of woman that desires her humiliation (there is no question that the story objectifies the woman). Other explanations might be sought in what Freud calls "the mysterious masochistic trends of the ego."[23] Losing the woman to another man is also threatening, because sexual knowledge of another man would provide the woman with experience for comparison. Other men might be "better," or know some things about sex he does not know, and perhaps she will enjoy with them what she does not experience with him. This takes us back to the patriarch's displaced fear. His fear for his life at the hands of other men disguises the fact that it is really the woman's sexual knowledge that is life-threatening for him. It is "safer" for him to fear other men than to acknowledge his fear of the woman's sexuality.

Patriarchy's Talking Cure

The fabula in which the wife is, in effect, offered to the other man is repeated until the conflict revolving around the woman's feared and desired sexual knowledge has been resolved. By managing fear and desire within an ordered discourse, the narrative functions as a textual working-out of unconscious fantasies, a semiotic cure for the neurosis.

Let us consider first the fundamental similarities between the three tales. All three raise the possibility that the matriarch have sex with a man other than her husband. The patriarch is not only willing for his wife to commit adultery; he invites it. The foreign ruler, on the other hand, will not willingly commit adultery. The patriarch might thus be viewed as a cipher for the unconscious desire, the foreign ruler as the embodiment of fear, and the story as the locus of the tension. The *difference* in the three tales is significant for resolving the conflict. In the first, Sarah is taken into the royal harem, and restored when the pharaoh learns that she is already another man's wife. But did she have sexual relations with the pharaoh? We cannot be sure, for this version of the story does not satisfactorily resolve the issue. It must, therefore, be repeated. The second time around, matters are different. In Genesis 20, Sarah is again taken, but Abimelech does not lay a hand on her. It is no doubt reassuring that what is unconsciously desired and feared does not take place, but the situation remains potentially threatening as long as the woman is allowed to enter another man's household. In the third version, Genesis 26, the possibility of what is both desired and feared taking place is ruled out from the start: Rebekah is not even taken into Abimelech's house.

In the working out of the neurosis, the realization of the fantasy is precluded. To describe this process as it is actualized in the narrative, I shall borrow some terms from Freud, without applying them in a strictly Freudian sense.[24] Instead I shall use a fundamental Freudian concept as a metaphor in order to clarify the contradictory impulses in the text. The foreign ruler, who expresses moral outrage at the deception Abraham has perpetrated, is a kind of super-ego, an enforcing, prohibiting agency, to Abraham's id, unconscious desire ready to give over the woman. In other words, the positions occupied in Freudian theory by the super-ego and the id, i.e. the self-observing, self-critical agency in the ego and the libidinous unconscious desire, are fantasized as characters in the story. The text is metaphorically in the position of the ego, where these contradictory impulses are finally resolved.

In the first version, the pharaoh is upset, but his response does not crystallize the moral issue; the super-ego is not yet highly developed.

> What is this you have done to me? Why did you not tell me that she was your wife? Why did you say, "She is my sister," so that I took her for my wife? (Gen. 12.18–19)

In the second version, in contrast, we find a virtual obsession with issues of sin and guilt, all signs of a highly active conscience. The pharaoh's "What is this you have done to me?" becomes Abimelech's

> What have you done to us? How have I *sinned* against you that you have brought on me and my kingdom a great *sin*? *Deeds that are not done* you have done to me. (Gen. 20.9)

This super-ego, however, needs external moral support, and thus the narrative begins with a lengthy dialogue between Abimelech and God in a dream.[25] God, as symbol and overseer of the moral order, passes judgment: "You are a dead man because of the woman you have taken; she is another man's wife" (v. 3). With continued emphasis on the issue of innocence versus guilt, Abimelech protests his innocence before the law, appealing to his ignorance of Sarah's status:

> Lord, would you slay a *righteous* people? Did he himself not say to me, "She is my sister"? And she herself said, "He is my brother." In the *integrity* of my intentions and the *innocence* of my hands I have done this.

Abimelech is "innocent" because God, the moral law, prevented him from "sinning": "It was I who kept you from sinning against me; therefore I did not let you touch her" (v. 6). Fear of punishment provides powerful motivation for adherence to the law: "If you do not return her, know that you shall surely die, you and all that is yours" (v. 7).

This ethical rationalization is carried through on every level of the narrative in Genesis 20. Just as Abimelech (in the position of super-ego) justifies himself to God (external moral law), so also Abraham (in the position of the id, the unconscious desire) justifies his deceit to Abimelech (super-ego):

> It was because I thought, There is surely no fear of God in this place, and they will kill me because of my wife. Besides she is indeed my sister, the daughter of my father but not the daughter of my mother; so she could be my wife.

Subtly he tries to shift the blame by implicating God:

> When God caused me to wander from my father's house, I said to her, "This is the kindness you must do me: at every place to which we come, say of me, 'He is my brother.'"

Abraham's protestations of innocence are like psychoanalytical negations: if he were innocent he would not need to protest so much. He undermines his defense—that he feared the lack of morality "in this place"—by adding that he told Sarah to claim he was her brother "at every place to which we come," indicating compulsive behavior and not a single aberration. This "Freudian slip" is a sign of a guilty conscience, the need to be caught in the lie—and commentators have caught him.[26] The libido still feels the need to be held in check against its own powerful impulses.

By the third time (Gen. 26), the super-ego functions independently of external restraints; it rejects the very notion of the woman having sex with another man. The moral issue is generalized. "One of the people," not the Self who no longer feels threatened, "might have lain with your wife"—but nothing happens. We are informed in v. 7 that the men of Gerar asked Isaac about Rebekah, so we know they have noticed her. We are also told (v. 8) that Isaac and Rebekah were in Gerar for a long period of time, so we also know they are not interested. The fascination with the fantasy has been abandoned. As on the previous occasions, the id is held accountable to the super-ego, but it is no longer viewed as threatening: "You"—the fascination with the woman's desired and feared sexual knowledge—"would have brought guilt upon us," Abimelech tells Isaac (v. 10), but (so the implication) I—the admonitory, judgmental agency in the ego—prevented it. In this version, the super-ego does not need God, the external source of morality, to tell it what to do. It makes its own law: "Whoever touches[27] this man or his wife shall be put to death" (*mot yumat*). In the Bible, this kind of apodictic formulation appears in the legal material. In psychoanalysis, the ability to internalize moral standards is a sign of maturity.

It can hardly be fortuitous that once the story ceases to entertain the fantasy of another man having the woman, the patriarch is pictured enjoying the woman sexually, and the other man witnesses it. Abimelech looks out his window and sees Isaac "fondling" (NRSV) or "caressing" (Westermann) Rebekah. Whatever the precise meaning of the verb *metsaheq*, a pun on Isaac's name, it has to refer to some form of sexual intimacy, since, on the basis of this activity, Abimelech recognizes that Isaac and Rebekah must be man and wife. In this final version of the tale, the fantasy of the woman's having sex with another man is rejected in favor of the (also fantasized) assurance that her sexuality belongs exclusively to the patriarch.

And what of the other man's watching? According to Girard's theory of triangular desire, the relation between the rivals in an erotic triangle is as important as their relationship to the object of desire.[28] Using the Girardian triangle as a model, I suggested above that the desiring subject (the position occupied in our narratives by the patriarch) needs the desire of other men to confirm the excellence of his sexual choice. The patriarch sees the matriarch as an object of beauty, and thus an object of desire ("I know that you are a beautiful woman," 12.11; cf. 26.7), but he needs to know that other men desire her too; so he sets up a situation that will elicit their desire: he presents her as an available woman.[29] The prestige of his rival only serves to affirm that the woman he has selected is worthy of desire.[30] The rival who takes the matriarch has the ultimate social prestige—he is the pharaoh or the king—and he has sexual prestige because he has a harem; he can have any woman he likes, and one assumes he chooses only the best. He is also willing to pay a high price for the woman, either to possess her (12.16) or as restitution (20.14, 16)—further testimony to her value. Girard examines stories, like ours, where the hero appears to offer the beloved wife to the rival, and concludes, "He pushes the loved woman into the mediator's arms in order to arouse his desire and then triumph over the rival desire."[31] Having Abimelech, the rival, witness his sexual activity with the matriarch is the patriarch's ultimate turn-on, his incontestable victory over rival desire. In this version of the fantasy, the roles are here reversed. The patriarch is no longer in the position of the fearing/desiring subject; the other man is. Fear of the woman's knowledge of other men is transformed into other men's envy of him.

Not a Woman's Story

I have argued that Genesis 12, 20, and 26 deal with an unacknowledged and unthinkable male fantasy. In the patriarch-matriarch-foreign ruler triangle, the matriarch never becomes a narrative presence. Though addressed by men—Abraham says, "Say you are my sister" (12.13); Abimelech says, "Look, I have given your brother a thousand pieces of silver; it is your vindication . . ." (20.16)—the matriarch never speaks and only once is she reported to have spoken (20.5). The woman has no voice in determining her sexual status and no control over how her sexuality is perceived or used. Susan Niditch calls Sarah in Genesis 12 a "tacit accomplice."[32] Sharon Pace Jeansonne considers her less an accomplice than a silent object.[33] In my reading, she is both accomplice and object because she, like the other characters, is a creation of the narrative unconscious. The male fantasy that created her character is not interested in the woman's point of view— her reaction to Abraham's suggestion, her willingness to be exchanged for her husband's well-being, or her experience in the harem of a strange man. The question of force versus consent, crucial for constructing the woman's perspective, is not raised.[34]

The woman is only an object in a story about male fears and desires. The possibility of the wife having sex with another man is taken out of the control of the woman and made solely an affair between men. This is the only way androcentric ideology can conceive of it, unless, as in the case of Potiphar's wife, the woman is a "bad woman,"[35] which, of course, the matriarch cannot be or else she would not qualify to be the matriarch. As it is posed in Genesis 12, 20, and 26, the question is not, Will the woman commit adultery, but, Will the other man commit adultery? The patriarch thinks not: he thinks the other man will kill him rather than commit adultery with a married woman. The foreign ruler also rejects the thought of adultery. The result is a kind of gentlemen's agreement about the other man's property, which reflects the biblical understanding of adultery as less a matter of sex than a violation of another man's property rights.[36] Legislating the husband's exclusive sexual rights to his wife is an effective way of controlling women's desired and feared sexuality. That the patriarch, the foreign ruler, and God all recognize the seriousness of adultery with a married woman is crucial to the ideology of all three versions (what the woman thinks is irrelevant).

"She Is Indeed My Sister"

Scholars generally deal with Abraham's claim that Sarah really is his half-sister in Genesis 20.12 by asking whether or not it is a lie. Clines and Miscall think Abraham is lying;[37] Westermann, von Rad, Speiser, and Skinner think he is telling the truth.[38] Some apologists call Abraham's claim that Sarah is his sister a "white lie."[39] Regardless of whether or not Sarah and Abraham are sister and brother, we know it is not true of Isaac and Rebekah. From a psychoanalytic-literary perspective, the important issue is not the veracity of Abraham's claim but the fact that in all three versions the brother-sister relationship is imagined. All three accounts raise the issue of consanguinity simply by having the patriarch tell the foreigners that the matriarch is his sister. Might we not see in this latent incest fantasy a desire to achieve unity with the other? In the Song of Songs, for example, the man uses the epithet "sister, bride" to refer to the woman as a sign of intimacy. Clearly the matriarch's kinship ties to the patriarch are important to these stories in Genesis 12–36; she must come from his own people, his own kind.[40] As a sibling, the matriarch is more "self" than "other"—more like the patriarch than different. Fantasizing her as his sister may represent a narcissistic striving toward completeness or wholeness, whose realization can only be imagined in his mirror-image from the opposite sex (she is what he would be if he were a woman). Oedipal desire, of which, according to Eve Kosofsky Sedgwick, the Girardian triangle is a schematization,[41] may be at work here as well. As his close female relative, the sister is a stand-in for the mother as object of desire (and Sarah is the arch mother). In this case, Abraham will have married a girl as much like the girl who married dear ol' dad as possible. Fear of the father's wrath may explain his willingness to give her back, symbolically, to the father—the subject position held in our tale by the powerful, foreign ruler–authority figure. In the end, his relationship to his mother-substitute is legitimized by the father. This is the significance of the fact that Abimelech *sees* Isaac and Rebekah engaged in sexual play: it represents the father's acknowledgment that this woman rightfully belongs to the "son" and the father's permission for him to have sex with her.

Who's Afraid of "The Endangered Ancestress"?

We have looked at the thrice-told tale in Genesis 12, 20, and 26 as a symptom of the narrative's intra-psychic conflict, a conflict between the unconscious desire that the wife gain sexual knowledge of another man and the fear that this could happen. The conflict appears in disguised and distorted form: the patriarch fears for his life because of his beautiful wife, and passes her off as his sister, thereby allowing another man to take her into his harem. In reality, the fear is of the woman's sexuality, which is both desired and feared. There is a compulsive need to repeat the story until the conflict is resolved. In Genesis 12, the super-ego (the pharaoh) is subject to the id (Abraham); he takes the woman. In Genesis 20, the super-ego (Abimelech) has external moral support (God). He is subject to the id (Abraham) in that he takes the woman, but subject to external law (God) in that he does not touch her. But morality based on external authority is not the best solution for the patriarchal neurosis. In the third version (Gen. 26), the moral code is internalized; the fascination with the woman's desired and feared sexuality no longer poses a threat; the neurosis is cured; the cure is believed.[42]

In the children's refrain, "Who's afraid of the big bad wolf, the big bad wolf, the big bad wolf?," we find a denial of fear that, as such, is also a recognition of fear. The thrice-told tale in Genesis 12, 20, and 26 functions similarly. It says, in effect, "Who's afraid of the woman's sexual knowledge?" And it answers by reassuring the patriarch that there is no need to fear. But it betrays itself, for, like the ditty about the big bad wolf, it acknowledges that there is something to be feared. If the danger in these three stories is woman's sexuality and woman's sexual knowledge, who or what is in danger? To the question, "Who or what is afraid of the woman's sexual knowledge?," the answer is "Patriarchy."

NOTES

1. E.g. Keller 1954; von Rad 1961: 162–65, 221–25, 266; Koch 1969: 111–32; Polzin 1975; Westermann 1985: 159; Coats 1983: 109, 149, 188; Biddle 1990.

2. Following the RSV. The translation of the obscure Hebrew is problematic, but this seems to be the sense; see Westermann 1985: 328; von Rad 1961: 224; Skinner 1910: 319.

3. Koch 1969: 125; Polzin 1975: 83; Miscall 1983: 35; Coats 1983: 111.

4. Koch 1969: 127; cf. Abou-Zeid 1966: 253–54, 256–57. For discussion of honor and its relationship to the politics of sex, see Pitt-Rivers 1977: esp. 113–70.

5. Clines 1990: 67–68.

6. See Van Seters 1975: 167–91; Koch 1969: 111–32; Noth 1972: 102–109; Westermann 1985: 161–62.

7. On the issue of literary dependency, see Van Seters 1975: 167–91; Westermann 1985: 161–62; cf. Alexander 1992. For an argument that the pentateuchal sources use the same (wife-sister) motif to develop different themes, see Petersen 1973. For discussions of the stories as oral variants, see Culley 1976: 33–41; and the more recent folkloristic approach of Niditch 1987: 23–66.

8. Most commentators agree with Koch (1969: 126), who thinks that "moral sensitivity becomes gradually stronger"; Polzin (1975: 84) argues that Genesis 12 is as sensitive to ethical issues as are chs. 20 and 26.

9. Von Rad (1961: 162) calls Genesis 12 "offensive," and speaks of the "betrayed matriarch" (p. 164); see also Vawter 1977: 181.

10. Clines 1990: 67–84; Fox 1989; Rosenberg 1986: 70–98; Steinberg 1984; to a lesser degree, Polzin 1975; Miscall 1983: 11–46.

11. Clines 1990: 67–84.

12. So Vawter 1977: 245; Miscall 1983: 32; Clines 1990: 75–76.

13. Freud 1961: 4.

14. Freud 1965: 299. I see little difference in my suggesting below that Abraham behaves as he does because of fear and desire that his wife gain sexual knowledge of another man and, say, Westermann's contention (1985: 164) that Abraham behaves this way because of insufficient trust in the divine promises. For insightful remarks about the way traditional scholarship disguises its subjectivity, see Miscall 1983: 40–42.

15. Freud 1961: 16–25 *passim*.

16. Brooks 1987: 10.

17. Rosenberg 1986: 77.

18. Lacan 1988: 41.

19. Indeed, one of the early arguments of source criticism for multiple authorship of the Pentateuch was the fact that the patriarch, and his son after him, would hardly have been so foolish as to repeat the ruse three times.

20. Clines 1990: 68.

21. Freud, Letter to Wilhelm Fliess of Oct. 15, 1897, cited by Felman 1983: 1022.

22. See Girard 1965: esp. 1–52.

23. Freud 1961: 12. We might also keep in mind that the repetition complex is related to the desire for death and the delaying of it, which is reflected in the patriarch's fear of death because of the woman.

24. I am offering neither a Freudian reading nor suggesting the superiority, or even validity, of Freudian analysis (in recent years there have been numerous important feminist critiques of Freudian theory). For basic distinctions between the ego, the id, and the super-ego, see Freud 1960; Freud used these terms differently and sometimes indiscriminately, and he changed his usage over time.

25. On the legal character of the dialogue, see Westermann 1985: 322–23. Interestingly, the locus for dealing with the conflict here is a dream. Freud saw dreams as fulfillments of unconscious wishes. Even anxiety dreams and punishment dreams, such as this one, perform this function, "for they merely replace the forbidden wish-fulfillment by the appropriate punishment for it; that is to say, they fulfill the wish of the sense of guilt which is the reaction to the repudiated impulse" (Freud 1961: 37).

26. E.g. Miscall 1983: 15; Westermann 1985: 326; Coats 1983: 150.

27. The verb *ngʿ* was used of approaching the woman sexually in 20.6. Here it has a double meaning, since it is also applied to the man in its more general sense of harming. The inclusion of "this man" in the edict may be taken as a sign of acceptance of the dangerous impulses as no longer capable of jeopardizing the Self.

28. Girard (1965) proposes that our desire for something does not really come from ourselves, nor does it lie in some kind of intrinsic worth in the object of our desire; rather it is based on looking at what other people find desirable. Other people become our models, "mediators of desire" in his theory, whose desire we copy. The positions in Girard's metaphorical triangle are: the desiring subject; the mediator of desire, who defines the subject's desire for him or her; and the object of the desire.

29. White (1991: 180–83) makes a similar point about the beautiful woman as an object of desire in Genesis 12, but he evaluates Abraham's desire differently, as different from and superior to that of his rivals.

30. Girard 1965: 50.

31. Girard 1965: 50. Girard also argues that "the impulse toward the object is ultimately an impulse toward the mediator" (p. 10) and that the desiring subject wants to become his mediator/ rival (p. 54). The patriarch becomes like his wealthy, powerful rival when he becomes wealthy at the foreign ruler's expense (12.16, 20; 20.14, 16; cf. 26.12–14, where the envy theme is continued), and when the ruler recognizes him as more powerful—for example, as a prophet who can pray for him, or simply as "much mightier than we are" (26.16).

32. Niditch 1987: 59.

33. Jeansonne 1990: 17. Jeansonne maintains that Sarah's silence is not evidence of complicity but rather a sign of her powerlessness, similarly Rashkow 1992. This is quite literally an argument from silence, and it too easily leads us into a victim-victimizer dichotomy that ignores women's complicity in patriarchy. On this point I agree with Niditch (1987: 59), but for a different reason: Sarah is an accomplice because her character is the creation of an androcentric narrator. Sarah is not, as White (1991: 185) would have it, an "innocent victim," because she is complicit.

34. This is also the case with Hagar in Genesis 16; see above.

35. See Bach 1993.

36. See Westbrook 1990. For an interpretation of Genesis 12 that sees the taboo against sex with a married woman exploited by Abraham to set up the pharaoh, see White 1991: 174–86. For an anthropological perspective, see Pitt-Rivers 1977: 159, who suggests the stories are about

"sexual hospitality," where women are used to establish relations among groups of men; see pp. 113–70.

37. Clines 1990: 76; Miscall 1983: 14–15.

38. Westermann 1985: 326; von Rad 1961: 222; Speiser 1964: 92; Skinner 1910: 318.

39. Anderson, annotations to the RSV; Fox 1989: 32.

40. For anthropological readings of the three accounts as representing a movement from incest to the preferred form of marriage, see Pitt-Rivers 1977: 154–55; Donaldson 1981. Pitt-Rivers offers a suggestive reading of these accounts in relation to the story of the rape of Dinah, Genesis 34, see pp. 151–71. On the matriarchs' role in Genesis 12–36, see also Exum 1993: 94–147.

41. Sedgwick 1985: 22. See her discussion (pp. 21–27), which, in contrast to Girard, takes gender into account as a constituent factor. Interestingly, Freud saw the repetition complex as going back to some period of infantile sexual life, to the Oedipus complex; see Freud 1961: 19.

42. Later retellings of these stories continue the process of filling gaps, thereby resolving some of the anxiety-provoking ambiguities (for example, did Abraham lie about Sarah's being his sister?; What happened to Sarah in the harem?; Did Abraham know what happened in the harem?) and some give Sarah a greater role (for example, Sarah prays for protection, and the ruler is afflicted "because of the word of Sarai" [ʾal debar sarai, Gen. 12.17]). On later versions of the tale in Jewish and Islamic sources, see Firestone 1991.

References

Abou-Zeid, Ahmed
1966   "Honor and Shame among the Bedouins of Egypt," in *Honour and Shame: The Values of Mediterranean Society* (ed. J.G. Peristany; Chicago: University of Chicago Press): 245–57.

Alexander, T.D.
1992   "Are the Wife/Sister Incidents of Genesis Literary Compositional Variants?" *VT* 42: 145–53.

Bach, Alice
1993   "Breaking Free of the Biblical Frame-up: Uncovering the Woman in Genesis 39," in *A Feminist Companion to Genesis* (ed. A. Brenner; The Feminist Companion to the Bible, 2; Sheffield: Sheffield Academic Press): 318–42.

Biddle, Mark E.
1990   "The 'Endangered Ancestress' and Blessing for the Nations," *JBL* 109: 599–611.

Brooks, Peter
1987   "The Idea of a Psychoanalytic Literary Criticism," in *Discourse in Psychoanalysis and Literature* (ed. S. Rimmon-Kenan; New York: Methuen): 1–18.

Clines, David J.A.
1990   *What Does Eve Do to Help? And Other Readerly Questions to the Old Testament.* (JSOTSup, 94; Sheffield: JSOT Press).

Coats, George W.
1983   *Genesis, with an Introduction to Narrative Literature* (FOTL, 1; Grand Rapids: Eerdmans).

Culley, Robert C.
1976   *Studies in the Structure of Hebrew Narrative* (Semeia Supplements; Philadelphia: Fortress Press; Missoula, MT: Scholars Press).

Donaldson, Mara E.
1981   "Kinship Theory in the Patriarchal Narratives: The Case of the Barren Wife," *JAAR* 49: 77–87.

Exum, J. Cheryl
1993   *Fragmented Women: Feminist (Sub)versions of Biblical Narratives* (JSOTSup, 163; Sheffield: JSOT Press; Valley Forge, PA: Trinity Press International).

Felman, Shoshana
1983   "Beyond Oedipus: The Specimen Story of Psychoanalysis," in *Lacan and Narration: The Psychoanalytic Difference in Narrative Theory* (ed. R. Con Davis; Baltimore: Johns Hopkins University Press): 1021–53.

Firestone, Reuven
1991   "Difficulties in Keeping a Beautiful Wife: The Legend of Abraham and Sarah in Jewish and Islamic Tradition," *JJS* 42: 196–214.

Fox, Everett
1989   "Can Genesis be Read as a Book?," *Semeia* 46 (*Narrative Research on the Hebrew Bible*, ed. M. Amihai, G.W. Coats, and A.M. Solomon): 31–40.

Freud, Sigmund
1960   *The Ego and the Id* (trans. Joan Riviere; rev. and ed. James Strachey; New York: W.W. Norton).
1961   *Beyond the Pleasure Principle* (trans. and ed. James Strachey; New York: W.W. Norton).
1965   *The Interpretation of Dreams* (trans. and ed. James Strachey; New York: Avon Books).

Girard, René
1965   *Deceit, Desire, and the Novel: Self and Other in Literary Structure* (trans. Y. Freccero; Baltimore: Johns Hopkins University Press).

Jeansonne, Sharon Pace
1990   *The Women of Genesis: From Sarah to Potiphar's Wife* (Minneapolis: Fortress Press).

Keller, Carl A.
1954   "'Die Gefährdung der Ahnfrau.' Ein Beitrag zur gattungs- und motivgeschichtlichen Erforschung alttestamentlicher Erzählungen," *ZAW* 66: 181–91.

Koch, Klaus
1969   *The Growth of the Biblical Tradition: The Form-Critical Method* (trans. S.M. Cupitt; New York: Charles Scribner's Sons).

Lacan, Jacques
1988   "Seminar on 'The Purloined Letter'" (trans. J. Mehlman), in *The Purloined Poe: Lacan, Derrida and Psychoanalytic Reading* (ed. J.P. Muller and W.J. Richardson; Baltimore: Johns Hopkins University Press): 28–54.

Miscall, Peter D.
1983   *The Workings of Old Testament Narrative* (Semeia Studies; Philadelphia: Fortress Press; Chico, CA: Scholars Press).

Niditch, Susan
1987   *Underdogs and Tricksters: A Prelude to Biblical Folklore* (San Francisco: Harper & Row).

Noth, Martin
1972   *A History of Pentateuchal Traditions* (trans. Bernhard W. Anderson; Englewood Cliffs, NJ: Prentice-Hall).

Petersen, David L.
1973   "A Thrice-Told Tale: Genre, Theme, and Motif," *BR* 18: 30–43.

Pitt-Rivers, Julian
1977   *The Fate of Shechem: Or, the Politics of Sex* (Cambridge: Cambridge University Press).

Polzin, Robert
1975   "'The Ancestress of Israel in Danger' in Danger," *Semeia* 3 (*Classical Hebrew Narrative*, ed. R.C. Culley): 81–98.

Rad, Gerhard von
1961   *Genesis* (trans. J.H. Marks; Philadelphia: Westminster Press).

Rashkow, Ilona N.
1992   "Intertextuality, Transference, and the Reader in/of Genesis 12 and 20," in *Reading between Texts: Intertextuality and the Hebrew Bible* (ed. D.N. Fewell; Louisville, KY: Westminster/John Knox): 57–73.

Rosenberg, Joel
1986   *King and Kin: Political Allegory in the Hebrew Bible* (Bloomington: Indiana University Press).

Sedgwick, Eve Kosofsky
1985   *Between Men: English Literature and Male Homosocial Desire* (New York: Columbia University Press).

Skinner, John
1910   *A Critical and Exegetical Commentary on Genesis* (Edinburgh: T. & T. Clark).

Speiser, E.A.
1964   *Genesis* (AB, 1; Garden City, NY: Doubleday).

Steinberg, Naomi
1984   "Gender Roles in the Rebekah Cycle," *Union Seminary Quarterly Review* 39: 175–88.

Van Seters, John
1975   *Abraham in History and Tradition* (New Haven: Yale University Press).

Vawter, Bruce
1977   *On Genesis: A New Reading* (Garden City, NY: Doubleday).

Westbrook, Raymond
1990   "Adultery in Ancient Near Eastern Law," *RB* 97: 542–80.

Westermann, Claus
1980   *The Promises to the Fathers: Studies on the Patriarchal Narratives* (trans. David E. Green; Philadelphia: Fortress Press).
1985   *Genesis 12–36* (trans. J.J. Scullion; Minneapolis: Augsburg Press).

White, Hugh C.
1991   *Narration and Discourse in the Book of Genesis* (Cambridge: Cambridge University Press).

Goddesses and
Women of Magic

A Heifer from Thy Stable
On Goddesses and the Status of
Women in the Ancient Near East

CAROLE R. FONTAINE

The question of how women relate to religious systems of signification is always a complex one. This is particularly true when we try to probe ancient texts concerning the relationship between the status of women and the presence of goddesses in a given culture. The standard feminist critique of history and its interpreters holds for any investigation of these issues in ancient Near Eastern societies: "history," as it has come down to us through cuneiform and hieroglyphic sources, is very much the province of the "winners"—elite males whose ideological interests were served by the "disappearing" of the voices of women and other subject peoples. Added to this inherent bias within the texts themselves is the problem of piecemeal survival, with some texts surviving the destructions of war or abandonment of sites and others perishing. Nor do all texts survive in good condition: clay tablets break or become worn down around the edges and outer sheets of papyrus rolls may be victims of decay and rough handling by graverobbers or inept restorers. Further, even where text critical work is able to establish a readable text, translation problems exist. Not all lexical items or contextual allusions are readily intelligible to translators, and considerable debate may ensue. In short, we do not have a complete record of past, even though biased, sources on which to base our studies, and what we do have to work with is often shrouded in ambiguity or limited in scope and value.

The situation is even more difficult should we try to trace the development of the "historical" goddess cults from their supposed Neolithic precursors. In the absence of texts from the Neolithic era, we are forced to rely on iconographic representations, and recovery of material culture through archaeological excavation. Archaeological reconstructions of culture are no more free from the biases and preconceptions of their excavators than literary readings of ancient texts are free from the values imposed on them by their modern critics. Hence, we may observe widely divergent interpretations of a single artifact:

Do Paleolithic and Neolithic "Venus" figurines represent a celebration of the sacrality of the female body with its life-creating and sustaining abilities, or do we have instead male art which finds its outlet in the creation of female "sex objects"? Both interpretations appear in the literature, and in the absence of epigraphic confirmation of either hypothesis, the anepigraphic evidence retains a mystery as it gestures toward a functional meaning we may imagine but cannot "prove." We may choose to endorse Mellaart's conclusions from the evidence of burial practices, grave goods, and iconography at Čatal Hüyük that women were held in high esteem, holding religious offices and participating in the vital activities of the community.[1] We may even relate this alleged high status for women to the overwhelming presence of goddesses in the community's cultic installations, but without corroborating texts and a thorough excavation of the site, as feminist historians we still find ourselves operating in the realm of scholarly conjecture. Excavations from Minoan Crete, covering a time period which ranges from the middle of the Early Bronze Age into the Late Bronze Age, are often used to support the presence of peace-loving matriarchies in the ancient world. Here we find another case in point where speculation sometimes outstrips solid reconstruction. Where evidence is embarrassing or contradictory to the matriarchal hypothesis, it is ignored or redated to reflect the warlike practices of the later Mycenaean invaders, thereby preserving the desired view of the Minoans.[2] What we *may* say about the Neolithic Anatolian and later Minoan communities mentioned here is that they appear to be *relatively* peaceful, compared to the later imperialistic, clearly patriarchal empires of the Nile Valley and the Fertile Crescent, and that this cultural configuration was enabled both by their geographical locations and socioeconomic adaptations to their ecosystems. Within this cultural matrix, it appears that the relations between the sexes may have been organized along more egalitarian lines, at least judging from iconography and burial practices, and that the presence of goddesses in these cultures may have served both to symbolize and legitimize the position of women.

No matriarchies can be proven to exist in the absence of genealogical texts, and we must pose the question of whether or not that is something to be mourned. Feminist critique of power relations suggests that a simple reversal of the roles of oppressed and oppressing groups is not enough, at least from an evolutionary perspective (even though such reversal must certainly appear advantageous to those in the oppressed group). What is needed is a thoroughgoing dismantling of the structures by which any group is able and allowed to oppress another. Matriarchal rule is not necessarily the answer, so that the failure to uncover such "ideal" cultures need not deter us from the task of envisioning an alternative future to patriarchal destruction of the earth.

Once we move into the historical periods of the Bronze and Iron Ages, the goddess cults known to us are well integrated into the patriarchal ideology of their cultures. Isis, the Egyptian redeemer, acts on behalf of Osiris her husband and Horus her son rather than for herself. The Hattic goddesses of pre-Hittite Anatolia are incorporated into the Hittite pantheon, and engage in activities which benefit the new imperial power structure. The Sumerian Inanna acts on behalf of her city Uruk (biblical Erech), and by the time she is identified with the Semitic Ištar, her divine power has been fully harnessed to support kingship.[3] While it is tempting to see this "domestication" of the ancient Near Eastern goddesses as an analog for the slow but steady decline of the status of women known to us from legal and economic texts, we are brought to another critical question in our attempts at reconstruction of women's past: What is the relationship of a text to the society that spawned it? Dare we assume a simple, one-to-one correspondence between literary symbol and social reality? Can a patriarchal text speak truth about the reality of women's lives?[4] This, of course, is not a question confined only to feminist discourse on history and literature, but one that consistently plagues all the disciplines.[5]

It might be helpful to propose here a model for sorting through the various types of texts preserved, with an emphasis on the amount of social verisimilitude likely to be preserved in them. The figure below represents a kind of sliding scale ranging from texts which are most likely to contain the highest degree of verisimilitude to those judged least likely to reflect social reality, at least in any direct way. It is important to remember that the creation of a text, even a humdrum economic or legal text, is still an imaginative, creative act undertaken by someone with the leisure or mandate to engage in such activities. Texts both *respond* to social reality and help to shape it.[6] Texts may be classed along a continuum of those which are based in purely referential discourse (high degree of verisimilitude) to those which are highly symbolic and expressive (small degree of verisimilitude), i.e., those which are mapped on the combinative, syntagmatic axis of language as opposed to those whose nature is more related to the associative, paradigmatic axis.[7] Further, anyone with experience of modern legal or economic texts knows that even such supposedly "neutral" texts as these may contain a large measure of wishful thinking or outright disinformation. The walls of Karnak give adequate testimony to the fact that ancient writers were no more adverse to casting recorded reality into their desired image than are modern lawyers and businesspeople.[8] Additionally complicating the task of judging a text's relation to society, types of texts may blend across genres, mixing elements that are referential and imaginative ("secular" love poetry developed from models of ritual performance of a "sacred marriage," for example, or imaginative tales which become embedded in annalistic or etiological narratives). Hence, the following model should be taken as a guide only. Texts must be evaluated for verisimilitude on an individual basis, in conjunction with study of material culture, parallel texts, and comparative ethnography.[9]

Even were we to solve the riddle of text-and-society, our problems in the use of ancient Near Eastern texts are still legion. Androcentric language was often used inclusively, so that we may not automatically assume the absence of women even when they are not explicitly mentioned as present. Further, as noted above, these texts reflect the

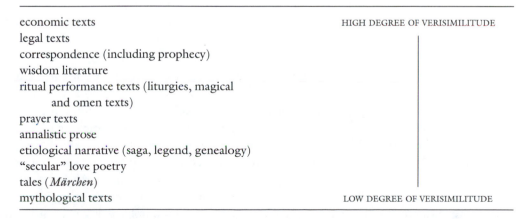

economic texts　　　　　　　　　　　　　　　　HIGH DEGREE OF VERISIMILITUDE
legal texts
correspondence (including prophecy)
wisdom literature
ritual performance texts (liturgies, magical
　　　and omen texts)
prayer texts
annalistic prose
etiological narrative (saga, legend, genealogy)
"secular" love poetry
tales (*Märchen*)
mythological texts　　　　　　　　　　　　　　LOW DEGREE OF VERISIMILITUDE

FIGURE 1.　Degree of verisimilitude in ancient Near Eastern texts, organized by genre agendas of their elite male authors and tend to focus on the public domain where male power is located and exercised. The private domain of the extended family, even though it functioned as the primary unit of economic production in antiquity,[10] is usually known to us only through hints or textual "asides" because it was not of particular interest to the authors. Since the private domain was the arena in which the lives of most women were lived out, we are generally left with a nebulous picture of women's everyday lives. Reflecting the class issues involved in the creation of "literary" and referential texts for the ruling classes, it is also the case that we know less about the lives of women of middle or lower class than we do about elite women. Generally, then, we have very little access to what women themselves actually thought about their lot in life, and scholarly models of reconstruction which are insensitive to the web of considerations involved in the formation and interpretation of these texts often do not advance our knowledge.

Models of the Past

In our search for answers, we must begin by posing the proper questions. In any consideration of the "status" of women, the researcher must be aware of the comprehensive difficulties involved in such a project. As Martin K. Whyte points out in *The Status of Women in Preindustrial Societies,* there is no such thing as the status of women, for there is wide variability both cross-culturally and within cultures, where women's "class" identity, with all its possible benefits and detriments, is linked to the class of their men.[11] Elite women may have a quite different status than do their out-group sisters. In his sample of 93 preindustrial cultures, covering a time period from 1750 BCE to 1800 CE, Whyte investigated the status of women through use of the following variables: property control, kin power, value of life, value of labor, domestic authority, ritualized female solidarity, control of sexuality, ritualized fear of women, joint participation with men, and informal influence. Despite the difficulties in use of the cross-cultural method (inability to deal with evolutionary change in the status of women in a given culture, inability to handle class variations in status in a sample, need to rely on data gathered in ways that reflected gender-bias in either informant or fieldworker, focus on formal rather than informal aspects of the status of women, etc.), significant hypotheses were tested and important findings made.[12] Whyte concluded that no one key factor could be used to predict the status of women for a particular culture, nor was there any one factor which, if improved, resulted in raising the entire status of women. In matrilineal and matrilocal societies, women enjoyed modest benefits in status in the area of property rights, female solidarity, kin power, sexual restrictions, and value of life. Male hunting, male bonding, and male strength did not account for the low status of women, but cultures which were dominated by the "classical" religions (Judaism, Christianity, Islam, Hinduism, and Buddhism) consistently displayed lower statuses for their women. This last finding may be related to the fact that these religions tend to appear in more culturally complex societies (in which women generally fare worse) rather than in simpler, less stratified, and diversified cultures.[13] Whyte's study did not offer any specific correlation on the relation of the presence of goddesses to women's status, and lack of explicit focus on the religious ideologies used to legitimate low or high status for women limits its usefulness for our purposes here. Nevertheless, this study alerts us to the incredible complexity involved in any investigation of the status of women.

LOW			HIGH
FEMALE			FEMALE
STATUS			STATUS
Female material control:	*Demand for female produce:*	*Female political participation:*	*Female solidarity groups:*
females create, act, allocate, dispose of land/produce/ crafts beyond the domestic unit	recognized value internally or exter- nally beyond the domestic unit	regular, official par- ticipation; influence policy beyond the domestic unit	for political or eco- nomic interests, females group in regular way to pro- tect or represent interests; are recog- nized and effective in doing so

FIGURE 2.   Peggy R. Sanday's analysis of female status in the public domain (192–93)

Specific attention to the variations in women's status when goddesses are present in a culture is found in Peggy R. Sanday's seminal study, "Female Status in the Public Domain."[14] Four variables are used to chart female power (the ability to act effectively) and authority (recognized and legitimized power) in a sample of twelve cultures: female material control, demand for female produce, female political participation, and female solidarity groups (see Figure 2). It was found that where women contributed approxi- mately 40 percent to the group's subsistence needs, their status generally improved, especially where they retained control over the allocation of their products.[15] Where sys- tems of religion and/or magic held a favorable view of female power, Sanday determined this to be a *response* to changes in production, rather than a cause. While there was no correlation between the number of female deities in a culture and women's status, there was a strong correlation between the percentage of goddesses and women's contribution to group subsistence needs. There were low but positive correlations between goddesses with general powers (i.e., power over both females and males) and female status.[16]

Sanday's results are intriguing for the questions raised with respect to the ancient Near East, but as she acknowledges, more work needs to be done in this area before we can propose hard and fast conclusions. Further, there are elements in Sanday's shaping of the study which deserve attention. By focusing on female status in the *public* domain, the entire sphere of women's role and status within the domestic unit is pushed aside. If one of the goals of feminist research in this area is to reclaim and revalue the worlds in which women actually live, the public domain cannot become our exclusive locus of inquiry. Similarly, by attending primarily to goddesses with "general powers" and excluding those with power exclusively over women, we see a subtle modern bias at work to devalue the role of fertility in women's lives and self-understanding. While it is true that a "full- service" goddess might be more appealing to modern people seeking to expand their horizons of divinity, the "fertility" goddesses of antiquity cannot be so easily dismissed without losing important insights into ancient women's concerns and religious sensibili- ties. Although it has rightly been pointed out that the designation "fertility goddess" is an appellation which has allowed predominantly male scholars to dismiss and discount

the role of goddesses in ancient religions,[17] it is still the case that the roles of these goddesses in promoting and sustaining fertility were significant aspects of their personalities
and functions. At this point, it becomes important to remain aware of how modern trends
in rethinking the "biological destiny" of women may be skewing our vision of the past.

In *Die Göttin und ihr Heros: die matriarchalen Religionen in Mythos, Märchen
und Dichtung* (München: Frauenoffensive, 1980), feminist philosopher and aesthetician
Heide Göttner-Abendroth uses world mythology in an attempt to reconstruct the
"matriarchal mythology" of early civilizations. She outlines three stages in the development of matriarchal religions, which she understands as "religions of rebirth" rather than
simply as "fertility religions" (see Figure 3).

While Göttner-Abendroth has performed a valuable service in calling our attention
to patterns which seem to extend across time and region in mythological texts, there are
a number of problems with her reconstruction. Even discounting a too-easy identification of matrilineal and matrilocal cultures as matriarchal ones and her reliance on the
scholarship of Bachofen and Graves, her simplistic assumptions of the way in which
mythology reflects out-group history must give pause to historians and literary critics
alike. As is typical of most attempts to develop a comprehensive, universal scheme, she is
obliged to "tinker" with the evidence from certain cultures which does not fit her patterns and this results in violation of some of the basic rules of good ethnography. A case
in point is her phase I.c. of developed urban matriarchies, where she sees battles with
nature demons (i.e., dragons and the like) as a feature of classical matriarchal mythology.[18]
This conclusion is certainly a questionable one for Mesopotamian myth, where the cosmic battle between the chaos-dragon Tiamat and the god-king Marduk represents not a
development from goddess-centered mythology but a patriarchal rejection of the ancient
goddess as the source of cosmic life. Others may be bothered not only by her historical
reconstructions based on myth, but also by the political position which affirms mother-
right and mother-rule without reflection on the possibilities of abuse inherent in any
such system of gender dominance. However, Göttner-Abendroth does see matriarchal
social organization as far more egalitarian and wholesome than any known to us under

I. Pre-Indo-European (matriarchal periods)
    a. early rural matriarchies: chthonic goddesses
    b. developed urban matriarchies: astral goddesses
    c. continued urban matriarchies: cyclic battle with nature demons
II. Indo-European transformations (imposition of patriarchy)
    a. sex change: Great Mother becomes All-Knowing Father
    b. role change: Goddess as God's "Wife"
    c. generational change: Goddess as Father's "Daughter"
    d. myths of rebellion against Father
    e. matriarchal cults survive in secret opposition
III. Patriarchal Major Religions (absolute father-god)
    a. abstract mythology
    b. philosophical abstractions

FIGURE 3.   Heide Göttner-Abendroth's stages of transformation in matriarchal religions
(adapted from *Die Göttin und ihr Heros,* 119–20)

patriarchy, but once again, this is a very complex argument to sustain when based primarily on imaginative texts.[19]

The brief review of these models for evaluating the status of ancient women and the relationship of that status to the presence of goddesses and their worship leaves us with some directions for inquiry and cautions about how we proceed. As we turn to women's texts from the ancient world then, we must beware of the temptation of generalization. Status of elite, goddess-identified women (see Enheduanna and Puduḫepa, below) may not extend to their lower-class sisters, nor should we assume that the presence of goddesses always implies a higher view of female authority and power. Questions of status should always be asked in conjunction with study of the economic power held by women. Future work should attempt to test Sanday's hypothesis about women's contribution to a culture's subsistence needs and the percentage of full-service goddesses in the society, although that is beyond the scope of the present essay. Further, insofar as possible given the texts with which we are working, we should attempt to press our questions about women's roles and status into the domestic sphere and not simply in the public domain where only a few exceptional women find a place. We should be alert to recurring patterns within the literature and cultures studied, while simultaneously resisting the easy assumption that a given motif or pattern will carry the same oncology and meaning in one culture as it does in another. Finally, we must be sensitive to the "literary" nature of the texts studied with respect to the proportion of cultural verisimilitude likely to be present, preferencing economic texts and correspondence, for example, more highly than tales and myths. With these injunctions in mind, let us now turn to the examination of texts by some ancient women of Mesopotamia and Anatolia.

"Be it known!": Ancient Women Speak

In the cuneiform sources reflecting the rise of the kingdom of Akkad in the last half of the third millennium we meet a truly remarkable woman: Enheduanna of Ur (ca. 2300–2230 BCE). Daughter of the great political leader Sargon of Akkad, Enheduanna combined the roles of princess, priestess, and poet to such an extent that centuries later her literary works were still being catalogued and held in great esteem by the cultures which had inherited them. One scholar has gone so far as to declare her the "first non-anonymous author in literature."[20]

The origins of her father Sargon, salient to our discussion here, have been mythologized: he claimed to be the son of the union between a high priestess and an unknown father. A water-drawer plucked him from the river where his mother had placed him after she secretly gave birth, and he later came into power when the goddess Ištar gave him her love as he worked as a gardener.[21] Some scholars take this to mean that he was aided by women, perhaps devotees of Ištar, in his rise to power. Subsequently, Sargon was able to unite the city-state kingdoms of Sumer (Ur and Uruk) with his own kingdom of Akkad. Several political and theological moves paved the way for and symbolized his consolidation of Sumerian and Akkadian culture. He appointed his daughter Enheduanna to a dual cultic role as high priestess-bride of the moongod Nanna in Ur and also installed her as a cultic functionary in Uruk, thus honoring the Sumerian traditions wherein a male deity was served by a female cult official or *en,* and vice versa. He synthesized Sumerian and Akkadian theologies by identifying his patron deity, the semitic

Ištar, with the Sumerian Inanna.[22] In the masterful Sumerian poetic compositions of his daughter Enheduanna, this identification is carried through with style and fervor, and constitutes one of the world's first efforts at a "systematic theology." Enheduanna's life and work are known to us through her seals, inscriptions, and the cycle of hymns to Inanna and the temples of Sumer which comes from her hand or has been attributed to her. We have her portrait preserved on a badly damaged disc from Ur.[23]

In her composition *nin-me-šar-ra,* or "The Exaltation of Inanna" as it has come to be known, Enheduanna moves beyond a mere propagation of her father's political theology to a personal identification with the fortunes of her beloved goddess. The same terms used to depict Inanna's past flights from the cities of Sumer are employed to describe the usurper Lugalanna's expulsion of Enheduanna from her priestly offices in Ur and Uruk. When appeals to the moon god Nanna and the sky god An prove futile (since Lugalanna now controls their cults), she turns hopefully to Inanna. She says of her own composition that inspiration came to her at night and that she "gave birth" to this song, "that which I recited to you at (mid)night/May the singer repeat it to you at noon!" (lines 139–140).[24] By casting her predicament in terminology which has been applied to the goddess's own past trials, Enheduanna forges a bond of compassionate empathy by which she hopes to return to her former position of service to the goddess. Given the reconstructed political context which informs the composition, it is not surprising that it is the martial aspects of Inanna, rather than the fertility functions, which receive the most emphasis:

> That you are lofty as Heaven—be it known!
> That you are broad as the earth—be it known!
> That you devastate the rebellious land—be it known!
> That you roar at the land—be it known!
> That you smite the heads—be it known!
> That you devour cadavers like a dog—be it known!
> That your glance is terrible—be it known!
> That you lift your terrible glance—be it known!
> That your glance is flashing—be it known! . . .
> That you attain victory—be it known! . . .
> Oh my lady beloved of An, I have verily recounted your fury!
> lines 123–130, 132, 135[25]

Since the text considered here is a prayer text which contains clear liturgical elements ("be it known!"), it can be rated fairly high on our scale of verisimilitude. While Enheduanna certainly makes use of hymnic convention and hyperbole, both in the invocatory epithets and the "complaint" section which details her humiliation at the hands of the usurper, since she is seeking redress of tangible wrongs we must assume that her account and plea bear some clear relationship to the historic events that occasioned them. Like the individual complaint psalms of the Hebrew Bible, we may not know the precise details of what has afflicted the psalmist, but we are generally on safe ground in concluding that *something happened.* She who had "carried the ritual basket" and "intoned the acclaim" has been "placed in the lepers' ward" (lines 68–69).[26] Enheduanna had encountered the "catch-22" in the status of women "elites": where status derives from the politics and pleasures of one's male relatives, one can be easily "de-classed" when new elite males take charge. When the gods to whom she had been espoused turned a deaf ear to her lament, she turned to the goddess Inanna-Ištar with the cry "O my divine impetuous wild cow, drive out this man, capture this man!" (line 91).[27] If we are to believe the composition's concluding lines, the goddess did not desert her as had her gods. It may have been Enheduanna's father who placed her in power, but it was her goddess who restored her and her own talents which insured her an enduring place in Sumerian literature.

"If truly you are my daughter . . ."

The opportunities and pitfalls associated with the role of princess in Mesopotamia are well attested in the literature from the city-state of Mari (Tell Hariri) in the Old Babylonian period.[28] During the reign of King Zimri-Lim (ca. 1780–1760 BCE, middle chronology) women in his court held a remarkable range of positions in both the public and private spheres. An able strategist, Zimri-Lim was often away from Mari while conducting his numerous campaigns to establish and maintain Mari's hegemony along the upper Euphrates. For this reason, he often had occasion to leave matters of state and religion in the capable hands of his head queen Šibtu, herself a princess from the court of Aleppo in Yamḥad. It was there that she apparently met and married Zimri-Lim when he had fled Mari in exile at his father's death. Although he had many wives and a large harem, Šibtu clearly held a preeminent place in his affections and trust. Scholars speculate that since no such broad role for the queen or queen-mother was known in Mari either before or after Zimri-Lim's reign, the extraordinary activity of the women in Zimri-Lim's family is an example of women claiming "unassigned power" when circumstances permit, rather than of any institutionalized "assigned power" in the city-state. Our main textual evidence for this period comes from correspondence from the royal archives.[29]

Šibtu's correspondence is quite varied, permitting some glimpses into personal life, even though most of it is economic and routine in nature, as she carries out tasks delegated to her by Zimri-Lim and updates him on the state of affairs in the palace and city. Much of the interchange between the pair which is private in nature consists of her inquiries about the king's health, reports of favorable omens which she had ordered taken for him, and his reassuring replies about his welfare and the fortunes of the army. In ARM X 26, she reports, "(To my lord) say: Thus Šibtu (your) maidservant: I have (just given) birth to twins—a son and a daughter. May my lord rejoice!"[30] Elsewhere (ARM X 17) she writes that she is sending Zimri-Lim a coat and other articles of clothing that she has made herself, requesting that he wear them. But apart from such typical domestic roles, Šibtu was involved in acting as an all-purpose factotum for her absent lord. She oversaw the direction of the palace, the harem, the temple, workshops, and the entire city, receiving and sending diplomatic correspondence to the outlying provinces, showing that her influence and authority extended well beyond the city of Mari itself. Aside from overseeing the city archives, she supervised the work of various officials, many of whom sought her influence in settling a variety of official and personal matters. She was also in contact with her father's court and acted to secure positive treatment for favorites. In the realm of cultic activity, she filled the role of king or governor as needed, escorting the cult statues, ordering sacrifices, and relaying divine oracles to the king.

That she was a concerned and thoughtful queen is evident from the number of appeals for help which she received and the letters from her which direct officials to give aid and comfort. In ARM X 153, one Kibri-Dagan was requested by her to discover what was causing a particular woman's "heartache"; in ARM X 160, she arranges for the release of women who had been given in pledge for a debt. In ARM X 114, Tarišḫattu, a woman of higher rank (perhaps a widow of Zimri-Lim's father?), writes to Šibtu to settle a matter of slander, saying "If truly you are my daughter and you love my health, then you will convey (this matter) to the king. . . ."[31]

Also evident from her letters is the fact that she had fully internalized the values of imperial patriarchy, among them the well-known "double-standard" that limits the sexual activity of women while allowing a full range of opportunities for men. So great is Zimri-Lim's trust in his queen's solidarity with his goals that he is able to direct her to select the most beautiful of the women taken in battle for his harem (ARM X 126), though he later decides to see to the matter himself. When an epidemic strikes the harem (X 129–130), it is Šibtu who carries out Zimri-Lim's instructions for limiting the spread of the disease.[32] From the correspondence available to us, we can conclude that Šibtu firmly understood that her welfare was tied to the fortunes of her lord; she does not grudge him a fine harem or lesser wives to oversee other palaces, for such arrangements were expected of a great king and testified to his prominence, hence augmenting her own. As is often seen in ethnographic data, a variety of factors determine whether or not the addition of another woman to the household is seen as threatening to personal status or as enhancing the available pool of workers.[33] The "other woman" only becomes a threat where the head wife's status or husband's affections are jeopardized by the addition of the new female—we may think here of the fates of Sarah and Leah in the biblical narratives. Unlike them, Šibtu, daughter of the powerful king of Yamḫad, was secure in her position and assured in her relationship with Zimri-Lim.

"Even if I am a woman . . ."

Not all of the princesses of Mari were so fortunate as Queen Šibtu and that we ought not to generalize from her position is brought home in letters concerning Zimri-Lim's daughters' struggles with their co-wives. Part of Zimri-Lim's plan for the maintenance of strong vassal alliances involved the giving of daughters in political marriages. Royal daughters in such positions also served their father by acting as trusted informants on political and socioeconomic conditions in their region, actions which predictably caused friction when vassal husbands were less than whole-hearted in their allegiance to Mari: one of Zimri-Lim's daughters, Inib-šarri, was given in marriage to Ibal-Addu of Ašlakka, only to discover, much to her dismay, that a previous wife still held the position of head wife and queen (ARM X 74). After writing to Zimri-Lim concerning her husband's potentially traitorous activities, she flees to a neighboring city and writes her father entreating him to return her to Mari (ARM X 77, II 112, 113). While in "exile" in Naḫur, she corresponds with an official on various matters, at one point invoking the blessing of Belet-ekallim (= Ningal?), her goddess, to protect him (ARM X 78).[34] We do not know the outcome of her requests to return home.

Another daughter who was successful in achieving the dissolution of a noxious political marriage was Kiru, married to one Ḫaya-Sumu of Ilanṣura. Again, the father's political motives set the stage for the daughter's misery: Zimri-Lim had not only given Kiru in marriage but had also established her as mayor in her own right; at the same time, he gave Ḫaya-Sumu another (adoptive?) daughter, Šibatum, perhaps by a lesser ranking wife, and this is the queen favored by Ḫaya-Sumu. Domestic battles escalate among the trio, until Ḫaya-Sumu threatens Kiru's life (ARM X 32). Desperate, Kiru writes home to daddy: "If he (the king) does not bring me back, I shall die; I will not live," and again, "If my lord does not bring me back, I will head toward Mari (and there) jump (fall) from the roof" (ARM X 33). Humiliated before guests, deprived of her rightful servants and prerogatives, and finally threatened with death, Kiru's pleas were finally heard. In ARM X 135, Zimri-Lim instructs Šibtu to make arrangements to return Kiru to Mari.[35]

Other examples of unhappily married daughters of Zimri-Lim exist, but not all marriages ended so unfortunately as Kiru's and Inib-šarri's. Other daughters found sufficient happiness in their politically motivated marriages to write to Zimri-Lim on their husbands' behalf (ARM X 98). At least one daughter was sent into the cloister as a *nadītu*-woman (ARM X 38), and we also hear the daughters of other kings mentioned in the Mari correspondence. While Zimri-Lim did not hesitate to make use of his daughters as instruments of foreign policy, he maintained contact with them, although we may wonder how much of his correspondence was due to fatherly affection, since the information obtained by his daughters was of great benefit to his own political maneuvering. Indeed, Kiru even writes Zimri-Lim reminding him of previous problems caused when he disregarded her reports (ARM X 31), concluding "And now, even if I am a woman, may my father and lord listen to my message."[36] Still, Zimri-Lim sought to influence the fate of his daughters for the good, occasionally even giving them assigned powers within the political structure. But if the rank of princess could bequeath special status and opportunities to a woman like Šibtu, it is clear it could also bring considerable hazards as in the cases of Kiru and Inib-šarri. Once again, the fate of royal women, like that of their lower-class sisters, was almost entirely dependent on the wishes and whims of the men who controlled their lives.

In the realm of religion, we are given intriguing hints from the Mari letters about how women related to the gods and goddesses of their regions. Women are often found offering prayers before the gods Šamas, Adad, and Dagan for the safety of the king and his armies. Women also offer sacrifices, commission oracles, and are found worshiping both the main gods of Mari, Dagan and Adad, as well as other gods (Šamas, Itur-Mer, Nanna, Tešub, etc.) and the goddesses of their own and surrounding areas (Ištar, Ištar.RA.DA.NA, Annunitum, Ḫebat, Belet-ekallim). Women served as lay and professional prophetesses for both gods and goddesses, and could be attached to specific cult centers (including cloisters) in a variety of capacities. While such a dedication provided status and authority to the women involved, it offered only moderate protection in time of war: in ARM X 126, we learn that some *ugbabātum*-priestesses were taken as war captives, but were not forced into the textile factories as slave labor as the other female captives were.[37]

Two tantalizingly brief events relating women to their goddesses might be mentioned. In ARM X 87, one Šattamkiyazi has left her own city to serve the king in another, apparently against the wish of her goddess, Ištar.RA.DA.NA, as expressed in a liver omen.

As a consequence, she has become quite ill ("the hand of Ištar.RA.DA.NA presses heavily against me"), and requests leave of the king to offer another sacrifice to her goddess in hope of restoring her health.[38] In ARM X 112, women servants of the palace tell the male palace servants that "we are constantly praying for you to Belet-ekallim."[39] While the evidence from Mari does not permit us to conclude that it was the presence of goddesses there that accounted for the relatively high status of elite women and widespread activities of women in the cult, it is clear that women had deeply felt "personal" relationships with their deities, goddesses as well as gods, and in official capacities could be regarded as legitimate representatives of the divine before the king, and vice versa.

"A Heifer from Thy Stable": Women of Anatolia

From the royal archives at Ḫattuša, capital of the Hittite empire which flourished in central Anatolia during the Late Bronze Age (ca. 1450–1200 BCE), comes a wealth of materials which shed light on the position of women in this most sophisticated of conqueror-kingdoms. Since space does not permit a thorough review of all the materials found at Ḫattuša, we will concentrate on two figures which represent the far ends of the social scale: Queen Puduḫepa and the MI.ŠU.GI of Hittite ritual texts.

Queen Puduḫepa was the wife and consort of Ḫattušili III, an able military and political leader who came to the throne through the irregular process of deposing his nephew. Ḫattušili later explains with some piety that this was all the idea of his personal goddess, Ištar of Šamuḫa, whom he was bound to obey since she had saved his life when he was only a sickly child. When the same Ištar told him to take Puduḫepa, a girl half his age, as wife, he naturally obeyed. That Puduḫepa was the daughter of a priest of Ištar in the southern province of Kizzuwatna, possibly of royal extraction, but certainly in a position to consolidate allegiances to the Hittites in a territory notable for its Hurrian and Mitannian ties, only made obedience to the goddess that much more satisfying. The marriage was apparently a happy and fruitful one: Puduḫepa bore four children that are known, and her prayers and intercessions for Ḫattušili's health in his old age suggest that her relationship to her husband was a positive and fulfilling one. Due to the peculiarities of Hittite succession in the Old Kingdom, the Queen (-Mother) retained a powerful position even after the death of her husband, and Puduḫepa continues to be mentioned during the reign of her son, Tudḫaliya IV.[40]

Because of her mention in her husband's "Apology" and the many vows, prayer-texts, and items of personal correspondence to and from the Hittite court, we know more about Puduḫepa than any other woman of the Late Bronze Age. Although Hittite queens were always active in the religious sphere through their position as high priestess of the cult of the Sun-goddess of Arinna, the head of the Hittite pantheon, Puduḫepa expanded her activities into the political and social realms. She had her own seal, carried on her own diplomatic correspondence, took a hand in arranging the settlements for her daughters in their political marriages (one married to Ramesses II, the other to the prince of Amurru), and is the only woman of the ancient world known to have received a divine "message" dream (as opposed to the "symbolic" dreams usually recorded for women).[41] She had her own chariot, probably to rush her to her cultic duties throughout the kingdom, and had access to temple treasuries, though she could not collect taxes.

She carried out normal cultic and administrative duties associated with her rank, even took part in a court case (which was highly unusual in Hittite legal proceedings), and ordered materials from her home province of Kizzuwatna copied and archived in Ḫattuša.[42]

In the realm of personal theology, this queen left us materials which allow a glimpse into the religious sensibilities of a Bronze Age woman. Puduḫepa's seal, like those of the Hittite kings and queens before her, shows her clasped in the embrace of the Sun-goddess of Arinna whose high-priestess she was. Both females wear strikingly similar costumes, and the seal reads GEME.DINGIR.LIM, "the servant of the goddess."[43] In KUB XXI, 27 Puduḫepa addresses this goddess to plead for the restoration of her husband's health. The tone of her prayer is intimate, persuasive, and trusting. She tells the goddess

> To the Sun-goddess of Arinna, my lady, the mistress of the Hatti lands, the queen of heaven and earth. Sun-goddess of Arinna, thou art queen of all countries! In the Hatti country thou bearest the name of the Sun-goddess of Arinna; but in the land which thou madest the cedar land thou bearest the name Hebat. I, Pudu-hepas, am a servant of thine from of old, a heifer from thy stable, a foundation stone (upon which) thou (canst rest). Thou, my lady, rearedst me and Hattušilis, thy servant to whom thou espousedst me, was closely associated with the Stormgod of Nerik, thy beloved son. . . .[44]

A number of features are of interest here. Puduḫepa, whose name means "Servant of Ḫebat," has made a clear connection between her patron goddess Ḫebat, a Hurrian mother goddess worshiped in her native "Cedar Land,"[45] and the Hattic mother-goddess (probably to be identified as Wuru(n)šemu) who heads the official Hittite pantheon. She further goes on to identify this Ḫebat/Wuru(n)šemu as the goddess who gave her in marriage to Ḫattušili, even though his "Apology" clearly states that it was Ištar of Šamuḫa who did so. In another portion of the "Apology" (12, ll. 7–15), we learn of one of Puduḫepa's dreams:

> Now, while My Lady Ishtar had even before this been promising me the kingship, at that time My Lady Ishtar appeared to my wife in a dream: "I shall march before your husband. And all Hattušas shall be led with your husband. Since I thought highly of him, I did not—no, not ever—abandon him to the hostile trial, the hostile deity. Now also I will exalt him, and make him priest of the sun goddess of Arinnas. Do you also make me, Ishtar, (your) patron deity."[46]

Since the prayer of Puduḫepa cited above (KUB XXI, 27) is usually dated toward the end of Ḫattušili's reign, we presume here that the dream appearance of Ištar occurred earlier since it is clearly narrated as taking place before Ḫattušili's seizure of the throne. Has Puduḫepa taken her husband's Ištar as her patron deity, thus fusing this militant goddess with the mother-goddesses of her youth and her official cultic roles? Though modern scholars are often apt to separate the military roles of the nubile "maiden" goddess from the nurturing roles of the "mother" goddess, it is clear that such distinctions did not hold for at least one ancient devotee.

Like Enheduanna's fusion of the Sumerian Inanna and the Semitic Ištar, Puduḫepa's thealogical move here can be understood as growing out of her experience of her goddesses. Both thealogical and political motivations are at work. The Hittites of the

New Kingdom were known for their syncretistic policies which incorporated the deities of conquered territories into the official pantheon rather than repressing indigenous worship. They were self-styled as "people of the thousand gods," and indeed, it seems they never met a diety they didn't like, which resulted in a cultic calendar so ridiculously full that wars had to be interrupted so that the king could perform his assorted ritual duties. Hence, Puduḫepa's syncretism takes place against a background of easy tolerance and official approval. While it is not too far a "stretch" to identify Ḫebat with the Sun-goddess of Arinna since they are both understood as consorts of the Weather-god of Ḫatti and mothers of the divine son, the Weather-god of Nerik (the Hurrian Šarruma), the immediate coherence between these mother figures and the battle-ready Ištar, the Weather-god's sister, is not so readily apparent. Politically, it was important that the official head of the Hittite pantheon, the Sun-goddess of Arinna, accept Ḫattušili, the favorite of Ištar, as an acceptable if irregular king. Puduḫepa's syncretism allows this by identifying the goddess who brought her husband to power with the goddess who sustains and authorizes Hittite kingship.[47] But the Queen's consolidation of these divine females moves beyond simple pragmatic politics into the realm of faith—could the power that moved her from her home into an unknown land actually be any different from the loving power she knew as a child and continued to experience as queen? Puduḫepa's Hurrian roots have been posited as an explanation of the marked Hurrian-Hittite theological syncretism during Ḫattušili's reign, though the beginning of this trend can be traced back further. However, it is to the common condition of women that we must turn for the deeper psychological motivation behind the politics. Like the royal daughters of Sumer and Mari, Puduḫepa probably had very little choice in her marriage partner or place of residence. Dedicated to Ḫebat by her very name, it is scarcely possible that a woman of faith would leave her native deities behind, and highly probable that she would identify the divine figures with whom she was familiar with those who populated her new world. Where women are moved and traded like game-pieces on the board of political hegemony, they cannot afford inflexible deities bound to a given location. The goddesses a woman worshiped had to be thealogically "portable" if they were to be of any use to the devotee—a goddess only effective in the "Cedar Land" was of limited value to the Queen in Ḫattuša. As Puduḫepa grew, changed residence, and social rank, her understanding of her goddess grew and traveled along with her. She can speak of herself as "a heifer from thy stable," a "foundation stone (upon which) thou (canst rest)," both metaphors which conjure up images of service, dedication, and long-term intimacy. Later in her prayer Puduḫepa goes on to draw parallels between the motherhood of the Sun-goddess and her own travail over Ḫattušili's illness. In a culture obsessed by ritual purity, Puduḫepa can speak to her divine helper, using images drawn from the world of women, from the time when a woman's body is presented in all its primal "otherliness" and potential impurity, and be guaranteed a positive hearing not in spite of her sex *but because of it*, since this gender marking is shared with the goddess. A reader of the biblical book of Leviticus can conceive of such a relationship between women and the exclusive male god of ancient Israel only with the greatest of difficulty, though to be sure, the female characters of the Bible are often presented as relating their birth-giving activities in some way to that same god they are not allowed to approach.[48]

"I am speaking the gods' words . . ."

A fascinating look at the role certain females might play that crosses the boundaries between the public and private domains can be found in the recorded rituals of the MI.ŠU.GI (Hittite: MI.ḫašauwaš), or "old women."[49] These women constitute the class of practitioners most often mentioned in Hittite ritual texts, and were truly indispensable to the functioning of that society. Many of the rituals by them are recorded in the first person, so we have a sense of a qualified informant bequeathing her "recipe" for the restoration of health, purity, and peace to the tradition for use in similar circumstance. Many of these women appear to be from the provinces of Kizzuwatna and Arzawa, and the Hurrian element in these rituals is especially pronounced.[50] An Old Kingdom edict of Ḫattušili I aims at curtailing the influence of the MI.ŠU.GI on the women of the palace, and it has been suggested that they, along with the Hattic city elders and the Tawananna (the king's wife in Hittite times, but originally the king's *sister* and mother of the heir-presumptive in the Hattic period), represented one of the indigenous groups attempting to resist the imposition of cultural changes brought by the Indo-European Hittite conquerors.[51] We know the names of thirteen women designated as MI.ŠU.GI, with many other women appearing as "authors" of magical rituals whom scholars also consider to be recognized practitioners.[52] Among these, the proposed MI.ŠU.GI Ayatarša is said to be the female slave of one Nawila; one Anniwiyani is called "mother of Armatis, the birdmaker, slave of Hurlus," so that we know that MI.ŠU.GI were not cloistered as the *nadītu* were.[53] Here, then, we have an exception which tests the rule by which modern scholars usually assume that slave-women are necessarily women of low status. The Hittite MI.ŠU.GI was endowed with powers so formidable that kings must legislate against them and tradition must encode her words, and yet she could be owned by another.

The MI.ŠU.GI performed her services in a number of areas. The rituals with whose authorship she is credited or those which may reasonably be attributed to her include evocation magic (calling enemy gods away from their towns and calling native gods back to their own place), countermagic against sorcery, removal of ritual impurity and quarrels, restoration of sexual functions, the healing of children, the interpretation of omens, and royal funerary rites.[54] An example of how authoritative were her words and actions comes from the preamble of Annanna's *mugawar* ritual designed to entice the Sungod's return to his own land: "I am speaking the gods' words and am evoking him" (VBoT 58 iv 9–10).[55] A full picture of the sphere of her activities emerges from a reading of the variety of rituals recorded. She selected rituals appropriate for a given situation, assembled or created necessary equipment (wax and clay figures, woolen thread, household items, food and drink, wooden pegs, stones, mud, herbs, dung), gave orders, made sacrifices, interpreted omens, and pronounced words of blessing and curse. She most frequently called upon the Sungod in her rituals, but invoked other deities as necessary for the given situation. She speaks decisively when her rituals are recorded, and her words and deeds were obviously considered efficacious enough to be recorded for posterity. An excerpt from the Ritual of Tunnawi gives some of the flavor of her words and deeds:

> If a person, either a man or a woman, has been placed in any impurity, or someone else has named him/her for impurity, or (if) her children repeatedly die within the woman, or (if) her children are born prematurely, or (if) in a man or woman the sexual organs

are disabled as a result of a formula of impurity, and that person is experiencing impurity, then that person, whether a man or woman, performs the ritual of impurity. . . .[56]

After various hex-breaking activities, she recites the incantation "Evil impurity, witchcraft, sin, anger of the god, terror of the dead, the wickedness of mankind, remove (all) that!"[57] Although the Hittites possessed other male and female ritual practitioners and physician-priests, it was the work of the MI.ŠU.GI which was most frequently called upon by society.[58]

"I am at peace and sisterly": Letters from Egypt

From the Hittite royal archives found at Boghazkoy also comes evidence of the correspondence carried on between "Naptera" (= Nefertari), the Great Royal Wife of Ramesses II, and "Petkhep" (= Puduḫepa) of Hattiland. After Ramesses and Ḫattušili (then serving his brother, the king Muwatalli) fought one another over Syrian hegemony at the battle of Kadesh (ca. 1286/85) with the Egyptian army only narrowly escaping an ignominious defeat at the hands of the Hittites, the two nations sought to come to agreement by treaty (ca. 1271) rather than through clash of arms. As usual, the agreements of nations were sealed "with a kiss"—by the exchange of appropriate females. In this case, M3ᶜT-HR-NFRW-Rᶜ ("Justice is the beautiful face of God (Re)"), the daughter of Puduḫepa and Ḫattušili was given to Ramesses as a wife, and the letters (KBo I 29; KBo I 21?) passing between to the two queens seem related to this occasion.[59] As was noted in the correspondence between Šibtu and Zimri-Lim, the head wife has little concern over the double standard which provides her husband with many wives as a political matter of course. Nefertari writes in response to Puduḫepa's routine inquiry over her health, and speaks of the "good brotherhood" which Re, the Sungod, will give to Ḫattušili and Ramesses. For her own part, she says "And I am at peace and sisterly with the great queen, my sister; I, now (and forever)."[60]

Along with these treaty texts comes an interesting reflection of the "gender" question regarding deities. The Egyptian copy of "Hittite treaty" contains a notice describing the seal of Puduḫepa which the treaty bears. The Egyptian scribe wrote

> Female figure in the likeness of (the great goddess) of the Khatti, clasping in her arms the figure of the Great Queen of Khatti. Circumscription: Seal of the Sun-god of the city of Arenna, (A-r-n-na) lord of the land; seal of Putu-khipa, Great Queen of Khatti, daughter of the land of Kizawaden, mistress (?) of the city of Arenna, mistress of the land, the ministress of the goddess. In the border: the seal of the Sun-god of Arenna, the lord of all the land.[61]

This is actually an excellent description of Puduḫepa's seal, known to us from other archaeological finds, but it seems clear that the Egyptian scribe, undoubtedly male, felt some confusion. In Egypt, the solar deity was clearly male, yet in Ḫatti, a different gender tradition about this deity obtains. While the scribe has dutifully described the goddess who clasps Puduḫepa, he has had trouble incorporating this female deity into his traditional theological language, choosing instead to translate by using the typical solar disc hieroglyph which stands for Re. While some scholars argue that this means that the hieroglyph must therefore carry an androgynous meaning, it also seems likely that the scribe, even while recording the outlandish Hittite view, reinforced his notion that the solar deity was male. That the disputes over appropriate gender designations for deity began at least as early as the Late Bronze Age should afford modern persons engaged in that struggle some comfort: obviously, these are not easy questions to decide.

Conclusion: Syncretistic Thealogy

In closing, this brief glimpse into the words and lives of ancient women has brought us closer to an understanding of the conditions that bounded their lives, and shown us the strength and wit with which they addressed and expanded the roles decreed for them by society. It was impossible to speak of the lives of these women, mostly elites, without also speaking of the menfolk to whom they were attached. Where we had access to the personal feelings of these women, we saw head wives generally content with their lot, and more attached to their men than to the less fortunate women, occasionally even their daughters, who surrounded them. Slavery was accepted as a matter of course; sexual exploitation of captives was regarded as routine. Women caught up in struggles with their co-wives or in conflict with elite males outside their kinship group seemed more conscious of their lower status as female, but even so, this concern did not extend to women of lower classes who frequently appear as pawns traded in the battle for prestige. Few women of other-than-elite status were available for study, due to the nature of the materials available.[62]

At least some of the women considered here could be designated as "goddess-identified," particularly Enheduanna, Šattamkiyazi, and Puduḫepa. In each case, the affiliation served as a basis for at least some of the high status each was accorded, and this, in turn, was tied into the political fortunes reflected in worship of that goddess. In the contexts where a relationship between women and the status-authorizing goddess could be discerned, the women in question also seemed fully engaged, at least in an administrative way, in the economic life of the temple, city-state, or kingdom in question, providing tentative support for Sanday's hypothesis.

A particular trend toward syncretism was recognized, in service of both politics and female religious sensibilities. Enheduanna could fuse the Sumerian Inanna to the Semitic Ištar; Puduḫepa found the goddess of her "Cedar Land" alive and well in the cult center of Arinna, and identified both with her husband's patron goddess. Egyptian women's names also reflect a similar syncretizing perspective: the Egyptian name of Puduḫepa's daughter identified the goddess "Maʾat," or "Justice" as the beautiful face of the sun-god Re; the throne name of Hatshepsut, M3ᶜT-K3-Rᶜ, makes a similar move, proclaiming "Justice (Maʾat) is the likeness of God (Re)." We might also think here of the Egyptian maidservant Hagar, who is narratively the first to identify the Hebrew patriarchal God-of-the-fathers with one of the indigenous gods of Canaan (Gen 16:13–14). As the women were moved from place to place, they found that their deities moved with them, and though both might acquire new names, the relationship of mutuality remained undisturbed.[63]

Notes

1. J. Mellaart, *Čatal Hüyük* (London: Thames & Hudson, 1967) 101; "Excavations at Čatal Hüyük, 1963: Third Preliminary Report," *Anatolian Studies* XIV (1964) 93.

2. The latest entry in the popular literature about Crete may be found in R. Eisler, *The Chalice and the Blade: Our History, Our Future* (San Francisco: Harper & Row, 1987) 29–41. For a critique of this popular view of the Minoans, see C.G. Starr, "Minoan Flower Lovers," *The Minoan Thalassocracy: Myth and Reality,* ed. R. Hagg and N. Marinator (Stockholm: Proc. Third International Symposium at the Swedish Institute in Athens, 31 May–5 June, 1982) 9–12.

3. C.J. Bleeker, "Isis and Hathor: Two Ancient Egyptian Goddesses," *The Book of the Goddess: Past and Present,* ed. C. Olson (New York: Crossroad, 1985) 29–48; J. Ochshorn, "Ishtar and Her Cult," Olson, *Goddess* 16–28. Obviously, phrasing comments on historical goddess cults in this way has already injected a modern perspective into our interpretation.

4. G. Greene and C. Kahn, "Feminist Scholarship and the Social Construction of Woman," *Making a Difference: Feminist Literary Criticism,* ed. G. Greene and C. Kahn (New York: Methuen, 1985) 18.

5. Jonathan Culler, *The Pursuit of Signs: Semiotics, Literature, Deconstruction* (Ithaca: Cornell Univ., 1981) 3–17.

6. M. Bal, *Lethal Love: Feminist Literary Readings of Biblical Love Stories* (Bloomington: Indiana Univ., 1987) 132.

7. R. Jacobsen, "Closing Statement: Linguistics and Poetics," *Style in Language,* ed. T.A. Sebeok (Cambridge, MA: M.I.T., 1960) 350–77; T. Hawkes, *Structuralism and Semiotics* (Berkeley: Univ. of California, 1977) 76–87.

8. Inscriptions from Ramesses II claimed that he won the battle of Kadesh against the Hittites. He lied: at the very least, it must be considered a draw, if not an actual Hittite victory. See below.

9. For a discussion of the use of comparative ethnographic data, see R.R. Wilson, *Genealogy and History in the Biblical World* (New Haven: Yale Univ. Press, 1977).

10. T.F. Carney, *The Shape of the Past: Models and Antiquity* (Lawrence, KS: Corondao, 1975) 149; C. Meyers, *Discovering Eve: Ancient Israelite Women in Context* (New York: Oxford Univ. Press, 1988) 139–57.

11. M.T. Whyte, *The Status of Women in Preindustrial Societies* (Princeton: Princeton Univ., 1978) 170; for an assessment of how women's class affiliation is derived from the men to whom they are attached, see G. Lerner, *The Creation of Patriarchy* (New York: Oxford Univ. Press, 1986) 9.

12. Whyte, *Status* 13–26.

13. Whyte, *Status* 167–84.

14. Woman, *Culture & Society,* ed. M.Z. Rosaldo and L. Lamphere (Stanford, CA: Stanford Univ., 1974) 189–206.

15. Sanday, "Female Status" 198–200.

16. Sanday, "Female Status" 203–206.

17. J. Hackett, "Can a Sexist Model Liberate Us? Ancient Near Eastern 'Fertility' Goddesses," *JFSR* forthcoming. For an analysis of the different roles filled by "fertility" deities, see J. Ochshorn, *The Female Experience and the Nature of the Divine* (Bloomington: Indiana Univ. Press, 1981).

18. Göttner-Abendroth, *Göttin* 118.

19. Göttner-Abendroth, *Göttin* 12–16.

20. W.W. Hallo, "Women of Sumer," *The Legacy of Sumer, BibMesop* 4, ed. D. Schmandt-Besserat (Malibu, CA: Undena, 1976) 29.

21. E.A. Speiser, tr., "The Legend of Sargon," *Ancient Near Eastern Texts Relating to the Old Testament,* 3rd. ed. with Supplement, ed. J.B. Pritchard (Princeton: Princeton Univ. Press, 1969=ANET) 119.

22. For a fuller portrait of the character of Inanna, see my study, "The Deceptive Goddess in Ancient Near Eastern Myth: Inanna and Inaraš," *Semeia* 42 (1988) 87–93.

23. W.W. Hallo and J.J.A. Van Dijk, *The Exaltation of Inanna, YNER* 3 (New Haven: Yale Univ. Press, 1968) 1–11. *contra* J. Ochshorn, "Mothers and Daughters in Ancient Near Eastern Literature," *The Lost Tradition: Mothers and Daughters in Literature* (ed. C.N. Davidson and E.M. Broner; New York: Frederick Ungar, 1980) 7; Enheduanna writes in Sumerian, not Akkadian.

24. Hallo and Van Dijk, *Exaltation* 33.

25. Hallo and Van Dijk, *Exaltation* 31–32.

26. Hallo and Van Dijk, *Exaltation* 23.

27. Hallo and Van Dijk, *Exaltation* 27.

28. For an English introduction to the materials from Mari, see *BA* 47 (1984), which is devoted to this topic.

29. G. Dossin, *Archives royales de Mari, X: La correspondence féminine* (Paris: Département des Antiquités Orientales, Textes cunéiformes, XXXI, Musée du Louvre, 1967) = ARM X; W.H. Ph. Römer, *Frauenbriefe über Religion, Politik und Privatleben in Mari: Untersuchungen zu. G. Dossin, Archives Royales de Mari X* (Paris 1967), *AOAT* 12 (Neukirchen-Vluyn, 1971); B.F. Batto, *Studies on Women at Mari* (Baltimore: Johns Hopkins Univ., 1974); P. Artzi and A. Malamat, "The Correspondence of Šibtu, Queen of Mari in ARM X," *Or,* n.s., 40 (1971) 75–89; J.M. Sasson, "Biographical Notices on Some Royal Ladies from Mari," *JCS* 25 (1973) 59–78.

30. Artzi and Malamat, "Correspondence" 81.

31. Artzi and Malamat, "Correspondence" 78–79.

32. Batto, *Studies* 27–28.

33. L. Lamphere, "Strategies, Cooperation, and Conflict Among Women in Domestic Groups," *Women, Culture, & Society* 97–112.

34. Batto, *Studies* 37–42, 131; Sasson, "Notices" 63–67.

35. Batto, *Studies* 42–48; Sasson, "Notices" 68–72.

36. Sasson, "Notices" 68.

37. Batto, *Studies* 79–139. Many of the women found in the service of the deities were elites, judging by their genealogical ties; where relationships to males are not mentioned it is difficult to decide whether or not lower-class women were involved in cult and religion in anything other than menial capacities.

38. Batto, *Studies* 128–29; Römer, *Frauenbriefe* 31.

39. Batto, *Studies* 131.

40. For Ḫattušili's version of the truth, see "The Apology of Ḫattušili III" in E.H. Sturtevant and G. Bechtel, *A Hittite Chrestomathy* (Philadelphia: Univ. of Penn. Press, 1935) 65–83. For a fuller discussion of Puduḫepa's career, see my "Queenly Proverb Performance: The Prayer of Puduḫepa (KUB XXI, 27)," *The Listening Heart: Essays in Wisdom and the Psalms in honor of Roland E. Murphy, O.Carm.*, ed. K.G. Hoglund, E.F. Huwiler, J.T. Glass, and R.W. Lee (Sheffield, U.K.: JSOT Press, 1987; JSOT Supp 58) 95–126, and H. Otten, *Puduḫepa: Eine hethitische Königin in ihren Textzeugnissen* (Mainz: Franz Steiner, 1975).

41. A.L. Oppenheim, *The Interpretations of Dreams in the Ancient Near East: With a Translation of an Assyrian Dream-Book* (Philadelphia: American Philosophical Society, 1956=*Trans. Amer. Philosophical Soc.* 46/3) 254–55.

42. M. Darga, "Puduhepa: An Anatolian Queen of the Thirteenth Century B.C.," *Mansel'e Armagan: Mélanges Mansel=Festschrift Arif Müfid Mansel* (Ankara: Turk Tarih Kurumu Basimevi, 1974) 2:944–45; I. Seibert, *Woman in Ancient Near East,* rev. G. Shepperson (Leipzig: Edition Leipzig, 1974) 47–49.

43. S.R. Bin-Nun, *The Tawananna in the Hittite Kingdom* (Texte der Hethiter 5; Heidelberg: Carl Winter, 1975) 193. For a picture of Puduḫepa's seal, see E. Akurgal, *The Art of the Hittites* (New York: Harry Abrams, 1962).

44. A. Goetze, "Prayer of Pudu-hepas to the Sun-goddess of Arinna and her Circle," *ANET* 393. KUB=*Keilschriften aus Boghazöi*, I–XX V (Berlin, 1921–24).

45. For Hebat's association with the biblical "Eve" (Ḥawwat), see V. Haas, *Hethitische Berggötter und Hurritische Steindämonen: Riten, Kulte und Mythen* (Kulturgeschichte der antiken Welt 10; Mainz: Philipp von Zabern, 1982) 30.

46. Sturtevant and Bechtel, *Chrestomathy* 79.

47. It should be noted, however, that elsewhere it is the Weather-god who commissions the king, and that the Sun-goddess of Arinna is absent from foreign treaties, but see discussion of Puduḫepa's seal by Egyptian scribes, below. Bin-Nun, *Tawananna* 203–204.

48. Gen 4:1; 21:1; 25:21; 29:31; Ruth 4:13; 1 Sam 1:19–20, 27; 1 Sam 2:1–10; Luke 1.

49. O.R. Gurney, *Some Aspects of Hittite Religion* (Oxford: Oxford Univ. Press, 1976) 44–45.

50. Gurney, *Aspects* 44; D.H. Englehard, "Hittite Magical Practices: An Analysis" (Ph.D. dissertation, Brandeis Univ., 1970) 13.

51. Bin-Nun, *Tawananna* 120–40.

52. Gurney, *Aspects* 45, n. 2. Designated as MI.ŠU.GI are Annanna Ḥebattarakki, Kueša, Malli, Mallidunna, Šilalluhi, Šušumanniga, and Tunnawiya; Allaiduraḫi, Alli, Anniwiyani, Maštikka, and Paškuwatti are referred to by the variant SAL.ŠU.GI.

53. Englehard, "Practices" 23; Sturtevant and Bechtel, *Chrestomathy* 107.

54. Englehard, "Practices" 6–24.

55. Cited in Englehard, "Practices" 11; VBoT=*Verstreute Boghazköi-Texte* (Marburg, 1930).

56. Englehard, "Practices" 72.

57. Englehard, "Practices" 74.

58. Englehard, "Practices" 7.

59. D.D. Luckenbill, "Hittite Treaties and Letters," *AJSL* 37 (1921) 194. KBo=*Keilschrifttexte aus Boghazköi,* Hefte 1–6 (Leipzig, 1916–23), Hefte 7–17 (Berlin, 1954-).

60. Luckenbill, "Treaties" 194.

61. J. Garstang, "The Sun-Goddess of Arinna," *Annals of Archaeology and Anthropology* 6 (1914) 109.

62. Slave-women do appear as literary "types" in various biblical and extrabiblical narratives and instructions. A further analysis of the literary use to which they are put will appear in *Holy Torch of Heaven: Goddesses, Queens and Ordinary Women in the Ancient Near East,* in progress.

63. The research presented here is an excerpt from my forthcoming book, *Holy Torch of Heaven: Goddesses, Queens and Ordinary Women in the Ancient Near East.* The study was made possible by a sabbatical grant from Andover Newton Theological School spent as a Visiting Research Scholar in the Near Eastern and Jewish Studies Department of Brandeis University. I wish to thank Dorothy Moore, Deborah Vickers, Gerry Brague, Cara Davis, and Connie Schütz for their technical assistance in the preparation of this manuscript.

The Queen Mother and the Cult in Ancient Israel

SUSAN ACKERMAN

I

In a 1991 issue of the *JBL,* Z. Ben-Barak published an article on the status and rights of the *gĕbîrâ,* or queen mother, in ancient Israel.[1] In it Ben-Barak argued that the *gĕbîrâ* was not an official functionary within the Israelite or Judean monarchy; that is, the *gĕbîrâ* did not lay claim to privilege in either the northern or southern court by virtue of an institutionalized position. To be sure, Ben-Barak noted that there were *gĕbîrôt* in the Hebrew Bible who did rise to places of prominence and influence during their sons' reigns, but she suggested that this was effected only by a few authoritative and powerful women through the force of their own personalities. Such authoritative and powerful women included in particular a queen mother who exerted herself in the matter of succession upon the death of her husband, the king, typically by promoting a younger son as heir to the throne in defiance of the generally acknowledged claim of the firstborn (or of the oldest surviving son if the eldest had died or had become unable to rule). Bathsheba, in advocating Solomon's claim to kingship over that of Adonijah, is the paradigmatic exemplar of the *gĕbîrâ* who schemed for succession on behalf of her younger son; elsewhere in the Hebrew Bible Ben-Barak cites Maʿacah, the queen mother of Abijam/Abijah[2] (a younger son according to 2 Chr 11:18–23); Hamutal, the queen mother of Jehoahaz (the younger brother of Jehoiakim according to the date formulas found in 2 Kgs 23:31, 36); and Nehushta, the queen mother of Jehoiachin (the younger brother of Zedekiah according to 2 Chr 36:9–11, but cf. 2 Kgs 24:17, where Jehoiachin is identified as Zedekiah's nephew). Further afield, Ben-Barak notes examples of the same phenomenon from Ugarit, from the Hittite empire, from Assyria, from Yʾdy (Yaʾdiyaʾ?) Śamʾal, from Babylon, and from Persia. Ben-Barak stresses that in all these examples there was no official role for the queen mother in the standard succession to the throne. It was only the ambitious *gĕbîrôt,* those who craved the highest office in the land for their sons, who used their influence to determine their husbands' heirs.

In advancing this thesis that the *gĕbîrâ* in the Hebrew Bible had no official position, Ben-Barak is arguing against, albeit not explicitly, another fairly recent article on the queen mother, this one published by N.-E.A. Andreasen in *CBQ*.[3] In that article, Andreasen quickly rejects the argument that the queen mother had no institutionalized status. He writes instead that, "it soon becomes obvious from the text that the queen mother was not merely treated with deference by the monarch, but that she held a significant official position superseded only by that of the king himself."[4] Andreasen describes this official position as that of "lady counsellor," with counsel being sought especially in regard to the royal succession and also, at least in the case of Bathsheba, in matters judicial and in mediations between political factions (1 Kgs 2:13–25). Andreasen, along with many other commentators, sees the roots of this institutionalized role for the queen mother in Hittite culture, where the queen mother or *tawananna* had significant responsibilities within the social and political affairs of the king's court.[5]

The Hittite *tawananna,* moreover, had responsibilities within the cultic life of Hittite society. Indeed, S.R. Bin-Nun, in her Oxford Ph.D. dissertation, the most recent and up-to-date study available on the *tawananna,* has argued that in the earliest periods of the Hittite Old Kingdom (and in pre-Hittite Anatolia as well), the title *tawananna* referred exclusively to a religious functionary. Only secondarily, she suggests, in the period of the Hittite empire, does the *tawananna* assume responsibilities within Hittite social, political, and economic spheres. Yet even then her cultic obligations persist.[6] Despite, however, this primacy of religious function in the duties of the Hittite queen mother, Andreasen argues that when the office was borrowed into Israel, the cultic role of the *gĕbîrâ* was eliminated.[7] On this point, then, Andreasen is in agreement with Ben-Barak, as both of them suggest that there was no official position for the queen mother within institutionalized Israelite religion.

In fact, as Andreasen points out, only a few scholars have advanced arguments supporting an official role for the queen mother in the cult. S. Terrien in 1970 proposed that the queen mother was one element in a constellation of religious beliefs and practices—the Jerusalem temple as the *omphalos mundi,* serpent worship, chthonian divination, a solar cult, and male prostitution involving homosexual and bisexual intercourse—all of which played a role "in the mystical or sacramental aspect of the principle of monarchic succession."[8] But Terrien finds today little support among historians of Israelite religion for his reconstructions: the notion of cult prostitution in Israel and throughout the ancient Near East, whether male or female, has been increasingly discredited, for example,[9] and fully developed solar worship such as Terrien describes seems to have come to Israelite religion only relatively late and from the east, in the eighth and seventh centuries, that is, through increasing Aramean and even Assyrian influence.[10] Also garnering only minimal scholarly support today is the 1963 proposal of G.W. Ahlström that the cultic responsibility of the queen mother in ancient Israelite religion was to play the role of the bride in the *hieros gamos*.[11] Currently, however, few historians of religion endorse any reconstruction involving a *hieros gamos* in Israel, and, to my knowledge, none among those who do allow for an Israelite sacred marriage would agree with Ahlström's contention that the queen mother (and not the queen or some priestess) functioned as the ritual consort.[12]

Still, despite the failure of Terrien and Ahlström to articulate a convincing role for the queen mother in Israelite religion and also despite the conclusions of Ben-Barak and

Andreasen that the *gĕbîrâ* had no official cultic function, I believe that the issue is far from settled. Moreover, I propose that the time is ripe to consider the question of the queen mother and the cult anew. The time is ripe because our understanding of what comprised cult in ancient Israel has changed considerably in the past fifteen years. Since the late 1970s, that is, we have seen multiple attempts to redefine the nature of Israelite religion both in the light of new archaeological discoveries and also in the light of more nuanced exegeses of the biblical text.[13] What we have learned from these numerous re-definitions is that the ancient cult allowed a far greater latitude in religious beliefs and practices than the exilic and postexilic editors of the biblical text would admit. We have thus come to doubt the rather homogeneous picture presented by the biblical writers of Israelite religion. Instead, we have increasingly broadened our parameters in describing what the Israelite cult encompassed. In this paper I propose to seek amid these broadened parameters evidence suggesting that the queen mother did play some role in Israelite religion.

To be sure, the data that will guide this exploration are sparse, since the male-dominated culture that gave us the Bible, still our primary piece of evidence concerning the Israelite cult, tended not to include significant information concerning women's religious activities; those female acts of devotion that are described, moreover, are more often than not denigrated (women's worship of the Queen of Heaven in Jeremiah 7 and 44, for example, or their wailing over Tammuz in Ezekiel 8). Comparative evidence from elsewhere in the ancient Near East, while essential, cannot truly compensate for this deficit in the biblical text, as the comparative material also typically stems from patriarchal societies that overlooked or devalued women's cult activities. From the start, then, I must admit that the reconstruction offered here is necessarily speculative. Still, while caution is advisable, I do hope to demonstrate that the queen mother did have an official responsibility in Israelite religion: it was to devote herself to the cult of the mother goddess Asherah within the king's court. I will also suggest that this cultic role was primary among other obligations required of the *gĕbîrâ*. Ultimately I conclude, with Andreasen and against Ben-Barak, that the queen mother did have sociopolitical responsibilities in ancient Israel, particularly with regard to succession upon the old king's death. But, unlike Andreasen, I believe that these sociopolitical functions cannot be divorced from a cultic role. In fact, I will propose that the queen mother's devotions to Asherah stand behind and are fundamental to the role accorded her in matters of succession.

II

The biblical text that most explicitly links the *gĕbîrâ* with a cultic activity of any sort is 1 Kgs 15:13 (2 Chr 15:16), in which Maʿacah, the queen mother of Asa,[14] is removed as *gĕbîrâ*[15] because she made a *mipleset lāʾăšērâ*,[16] to be translated either "an abominable image for Asherah [the goddess]" or "an abominable image of the asherah [the stylized tree that symbolized the goddess in the cult]."[17] The former translation, "an abominable image for Asherah [the goddess]," is in my mind preferable: the definite article prefixed to ʾăšērâ need not preclude our understanding of ʾăšērâ as a proper name since it is easily explained as appellative, as elsewhere in Deuteronomistic prose (Judg 2:11, 13; 3:7; 10:6). Certainly the Chronicler understood ʾăšērâ in this passage to be a proper name since he transposed *mipleset* and ʾăšērâ (*lāʾăšērâ mipleset*), leaving us no option but to translate "she made for Asherah [the goddess] an abominable image."[18] Moreover, the alternate translation of the Kings text, "she made an abominable image of the asherah [the stylized cult symbol]" borders on the nonsensical: What does it mean, after all, to make an image of an image? In fact, elsewhere in Deuteronomistic prose when *ʾăšērâ*, the image, is referred to, the noun *ʾăšērâ* stands alone without *mipleṣet* or similar modifier:[19] *wayaʿaś ʾahʾāb ʾet-hāʾăšērâ*, "and Ahab made the asherah" (1 Kgs 16:33), for example (note the similar use of *ʿśh*, "to make," in both this passage and 1 Kgs 15:13 while contrasting the treatment of *ʾăšērâ* as object). Maʿacah, the queen mother, we conclude, is described in 1 Kgs 15:13 as worshiping the goddess Asherah by making a cult statue for her.[20]

It has been suggested that Maʿacah's worship of Asherah was an alien element introduced by her into the Judean cult.[21] The primary piece of evidence supporting this claim is Maʿacah's presumed foreign ancestry: elsewhere in the Hebrew Bible the personal name *maʿăkâ* does appear as the name of a non-Israelite (Maʿacah, the daughter of King Talmai of Geshur and mother of Absalom; 2 Sam 3:3 and 1 Chr 3:2); this Maʿacah of Geshur, moreover, is apparently the grandmother of the Maʿacah of 1 Kgs 15:13, who is identified in 1 Kgs 15:2 and 2 Chr 11:20–22 as the daughter of Absalom. Maʿacah's foreign heritage, however, need not predicate the conclusion that the Asherah cult Maʿacah promoted was foreign; nor does the fact that King Asa regarded Maʿacah's worship as heterodox necessarily imply such. In fact, certain biblical and archaeological evidence suggests that Asa's opinion was not normative in Judah. A case can instead be made that Asherah worship was customary among the populace. S.M. Olyan has even argued that the worship of Asherah may have been part of the state cult; Asherah may have been worshiped, that is, along with Yahweh in official Judahite religion.[22] Note in this regard that Maʿacah's image devoted to Asherah stood in all likelihood in Yahweh's Temple in Jerusalem; the Jerusalem Temple is at least the logical place for a member of the royal family to erect a cult statue, first, for reasons of proximity, as Temple and palace stood side by side in Jerusalem, and, second, because the Temple essentially functioned as the private chapel for the monarch.

Moreover, we would be wrong were we to assume that Maʿacah's worship of Asherah in Yahweh's Temple was an anomaly, eliminated when Asa destroyed the cult statue that Maʿacah had made. Rather, by all indications, Maʿacah's cult statue of Asherah was replaced in the Jerusalem Temple after Asa's reforms. Such is at least suggested by 2 Kgs 18:4, in which Hezekiah removes an *ʾăšērâ* from Jerusalem as part of his own reforms; this *ʾăšērâ*, like Maʿacah's and for the same reasons, presumably stood in Yahweh's Temple. The biblical text is indeed explicit that a third *ʾăšērâ*, the one that replaced the statue Hezekiah destroyed, stood in the Jerusalem Temple. Thus 2 Kgs 21:7 describes how Manasseh erected an *ʾăšērâ* in Yahweh's Temple in Jerusalem. This *ʾăšērâ* stood there until destroyed by yet another reformer, Josiah (2 Kgs 23:6). Josiah also removed from the Jerusalem Temple the vessels made for Asherah as part of her sacrificial cult (2 Kgs 23:4) and tore down the structures within the Temple compound where women wove garments to be draped as clothing over Asherah's cult statue (2 Kgs 23:7).

These multiple texts suggest that it was the norm in the southern kingdom in the ninth century, the eighth century, and the seventh century to worship both Yahweh and Asherah in the state temple in Jerusalem. The zeal of the reformer kings, Asa, Hezekiah, and Josiah, to remove the Asherah cult was the exception. This conclusion is supported by archaeological evidence, namely by the much-discussed eighth-century inscription from Khirbet el-Qôm, some ten kilometers east-southeast of Lachish.[23] While this inscription has proven difficult to read, commentators do agree that paired in it we have from a southern provenance the cult of Yahweh and some allusion to the cult of Asherah.[24] The most satisfying attempt at translation is P.D. Miller's:

> *brk ʾryhw lyhwh*
> *wmṣryh lʾšrth hwšʿ lh*

> Blessed is Uriyahu by Yahweh;
> Yea from his adversaries by his asherah he has saved him.[25]

Despite Asa's censure, then, we cannot conclude that the *gĕbîrâ* Maʿacah introduced a foreign cult into the Jerusalem court. Nor, I would argue, should Jezebel, another queen mother who is often regarded by commentators as introducing an alien cult of Asherah into Israel, be so accused. Instead, I suggest that she, like Maʿacah, worshiped Asherah while *gĕbîrâ* as part of the state cult of the northern kingdom.

Here, however, the data are somewhat ambiguous, first because we tend to think of Jezebel only as queen, the wife of Ahab, rather than assigning to her the title of queen mother. But in fact in 2 Kgs 10:13 she is labeled *gĕbîrâ* after Ahab's death by relatives of King Ahaziah of Judah. At a minimum, then, Jezebel filled the role of *gĕbîrâ* in the minds of the editors who included 2 Kgs 10:13 in the biblical text. If, moreover, 2 Kgs 10:13 is historically reliable, she was considered *gĕbîrâ* by members of the southern royal family.

But whether Jezebel as queen mother devoted herself to the cult of Asherah as did Maʿacah is a second ambiguity. Indeed, scholars disagree on whether Jezebel, even when queen, worshiped Asherah in addition to her well-attested allegiance to Baal. The crux of the matter is 1 Kgs 18:19, where Elijah summons to his contest on Mount Carmel the "four hundred and fifty prophets of Baal and the four hundred prophets of Asherah who eat at Jezebel's table." This text seemingly does associate Jezebel with the cult of Asherah; however, subsequent to this passage the four hundred prophets of Asherah do not again appear, at least in the Masoretic tradition. They do appear in v. 22 of the LXX, but as several recent commentators have noted, the phrase *hoi prophētai tou alsous*[26] is marked by an asterisk in Origen's *Hexapla*, indicating a secondary addition in the Greek.[27]

But this evidence simply means that *nĕbîʾê hāʾăšērâ* in 1 Kgs 18:19 is most probably a gloss; it need not mean that Queen Jezebel did not worship the goddess Asherah. Certainly there were opportunities in Samaria for her to do so. As we have already noted, 1 Kgs 16:33 reports that Ahab erected an *ʾăšērâ* in Samaria. Moreover, since 1 Kgs 16:33 occurs at the beginning of the long cycle of narratives concerning Ahab, we can presume that he erected the *ʾăšērâ* early in his reign. There was, that is, an Asherah cult of some sort in Samaria during the bulk of Ahab's monarchy, and the king participated in it. Jezebel, as Ahab's wife, may well have also participated in it as part of her obligations of marriage.

The inscriptional evidence from Kuntillet ʿAjrûd in the eastern Sinai, fifty kilometers south of Kadesh Barnea, also locates a cult of Asherah contemporaneous with Ahab's reign (the inscriptions are ninth or eighth century) in Samaria.[28] An Asherah cult in the northern capital is at least strongly implied by the inclusion of the geographical name Samaria in one of the inscriptions found on the site: *brkt ʾtkm lyhwh šmrn wlʾšrth,* "I bless you by Yahweh of Samaria and by his Asherah/asherah."[29] This inscription, so like the Khirbet el-Qôm material, has also suggested to many that at least among certain religious circles in Samaria the cult of Yahweh and the cult of Asherah were paired; this pairing is also suggested by two other inscriptions found at Kuntillet ʿAjrûd, *lyhwh htmn wlʾšrth,* "by Yahweh of the South and by his Asherah/asherah," and *brktk lyhwh tmn wlʾšrth ybrk wyšmrk wyhy ʿm ʾdny,* "I bless you by Yahweh of the South and by his Asherah/asherah. May he bless and keep you and may he be with my lord."[30]

Again, moreover, Olyan has argued that this pairing of Yahweh and Asherah at Kuntillet ʿAjrûd and in Samaria should not be regarded as "syncretistic" or "heterodox" within Israelite religion; he proposes instead that the worship of Asherah was a part of the normative religion of the northern kingdom.[31] Olyan notes several data in support of this conclusion: first, that Jehu in his purge of Samaria is not described as destroying the *ʾăšērâ* that Ahab had previously erected; indeed, according to 2 Kgs 13:6, this *ʾăšērâ* remained standing in Samaria after Jehu's death. Since Jehu's targets in his reform were non-Yahwistic elements in the cult, the fact that the *ʾăšērâ* was allowed to survive suggests it was perceived as appropriate within official Yahwism.[32] That there was an *ʾăšērâ* in the state temple devoted to Yahweh at Bethel according to 2 Kgs 23:15 likewise suggests the *ʾăšērâ* was considered legitimate in the Yahwism of the northern monarchy.[33] Olyan also suggests that despite the virulent attacks on non-Yahwistic cult elements in the northern prophet Hosea, the cult of Asherah is never condemned,[34] implying that the prophet had no objections to an Asherah cult as part of the official religion of the north. Olyan argues that Amos's silence with regard to Asherah worship is equally of significance.[35] He concludes, "Based only on an examination of the biblical sources, we argue that the asherah was a legitimate part of the cult of Yahweh . . . in the north . . . in state religion and in popular religion."[36]

If Olyan is correct that the biblical evidence does suggest that the cult of Asherah was paired with the cult of Yahweh in the state religion of the northern kingdom, and if in particular the cults of Asherah and Yahweh were paired in Ahab's Samaria, as indicated by the Kuntillet ʿAjrûd material in addition to the biblical text, then Jezebel may well have participated in the cult of Asherah as part of her obligations to state Yahwism. Note here that despite the Deuteronomistic condemnations of Ahab's state cult as syncretistic or even non-Yahwistic because it incorporated Jezebel's worship of Baal, the state religion of Ahab's monarchy in fact remained Yahwism: the sons of Jezebel and Ahab, Ahaziah and Jehoram, both bore Yahwistic names (*ʾăḥazyāhû,* "Yahweh has grasped"; *yĕhôrām,* "Yahweh is exalted"), as did their daughter,[37] Athaliah (*ʿătalyāh,* "Yahweh is great"),[38] Athaliah's son Ahaziah, her daughter Jehosheba (*jĕhôšebaʿ,* "Yahweh is abundance"),[39] and her grandson Joash (*yôʾāš,* "Yahweh has given").

There is every possibility, in short, that Jezebel participated in an Asherah cult during her tenure as Ahab's queen both as part of her marital responsibilities and as part of her obligations of state. Moreover, although we can only speculate, I would argue that it is not unlikely that Jezebel continued to participate in an Asherah cult after Ahab's death when she assumed the role of queen mother. To be sure, the only narrative in Kings that describes the widowed Jezebel is the story of her death in 2 Kings 9. But it may be significant for our purposes that Jezebel is lodged during that scene in her royal residence in

Jezreel (1 Kgs 18:45–46) and not in Samaria. She is distanced, that is, from the Baal temple in Samaria most typically associated with her religious allegiances.[40] Her cultic attentions in Jezreel thus may have been focused on the state religion of the northern kingdom that paired the cult of Yahweh and the cult of Asherah. It is at least possible, we conclude, that Jezebel as *gĕbîrâ* participated in the worship of Asherah.

It is also possible that one of the most memorable *gĕbîrôt* described in the Hebrew Bible, Athaliah, the daughter of Jezebel and Ahab, participated in the cult of Asherah. Athaliah was given by her parents to Jehoram, the king of Judah, as wife, presumably as part of a treaty between the northern and southern kingdoms (2 Kgs 8:18). She became *gĕbîrâ* to their son Ahaziah after Jehoram was killed in battle against the Edomites (2 Kgs 8:20–24), but this arrangement was short-lived since Ahaziah was killed while on a visit to Jezreel as part of Jehu's bloody coup (2 Kgs 9:27–28). Athaliah then assumed the throne of Judah for six years until she was deposed as part of a popular uprising led by the high priest Jehoiada (2 Kgs 11:1–20).

Part of Jehoiada's popular uprising involved destroying the Baal temple that was in Jerusalem[41] and killing its priesthood. Although the text does not specify that it was in fact Athaliah who was responsible for having this temple built, commentators unanimously assign it to her reign and are also unanimous in suggesting that Athaliah promoted the Baal cult in Judah under the influence of Jezebel and her patronage of the Baal cult in the north. If this is indeed the case, then we might as well expect that Athaliah allied herself with other cults favored by her mother. If, moreover, we have been correct in our assumptions above that Jezebel both as queen and queen mother participated in the cult of Asherah, we can suggest that Athaliah would have done the same. Indeed, we would expect as much, given our earlier conclusion that devotion to Asherah was a normative aspect of Yahwistic religion in the south. Note in this regard that, as in the case of Jezebel, the Yahwistic names of Athaliah's descendants prove that she participated as required in the state cult.

One final queen mother may have been a participant in the cult of Asherah: this is Nehushta, the queen mother of Jehoiachin (2 Kgs 24:8). The primary piece of evidence here is the *gĕbîrâ*'s name; *nĕḥuštāʾ* derives most probably from the root *nāḥāš*, "serpent."[42] (The alternative, which would derive *nĕḥuštāʾ* from *nĕḥōšet*, "bronze," is much less likely,[43] for while human names taken from the animal kingdom are common in the Semitic world for both males and females, male names based on metals are rare[44] and female names are to my knowledge unattested.) Moreover, as the "serpent lady," the *gĕbîrâ* Nehushta bears, I would suggest, an epithet of Asherah, whose associations with snakes are attested in multiple sources. From Egypt comes a Nineteenth Dynasty plaque showing a goddess, identified as "Qudšu, the beloved of Ptah," astride a lion and holding serpents in both hands;[45] a similar stele reads "Qudšu, lady of the sky and mistress of all the gods" and shows a goddess standing astride a lion holding a serpent in her left hand.[46] These data suggest that the lion-straddling, snake-bearing goddess depicted on the plaque from the Winchester College collection published by I.E.S. Edwards, although identified as a composite deity Qudšu-Aštart-Anat, is Qudšu.[47] Qudšu, "the holy one," is well known from Ugaritic sources as a standard epithet of Asherah. Numerous other Egyptian and some Canaanite representations of a snake-bearing goddess astride a lion, while uninscribed, presumably also depict Qudšu/Asherah;[48] even without the inscribed *comparanda*, indeed, we would suggest this because of Asherah's well-known associations with lions[49] (at Ugarit the children of Asherah are called her "pride of lions," *ṣbrt ary* [*CTA* 3.5.45; 4.1.9; 4.2.25–26]; F.M. Cross has argued that Asherah herself is called *labiʔtu*, "lion lady";[50] the naked goddess on the bottom register of the tenth-century Taʕanach cult stand who grasps lions with her right hand and her left is surely to be taken as Asherah).[51]

Inscriptional evidence also demonstrates Asherah's association with serpents. In the proto-Sinaitic texts she is called *dt bṭn*, "Lady of the Serpent";[52] Cross has interpreted her standard epithet at Ugarit, *rbt atrt ym*, similarly, translating "the Lady who treads on the Sea (-serpent)."[53] If, moreover, Cross is correct in identifying Phoenician/Punic *tnt* as Asherah,[54] and if he is further correct that *tnt*, which he vocalizes *tannit*, means "serpent" (<*tannīn*), this too would demonstrate Asherah's association with serpents.[55] Finally, we note *KAI* 89, a Punic devotional tablet on which Asherah bears the epithet *ḥwt*.[56] It is possible that *ḥwt* as an epithet means "serpent," cognate with Old Aramaic *ḥwh* (Sefire I, A, 31), later Aramaic *ḥiwâ*, *ḥiwyāʔ*, *ḥewyāʔ*, and Arabic *ḥayya*. If such an etymology is correct, it would surely connect Asherah with snake imagery.[57]

These materials showing the association of Asherah and serpents suggest, as we posited above, that the queen mother Nehushta, "the serpent lady," is like Maʕacah, Jezebel, and Athaliah to be understood as a devotee of Asherah. She shows her allegiance to the goddess through the very name she bears.

III

Of the four queen mothers in the Hebrew Bible whom we have identified as devotees of Asherah, three—Maʕacah, Athaliah, and Nehushta—are queen mothers in the southern kingdom of Judah. Moreover, while the fourth, Jezebel, is a northerner, it is important to realize that it is in the words of southerners that she is labeled *gĕbîrâ* (2 Kgs 10:13). Also significant in this regard is that Jezebel reigns in a court much more characterized by a "southern" style of kingship than by typical "northern" fashion: a court, that is, based on a principle of dynastic succession rather than charismatic leadership, a court that builds itself a royal citadel in Samaria modeled after the Davidic/Solomonic fief in Jerusalem, a court involved in foreign alliances and foreign marriages, a court that persecutes dissenters (Elijah), and a court known for its palace intrigues (the trumped-up charges of the Naboth incident, for example).[58] Furthermore, Jezebel is the only northern queen mother whose name we know. Conversely, we know the names of the queen mothers of all the Judean kings except for Ahaz and Jehoram. To put it another way, of the nineteen queen mothers who are named in the Bible, one comes from the period of the united monarchy (Bathsheba), one is a northerner whose court is more "southern" in style than northern and who is called *gĕbîrâ* by visitors from the south (Jezebel), and the remaining seventeen are *gĕbîrôt* in Judah during the period of the divided monarchy. The names of the seventeen *gĕbîrôt* of Judah, moreover, are routinely preserved for us as part of the Judean royal archives. The names, that is, are included in the formulaic notices that begin the description of the reign of each king of Judah. For kings who reigned before the fall of Samaria, the standard pattern reads, "In the XX year of King PN of Israel, PN began to rule over Judah. He reigned for XX years in Jerusalem; his mother's name was PN, daughter of PN" (1 Kgs 15:1–2, 9–10; 22:41–42; 2 Kgs 8:25–26; 12:1; 14:1–2; 15:1–2, 32–33; 18:1–2; similarly, 1 Kgs 14:21). After the fall of Samaria, the basic pattern remains, although the synchronization with the king of Israel is obviously eliminated (2 Kgs 21:1, 9; 22:1; 23:31, 36; 24:8, 18). We should compare to these texts the archival notices for the kings of the northern kingdom (1 Kgs 14:20; 15:25, 33; 16:8, 15, 23, 29; 22:51; 2 Kgs 3:1; 10:36; 13:1, 10; 14:23; 15:8, 13, 17, 23, 27; 17:1), which in the main parallel their southern counterparts, but fail to name an Israelite queen mother.

These data, as many commentators have noted, suggest that the queen mother figured much more prominently in the royal court in the south than she did in the north. To explain this, I propose to turn to the differing ideologies of kingship found in Israel, on the one hand, and in Judah, on the other. These two contrasting ideologies were initially described by A. Alt in his 1951 article "Das Königtum in den Reichen Israel und Juda."[59]

To be sure, in the forty years since Alt's article first appeared, there have been modifications and refinements of his thesis. Of particular interest to us is the work of F.M. Cross and the description he offers of sacral kingship as one feature in the contrasting ideologies of north and south. Here, in addition to depending on Alt for a theory of north/south dichotomy, Cross also draws profitably on basic descriptions of sacral kingship in Israel provided by the British and Scandanavian "myth and ritual" schools (while prudently ignoring these schools' more controversial conclusions concerning, for example, the annual New Year's festival).[60] Cross's synthesis argues that part of the ideology of Judean but not Israelite kingship involved seeing the Davidic king as the adopted son of Yahweh, the divine father;[61] the pertinent texts, all of which Cross assigns to a Jerusalem provenance, are well known: 2 Sam 7:14a; Pss 2:7; 89:20–38 (Hebrew); 110:1–7; Isa 9:5 (Hebrew). We quote only the adoption formula of Ps 89:27–28, to Cross the "ultimate statement"[62] of the Judean royal ideology:

> He [the king] will cry out to me [Yahweh], "You are my father,
>> My god and the rock of my salvation."
> I surely will make him my first-born,
>> the highest of the kings of the earth.

It is this motif of divine sonship in Judean royal ideology that I believe can provide a clue for understanding the role of the queen mother in the southern monarchy. For if the Judean royal ideology holds that Yahweh is the adopted father of the king, then is it not possible that the adopted mother of the king is understood to be Asherah, given, as we have noted above, that Asherah was seen by many—in both the state and popular cult— as the consort of Yahweh? The language of divine adoption, that is, may imply not only Yahweh, the male god, as surrogate father, but also Asherah, the female consort, as surrogate mother.

If this is so, the implications for the Judean queen mother are enormous. As the human mother of the king, the queen mother could be perceived as the earthly counterpart of Asherah, the king's heavenly mother. The queen mother might even be considered the human representative, even surrogate, of Asherah. Assuming such a correspondence would explain why those queen mothers for whom cultic allegiances are described or hinted at in the Bible are depicted as patronesses of the goddess Asherah. Indeed, according to the logic we have described, it is nothing but appropriate that these women direct their homage to their divine alter-ego. To do so could in fact be construed, within the royal ideology of Judah, as their cultic obligation.

In addition, I would argue that if my hypothesis is correct, we should see the cultic functions undertaken by the Judean queen mothers on behalf of the goddess Asherah as standing in close relationship to the political responsibilities assigned to the *gĕbîrôt* within their sons' courts. As I have already indicated, I do agree with Andreasen, against Ben-Barak, that the queen mother in Judah did have an official position within the palace, and I would further agree with Andreasen's description of that position as "lady counsellor." I would, however, differ with Andreasen by suggesting that one reason the queen mother can fulfill this official role of counselor may stem from the belief that she represents the goddess Asherah within the monarchy. An identification of the queen mother with Asherah, that is, could give to the *gĕbîrâ* power and authority which, like the king's, originate in the world of the divine. Such a divine legitimization would then allow the queen mother to function as the second most powerful figure in the royal court, superseded only by her son, the king. Consider in this regard the issue concerning which the queen mother most often exercises her authority: the matter of the royal succession. Could not the crucial role the *gĕbîrâ* plays in this transition of power be intimately connected to the cultic function I have proposed for the queen mother as devotee of Asherah? More specifically, if the queen mother is considered the human representative of Asherah in the royal court, she should be able to legitimate her son's claim to be the adopted son of Yahweh. Indeed, the queen mother, assuming that she speaks as the goddess and thus as Yahweh's consort, is uniquely qualified to attest to her son's divine adoption. Thus the right to determine the succession would most naturally and properly fall to her.

I conclude, then, that it may be artificial to seek to divorce the political role of the Judean queen mother from a cultic function. I also suggest that it may be artificial to deny the primacy of the queen mother's cultic responsibilities.

NOTES

1. Z. Ben-Barak, "The Status and Right of the *Gĕbîrâ*," *JBL* 110 (1991) 23–34; see also Ben-Barak's earlier article, "The Queen Consort and the Struggle for Succession to the Throne," in *La femme dans le Proche-Orient antique* (Compte rendu de la XXXIIIe Rencontre assyriologique internationale [Paris, 7–10 juillet 1986]; ed. J.-M. Durand; Paris: Recherche sur les Civilisations, 1987) 33–40.

The term *gĕbîrâ/gĕberet* is used fifteen times in the Hebrew Bible. In Gen 16:4, 8, and 9 it means "mistress" (describing Sarah's relationship with Hagar), and this translation is also required in 2 Kgs 5:3; Ps 123:2; Prov 30:23; and Isa 24:2; 45:5,7. In 1 Kgs 1:19 *gĕbîrâ* should be translated "queen," referring to the wife of the Egyptian pharaoh. Elsewhere in Kings, and also in Chronicles and Jeremiah (1 Kgs 15:13; 2 Kgs 10:13; 2 Chr 15:16; Jer 13:18; 29:2), the term means "queen mother."

2. The variant names Abijam and Abijah are most probably the result of textual confusion; see M. Noth, *Die israelitischen Personennamen im Rahmen der gemeinsemitischen Namengebung* (Hildesheim: Georg Olms, 1980) 234 #117.

3. N.-E.A. Andreasen, "The Role of the Queen Mother in Israelite Society," *CBQ* 45 (1983) 179–94.

4. *Ibid.*, 180.

5. G. Molin, "Die Stellung der Gᵉbira im Staate Juda," *TZ* 10 (1954) 161–75; H. Donner, "Art und Herkunft des Amtes der Königinmutter im Alten Testament, in *Festschrift Johannes*

Friedrich zum 65. Geburtstag am 27. August gewidmet (ed. R. von Kienle et al.; Heidelberg: Carl Winter, 1959) 105–45; R. de Vaux, *Ancient Israel: 1, Social Institutions* (New York/Toronto: McGraw-Hill, 1961) 118.

6. S.R. Bin-Nun, *The Tawananna in the Hittite Kingdom* (Heidelberg: Carl Winter; Universitätsverlag, 1975) 34–50, 107–59.

7. Clearly we cannot speak of direct borrowing, given the time gap between the fall of the Hittite empire and the rise of the Israelite monarchy. Still, H. Donner has argued that the political structures of Hittite society survived in first-millennium Syria and Canaan and from there came to influence the united monarchy in Jerusalem. See Donner, "Art and Herkunft," 123–30; also Andreasen, "Queen Mother," 181.

8. S. Terrien, "The Omphalos Myth and Hebrew Religion," *VT* 20 (1970) 315–38; quotation from p. 331.

9. See E.J. Fisher, "Cultic Prostitution in the Ancient Near East? A Reassessment," *BTB* 5 (1976) 225–36; R.A. Oden, "Religious Identity and the Sacred Prostitution Accusation," in *The Bible Without Theology: The Theological Tradition and Alternatives to It* (San Francisco: Harper & Row, 1987) 131–53; J. Westenholz, "Tamar, *Qĕdēša, Qadištu,* and Sacred Prostitution in Mesopotamia," *HTR* 82 (1989) 245–65.

10. See M. Cogan, *Imperialism and Religion: Assyria, Judah, and Israel in the Eighth and Seventh Centuries B.C.E.* (SBLMS 19; Missoula, MT: Scholars Press, 1974) 84–87.

11. G.W. Ahlström, *Aspects of Syncretism in Israelite Religion* (Horae Soederblomianae 5; Lund: Gleerup, 1963) 57–88.

12. See the criticisms of Andreasen, "Queen Mother," 182.

13. While by no means the only attempts at such redefinitions, many of the articles collected in the Cross *Festschrift* (*Ancient Israelite Religion: Essays in Honor of Frank Moore Cross* [ed. P.D. Miller, P.D. Hanson, and S.D. McBride; Philadelphia: Fortress, 1987]), especially those of B. Peckham, M.D. Coogan, J.A. Hackett, P.K. McCarter, N. Avigad, W.G. Deever, J.S. Holladay, and P. Bird, are characteristic of the reevaluations to which I refer.

14. Ma°acah is identified in 1 Kgs 15:2 and in 2 Chr 11:20–22 as the queen mother of her son Abijam/Abijah (see n. 2 above) and in 1 Kgs 15:10 and in 2 Chr 15:16 as the queen mother of her grandson Asa. Ma°acah, that is, continued to function as queen mother even after her son the king had died. This should suggest that the *gĕbîrâ* commanded at a minimum a semi-independent position in the court, one that was not exclusively dependent on her son the king. This anticipates our conclusion below that the queen mother did have an institutionalized position in the ancient Israelite monarchy.

15. The fact that Ma°acah can be deposed (*swr*) as *gĕbîrâ* also, as in n. 14 above, anticipates our conclusion that the queen mother did hold some sort of official position within the court.

16. The noun *miplešet* which occurs only in 1 Kgs 15:13 and in the Chronicles parallel, comes from the verb *plṣ,* "to shudder." Presumably it means "a thing to be shuddered at," "a horrid thing," or, as here, "an abominable image."

17. The biblical tradition is quite emphatic in its understanding of the *°ăšērâ* as a stylized wooden tree. Deut 16:21 speaks of "planting" (*nāta°*) the *°ăšērâ;* elsewhere in the Bible the cult object is "made" (*°āśâ*), "built" (*bānâ*), "stood up" (*°āmad*), or "erected" (*hiṣṣîb*). If destroyed, the *°ăšērâ* is "burned" (*bi°ēr* or *śārap*), "cut down" (*kārat*), "hewn down" (*°gāda°*), "uprooted" (*nātaš*), or "broken" (*šibbēr*). See also below, n. 26.

18. The Greek of 2 Chr 15:16 reads *tē Astartē* for MT *lā°ăšērâ.* The MT is clearly primitive.

19. I understand 2 Kgs 21:7, *pesel hā°ăšērâ,* in the same way I have analyzed 1 Kgs 15:13 and thus would translate "an image of Asherah."

20. In a certain sense, to be sure, to argue about translating "asherah [the cult symbol]" or "Asherah [the goddess]" is to quibble over semantics. Most practitioners of ancient Israelite

religion, evidence suggests, would interpret the cult object asherah as something that is a symbol of the goddess and is in effect synonymous with her. One has only to compare the ancient Israelite understanding of Yahweh's primary symbol in the league cult and in the Jerusalem Temple, the ark, to see how close the relationship was in Israelite religion between cult object and deity. Num 10:35–36, the so-called Song of the Ark, illustrates perfectly the simultaneity of symbol and god in Israelite imagination: "whenever *the ark* set out, Moses said, 'Arise, *O Yahweh*'"; similarly, "when *it* [the ark] rested, he [Moses] said, 'Return, *O Yahweh*.'" We would expect that the *ʾăšērâ*, the cult symbol, and Asherah, the goddess, would likewise have been understood by the ancient Israelites as one and the same.

21. See Ahlström, *Aspects of Syncretism*, 59, 61, who cites also W.F. Albright, *Archaeology and the Religion of Israel* (2d ed.; Baltimore: Johns Hopkins University Press, 1946) 157–59; and S. Yeivin, "Social, Religious, and Cultural Trends in Judaism under the Davidic Dynasty," *VT* 3 (1953) 162–64. See too the remarks of P.R. Ackroyd, "Goddesses, Women, and Jezebel," in *Images of Women in Antiquity* (ed. A. Cameron and A. Kuhrt; London/Canberra: Croom Helm, 1983) 255, although note that Ackroyd himself does not agree with the conclusion of Ahlström, Albright, and Yeivin.

22. S.M. Olyan, *Asherah and the Cult of Yahweh in Israel* (SBLMS 34; Atlanta: Scholars Press, 1988) 9.

23. The *editio princeps* was by W.G. Dever, "Iron Age Epigraphic Material from the Area of Khirbet el-Kôm," *HUCA* 40/41 (1969–70) 158–89. The inscription was restudied by A. Lemaire, "Les inscriptions de Khirbet el-Qôm et l'Ashérah de Yhwh," *RB* 84 (1977) 597–608; idem, "Date et origine des inscriptiones hébraïques et pheniciennes de Kuntillet ʿAjrud," *Studi epigraphie e linguistici* 1 (1984) 131–43; idem, "Who or What was Yahweh's Asherah?" *BARev* 10/6 (1984) 42–51. In his reassessment Lemaire proposed reading in the second and third lines of the text a reference to Asherah, a reading Dever now accepts; see Dever, "Asherah, Consort of Yahweh? New Evidence from Kuntillet ʿAjrûd," *BASOR* 255 (1985) 22; less completely, idem, "Recent Archaeological Confirmation of the Cult of Asherah in Ancient Israel," *Hebrew Studies* 23 (1982) 40; idem, "Material Remains and the Cult in Ancient Israel: An Essay in Archaeological Systematics," in *The Word of the Lord Shall Go Forth: Essays in Honor of David Noel Freedman in Celebration of his Sixtieth Birthday* (ed. C.L. Meyers and M. O'Connor; Winona Lake, IN: Eisenbrauns, 1983) 570, 58 n. 17. Other studies of the el-Qôm material include J.M. Hadley, "The Khirbet el-Qom Inscription *VT* 37 (1987) 50–62; K. Jaroš, "Zur Inschrift Nr. 3 von Ḥirbet el-Qôm," *BN* 19 (1982) 31–40; W.A. Maier, *ʾAšerah: Extrabiblical Evidence* (HSM 37; Atlanta: Scholars Press, 1986) 172–73; B. Margalit "Some Observations on the Inscription and Drawing from Khirbet el-Qôm," *VT* 39 (1989) 371–78; P.D. Miller, "Psalms and Inscriptions," in *Congress Volume: Vienna 1980* (VTSup 32; Leiden: Brill, 1981) 311–32; S. Mittmann, "Die Grabinschrift des Sangers Uriahu," *ZDPV* 97 (1981) 139–52; J. Naveh, "Graffiti and Dedications," *BASOR* 235 (1979) 27–30; M. O'Connor, "The Poetic Inscription from Khirbet el-Qôm," *VT* 37 (1987) 224–29; Olyan, *Asherah*, 23–25; M.S. Smith, *The Early History of God: Yahweh and the Other Deities in Ancient Israel* (San Francisco: Harper & Row, 1980) 88; Z. Zevit, "The Khirbet el-Qôm Inscription Mentioning a Goddess," *BASOR* 255 (1984) 39–47.

24. There have been four main proposals on how to understand the crucial reading *ʾšrt* at Khirbet el-Qôm and also in the closely related inscriptions from Kuntillet ʿAjrûd. The first, to understand *ʾšrt* as "shrine," cognate with Phoenician *ʾšrt*, Aramaic *ʾtrtʾ*, and Akkadian *aširtu*, as proposed by E. Lipiński, "The Goddess Aṯirat in Ancient Arabia, in Babylon, and in Ugarit," *OL* 3 (1972) 101–19, is unviable; see particularly J. Emerton, "New Light on Israelite Religion: The Implications of the Inscriptions from Kuntillet ʿAjrud," *ZAW* 94 (1982) 2–20, who points out that *ʾăšērâ* never means "shrine" in the Hebrew of the Bible and thus should not have such a meaning in the Hebrew epigraphic corpus. Emerton and others discuss instead two options: (1) to read *ʾšrt*

as "asherah," that is, the cult object sacred to the goddess Asherah, or (2) to read *ʾšrt* as "Asherah," the divine name. P.D. Miller ("The Absence of the Goddess in Israelite Religion," *HAR* 10 [1986] 246) and P.K. McCarter ("Aspects of the Religion of the Israelite Monarchy: Biblical and Epigraphic Data," in *Ancient Israelite Religion,* 149) have further suggested that *ʾšrt* should be understood as a hypostatized aspect of the female side of Yahweh. To choose between these options, while an important task for those concerned with the morphology of the el-Qôm and ʿAjrûd inscriptions, need not overly concern us here. For the historian of religion, the attempt to differentiate between asherah a sacred symbol, Asherah the goddess, or Asherah a female hypostasis of Yahweh is again, as in n. 20, to quibble over semantics. I believe that in the ancient Israelite imagination the cult symbol of the goddess or a female hypostasis would have been perceived as Asherah herself.

25. Miller, "Psalms and Inscriptions," 317.

26. The Greek text almost always renders Hebrew *ʾăšērā* as *alsous,* "grove," evidence that supports our understanding of the *ʾăšērā* or cult symbol as a stylized tree (see n. 17 above).

27. J. Day, "Asherah in the Hebrew Bible and Northwest Semitic Literature," *JBL* 105 (1986) 400–401; Emerton, "New Light," 16; Lipiński, "Aṯirat," 114; these references are pointed out by Olyan, *Asherah,* 8 n. 24.

28. The bibliography is vast. Preliminary reports can be found in Z. Meshel and C. Meyers, "The Name of God in the Wilderness of Zin," *BA* 39 (1976) 6–10; Z. Meshel, "Kuntillet ʿAjrûd—An Israelite Site from the Monarchical Period on the Sinai Border," *Quadmoniot* 9 (1976) 118–24 (Hebrew); idem, "Kuntillet ʿAjrûd—An Israelite Religious Center in Northern Sinai," *Expedition* 20 (1978) 50–54; idem, *Kuntillet ʿAjrûd: A Religious Center from the Time of the Judean Monarchy* (Israel Museum Catalogue 175; Jerusalem: Israel Museum, 1978); idem, "Did Yahweh Have a Consort? The New Religious Inscriptions from Sinai," *BARev* 5/2 (1979) 24–35. Significant studies include P. Beck, "The Drawings from Horvat Teiman (Kuntillet ʿAjrûd)," *Tel Aviv* 9 (1982) 3–86; Dever, "Asherah," 21–37; idem, "Archaeological Confirmation," 37–43; Emerton, "New Light," 2–20; D.N. Freedman, "Yahweh of Samaria and his Asherah," *BA* 50 (1987) 241–49; M. Gilula, "To Yahweh Shomron and to his Asherah," *Shnaton* 3 (1978/79) 129–37 (Hebrew); J.M. Hadley, "Some Drawings and Inscriptions on Two Pithoi from Kuntillet ʿAjrûd," *VT* 37 (1987) 180–211; Lemaire, "Date et origine," 131–43; idem, "Yahweh's Asherah," 42–51; Lipiński, "Aṯirat," 101–19; McCarter, "Aspects of the Religion," 137–49; Maier, *ʾAšerah,* 168–72; Miller, "Absence of the Goddess," 239–49; Olyan, *Asherah,* 25–37; Smith, *Early History,* 85–88; J. Tigay, "Israelite Religion: The Onomastic and Epigraphic Evidence," *Ancient Israelite Religion,* 173–75; idem, *You Shall Have No Other Gods: Israelite Religion in the Light of Hebrew Inscriptions* (HSS 31; Atlanta: Scholars Press, 1986) 26–30; M. Weinfeld, "A Sacred Site of the Monarchic Period," *Shnaton* 4 (1980) 280–84 (Hebrew); idem, "Further Remarks on the ʿAjrûd Inscription," *Shnaton* 5–6 (1981–82) 237–39 (Hebrew); idem, "Kuntillet ʿAjrud Inscriptions and their Significance," *Studi epigraphici e linguistici* 1 (1984) 121–30.

29. In the original announcements of the ʿAjrûd materials ("Kuntillet ʿAjrûd—An Israelite Site," 118–24; "Kuntillet ʿAjrûd—An Israelite Religious Center," 50–54; *Kuntillet ʿAjrûd*), the excavator, Z. Meshel, understood *yhwh šmrn* as "Yahweh our guardian" (*šōměrēnû*). But in 1979 M. Gilula ("Yahweh Shomron," 129–37) proposed reading instead "Yahweh of Samaria" (*šōměrōn*), and almost all commentators, including now Meshel ("Consort," 31), prefer this translation. See in particular Emerton, "New Light," who points out that a second ʿAjrûd inscription reading *yhwh tmn,* which can only be translated "Yahweh of the South," gives credence to the translation "Yahweh of Samaria." Emerton also assembles other evidence suggesting that our traditional understanding of Hebrew grammar, which would not permit proper names such as Yahweh to serve as the *nomen regens* in a construct phrase, is flawed.

30. The official publication of the Kuntillet ʿAjrûd material has not yet appeared, and various commentators differ on the number of relevant inscriptions and their precise readings. We rely here on Tigay, "Israelite Religion," 173–74, and 189 n. 85. Tigay's sources are Meshel's remarks in *Kuntillet ʿAjrûd* and information provided by Meshel to M. Weinfeld and published by Weinfeld in "Further Remarks" (Hebrew), and in "Kuntillet ʿAjrud Inscriptions."

31. Olyan, *Asherah,* passim.

32. See also on this point Ackroyd, "Goddesses," 255–56; Ahlström, *Aspects of Syncretism,* 51; Freedman, "Yahweh of Samaria," 248.

33. Ahaziah in Amos 7:13 calls the Bethel temple "a king's sanctuary" and "a dynastic temple" (for notes on translation, see Albright, *Archaeology,* 139).

34. Hos 4:13 does describe the daughters of Israel who play the harlot "under evergreen oak, styrax tree, and terebinth," but the *ʾăšērâ* is not explicitly mentioned.

35. Olyan, *Asherah,* 6–8.

36. *Ibid.,* 13.

37. There has been some debate on the relationship of Athaliah to Ahab and Jezebel; in 2 Kgs 8:26 and 2 Chr 22:2, Athaliah is called the *bat ʿomrî,* "the daughter of Omri," whereas in 2 Kgs 8:18 and 2 Chr 21:6, she is called the *bat ʾaḥʾāb,* "the daughter of Ahab." It is generally conceded that *bat* in *bat ʿomrî* should be understood in a more general sense of female descendant; the NRSV, in fact, translates "granddaughter." But cf. H.J. Katzenstein, "Who Were the Parents of Athaliah?" *IEJ* 5 (1955) 194–97.

38. Based on Akkadian *etellu,* "to be great, exalted"; the root *ʿtl* is otherwise unknown in Hebrew.

39. Jehosheba is the daughter of Joram, Athaliah's husband, according to 2 Kgs 11:2. Her mother's name is not given. But since the names of no other wives of Joram are known, it is reasonable to presume that Jehosheba was Athaliah's daughter.

40. But cf. Y. Yadin, "The 'House of Ba ʿal' of Ahab and Jezebel in Samaria, and that of Athaliah in Judah," in *Archaeology in the Levant* (Kathleen Kenyon Festschrift; Warminster: Aris & Phillips, 1978) 127–29.

41. Or possibly in its outskirts; see Yadin, " 'House of Ba ʿal,' " 130–32.

42. See D. Harvey, "Nehushta," *IDB* 3, 534b.

43. *Pace* BDB 639a, s.v. *nḥš* III. *Pace* also *HALAT* 3. 653b, s.v. *nĕḥuštāʾ*, which derives *nĕḥuštāʾ* from the Akkadian root otherwise unattested in Hebrew, *nḥš,* "to be luxuriant."

44. In the Hebrew Bible, see only the three individuals named Barzillai (‹*barzel,* "iron"): the first an ally of David in 2 Sam 17:27–29; 19:31–40; and 1 Kgs 2:7; the second a priest according to Ezra 2:61 (= Neh 7:63); and the third the husband of Merab according to 2 Sam 21:8.

45. *ANEP* #470.

46. *ANEP* #474; see also #473.

47. I.E.S. Edwards, "A Relief of Qudshu-Astarte-Anath in the Winchester College Collection," *JNES* 14 (1955) 49–51; pictured also in *ANESTP* #830.

48. Egyptian: Edwards lists a total of thirteen *comparanda,* now in museums in Cairo, Turin, Vienna, Moscow, Copenhagen, Paris, and London, to the Qudšu-Astarte-Anat plaque ("Relief," 49). See also *ANEP* #471 and #472. Canaanite: See, e.g., the reference in K.R. Joines, "The Bronze Serpent in the Israelite Cult," *JBL* 87 (1986) 246–47 and 247 n. 12; cf. J.B. Pritchard, *Palestinian Figurines in Relation to Certain Goddesses Known Throughout Literature* (New Haven: American Oriental Society, 1943) #36. See also P. Amiet, *Art of the Ancient Near East* (New York: H.N. Abrams, 1980) pl. 511; S. Mitchell, "Archaeology in Asia Minor, 1985–1989," *Archaeological Reports for 1989–90 (Journal of Hellenic Studies,* Supplement) 86 fig. 5.

49. In addition to the discussion here, see W.G. Dever, "Archaeological Confirmation," 39–40 and figs. 3–4; idem. "Asherah," 28.

50. J.T. Milik and F.M. Cross, "Inscribed Arrowheads from the Period of the Judges," *BASOR* 134 (1954) 8–9; F.M. Cross, *Canaanite Myth and Hebrew Epic: Essays in the History of the Religion of Israel* (Cambridge, MA: Harvard University Press, 1973) 33. But cf. idem, "The Origin and Early Evolution of the Alphabet," *Eretz-Israel* 8 (1967) 13* and n. 33; idem, "Newly Found Inscriptions in Old Canaanite and Early Phoenician Scripts," *BASOR* 238 (1980) 7, where Cross suggests that *labiʔtu* should be understood as a title of Anat or perhaps refers to a fusion of Anat and Asherah. See further on this Dever, "Asherah," 28.

51. The stand has four registers; on its bottom register is depicted the lion-grasping goddess. The lions are represented again on the third register from the bottom, but in that register they flank a sacred tree. These two lion-flanked icons are best understood as variant representations of the same divine power. That the divine power in question is Asherah is indicated by her association with sacred trees (above, nn. 17 and 26).

52. Cross, *Canaanite Myth*, 33.

53. *Ibid*.

54. There is much doubt here. Certain first-millennium evidence argues that *tnt* may be Astarte, in particular the reading *ltnt ʕštrt*, "to *tnt*-Astarte," in the Sarepta inscription (for discussion, see Day, "Asherah," 396–97, 401). Or *tnt* may be a conflation of Asherah and Astarte (see R.A. Oden, *Studies in Lucian's De Syria Dea* [HSM 15; Missoula, MT: Scholars Press, 1977] 98). Cf. the identity of the goddess of Sidon, who is identified as Elat (= Asherah) in the Ugaritic texts (*CT*/14.4.198–199, 201–202) and as Astarte in the Hebrew Bible (1 Kgs 11:5, 23; 2 Kgs 23:13). Also note the way in which Astarte and Asherah interchange as consorts of Baal in the Deuteronomistic history.

55. Cross, *Canaanite Myth*, 32–33.

56. See H.N. Wallace, *The Eden Narrative* (HSM 32; Atlanta: Scholars Press, 1985) 152–57; see also M. Lidzbarski, *Ephemeris für semitische Epigraphik* 3 (Giessen: Töpelmann, 1915) 284–85.

57. Even if this etymology is incorrect (an alternate etymology would associate *ḥwt* with the root *ḥyh*, "to live"), Asherah's association with serpents on the basis of *KAI* 89 is not severed, since Punic *ḥwt* is the equivalent of Hebrew *ḥawwâ*, Eve. This is significant since it has been argued that Eve in Gen 2:4b–3:24 is a demythologized Asherah figure (Wallace, *Eden Narrative*, 111–14, 158). At a minimum Eve, like Asherah, represents fertility ("the mother of all the living"; Gen 3:20). And significantly for our thesis, this Asherah-*cum*-Eve is associated with a serpent.

A second biblical text might also be adduced in support of Asherah's association with serpents: 2 Kgs 18:4, 2 Kgs 18:4 describes Hezekiah's reforms as he purges the cult of elements he perceives to be non-Yahwistic. Two of these elements are the *ʔăšērâ*, which we argued above sat in the Temple in Jerusalem, and Nehushtan, "the bronze serpent that Moses had made" and to which "the Israelites made offerings." This Nehushtan must, like the *ʔăšērâ*, have been located in the Temple, given its Mosaic origins and its place in the sacrificial cult. Can it be that these two objects singled out by Hezekiah as non-Yahwistic elements within the Temple are unrelated? I am inclined to think not. Both the *ʔăšērâ* and Nehushtan, I would suggest, are cult images devoted to Asherah (see similarly Olyan, *Asherah*, 70–71).

58. See A. Alt, "The Monarchy in the Kingdoms of Israel and Judah," in *Essays on Old Testament History and Religion* (Garden City, NY: Doubleday, 1967) 321–26.

59. A. Alt, "Das Königtum in der Reichen Israel und Juda," *VT* (1951) 2–22; reprinted in *Kleine Schriften zur Geschichte des Volkes Israel* (Munich: Beck, 1959) 2. 116–34; English trans. "Monarchy," in *Essays*, 313–15.

60. The debate concerning the "divine" character of Judean kingship is, of course, an extensive one; for bibliography and for the history of scholarship, see P.D. Miller, "Israelite Religion," in *The Hebrew Bible and Its Modern Interpreters* (ed. D.A. Knight and G.M. Tucker; Philadelphia: Fortress; Chico, CA: Scholars Press, 1985), 218–20; more fully but less up-to-date, the survey of

A.R. Johnson, "Hebrew Conceptions of Kingship," in *Myth, Ritual, and Kingship: Essays on the Theory and Practice of Kingship in the Ancient Near East and in Israel* (ed. S.H. Hooke; Oxford: Clarendon, 1958) 204–35.

61. Cross, *Canaanite Myth*, 241–65.
62. *Ibid.*, 258.

The Wise Women of 2 Samuel
A Role Model for Women in Early Israel?

CLAUDIA V. CAMP

Since the 1960s, biblical studies has focused a good deal of attention on the wisdom literature of the OT. Among the important questions that have been raised and variously answered are those concerning the locus of origin of early Israelite wisdom (whether clan or court) and the place of wisdom's faith expression within the context of Yahwistic theology. More recently, a raised consciousness with regard to sexual equality has prompted a re-evaluation of the Bible's attitude toward women and an increased critical appreciation of the value of feminine imagery, both in biblical and modern theology. At the confluence of these two streams of interest stand the passages in the Succession Narrative that tell the tales of two wise women of early Israel.

The thesis of this paper is that the wise women of Tekoa and Abel, portrayed in 2 Samuel 14 and 20 respectively, are representatives of at least one significant political role available to women in the years preceding the establishment of the kingship in Israel, a role that continued to exist into the monarchic era, but of which we have no evidence after the time of David.[1] It was a role that we might classify as a regularized set of functions rather than an official position, a definition that accords well with what we can ascertain of that society's tendency toward the diffusion of political functions throughout the community.[2] As we shall see, it was a role that was firmly rooted in the tribal ethos. Thus, this study will provide a basis also for a further refinement of the thesis associated with Audet[3] and Gerstenberger[4] that this ethos was the locus of origin both of the traditions underlying what we now call "old wisdom" and most of the basic ethical underpinnings of nascent Yahwism as well. In the conclusion, we shall articulate the symbolic value such a role might have carried, and its function in our understanding of the intertwined theology of wisdom and Yahwism.

I

Let me briefly summarize the situations presented in these two stories. Chap. 13 has described the rape of Tamar, David's daughter, by her brother Amnon and Amnon's subsequent murder by the infuriated Absalom. Absalom flees from David's wrath, but, three years later, David is "comforted concerning Amnon," and longs to see Absalom once more. Whether it is pride or legality that prevents David from acting at once is unclear, but in 14:1–3 we see that Joab finds it necessary to devise a ruse to bring Absalom home. He summons a wise woman from Tekoa and instructs her to go to David dressed in mourning and to present him with the following tale: She is presumably a widow with two sons, one of whom has murdered the other in anger. Her family demands the death of the murderer, ostensibly for appropriate revenge, but, in reality, so that they might eliminate the sole heir of her husband's family. When David promises to look into the case, she presses him further, gaining for herself a promise of immunity from persecution. Pressing again, she receives David's word that "the avenger of blood" would not destroy her son. With these words, David has unwittingly passed judgment on his own case as well, and the woman can now make her accusation against him for "planning against the people of God," and make her poignant plea for Absalom's restoration. This plea is formulated in an identificational proverb followed by a rhetorical question: "We will indeed die, like water spilt out on the ground which cannot be gathered up; but will God not dedicate himself to seeing that a banished one does not remain exiled from him, and will he not find ways to do so?" (v. 14).[5] In vv. 15–17, she again makes reference to her own fabricated story, the destruction of her and her son "from the heritage of God," in a manner that has led commentators to question either the coherence of the story or the woman's intelligence. This is an issue I shall address below. In any case, the sudden switch raises the king's suspicions, and he asks whether Joab has put her up to the ploy. Whether in spite of or because of her confirmation of this fact, the trick succeeds and Absalom is restored.

David's troubles did not end, of course. Absalom's restoration was followed by his revolt. The crushing of this insurrection was succeeded by that of Sheba the Benjaminite who, as related in chap. 20, called the men of Israel to their tents, claiming "no portion in David, no inheritance in the son of Jesse" (20:1). Pursued by Joab, Sheba flees to the far north of Israel, into the city of Abel Beth Ma'acah. Joab besieges the city but is stopped in the midst of his efforts by the voice of a woman, a wise woman, calling to him from the city. By the use of a proverb not fully recoverable from the present text, she reminds him of Abel's reputation of counsel, peace, and faithfulness, and then asks rhetorically whether he would "destroy a city which is a mother in Israel," if he would "swallow up the heritage of Yahweh" (v. 19). Joab hastily demurs and tells her his mission. The woman promises him Sheba's head. She then goes "to all the people in her wisdom" and they comply with Sheba's execution (v. 22).

There are a number of elements implicit in these texts that point to both the existence and nature of a role of the "wise woman" in Israel, at least for the time period of the Judges and during the early monarchy. In order to sketch out the parameters of such a role, we must first turn to the question of what the narrator of these stories meant when he described his female characters as "wise." The fact that they are identified by no more than this adjective and the names of their respective towns suggests that the audience who heard these accounts must have had some prior image of these two nameless figures who stand so boldly before a king and a general; that when the words *ʾiššâ ḥăkāmâ* were used, features of a culturally stereotyped character arose in the hearers' minds, thus obviating the need for further description. This makes it difficult to subscribe to Whybray's assessment that the wisdom depicted by the Succession-Narrative author is primarily "the politically oriented wisdom of the trained official, or king."[6] I shall return at a later point to both the ideas of training and of the political nature of wisdom, but it is clearly problematic with respect to the wise women to view wisdom narrowly as a phenomenon of the court and its habitués, for they are presented as having little contact with that environment.

The women do, however, exhibit two traits often associated with that somewhat amorphous concept "wise." They speak, first of all, with the voice of authority. De Boer has demonstrated the close connection between the wise person and words of counsel that are not mere advice but are meant to be followed on penalty of death.[7] Although the woman of Tekoa presents her false tale humbly at first, her accusing rhetorical question in 14:13 is spoken by one who seems accustomed to making and delivering such judgments. "Why then have you planned such a thing against the people of God?" she asks David. "For in giving this decision the king convicts himself. . . ." The fact that the narrator tells us in v. 3 that Joab has "put the words in her mouth" does not mitigate this assessment of her hearing. It would be hard to imagine a person with the courage and mien to execute such an audacious act if she lacked the practical experience of the exercise of authority.[8]

As for the wise woman of Abel, her authority is without question, both in her commanding stance before Joab and in her obvious influence among her people. We can, in fact, probably interpret her "going to all the people in her wisdom" as an act of counsel similar to that which a court advisor may give a king. Her advice is apparently taken, moreover, with the same seriousness that a respected royal advisor expected his to be heard.[9] The people act with unquestioning alacrity.

Authority is not, of course, the exclusive domain of wise persons. It is combined in both our passages, however, with a second characteristic commonly associated with "wisdom," viz., the utterance of proverbs (14:14; 20:18). Given the brevity of these two pericopes and the lack of other descriptive material about the women, I think this fact is of great significance in trying to ascertain their position in their communities. Who speaks in proverbs and what is the intended effect of such speech? It is precisely this question that leads directly into the heart of the debate on the locus of the origin of wisdom, a debate that is very much to the point in this examination of the nature of the role of the wise women. The author of these two passages has placed proverbs in the mouths of two female figures designated "wise," whose usual arena of activity was apparently the local town setting, if we may judge from the narrative's presentation. This fact compels us to consider very carefully the hypothesis that a significant "wisdom" influence arose outside the courtly setting. We will consider the exact nature of this other setting in the second portion of this paper, but let us first examine the proverbs themselves.

The wise woman of Abel introduces her challenge to Joab with what might be described as a classic application of the wisdom of the ages as a basis for authority: "They were wont to say in olden times. . . ." She then quotes a traditional saying whose precise content is somewhat uncertain because of textual difficulties. Following the LXX, Eissfeldt translates: "Let them ask in Abel and Dan whether what the faithful of Israel have ordained has come into disuse."[10] The MT, "Let them but ask in Abel and so they settled a matter," is regarded by most commentators as secondary. In either case, the saying clearly refers to the heritage of Abel as a place where one might receive counsel of peace and faithfulness.

Important for our discussion is not only the fact that such a saying appears on the lips of a woman who is called wise, but also the weight of authority that the saying obviously bears. It provides the focal point of an argument sufficient to cause Joab to reconsider his attack on the city. Thus, what is significant about this saying is the *use* that is made of it. It has often been assumed that the saying-form, over against that of the admonition, does not inherently make a moral judgment, that it merely makes a statement of what *is,* according to a wise person's astute observation. It is not the case, however, that such statements are made so that the sage may take delight in his or her retrospective summary of experience. They are, rather, formulated to be used in one or other particular situation. The saying, furthermore, even when it does not place an explicit value judgment on its object, would have no purpose in being made if it did not, by the knowledge it imparted, indicate an *appropriate* attitude or behavior in response to it. Right knowledge mandates right action. A saying, then, is employed by a wise person for a particular purpose, possibly to educate another (which always involves some implicit directing as to what is "right" or "wrong") or, as in this case, to exert influence over another's action in a way that carries some authority. Thus, the proverb about Abel, when spoken by this wise woman, constitutes a directive to Joab that to attack the city would certainly be a wrongful deed. She is a wise person utilizing the art of wisdom speech to an end often associated with ancient Near Eastern wisdom literature, viz., the persuasion of a ruler by a soft tongue in a delicate situation (cf. Prov 25:15; 15:1). Without intending to limit our view of the wise person to this one function, it is important to note that the skill and necessity of persuasive counsel is as at home in the village as it is in the royal court, and that Joab, the king's advisor, has been turned aside by precisely the same technique he himself would have used in another situation.[11] Politics is indeed a part of the wisdom tradition, as Whybray contends, but there is no warrant for setting the wisdom of the woman of Abel over against, rather than within, this arena.[12]

The wise woman of Tekoa also employs a proverb for purposes of persuasion, but in a somewhat different manner than did the wise woman of Abel. "We will indeed die," she says to David, "like water spilt on the ground which cannot be gathered up." This saying falls into the category of "identificational proverb," that R.B.Y. Scott has enumerated as one of the proverb idioms or idea patterns characteristic of folk wisdom not only in the ancient Near East but also in the classical world and modern Europe.[13] A similar image is also found in Prov 17:14: "The beginning of strife is like letting out water." This proverb concludes with the moral: "So quit before the quarrel breaks out." Although the applications diverge radically, the import of the image of wasted water remains constant. And consider its impact in the midst of a Palestine summer! The point to be made from the comparison of these two proverbs is that this image was apparently part of common usage, perhaps "originally" couched in a particular set saying of its own, but so useful as to receive many applications. The second line of Prov 17:14 is clearly a later moralizing addition. What we have here, then, is a shining example of a proverb "in action," perhaps a reference to a well-known saying rather than a full citation. It is a proverb not nestled quietly in a collection but employed by a person of agile mind and persuasive tongue to influence a situation, suggesting once more that neither "wisdom speech" nor its effective utilization was the sole domain of the royal court.

The precise meaning of the proverb is curiously ambiguous in the context, with various commentators applying it in different manners to Amnon, Absalom, and the nation Israel, as well as to the woman's own story.[14] A firm decision on the "correct" interpretation may not be possible. It may, furthermore, be unnecessary. Given the cunning with which the woman has presented her story, established the king's involvement in it, and then made her accusation, it seems that the ambiguity may have been fully intentional. It is a characteristic of poetic speech to intend more than is actually stated, to carry a surplus of meaning. Thus, spoken right at this point when the woman is about to recast her own story in light of her open accusation of David, it is fully in keeping that she would make such a loaded remark, one that encapsulates the bathos of the many lives and situations that are involved in the dilemma that currently faces the king. The woman of Tekoa is wise not only in her cunning, not only in her ability to deal handily with a superior, but also in that particular sense that is so often noted in the wisdom literature of the ancient Near East, viz., in her ability to speak the right word at the right time, to capture the essence of a situation in a few, but pleasing, words and thereby to redirect the course of events.

In the wise women's use of proverbs to lend incisiveness and authority to their arguments, we have seen the kind of persuasive counsel, presented in a compelling manner, that a royal advisor may have employed. The episodes in which the narratives present the women also aid in filling out our developing model of this role. When the wise woman of Tekoa encounters King David, she spins for him a dramatic yarn very similar to two other tales in the historical writings, one told to David by the prophet Nathan (2 Sam 12:1–15) and one by an unnamed prophet to Ahab (1 Kings 20:38–43). The purpose of these parables does not seem to be the creation of a binding legal precedent but, rather, in the words of David M. Gunn, to provide "a sufficiently apt parallel to the addressee's situation that he might make the right judgment (i.e., the one that suits the deceiver's purpose) and that when the key is provided he cannot escape the force of its application to his own case."[15] It is not so much juridical trickery as psychological manipulation that is applied by the prophets and wise woman, who use the parables to create the two conditions—of distancing and of re-involvement—necessary for a person blinded by proximity to a problem to achieve a new perspective on it. Although they did not apply our modern terminology of "literatherapy" to this technique, there can be little doubt that these OT "psychologists" had full awareness of its efficacy.[16]

The wise woman of Abel also employs a form of psychological pressure to attain her goal of halting Joab's siege. Her appearance on the city wall[17] with a verbal challenge to the attacker is not, however, without precedent in the OT. There are three similar episodes that we might compare with the present text: the confrontation of the Chief of the Assyrian army with the representatives of Hezekiah near the Jerusalem wall in 2 Kgs 18:17–36 and the two separate incidents involving Abner as he was pursued first by Asahel (2 Sam 2:18–23) and then by Joab (2 Sam 2:24–28). These three episodes and that of the woman of Abel show four important parallels in narrative-structure that I assume would have found some basis in the actual unfolding of events in such cases of confrontation.[18] The common narrative elements are as follows:

1. In all four stories, we have the person who wishes to make a speech call out to the leader of the opposing side. Because the speechmaker is the leader of one faction in the other three stories, we can assume that the wise woman of Abel is also filling such a

role in her case. In two of the stories, this summoning is presented as direct discourse (2 Sam 2:20; 20:16–17), with the speaker making a certain identification that he or she will be addressing the right person.

2. In every case but one, the speaker takes up some sort of topographical position, however *ad hoc,* from which to deliver his or her allocution: the woman of Abel from the city (2 Sam 20:16)[19]; Abner (to Joab) on the hill of Ammah (2 Sam 2:24–25); and the Assyrian chief "by the conduit of the upper pool which is on the highway to the fuller's field" (2 Kgs 18:17). Only when Abner speaks to Asahel does a speaker fail to establish such a position. Abner's attempt to distract Asahel ("Turn aside to your right hand or your left hand . . ." v. 21) may have been an unsuccessful ploy to buy time to do so. We might interpret this element in the narrative-structure as a symbolic claiming of space that lends, if not credence, at least psychological force to the leader's speech.

3. The speaker in every case employs rhetorical devices in the course of the speech to attain his or her ends. The wise woman of Abel uses a proverb. (See the discussion above in the body of this article.) Abner, in his confrontation with Asahel, first tries distraction (which cannot properly be considered rhetorical), and then an appeal, also unsuccessful, to the loyalties of blood and friendship: "Why should I smite you to the ground? How then could I lift up my face to your brother Joab?" (v. 22). We might conjecture that at least part of the reason these verbal ploys fail to effect their purpose is that they fail as rhetoric; they do not sufficiently re-orient Asahel in the given situation to "turn him aside" from his quarry. Abner's speech to Joab, on the other hand, incorporates a more universal appeal to brotherhood, framed in escalating rhetorical questions: "Shall the sword devour forever? Do you not know that the end will be bitter? How long will it be before you bid your people turn from the pursuit of their brethren?" (v. 26). Here, Abner succeeds in redefining the situation for Joab, and hence, Joab's attitude toward it. We should note that Joab responds to Abner in *exactly* the same manner as he does to the wise woman of Abel, first with a self-defensive demurral (cf. 2:27 with 20:20), and then with acquiescence to the speaker's plea.

When the Assyrian chief speaks to Hezekiah's officials, however, he uses quite a different rhetorical device. Unlike the other three speechmakers, he is in the position of power, rather than that of the underdog. Therefore, his tone and intent are those of taunting rather than direct persuasion (2 Kgs 18:19–25, 27). He may have undermined his own cause by this approach, however, for when he turns his attention to the people on the wall (vv. 28–35), they "were silent and answered him not a word" (v. 36), in spite of his promises of wealth and security.

4. The final element in the common narrative-structure of the four stories is the report of the success or failure of the leader's speech which, as we have already indicated, depends, at least in part, on the success or failure of their verbal diplomacy. In the two cases that are most similar, both involving Joab, the obvious underdogs, Abner and the wise woman, come out on top. Abner, on the other hand, when he has no time to take up a position from which to speak to Asahel, makes a hurried, half-baked essay into diplomacy and fails. The Assyrian has mixed success, instilling fear into the Jerusalem leadership, but not altogether intimidating the populace.

In all of these episodes, what appears to be a common form of psychological warfare is carried out by means of confrontational speeches made by the leader of one side or the other in a situation of pending conflict. We can readily assume, then, that the words and actions of both the military leaders and the similar ones of the wise woman resonated with the images the stories' hearers had of each of these figures and their customary tactics.

The wise women of Tekoa and Abel, then, appear in situations in which they act in a manner associated with a prophet and a military leader, respectively, while using forms of language associated with the wisdom tradition. There is no evidence at all to suggest that these women either prophesied or performed military leadership functions on a regular basis. What we can more readily infer from these stories is that wise women were customarily granted a similar *kind* of authority on such a regular basis that it would not have been surprising for them to assume those roles when the need arose. Their adroitness in dealing with these delicate and even dangerous situations also raises the possibility that they were not, as Whybray contends, persons without training, but that they had, in fact, been prepared at some point in life to fulfill such consequential responsibilities in their local settings, in spite of what some scholars assume to be their second-class status as women.[20]

II

Given this inferential picture of the status of the wise woman that we are able to draw from the 2 Samuel texts, we must now ask what the source and scope of her authority might have been. Here the texts supply a clue in their use of the image of the *mother*, in one case a role enacted by the wise woman of Tekoa, in the other case a metaphor applied to her city by the wise woman of Abel. We will return in our conclusion to the symbolic value of the mother-image, but here we will consider the literal case of the mother in Israel.

The Book of Proverbs gives us an important indication of the mother's role in the training of her children, not only as infants and toddlers, but also in the proper attitudes and actions of adult life. The mother's *tôrâ* is placed in parallelism with the father's *mûsār* in Prov 1:8, and with his *miṣwâ* in 6:20. Although these instructions are similar in some respects to works from Egyptian wisdom, it is unique to Israel that the mother as well as the father is cited as the bearer of this tradition. (Cf. the instruction to Lemuel by his mother in 31:1–9.) Thus we see that the child-rearing function that Phyllis Bird has elucidated as a source of authority for women in Israel[21] acts as this source in a very significant sense. For the authority that it renders is not qualified by the "higher" authority of the father, but, rather, places a woman on exactly the same footing as her husband in at least this one area of endeavor.[22]

The use of wisdom's admonition-form in the educational setting of the family has been clearly demonstrated by Erhard Gerstenberger.[23] We might also conjecture that the saying-form, though less directly pedagogical, was also used in this arena. At the very least, such maxims must have been passed from parent to child, undoubtedly in an applied form rather than as part of a collection. Thus, whatever her subsequent training, the wise woman probably gained her first experience in the use of such language (and the recognition of her peers) in the training of her immediate family. It would seem also, then, that as the father became grandfather and approached that chronological time when he might be considered "elder," with power over and responsibility for a larger community, so too would the status of the mother, now grandmother, now matriarch,

increase in honor and authority. This assumes, of course, both that she survived the aver-
age female life expectancy of 30 years[24] and that she demonstrated the same skills and
acumen with regard to her own family that a man would presumably have to have
achieved before attaining the honor as well as the age of elder.

I have made reference to Gerstenberger's work that draws our attention to the
Sippenethos as the locus of origin, not only of the wisdom admonition, but also of the
prohibition-series in the Pentateuch. The conclusions of Norman Gottwald's several
articles and book on the sociology of Israel[25] add depth and substance to this reconstruction. Whereas Gerstenberger rather vaguely presupposed the tribe to be a nomadic or
semi-nomadic extended family unit, Gottwald has given us a much more concrete and
sociologically plausible description of a village-peasant population—the very home of
the wise women!—whose residential units were connected by a variety of *interkinship,*
"cross-cutting sodalities."[26] The potential scope of the wise mother's authority is,
through this analysis, expanded from the realm of the immediate or extended family to a
more comprehensive political unit. She becomes a tribal (= village) wise woman, concerned not only with education, but also with governance. The existence of such a role
for women would suggest that the egalitarian attitude of early Yahwism, stressed by
Gottwald, allowed for a functional, if not always explicit, egalitarianism with respect to
sex as well, particularly under the rigorous conditions endured by the newly wrought
federation.[27]

It is in precisely this manner that I should explain the appearance of a wise *woman*
on the wall of Abel confronting the army of a king. She is not called a "judge," although
it is clearly in her power to make decisions in the face of a military threat; nor is she a
"prophetess," imbued with the power of the spirit to deal with an overwhelming situation. *Charisma* she may or may not have had; but, as the narrator so explicitly relates, it is
"in her wisdom" that she advises "all the people" of the town. Sagacity, faithfulness, a
commanding presence, and readily acknowledged influence with her peers—these are
the attributes that clearly mark this woman. They are, moreover, attributes which any
number of women might have exhibited. In the early years of Israel, with its egalitarian
principles and desperate need for able minds as well as bodies, such qualities might have
placed women not uncommonly in positions of authority in the village-tribal setting.

III

Both the form-critical and sociological perspectives have demonstrated the vital
influence of the tribe (or, in Gottwald's terms, the re-tribalized social structure) of pre-
monarchic Israel as the source and setting of the tenets of early Yahwism. The speeches
of the two wise women of 2 Samuel allow us, however, to move another step closer to an
understanding of the interrelationship of wisdom and Yahwism in the tribal-village setting. This understanding finds a focus in the image of the mother which, as we have seen,
is the initial source of the wise woman's authority. Both of the women are particularly
concerned with the possible destruction of "the heritage of Yahweh (or God)" (*naḥălat
ʾĕlōhîm* in 14:16; *naḥălat yhwh* in 20:19), an entity somewhat differently conceived in
each case but, in both cases, associated by a parable or metaphor (i.e., symbolically) with
a "mother." To speak of a symbolic value carried by female imagery is, in one sense, to
move a step beyond the scope of the problem suggested by the title of this article, a

problem defined by a historical or, even more, a sociological inquiry. Yet, as we see here, the literary forms in which these references to women are couched already point toward a movement in the direction of symbolic meaning which must be given some consideration, however tentative.

The parable in 2 Samuel 14 depicts a biological mother, concerned for the preservation of the name of her dead husband and for the right of the widow and orphan to be free from persecution. In v. 16, she challenges David to deliver her and her son from the one who would undo this divinely mandated guarantee, who would "destroy" them "from the heritage of God." Thus, having already accused David of planning against the people of God (v. 13), she has returned to her now apparent false pretext for approaching him. The development of her story, with its carefully graduated intensity, does not, however, fall apart in this verse. Rather, the artistically wrought ambiguity of her speech, noticeable first in the proverb of v. 14, militates against an interpretation that reduces her dual purpose to a single one, the return of Absalom. The entire parable, as well as the proverb itself, is a poetic form and thus is susceptible of multi-reference. Evident in this tale are not only a royal advisor's fear about the royal succession, but also a concern for the preservation of family name and for the protection of society's weak—concerns that we would expect from a mother and a leader in the Yahwistic tribal-village setting,[28] as well as from one of the first mouthpieces of Israel's wisdom tradition.[29]

In 2 Samuel 20, the city of Abel is called "a mother in Israel," and identified by parallelism with the *naḥălat yhwh* by the wise woman in her defiance of Joab. "You seek to destroy a city which is a mother in Israel," she accuses him, "why will you swallow up the heritage of the Lord?" We should note, however, that *naḥălat yhwh* is never used to affirm the integrity of a mere plot of ground without reference to the people whose inheritance it is.[30] Thus when the "heritage of Yahweh" is placed in parallelism with "a mother in Israel," we might expect the latter term to carry a metaphorical surplus of meaning beyond the obvious "biological" association of city and surrounding towns. The fact that the same title, "mother in Israel," is accorded to the judge and prophetess Deborah (Judg 5:7) reinforces this expectation. Deborah earns this accolade for her good and effective counsel of faithfulness and unity in Israel.[31] The proverb quoted by the wise woman immediately preceding her challenge to Joab confirms the connection between this epithet and such counsel. Abel is characterized in the proverb as a city with a long reputation for wisdom and faithfulness to the tradition of Israel. It is, therefore, a mother in the same way Deborah was: a creator and hence a symbol of the unity that bound Israel together under one God Yahweh.[32] And it is the wise woman's implicit appeal to this unity that stops Joab in his tracks.

The plea for unity by the wise woman of Abel is one further manifestation of the concern for the shalom of individual and society to which the Tekoite "mother" also appeals. These concerns lie at the heart of early Yahwism. When we consider that they are placed in the mouths of wise women, and expressed through the image of the mother, we have added a significant dimension to any discussion of the wisdom-Yahwism nexus in Israel. For as we have seen, representatives of a female role embody and proclaim the ideals of both realms, and female imagery constitutes one symbolic link between them.

I suggested at the outset that this consideration of the symbolic value of the female imagery in these stories must remain tentative in the limited context of this article. This tentativeness is warranted for at least three reasons.[33] In the first place, we have examined only one female image other than the wise women themselves, that of the mother; and that only in a limited number of texts. Second, we have made only one attempt (in looking at the "heritage of God") to show the relationship between female imagery and other important, biblical motifs. Because individual symbols function meaningfully only in the context of a larger symbol system, the extension of such an inquiry would be vital to drawing out the full import (and possible limitations) of the female images. Finally, we are faced with the unassailable fact that female images, either in the form of significant "historical" persons or of symbolic figures, are relatively rare in the OT.

It is important to note, however, that female imagery does become very prominent in the first nine chapters of the Book of Proverbs, where wisdom itself is personified as a woman. The relationship of the historical wise woman to this poetic figure will bear future consideration. The "domain assumption"[34] of past scholarship has been that this concentration on women in Proverbs 1–9 is a mark of wisdom's isolation from the mainstream of OT theology. This article has made but a preliminary step towards a new working hypothesis, viz., that the emphasis on female imagery associated with wisdom (*both* in Proverbs and in the 2 Samuel texts) reveals a latent tendency in Israel's theological reflection, underdeveloped because of the male-dominated priesthood and generally patriarchal milieu, but not insignificant in Israel's understanding of the relationships between persons in community and between the community and Yahweh.

NOTES

1. Any sociological analysis of these female figures is lacking in the literature on the 2 Samuel passages. Many scholars refer to the wise women with condescension. H.W. Hertzberg (*I and II Samuel* [Philadelphia: Westminster, 1964] 333) calls the stories "charming" and "delightful," ascribing the Tekoite woman's "wisdom" to the fact that she allows her male adversary to think he has won. R.N. Whybray (*The Succession Narrative* [Naperville, IL: Allenson, 1968] 59) ascribes to her no wisdom at all, attributing her success to Joab. J. Hoftijzer rightly refutes Whybray's claim, acknowledging that the success of the ploy depends on her wisdom and capability ("David and the Tekoite Woman," *VT* 20 [1970] 419–44, esp. p. 444). He considers her doubly "vulnerable," however, insofar as he categorizes her as an "ordinary" person as well as a woman. He fails to raise the questions of what kind of woman she must have been to pull off the gambit, and what the implications of her use of proverbial language would be in determining her role.

2. See N.K. Gottwald, "Domain Assumptions and Societal Models in the Study of Pre-Monarchic Israel," *Congrès international pour l'étude de l'Ancien Testament* (ed. G.W. Anderson, et al.; VTSup; Leiden: Brill, 1975) 89–100, esp. p. 95.

3. J.-P. Audet, "Origines comparées de la double tradition de la loi et de la sagesse dans la proche-orient ancien," *Trudy XXV Mezhdunarodnogo Kongressa Vostokovedov* [Transactions of the 25th International Congress of Orientalists] (Moscow: Izd-vo Vostochnoi lit-ry, 1963), I. 352–57.

4. E. Gerstenberger, *Wesen und Herkunft des sogenannten "apodiktischen" Rechts* (WMANT 20; Neukirchen: Neukirchener, 1965).

5. I accept here Hoftijzer's reading of the rather difficult second half of this verse ("David," 434–37). His reading does not require textual emendation and it recognizes the difficulty in translating *nsʾnpš* as "to take away a (the) life (of)" (contra the *RSV* and most commentators). He proposes instead the translation "to aim (his) activities at" (cf. Prov 19:18; Ps 24:4), a possible contextual connotation of the usual "to long or yearn for."

6. R.N. Whybray, *The Intellectual Tradition in the Old Testament* (New York: de Gruyter, 1974) 90–91.

7. P.A.H. de Boer, "The Counsellor," *Wisdom in Israel and the Ancient Near East* (ed. M. Noth and D.W. Thomas; VTSup 3; Leiden: E.J. Brill, 1955) 42–71, esp. 56.

8. The phrase "put the words in (someone's) mouth" occurs nine times in the OT other than in 2 Samuel 14, usually with the sense of "to tell someone what to say in a forthcoming situation." There can be no doubt that in this sense, Joab "fed the woman her line"; certainly it was his trick, not hers. My argument with Whybray (see n. 1) arises from his refusal to admit that the woman, as bearer of this story, can be accorded any merit for its success. There are, on the contrary, at least three bases on which to argue for the authoritative role of the Tekoite woman in this situation.

First, the authority that comes from wisdom is not simply a matter of knowing what to say, but also of knowing when and how to say it; execution is not separable from insight for the wise person. Even the fool can be mistaken as wise, but only if he keeps his mouth shut (Pros 17:28). The sequence of David's responses to the woman's (or, if you prefer, Joab's) tale was unpredictable; thus, quick-wittedness on her part was indispensable. The delivery of her accusation had to be carefully timed and forcefully executed, but also accurately modulated so as to effect the desired response. It is improbable that any but a person practiced in the art of confrontation (and manipulation?) could have managed this situation effectively. Furthermore, as I shall suggest later in this article, it is at least possible that the woman, in part, used this encounter with the king to make her own point.

The second argument for the wise woman's authority, over against that of Joab, comes from an examination of the use of the phrase "put the words in (someone's) mouth" in the OT. Exod 4:10–16 provides the clearest example of the fact that the authority which inheres in the words put in someone's mouth can be considered separately from the personal authority that that individual carries. In Exodus, Moses's slowness "of speech and of tongue" (v. 10) cannot be overcome even by Yahweh's promise to "be with (his) mouth" (v. 12). For this reason the burden of speech-making is put on Aaron, whom Yahweh *already knows* "can speak well" (v. 14). Aaron's eloquence and personal bearing are thus separately constituted from the words that Moses, instructed by Yahweh, will later "put in his mouth" (v. 15). Although this distinction between the speaker and the dictated speech is not so explicit in the other eight occurrences of this phrase, it is worth noting that in five of these cases, the bearers of the words *are* persons of authority (Balaam in Num 22:38; 23:5, 12, 16; and "leading men" and "men of insight" in Ezra 8:17). In the cases of the three exceptions, Deut 31:19, Isa 51:16 and 59:21, the words are apparently "put in the mouth" of Israel as a whole. It is only by implication in these instances that we can call Israel an "authoritative" bearer who will pass on Yahweh's words in a forthcoming situation. In any event, these three exceptions do not damage the case made above, even if they do not support it.

The third argument for the authority of the wise woman of Tekoa will be made in the text below in the examination of her use of proverbial language. Cf. Prov 26:7.

9. Cf. 2 Sam 17:23, where Ahitophel commits suicide because his advice is not followed by Absalom.

10. O. Eissfeldt, *The Old Testament: An Introduction* (New York: Harper & Row, 1965) 149.

11. Cf. the proverb-laced speech of other of the king's advisors, Ahitophel and Hushai (2 Sam 17:3a, 8, 10, 12).

12. Evidence which strongly correlates with this assertion may be found in C.R. Fontaine, "The Use of the Traditional Saying in the Old Testament" (Sheffield: JSOT Press, 1985). A comparison of the proverbs spoken by the tribal leader Gideon (Judg 8:2, 21) in Fontaine's study with those of the wise women shows a remarkable similarity in context of use and effectiveness.

13. R.B.Y. Scott, "Folk Proverbs of the Ancient Near East," *Studies in Ancient Israelite Wisdom* (ed. J.L. Crenshaw; New York: Ktav, 1976) 417–28, esp. pp. 419–20.

14. Hertzberg (*I and II Samuel*, 332), e.g., applies it "probably" to Absalom or, "perhaps," to Amnon. The logic here is that death inevitably awaits Absalom (as it has already found

Amnon) and that God therefore wills David to show his son the same measure of mercy he has shown the woman. Hoftijzer, however, argues for a more legalistic interpretation ("David," 430–33), citing evidence that the grammatical construction of *mwt nmwt* refers to untimely death that is the result of punishment. He then interprets the proverb to mean that it is the nation Israel (cf. "the people of God," 14:13) who will die as punishment for David's refusal to comply with his own ruling. This interpretation is called into question, however, insofar as it assumes that David's response to the woman's parable creates a binding legal precedent. This assumption is challenged by D.M. Gunn on the basis of literary analysis of the text (see n. 15).

15. D.M. Gunn, "Traditional Composition in the Succession Narrative," *VT* 26 (1976) 214–229, esp. p. 219.

16. For a discussion of the use of literatherapy by OT figures, see M. Shiryon, "Biblical Roots of Literatherapy," *Journal of Psychology and Judaism* 2 (1977) 3–11, esp. pp. 5–7.

17. The precise vantage point from which the woman spoke to Joab is conjectural. The text says simply that it is "from the city" (2 Sam 20:16). *BH* makes the suggestion (omitted in *BHS*) that the awkward (and unique) *watāʿamōd baḥēl* applied to the siegemound in v. 15 be transposed to the beginning of v. 16 so that that verse would read: "And a wise woman stood on the rampart and called out from the city. . . ." This emendation of the MT has the advantage of added clarity in both v. 15 and v. 16 and is at least a possibility in a text that shows evidence of corruption else-where as well. (Cf. the discussion above on the proverb in v. 18.) Even if we eschew emendation, however, it seems logical to envision the woman assuming some position from which she could be seen as well as easily heard.

18. A strict structuralist would, of course, condemn any attempt to connect narrative structure with historical events. My point in doing so here is not to claim that all of these particular encounters actually occurred, but only that any of them *might* have happened and, if they did, that they would have been played out in approximately the same manner as recorded here. The effort here is to take historical narrative seriously for what it is: not necessarily as a verifiable report of actual events, but as stories representative of a people's "real life" that would have rung true as they listened to them.

19. See n. 17.

20. Eissfeldt is one of the few scholars who recognizes this possibility. See *The Old Testament*, 12.

21. P. Bird, "Images of Women in the Old Testament," *Religion and Sexism* (ed. R.R. Ruether; New York: Simon and Schuster, 1974) 41–88, esp. pp. 62–63.

22. See Gen 28:7, 37:10; Judg 14:2–3; Prov 4:1; 10:1; 15:20; 17:25; 23:22, 24–25; 30:11 for further evidence or the respect shown mutually to father and mother. R.N. Whybray (*Intellectual Tradition*, 42) notes that "it is difficult to avoid the conclusion that this feature [the mention of the mother as well as the father in the instruction] is an example of the adaptation of the Egyptian tradition to the peculiar situation in which the Israelite instructions were composed: a domestic situation in which the father and mother together shared the responsibility for the education of the child."

23. E. Gerstenberger, *Wesen und Herkunft*, esp. pp. 110–20.

24. Cf. C.L. Meyers, "The Roots of Restriction: Women in Early Israel," *BA* 41 (1978) 91–103, esp. p. 95.

25. N.K. Gottwald, *The Tribes of Yahweh* (Maryknoll, N.Y.: Orbis, 1979); "Biblical Theology or Biblical Sociology?" *Radical Religion* 2 (1975–76) 42–57; "Domain Assumptions."

26. N.K. Gottwald, "Domain Assumptions," 95.

27. Described in detail by C.L. Meyers, "Roots of Restriction."

28. N.K. Gottwald, "Biblical Theology," 50.

29. Cf. Prov 13:22; 14:21, 31; 15:25; 17:5, 6; 19:17; 20:20; 22:16; 22:22–23; 23:10–11; 28:27; 29:7. See also E. Gerstenberger (*Wesen und Herkunft*, 146–47) for a discussion of the basic

congruence and continuity of the substance (as well as the form) of the more explicitly Yahwistic pentateuchal legal commandments and wisdom's admonitions.

30. N. Gottwald, "Biblical Theology," 48.

31. P.A.H. de Boer, "Counsellor," 59.

32. N. Gottwald has elaborated the significant symbolic interrelationship between the "singularity of the divine manifestor" and the "singularity of the social entity Israel." See "Biblical Theology," esp. p. 49.

33. My forthcoming book "Wisdom and the Feminine in the Book of Proverbs" expands the scope of this investigation with regard to these three problematic areas.

34. The sociological concept of domain-assumptions was introduced by N. Gottwald, and defined as "the key or master conceptual frames of reference which affect the kinds of models and hypotheses that are imaginable—and therefore possible—in an epoch or circle of scholarship" ("Domain Assumptions," 89). Wisdom scholarship, no less than the research in the history of Israel with which Gottwald is concerned, needs to examine and make explicit many of the "half-or-unexpressed and unargued" assumptions on which it bases its conclusions.

Rereading Women
in the Bible

Reading Strategies
and the Story of Ruth

EDWARD L. GREENSTEIN

It was said in the name of Rabbi Benaʾah:
"There were 24 dream interpreters in Jeru-
salem. Once I had a dream and consulted
with every one of them. This one interpreted
for me one thing, and that one another.
And they all came true."

BABYLONIAN TALMUD, *BERAKHOT* 55B

The history of interpretation is the history of readers reading and making sense of texts. No one is born reading; every literary experience involves the exercise of learned behavior. Each reader applies the conventions of reading and methods of interpretation that one has acquired or creatively developed. Looking back on the many diverse readings of a well-worn text, such as a popular biblical narrative, one often appreciates the value of many different types of reading. Like the ancient rabbis and others,[1] one may remain convinced that a narrative means all of a number of things.[2] In that case, one may take a lesson from the history of interpretation and decide to read differently, according to one or several of a variety of hermeneutical strategies.

I take the position that different theoretical approaches to literature serve the useful function of generating diverse strategies by which to read and interpret texts. Rather than choose to delimit meaning by adhering to one particular school or method of criticism, readers may elect to adopt and adapt reading approaches from a variety of theories. One of the beneficial lessons of poststructuralist, and especially deconstructive, writing is that no theory can stand up to all critical challenge and monopolize the way we read. Unless we uncritically ground our textual object in an absolute metaphysical framework, the center cannot indefinitely hold—for we can always shift the center and regard our reading from a different angle. Seen differently, texts appear different, meaning that, insofar as we can know and for all intents and purposes, they are different. The text, then,

211

can be empirically known not as a material object but only as the tentative projection of a process of reading.[3] The meaning of a text is not self-evident but is made by readers, and the same reader may find a number of different reading strategies both valid and enriching by making meaning on many levels alternatively.

The point has been incisively and exquisitely articulated by Borges:

> Even for the same reader the same book changes, for we change; we are the river of Heraclitus, who said that the man of yesterday is not the man of today, who will not be the man of tomorrow. We change incessantly, and each reading of a book, each rereading, each memory of that reading, reinvents the text. The text too is the changing river of Heraclitus.[4]

Each reading is influenced by different circumstantial factors and by different practical procedures. One may revise one's interpretations over time, but one does not in doing so necessarily invalidate the earlier readings one has produced. They may all share a measure, if not an equal measure, of validity and conviction. If that is so, the resourceful reader will become open to an array of possibilities for making good sense of texts.

In order both to argue that thesis and to illustrate it, I shall review a number of critical readings of the little Book of Ruth. I hope to show that a number of interesting and (in their own way) convincing readings of the story rest on or derive from diverse theoretical premises, as well as different ideological objectives. Each reading applies or adapts strategies that are associated with one or another school of literary criticism. In each case the proof of the pudding will be in the eating. That is, the value of each reading, each application of some theory or theories, will be judged by the extent of its hermeneutical interest and use. The benefit of acknowledging a variety of theoretical approaches is that it enables the reader to choose, to make good matches, good "chemistry," between reading strategies and texts. One method may work "better" on one text, or type of text, than it would on another. The "better" reading is the one that satisfies the goals that one (consciously or unconsciously) seeks, using the evidence and argumentation that one finds most convincing or effective.[5] New and interesting readings are produced by trying out a fresh approach on a familiar tale, in this case, the story of Ruth.

To read from a literary perspective means to read in the way that we read what we, by whatever traditions and conventions, call literature.[6] Most literary readings of the Ruth narrative operate within the theoretical principles of the New Criticism. The text is approached as an object of art each element of which contributes to a coherent, if often ambiguous and polyvalent, sense. A poem offered in response to a Grecian urn is itself viewed as an object, albeit a verbal one.[7] Beginning with the assumption that the Book of Ruth "is a unity,"[8] each part of the whole is treated as deliberate and integral to a meaningful design.[9] The meaning can be inferred from the harmonies among the various textual components. In the Book of Ruth, as Phyllis Trible puts it, "Th[e] total symmetry [of its overall structure] lends integrity to the story; it sets it apart as an aesthetic object; and it embraces meaning as inseparable from form and content."[10] We shall see later on that literature, like the language of which it is made, may indeed turn out to be unruly. The New Critic, however, looks for, and finds, some sort of pattern or patterns in reading. The pattern is interpreted as the architecture of the literary work, a structure that guides the reading subject in making sense.[11]

More complex literary works may be found to manifest a number of patterns, so that the critic inevitably plays a role in identifying of what the pattern consists and in deciding which pattern to highlight in interpreting a text. Most exegetes will suggest only one reading at a time, giving the impression that one particular meaning stands out above all others. By contrast, D.F. Rauber, who follows the fashion of developing a single primary line of interpretation, insists that his own reading "is not intended to be exhaustive. There are," he adds, "numerous other patterns and progressions" in the Book of Ruth.[12] In first surveying some different analyses of the Ruth narrative that are all more or less sympathetic to the New Criticism, we shall see that elements of one pattern may function differently when connected to a different pattern. Whether this is because there are overlapping patterns within the literary design or because different critics draw the patterns differently is a theoretical issue that can only be settled by adopting one philosophical position or another. But in either event, it is clear that no reading incorporates all the textual facts. The critic draws some of the language into the pattern, and in doing so leaves other language out. Interpretation is necessarily selective, and selection is necessarily motivated differently for different readers.

For S.D. Goitein, the story of Ruth is a virtually perfect work of literary art, unparalleled in its structural harmony.[13] It is composed of four main scenes, bridged by transitions in which women engage in dialogue, reflecting on the progress of the plot and/or plotting to advance it.[14] The first scene presents Naomi and Ruth on their return to Bethlehem. Upon her arrival back home, Naomi reacts to the townswomen who ask, "Is this Naomi?" (1:19). Playing on her name, she says: "Call me not Naomi [Pleasant One]; call me Mara [Bitter One]" (1:20).[15] In the course of the narrative, from chapter 1 to chapter 4, Naomi is transformed from embittered to happy.[16] The cause of that transformation, for Goitein, lies at the heart of the tale's meaning. To locate the factors responsible for that transformation, Goitein examines the intervening chapters.

The two middle chapters, or scenes, feature encounters between Ruth and Boaz. In the first of these, or scene 2, Ruth "chances" upon Boaz while gleaning in his field; in the second, or scene 3, Ruth invades Boaz's privacy on the threshing floor. The widely noted parallel between these scenes is variously adduced to support a theological interpretation. In scene 2, Boaz explains his special attention to Ruth: he had heard of Ruth's dedication to her mother-in-law Naomi (2:11); referring back to Ruth's beneficence toward Naomi, Boaz will in scene 3 call it her "first" *hesed*—act of personal devotion (3:10). But in scene 2 Boaz invokes the deity to provide an ultimate reward to the woman (2:12); he himself shows her modest kindness. In scene 3, Boaz is made to realize that Ruth seeks to show *hesed* not only to Naomi but also, and perhaps especially, to her late husband Mahlon. He understands that Ruth is pursuing him in order to redeem Naomi's land and produce an heir through him, a relative, in a quasi-levirate procedure.[17] That, it dawns on him in the middle of the night, is why she prefers him to a more appropriate younger man (3:10). Boaz senses that he must act as an agent for God. The *hesed* that YHWH will repay Ruth will be delivered through Boaz.

Goitein observes that the quiet tone of the narrative suits the book's theology.[18] God functions by implication, not by dramatic intervention.[19] Characters invoke God in blessings; Naomi explains her sorry life as a divine affliction. When, on her first day out to glean, Ruth enters the field of Boaz, the narrator says that "her occurrence occurred" (2:3). As Trible comments, "It is a felicitous expression . . . , reporting chance and accident while hinting that chance is caused. Within human luck is divine intentionality."[20] A number of critics reinforce the sense that Boaz is acting on behalf of God by noting an unusual turn of phrase in the threshing floor scene and interpreting it as a literary allusion.[21] Ruth instructs Boaz to "spread [his] wings [i.e., robe] over [his] maidservant, as [he] is the redeemer" (3:9). This recalls 2:12, where Boaz tells Ruth that he knows she has "come for shelter under the wings" of YHWH. YHWH's wings take the form of Boaz's wings, symbolizing Boaz's enactment of the deity's role.

What has brought about the transformation of Naomi, then, is a transformation of Boaz, from nice guy to angel. But what precipitates the change in Boaz? What makes the plot tick? The narrative's dynamic will, in a unified work—and Ruth is for Goitein as for others an artistic unity—correlate with all major elements of the story. Goitein delineates six components of a successful narrative: an engaging plot, a tight structure, a familiar setting (real or imagined, but one that elicits associations), realistic characters, a pervasive yet subtle message (spread lightly but all over, like salt on a meal), and a reinforcing style.[22] In Goitein's reading these components all come together in relation to the theme of *hesed*. He aligns his interpretation with that of the Talmudic sage, Rabbi Zeʾeira: the Book of Ruth was composed to model the rewards of doing *hesed*.[23] Those who show generosity to others will providentially receive the same. The chief protagonists, Ruth and Boaz, are for Goitein embodiments of *hesed*. The story's characters, then, express the book's preeminent concern.

The plot is organized around a lucid structure in which Ruth's acts of *hesed,* to the living (Naomi) and the dead (Mahlon), stir Boaz to reciprocate, first to the living (Ruth and Naomi) by offering Ruth preferential treatment in the field, and then to the dead (Mahlon) by purchasing Naomi's estate and marrying Ruth. The book climaxes—when Obed is born—not following the scene on the threshing floor but following the legal process at the city gate. Through the quasi-levirate ceremony Boaz makes it possible "to establish the name of the dead on his estate" (4:5).[24] The relative who refuses to marry Ruth is, as a number of commentators note, left nameless himself.[25] The narrative punishes him as it were for rejecting the opportunity to memorialize his late kinsman, Mahlon. The scene is critical because it manifests Boaz's ultimate show of *hesed*. He, whose name suggests personal "strength," will perpetuate the name of Mahlon and its attachment to his patrimony.[26] It is *hesed*—Boaz's *hesed* for the dead—that figures prominently at the dramatic height of the tale.

Hesed accounts, too—in Goitein's reading—for the settings of the Ruth story. Naomi and Ruth return to Bethlehem at the time of the harvest, and the progress of the harvest receives explicit notice at the end of chapter 2. In addition to providing the sites for Ruth and Boaz to meet, the field at harvest time conditions the practice of gleaning.[27] The Torah, both in Leviticus 19 and in Deuteronomy 24, enjoins the Israelites to leave part of the harvest for the disadvantaged to collect. The gleaning law, then, like the characters Ruth and Boaz, betokens *hesed*; the institution of gleaning is suggested, to Goitein, by the story's agricultural setting.

The didactic theme of Goitein's (and others') reading of Ruth—the promotion of *hesed*—does in this analysis pervade the entire length of the text and its several narratological elements. This interpretation, however, does not evenly draw all parts of the story into its orbit. The text begins by describing the migration of Naomi's family to Moab on account of a famine in the land of Judah. This entire episode, which goes on to recount the deaths of Naomi's husband and sons in Moab, Goitein diminishes in importance by excluding it from the narrative proper. Rather than see these events as integral to the main plot and, consequently, to the theme of the story, Goitein regards them as "exposition," a prelude to the story itself.[28] Goitein buttresses his decision by appealing to the repetition in 1:7 of Naomi's exodus from Moab in 1:6. The repetition signifies to Goitein that the key narrative starts here. By construing the central structural pattern of the story in this way, Goitein must play down or miss patterns that many other readers perceive. In the readings of D.F. Rauber and Jack Sasson that will be discussed below, the famine in Bethlehem functions as an initial lack that must be made up in the course of the ensuing narrative. Others understand that the story begins and ends with the account of a lineage—the line of Elimelech that would seem to die out and the line of Boaz that retrieves one link in Elimelech's line and ties it to the Davidic monarchy.[29] As Porten remarks,[30] the prominence of this framework is underscored by the ten-fold mention of names at the beginning of chapter 1 and the ten-generational genealogy at the end of chapter 4; and by the fact that the story begins with Elimelech, whose name means "God is King," and ends with the birth notice of Judah's first king, David.[31] Note, too, that the birthplace of David, Bethlehem, and his social (?) group, Ephrath (1 Sam. 17:12), are mentioned at the beginning and near the end of the Ruth story (Ruth 1:1–2; 4:11).[32] What for Goitein is background exposition is for Porten and others the presentation of a central thematic concern.

Virtually all readers comment on the book's reiteration of Ruth's Moabite origin; she is repeatedly referred to in this otherwise laconic narrative as "the Moabite."[33] In 2:10 an extended wordplay and assonantal chain highlights Ruth's foreignness. She asks Boaz why he has shown her such favor while she is a "foreigner"—*lehakkireni* (root: *n-k-r*) *veʾanokhi* (*n-k*) *nokhriyya* (*n-k-r*). A repetition of the consonants *n*, *k*, and *r* echoes the word for "foreigner," *nokhriyya* (root: *n-k-r*).[34] To many, Ruth's particular ethnicity is crucial to the story and its theme, especially because Deut. 23:4–7 makes a point of excluding Moabites from the Israelite community.[35] Goitein contends that Ruth's nationality is peripheral to the narrative, necessary only as a kind of prop. In order to bind herself to Naomi, Ruth had to abandon her homeland, which in this instance happens to be Moab.[36] It is evident why Goitein seeks to marginalize Moab: he has an ideological axe to grind. He wants to delegitimize two widespread claims concerning the meaning of Ruth. According to one, the Book of Ruth was composed in order to oppose the measures taken by Ezra and Nehemiah in the fifth century B.C.E. against Judean intermarriage.[37] In the other, found in many traditional Jewish commentaries, Elimelech and his sons were punished by God for having left the land of the Covenant for the abominable Moab and for having married forbidden Moabite women.[38] Goitein did not consider the positive function that Rauber finds in making Ruth a Moabite.[39] The Torah everywhere enjoins Israelites to treat the stranger with compassion. Boaz's kindness to Ruth is magnified by his extending generosity to Ruth even though she is a stranger, a Moabite.

Porten sees the Moabite association as essential to a major theme of the book.[40] Abraham, the first Hebrew, had two brothers, Nahor and Haran. Abraham's lineage is reunited with Nahor's when in the next generation Isaac marries Rebekah, Nahor's granddaughter (Gen. 22:23). The reunification of Abraham's genealogical line and Haran's is achieved in the coupling of Boaz and Ruth. Boaz is descended from Judah, Abraham's greatgrandson (Ruth 4: 18ff.; cf. Gen. 38:29); and Ruth is a "daughter" of

Moab, the son of Lot and grandson of Haran (Gen. 19:37). David, the climactic scion of the Judean genealogy, then represents a consummation of the Abrahamic covenant, the one who reestablishes the family of Abraham.

Indeed, carrying Porten's line of interpretation further, one can identify a political motive for leading all the blood lines to David. King David is first made king of Judah (David's tribe) and then, seven and a half years later, he is accepted as king of northern Israel (Jacob's legacy), too. Among his conquests are the Aramean states (descendants of Abraham's brother Nahor), the Edomites (descendants of Jacob's brother Esau), and the Ammonites and Moabites (sons of Lot, the son of Abraham's brother Haran). David in his person, therefore, incorporates the various peoples he governs. Their blood runs in his veins. He is the one person who can legitimately reign over them all. LaCocque has asked, "Why would a piece of propaganda for David repeat so many times that Ruth was a Moabite . . . ?"[41] Porten's analysis provides the answer: Ruth's position in David's genealogy brings the Ammonites and Moabites under his imperial claim.[42]

Depending on where one draws the lines of interpretation, Moab may belong to the center or the margins of the narrative structure.

Goitein, we saw, relegated the opening verses of the book to secondary "exposition." In Rauber's literary reading the pivotal theme of the story is introduced in the very first verse, and in the ensuing verses that theme is elaborated.[43] Rather than entail a prologue, the opening unveils the heart of the matter. Barrenness and loss, both for the land—in the form of famine—and for people—in death—represent half a cycle, the other half of which is fertility and birth. The "controlling pattern" of the Ruth narrative, Rauber writes, "can be stated abstractly as emptiness-fullness."[44] The cycle runs along two parallel, but unsynchronized—staggered—planes: that of nature, and that of personal history. The anxiety produced by emptiness and loss can only be mitigated by fullness and gain. When the means of achieving that resolution are unknown or out of reach, we feel tension, desperation, and expectation. Those uneasy feelings form the dynamic subtending the story. When the land of Judah enjoys renewed fertility, we hope the same for the miserable Naomi. Our hopes are fed by Ruth's decision to stand by Naomi and her fortunate encounter with Boaz in his field. The quiet suspense of the narrative hinges on Ruth and Boaz overcoming the mundane obstructions of tradition and convention and becoming a couple.

Rauber can delineate many features of the text that conform to the hermeneutical design he has sketched. Some of them functioned within Goitein's scheme, too. "Famine" and "harvest" are noted at various points as markers of narrative time.[45] Harvesting provides the setting of chapter 2, and the threshing floor serves as the scene of chapter 3. On the human side, Naomi innocently announces the story's theme when in 1:21 she says: "I had gone out full, but empty has YHWH returned me."[46] Chapter 1 had underlined the deaths in Naomi's family, and she herself had foregrounded the problem of barrenness when she told her not incidentally childless daughters-in-law that she could no longer bear sons (1:13). Naomi's emptiness is filled by Ruth, when Boaz makes all arrangements to marry her and they count their first son as Mahlon's. If making up Naomi's loss is indeed the story's chief concern,[47] it makes perfect sense that the townswomen bless God for having provided Naomi a "redeemer" in the form of Ruth's son (4:14–15). Naomi pulls the child to her own bosom and, wonder of wonders, nurses him (v. 16).[48] The women, who function as a sort of Greek chorus,[49] declare: "A son has been born to Naomi!" (v. 17). Rauber aptly explains:

> The fertility of Ruth and the fruit of her womb are triumphant rejoinders to the barrenness which darkened the first chapter. Here also is the human manifestation of the theme of harvesting which has pervaded the work from chapter 2 on. Here also is the re-establishment of the full family and social harmony.[50]

The allusion in 4:11 to the matriarchs Leah and Rachel, "who the two of them built up the House of Israel," similarly evokes, as Rauber observes, "the strong patriarchal emphases on fertility and 'the seed.'"[51]

The fertility cycles of nature and people come together stunningly in the overdetermined image of Boaz filling Ruth's apron with grain on the threshing floor (3:15). The grain, as was noted already in an ancient midrash,[52] symbolizes Ruth's future impregnation.[53] Boaz supplies Ruth with this concrete token, saying she should not return "empty" to her mother-in-law (3:17). It is Naomi's emptiness the anticipated birth is to fill.[54]

In analyzing the story's theme as the revolution of the emptiness-fullness cycle, and demonstrating its application to Naomi, Rauber is mindful of the theological underpinning that Goitein and others had stressed. The verse 3:9, in which Ruth beckons Boaz to spread his "wings" over her as "redeemer," is for Rauber the "exact center" of the narrative.[55] Nevertheless, in presenting so abstract a reading Rauber must pay less attention to the legal process that occupies a large part of the book's climactic scene.[56] He must also pass quickly over the particulars of the genealogy that concludes the book; the Davidic imperial politics that would seem to lie behind what Porten finds at play within Ruth barely figure at all for Rauber. It is clear that Rauber's emphasis on an abstract pattern serves a purpose that is virtually antithetical to the ethnocentric concerns that are so crucial in Porten's reading. Rauber had been looking chiefly for macro-patterning, while Porten had been seeking out micro-designs; the one's concerns are more global, the other's more specific.

The last New Critical reading of Ruth we shall discuss, before turning to structuralist analysis, is the feminist interpretation of Trible.[57] Trible's reading all leads to her explicit goal: "a theological interpretation of feminism: women working out their own salvation with fear and trembling, for it is God who works in them."[58] Here Trible adds her own nuance to the widely noted theology of the book, in which human agents manifest divine providence by their own acts. The female characters are, for Trible, the ones that model the story's thematic interests: "Naomi works as a bridge between tradition and innovation. Ruth and the females of Bethlehem work as paradigms for radicality."[59] To advance her interpretation, Trible highlights the interaction of women in the narrative. Within the context of the Hebrew Bible, and for all we know ancient Israel in general, women functioning in collaboration as major protagonists in a story is a radical concept that justifies special attention.[60] Trible exploits this to her hermeneutical advantage as a basis for ascribing to the female characters feminist motivations. In order to accomplish this, as we shall see, Trible must (like everyone else) read selectively.

Trible focuses intensely on Ruth's bonding to Naomi in chapter 1. In contrast to a more recent reading by Danna Nolan Fewell and David M. Gunn,[61] Trible regards this bonding in a positive light. Like the patriarch Abraham, Ruth departs from her native land for a different life.[62] She makes a radical decision to follow another God by choosing the company of a woman over a conventional existence at home. To reinforce this reading, Trible points to the mention of matriarchs in chapter 4: "Comparison of Ruth [in vv. 11–12] to the ancient mothers Rachel, Leah, and Tamar recalls the parallel between Ruth and Abraham. . . ."[63] A further parallel to the patriarchal narratives is the migration from the land of Israel on account of famine, the event that triggers the story's initial action. Such a migration occurs in each generation of Israel's ancestors in Genesis.[64] The narrative in chapter 1 in typical fashion does not externalize Ruth's motivation in clinging to Naomi. Trible introduces a motive: "A young woman has committed herself to the life of an old woman rather than to the search for a husband. . . ."[65] By casting Ruth's decision in this way, Trible has made a fateful hermeneutical choice; it affects her reading of the balance of the story.

The boldness of Ruth's action may account for Trible's strategy of treating it somewhat hermetically. Other readers, with different objectives, interpret Ruth's decision, at least retrospectively, in the context of the book's final chapter. All along, Ruth had intended to return to Judah with Naomi in order to marry a kinsman of her late husband and produce an heir to his estate. That is what the legal procedure in chapter 4 is all about: "to establish the name of the dead on his estate" (see above). Trible plays down the significance of this chapter as a deviation from the largely female concerns of the preceding three.[66] In fact, rather than understand that Ruth had, following Naomi's advice, manipulated Boaz into redeeming Mahlon's land and marrying Ruth, Trible views Boaz as the one who uses Ruth as an instrument to accomplish the patriarchal duty of restoring the name of Mahlon to his patrimony.[67] This interpretation can succeed only by devaluing what Boaz declares to be Ruth's ulterior motivation. The nature of this "latter *hesed*" can be clarified by reading the first scene retrospectively, in view of the final scene in which Boaz both marries Ruth and redeems the estate. When Boaz on the threshing floor praises Ruth for her "latter *hesed*" (3:10), Trible does not explain its reference.[68] When Naomi in chapter 1 had referred to the *hesed* Ruth and Orpah had shown to "the dead" (v. 8), she was then clearly speaking of the past.[69] Boaz, however, places the "latter *hesed*" in the context of Ruth's preferring him to a younger, more appropriate husband. From what Boaz does in consequence of that meeting, it becomes evident that he understood that Ruth intended to join him in an act of *hesed* for the late Mahlon. The idea is suggested already in Naomi's remark to her daughters-in-law in 1:13–14: the women should not stay with Naomi because she can produce no more sons. Had Ruth and Orpah wanted to remain with Naomi because they could thereby provide sons for their husbands posthumously through as yet unconceived brothers-in-law, it is hopeless, says Naomi. Although this statement might well establish the motivation for Ruth's clinging to Naomi, Trible, in conformity with her overall reading, passes over the remark in haste.[70] Even so, Trible's reading accounts a preponderance of weight to the first chapter, and to the conversation between Naomi and Ruth there in particular.

In contrast to Trible's reading, which focalizes scene 1 and only such other points within the narrative that underscore the bonding and assertiveness of the female protagonists, Rauber had suggested that the interpretation of Ruth should rest on the recurrent patterns within the text. For him "chapter 1 is concerned with establishing a dominant pattern for the work."[71] That pattern, as we saw, Rauber identified as the "emptiness-fullness" cycles. Rauber maintains that "the great key to the reading of Hebraic literature is sensitivity to pattern."[72] Operating in the New Critical tradition, Rauber found the pattern on the narrative surface, in the overt design.

The structuralist approach, too, capitalizes on patterns; but in structuralism the patterns are not only abstract but beneath the surface of the text.[73] The text, from a structuralist perspective, is but the superficial concrete manifestation of underlying conceptual relations. Analogous to language in general, the text is a surface representation of "deep" structures. The goal of interpretation is, in this view, to lay bare the underlying sense. Typically, structuralists understand deep-structure relationships to take the form of the opposition of two concepts in tension with one another. A narrative projects these binary oppositions in a variety of guises or transformations in the text and seeks to resolve their contradiction or opposition in some way. Because significance inheres not in the surface representations—the narrative action and the particular characters, for example—but in the deep structure oppositions, the analyst—or narratologist—looks for, or finds significance in, those relations that seem to recur throughout a text. The structuralist will accordingly favor those elements that repeat and devalue those that stand out by their extraordinariness. Indeed, taking a lesson from Freud, who taught us that the unconscious transforms or disguises objects of the greatest anxiety and concern,[74] seemingly minor and extraneous elements may in a structuralist reading receive the greatest attention.

Rauber had observed a pattern of "emptiness-fullness" throughout the Ruth story. This pattern, however, is explicitly articulated and symbolically represented in the surface structure of the narrative. Rauber's analysis does not purport to reveal an otherwise hidden set of underlying relations. Both the New Critic and the structuralist regard the text as a semiotic object that must be subjected to analysis by the interpreter.[75] But the former seeks significance more in the specific language of a text while the latter finds meaning more in its abstract patterning.

Looking at Ruth, a structuralist might focus on the widely noted cross-cultural problem of endogamy (marriage within the group) versus exogamy (marriage with someone from outside the group).[76] The contradiction between the biblical ideal of endogamy (see Deuteronomy 23) and the well-known reality of rampant exogamy (see Judges 3) is mitigated by the descent of King David from an exogamous coupling, Boaz and Ruth. From this perspective, the unreproductive marriages of Naomi's sons to Moabite women emblematize a problem that is resolved only when the Moabite widow Ruth migrates to Judah and marries a Judean. In such a reading, the Moabite origin of Ruth is, contra Goitein (see above), central to the message. The concluding genealogy—a linkage of ten Israelite men—is not an afterthought but the very point: not the dramatic climax but the thematic resolution.

The structuralist will find special significance in this aspect of the Ruth narrative not because it figures prominently in the plot—it is barely perceptible, after all, in the middle scenes—but because the same binary opposition between endogamy and exogamy can be located in a large number of biblical texts. Those matters that most worry a society, say Lévi-Strauss and other structural anthropologists,[77] will tend to appear ubiquitously in that society's mythology and folk literature. Truly to investigate the meaning of a narrative, then, a structuralist should examine it within a larger corpus of texts. It is not the individual story but the recurrent relations within a body of texts that carry the greatest significance.[78]

Harold Fisch studies the Book of Ruth in conjunction with two other biblical narratives, the cycle of stories about Lot between Genesis 13 and 19—culminating in the rape of Lot by his daughters—and the story of Judah in Genesis 38—culminating in the seduction of Judah by his daughter-in-law Tamar.[79] Fisch's selection of these two texts is not arbitrary; Ruth is ultimately descended from Lot (Moab issued from the rape), and Ruth 4:12 refers to Judah and Tamar. From these three texts Fisch abstracts a common story: a family is divided; some tragedy ensues; "the hope of the family is preserved in a woman/women"; "a near kinsman is made to accept responsibility for the continuation of the family"; "the woman takes the initiative"; the male protagonist loses self-control through gaiety (intoxication except in the case of Judah); the woman/women and the male protagonist are coupled (through a quasi-levirate procedure except in the case of Lot); and there is a significant male issue.[80] The tension in this synthetic synopsis of the parallel narratives revolves around the opposition of family continuity/discontinuity. The tension is resolved through the female protagonist's taking matters into her own hands. The woman's act in the three stories runs the gamut from grossly illegal (rape) to scrupulously licit (the procedure at the city-gate in Ruth 4). Of all the possible oppositions and relations on which Fisch could have fixed, it is this theme of legality that for him stands out in significance. That is because Fisch is interested in connecting his reading with the general biblical theme of the Covenant and the history that embodies it.

Fisch acknowledges the potential to abstract themes from what he calls the Ruth-corpus: "Ultimately, we are concerned with the articulation of a dialectical pattern of order and disorder, life and death, fullness and emptiness."[81] But in contrast (or opposition) to conventional structural analysis, by which patterns are studied and deep structures disclosed synchronically, without respect to historical sequence, Fisch turns his synchronic analysis of the Ruth-corpus into a tool for tracing what he contends is a diachronic movement from lesser to greater degrees of legality or propriety. "One is tempted to claim," Fisch writes, "that the real value of the synchrony, i.e., the exhibition of the structural pattern which unites the stories, is in lighting up the social and moral differences between them in the diachronic scale."[82] Fisch arranges the three narratives in the corpus in a sequence corresponding to the biblical tradition: Lot and his daughters, Judah and Tamar, Boaz and Ruth. The first episode reflects a primitive, amoral stage of development; the second a questionable but socially negotiated transaction; and the third "a careful observance of the proprieties."[83] The story of Ruth, in Fisch's rather didactic interpretation, " 'redeem[s]' the previous episodes in the corpus," an altogether appropriate function for a text in which "redemption" (geʾulla) is a key term and value.[84]

Fisch is able to place his analysis within the tradition of structuralism by associating its theme with that of a fundamental paradigm of Lévi-Strauss, "the raw and the cooked."[85] In the South American Indian myths he studied, Lévi-Strauss found that psychosocial tensions between the competing attractions of life in a state of nature and life in a state of culture were represented in the surface structure by images of raw and cooked food.[86] In biblical society, as Fisch reads, the same abstract opposition between nature and culture is represented in the area of sexual liaisons.[87] The three narratives of the Ruth-corpus reflect a continuum between the almost state-of-nature cohabitation of Lot and his daughters, the half-way character of Tamar's prostitution, and the fully civilized marriage of Ruth to Boaz.

Now although Fisch has formulated his analysis in terms of an abstract thematic opposition, for the most part his interpretation remains close to the plot and other aspects of the textual surface structure. The tensions between nature and culture, or familial continuity and discontinuity for that matter, are interpreted only in specific relation to particular biblical texts. One could alternatively relate the generalities Fisch observes to more widely applicable themes. The broad issue of endogamy and exogamy as a trans-biblical theme was mentioned above. For another example, we turn to that episode of the common Ruth-corpus plot Fisch calls "the bed-trick." Within the corpus, Lot's daughters get their father drunk and sleep with him; Tamar pretends to be a prostitute and with no difficulty has her father-in-law Judah; and Ruth creeps up to Boaz when he is in a stupor, uncovers his legs, and suggests what she suggests.[88] A scene in which a woman, alone or in collusion, tricks a man into sleeping (or lying down) with her occurs in other biblical passages, too. The best known instance is perhaps the deception of Jacob by Laban, when Jacob thinks he is bedding down with Rachel but discovers in the morning it is her older sister Leah (Genesis 29). The so-called bed-trick, in fact, belongs to the larger biblical category of deception tale.[89] On a global level, the general theme of deception has been taken to convey a critical biblical message: looks are deceiving.[90] Ravaged by catastrophe, the Israelites should not infer that they are abandoned by God and undone. Israel, the message goes, should not be misguided by appearances.

Fisch, then, interprets the structure of the Ruth-corpus in relatively narrow fashion, for a structuralist. It suits his didactic purpose, as does the structuralist analysis he applies. Like all readers, he employs his method insofar as and to the extent that it satisfies his hermeneutical objective.

Structuralist analysis searches for abstract deep structures. It is often assumed that such deep structures represent not merely the thinking of a particular mind or cultural mindset but the very process of human thought itself.[91] There is accordingly a tendency to deduce that true deep structures are potentially universal. That is, there is a finite set of possible patterns and processes from which are derived all ideas and the mechanics of thought. Early structural, one might even call it proto-structural (more technically "formalist"[92]), analysis of narrative sought to identify universal story patterns for different genres of literature. Most famous among such attempts is the analysis of the Russian fairy tale by Vladimir Propp.[93] Propp observed that he could isolate a relatively limited number of actions, or "functions," some obligatory and some optional, that in a controlled set of sequences would combine to form each of a short list of folktale types. It's a little like a complex Chinese menu. Sasson has tried to fit the story of Ruth into the Procrustean bed of the Russian folktale.[94] The advantage of such an approach is that it makes universal claims; it confirms interpretation for those who accept the premises of the analysis and approve the manner of its application. (The disadvantage is that such fittings are apt to appear arbitrarily selective, hence artificial, and may convey little conviction.)[95] Because the theory prescribes, or predicts, certain elements in the narrative, it can be appealed to in the event of an exegetical dispute.

Matching Ruth and Boaz to specific fairy tale character functions, Sasson interprets Ruth's conduct in chapter 2 as that of a calculating and aggressive seeker of gain,[96] and he sees Boaz in chapter 3 transformed into an active, supremely helpful "magical agent."[97] Boaz is Ruth's "donor," the one-way bestower of favors; Ruth is therefore the receiver. Similarly, in a structural analysis of Ruth employing the narrative model of A.J. Greimas,[98] in which the structure of a story is understood by analogy to the syntax of a sentence, Ruth is the "object" to be conveyed to a "receiver," while Boaz is the "subject" at the center of the struggle.[99] I underscore this point because it is diametrically opposed in a significant poststructuralist and feminist reading of Ruth, that by Mieke Bal.[100]

Structuralism, like New Criticism, as was said above, views the text as a semiotic object the meaning of which can be got by means of proper analysis. Analysis, as we have seen, is made by readers each of whom brings different interpretive strategies and sensibilities to bear in making sense. If, as many now claim, even the most fundamental perceptions—of texts or anything else—are already conditioned by prior experience and conceptualization,[101] we might do better to locate the making of sense not in the object of attention but in the perceiver, in the person. To return to Borges's metaphor, cited above, the river of Heraclitus is not a stable object but the locus of everchanging waters. Analogously, a text is not a fixed object but rather a common reference point for all those who read it.[102] Meaning is not extracted from the text but projected onto a common screen, which to facilitate discourse we reify as "the text." Poststructuralist criticism is preoccupied with the politics of reading more than the politics of the text.[103]

In her poststructuralist feminist treatment of biblical narrative, Mieke Bal contends that the patriarchal interpretations that have characterized most readings of the Hebrew Bible result from projecting the often unconscious male biases of Western culture onto the text.[104] Sasson's formalist reading of Ruth endows Boaz with a somewhat one-sided status as the heroic helper. This is not surprising, since the fairy tale model Sasson superimposes on the Ruth story comes from a male dominant culture and calls for a male hero—more specifically, it calls for a "magical agent" to assist the initial hero, who is in this instance Ruth. As Ruth's "donor," too, Boaz must be seen as giving to Ruth and not getting. A reading need not assume, however, that generosity runs in only one direction.

Bal focuses on Ruth 3:10, in which Boaz expresses appreciation for Ruth's own graciousness: "Blessed may you be to YHWH, my daughter; your latter *hesed* you have made finer than your former one, by not going after younger men, be they poorer or richer." Boaz is quite clearly evoking Ruth's giving and not his own.[105] Moreover, Bal, who routinely adopts a pyschoanalytic perspective, detects in Boaz's reference to younger men an expression of anxiety about his own sexual potency. Boaz's fear can be corroborated by his trembling at the unexpected approach of a woman in 3:8.[106] Like other commentators,[107] Bal places great significance in the narrative's use of personal names. Boaz's name, Bal observes, is ironic. While it is meant to signify "strength,"[108] Boaz is encountered in weakness. He appears to have taken no initiative to help Naomi upon her return from Moab,[109] and at his fateful meeting with Ruth on the threshing floor he is caught sleeping and unaware.[110] Boaz becomes sexually energized and socially activated only through the assertions of Ruth. Although in other readings Boaz's indebtedness to Ruth who has empowered him as a man would be treated as a subtext at best and has in fact been almost entirely ignored. Bal chooses, for her own explicit reasons, to highlight it.

Bal's innovative reading is not only feminist in orientation. It regroups elements of the narrative noted by others, too, into a different pattern, thereby suggesting an altogether different theme.[111] Bal overlooks or slights the statement of the redeeming kinsman, the *goʾel,* in 4:6 to the effect that he refuses to purchase Naomi's estate because he would by doing so "ruin" his own estate. That is, since Boaz has announced his intentions to marry Ruth,[112] the son of that union would be considered as the son of the late Mahlon and would take full possession of Naomi's estate. The redeeming kinsman would lose the entire purchase price. For Bal what stands out is the story's concern here with law and legality. Deuteronomy (22:22; 23:2) forbids Israelites from marrying Moabites. Bal suspects that the kinsman refuses to marry Ruth and redeem Naomi's estate because that would violate established law.[113] The namelessness of the redeemer Bal explains within this framework. Boaz will not address his kinsman by name because by doing so he would have to acknowledge his intersubjectivity, his legitimate participation in the legal procedure. Boaz realizes that in order to achieve his aim of marrying Ruth and taking title to the late Mahlon's estate, which is the right thing to do, he must transgress the law. Like a structuralist, the poststructuralist Bal seeks to abstract a universal theme. The story's climax, Bal suggests, problematizes the tensions "between law and legitimacy."[114]

When one thinks about some of the issues in Ruth, one may agree that what Bal calls the "trial between law and legitimacy" is one of them. Without tying various elements of the narrative together as Bal has, one would not, however, be likely to articulate this theme. Each of the readings of Ruth we have treated has by taking a different tack featured a different aspect of the story. For different purposes, one would choose to read differently. To stress the particularly Israelite themes of the story, one might highlight the genealogical components of the narrative, dealing with Ruth's Moabite background in a political manner. One might also point to the parallel cycles of rebirth in the land and the family, seeing the intimate connection of people and their ancestral land on a national scale—concerning the relations of the Israelite people to their homeland.[115] On the other hand, one may use Ruth for its moral or theological lesson about the virtues of personal kindness. On a higher level of abstraction, one may read this narrative as a tale that sublimates universal human insecurities about fertility and order. Thinking politically, one may appeal to Ruth for confirmation of a male dominant social system—after all, it is in an all-male forum that personal fates are decided. Or one may adduce the Ruth narrative to demonstrate the benefits that may accrue to a society from the collaboration of independent and assertive women.

Considering the multiple possibilities of meaning in Ruth, as in other great stories, one might speak vaguely of the rich texture of the text or the depths of meaning in the narrative. But when upon further reflection it becomes evident that the varieties of meaning are gotten by different means, increased importance or value is ascribed to the ways that we read. Meaning is enhanced by shifting perspective as colors are multiplied by turning a prism.

Notes

This essay was presented in an earlier form at the conference "The Hebrew Bible: Sacred Text and Literature," held at Wayne State University and the University of Michigan, October 30–November 2, 1988. I am grateful to the participants for their helpful comments and stimulating discussion; to Prof. Peter Machinist for his editorial suggestions; and to the Abbell Research Fund of the Jewish Theological Seminary for support of my research on the topic.

1. For an important clarification of the relations between classical rabbinic hermeneutics and current literary theory, see now David Stern, "Midrash and Indeterminacy," *Critical Inquiry*

15 (1988), pp. 132–61; cf., too, David Weiss Halivni, *Peshat and Derash: Plain and Applied Meaning in Rabbinic Exegesis* (New York: Oxford University Press, 1991), pp. 158–62.

2. Cf., e.g., D.F. Rauber, "The Book of Ruth," in Kenneth R.R. Gros Louis, James S. Ackerman, and Thayer S. Warshaw, eds., *Literary Interpretations of Biblical Narratives* (Nashville: Abingdon Press, 1974), pp. 163–76, at 174–75: "The task of the literary critic is to explore the complex world of the artist and to suggest ways in which we can respond as fully as possible to its multiplicity, its suggestiveness, its richness."

3. See further Stanley Fish, "Why No One's Afraid of Wolfgang Iser," *Doing What Comes Naturally: Change, Rhetoric, and the Practice of Theory in Literary and Legal Studies* (Durham, NC: Duke University Press, 1989), pp. 68–86.

4. Jorge Luis Borges, *Seven Nights,* trans. Eliot Weinberger (New York: New Directions, 1984), pp. 76–77.

5. For this pragmatic understanding of interpretation and argumentation, cf., e.g., Fish, *Doing What Comes Naturally;* Richard Rorty, *Objectivity, Relativism, and Truth* (Cambridge: Cambridge University Press, 1991), esp. part 1; and cf. idem, *Consequences of Pragmatism* (Minneapolis: University of Minnesota Press, 1982), esp. pp. 160–75, for the distinction of pragmatism from relativism. For a modification of Rorty's perspective, see Joseph Margolis, *Pragmatism without Foundations* (New York: Basil Blackwell, 1986), esp. pp. 164–86.

6. Cf., Stanley Fish, *Is There a Text in This Class?* (Cambridge, MA: Harvard University Press, 1980), esp. "How To Recognize a Poem When You See One," pp. 322–37; Terry Eagleton, *Literary Theory: An Introduction* (Minneapolis: University of Minnesota Press, 1983), pp. 1–16; and cf. my "Literature, the Old Testament as," in Paul J. Achtemeier, ed., *Harper's Bible Dictionary* (San Francisco: Harper & Row, 1985), pp. 567–71, at 567.

7. Cf. this representative statement: "A verbal composition, through being supercharged with significance, takes on something like the character of a stone statue or a porcelain vase. Through its meaning or meanings the poem *is.* It has an iconic solidity"; W.K. Wimsatt, Jr., *The Verbal Icon: Studies in the Meaning of Poetry* (Lexington: University of Kentucky Press, 1954), p. 231.

8. Rauber, "The Book of Ruth," p. 175.

9. Cf., e.g., Jacob M. Myers, *The Linguistic and Literary Form of the Book of Ruth* (Leiden: E.J. Brill, 1955), p. 6; Stephen Bertman, "Symmetrical Design in the Book of Ruth," *Journal of Biblical Literature* 84 (1965), pp. 165–68, at 165; Bezalel Porten, "The Scroll of Ruth: A Rhetorical Study," *Gratz College Annual of Jewish Studies* 7 (1978), pp. 23–49, at 23; Alexander Globe, "Folktale Form and National Theme, with Particular Reference to Ruth," in Barry N. Olshen and Yael S. Feldman, eds., *Approaches to Teaching the Hebrew Bible as Literature in Translation* (New York: Modern Language Association, 1989), pp. 127–32.

10. Phyllis Trible, "A Human Comedy: The Book of Ruth," in Kenneth R.R. Gros Louis with James S. Ackerman, eds., *Literary Interpretations of Biblical Narratives, Volume II* (Nashville: Abingdon Press, 1982), pp. 161–90, 314–17, at 161.

11. For a critical overview of the New Criticism in its various forms, see Vincent B. Leitch, *American Literary Criticism from the Thirties to the Eighties* (New York: Columbia University Press, 1988), pp. 24–59.

12. Rauber, "The Book of Ruth," p. 173.

13. Shlomo Dov Goitein, "Megillat Rut" [The Scroll of Ruth], ʿ*Iyyunim bammiqraʾ* [Studies in the Bible], 2nd ed. (Tel Aviv: Yavneh Publishing, 1963), pp. 49–58, esp. at 50 [in Hebrew].

14. On the symmetrical construction of the book in scenes, see further Bertman (n. 10 above).

15. For this and other plays on proper names in Ruth, see now Moshe Garsiel, *Biblical Names: A Literary Study of Midrashic Derivations and Puns* (Ramat Gan: Bar-Ilan University Press, 1991), pp. 250–53.

16. Goitein, "Megillat Rut," pp. 52–53. For Naomi's central role in the narrative, cf., e.g., Edward Robertson, "The Plot of the Book of Ruth," *Bulletin of the John Rylands Library,* 32 (1949–1950), pp. 207–28; Vincent L. Tollers, "Narrative Control in the Book of Ruth," in idem and John Maier, eds., *Mappings of the Biblical Terrain: The Bible as Text* (Lewisburg: Bucknell University Press; Toronto: Associated University Presses, 1990), pp. 252–59; Ilana Pardes, *Counter-traditions in the Bible: A Feminist Approach* (Cambridge, MA: Harvard University Press, 1992), pp. 108–12.

17. The evident purpose of the quasi-levirate procedure in chapter 4 is entirely lost on Northrop Frye, *Words With Power, Being a Second Study of the Bible and Literature* (New York: Harcourt Brace Jovanovich, 1990), p. 212, who explains that Boaz's "motive in doing this was apparently to give Ruth full status as an Israelite widow instead of merely a foreigner."

18. Goitein, "Megillat Rut," pp. 54–55.

19. Cf., e.g., Hermann Gunkel, "Ruth," *Reden und Aufsatze* (Göttingen: Vendenhoeck & Ruprecht, 1913), pp. 65–87, at 87; Edward F. Campbell. Jr., *Ruth,* Anchor Bible 7 (Garden City, NY: Doubleday, 1975), pp. 28–29.

20. Trible, "A Human Comedy," p. 173 and passim; cf., e.g., Robertson, "The Plot," 213; Ronald M. Hals, *The Theology of the Book of Ruth* (Philadelphia: Fortress Press, 1969), pp. 11–12; Gabriel H. Cohn, *ʿiyyunim bimgillat rut* [Studies in the Scroll of Ruth], 2nd rev. ed. (Jerusalem: Ministry of Education and Culture, 1980), pp. 20, 28.

21. Cf. Hals, *Theology,* pp. 7–8; Rauber, "The Book of Ruth," p. 171; Trible, "A Human Comedy," p. 178. Garsiel interprets the association ironically: Boaz invoked a divine blessing upon Ruth, but Ruth sought human help; Moshe Garsiel, "The Literary Structure, Plot Development, and Narrator's Aim in the Scroll of Ruth," in Ezra Hamenahem, ed., *Hagut bammiqraʾ* [Reflections on the Bible], vol. 3 (Tel Aviv: Don, 1979), pp. 66–83, at 75 [in Hebrew].

22. Goitein, "Megillat Rut," pp. 49–50; cf. Beattie's three narratological principles: narrative coherence, credibility, and "self-sufficiency," i.e., that the narrator provides all the necessary facts for comprehending a story; D.R.G. Beattie, "Ruth III," *Journal for the Study of the Old Testament* 5 (1978), pp. 39–48.

23. *Midrash Ruth Rabba* 2:14; cf. *Midrash Ruth Zuta* 1 (ed. S. Buber, p. 42); Goitein, "Megillat Rut," p. 57. Cohn (*ʿIyyunim,* pp. 34–36), too, suggests that the virtue of doing *hesed* is "the overall meaning" of the story.

24. Cf., e.g., Johannes Pedersen, *Israel: Its Life and Culture,* vol. 1–2 (London: Oxford University Press, 1926), pp. 80–81; Oswald Loretz, "The Theme of the Ruth Story," *Catholic Biblical Quarterly* 22 (1960), pp. 391–99. On the nature of the levirate-like transaction and its social function, see Susan Niditch, "The Wronged Woman Righted: An Analysis of Genesis 38," *The Theological Review* 72 (1979), pp. 143–49.

25. Cf., e.g., Campbell, *Ruth,* pp. 141–42; Porten, "The Scroll of Ruth: A Rhetorical Study"; Trible, "A Human Comedy," p. 184. Contrast the treatment of *peloni ʾalmoni* in, e.g., Adele Berlin, *Poetics and Interpretation of Biblical Narrative* (Sheffield: The Almond Press, 1983), pp. 99–101; Athalya Brenner, *Ruth and Naomi: Literary, Stylistic and Linguistic Studies in the Book of Ruth* (Tel Aviv: Sifriat Poalim, 1988), pp. 90–91 [in Hebrew].

26. Porten, "The Scroll of Ruth: A Rhetorical Study," p. 46, observes that this thematic connection can be reinforced by noting the assonance in the Hebrew between the name Mahlon and the word for patrimony, *nahala.*

27. Goitein, "Megillat Rut," p. 57.

28. Goitein, "Megillat Rut," pp. 51–52; cf., e.g., Gunkel, "Ruth," p. 65; Yosef Tsamudi, "On the Scroll of Ruth," *Beth Mikraʾ* 35 (1989–1990), pp. 202–15, at 203–4 [in Hebrew]; Yair Zakovitch, *Ruth: Introduction and Commentary* (Tel Aviv/Jerusalem: Am Oved/Magnes Press, 1990), p. 3 [in Hebrew]: Garsiel, "The Literary Structure," p. 66. Garsiel suggests an interpretation of the narrative along the lines of a text-controlled reader response: the action comprises

episodes each of which presents a problem that frustrates the reader's expectation of an easy resolution; the "message" (Garsiel himself places the word in quotation marks) is that personal salvation, too, demands perseverance and effort (p. 67).

29. Cf., e.g., Bertman, Porten, Sasson, Berlin, Globe.

30. Porten, "The Scroll of Ruth: A Rhetorical Study," pp. 24–25, 47–48; idem, "Theme and Historiosophic Background of the Scroll of Ruth," *Gratz College Annual of Jewish Studies* 6 (1977), pp. 69–78, at 71–72.

31. Cf. Beattie, "Ruth III," p. 46; Hillel Barzel, "Hasheʾeilah ketavnit ʿomeq (II): Qeriʾa lefi hanahot shel Lévi-Strauss battenakh uvassifrut" [The Question as a Deep Structure (II): Reading according to the Assumptions of Lévi-Strauss in the Bible and Literature], ʿIton 77 46 (Oct. 1983), pp. 36–39, at 36; Globe, "Folktale Form," p. 132; lacking in Garsiel, *Biblical Names,* pp. 250–53.

32. Cf., e.g., Zakovitch, *Ruth,* p. 32.

33. An exception is Robertson, "The Plot," who, in making the story out to be little more than the struggle of Naomi to triumph over her distress, excludes from consideration both Ruth's Moabite background and the kindnesses performed and enjoyed by Ruth.

34. Cf., e.g., Campbell, *Ruth,* pp. 98–99; Porten, "The Scroll of Ruth: A Rhetorical Study," p. 34.

35. For extensive discussion of Ruth's Moabite association in the biblical context, see Brenner, *Ruth and Naomi,* pp. 65–70 [in Hebrew]. The negative side of Ruth's Moabiteness is also played up in Danna N. Fewell and David M. Gunn, *Compromising Redemption: Relating Characters in the Book of Ruth* (Louisville: Westminster/John Knox Press, 1990); and in André LaCocque, *The Feminine Unconventional: Four Subversive Figures in Israel's Tradition* (Minneapolis: Fortress Press, 1990), pp. 84–116, esp. 85–86.

36. Goitein, "Megillat Rut," pp. 51, 55.

37. On this well-known view and its rejection by various authors, cf., e.g., Roland E. Murphy, *Wisdom Literature: Job, Proverbs, Ruth, Canticles, Ecclesiastes, and Esther,* Forms of the Old Testament Literature, vol. 13 (Grand Rapids, MI: W.B. Eerdmans, 1981), pp. 86–87. For recent presentations of this interpretation, see, e.g., LaCocque, *The Feminine Unconventional,* pp. 84–116; Zakovitch, *Ruth,* pp. 19–20, 24.

38. Cf. the Targum at 1:4–5 (text interpolated into the Hebrew source appears in italics): "They [viz., Mahlon and Chilion] *transgressed the decree of the Lord's word and* took for themselves *foreign* wives *from daughters of Moab* [Heb., Moabite wives] . . . and *because they transgressed the decree of the Lord's word and intermarried with foreign peoples, their days were curtailed and* they both died. . . ." See also TB Bava Batra 91a; and cf. now Fewell and Gunn, *Compromising Redemption,* p. 121, n. 6.

39. Rauber, "The Book of Ruth," pp. 167–69.

40. Bezalel Porten, "Megillat rut—mivneha, noseʾeha vesignona" [The Scroll of Ruth—Its Structures, Themes, and Style], *Beth Mikra* 69 (1977), pp. 224–29, esp. 227 (= "Structure, Style, and Theme in the Scroll of Ruth," *AJS Newsletter* 17 [June 1976], pp. 15–16, at 16); idem, "Theme and Historiosophic Background," esp. p. 72. Cf. also Harold Fisch, "Ruth and the Structure of Covenant History," *Vetus Testamentum* 32 (1982), pp. 425–37, esp. 435.

41. LaCocque, *The Feminine Unconventional,* p 107. Jacob Licht, *Storytelling in the Bible* (Jerusalem: Magnes Press, 1978), p. 125, contends that the story "endeavors to show how the apparently reprehensible female ancestor has been absorbed into the thoroughly respectable family of Boaz in a perfectly proper way, and for irreproachable reasons."

42. I am not implying that the Book of Ruth should be dated to the era of David. The Davidic imperial claim could and might have been made by any Judean king. I would concur with Sasson in attributing the composition of Ruth to the late 7th century B.C.E., the reign of Josiah, the Judean king who sponsored a neo-classical, nationalist renaissance and tried to revive the Davidic

regime; cf. my "The Formation of the Biblical Narrative Corpus," *AJS Review* 15 (1990), pp. 151–78, at 162–63 with n. 47 and references there.

43. Rauber, "The Book of Ruth," pp. 165ff.

44. Rauber, "The Book of Ruth," p. 165.

45. The fertility reading is elaborated and attenuated to a theological allegory in Barbara Green, *A Study of Field and Seed Symbolism in the Biblical Story of Ruth* (Ph.D. diss.: Graduate Student Union, Berkeley, 1980; Ann Arbor: University Microfilms, 1982).

46. Rauber, "The Book of Ruth," p. 166.

47. Cf. the references in n. 17 above and, e.g., Edward Robertson, "Old Testament Stories: Their Purpose and Their Art," *Bulletin of the John Rylands Library* 28 (1944), pp. 454–76, at 465–66; Berlin, *Poetics and Interpretation*, p. 83; Basil Rebera, "Lexical Cohesion in Ruth: A Sample," in Edgar W. Conrad and Edward G. Newing, eds., *Perspectives on Language and Text* (Winona Lake, Indiana: Eisenbrauns, 1987), pp. 123–49, at 147–48.

48. Whether Naomi acts as nursemaid (ʾomenet, the term used here) or actually functions as wetnurse (*meneqet*) remains ambiguous; cf. Fewell and Gunn, *Compromising Redemption*, p. 82. The possibility that Naomi might actually nurse the baby may be reinforced by noting the parallel with the early life of Moses, who is nursed by his natural mother at the somewhat unwitting invitation of his adoptive mother, the daughter of Pharaoh (Exod. 2:7–9); see Gillian Feeley-Harnik, "Naomi and Ruth: Building Up the House of David," in Susan Niditch, ed., *Text and Tradition: The Hebrew Bible and Folklore*, Semeia Studies (Atlanta: Scholars Press, 1990), pp. 163–84, esp. 173.

49. So, e.g., Gunkel, "Ruth," p. 86; Robertson, "The Plot," p. 225.

50. Rauber, "The Book of Ruth," p. 172.

51. Loc. cit.

52. *Midrash Ruth Zuta* 3 (ed. S. Buber, p. 47).

53. So Rauber, "The Book of Ruth," p. 173; cf., e.g., Feeley-Harnik, "Naomi and Ruth," p. 171.

54. Cf., too, Johanna W.H. Bos, "Out of the Shadows: Genesis 38; Judges 4:17–22; Ruth 3," in J. Cheryl Exum and J.W.H. Bos, eds., *Reasoning with the Foxes: Female Wit in a World of Male Power* = *Semeia* 42 (1988), pp. 37–67 at 58–64.

55. Rauber, "The Book of Ruth," p. 171.

56. Rauber, "The Book of Ruth," p. 175, seems almost to rationalize this neglect by noting that "in most scholarly treatments discussion of the legal problems tends to occupy center stage and to push into the wings what most deeply concerned the artist."

57. Trible, "A Human Comedy" (see n. 10 above).

58. Trible, "A Human Comedy," p. 190.

59. Loc. cit.

60. As pointed out by Trible and Feeley-Harnik (see n. 48 above), a rare parallel may be found in the story of the Exodus, where women stand up to Pharaoh and initiate the movement toward liberation.

61. Fewell and Gunn, *Compromising Redemption*, esp. pp. 12, 74, and passim.

62. Robert Alter, *The Art of Biblical Narrative* (New York: Basic Books, 1981), p. 59, calls the language describing Ruth's departure in Ruth 2:11 "a pointed allusion" to Gen. 12:1.

63. Trible, "A Human Comedy," p. 186. A similar comparison of Ruth and Abraham, pointing to parallels between Ruth and Genesis 24, is made by Cohn, ʿIyyunim, pp. 24–28.

64. Cf., e.g., Robertson, "The Plot," p. 208.

65. Trible, p. 168. Brenner finds this love expressed toward the end of the story, too, when Ruth surrenders her biological son to Naomi; Athalya Brenner, "Female Social Behaviour: Two Descriptive Patterns within the 'Birth of the Hero' Paradigm," *Vetus Testamentum* 36 (1986), pp. 257–73, at 266–67.

66. Trible, "A Human Comedy," p. 187.

67. Trible, "A Human Comedy," pp. 186–87.

68. See Trible, "A Human Comedy," p. 179.

69. So Trible, "A Human Comedy," p. 165.

70. Trible, "A Human Comedy," p. 165.

71. Rauber, "The Book of Ruth," p. 165.

72. Loc. cit.

73. On structuralism, especially with regard to language and literature, cf., e.g., Andre Martinet, "Structure and Language," in Jacques Ehrmann, ed., *Structuralism* (Garden City, NY: Anchor Books, 1970), pp. 1–9; Jean Piaget, *Structuralism,* ed. and trans. Chaninah Maschler (New York: Harper & Row, 1971), esp. pp. 74–96; Philip Pettit, *The Concept of Structuralism: A Critical Analysis* (Berkeley: University of California Press, 1975); and Jonathan Culler, *Structuralist Poetics: Structuralism, Linguistics and the Study of Literature* (Ithaca: Cornell University Press, 1975).

74. Cf. esp. Sigmund Freud, *The Interpretation of Dreams,* trans. James Strachey (New York: Avon Books, 1965), esp. pp. 194–95.

75. Cf. John Barton, *Reading the Old Testament* (Philadelphia: Westminster Press, 1984), pp. 180–84.

76. Cf. Barzel (n. 32 above), p. 36; and in general Edmund Leach, *Genesis as Myth and Other Essays* (London: Jonathan Cape, 1969). Fewell and Gunn, *Compromising Redemption,* suggest that even Naomi looks unkindly upon Ruth for her Moabite origins. Barzel understands the problem the Ruth narrative seeks to resolve by analogy to Lévi-Strauss's analysis of the Oedipus story in "The Structural Study of Myth." Lévi-Strauss takes the Oedipus story to concern the origins and nature of humanity. Barzel takes the Ruth narrative to concern the nature of a great leader, in this instance, David: Are his origins ordinary or unusual? Ruth's Moabite background provides an extraordinary ingredient in David's genealogy.

77. Cf., e.g., Alan W. Miller, "Claude Lévi-Strauss and Genesis 37–Exodus 20," in Ronald A. Brauner, ed., *Shivʾim* (Philadelphia: Reconstructionist Rabbinical College, 1977), pp. 21–52; Nathaniel Wander, "Structure, Contradiction, and 'Resolution' in Mythology: The Treatment of Women in Genesis 11–50," *Journal of the Ancient Near Eastern Society* 13 (1981), pp. 75–99.

78. Cf. esp. Claude Lévi-Strauss, "The Structural Study of Myth," *Structural Anthropology* Garden City, NY: Anchor Books, 1967), pp. 202–28.

79. Fisch (n. 41 above); for some detailed comparisons between these stories and Ruth, see also Yair Zakovitch, "The Threshing-Floor Scene in Ruth," *Shnaton* 3 (1978–1979), pp. 29–33 [in Hebrew]; and idem, *Ruth,* pp. 24–28.

80. Fisch, "Ruth and the Structure," pp. 430–31. I have modified some of Fisch's formulations to make them less objectionable (at least to me). Since I accept the validity of Fisch's approach, I do not want to weaken its conviction by formulating the evidence in what strikes me as a less cogent manner. Fisch represents the separation between Abra(ha)m and Lot as Lot's departure from his uncle, but Gen. 13:11 reads: "they departed one from the other." I would not categorize the deaths in the families of Judah and especially Naomi as "disasters," as Fisch does. Nor does his "ʿagunah-theme" apply to Lot's daughters, who were not really widowed without hope of remarriage. I also think that my usage, "there is a significant male issue," is more to the point than his emphasis on the "father or father-figure," an overly androcentric perspective.

81. Fisch, "Ruth and the Structure," p. 432.

82. Fisch, "Ruth and the Structure," p. 433.

83. Fisch, "Ruth and the Structure," p. 434; cf., e.g., Licht, (see n. 42 above); Zakovitch, *Ruth,* p. 26.

84. Fisch, "Ruth and the Structure," pp. 435–36.

85. Claude Lévi-Strauss, *The Raw and the Cooked,* trans. John and Doreen Weightman (New York: Harper & Row, 1969).

86. For reference to some biblical narratives in which this theme may figure, see David Damrosch, *The Narrative Covenant: Transformations of Genre in the Growth of Biblical Literature* (San Francisco: Harper & Row, 1987), p. 88. For an analysis of the Mesopotamian Epic of Gilgamesh with respect to this theme, see G.S. Kirk, *Myth* (London: Cambridge University Press, 1970), pp. 132–52.

87. Fisch, "Ruth and the Structure," p. 434.

88. The nocturnal scene on the threshing floor is certainly not explicit and is generally interpreted as deliberately ambiguous; cf., e.g., Campbell, *Ruth*, pp. 130–32; Moshe J. Bernstein, "Two Multivalent Readings in the Ruth Narrative," *Journal for the Study of the Old Testament* 50 (1991), pp. 15–26, at 16–20.

89. Cf. now Susan Niditch, *Underdogs and Tricksters: A Prelude to Biblical Folklore* (San Francisco: Harper & Row, 1987). For deception as a woman's strategy in biblical narrative, cf. Esther Fuchs, "'For I Have the Way of Women': Deception, Gender, and Ideology in Biblical Narrative," *Semeia* 42 (1988), pp. 68–83. The specific relation of biblical women and deceptive tactics diminishes if not dissolves, however, when the latter are viewed within the Bible more globally; see the dissertation of my student, Ora Horn Prouser, "The Phenomenology of the Lie in Biblical Narrative" (Jewish Theological Seminary of America, 1991).

90. See Miller (n. 77 above); cf. my discussion in "The Torah as She Is Read," *Essays on Biblical Method and Translation* (Atlanta: Scholars Press, 1989), esp. p. 47.

91. Cf., e.g., Lévi-Strauss, *The Raw and the Cooked,* pp. 1–32, esp. 10–12, who contends that myths manifest "objectified thought." Contrast, however, perspectives such as that of Piaget, *Structuralism,* who regards structural systems as basically constructed, not predetermined or innate.

92. On formalism in the context of structural poetics, see, e.g., Robert Scholes, *Structuralism in Literature* (New Haven: Yale University Press, 1974), pp. 59–141; Culler, *Structuralist Poetics,* pp. 205–24, 232–34.

93. Vladimir Propp, *The Morphology of the Folktake,* rev. ed. by Louis A. Wagner (Austin: University of Texas Press, 1968).

94. Jack M. Sasson, *Ruth: A New Translation with a Philological Commentary and a Formalist-Folklorist Interpretation* (Baltimore: Johns Hopkins University Press, 1979). Cf. also Globe (n. 9 above). For an extensive critique of Sasson's application of Propp to Ruth, see now Pamela J. Milne, *Vladimir Propp and the Study of Structure in Hebrew Biblical Narrative* (Sheffield: Almond Press, 1988), esp. pp. 144–54, 172–73.

95. Cf. esp. Milne, *Vladimir Propp,* pp. 153–54, 172; also Brenner, *Ruth and Naomi,* p. 38.

96. Sasson's interpretation of Ruth's arriving at Boaz's field as a deliberate move runs up against the virtual consensus that "her occurrence occurred" (2:3) refers to chance, albeit the apparent result of divine providence (see above). Cf. the remarks of the great 10th c. Karaite commentator, Yefeth ben Ali: "[the expression] *And it so happened to her* shows that it was a matter of pure chance and was not done deliberately by her, since she did not know Boaz as yet, and had gone there not because of her own intention concerning this matter but because the Lord of the worlds guided her to what was to be her future good fortune . . ."; Leon Nemoy, *Karaite Anthology: Excerpts from the Early Literature* (New Haven: Yale University Press, 1952), p. 98.

Northrop Frye proposes that in a "more primitive" version of the scene on the threshing floor Ruth seeks out Boaz as part of a fertility rite; *Words with Power, Being a Second Study of the Bible and Literature* (New York: Harcourt Brace Jovanovich, 1990), pp. 210–11.

97. Cf. Sasson, *Ruth,* esp. p. 208.

98. See, e.g., Algirdas Julien Greimas, *On Meaning: Selected Writings on Semiotic Theory,* trans. Paul J. Perron and Frank H. Collins (Minneapolis: University of Minnesota Press, 1987), esp. pp. 63–120; cf. Mieke Bal, *Narratology: Introduction to the Theory of Narrative* (Toronto: University of Toronto Press, 1985), pp. 11–12, 26–30. For an introduction to Greimas's semiotic theory and its application to biblical exegesis, see Daniel Patte, *The Religious Dimensions of Bibli-*

cal Texts, Semeia Studies (Atlanta: Scholars Press, 1990). For an exemplary illustration of Greimas's analytic model in the interpretation of a Hebrew Bible narrative, see David Jobling's study of the Garden of Eden story in his *The Sense of Biblical Narrative: Structural Analyses in the Hebrew Bible II,* JSOT Supplement Series 39 (Sheffield: JSOT Press, 1986), pp. 17–43.

99. Tollers (see n. 16 above), esp. pp. 255–58.

100. Mieke Bal, *Lethal Love: Feminist Literary Readings of Biblical Love Stories* (Bloomington: Indiana University Press, 1987), pp. 68–88. Bal does not refer to Sasson's work.

101. Cf. my "Theory and Argument in Biblical Criticism," *Essays on Biblical Method and Translation,* pp. 53–68; and Fish, "Why No One's Afraid" (see n. 3 above).

102. This understanding of "text" is not very different from the definition of a poem by I.A. Richards, first published in 1925. For Richards, a poem is "a class of more or less similar experiences" that result from reading "the poem"; I.A. Richards, *Principles of Literary Criticism* (San Diego: Harvest Books, n.d.), p. 226. Richards would rein in the possibilities of reading by measuring all "experience" by "the relevant experience of the poet when contemplating the completed composition" (p. 227)—as if such an experience could be any more handily and decisively conveyed and known than "the poem" itself. Nonetheless, Richards underscores the critical role of the reader in constructing, and not only deconstructing, the literary work.

103. Cf., e.g., Gary A. Phillips, "Introduction," *Poststructural Criticism and the Bible* = *Semeia* 51 (1990), pp. 1–5, esp. 2; idem, "Exegesis as Critical Praxis: Reclaiming History and Text from a Postmodern Perspective," ibid., pp. 7–49.

104. Cf. my review of Bal, *Lethal Love,* in the *Journal of Religion* 69 (1989), pp. 395–96: and cf. also Mieke Bal, "Reading as Empowerment: The Bible from a Feminist Perspective," in Olshen and Feldman, eds., *Approaches to Teaching the Hebrew Bible* (see n. 9 above), pp. 87–92.

105. Cf., e.g., Jacob Fichman, 'Arugot (Jerusalem: Mossad Bialik, 1954), p. 282 [in Hebrew; translated in part into English in Alex Preminger and E.L. Greenstein, eds., *The Hebrew Bible in Literary Criticism* (New York: Frederick Ungar, 1986), p. 539].

106. Bal, *Lethal Love,* p. 78.

107. Cf., e.g., Campbell, *Ruth,* ad loc.; Beattie, "Ruth III," p. 46: E.L. Greenstein, "Biblical Narratology," *Prooftexts* 1 (1981), pp. 201–8; and Jack M. Sasson, "Ruth," in Robert Alter and Frank Kermode, eds., *The Literary Guide to the Bible* (Cambridge, MA: Harvard University Press, 1987), pp. 320–28, esp. 322.

108. Cf., e.g., Barzel (see n. 31), p. 26; Garsiel, *Biblical Names,* p. 251.

109. Bal, *Lethal Love,* pp. 78–79. For a perspective aligned with Bal's using classical rabbinic material, see Eliezer Diamond, "Chronology or Characterization? The Case of Midrash Ruth," *Proceedings of the Rabbinical Assembly 1990* (New York: Rabbinical Assembly, 1991), pp. 159–69, at 164–65.

110. Bal, *Lethal Love,* p. 75. Tsamudi (n. 28 above), p. 210, observes that Boaz takes no steps of his own to marry Ruth.

111. There are some connections with the covenantal reading of Fisch, "Ruth and the Structure," discussed above.

112. Reading the *ketiv*—*qaniti,* "I am acquiring"—in 4:5 with Sasson, *Ruth,* pp. 119–36; cf. D.R.G. Beattie, "Kethibh and Qere in Ruth iv 5," *Vetus Testamentum* 21 (1971), pp. 490–94; idem, "The Book of Ruth as Evidence for Israelite Legal Practice," *Vetus Testamentum* 24 (1974), pp. 251–67, esp. 263–64. I cannot accept Beattie's argument, however, as I differ significantly in understanding Mr. So-and-So's motives for refusing to buy (see immediately below). Even if one were to read the *qere* (*qanita,* "you must buy/are buying"), the same ultimate explanation of the redeemer's reasoning would hold. The son of So-and-So and Ruth would not be considered his own son, and the value of his estate would decrease by the amount he paid for Naomi's land because the son he would have by Ruth would alone have title to that land. That is, in purchasing what is in effect the estate of the deceased Mahlon, So-and-So would reduce the value of his own

estate by the amount of that purchase. See my "On Feeley-Harnik's Reading of Ruth," in Niditch, ed., *Text and Tradition*, pp. 185–91, esp. 187–88; cf., e.g., Yehoshua Amir, "The Scroll of Ruth," in Ezra Hamenahem, ed., *Hagut bammiqraᵓ* [Reflections on the Bible] 2 (Tel Aviv: Am Oved, 1976), pp. 187–99, at 191 [in Hebrew].

For a recent argument connecting the marriage of Ruth to the redemption of the inalienable patrimony, see André Lemaire, "Une inscription phénicienne decouvert recemment et le mariage de Ruth la Moabite," *Eretz-Israel* 20 (1989), pp. 124*–29*.

113. Zakovitch maintains that Mr. So-and-So refused to marry Ruth because she was a Moabite (*Ruth*, pp. 8, 20, 106–7; cf. Pardes, *Countertraditions in the Bible*, p. 114). Like Bal, Zakovitch slights the economic loss the kinsman would thereby incur (see preceding note). This reading serves Zakovitch's larger purpose since he understands the narrative presentation of Ruth as a positive model, calculated to counter Ezra and Nehemiah's measures against Judean intermarriage (see n. 35 above).

114. Bal, *Lethal Love*, p. 81. In another poststructuralist reading of Ruth, Fewell and Gunn, *Compromising Redemption*, also stress the negative inner-biblical associations of Ruth's Moabite origin (esp. pp. 69–70 and passim).

115. Cf. Cohn, ῾*Iyyunim*, p. 16, who highlights the narrative's movement from "exile" (first famine, then Moab) to "redemption" (first Israel, then family) in what one might regard as a Zion-centered reading.

"A Son Is Born to Naomi!"
Literary Allusions and Interpretation in the Book of Ruth

Danna Nolan Fewell and David M. Gunn

This paper moves between two focal points, character and allusion. We wish to explore the character of Naomi, an exploration which will inevitably center on her relationship to Ruth. We also wish to suggest that attention to literary allusion in the text can help us considerably in our understanding of her character. Indeed, it is our conviction generally concerning the book of Ruth that it owes significant depth and complexity to the author's use of literary allusions. Literary allusions help to construct the worldview of the narrative. They provide clues to understanding ambiguous events and situations. They illuminate the attitudes and motivations of characters when the surface of the narrative is reticent.

Our general starting point is Phyllis Trible's fine reading of the book in *God and the Rhetoric of Sexuality*. Her reading is both literary critical and feminist; so, too, our own—which is why we have chosen to begin here as opposed to one or another of the several excellent studies that have appeared in recent years (Sasson is a case in point). Yet our reading noticeably diverges from hers on the character of Naomi. Like many other commentators, Trible finds Naomi to be a model of selflessness, her dominant concern being for the welfare of her daughters-in-law. Her support of Ruth, like Ruth's devotion to her, is exemplary. We would suggest a less sanguine reading.

A. Five Silences

Of particular interest to us are five notable silences in the book of Ruth, all having an important bearing on the reader's understanding of Naomi. Let us consider these gaps and Trible's response to them. They are: 1. Naomi's silence at Ruth's final determination to go on with her to Bethlehem; 2. Naomi's silence about Ruth on her arrival in Bethlehem; 3. Naomi's silence about her kinsman Boaz, until prompted by Ruth's story of success at gleaning; 4. Ruth's silence about her own part in the threshing floor scene when she returns to Naomi the next morning; 5. Naomi's silence about Ruth at the birth of Obed.

1. In the exchange between Naomi and the daughters-in-law in chapter 1, Trible observes that ironically Orpah's separation from Naomi stems from her agreement with her, whereas Ruth's unity with Naomi stems from her opposition to her: "Ruth's commitment to Naomi is Naomi's withdrawal from Ruth" (p. 173). But *why* does Naomi so withdraw, if she is so selfless, so wholly motivated by her regard for others? "Throughout the exchange," writes Trible, "her counsel is customary, her motive altruistic, and her theology tinged with irony" (p. 171). Let us accept the conventional counsel and the caustic theology. But why should the altruism of Ruth reduce an altruistic Naomi to silent withdrawal? For she speaks not a word either to, or about, Ruth, from this point to the end of the scene in the arrival at Bethlehem. If Ruth's famous "Where you go, I go; your god, my god" speech can melt the hearts of a myriad preachers and congregations down the centuries, why not Naomi's heart?

2. This withdrawal from Ruth is particularly marked in the scene of arrival among the women of the town. Naomi proclaims that she had gone away full, she had returned empty. She speaks as though her loyal companion Ruth were invisible. Trible is also struck by this oversight and suggests, a little limply, that it is because "this aged widow" is "overpowered" by her sense of divinely inspired calamity (p. 174). Yet as chapter 2 begins *we* might begin to wonder why it is that still the only words she can find for her daughter-in-law are "Go, my daughter!," echoing her insistence earlier on the journey: "Go! Return (v. 8) . . . Return! (v. 11) . . . Return! Go! (v. 12) . . . Return!" (v. 16).

We might also do well to read more closely Naomi's impassioned speeches in chapter 1, to her daughters-in-law (1.8–9, 11–13) and to the women of the town (1.20–21). To be sure, the surface rhetoric of the first is directed outwards to the young women. But at the heart of all her utterance in this chapter (as can be shown by a close rhetorical analysis of the passages) is Naomi's bitter sense of deprivation. She has been left without husband or son. "May Yahweh deal loyally with you, as you [not Yahweh!] have dealt with the dead and me!" "Have I yet sons in my womb?" she cries bitterly. "I am too old to have a husband!" "No, my daughters for it is more bitter for me than for you [cf. Campbell, 70–71], for the hand of Yahweh has gone forth against me." "I went away full, and Yahweh has brought me back empty!" Her worldview is theistic. She lays blame for her calamity at Yahweh's door and her language echoes that of Job (especially 1.19–20). She sees herself alone. Her speech to the daughters wears them on its sleeve. At the heart of Naomi's speech is Naomi.

3. At the end of chapter 2, Naomi replies to Ruth's report of Boaz with the information that Boaz is a "relative," one of their "redeemers." "Yet how very strange is her disclosure," writes Trible. "Naomi knows that Boaz is a close relative, but she has not sought his help. Why we do not know. Is it that emptiness has so overpowered her [again!] that she forgot his existence, even as earlier she failed to understand that Ruth was with her? Or is it that calamity paralyzed her will to act? Or is Naomi in this instance a woman of her culture who waits for the man to act first?" (p. 179). We shall return to this last suggestion shortly.

4. The fourth silence is Ruth's—on her return to Naomi after her night at the threshing floor the narrator tells us that

she told [Naomi] all that the man had done for [to?] her, saying "These six measures of barley he has given me, for he said, 'You must not arrive empty [cf. 1.9] to your mother-in-law.'" (3.17)

Yet we know that those words purporting to come from Boaz are in fact Ruth's. Boaz had not mentioned Naomi. Nor does the narrator indicate that Ruth told Naomi anything of what Ruth herself had done and said at the threshing floor, though that speech we know to have been crucial. "Would a disclosure of what she said be too much for Naomi to bear?" wonders Trible (p. 186). "After all, Naomi had expected Boaz to tell Ruth what to do" [i.e., not the other way round]. Too much to bear? That suggests a sensitive, fragile character. Is the Naomi who sent Ruth out into the night such a person? But leaving that question aside for a moment let us ask another. What *did* Naomi expect Boaz to tell Ruth to do, that she could not bear to be told a different story? Trible is more reticent than the text here.

And why should Ruth make such a point of turning her reply into a reply about *Naomi*? Perhaps she knows that Naomi cannot bear to hear anything other than what she *wishes* to hear. We would suggest, then, that she fabricates an expression of Boaz's concern for Naomi in order to mirror what she knows to be Naomi's chief concern—namely, Naomi!

5. The fifth silence is again Naomi's, at the end of the book—not a word about Ruth from her. "That Ruth may now find a husband," writes Trible on the conclusion of chapter 3, "satisfies Naomi's original concern" (p. 187). But this expression of her concern has never been the narrator's, only Naomi's. And if Ruth's welfare had been her sole interest, how odd that she should not be seen to celebrate that welfare. Instead she is silent at marriage and birth, a silence that strikes the women of the city no less than the reader, so much so that they gently chide her by reminding her about the baby's mother, "your daughter-in-law, who loves you, who is more to you than seven sons" (4.15). Naomi's perception of the event is again mirrored through the speech of others: "A son is born to Naomi!" exclaim the women as she presses the child to her bosom (4.16–17).

At the heart of Naomi's impassioned speeches in chapter 1 had been her sense of deprivation. She had been left without husband or son. "Have I yet sons in my womb?" she had cried bitterly. "I am too old to have a husband!" "I went away full, and Yahweh has brought me back empty!" Now as the story draws to a close she has, at last, a son. That, for her, would appear to be the story's resolution. Of Ruth, no mention. And on this silence, Trible is silent.

The character and motivation of Naomi is indeed a matter on which the narrator exercises considerable reticence. Yet a character of complexity *is* built, in the "gaps" as much as in the "given." Those silences drew us into them to ponder her more critically, to wonder less at her apparent altruism and more at her own self-interest. The "given" can chart our course a little further: let us now take a different tack and attend to a dimension of the text that we believe can crucially inform our reading. We refer to literary allusions.

B. Literary Allusions

1. We begin with the setting of the story. What is the significance of Moab? Why not Egypt, Edom, Paddan-Aram, Philistia? What connotations does Moab carry for the

Hebrew characters of the story, and how might a Hebrew audience feel about Moabites? The story of Lot and his daughters (in Genesis 19) suggests, for a start, that feelings of moral superiority, a righteous chauvinism, might be characteristic of attitudes to this near neighbor. Furthermore, the story of Moab's hostility to Israel's advance toward the promised land is capped by the tale of the sin of Baal-Peor: "When Israel dwelt in Shittim the people began to play the harlot with the daughters of Moab. These invited the people to the sacrifices of their gods, and the people ate (!), and bowed down to their gods." This resulted in the kindling of Yahweh's anger and the death of many of the chiefs of the people (Numbers 25).

So Elimelech sets out to find food, to eat in Moab! Not, perhaps, the most propitious beginning to a story.

2. The exposition describes a situation structurally reminiscent of the exposition to the Judah-Tamar story (Genesis 38). There is a separation from family/homeland, a sojourning elsewhere, marriages to foreign women, deaths of spouse and two sons—all told in rapid succession. In the Judah-Tamar story Judah regards Tamar the Canaanite with suspicion, considering her to be the cause of the trouble (namely, the deaths of his two sons). He does not accuse her of this openly, however; rather, he urges her to return to her father's house.

Naomi's attitude toward her daughters-in-law is cloaked by an ambiguous text; but she does urge them to return to their mothers' houses. The allusion to the Genesis tale prods us. Might she perhaps be like Judah, not expressing her suspicion directly to the young women, but insisting nevertheless that they belong not with her but with their own families in Moab? Ruth, then, would be to Naomi as Tamar is, to Judah, an albatross around her neck. Read thus, her blessing, "May Yahweh deal *hesed* with you . . . May Yahweh grant that you find a home" (1.9) is two-edged: it may well convey her recognition that the women have treated her kindly; yet it is at the same time a way of distancing herself, as it wraps in piety her message to them to part from her. But even the piety is a little strained—for her perception is that these Moabite women have their own gods (cf. 1.15: "See, your sister-in-law has gone back to her people and her gods"). We sense the possibility that her verbal generosity is but polite rhetoric.

On this reading, Naomi's silence at Ruth's unshakeable commitment to accompany her emerges as resentment, irritation, frustration, unease. Ruth the Moabite is to her an inconvenience, a menace even. By the same token, her ignoring of the younger woman before the women of the city is readily understood. It is the silence of resentment. It is also, perhaps, the silence of embarrassment. The Moabite who stands alongside her embodies Naomi's (though in actuality Elimelech's) abortive flirtation with foreignness, a failure more than tinged with cultural and religious guilt. Trible (along with most commentators) noted the conventionality of Naomi's advice to her daughters-in-law to return to their own people. That conventionality sits well with our reading.

3. A woman who buys the conventional prejudices of a society is also one who will impute those to others and who will adhere to the fundamental value systems of the social structure. In this case the dominant system is patriarchy. It creates Naomi's sense of total deprivation and, as already observed, it structures the story as a whole through the mechanisms of female economic dependence. Such a woman is also likely to buy into the convention of male initiative. Perhaps, then, as Trible suggests, she makes no approach to Boaz or any other redeemer because to act thus would be to set her outside

the bounds of convention. When she does act radically, in chapter 3, it is not in fact her, but her daughter-in-law who has to do the acting! Naomi sits at home [cf. 2.7!], distancing herself from culpability (not to mention danger).

Here we might ask another question. Why does Naomi stay at home while Ruth gleans? Is she too old? (But she managed to walk all the way from Moab.) Is she waiting for someone, Yahweh perhaps, to take care of her? Whatever the case, she is noticeably ready to break her reticence before Ruth when the younger woman presents her with food, showing her the grain from the gleaning, at the end of chapter 2.

4. A Naomi with a prejudice against foreigners, a Naomi who thinks like Judah, is also consistent with a Naomi who sends Ruth to the harvest field without advice or warning. The field is a place of some menace for an unattached young foreign woman, as the constant reference to the risk of unwelcome attention and molestation makes clear, and this is something of which Naomi herself is aware. At the end of Ruth's first day in the fields, when she perhaps teasingly reports that Boaz had urged her to stick close to the young men, Naomi replies belatedly that it would be better if she went out with the young women, lest she be molested in another field (2.22). Why the sudden concern? Because Ruth has become her bread-winner? Because she has sensed the possibility of bounty near at hand (through Boaz's obvious interest in Ruth) and does not want Ruth to run off with a young, unrelated and poor, man? Her feelings about Ruth at this point are ambivalent still—she is uncomfortable about her and yet perceives her to be useful.

Her concern for Ruth's safety, however, has its limits. With winter at hand, she is not averse to launching Ruth in chapter 3 into a dangerous action, again uncautioned. The Song of Songs tell us of the risk a woman takes when she goes into the streets at night alone:

> I sought him, but found him not;
> I called him, but he gave no answer.
> The watchmen found me,
> As they went about the city;
> They beat me, wounded me,
> They took away my mantle,
> Those watchmen of the walls. (5.6–7)

And discovered on the threshing floor, how might she be perceived by the men there?

> You have loved a harlot's hire
> Upon all threshing floors,

declaims Hosea (9.1), pointing us to one likely perception among men who have been drinking and who are inclined to molestation.

5. So what precisely does Naomi wish to happen on the threshing floor? As is generally recognized, the course of action proposed and undertaken is heavily laden with sexual potential. Ruth is directed to make herself attractive and go down to the threshing floor to "sleep" (*shakab*) with the man (3.4). The motif of the young woman introduced into the bed (so to speak) of an inebriated man, at night so that her identity goes unrecognized, brings strongly to mind not only the story of Lot and his daughters once more, but even more strikingly Laban's tricking of Jacob with Leah (Genesis 29). Naomi tells Ruth explicitly to wait until Boaz has finished drinking. She never tells her to identify herself. It is the man who will say what to *do* (not speak!). Again the incognito motif

points us to the Judah-Tamar story and Tamar's drastic ploy to force Judah to recognize her right to motherhood. She tricks him, of course, by "playing the harlot."

Why should Naomi set up such an arrangement? The literary allusions suggest that entrapment is the goal. Sexual intercourse, if not pregnancy, will enforce either marriage or a pay-off. The man, remember, is a "man of substance" (a "man of property," we might say, or a "man of worth"—ʾish gibbor hayil [2.1]). He is also a relative (at least by marriage); all the more reason for him to wish to avoid a public scandal.

But why not approach Boaz directly? And why has Boaz not approached Ruth himself? (Our assumption here is that he is, indeed, interested in her—to that we return shortly.) What is wrong with Ruth as a prospective wife? We must leave aside for now that question as it applies to Boaz. But we can address it with regard to Naomi's perception.

What stands as a barrier between Ruth and marriage to Boaz, in Naomi's view? The answer must lie in the fact that Ruth is a Moabite woman. The text constantly offers us this point of view through persistent and carefully placed use of the epithet "Moabite woman." Allusion to Lot's daughters and (perhaps) the women of Baal-peor compounds it. And that perception fits well with what we have suggested earlier regarding Naomi's values. She understands the conventions only too well. A pillar of society like Boaz cannot afford to pursue his interest in a Moabite woman in terms of marriage, unless under some kind of cloak or compulsion. Naomi decides to go for compulsion.

6. Leah and Tamar come into view again in chapter 4, where the people and elders allude to them explicitly in the course of invoking a blessing upon Ruth and Boaz. "May Yahweh make the woman who is coming into your house like Rachel and Leah, who together built up the house of Israel," they say. "And may your house be like the house of Perez, whom Tamar bore to Judah, because of the children that Yahweh will give you by this woman" (4.11–12). The explicit allusive reference here confirms our sense of implicit presence in chapters 1 and 3. At the same time the allusions would appear to carry a force here that reaches beyond what the people and elders seem to have in mind as models of fruitfulness and architects of a male dynasty. The message of the women, that "a son is born to Naomi," interprets Ruth to be a surrogate, which brings into focus other dimensions of the Rachel and Leah story, dimensions of jealousy and resentment that come when other women bear children for the barren. We are reminded also of Sarah and Hagar. Though establishing Naomi within the tradition, these narratives also undermine her triumph, for they reveal the solution of the surrogate to be an unsatisfactory one.

Savored thus, Naomi's silence is bittersweet. To be sure, she appears to have within her grasp the security of a son and a (surrogate) husband; Naomi is no longer "empty." But the image of the woman with the child at her breast is ambiguous—is she mother or only nurse? "A son is born to Naomi," say the women of the neighborhood, attempting to force the issue, sensing Naomi's need. But Naomi must know, as the reader knows, that despite its metaphoric appeal, this ascription of motherhood is only rhetoric. Any reality that it might have lies in the gift of her daughter-in-law—the daughter-in-law who is, in the words of the women, "better than seven sons."

So where does that leave Naomi? As she seeks to restore her hold on the patriarchal system, the narrative exposes the precariousness—and the irony—of her position. She owes her restoration to a woman, to Ruth the Moabite woman, to Ruth the woman whose radical action challenges the male-centered values that permeate both the story and Naomi's worldview. Little wonder that to the message, "your daughter-in-law who loves you is better than seven sons," her response is silence.

Oh, how we hate to be saved by Samaritans!

REFERENCES

Campbell, Edward
1975   *Ruth. A New Translation with Introduction and Commentary* (Anchor Bible; Garden City, NY: Doubleday).

Sasson, Jack M.
1979   *Ruth. A New Translation with a Philological Commentary and a Formalist-Folklorist Interpretation* (Baltimore and London: Johns Hopkins University).

Trible, Phyllis
1978   "A Human Comedy," in *God and the Rhetoric of Sexuality* (Overtures to Biblical Theology; Philadelphia: Fortress), ch. 6. [Reprinted in Kenneth R.R. Gros Louis, ed., with James Ackerman, *Literary Interpretation of Biblical Narratives, Vol. II* (Nashville: Abingdon, 1982), pp. 161–90].

The Seduction of Eve and the Exegetical Politics of Gender[*][1]

Reuven Kimelman

First Reading

Although various literary methods have shown how the multidimensionality of the Eden story can be explicated in different ways, indeed in competing ways, there is hardly a reading that does not leave a remainder. If no single reading perspective can account for all the data, the only question is whether one reading can account for more of the data than another in a coherent way. In any case, it may take multiple readings to account for all the data. The claim to significance of the following reading lies in its capacity to minimize the remainder by providing a structure for illuminating the narrative that explains its overall thrust, accounts for the interaction of its characters, and sheds light on interpretational difficulties.[2] Although the reading is primarily synchronic, focusing on the narrative as a whole, it takes into account literary issues raised by a diachronic reading.[3]

Minimally, a reading worthy of the name has to deal with the reasons for the Bible beginning its account of human history with a tree of knowledge, humans seeking to acquire divine-like knowledge, and serpents talking to women. In doing so, it must focus on the role of sexuality and birth pangs, blaming and guilt, nakedness and clothing as part of the human debut on the stage of life. Such a focus needs to account for the shift in the relationship between man and woman from parity to domination and for the link between morality and mortality within a revised divine-human relationship. Any reading which deals with a lesser range of issues is inadequate.

In addition, in the light of the contemporary debate on androcentrism versus egalitarianism, a reading should spell out its implications for one or the other. In our case, the interpretation points in the direction of an egalitarian reading,[4] but for reasons different from those frequently advanced for such a reading.[5]

241

The biblical stage for exploring these issues is a luxuriant, divinely planted, well-watered garden. The opening scene is the first in a series of bouts in which humanity struggles to break out from its subdivine status only to come upon the chasm separating the human from the divine. Its organizing concern is therefore the links and barriers between the human and the divine. This theory will be argued through a series of readings and interpretations followed by a close examination of the interplay among tree, serpent, and Eve.

The disarmingly simple manner in which these complex issues are presented in the biblical narrative contributes to the difficulty of interpretation. The simplicity and lack of explicit comment on the meaning(s) of the story have invited readers to fill in the gaps from personal knowledge and experience. Such gaps have elicited such a variety of interpretations, however, that there is little consensus on even the central concerns of the narrative.[6] The following analysis seeks to provide a reading experience that embraces many of the issues involved as well as to supply criteria for validating interpretations.

The initial frame of our reading is the Massoretic division which begins with 2:4 and ends with 3:24 except that we follow most moderns in allocating 2:4a to the conclusion of the previous narrative. This is based on the assumption that 2:4a recapitulates whereas 2:4b introduces. Such an understanding forms the basis of some of the better-known modern divisions of the narrative. So, for example, S.R. Driver, *The Book of Genesis*, entitles 2:4b–3:24, "The Creation and Fall of Man." E. Speiser, *Genesis*, entitles the first part (2:4b–24), "The Story of Eden," and the second part (2:25–3:24), "The Fall of Man." Claus Westermann, *Genesis 1–11*, entitles the whole unit, "The Creation of Man and Woman and the Expulsion from Paradise," whereas Nahum Sarna, *Genesis*, entitles it, "Eden and the Expulsion: The Human Condition." *The Jerusalem Bible* entitles 2:4b–25, "The second account of the creation. Paradise," and ch. 3, "The Fall." *The New Oxford Annotated Bible* entitles 2:4b–25, "The Garden of Eden," and ch. 3, "The First Sin and Its Punishment."

The nature of these works militates against their providing an explanation of their titles. Nonetheless, since the splitting of 2:4 is a literary judgment—even source judgments are literary judgments, however disguised—it would have been helpful to have had the titles of the chapter explained along the lines of some explicit literary criterion for framing the story rather than serving only as a summary of the major event(s) of the narrative.

One such way of framing the narrative consists of linking the beginning with the end and viewing the intervening material as an explanation for the transition. For example, since the identical expression, "to till the soil," appears in both Gen. 2:5c and 3:23b, it creates an *inclusio* that frames the narrative. This way of reading allows for the assumption that, since 2:5 points out that "there was no human to till the soil" whereas 3:23b states that man was banished "to till the soil," the intervening material explains how man came to till the soil. Although ostensibly outside the frame, both 2:4b and 3:24 can be seen as introducing and extending 2:5 and 3:23 respectively. A reading based on such surface patterning alone could then conclude that "Genesis 2–3 is basically a story about how land became vegetated and human beings became tillers of the soil."[7]

Even a cursory reading would find this account of the complexity of the intervening material inadequate and thus unqualified to be the framing idea.[8] The problem does not lie in the technique of linking beginning and ending in order to get a handle on the narrative, but in the belief that meaning can be generated by poetics alone. Structures of narratives are not self-evident data, but results of interpretation. There is no automatic transition from poetics or surface patterning to underlying meaning. The more sophisticated the literature, the more difficult it is to correlate form and meaning in some regular systematic and ultimately mechanical fashion. In actuality, the relationship between the two is more dialectical, whereby change in one induces change in the other. In this sense, it is almost always the case that "interpretation both precedes and follows poetics."[9] That is to say, just as specific modalities of interpretation highlight specific structures or frames, so the highlighting of specific features renders possible specific interpretations. Just as some inkling of meaning precedes the determination of form, so the determination of form extends the quest for meaning and back and forth.[10]

In this case, it is the forthcoming interpretation that induces us to see these verses as framing ones. Once they are highlighted as framing verses, they in turn support and extend our interpretation. This can be illustrated by structuring the framing verses as follows:

A. No bush of the field was yet on earth,
B. no plant of the field had yet sprung up,
C. for *the Lord God* had not made it rain upon earth,
D. and there was no human *to till the soil* (2:5).
E. So *the Lord God* sent him away from the garden of Eden
F. *to till the soil* from which he had been taken (3:23).

This structuring makes clear that A and B are parallel in function, as are C and D. The former note what is missing, the latter explain why. Since C explains the deficiency of B as D does to A, that means that C is to B as D is to A, making for a structure of *abba*. This way of seeing allows structure and content to converge in order to make the point that there is no growth from the ground because God has not brought rain and there is no human to work it.[11] Such a reading advances the thesis of the human role being a complement to that of the divine.

Initially, the tilling of the soil was to underscore the human role in the divine-human enterprise. E and F, however, have "the Lord God" and human acting not in consort, but in conflict. According to the previous verse (3:22), the crisis in the relationship is due to humanity becoming too much like the divine. Lest humanity become even more like the divine, they are expelled. This reading sees the shift in the narrative from one of partnership to one of disengagement. The crisis is precipitated by the junior partner seeking to play the role of the senior partner. The intervening material explains how the initial balance between the divine and the human went awry. The advantage of this reading over the previous one lies in it not being predicated on surface pattering alone. Instead, the problematic of the narrative is thrown into relief by the frame, as the frame is thrown into relief by the problematic of the narrative.

Second Reading

Our second reading adheres to the frame created by the speech elements from 2:15 to 3:19. This dialogic part of the narrative is characterized by the simplicity of its structure. Not only is each character introduced individually, but up to the denouement, where all three characters reappear together, each scene has only two participants, whereas the concluding punishment scene brings all four speaking parts back on stage. The structure is as follows:

Ch.	2:15–21	God and Adam
	22	transition
	22–25	man[12] and woman
Ch.	3:1–5	serpent and woman
	6–8[13]	God, man, and woman
	14–19	God, serpent, woman, and man

It is clear from this way of structuring the narrative that there is a subdivision of the text based on the presence of the serpent. The serpent appears on the scene in 3:1 and leaves in 3:15, whereas God, man, and woman remain constant. In addition, the serpent is the only character to have a specific designation. By being introduced as "shrewd," attention is focused on its significance for the turn of events. By the next verse, the focus is on the woman and the serpent. The reader watches to see whether she will be beguiled by the serpent's shrewdness or continue to comply with the divine prohibition against eating from the tree of the knowledge of good and evil.

The seduction of Eve, as she was to be called, occurs so rapidly and smoothly that it raises doubts about the idea of disobeying God being exclusively that of the serpent. If the serpent gets Eve and subsequently Adam to act out of character, then he, of course, functions outside of them. If, on the other hand, he is seen as providing them with an opportunity and rationale to extend previous inklings on their part, then he functions, dramatically that is, as an extension of them.

To answer the question regarding the relationship of the character of the snake to that of Eve, we need to compare the differences between God's enjoining of the primordial human and the subsequent report of the woman. Originally, Scripture says, "And the Lord God commanded Adam, saying, 'Of every tree of the garden you [singular throughout] may eat, yea freely eat, but as for the tree of knowledge of good and evil, you must not eat of it, for on the day that you eat of it, you will die, yea surely die'" (Gen. 2:16–17). Correcting the serpent by emphasizing that God had not prohibited all of the trees of the garden, the woman says, "From the fruit of the other trees in the garden we may eat, but from the fruit of the tree that is in the midst of the garden, God has said: You [plural throughout] are not to eat from it and you are not to touch it lest you die" (3:2–3).

The differences between the original command and Eve's version are as follows:

Original (2:16–17)	*Eve's version* (3:2–3)
1. God commanded	God said
2. freely eat from every tree	may eat
3. tree of knowledge of good and evil	tree in the midst of the garden
4. you (singular)	we and you (plural)
5. no eating of it	no eating or touching
6. surely die that day	lest you die

These differences are either the type of revisions characteristic of recapitulations, or they reveal the inner workings of Eve's mind.[14] The latter position gains credence by noting the direction of the following six changes:

1. The "command" of God has been diluted to the "saying" of God (cf. 3:17).
2. God's generosity has been reduced to a general permission.
3. The ominous tree of good and evil becomes a nondescript tree in the midst of the garden.
4. The singular has become plural, making one into two (see below).
5. Touching has been added to the prohibition of eating.
6. The imminent penalty of death gives way to some future threat.

The differences add up to a diminishment of divine authority, a shift from generosity in the direction of arbitrariness, a reduction of the import of the tree to a location, a tinkering with the extent of the prohibition,[15] and a belittling of its gravity. Such changes and omissions are too consequential and systematic to be accidental. They point to a tendentious reformulation. Through them, the narrative signals Eve's suggestibility if not susceptibility to the snake's argumentation by showing the movement she has already made in that direction.[16] In this sense, the snake functions to extend the direction of Eve's thinking rather than to instigate it. The idea that the snake serves to extend Eve's character becomes the basis of the interpretation below of the role of the snake in the story.

Once the awesomeness of the prohibition has been punctured, its severity downgraded, and the sense of indebtedness to the divine diminished, Eve becomes fertile soil for the serpent's seeds of doubt. Listen to his deft attack: "Die, you will not die!" he says reassuringly. On the contrary, "On the day that you eat from it, your eyes will be opened and you will become like God, knowing good and evil" (3:5). By linking the knowing of good and evil with becoming like God, the serpent dangles before Eve a grand future in order to persuade her that God is a god who begrudges their potential godliness rather than one who graciously grants them life and sustenance.

Discovering grounds for attributing the ban to a self-serving ruse to withhold divinity rather than a protective barrier to safeguard her life, Eve now finds the tree to be "(1) good for eating, (2) lustful to the eyes, (3) and desirable for wisdom/viewing" (3:6).[17] These three characteristics contrast with the trees, which were originally designated as only "(1) desirable to look at and (2) good to eat" (2:9). The anticipated gain from eating has reversed the order, making it first appeal to the palate and then to the eye. More than delectable and visually pleasing, the tree has become downright "lustful to the eyes." Clearly, this tree is far more than merely a tree in the middle of the garden.

What has changed, however, is not the tree but Eve's beholding. With eyes fixed on the tree, she is not able to banish the snake-implanted thought of being but a bite away from divinity. Lest the point be missed, the narrative describes her in words—"And she saw that it was good . . ." (3:6a)—which evoke the language of God's work of creation: "And He saw that it was good." Thinking she was verging on the divine, "She took from its fruit and ate and gave also to her husband beside her, and he ate" (3:6b). Straightaway, "The eyes of the two of them were opened"—just as the serpent had said. "And they knew"—seeing how the serpent had correctly predicted the first part, the response of the reader is primed for similar precision with regard to the second, namely, that they "knew that they were God(like) knowing . . ." What a letdown to find out that they only "knew that they were nude" (3:7).

Since frustration of expectation calls attention to itself, the sudden awareness of their nudity must be a pivotal point in the story. The meaning of this awareness, however, is unclear since the fact of their nudity was pointed out at the outset. Those who argue that the awareness of nudity is what produces shame and that the tale can be reduced to a story about the introduction of shame into human consciousness should find the absence of the word "shame" in v. 7 bothersome. They should also be perplexed at why disobeying God should produce the type of shame between male and female that calls for covering up of nakedness. A shame-focused plot would have them covering up themselves from God, not from each other. The issue at this moment, however, cannot be nakedness before God, since they only flee from God afterwards, upon believing that they heard the sound of God. Since the eating of the tree itself does not make them shameful before God, there is no strict theological sin-shame linkage here. The objections against the explanatory power of the shame theory can also be adduced to counter the conscience theory.

What is the tree of knowledge if strictly speaking it is neither a tree of shame nor a tree of conscience? To get a handle on this question, it is preferable to see how it functions in the story rather than asking about its essential nature. Accordingly, it is necessary to compare the reality before the act of eating with that afterwards. The differences should help explain its significance.

Let us first focus on the events immediately following the act. When Adam first saw Eve, he so focused on similarities—"she is bone of my bones; flesh of my flesh" (2:23)—that he called her *ʾišah* (woman), which, in the popular etymology of assonance, is nothing more than *ʾiš* (man) with a feminine ending. As (wo)man is a prefixed man, so *šah* is a suffixed *ʾiš*. The consciousness of difference, however, now creates division, requiring a loincloth of fig leaves to mask what sets them apart.[18] At that very moment, "They heard the sound of the Lord God moving about in the garden at the breezy time of day" (3:8). Whence the sound of motion, if hitherto God had not been identified by any physical dimension?[19] Thus the presence of the phrase "the breezy time of day." By informing the reading that "the sound of God" is really the rustle of the wind, the reader is informed that they heard only what they thought was the sound of God. This introduction of irony makes the reader more knowledgeable than the heroes. As such, it plants the seeds of doubt about the reliability and judgment of the two. We are not surprised, hence, to find our guilt-ridden couple hiding in "the midst of the tree(s) of the garden"—the very place of the crime!

The stage is set. God asks Adam, "Where are you?" (3:9). Although this double-barreled question possesses both geographical and psycho-moral coordinates, Adam retorts, "I heard the sound of You in the garden, and I was afraid because I was naked, so I hid" (3:10). This does not answer the question, "Where are you?," but rather, "Why are you hiding?"[20] What could have been taken as an innocent geographical inquiry was taken as an accusation, so brittle is Adam's confidence. With regard to the content of Adam's response, we have to ask what he means by relating his fear to his nakedness. Had he not just covered himself? Apparently, the nakedness of Adam cannot be covered by clothes.[21] Within nine (Hebrew) words, Adam's "I" reverberates self-consciously fourfold. Such are the contours of guilt: rustles become sounds of God and cover-ups leave the exposed naked and alone. Loincloth or no loincloth, Adam felt naked, unmasked and vulnerable,[22] condemned out of his own mouth. Giving Adam a second chance to own up, God asks whence he knows of his nakedness and whether he had eaten of the prohibited tree. Caught, Adam counterattacks by implicating both God and

Eve together. It was "the woman You put at my side—she gave me of the tree, and I ate" (3:12). Following suit, Eve also shifts the blame one level down, protesting, "The serpent enticed me, and I ate" (3:13). Both adopt a strategy of letting the perpetrator feign victim.

Expanded Interpretation

The differences in the human situation before and after the eating take on an added dimension by widening the frame to include all three opening chapters.[23] *Before* the transgression, humanity had been described as being created "in the image of God." In ancient Near Eastern literature, "the designation of the king as 'image of the god' serves to emphasize the godlike nature of the king in his ruling function and power."[24] In its biblical context, the designation of humanity as "the image of God" serves to emphasize their godlike nature in being able to function as rulers.[25] It is that which enables and authorizes them to fulfill the mandate to subjugate and bring under control the physical world. As such, they are called upon to assume heretofore exclusive divine prerogatives. Humanity's first step in assuming the divine mantle, in ch. 2, consists in categorizing creation through the giving of names. Adam speaks and names the animals just as God had spoken and designated the place and the function of the elements of creation. What was once an exclusive divine prerogative becomes Adam's way of exercising the divinely granted power of mastery.

After the sin, man and woman shrink from the majesty of rulers to the pitifulness of rebellious subjects squirming in the presence of authority. Those who stood unflinchingly before the divine charge now cringe in God's presence, shirking all responsibility. What accounts for this shrinkage, as it were, in human stature? They who were once the climax of creation now slink about as whimpering earthlings. *Before* the transgression, the original couple together constituted the divine image as well as the primordial earthling, *ha-ʾadam,* who was apparently neither exclusively male nor female; as it says, "in the image of God He created *it,* male and female He created *them*" (1:27, emphasis added). The word for "it" is normally translated as "him," but that makes little sense since what is called *ha-ʾadam* is male and female and referred to as *them*. Part of the problem is the absence of the neutral "it" in Hebrew. The shift from "it" to "them" may be indicating the paradoxical nature of a potential plural within a singular. As such it functions proleptically: what is now "it" is to become "them." The "it" is thus best understood as "humankind" which subsequently underwent differentiation to become "them," as it says, "Male and female He created them, and He blessed them, and He called their name Adam on the day of their creation" (5:3).[26]

Although this reading is not without its difficulties,[27] the advantage lies in assuming that female was as much a part of the original command as was male. This explains the woman's recapitulation of the original prohibition in the plural. With hindsight it verily was "we." It also explains why she does not exculpate herself under the pretext of not having heard the original prohibition.[28] Although the male—being a male—underscores his priority and sees the female as emerging from him—"this one shall be called Woman, for from man was she taken" (2:23)—there is no reason to identify the narrative with one of its characters, even that of the male. Once the verse is seen as the narrative's way of representing a male perspective, the argument that male must precede female to explain whence she was taken is rebutted.[29] The fact that man views woman as his physical and etymological extension does not itself negate the position that male and female are coeval in the primordial earthling, or that the image of male-female creation provides a "minimal base for an anthropology of equality."[30] Such a non-sexist reading also coheres with the allocation of one side (*ṣela*, 2:22)[31] to what became her and the other to what became him[32] as well as with a birth model based on female parturition. It also helps account for the designation of female as "counterpart" or as the "one corresponding to him."[33]

The argument against the parity model—based on the translation of the female designation as "helper" and the contention that her role is solely to help fulfill the command of Gen. 1:28, "be fruitful and multiply"—is inadequate on both linguistic and literary grounds.[34] First, it separates the *ʿezer* from *kᵉnegdo*. Such a move is unwarranted, for together they form an idiom which can only be illuminated by context as it lacks any biblical parallel. Second, to explain chs. 2 and 3 in their own terms and then complement it by reference to ch. 1, as I have been doing, is one matter, since the final redaction took both into consideration; to make the meaning of ch. 2, however, dependent totally upon ch. 1 is a different matter, for it assumes that chs. 2 and 3 lack any self-referentiality. Chapter 2 explicitly states that the splitting of *ha-ʾadam* comes to resolve the problem of loneliness, a problem more likely to be resolved by a counterpart than by a helper. This role for woman also matches the part she plays in ch. 3, a part that resembles more that of male complement than that of helper in any subordinate sense. The parity model as opposed to the subordination model is further supported by the reference to the male as "her man/husband" (3:6).

Since the original human was one, the narrative promotes the idea of male-female union as a restorative act. Nonetheless, it is the male who is charged with overcoming the obstacle to their reunification. He is to leave "father and mother and cling to his wife." With the umbilical cord severed, man may cleave to woman to "become one flesh" (2:24). Marriage becomes the rite of passage that makes the man. Note that sexuality is not a consequence of recognition of difference, but of familiarity short of identicalness. It is precisely this "tension between the *same* and the *different* that creates sexuality."[35] For life to continue, the conjugal link must replace the filial bond.[36]

After the sin, awareness of their differences induces man and woman to cover themselves in the hope of achieving at least visual similarity. To no avail, the cover-up fails and the distance between them continues to grow. True, they hide together, but once found (out) they are on their own. Adam iterates, "I, I, I, I," without so much as a hint of "we." Man not only fingers woman in order to exonerate himself, but the ingrate also accuses God of placing at his side a Trojan horse. His feminine complement is no longer "bone of my bones and flesh of my flesh," but "the woman." Instead of being a source of union, difference becomes a source of division. What was once complement is now the other.[37]

The absence of remorse of either party shuts the door on any possibility of pardon albeit leaving it ajar for retribution. The punishment widens further the gap between man and woman. What once made them one flesh will now underscore their difference both physically and emotionally. Child-conceiving and childbearing become pregnant with pain.[38] At the greatest fulfillment of womanhood will be the greatest experience of pain. Tragically, it takes the pain of near death to bring about life. Precisely in the act of establishing social immortality, the fragility—and therefore nondivinity—of human continuity is highlighted.

Alas, female desire now makes for male dominance, albeit conditionally, as we shall see. The new connubial situation raises questions about whether conjugality is potentially a stage for aggression. It also raises the issue of whether inequality is an erotic necessity. If so, the intimacy of two bodies fitting so perfectly together to exchange life could double as a form of conquest. Once being on top is seen as an expression of dominance,[39] becoming one flesh, according to one reading, can spark memories of origins, with man looking down at the earth and woman looking up at man.[40]

According to the popular etymology of assonance, man, *ʾadam*, is a contraction of the term for earth, *ʾadamah*,[41] whereas woman, *ʾišah*, is an extension of the term for male, *ʾiš*.[42] If etymologically the trajectories behind the words for man and woman are moving in different directions, it should not be surprising to find a play on assonance used to indicate how often male and female are psychologically at cross purposes. It thus seeks to deal with the question why that which fits so well physically is so often at odds psychically. In doing so, the all-too-frequent failure of the union of flesh to cover up the division of minds is amplified.

Does this mean, as psychoanalysis claims, that as sexual relations are tinged with subjugation, so marriage is characterized by dominance-submission pacts? Apparently so, for in our case the covenant of trust is so broken that, in the subsequent cursed world, males need to establish control before entrusting themselves to females. In the light of the cycles of intergenerational conflict, sibling rivalries, and conjugal misunderstandings throughout Genesis, it may not be too farfetched to portray its understanding of marriage as a stage for the working out of these conflicting feelings. At any rate, it is clear that henceforth sex is never just sex, but an encounter between two people lugging their past right into their carnal encounter. Bodily fusion is insufficient to overcome psychic combat. To become physically united with him, Eve, of course, must absorb what Adam offers. But it is now quite unclear what is being offered. Such are the wages of love east of Eden.

What accounts for such comeuppance? Maybe there is a connection between Adam's irresponsible blaming of Eve and his subsequent dominance of her. After all, it is only after man emerges as a moral midget that female subservience is called for. It is worth considering whether this link between moral smallness and the need for control is what makes male dominance dependent upon female subservience. Alternatively, the need for dominance becomes an erotic necessity because sex now displaces feelings of powerlessness at least as much as it previously displaced feelings of loneliness. To claim that Adam's unresolved anger at Eve for precipitating his expulsion from Eden is what prevents him from fully facing Eve as an equal is anachronistic. It assumes that the information derivative of 3:17 is available to explain 3:16, something impossible in a first reading. In any event, moral failure provides an etiology for sexual imposition.[43]

At any rate, man now has an authority problem. Those who presume that woman was totally a new creation from male can assume that repetition of the divine prohibition on his part sufficed to secure her compliance. Those who assume, and I believe correctly, that both together made up the primordial human lack evidence for any hierarchy of command and compliance. Whatever the case may be, the maintenance of authority now involves power plays. Such is the gap that separates the divine vision of parity from the human machinations of dominations.[44]

The implications of sexual subservience are not all that clear, since Eve's relationship with Adam does not otherwise undergo major alteration. *Before* the transgression, Eve's prominence is illustrated by the fact that it was she who talked with the snake and she who made the decision to eat and share with the man beside her, who seems to have been silently standing by all along. He just eats. The alibi that he ate unknowingly never stocks his arsenal of excuses. *After* the sin, she continues to maintain her prominence, as is pointedly illustrated by the ceremony of naming. As long as there was only *ha-ʾadam*, it did the naming. Admittedly, the male names woman (2:23) and calls her Eve (3:20), as she cannot very well name herself. In the very next scene, however, where either could do the naming, it is Eve who names Cain and Abel (4:1) and subsequently Seth (4:25).[45] The significance of this is evident from the fact that Genesis takes pains to note that Abraham named his sons Ishmael (16:15) and Isaac (21:3); that Isaac named Jacob (25:25), as underscored by the singular use of the verb; and that Jacob's wives named each of their sons, with Jacob adding only the name of Benjamin to his last son. As namegiver, Eve maintains her prominence.[46]

Male sexual dominance does not seem to be easily transferable to other domains. Domination in sexual interaction is no guarantee for domination in social interaction. On the contrary, it may incite compensatory moves in the opposite direction.[47] In this case, male sexual domination seems to be contingent upon female passion. As such, the copula *waw* that begins the verse, "*waw*your passion shall be toward your husband, *waw*he shall rule over you" (3:16), should be understood as introducing a protasis with the sense "if," just as it regularly introduces the apodosis with the sense of "then." This understanding would allow the *waw* to indicate "as long as."[48] Thus, as long as she is the more passionate, he would rule, but were he to be, she would rule. Passion and manipulation are seen as sides of the same coin. The reversal of one engenders the reversal of the other. In short, the greater the desire, the greater the subservience.[49] Since woman has to overcome the pain of childbearing, her desire appears to outweigh man's, whose comparable experience lacks pain. Thus it can be said, in a type of measure for measure scheme, that she is subjugated initially for instigating the compromising of divine dominion.[50]

There is inadequate warrant for subsuming the total male-female situation under the terms of domination. Were the interest in the total situation, there would have been an observation indicating woman's inferiority rather than an exclusive focus on the issue of passion. Moreover, since subservience is presented in the context of punishment, it is not surprising to find, in what may be an inner biblical exposition of this theme, a time when mutuality replacing subservience is destined to be restored to its pristine glory. As the woman says in the Song of Songs, in the only extra-Genesis occurrence of the term for passion (*tešuqah*), "I am my beloved's, and his passion is for me" (7:11).[51] As at the beginning, the issue is passion and only passion.

As with woman, so man's punishment is increased toil, physical and mental. Only in painstaking labor can he eke out his daily bread from a now refractory ground that incessantly reminds him of both origin and end. The etymology that originally underscored commonality, *ʿadam* from *ʿadamah,* and *ʾišah* from *ʾiš,* now points to difference.

With the former, this difference will ultimately lead to death; with the latter to pain—life-giving pain that is.

The change is also reflected in the two uses of the expression "plants of the field," in Gen. 2:5 and 3:18. Its reappearance in Gen. 3:18 makes the point that what was to have been a divine-human endeavor in 2:5 has become a human burden. Henceforth, the struggle for life will be shot through with the consciousness of death. Life-sustaining acts of eating and life-giving acts of procreation will both be characterized by toil and pain. In their cultural context, both punishments underscore the gap between the human and the divine. That which was to have been divinely blissful is now a constant reminder of their mortal status. The confounding of expectation is again refracted through a measure for measure scheme. In sum, the disruption of the divinely created harmonies—which embraced God and humanity, humanity and nature, male and female, humanity and the animal kingdom—will signify the disharmonious world from the expulsion on.

The Meaning of the Story

Although there is little agreement on the precise meaning of the Eden episode, there is a general tendency to present the first act of disobedience as a necessary development in the growth of humanity. Such a tendency is reflected in the theories that deem the theme to be one of sexual awakening, of transition from childhood to adulthood, or that of growth in human culture. Common to all of them is the assumption that the first couple had to sin in order to grow up. In this sense, all three theories are taken in by the linkage between phylogeny and ontogeny. The act of Adam and Eve, according to them, epitomizes what humanity had to undergo in order to come into its own maturity. These theories tend to point to the transition from nakedness to clothes as indicating the Rubicon over which humanity had to pass. This rite of passage, as it were, is for them so evocative of childhood that it dominates their whole reading.

Besides the problems of the overall reading, which will be dealt with later, each theory has its own difficulties. We shall start with the objections to the theme of sexual awakening and to the attendant idea that the knowledge gained was that of sexuality.[52] First, the prohibition against eating from the tree of knowledge of good and evil was mentioned before the event of gender differentiation and therefore cannot be a result thereof. Second, male's awareness of the female as counterpart precedes rather than succeeds the event of disobedience, as does the image of man and woman becoming one flesh (2:24); thus gender differentiation precedes the act of eating. Third, the punishment of increased pain in sexuality implies experience of a less painful sexuality. Moreover, both times the expression "to know good and evil" appears, it is associated with divinity (3:5, 22) not with sexuality. In fact, had it been associated with sexuality it would have implied that sexuality had heretofore been banned. To argue that "the Divine command to abstain from the fruit of the tree of knowledge of good and evil is . . . designed to preclude the human discovery of procreativity,"[53] not only lacks textual support, but goes against the grain of the images of male-female relationships in chs. 1 and 2 and the stated positive attitude to procreation that involves both commandment and blessing. Finally, there is the simple cultural assumption that man and woman together naked would act accordingly.[54] All these considerations undermine the nexus between sin and sexuality.

Nonetheless, though not determinative of the narrative, sexual motifs, as noted since antiquity, do figure prominently in the background.[55] Rather than focusing on the prominence of these motifs, however, it is more important to note how a background so fraught with potential sexual/fertility symbols ends up producing a foreground of such ethico-religious content. The sexual flow, as it were, has been channeled into the religious and moral furrows that determine the course of the narrative. This needs to be underscored since those who conflate antiquity and modernity through retrojection find it so difficult to shake off the sexual reading.

The thesis that the generative idea of the story is that of humanity rising from childhood to adulthood also has its difficulties. The overall evidence points more in the direction of movement to puerility than in that of maturity. Note how, before eating from the tree, humanity receives and complies with the original command, classifies the animal kingdom, interprets their relationship correctly, realizes that loneliness cannot be resolved by identification with the animal kingdom, and has the capacity to cultivate the earth. This is not the profile of an innocent being in the state of nature. On the contrary, it is only after eating of the tree that humanity adopts the juvenile behavior of fleeing authority, dissembling, and faulting all but themselves. If the model of human growth is applicable at all, it is more in the direction of regression to childhood than progress to adulthood.[56]

One effort to salvage the growth thesis contends that Eve loses her "childlike innocence" and "acquires the knowledge of things—cultural knowledge." "In this way," it is argued, "Eve wrests knowledge from the realm of the divine, takes the first step toward culture, and transforms human existence." Besides the ambiguous nakedness issue, the evidence for this conclusion is that they "are now able to sew themselves loincloths out of the available fig leaves."[57] This reading supposes that the expression "the knowledge of good and evil" is a merism implying a knowledge of all things (and therefore the knowledge of culture) and that the first act of culture is sewing. The same objections that were leveled against the "innocence to maturity" thesis surely apply here. In addition, this thesis is faced with the problem of the pertinence of God's declaration, "Now the human has become like one of us knowing good and bad" (3:22), a declaration that is quite oblivious to the alleged portentous implications of learning how to sew. It is hard to believe that anyone would consider the act of sewing of sufficient theological import to provoke such a comment, especially since the act elicits no comment of its own. Moreover, if the story wanted the making of clothes to symbolize techogony, it would not have them making clothes of leaves, and surely would not have the clothes they wear upon being sent out to the real world made by God. If techogony or human culture is an issue, it only becomes so at the end of ch. 4. If ch. 3 does anticipate ch. 4, it does so, as shall be discussed, on the religioethical level and not on the technological level.

Seeking to maintain the model of human growth, some propose that knowledge of evil is a prerequisite for moral growth. The assumption is that knowledge of evil is predicated upon the experience of sin, and since Eve had not yet sinned she could have no knowledge of evil. This interpretation is subject to objections on both philosophical and literary grounds. On philosophical grounds, as Plato argued in the *Republic,* there is no necessity for moral knowledge to be predicated upon the experience of evil. One need not commit murder to know it to be wrong. On literary grounds, the narrative does not attest to any growth in moral knowledge on the part of Eve. Moreover, since the tree is that of the knowledge of *good and evil,* whatever applies to good necessarily applies to evil. If she were bereft of the knowledge of one, then so of the other.

But did she lack such knowledge? In actuality, before she ate Eve was capable of telling the serpent about the interdiction, who prohibited it, and the dire results. Now, if one knows what is wrong, the authority behind it, and the consequences, where is the deficiency in the knowledge of good and evil? In terms of the narrative, by desisting and complying with the divine command, she had been good; by transgressing it, she commits evil. Heretofore, her Creator's prohibition, along with the threat of death, had deterred her. Once the serpent undermines both, she unrestrainedly seeks her putative benefit.

Then what was Eve missing, and what did she hope to gain by eating of the tree? Apparently, knowing what is wrong, acknowledging its authority, and being cognizant of the sanctions were insufficient. What was missing was an explanation for the proscription. Were such an explanation forthcoming it would remove the arbitrariness of the command, but at the price of sacrificing its divine authority. If her understanding were to determine the status of the prohibition, she would become the arbiter of its rightness. As such she would be the knower, i.e. the source of the knowledge of good and evil.[58] This was not to be so.

In the creation narrative, God makes the rules. Humanity can aspire to be vice regent but may not usurp the divine role of determining what is right and wrong. In the garden, divine authority is established precisely by what appears to be arbitrary. By eating from the tree, Eve changes the rules of the garden and becomes, if only momentarily, as God—the arbiter of right and wrong. Not satisfied with the role of servant of the law, she aspires to be its master and maker. By becoming maker of the rules, divine authority is displaced by her own.

Note that godlikeness here is not depicted in terms of immortality[59] or omnipotence,[60] but in terms of knowing. Eve fails not because of her frailty or mortality, but because of her deficiency in knowing; not, mind you, of right and wrong, which she does know, but in realizing the consequences of her act. As the source of the knowledge of good and evil, God alone makes such distinctions.

Scripture is walking a tightrope. Although it grants to humanity the right, indeed the duty, to play God in the subduing of the physical universe along with the ruling and classification of the animal kingdom, it withholds this prerogative in the realm of right and wrong. In this realm, calculations are not reducible to human considerations.

It is precisely human mastery of the physical universe that makes it so tempting to extend control to the moral universe. Indeed, were it not for the Sabbath at the beginning of ch. 2 intervening between the mandate of executive power in the physical universe and the subsequent limitations in the moral universe, we would have all the makings of that pathology of power that has haunted human achievement down through the generations. The Sabbath, which serves as an armistice in the struggle with nature, and mortality, which serves as a check on human endeavor, together can serve as brakes on the tendency of human power to go amok. Without the Sabbath, there would be no experience of the restraint of power; without mortality, as Gen. 3:22 notes, there would be no cause for restraint.

This issue of immortality is not all clear in the story. Three possibilities have garnered support: (1) humanity was originally intended to be immortal, but lost immortality through disobedience; (2) humanity was mortal from the start, but could have gained immortality through ingestion of the tree of life; and (3) humanity's immortality was dependent upon a diet of the tree of life.

The first option follows those codices of *The Wisdom of Solomon* (2:23–24) that read:

> God created man for incorruption/immortality (*aphtharsia*) and made him in the image of his own eternity (*aidotētos*) but through the devil's envy death entered the world.

This reading sees human immortality as a correlate of the image of God.

The second possibility has been championed recently by Barr.[61] Among his arguments is the assumed cultural assumption of human mortality and the explicit explanation for the expulsion. Barr argues that the case for mortality like that of sexuality can be culturally assumed. Such an assumption is apparently based on the proposition that the characters in a narrative are like their readers unless otherwise noted. Although this literary assumption is probably generally true, it begs the question whether the first humans are meant to be like their readers. It is just as possible that the narrative aims to show how the first couple became like their readers. After all, much of the primeval narrative shows how the world created by God became the world as experienced by the reader. Barr's assumption of the sexuality of the first couple may be more valid precisely because of the many notices of male-female interaction, including the very rationale for constructing a distinct woman. Since there are no such notices with regard to mortality, nothing can be said on the subject based on cultural assumptions or reader expectations. Thus the reading of *The Wisdom of Solomon* (2:23) that correlates human immortality with the image of God may be as valid as the reverse. Barr's explanation for the expulsion is also questionable since it overemphasizes the fear expressed in 3:22 that man may take of the tree of life and go on living forever. Even Barr concedes the availability of another explanation for the expulsion, namely, to fulfill the punishment mentioned in 3:17–19. Thus, just as 3:22 and 3:24 correspond to each other as problem and solution, so 3:19 corresponds to 3:23. By bracketing 3:20–21, which deal with other issues, there emerges an *abab* structure with $a = 19$, $b = 22$, $a = 23$, $b = 24$. This structure shows, as the story now stands, that there are insufficient grounds for privileging one explanation for the expulsion over the other.

The question then is why was the path to living forever now blocked? Divine envy does not explain it. The evidence of divine power over these squirming humans is so overwhelming that any thought of divine-human equality or competition as a motif may be dismissed. Moreover, it has already been noted twice that all the other trees may be eaten, so why not the tree of life? We are left with the aforementioned third explanation and the conclusion that living forever presents a threat it did not as long as they complied with the prohibition. According to 3:22, the threat rises now precisely because they do know good and evil. Had they not eaten of the tree of knowledge, there would not be the necessity to keep them from eating of the tree of life. Believing that they can determine good and bad, they are not allowed to live forever lest that motivation for submitting to divine authority be vitiated.

By expanding the frame forward to include ch. 4, it is clear that even without immortality there are few constraints. In the very next scene Cain follows through on the logic of his parents' act. The narrative makes this point by structuring the episodes of parental disobedience and sibling murder along parallel lines. In both cases there is human willfulness, cover-up (by loincloth or by burial), and spurning of responsibility. Both begin with the identically formulated rhetorical question, "Where are/is?" (3:9; 4:9). In fact, when God queries Cain, he asks both "where?" and "what have you done?" (4:10) thereby conflating the previous "where?" to man and the "what is this you have done?" to woman. Both use the words "dominate" and "passion" in a single verse (3:16; 4:7). This is all the more telling since the term for "passion" (*tešuqah*) has only one other biblical witness, which, as noted above, may be playing on Gen. 3:9. The link between the two episodes is forged ever more tightly by having Cain's punishment (4:11) recall that of Adam (3:11), except for the noose being tightened one more hitch. For Adam, the earth could at least be coerced into yielding its strength, whereas for Cain it will remain cursedly closed. Both experience a diminution of the presence of God and both are driven from their place eastward.[62] By having the second evoke the first, the narrative warns the reader of the slippage between sins on the divine-human plane and those on the interhuman plane. When the religious sin between humanity and God is replayed on the moral plane, Adam and Eve inevitably beget a Cain.

If human beings believe that they can displace divine authority by laying claim to be knowers, in the sense of being the source of the knowledge of good and evil, they can fall prey to the belief that the measure of good and evil is human. As the multiplication of people, however, brings about the multiplication of standards, it becomes convenient to believe that what is good for one is good, and what is bad for one is bad. It is not difficult for the idea of moral autonomy to deteriorate into the excuses of a facile conscience. In a universe of morally autonomous individuals, there is the ever present danger that Cain will believe that the elimination of his competitor, even brother Abel, is warranted and therefore good.

Whatever time is needed for the rejection of divine authority to precipitate moral chaos, the narrative telescopes this process into one generation. For Genesis, this telescoping accentuates the idea that the social dimension of sin is, within a generation, moral breakdown. In a world devoid of divine authority, warns the narrative, the threat of fratricide ever crouches at the door.

Tree, Serpent, and Eve

With this construction of the story in mind, let us now return to the question of the meaning of the tree, serpent, and Eve on the assumption that our reading can be supported through a careful construing of the interplay among them. First the tree: frustrated by a story so fraught with ambiguity, many have turned to ancient literature in search of parallels. The search has been singularly unilluminating.[63] Not only are trees of knowledge absent in the cognate literature, but even parallels to the tree of life are limited references to plants, food, and water which bestow immortality or at least eternal youth. Indeed, the closest verbal parallel is the biblical tree of life in Proverbs (3:18; 11:30; 13:12; 15:4) and in the Septuagint of Isaiah (65:22). But even if there were a parallel to the tree of life, it would be of little help since that tree has been marginalized to the borders of the story (2:9 and 3:22) and is totally absent from the central scene of the drama. For the purposes of Scripture, it is not the tree of life that is front and center, but the tree of knowledge (3:3), which has no ancient parallel. Its meaning is thus a factor of its role in the narrative, which, as we shall see, is part of the verbal play that characterizes both "serpent" and "Eve."

What about the serpent? Here the problem is the reverse. Abounding in mythology, literature, and culture, serpents symbolize too much.[64] Although polysemous symbols resist being bound to any single interpretation, it is unclear which, if any at all, of the interpretations based on ancient mythology can be worked into the literary structure without doing violence to the narrative. Those who see the serpent as a symbol of fertility or immortality should be surprised to find it associated first with the tree of knowledge of good and evil as opposed to the tree of life, and then with pangs of childbirth, expulsion from the life-giving waters of Eden, and ultimately death.[65] Those who find in it a symbol of healing, as associated with the likes of Aesclepius, should be struck at its capacity for precipitating the sicknesses of humanity. Those who perceive in it a symbol of wisdom should find it hard to believe that such a sapiential figure could induce such folly. Even its vaunted mantic qualities turn out to be disappointing.[66]

So many of the alleged associations for the serpent have been undermined by a reversal of expectations that many have given up on explaining the behavior of the serpent.[67] An alternative to explicating the symbolic valence of serpents and then applying it to the one in the story is to propose a construction of the story in which the presence of specifically a "serpent" becomes meaningful.

In order to arbitrate among the conflicting interpretations, it is necessary to focus on the given data rather than on some general theory for the role of serpents in mythology or culture. General theories tend to spawn conflicting interpretations without providing the means for resolution precisely because they lack anchorage in the text. Examples of such are theories about the meaning of the serpent that depend upon the symbolism of its shape. Such interpretations expatiate on how Eve was taken in by the serpentine reasoning that makes moral autonomy the most seductive of human blandishments. Although such twisted, as it were, arguments made palpable by the suggestiveness of the reptilian form do support the thrust of our reading, there is no indication that the shape of the serpent is the key to its presence.[68]

Since the issue is not the meaning of serpents in general, but the function of the serpent-image in the narrative, any interpretation has to account minimally for what is noted in the text. The narrative specifies three elements, namely, that the serpent is referred to as *naḥaš*, it is *ʿarum* (shrewd), and it talks. The choice of the term *naḥaš* for serpent, from among its biblical alternatives, generates three biblically attested images: a poisonous snake,[69] a metaphor for venomous speech,[70] and, by homonymy, divination and bewitchment.[71] By coalescing all three in the context of the narrative, an image of the venomous words of the serpent bewitching Eve by claiming to divine her future can be conjured up. Such use of equivoques allows the disparate meanings of the term to become equally relevant. Deploying a homophone as well as homograph for nude (*ʿarum*) in the very next verse to identify the serpent as shrewd (*ʿarum*) also links "nude" and "shrewd" both phonically and visually. In the actual reading experience the overlap is extended. When the term appears in the adjacent verse, it initially or retrospectively continues the "nude" valence. By recognizing a sound already echoing in his consciousness, the reader automatically links the two. Prospectively, however, and even this only fully in the light of the subsequent functioning of the serpent, the mind settles on the meaning of "shrewd" for *ʿarum*. It is only through such retroactive reading that the potential double meaning can be reduced to a single meaning.[72] Nonetheless, since prior to the emergence of the "shrewd" meaning the "nude" meaning was entertained, nudeness and shrewdness are interlocked in the mind of the reader. As in a palimpsest, erased meanings remain just below the surface.

This play of sound and sense prompts the thought that the serpent was called *ʿarum* for engineering the realization of the significance of being *ʿarum*.[73] Once the association is made, the reader is not surprised to find that, upon realizing the import of being nude, Adam and Eve become shrewd in their venal efforts to shift blame.[74] This rhetorical phenomenon of playing with homonyms through the use of more than one sense, both physically and lexically, to enrich the reading experience has been astutely called "polysensuous polyvalency."[75]

A similar rhetorical phenomenon lies behind the third association, which involves an intricate play on Eve's name. According to Gen. 3:20, the woman is named *Ḥavva* ostensibly for being the progenitress of all living.[76] But if that were all, she would have been named *Ḥayya*, i.e. life-bearer. What *ḥavva* adds to *ḥayya* is an allusion to the serpent, for in Aramaic and other cognate languages "serpent" is *ḥivya*.[77] Since there has not yet been found a Semitic source for the word *ḥavva*,[78] it may be adjudged a neologism, created to stand phonologically between *ḥayya* and *ḥivya* in order to encompass both. Such portmanteau-like words are coined to telescope two terms into one by exploiting the overlap between homonymy and synonymy.

This understanding of the fusion of *ḥivya* and *ḥavva* is reflected in the post-biblical paronomastic Hebrew comment that "the serpent is Eve's serpent and that Eve was Adam's serpent,"[79] which was taken to mean that "the serpent was the Satan of Eve and Eve was the Satan of Adam."[80] Although capturing superbly the biblical play on "Eve" and "serpent," the remark overextends the conniving of the serpent to Eve vis-à-vis Adam. The text never says that the tempted became the tempter. In fact, whereas Eve protests that she was duped, Adam makes no such claim. In short, there was a seduction of Eve, but no seduction by Eve.[81]

Nonetheless, these observations do provide the basis for an interpretation that can capture the richness of the double entendre through the suggestion that the serpent is Satan who is the evil impulse.[82] By identifying the serpent with Satan[83] and Satan with the evil impulse, the struggle is introjected into the interior life of Eve.[84] Although the identification with Satan is here inappropriate and likely anachronistic, the identification with the evil impulse is attractive. Such usage is paralleled in ancient Egyptian literature where "the serpent . . . may well represent the Egyptian king's alter-ego."[85] More importantly, it coheres with the observation in part two that sees the serpent in terms of an extension of human character rather than totally at odds with it. Here, the vehicle of the serpent achieves for us visually what the tenor of the evil impulse does for us psychologically. Together, the beguiling quality of the evil impulse can be imagined in all its stark reality. Once the metaphor works for the reader, Eve's plight is liberated from the restraints of past history in order to adumbrate the future struggles of humanity.

With the wiles of the serpent serving as a metaphor for the connivance of the evil impulse, it becomes explicable why this ancient symbol for primeval chaos is used to instigate the chaos in the individual soul that occurs upon usurping divine authority. The source of the opposition to divine structure, to repeat, is not some primordial monster but the human arrogation of authority.

The standard objection against the interiorization of the serpent is that the serpent is actually cursed. That, however, occurs prior to its literary metamorphosis into the human drive for divinity. Until the woman is designated by the serpent-sounding *Havva,* the serpent is to be grasped in all its vivid animality. That is what gives it its punch. Only at the end, in a moment of self-revelation, does the reader realize she has been had. This movement of the serpent from ontology to psychology helps explain why, of the three, God does not demand of the serpent an accounting. A separate accounting by the serpent would preclude its passage from external to internal reality. It also explains the reason for the punishment being so closely linked to humanity, and the reason the curse is not pronounced on it alone but on the ongoing relationship between its descendants and that of humanity.

This reading strategy is predicated upon the integration of temporality into meaning. What a story means is dependent on "when" a story means. Since individual images appear on a temporal axis, they are conditioned first by what precedes them and then by what succeeds them. Narratives are not taken in all at once, rather they are articulated through the past, present, and future of the reading experience. New meaning is therefore constantly coming into being as old meaning recedes in the face of emerging meanings. Although final meanings do not exhaust the meaning of the reading experience, they surely have a privileged position in the meaning that accompanies the reader as the next narrative is encountered.[86]

To return to our reading: it is clear that our temporal reading of our heroine shows her to be nothing less than Every(wo)man.[87] She embodies the human condition. Her representative status explains why the story features both woman and serpent, why the serpent talks specifically to woman, why of all the ancient epics of origins Genesis alone gives the creation of woman separate billing, and why Genesis underscores the commonality between man and woman. By highlighting the significance of the woman, this reading makes for the remarkable combination of authoritarian theology and egalitarian anthropology.[88]

To compound, if not to enrich, matters, note that *havva* can also denote "speech," or "declare."[89] An allusion to speech in the word *havva* would make it possible to hear, as it were, a speaking serpent in her name. Such charactonyms reflect the correspondence between name and deed or theme. Aware now that serpent, speech, and woman as life-giver can converge in the same word, the reader is provoked to consider the linkage among them.[90] These interanimations, or interpenetrations, of a single term can spark the idea that the serpent is hypostatically Eve's other and that the scene is one of Eve struggling with her own susceptibilities. As is so often the case, protagonist and antagonist constitute two sides of the same coin.

The reader realizes all this only at the end, upon hearing that the woman is to be called "Havva" (3:20) and not, as expected, "Hayya." The new name draws in the reader in two ways: the reversal of expectation piques the curiosity of the reader to reflect on its significance, whereas its hybrid morphology stirs the reader to seek out an explanation.

This also underscores the significance of the timing or location of Gen. 3:20 on the naming of Havva. Since the verse does not flow from the preceding verse nor flow into the succeeding one, its absence would not be noticeable. In terms of content, it could just as easily have been placed near the end of ch. 2, where the female was designated "woman." The meaning of the verse is therefore as much a function of its timing or location as it is of its content. If it had appeared at the end of ch. 2, the subsequent association with the serpent would have been aborted. Coming near the end of the story, it necessarily functions as part of the climax. By reverberating with the sounds of "serpent" and "speech" the name causes the ears to tingle with past sounds. By blending both sounds, the demarcation between Ḥavva and the serpent becomes blurred. It becomes fuzzy. Why, one would ask, was she almost called "serpent?" What actually happened back there? Was it a woman speaking to a serpent (Did you say a talking serpent?) to her namesake, or perhaps to herself?

Through such questioning the reader becomes aware of being privy to a give-and-take resonating in the deepest recesses of Eve's being. Of course, only a reader attuned to the serpentine wiles of human presumptiveness will comprehend how much one has been presented with the workings of one's own inner life where so often the borders between protagonist and antagonist become blurred. Others less conscious of the multitudinous times they have pleaded innocent under the pretext of irresistible temptation will see only a snake. Seeing only an ancient tale, they will remain oblivious to having witnessed the first bout of the ongoing struggle between human willfulness and divine authority.

This reading would have the reader see him/herself in Eve. It thus contrasts drastically with all those readings that view the story as one of humanity growing up. The ramifications for the reading experience are significant. Those readings that focus on the first use of clothes engender an air of superiority in the reader. Such a stance prevents identification with the characters in the belief that whatever happened happened only to them, and even then only at the dawn of creation, indeed at the dawn of their maturation.

Conclusion

Reader-response theory is helpful in illuminating the process of understanding illustrated in this study. It shows how much the response of the reader makes its mark on the creation of meaning. Predicated upon the convergence of reader and text, meaning is actualized through the reader's response. Upon transforming the textual signals into a coherent matrix, the meaning of the story is constituted. Several such signals are transmitted through the paronomasias on the Hebrew words for "tree," "pain," "serpent," "nude," and "Eve," as well as those for "earthling" and "woman." Without an exegesis of assonance, an exegesis that demands considerable reader involvement, many of the keys to the story's meaning would be missing. There is nothing like a pun for covering up complexity by the illusion of simplicity. Moreover, without the imagination of the reader and his or her self-understandings coming into play, the full significance of Ḥavva's name would remain opaque and much of the meaning of the story unfathomed. By bringing to bear the full complement of meanings, the skeleton of the text becomes enfleshed while the reader's self-understanding grows through understanding a Ḥavva who has been reconstituted in the mind of the reader. "This structure pinpoints the reciprocity between the constituting of meaning and the heightening of self-awareness which develops in the reading process . . ."[91] Standing in the penumbra of Ḥavva's shadow, the reader's shadow is cast over hers, for while dressing Ḥavva psychologically the reader becomes undressed morally. The more the reader enrobes Ḥavva in meaning the more she, as Adam, moves from historical prototype to moral and literary archetype.[92] The result is a story that is as much the reader's as it was theirs.

NOTES

*The biblical translations frequently follow the renderings of the *NJPS The Torah* or that of Everett Fox, *In the Beginning* (New York: Schocken, 1983), whose translation seeks to retain the exegetical possibilities of the Hebrew.

1. I am indebted to my colleague, Marc Brettler, and students, Michael Carasik and Aryeh Cohen, for their probing questions and helpful suggestions.

2. An alternative reading is that of Jerome T. Walsh, "Genesis 2:4b–3:24: A Synchronic Approach," *JBL* 96 (1977), pp. 161–77. Coming across this after composing mine, I was pleasantly surprised to find a reading that diverges so much in detail converge so much in conclusion.

3. Such a reading is becoming increasingly necessary in the light of the difficulty of source-critical readings at achieving consensus on either the literary unity or the genre of Gen. 2:4b–3:24; see John Van Seters, *Prologue to History* (Louisville: Westminster/John Knox Press, 1992), pp. 109–19.

4. The phase "points in the direction of an egalitarian reading" is chosen carefully to avoid over-reading in any single direction. Too many modern narrative studies of Gen. 2–3 read like ideological tracts. The situation is comparable to the argument over whether 1 Sam. is to be read as pro- or anti-monarchial, rather than reading it as a struggle with the pros and cons of monarchy in literary terms. Similarly, Gen. 2–3 should be read as an effort, *inter alios,* to understand the multidimensionality of the male-female relationship. It is rare that the complexities of such narratives can be reduced to single issues, such as patriarchy or androcentrism. Good literary texts are most multivalent when exploring multidimensional issues. As a text becomes politically charged, however, it tends to lower the threshold for ambiguity and to increase the pressure to reduce the spectrum of options to their binaries.

5. The arguments most often advanced for an egalitarian reading are those of Phyllis Trible, *God and the Rhetoric of Sexuality* (Philadelphia: Fortress Press, 1978). Her thesis has proven so provocative that much of the subsequent literature on the creation narrative has felt impelled to take sides on the issues she raises including the studies cited below by Bal, Bird, Burns, Carr, Clines, Dragga, Eilberg-Schwartz, Frymer-Kensky, Hess, Lanser, Magonet, Meyers, Ramsey, Schmitt, and Stordalen.

6. See the survey of recent interpretations by Terge Stordalen, "Man, Soil, Garden: Basic Plot in Genesis 2–3 Reconsidered," *JSOT* 53 (1992), pp. 3–26 (3–4, n. 2). He categorizes them as "religio-historical, social, psychoanalytical and feminist approaches, and several 'structuralist' and semiotic approaches."

7. Stordalen, "Man, Soil, Garden," p. 24.

8. The same stricture applies to the efforts recorded in Dan E. Burns, "Dream: Form in Genesis 2.4b–3.24: Asleep in the Garden," *JSOT* 37 (1987), pp. 3–14(7).

9. T. Todorov, *Introduction to Poetics,* p. 7, cited in Adele Berlin, *Poetics and Interpretation of Biblical Narrative* (Sheffield: Almond Press, 1983), p. 17.

10. See chapter 5, "Grasping a Text," of Wolfgang Iser, *The Act of Reading: A Theory of Aesthetic Response* (Baltimore: Johns Hopkins University Press, 1978).

11. So Stordalen, "Man, Soil, Garden," pp. 12–13.

12. The difference between "Adam" and "man" will be explained below.

13. Although 3:8 mentions God, man, and woman, as does the next unit, it still belongs in this section because there is no speaker and the subjects of the verbs remain man and woman except for the sound of God, which, as will be shown, is ambiguous.

14. On the whole question of biblical recapitulations, see George W. Savran, *Telling and Retelling: Quotation in Biblical Narrative* (Bloomington: Indiana University Press, 1991). According to him, the question that the serpent "puts to the woman in 3:1 is a deliberate misstatement" (p. 63).

15. Which is the same whether adding or subtracting, see Prov. 30:6 along with Deut. 4:2 and 13:1.

16. So Neḥama Leibowitz, *Studies in the Book of Genesis* [Hebrew] (Jerusalem: World Zionist Organization, 1969), pp. 23–24.

17. Both translations of להשכיל are noted since either one commits the reader to some overall scheme. The "viewing" translation keeps the issue open. According to Nahum M. Sarna, "The Targums as well as the Septuagint, Latin, and Syriac versions all derive the verb from the stem *s-k-l*, 'to see, contemplate'" (*The JPS Torah Commentary: Genesis* [Philadelphia: Jewish Publication Society, 1989], p. 25, line 6). He endnotes 1 Sam. 18:14, 15; Jer. 10:21; 20:11; and 23:5 (355 n. 5). Howard N. Wallace, however, states that the ancient translations "are all too ambiguous . . . The words they use could mean simply 'to look at' but often carry connotations of understanding or perceiving with the mind" (*The Eden Narrative* [HSM, 32; Atlanta: Scholars Press, 1985], p. 140 n. 97). Those who understand the word in terms of wisdom, as do most commentators from at least *Gen. Rab.* (19:5) on, do so retrospectively in the light of their understanding of the point of eating from the tree. Thus wisdom-based interpretations should tread carefully.

18. Mieke Bal's statement that it is God's "appearance, not nakedness itself that gives shame" (*Lethal Love: Feminist Literary Readings of Biblical Love Stories* [Bloomington: Indiana University Press, 1987], p. 120) disregards the fact that the effort to cover up their nakedness precedes their awareness of the presence of God.

19. See Deut. 4:12. In the same vein, James Barr argues that *d'mut* is added to *ṣelem* in Gen. 1:27 to avoid any attachment to a physical image and to emphasize a likeness to God ("The Image of God in the Book of Genesis: A Study of Terminology," *Bulletin of the John Rylands Library* 51 [1968–69], pp. 11–26 [24–25]).

20. Apparently noticing this discrepancy, the Ethiopic *Book of Adam and Eve* 1:36 has Adam answering, "O God, here am I. I hid myself among the fig trees . . ."

21. Sarna's understanding of "I was naked" as "another evasion of the truth" demonstrates the pitfalls of taking the figurative literally. This literalness is continued in his follow-up comment, "The statement itself voices the Israelite ethos that it is improper for man to appear naked before God" (*Genesis*, p. 26). Neither comment coheres with the flow of the narrative nor do they explain how Adam could possibly have thought that he could fob off God with a barefaced lie about something so blatant.

22. Jonathan Magonet argues "that the primary significance of the Hebrew word ערום 'nakedness' is not sexuality at all but a state of defenselessness and helplessness"; see "The Themes of Genesis 2–3," in P. Morris and D. Sawyer (eds.), *A Walk in the Garden: Biblical, Iconographical and Literary Images of Eden* (JSOTSup, 136; Sheffield: JSOT Press, 1992), pp. 39–46 [42].

23. Among those who argue for the unity of the first three chapters are Isaac M. Kikawada and Arthur Quinn, *Before Abraham Was: The Unity of Genesis 1–11* (Nashville: Abingdon, 1985), who stress the unity of the whole first eleven chapters. Gary Rendsburg sees the first three chapters as a single redactional unit (*The Redaction of Genesis* [Winona Lake, IN: Eisenbrauns, 1986], p. 8). According to Bal, Gen. 1–2 form "one coherent creation story," whereas Gen. 3 "elaborate[s] laterally upon the implications of the other specification of Gen. 1:27: he created them to his likeness" (*Lethal Love*, p. 119). Sarna notes some seven "leading ideas in the earlier account [which] are here reiterated" (*Genesis*, p. 16). To this list add the concept of a divine-human partnership intimated in both 1:27–28 and 2:5. In the former they share ruling responsibilities, in the latter they share vegetation growing responsibilities.

24. Phyllis Bird, "'Male and Female He Created Them': Gen. 1:27b in the Context of the Priestly Account of Creation," *HTR* 74 (1981), pp. 129–59 [143].

25. For the difficulties with the expression "image of God," see Bird, "'Male and Female He Created Them,'" p. 139 n. 23; and Howard Eilberg-Schwartz, "The Problem of the Body for the People of the Book," in idem (ed.), *People of the Body: Jews and Judaism from an Embodied Perspective* (Albany: SUNY Press, 1992), pp. 17–46 [26–31, 36–37]. The idea that humanity is the divine deputy for administering the world can be traced at least as far back as *The Wisdom of Solomon* 9:2–3 (see David Winston, *The Wisdom of Solomon* [AB, 43; Garden City, NY: Doubleday, 1979], pp. 201–202) if not further (see J. Van Seters, "The Creation of Man and the Creation of the King," *ZAW* 101 [1988], pp. 335–41).

26. There is no single way of accounting for all thirty-four ʾ*adam* occurrences in Gen. 1–5. Deciding whether an occurrence is a generic expression for humanity, the male, or a personal name cannot be resolved by any single formula. Each case involves a judgment that is as much contextual as it is philological; see Richard S. Hess, "Splitting the Adam: The Usage of ʾ*Adam* in Genesis I–V," in J.A. Emerton (ed.), *Studies in the Pentateuch* (Leiden: E.J. Brill, 1990), pp. 1–15. It should be noted that the issue was already a *cause célèbre* among medieval commentators. In his *Commentary to Genesis* 2:5–7, Abravanel says, "Ibn Ezra stirred the world by saying that the definite article which precedes the word *adam* contains a secret. By this he means that if *adam* were a proper noun, the definite article could not be prefixed, and therefore *adam* should be understood as a noun designating the genus of mankind, rather than an individual. To this I answer that *adam* represents a single man and at the same time mankind as a whole, since there was no one else of his kind. This is why the definite article was added" (translated by B. Netanyahu, *Don Isaac Abravanel* [Philadelphia: Jewish Publication Society, 1968], p. 301 n. 46).

27. As it is presented by Trible, *Rhetoric of Sexuality,* it has been accused of being anachronistic or ahistorical for ignoring "the findings of historical biblical criticism" (Ilana Pardes, *Countertraditions in the Bible: A Feminist Approach* [Cambridge: Harvard University Press, 1992], p. 22). Trible would have been more historical, it is charged, had she considered the larger context of priestly writings or how different documents have been meshed together as does for example, Bird in "'Male and Female He Created Them.'" The decision to link chs. 1 and 2 together or to link ch. 1 with later priestly writings in order to understand 1:27 is a question of literary framing. Since both moves are literary judgments, whether it be the issue of framing or the reading of its strands, it is unclear why one should be dubbed "historical" and the other "literary." In actuality, the debate is not about being historical versus being literary, but about two interpretive strategies whose differences are not resolvable on historical grounds alone without the introduction of literary considerations.

An illustration of the mixing of literary and historical analyses is the study of Bird, "'Male and Female He Created Them.'" She says in n. 13, for example, that "the present form of the composition of Genesis 1 is the result of a complex history of growth, stages of which are apparent in the received text, but can no longer be isolated or fully reconstructed." She never clarifies how stages of growth in a text can be apparent but not be isolated. If the phenomenon is not isolable, it is probably not apparent. In any event, no criterion is provided for either. She then goes on to say, "the framing structure . . . belongs to the final editor and gives evidence of selection, shaping and expansion of older material. I am less certain about the recovery of the underlying tradition or of the relationship of . . . Announcement to . . . Execution Report." This assumes that she can distinguish between older and newer material. If so, then why is she "less certain about the recovery of the underlying tradition"? Again we have the claim of a historian to be able to get behind the literary text to its "preliterary" history without providing a single criterion for doing so. The same kind of unsupported claim underpins her conclusion, "I find it necessary, in any case, to posit a prehistory of Israelite usage; Genesis 1 is in my view neither a 'free' composition nor a direct response to any known Mesopotamian or Canaanite myth, despite clear evidence of polemical shaping." There is again no explanation of why she finds it necessary to posit such a prehistory nor why "polemical shaping" is not clear evidence of a response to ancient myth. The result is not a historical analysis, but a series of assertions in the guise of history that are really literary judgments.

To claim a "historical" or "scientific" reading for one's literary judgment is a tactical move and should be recognized as such. The fact that this is rarely acknowledged witnesses to the broad acceptance of certain interpretive strategies, so much so that they have achieved a taken-for-granted status. But as Stanley Fish has repeatedly pointed out, "Interpretive strategies are not put into execution after reading; they are the shape of reading, and because they are the shape of reading, they give texts their shape, making them rather than, as is usually presumed, arising from them" (*Is There a Text in This Class?* [Cambridge: Harvard University Press, 1980], p. 13). "Indeed," he continues, "it is interpretive communities, rather than either the text or the reader, that produce meanings and are responsible for the emergence of formal features" (p. 14). It would be worthwhile ascertaining how pervasive an interpretive strategy within the academic community has to be before its judgments are stamped "historical" or "scientific" in order to privilege them.

28. See Nahmanides to Gen. 3:13.

29. As opposed to Susan Lanser, "(Feminist) Criticism in the Garden: Inferring Genesis 2–3," *Semeia* 41 (1988), pp. 67–84 [80 n. 7]. Her other argument that any ancient reader coming from an androcentric culture would just assume the primacy of the male is belied by the fact that already in late antiquity *ha'adam* was often referred to androgynously as male and female; see Louis Ginzberg, *The Legends of the Jews* (7 vols.; Philadelphia: Jewish Publication Society, 1968), V, pp. 88–89. It is rare that the ancients turn out to be as flat as modernist theories would have them be. Indeed, in the Sumerian story, "The Birth of Man," there appears already a deformed sexless creation. It says that Nirmat moulded "man-in-the-body-in-which-no-male-and-no-female-organ was placed (lú-suba-giš-nuǧar-ǧalla-nuāar)" (Thornkild Jacobson, *The Harps That Were . . . Sumerian Poetry in Translation* [New Haven: Yale University Press, 1987], p. 161). I owe this reference to my colleague, Tsvi Abusch.

30. Bird, "'Male and Female He Created Them,'" p. 151. See Bal, *Lethal Love,* p. 118.

31. It is not clear what has driven translators to the word "rib." Its other occurrences are all translated as "side," including 1 Kgs 6:15–16 where כנה again appears with צלע. *Gen. Rab.* 8:1 and 17:6 note the rendering "side" as does Rashi *ad loc.* (see Menahem Kasher, *Torah Shelemah* 2:241 n. 275). Although the translation that S.R. Driver works with reads "rib," he nonetheless notes, "The woman is formed out of the man's *side:* hence it is the wife's natural duty to be at hand, ready at all times to be a 'help' to her husband" (*The Book of Genesis* [London: Methuen, 1907], p. 42 n. 21, emphasis added). Sarna says, "The rib taken from man's side thus connotes physical union and signifies that she is his companion and partner, ever at his side" (*Genesis,* p. 22 n. 21). Both comments in underscoring the time factor ("ready at all times," "ever at his side") continue the male overreading of the meaning of woman emerging from the side of the earthling. *Jubilees* 3:6, which may be the earliest "rib" reading, makes no comment on its significance. Philo, more circumspectly, notes that the side indicates a half of a harmonious whole (*Genesis Questions* 1:25).

32. Bal allows for the possibility that since woman "appears first. It is . . . [she] who changes the meaning of *ha'adam* from earth-being into earth-man. In this semiotic sense, the woman was first formed, then the man" (*Lethal Love,* p. 116). The *Talmud* (b. *Berakhot* 61a) also asks the question of priority, but concedes the absence of scriptural evidence.

33. עזר כנגדו (2:20. So Claus Westermann, *Genesis 1–11: A Commentary* (Minneapolis: Augsburg, 1984), p. 227, citing Gunkel and Speiser. Carol Meyers suggests "suitable counterpart" (*Discovering Eve: Ancient Israelite Women in Context* [New York: Oxford University Press, 1988], p. 85). Admittedly, these translations serve, as Lanser says, "to validate what are in fact interpretive choices, not necessities of the Hebrew text" ("[Feminist] Criticism in the Garden," p. 81 n. 13),

but so is much of the story. Indeed, few interpretational difficulties here can be resolved by the "necessities of the Hebrew text." Translations, willy-nilly, are forced to make sense in view of some general understanding. Given the frequent indeterminate nature of the Hebrew, its meaning is more likely to be resolved on literary grounds rather than solely on grammatical or linguistic ones. Often the more subtle the literature the more oblique the relationship between grammar and meaning.

Nonetheless, it is important to note that the more egalitarian "counterpart" reading is not just a *Zeitgeist* phenomenon. It is anchored in ancient, medieval, and modern commentary. The Septuagint underscores the idea of suitability by translating βοηθὸν κατ' αὐτόν (see *Jubilees* 3:5a). Philo sees the idiom as referring to partnership (*Genesis Questions* 1:17, see his use of κοινωνίᾳ in 1:29) and uses the analogy of the lover as "another self." Commenting on 2:20, he uses the expression "a helper like himself," which he interprets to mean "a succorer and co-operator . . . showing complete similarity in body and soul" (1:23). Peshitta translates אכותה, *Targum Yer* translates כרנפיק כיה כר זונ, and *Targum Neof* translates זונ כד נפק ביה i.e. a partner like himself. Kimḥi and Ḥizkunni, *ad loc.*, both underscore the element of equality in the idiom. The former uses the expression שווה כבריאה, and the latter the expression כננדו מן הרומה לו כצלם דמות ורקמה. Westermann sees 2:20 as reinforcing the point of 1:27. On 1.27b he comments, "Humanity exists in community, as one beside the other, and there can only be anything like humanity and human relations where the human species exists in twos" (*Genesis* 1–11, p. 160), whereas on the literary form of ch. 2 he states the following as the "real meaning" of "the narrative as a whole (*Geschehensbogen*) . . . From beginning to end it is a question of the creation of humankind which is only complete when the man is given a companion who corresponds to him in the woman. The creation of woman completes the creation of humankind" (*Genesis* 1–11, p. 192).

34. *Pace* David J.A. Clines, who argues צזר "helper" points "to a secondary, a subordinate position"; see *What Does Eve Do to Help? and Other Readerly Questions to the Old Testament* (JSOTSup, 94; Sheffield: JSOT Press, 1900), pp. 25–48 [32]. Following Ambrose and Augustine he objects to any interpretation that smacks of parity. By opposing his former belief in the egalitarian reading, Clines shrewdly reverses the Pauline rhetoric of ingratiation from former persecutor to present believer.

35. Bal, *Lethal Love*, p. 115.

36. Meyers sees this as further evidence of the parity model: "Only in marriage are male and female complementary parts of the whole, for the parent-child relationship is an intrinsically hierarchical one in a way that the wife-husband one is not" (*Discovering Eve,* p. 96).

37. Trible's description of the narrative as "A Love Story Gone Awry" has its problems. In an effort to underscore that woman was present in the original earthling as much as man, she asserts that the woman speaks and acts for them both. As shown, this point can be made without overemphasizing the pristine harmony, just as the discrepancies between the original prohibition and the woman's recapitulation can be accounted for without assuming that she speaks and acts for them both.

38. For the difficulties in pinning down the meaning of 3:16a, see Meyers, *Discovering Eve,* pp. 99–109; and John J. Schmitt, "Like Eve, Like Adam: *mšl* in Gen. 3, 16," *Biblica* 72 (1991), pp. 1–22.

39. So *Alpha Beta De-Ben Sira* in *Ozar Midrashim* (ed. J.D. Eisenstein; New York: Reznick, Menschel, 1928), 1:47.

40. *B. Niddah,* 31b, *ʾAbot de-Rabbi Natan B,* 9 (ed. S. Schechter; New York: Feldheim, 1967), p. 25.

41. Based on Quintilian's linking of the Latin *homo* and *humus* (*Institutes* 1:5.34), the English equivalent would be to dub Adam a humanoid. For other such suggestions, see Tikva Frymer-Kensky, *In the Wake of Goddesses: Women, Culture, and the Biblical Transformation of Pagan Myth* (New York: Free Press, 1992), pp. 249–50 n. 4.

42. These two explicit word plays alert the reader to be on the lookout for other word plays; see *infra*. David Carr, "The Politics of Textual Subversion: A Diachronic Perspective on the Garden Or Eden Story," *JBL* 112 (1993), pp. 577–95, sees these two word plays as pivots around which much of the story revolves (pp. 579–80, 584–85).

43. This discussion, which is informed by the work of Avodah K. Offit, *The Sexual Self* (New York: Congdon & Weed, 1983), is well aware of the dangers of such analysis being subject to the charge of retrojection. Nonetheless, since it is rare that scholarly analyses of the Adam-Eve relationship are not informed somehow by the psychological assumptions of the writer, it is better to state them explicitly rather than inserting them surreptitiously in the course of the discussion.

44. Nonetheless, Trible's emphasis on woman "becoming a slave" (*Rhetoric of Sexuality*, p. 128) serves her contemporary polemic more than her biblical exegesis.

45. Pardes sees this as representing the pinnacle of Eve's position. Indeed, she dedicates the third chapter of *Countertraditions in the Bible* to "The Politics of Maternal Naming."

46. George W. Ramsey's critique ("Is Name-Giving an Act of Domination in Genesis 2:23 and Elsewhere?" *CBQ* 50 [1988], pp. 24–35 [29]) and that of Lanser ("[Feminist] Criticism in the Garden," pp. 72–73) of Trible agree that calling is equivalent to naming, but cannot agree on the import of either. According to Lanser, they both imply mastery; thus the naming of female by male implies domination. According to Ramsey, naming does not determine what an entity should be nor extend any control, rather it "*results from* events which have occurred" (p. 34) and is simply "an act of discernment" (p. 35) of what is. If Lanser is right and naming implies mastery, then the sign of mastery shifts here from the Adam to Eve. If Ramsey is right and the act of naming is politically insignificant, then who names whom establishes no hierarchy. It is thus safer to use the term "prominence" not "dominance" with regard to the namer.

47. Thus the argument of Schmitt ("Like Eve, Like Adam," pp. 2–4) that the husband does not function as ruler in Genesis is not counter-evidence.

48. Every translator has to struggle with the force of the copula *waw*. As noted, knowledge of philology and syntax will not suffice. Translations thus turn out to be derivative of the translator's overall sense of what is involved. This is clearly the case of those, such as NJPS and old RSV, who render the *waw* as "yet"; see Meyers, *Discovering Eve*, pp. 96–97.

49. Thus Trible's and Bal's readings can be maintained without their contortions of Gen. 3:16, *pace* Lanser, "(Feminist) Criticism in the Garden," p. 75.

50. Lanser faults both Bal's and Trible's readings, saying, "For finally neither can explain why male dominance should be the particular consequence of a transgression for which both man and woman are equally, as they argue, responsible" ("[Feminist] Criticism in the Garden," p. 75). Although both, as she says, are blameworthy, the woman still bears primary responsibility for initiating the incident. On early attitudes to the culpability of the two, see R.H. Charlesworth, "A History of Pseudepigrapha Research: The Reemerging Importance of the Pseudepigrapha," *ANRW* (ed. H. Temporini; Berlin: de Gruyter, 1979), 19.2, pp. 77–81.

51. For the speculations that the Song of Songs is an exposition of the Eden narrative, see Trible, *Rhetoric of Sexuality*, pp. 145–65.

52. For recent literature defending the thesis of sexual knowledge, see Sam Dragga, "Genesis 2–3: A Story of Liberation," *JSOT* 55 (1992), pp. 3–13 [4 n. 3].

53. Dragga, "Genesis 2–3," p. 5. He goes on to argue that the first couple becomes "creators themselves" by multiplying, but fails to cite any evidence in the text for his thesis that human procreation constitutes a threat to the divine. Dragga's thesis illustrates the pitfalls of importing ancient Near Eastern motifs without considering their appropriateness for the biblical narrative. The fact is, as Frymer-Kensky has noted, "Unlike Mesopotamia, Israel is never concerned with the danger of overpopulation" (*In the Wake of the Goddesses*, p. 97).

54. So James Barr, *The Garden of Eden and the Hope of Immortality* (Minneapolis: Fortress Press, 1993), ch. 3.

55. For the sexual nature of the serpent-Eve relationship in ancient interpretation, see Ginzberg, *The Legends of the Jews,* V, p. 122.

56. Thus there is no basis for the description of the human couple as "the naïve children [who] have passed through rebellious adolescence, emerging as responsible adults" (Dragga, "Genesis 2–3," p. 11). U. Cassuto's extension of such a modernist reading has even less to say for it. He writes that Adam "did not want to remain in the state of a child under the supervision of his father and always dependent upon him, but wanted to know on his own the world around him and to act independently on the basis of this knowledge" (*From Adam to Noah* [Hebrew] [Jerusalem: Magnes Press, 1959], p. 74). The reverse tactic is taken by E.A. Speiser who argues that *after* the eating God "speaks to him as a father would do to his child: 'Where are you?'" in order to evoke "the childhood of mankind itself" (*Genesis* [AB; Garden City, NY: Doubleday, 1964], p. 25). More recent readings of the story as one of maturing include Susan Niditch, *Chaos to Cosmos: Studies in Biblical Patterns of Creation* (Chico: Scholars Press, 1985), pp. 30–31; Burns, "Dream Form in Genesis 2.4b–3.24," pp. 3–14; and E.J. van Wolde, *A Semiotic Analysis of Genesis 2–3: A Semiotic Theory and Method of Analysis Applied to the Story of the Garden of Eden* (Studia Semitica Neerlandica, 25; Assen: Van Gorcum, 1989), pp. 214–27.

57. Frymer-Kensky, *In the Wake of the Goddesses,* p. 109. Strangely enough, the same author later states that it is the "thirst for knowledge and divinity that makes her listen" (p. 209) to the serpent. Were the phrase "knowledge and divinity" understood as a hendiadys, there would then be agreement.

58. The expression "to know good and evil" is another one of those expressions that remain indeterminate based on philological and syntactical analysis alone. Any understanding is predicated on a grasp of the overall meaning of the narrative, as is evident from the various options that have garnered support; see Westermann, *Genesis 1–11,* pp. 242–45; and Bal, *Lethal Love,* pp. 122–23. The closest parallel to our use is that of 1 Sam. 14:17, where David is compared to an angel of God because of his capacity "to discern good and evil." For a comparative analysis of the term as an expression of authority with a conclusion that the theme here is the usurpation of divine authority, see Clark W. Malcolm, "A Legal Background to the Yahwist's Use of 'Good and Evil' in Genesis 2–3," *JBL* 88 (1969), pp. 266–78 [277–78].

59. There is no basis for Bal's assertion that the humans were tricked "into renouncing the childish fantasy mf individual immortality" (*Lethal Love,* p. 124).

60. *Pace Pirqe de-Rabbi Eliezer* 13, that "becoming like God" implies the power to create and destroy worlds as well as to slay and resurrect.

61. Barr, *The Garden of Eden,* pp. 57–60.

62. For a listing of most of these similarities, see Michael Fishbane, *Text and Texture: Close Reading of Selected Biblical Texts* (New York: Schocken, 1979), pp. 26–27.

63. See Wallace, *The Eden Narrative,* ch. 4.

64. See Westermann, *Genesis 1–11,* pp. 238–39.

65. See Westermann, *Genesis 1–11,* p. 244. For the association of the serpent with life and youthfulness in cognate literature, see Karen R. Joines, "The Serpent in Gen. 3," *ZAW* 387 (1975), pp. 1–11 [1–3].

66. See Joines, "The Serpent in Gen. 3," pp. 4–7. As the above analysis shows, it is misleading to aver that "the "wise" snake turns out to be more right than God . . . about the knowledge that would come with eating the fruit" (Carr, "The Politics of Textual Subversion," p. 590).

67. Thus B. Vawter states, "No explanation is given why the serpent chose to interfere in the affairs of men or to assist in the disruption of good relations between God and man . . . The serpent remains as a consequence the symbol of an unexplained source of mischief and wrong for which no accounting is given" (*Genesis: A New Reading* [New York: Doubleday, 1977], p. 81).

Also Trible underscores her inability to explain the snake, saying, "The motives of this animal are obscure . . . he is a literary tool used to pose the issue of life and death, and not a character of equal stress. A villain in portrayal, he is a device in plot. The ambiguity of his depiction highlights the complicated dimensions of his nature without explaining or resolving them" (*Rhetoric of Sexuality,* p. 111). Calum Carmichael says, "Why, we might ask, must the serpent be given a rule at all?" and answers, "To depict the mystery of human curiosity whose origin is beyond comprehension." He then goes on to explain, "That the serpent is specifically chosen probably reflects the use of reversal in the construction of the story—the serpent, perceived as the lowest of creatures, is chosen to depict the creature originally enjoying a status halfway between God and humankind—rather than perhaps any influence from Near Eastern mythology" ("The Paradise Myth: Interpreting without Jewish and Christian Spectacles," *A Walk in the Garden,* pp. 47–63 [61 n. 9]). Meyers's reduction of the snake to "the etiological workings of the human mind" (*Discovering Eve,* p. 88) also promises much, but explains little.

68. A similar lack or textual support characterizes Bal's suggestion that "the serpent with its double-tongue, evolving into the dragon with its flaming tongues, may be read as the same creature as the cherubim with naming sword of Gen. 3:24. It has similar features and similar function" (*Lethal Love,* p. 124). Although this comment could be applied to *The Apocalypse of Abraham* 23: 7 (*The Old Testament Pseudepigrapha,* ed. J. Charlesworth, I, p. 700), it has no basis in the biblical story. There is also nm basis for the contention that "the movement of the serpent . . . is intended to convey the mystery of sexual attraction" (quoted by Carmichael, "The Paradise Myth," p. 62 n. 20). On the whole issue of the serpent's physical characteristics, see Karen R. Joines, *Serpent Symbolism in the Old Testament* (Haddonfield, NJ: Haddonfield House, 1974).

69. E.g. Jer. 8:17.

70. As it says, "They sharpen their tongues like serpents; spider's poison is on their lips" (Ps. 140:4); see also Ps. 48:5 and Isa. 14:29.

71. See, e.g., Gen. 44:5, 15 and Num. 23:23.

72. Resolving the problem in the reverse order, *Targum Ps. Jonathan* translates in both cases חכים.

73. See Carmichael, "The Paradise Myth," p. 49.

74. In the *Talmud* (*j. Qiddushin* 4:1, 65c) "the act of the serpent" (מעשה חיוי) becomes a metaphor for deception.

75. Shalom Paul, "Polysensuous Polyvalency in Poetic Parallelism," in M. Fishbane and E. Tov (eds.), *"Sha'arei Talmon": Studies in the Bible, Qumran, and the Ancient Near East Presented to Shemaryahu Talmon* (Winona Lake, IN: Eisenbrauns, 1992), pp. 147–163 [148–49]. He cites the following definition of R. Gordis for its Arabic equivalent, the *talḥin,* "In *talḥin* the author's choice of a particular word instead of its synonym is dictated by his desire to suggest both meanings simultaneously to the reader. The one serves as the primary or dominant meaning and the other as the secondary concept, thus enriching the thought or emotion of the reader" (p. 148 n. 7). For some of the other paronomasias in Genesis, see A. Guillaume, "Paronomasia in the Old Testament," *JSS* 9 (1964), pp. 282–90; for the prophets, see J.J. Glück, "Paronomasia in Biblical Literature," *Semitics* 1 (1970), pp. 50–78.

76. Bal's statement that through this name "Eve is imprisoned in motherhood" (*Lethal Love,* p. 128) verges on being a projection of mother hatred, or, to put it more delicately, "Bal both mystifies the power of proper names and exaggerates the restrictive nature of Eve's motherhood" (Pardes, *Countertraditions in the Bible,* p. 41). More in tune with the biblical perspective is Bird's comment that sees "sexual reproduction as blessing . . . It is God's gift and it serves God's purpose in creation by giving to humans the power and the responsibility to participate in the process of continuing creation by which the species is perpetuated" ("'Male and Female He Created Them,'" p. 157).

77. See Wallace, *The Eden Narrative,* p. 150; and especially *Targum Onquelos* and *Targum Ps.-Jonathan* to Gen. 3:1. The same bilingual punnings on "serpent" are found in 1 Kgs. 4:13 as well as in Josh. 9:7, 15, 20, and 21; see Moshe Garsiel, *Biblical Names: A Literary Study of Midrashic Derivations and Puns* (Ramat Gan: Bar-Ilan University, 1991), pp. 71, 222. On the issue in general, see Gary A. Rendsburg, "Bilingual Wordplay in the Bible," *VT* 38 (1988), pp. 354–57. On the nature of the vocabulary of 2:4b–3:24, see Joseph Blenkinsopp, *The Pentateuch: An Introduction to the First Five Books of the Bible* (Garden City, NY: Doubleday, 1992), p. 65.

78. See Wallace, *The Eden Narrative,* pp. 147–50.

79. *Gen. Rab.* 20:11.

80. *Midr. Tanḥuma,* ed. S. Buber, Introduction 78b; see the *Apocalypse, The Life of Adam and Eve* 21:5 (*The Old Testament Pseudepigrapha,* ed. J. Charlesworth, II, p. 281).

81. As 1 Timothy makes explicit, saying, "Adam was not deceived, but the woman was deceived" (2:14); see Jean Higgins, "The Myth of Eve: Temptress," *JAAR* 44 (1976), pp. 639–47; and J.A. Phillips, *Eve: The History of an Idea* (San Francisco: Harper & Row, 1984).

82. *Zohar* (I, 35b), based on *b. Babba Batra,* 16a.

83. As do *Wis. Sol.* 2:24, *2 En.* 31; *3 Apoc. Var.* 4:8; *Rev.* 12:9, 20:2. For a survey of the role of Satan or the devil in the history of interpretation of the story, see Winston, *The Wisdom of Solomon,* pp. 121–22.

84. Which is not the case if the serpent is only the instrument of Satan (*pace Pirqe de-Rabbi Eliezer* 13).

85. Betsy M. Bryan, "The Hero of the 'Shipwrecked Sailor,'" *Serapis* 5 (1979), pp. 3–13 [3]. I owe this reference to Gary Rendsburg of Cornell University.

86. Based on Iser, *The Act of Reading,* pp. 148–49.

87. Meyers links this representative nature of the character of Eve to the wisdom motif of the story, a motif often associated with women in the Bible. It appears, however that she overstates the case in saying, "It [Genesis] portrays the female rather than the male as the first human being to utter language, which is the utterly quintessential mark of human life" (*Discovering Eve,* p. 91). It is true that the female is the first and dominant speaker in ch. 3, but the male clearly has the first word in Gen. 2:23. As Bal notes, "If the woman is the first to be signified, the man is the first to speak" (*Lethal Love,* p. 116). Nonetheless, it may be significant to note that it is the presence of woman that renders speechless earthling into eloquent man.

88. I owe this formulation to Philip R. Dies (private communication).

89. As it does in Ps. 19:3; Job 13:17; 15:17; 32:6, 10, 17; 36:2, and as understood, *inter alios,* by *Gen. Rab.* 20:20 (see ed. J. Theodor and Ch. Albeck 1:195 n. 1) and by Rabbenu Baḥye to Gen. 3:20 (see ed. H. Chavel, pp. 81–82 n. 20).

90. As he would upon noting the triple play on "tree," "pain," and "birth pangs" (עץ, עצב and עצבון). Cassuto (*From Adam to Noah,* pp. 109–10) argued that this unusual term for the pangs of childbirth was deliberately chosen to link up the *tree* with its ultimate fruit, the pain and pangs. Similarly, the term עצבון is used for both her pangs (3:16) and his toil (3:18). For other such biblical triple puns, see Isa. 14, with Robert Alter, *The Art of Biblical Poetry* (New York: Basic Books, 1985), p. 147.

91. Iser, *The Act of Reading,* p. 157.

92. See Meyers, *Discovering Eve,* pp. 80–81. Westermann may be broaching the same idea in saying, "The man and the woman are not individuals in our sense but represent humankind in its origin" (*Genesis 1–11,* p. 241). According to Celsus (Origen, *Contra Celsum* 4:38), there were already Jews and Christians back in the second century who allegorized the story of human creation. Rabbinic literature attests to a similar effort to allegorize Job (*Gen. Rab.* 57:2; *j. Sotah* end of 5; *b. Babba Batra* 15a); see Moshe Greenberg, "Did Job Really Exist?" [Hebrew] in M. Fishbane and E. Tov (eds.) *"Shaʿarei Talmon": Studies in the Bible, Qumran, and the Ancient Near East*

Presented to Shemaryahu Talmon (Winona Lake, IN: Eisenbrauns, 1992), pp. 3–11. By medieval times, the allegorical nature of the Garden story was widespread, see Maimonides, *The Guide of the Perplexed* 2:30; Naḥmanides, *Kitvei Rabbenu Moshe ben Naḥman* (ed. Chavel; Jerusalem: Mossad Harav Kook, 1964), II, p. 296; and Shalom Rosenberg, "The Return to the Garden of Eden," in *The Messianic Idea in Jewish Thought: A Study in Honour of the Eightieth Birthday of Gershom Scholem* [Hebrew] (Jerusalem: Israel Academy of Sciences and Humanities, 1982), pp. 37–86, esp. 78ff.

Genesis 22
The Sacrifice of Sarah

Phyllis Trible

This essay plays with tradition and innovation. It interprets Genesis 22 in context, as it appears and as it subverts appearances.[1]

A Prologue for Orientation

Traditionally, two topics identify the story: the sacrifice or binding (Akedah) of Isaac and the testing or trial of Abraham. The first focuses on the son as object and potential victim of a divine command; the second on the father as subject and potential perpetrator of the command. These topics provide the common ground upon which author and reader stand.[2] We proceed, then, from familiar terrain. But our subtitle indicates a movement into unknown territory: "The Sacrifice of Sarah" yields surprise, elicits puzzlement, and builds suspense. Innovation separates reader from author because it indicates that the latter knows what the former does not. Near the end we regain parity, only to face another challenge.

A rhetorical critical method and a feminist hermeneutic shape the study.[3] Though insightful analyses of Genesis 22 are already available,[4] a nonpatriarchal perspective requires a thorough rereading. At first method prevails, but in the end hermeneutics. This skewed interplay orients the reader while subtly disorienting the text.

Introduction

With the narrator as interpreter, continuation and surprise begin the story, "And it came to pass after these events that God, indeed God, tested Abraham" (22:1).[5] The little phrase, "after these events," collects a tortuous saga of multiple dimensions. Long ago and far away, a preface of genealogy and geography initiates the action. Terah, descendant of Shem, takes his son Abram, his barren daughter-in-law Sarai, and his grandson Lot from Ur of the Chaldeans to Haran (11:10–32). There Terah dies, and the narrative proper commences. Swiftly the story moves: the call of Abram, his journey with Lot and Sarai to the promised land, a sojourn in Egypt, struggles to secure the land, the rejection of Ishmael, the destruction of Sodom and Gomorrah with its aftermath, the debacle in Gerar, and throughout it all the haunting specter of no heir. But at long last God keeps promise. Sarah conceives and bears Isaac, the child Laughter. Then life resumes with the expulsion of Hagar and Ishmael, his near death in the wilderness, and a dispute over wells in Beersheba. Barrenness, deception, warfare, surrogacy, manipulation, destruction, incest, jealousy, envy, rivalry, and malice (12:1–19:34)—all press upon a single line, fraught with the burden of continuity. "And it came to pass after these events. . . ."[6]

Surprise joins that burden. "God, indeed God, tested Abraham." Though such a procedure is implicit throughout the preceding stories, only here does the verb *test* (*nissāh*) appear.[7] The explicit use startles the reader. It portends a crisis beyond the usual tumult. How many times does Abraham have to be tested? Enough is enough is enough. After delays and obstacles Isaac, the child of promise, has come. Let the story now end happily, providing readers and characters respite from struggle and suspense. But vocabulary and syntax prevent such a respite. The divine generic *Elohim* occurs with the definite article *hā*, suggesting "the God, the very God." Reversing the usual order of a Hebrew sentence, this subject precedes its verb. The narrator makes clear that an extraordinary divine act is taking place. "God, indeed God, tested Abraham."

As the narrator's interpretation of what follows, the verb *test* evokes ambiguous responses. What kind of God tests human beings?[8] The kind who remains faithful even when Abraham fails? If so, the reader need not fear the outcome of this episode. Why, then, have the test at all? Does it imply that this time God might punish failure? Or have the advent of Isaac and the expulsion of Ishmael brought a new dynamic to the story, an unprecedented crisis of faith? Whatever, by using the verb *test,* the narrator poses a problem rather than providing an explanation. The ambiguity of surprise joins the burden of continuation. "And it came to pass after these events that God, indeed God, tested Abraham."

God's Command

In this exquisitely wrought narrative, the introduction leads to three sections (22:1b–2; 22:3–10; 22:11–18) plus the conclusion (22:19). The first section is divine command, where the narrator recedes, giving only verbal indication of dialogue. God calls (ʾmr) Abraham to attention by speaking his name: "Abraham." Matching the divine utterance comes the human response: "And Abraham said (ʾmr), "*Hinnēnî*." This is no simple reply, but a strong word of immediacy, even obedience. Older translations use the interjection, "Behold, I."[9] If we reject that archaism, let us retain its power. "Here now am I," at your service, giving full and total attention. Simply, even naively proclaimed, this obedient stance precedes a command of terror. It is carefully constructed, with the particle *nāʾ* joining the imperative "take" (*lqḥ*) to suggest consequence: "Take, so I require of you." The grammatical combination indicates that God knows well what is coming. Soon Abraham also will know because the object of the verb is not a simple word but heavy-laden language. It moves from the generic term of kinship, "your son," through the exclusivity of relationship, "your only one," through the intimacy of bonding, "whom you love," to climax in the name that fulfills promise, the name of laughter and joy, the name *yishāq* (Isaac). Language accumulates attachments: "your son, your only one, whom you love, Isaac." Thus far every divine word (imperative, particle, and objects) shows the magnitude of the test. Yet the horror awaits disclosure.

After the divine imperative *take* comes a second command, *go*. Familiar language harks back to the call of Abram in Genesis 12:1. There in a two-word formula, *lēk-lᵉkā*, God orders Abraham, "Go you." The prepositional phrases that follow move from generic identification of land through particular designation of clan to intimate specification of family, thereby isolating Abram. (He is not, however, cut off from Sarai and Lot.) "Go you from your country, and from your clan, and from your father's house to a land that I will show you." Abram receives no security for the present, only promise for the future. "I will make of you a great nation." The divine assurance vies with the narrated preface that "Sarai is barren; she has no child" (11:30). Threatened by barrenness, the verb *go* constitutes a radical act. Trials and troubles ensue, but the outcome is fruitful, as subsequent episodes relate. Now, after all these events, the same words *lēk-lᵉkā* occur again. "Go you," this time "to the land of Moriah." As it was in the beginning, so now in the end, "Go you."

At the beginning, this command, though scary, held promise and hope; at the end, how different is the implication. Yet the reader and Abraham do not immediately know the difference. Allusions to Genesis 12 may mislead. Only with the third imperative and its cognate object does the shock come: "Offer him there as a burnt offering upon one of the mountains which I shall tell you." The "him" is "your son, your only one, whom you love, Isaac." In other words, sacrifice the one to whom you are attached; "offer him upon one of the mountains of which I shall tell you." The non-specificity of the location matches the non-specificity in the call "to a land that I shall show you." But the meanings of the two occasions, the call and the test, decisively oppose each other. The promise of the beginning, "I shall make of you a great nation," and its potential fulfillment through Isaac unravel in the test. As Abraham once broke with the past, so now he must destroy the future.[10] Genesis 22:1b–2 intends and portends the unwriting of Genesis 12:1–3. If the imperative of the call be radical, how ominous is the imperative of the test. It awaits the response of Abraham, to be given in the second section of the story.

Abraham's Response

In the call episode Abram's answer is succinct and unequivocal. "So Abram went as Yhwh had told him" (12:9a RSV). In the sacrifice story his response is lengthy and hesitant. It alternates between narrated and direct discourse to vary the perspective of text and reader (22:3–10). Four units constitute this section of mounting suspense as murder draws near (22:3, 4–6, 7–8, 9–10).

1. Obedience Begins

Within the opening unit (22:3), the divine imperatives of section one, *take* and *go*, reappear as indicatives. "Take your son" becomes "Abraham took . . . his son." "Go yourself to the land of Moriah" becomes "Abraham went to the place of which the-God had told him." So far obedience prevails; its fulfillment depends upon the third verb, *offer* or *sacrifice*. No indicative match for that verb appears here, but a link occurs through the noun *ᵓolāh*, burnt offering. The connection suggests yet does not confirm perfect obedience. Besides responding to vocabulary in section one, verse three is an art-fully arranged sentence that harbingers the destiny of Isaac:

> So-rose-early Abraham in-the-morning
>   and-saddled his-ass
>   and-took two-of his-young-men with-him
>   and Isaac his-son
>   and-cut wood-for a-burnt-offering
>   and-arose
>   and-went to-the-place which God, indeed God, said-to-him. (22:3)[11]

At the beginning three indicative verbs describe Abraham's meticulous activity: rose, saddled, and took. An appropriate object or adverbial phrase attends each verb, though significantly the last of these verbs, *took,* has two objects: "two of his young men with him" and "Isaac his son." Content and structure indicate that stress comes at the end: "Isaac his son." These words stand apart for emphasis. The remainder of the sentence underscores the point. Like the beginning, three indicative verbs describe Abraham's preparation: cut, arose, and went. In the center, framed by six verbs that signal terrible obedience (rose, saddled, took; cut, arose, went), is the phrase "Isaac his son." The father's activity surrounds his son not to protect him in life but to prepare him for death.

2. Obedience Continues

Unit two (22:4–6) begins by advancing the story three days but still falls short of the destination. "On the third day Abraham lifted up his eyes and saw the place from a distance" (22:4). References to sight, especially the verb *see (r'h),* are proleptic, anticipat-ing a major motif. For the time being, however, the story turns to other vocabulary. It also switches to dialogue. Abraham speaks (*'mr*) to his young men (*na'ar*). "Stay-your-selves here with-the-ass" (22:5a). They are not to witness the deed. He continues, "I and-the-young man (*na'ar*), we-will-go over-there, and-we-will-worship, and-we-will-return to-you" (22:5b). The speech achieves ambivalent effects. Separation and union contend; detachment and attachment compete. Opposing the category young men (you) is the set Abraham and Isaac (we). Yet use of the term *na'ar* (young man) connects the two groups. Abraham identifies his companion by the same word that the narrator has employed to cite the attendants. "I and the young man," he says, not "I and my son" or "I and Isaac." Otherness undercuts oneness; detachment vies with attachment. Estab-lishing distance, *na'ar* avoids the pain of paternal bonding. "Your son, your only son, whom you love, Isaac" in the language of God has become in the speech of Abraham "the young man," like the other "young men."

Father and son are united, however, in three first person plural verbs that follow one upon the other: "we will go, and we will worship, and we will return to you." If the young men, the attendants, are suspicious, the last verb reassures them that the end will restore the beginning. Abraham makes no distinction between the subjects of the three verbs. Separation will return to union. While allaying suspicion, his speech also promotes deception. Abraham may misrepresent what will happen in order to accomplish it. Or perhaps he misunderstands what is at stake. Or perhaps he knows what the reader does not. In any event, his first words confound characters and readers.

These words yield to the narrator whose structure, syntax, and vocabulary sound familiar rhythms:

And-<u>took</u> Abraham the-wood-of the-burnt-offering
    and-laid [it] upon-<u>Isaac his-son</u>
and-<u>took</u> in-his-hand the-fire and-the-knife. (22:6abc)[12]

Three verbs provide the action. The first and last are identical, "took" (*lqḥ*). They allude to the divine command, "take" (22:2), and the response "he took . . . his son Isaac" (22:3). This time the objects, wood of the burnt offering and fire and knife, surround "Isaac his son." Ironies abound. Isaac carries the wood that will ignite him. Yet unkindled it is not dangerous material, unlike the fire and the knife that Abraham takes in his own hand.[13] The father embraces his son with potential destruction even as he protects him from immediate danger. Syntactically and thematically this sentence echoes verse three to trap Isaac. A narrated conclusion pairs unequals as it unites father and son: "So-they-went, the-two-of-them, together" (22:6d). The report plays on the theme of union and separation. "I and the young man, we will go," Abraham said earlier in a speech that established both distance (detachment) and inseparability (attachment). That ambivalence hovers subtly in the juxtaposition of "two" and "together." "Two" designates separate entities while "together" merges them. "So they went, the two of them, together." Silence speaks.

3. Isaac Interrupts

The poignant conclusion of unit two also advances the story. "They went." But Isaac interrupts, initiating unit three (22:7–8). Structurally, the narrator shows this break in Abraham's obedient journey by repeating the entire conclusion of unit three at the end of unit four (22:8b) so that the narrative later resumes by returning to the place before interruption. Thus, the sentence, "So-they-went, the-two-of-them, together," forms an inclusio around the words of Isaac and Abraham. It holds together these two, son and father.

Relational language within heightens the unfolding terror. "And-said (*ʾmr*) Isaac to-Abraham his-father. And-he-said: 'My-father!'" (*ʾābî*). Once God addressed the patriarch by name (22:1); now Isaac employs a term of intimate possession. Replying as he did to God with a strong word of immediacy, *hinnēnî,* Abraham adds the possessive vocative, "my-son" (*bᵉnî*). Again, the language suggests full attention, bound this time to a precious relationship. "Here now am I" [here for you], my son." Isaac's next words play on that particle of attention and immediacy. "Look (*hinnēh*)," he speaks, "the fire and the wood, but where is the lamb for a burnt offering?" Two ingredients he specifies, fire and wood. The absence of another, lamb, he questions. Never does he acknowledge the knife, the instrument that will be raised to murder him.

Abraham's reply pits touching evasiveness against terrifying subtlety: "And-said (*ʾmr*) Abraham, 'God will-see-for-himself the-lamb for-a-burnt-offering, my-son'" (22:8). The Hebrew sentence, like the English, begins with God and ends with son, the two poles in Abraham's life. These boundaries conflict rather than harmonize. And indeed they must. Divine and human do not balance. God is the subject of action, power, and authority. This recognition may mean either good or bad news. To say that God will see to the lamb evades the choice, at least for a time. If the narrator has Abraham seeing (*rʾh*) the place from afar off, Abraham has God seeing (*rʾh*) to the sacrificial lamb before the place is reached. So God dominates the reply in this sentence where syntactic order reverses with subject preceding verb: "God, indeed God, will see to it. . . ."[14]

At the opposite end comes "my-son." Besides rounding off the sentence, this vocative reverberates with the companion address, "my-father." Thus the first word spoken in
this entire unit (my-father) finds resonance in the last (my-son). The bonding of parent
and child encircles their conversation. Nevertheless, the meaning of "my-son" remains
indeterminate. Its juxtaposition to ⁽olāh, burnt-offering, allows the horrendous reading
of apposition. "God will see to the lamb for a burnt-offering," namely, "my-son." The
language functions on two levels. "My-son" is both speech to and speech about, direct
address and direct reference. What it gives in poignancy, it retracts in cruelty. With this
word, dialogue ceases. The refrain that concludes the unit locks in the tenderness and the
terror. Both father and son are trapped; they are snares for sacrifice. "So they went, the
two together." Silence shouts.

4. Obedience Climaxes

In unit four (22:9–10) the journey continues, with the narrator repeating vocabulary, changing nuances, and achieving destination. The opening sentence belongs to a
pattern woven through the units. At the end of unit one, Abraham "went (hlk) to-the-
place which the-God had-told him" (22:3). At the end of unit two (22:6) the singular
verb becomes plural, "they-went (hlk), the two of them together," while the clause of
destination is dropped. The end of unit three repeats "they-went (hlk), the two of them
together." Now at the beginning of unit four, the verb came (b²) in the plural, rather than
went, signals completion of the journey, along with repetition of the theological destination. "And-they-came to-the-place which the-God had-told him" (22:9).

Immediately separation occurs. Syntax and content tell the tale. Abraham alone is
subject of six verbs, with Isaac appearing as object after each group of three. He receives
center-stress and end-stress:

> And-<u>built</u> there Abraham the-altar,
>   and-<u>arranged</u> the-wood,
>   and-<u>bound</u> Isaac his-son.
> and-<u>laid</u> him on-the-altar, from-upon-the-wood.
>   And-<u>put-forth</u> Abraham his-hand
>   and-<u>took</u> the-knife to-slay <u>his-son</u> (22:9b–10)

Irony, poignancy, and suspense abound. The reader remembers Isaac's innocent question "Where is the lamb?" and Abraham's ambiguous reply (22:7–8). Now the narrator
equates burnt offering and son, an equation that Abraham's words previously suggested.
Isaac the questioner is the answer burnt offering. He is the lamb for sacrifice. Further,
the knife that he omitted in his list of sacrificial equipment reappears. When Abraham
first "took [it] in his hand," along with the fire, he protected Isaac from the dangerous
weapon (22:6). Now, by contrast, Abraham put forth "his hand" and "took the knife to
slay his son."[15] Protection yields to destruction. The moment, not just the hour, is at
hand. And yet the fire is missing. Does the omission thwart the ritual? Or is the fire next
time? An attentive reader permits the ambiguity. But no ambiguity characterizes the
action of Abraham. In obedience to the divine command, he stands poised to plunge the
knife. His response is complete; the suspense, insurmountable. Thus ends the second
section of the story.

God's Resolution

With variations, the third section corresponds to the first and the second. It comes, however, as a doublet, for a single resolution cannot embrace both characters evenly. Parallel units (22:11–14 and 22:15–19) contain a three-fold pattern: the narrated appearance of deity, a speech to Abraham, and the narrated response.[16] These two units do not introduce God speaking (ʾmr) directly to Abraham, as in section one, but rather the messenger of Yhwh calling (qrʾ) to him from heaven. If the difference connotes distance, it also bespeaks transcendence. From beyond, deity interprets the text. The responses of Abraham indicate that he understands.

1. *Yhwh Provides*

The first unit (22:11–14) begins just as Abraham is poised, knife in hand, to slay his son. The messenger of Yhwh diverts his attention by uttering his name (22:11a).[17] This time the verb *say* (ʾmr) comes from heaven. Further, it leads not to a single vocative, as in the beginning of the story, but to a repeated one. The emphasis reinforces the diversion, to compel a response, the familiar reply of obedience:

And-he-said, "Abraham, Abraham"!
And-he-said, "*Hinnenî*" (Behold,-here-am-I). (22:11b)

Abraham has not swerved in all the story; steadfastly he has remained faithful. Parallel commands now relieve the dreadful suspense. The first negates verbatim the narrated action in the climax of section two. "And Abraham put-forth (*slh*) his-hand" (22:10a) becomes "Do-not-put-forth (*slh*) your-hand . . ." (22:12a). At this point the vocabulary reverts to the word *naʿar*, young man, that Abraham earlier used for the child (22:5). The reversion hints at a shift in perspective yet to be realized. "Do not-put-forth your-hand to-the-young-man." In contrast to this specificity, the second negative generalizes, thereby ensuring the total safety of Isaac. "Do-not-do to-him anything." No harm shall befall the young man. These two prohibitions remove terror and relieve suspense. Yet the meaning remains obscure, awaiting a special word.

A deictic clause announces that word. "For (*kî*) now I-know that (*kî*). . . ." The formula signals climax, consequence, and conclusion.[18] "For now I know that a fearer of God are you because you have not withheld your son, your only one, from me" (22:12b). Fearer of God! To fear God is to worship God. The term "fearer of God" embodies awe, terror, and devotion in the presence of *mysterium tremendum*.[19] And the worship of God abolishes all idolatries, specifically now the idolatry of the son. "You have not withheld your son, your only one, from me." This interpersonal language takes the reader back to the beginning of the story, to the words, "your son, your only one, whom you love, Isaac." The repetition underscores the issue to clarify the test. Abraham had formed an attachment to his son. Attachment threatened the obedience, the worship, the fear of God. Thus the test offers Abraham an opportunity for healing, an opportunity to free both himself and his son.[20]

To attach one's self to another is to negate love through entrapment. In surrounding Isaac, Abraham binds himself and his son. To attach is to know the anxiety of separation. In clinging to Isaac, Abraham incurs the risk of losing him—and Isaac suspects it.

To attach is to practice idolatry. In adoring Isaac, Abraham turns from God. The test, then, is an opportunity for understanding and healing. To relinquish attachment is to discover freedom. To give up human anxiety is to receive divine assurance. To disavow idolatry is to find God. "Do not lay your hand on the young man or do anything to him, for now I know that you fear God because you have not withheld your son, your only one, from me."

The divine vocabulary of "young man" and "your son" discloses in retrospect a subtle truth hidden in Abraham's speech to his young men. At that time, he distanced himself from Isaac while affirming their unity. "Then Abraham said to his young men, 'Stay here with the ass. I and the young man, we will go yonder and we will worship and we will return again to you'" (22:5). The term "young man" undercut the bonding in the pronoun "we"; in turn, the pronoun "we" undercut the aloofness in the designation "young man." By neutralizing each other, these identifications allowed, though they did not compel, movement beyond attachment-detachment to nonattachment. Thus Abraham's words held potent meaning. Realization of that meaning comes now as the divine messenger juxtaposes the two ways of identifying Isaac: "young man" (detachment) and "your son, your only one" (attachment). Separating these two identifications is the crucial affirmation, "for now I know that a fearer of God are you." Structure and content together break the dangerous dialectic; it is transcended in the worship of God:

> Do not lay your hand on the young man or do anything to him,
> > for now I know that you fear God
> because you have not withheld your son, your only one, from me. (22:12)

The inseparability of what is said and how it is said yields the meaning. Fear of God severs the link between detachment and attachment to save both Abraham and Isaac.

Fear of God also brings vision. "Abraham lifted up his eyes and saw (*r'h*). . . ." Whereas earlier these words introduced "the place from afar" (22:4), this time Abraham sees differently: not afar off but, at hand, behind him an animal. Freed of attachment, he beholds an answer to Isaac's question, "Where is the lamb for a burnt offering?" (22:7d).

> And-lifted-up Abraham his-eyes and-saw.
> Lo-behold (*ḥinnēh*), a-ram behind-him
> > was-entangled in-a-thicket by-his-horns. (22:13a)

Right vision inspires proper action. Three indicative verbs now answer the divine imperatives spoken to Abraham at the beginning of the story. "Take, go, and sacrifice" (22:2) become "Abraham went, took, and sacrificed." Between these grammatical pairings, however, Abraham's world has changed. Contrasting objects, *ram* and *son,* establish the dissonance:

> and-went Abraham
> > and-took the-ram
> > and-sacrificed-it for-a-burnt-offering
> > > instead-of-his-son, (22:13b)

Strikingly unlike the syntactic patterns of previous sentences,[21] the son stands here outside the action of the father. Further, this sentence eliminates the ambiguity of apposition that once linked "burnt offering" and "my son" in Abraham's speech (22:8). By location and meaning, the preposition *taḥat,* "instead of," separates the two nouns.

As substitute for Isaac (and for the lamb), the ram vindicates Abraham's prediction that "God will see to" the sacrifice (22:8). The ram symbolizes the successful completion of the test.[22] Accordingly, an appropriate etiology concludes this unit of section three.

> So Abraham called the name of that place
> > "The Lord will see"
> As it is said to this day,
> > "On the mount of the Lord it will be seen." (22:14)

What is seen is that God provides. To be a God-fearer is to have this vision.

2. God Blesses

But the story cannot and does not end here. While the substitution of a ram for Isaac brings comfort and closure, it also reopens the issue that the test was designed to resolve. Is the sparing of Isaac license for Abraham to reattach himself to his son? If Abraham has demonstrated willingness to relinquish attachment, is he now allowed to keep it? In assuring the reader that Isaac is safe, this first of two resolutions allows misunderstanding. It invites betrayal and folly. Precisely to prevent such an interpretation, the story provides a second resolution in tandem with the first (22:15–19).[23]

The clue for parallel units is the little word *she*ʾ*nith,* "second time." "The messenger of the Lord called to Abraham a second time from heaven." An oath empowers the divine speech: "By myself I have sworn, utterance of the Lord." Two motivational clauses frame four promises:[24]

Motivation

Now (*kî*) because (*yaʿan*) you have done this thing
and-not withheld your-son, your-only-one

Promises

1. Therefore (*kî*) surely I-will-bless-you
2. and-surely I-will-multiply your-descendants
   as-the-stars-of-the-heavens
   and-as-the-sand that (is) on-the-seashore.
3. And-will-possess your-descendants the gate-of their-enemies,
4. and will-bless-themselves by-your-descendants all the
   nations-of the-earth.

Motivation

Because (*ʿeqēb* ʾ*asēr*) you-have-obeyed my-voice (22:16b–18)

In the opening motivation (22:16b), the introductory particles *kî yaʿan*[25] point back to the deictic words "for now (*kî ʿatah*) I know that" (22:12). And the content of this clause also recalls earlier divine speeches. The assertion "you have done this thing" alludes reversely to the prohibition "Do not do to him anything" (22:12). The recognition "you have not withheld your son, your only one" contains a direct quotation (22:2). Verification of these emphases comes in the concluding line, "because you have obeyed my voice" (22:18b). Framing promises of blessing, these motivational clauses underscore not just Abraham's willingness but indeed his relinquishment of idolatry. No longer is he attached to Isaac. He has not withheld his son; he has obeyed the divine voice.

Conclusion

By structure, use of particles, and repetition, the narrator has relentlessly secured meaning. Abraham fears God, worships God, obeys God. Alone Abraham returns from the place of sacrifice. It can be no other way. If the story is to fulfill its meaning, Isaac cannot, must not, and does not appear.[26] Abraham, man of faith, has learned the lesson of non-attachment. Before the crisis he asserted that "we will return" (*šûb*, 22:5). But now the narrator perceptively returns to the verb in the singular: "So Abraham returned . . ." (*šûb*, 22:19). To go yonder and worship (cf. 22:5) returns one to social discourse healed of interpersonal idolatry. A narrated report concluding this unit likewise ends the entire story:

> So-returned Abraham to-his-young-men
> > and-they-arose
> > and-they-went together to-Beersheba
> And-lived Abraham in-Beersheba. (22:19)

So much has been at stake that the story requires two conclusions. They give parallel messages: All is well with Isaac; God provides (22:11–14). All is well with Abraham; God blesses (22:15–19).

The Sacrifice of Sarah

Our rhetorical-critical reading demonstrates the ways structure, vocabulary, and content embody meanings. What a piece of work is Genesis 22! And yet, hardly do I complete the first two verses before a great uneasiness descends. So attached to patriarchy is this magnificent story that I wonder if it can ever be what it purports to be, namely a narrative of nonattachment.[27]

With all-consuming power, the patriarchal bonding of father and son threatens to destroy not only Abraham and Isaac but also another—Sarah. Why is she not in this story? Where is she? What does it all mean for her? Over centuries, many commentators have answered such questions by composing stories outside the text to fill gaps within it.[28] Another approach wrestles from within, using scripture to interpret scripture. Adopting this procedure, I should like to show how the biblical depiction of Sarah works to expose the patriarchy of Genesis 22, how that exposure alters the meaning of the story, and how the resultant interpretation challenges faith. A feminist hermeneutic takes over the rhetorical analysis to yield a different reading.

In the genealogical preface to the so-called Abrahamic narratives, Sarai receives special attention. A recital of descendants originating with Shem lists, in each case, a single male heir followed by reference to "other sons and daughters" (11:10–25). The pattern ceases with the introduction of Terah, "father of Abram, Nahor, and Haran" (11:26). Of the three sons named, only Haran, who dies early, is identified by a male descendant, his son Lot. All three, however, are associated with women:

> And Abram and Nahor took wives.
> > The name of Abram's wife was <u>Sarai</u>,
> > and the name of Nahor's wife, <u>Mil</u>cah,
> > > the daughter of Haran the father of
> > > <u>Mil</u>cah and Iscah.
> Now <u>Sarai</u> was barren; she had no child. (11:29–30)

Here male genealogy relinquishes structure and content to herald a story that names characters.

Contrast emerges between Sarai and Milcah, whose names appear in alternating sequence. The contrast moves between the silence and voice of the text. Nothing is said of Sarai's lineage, but Milcah is "the daughter of Haran"; she also has a sister. On the other hand, nothing is said about Milcah's fertility (cf. 22:20–23), but "Sarai was barren; she had no child." These ominous words haunt the narrative to come. They bring Sarai to center stage while Milcah recedes, as does her husband Nahor. The three remaining men, Terah, Abram, and Lot, go forth with the lone woman Sarai, the one who has neither pedigree nor fertility, neither past nor future.

> Terah took Abram his son and Lot the son of Haran, his grandson,
> > and Sarai his daughter-in-law, his son Abram's wife,
> and they went forth together from the Chaldeans . . . to Haran. . . .
> (11:31)

Unique and barren, Sarai threatens the demise of genealogy. The death of her father-in-law Terah in Haran reduces the generations to two. The generational preface stops (11:32), and the call of Abram begins (12:1–3).

In his journey from Haran to the promised land, Abram takes Sarai his wife as well as Lot his brother's son (12:5). Upon their arrival, Yhwh assures Abram descendants but does not take account of Sarai's condition. When famine sends the group to Egypt, the tension builds. Speaking for the first time, Abram addresses Sarai (12:11–13). With flattery he manipulates her to justify deception and protect himself. He disowns the beautiful Sarai as wife, calls her his sister, and allows Pharaoh to use her, thereby ensuring his own survival, even his prosperity. For her sake Pharaoh dealt well with Abram (12:16) but also for her sake Yhwh afflicted (*ngʿ*) Pharaoh (12:17). Sarai remains the pivot in the story. At the end, Pharaoh reprimands Abram and holds him accountable for the use of his wife (12:18–20). Pharaoh respects another man's property. Throughout it all, Sarai has neither voice nor choice. Though she is central in the episode, patriarchy marginalizes this manhandled woman.

Object of special attention, Sarai eventually speaks, seeking to fulfill herself within cultural strictures. Her words concern fertility and status; they also reveal her as a voice of realism, decisiveness, and command:

> And Sarai said to Abram,
> > "Because Yhwh has prevented me
> > > from bearing children,
> go to my maid.
> Perhaps I shall be built up from her." (16:2a)

Thus this barren woman proposes a plan whereby she may obtain children through her Egyptian maid Hagar (15:1–6). As property of Sarai, Hagar is female enslaved, used, and demeaned. Abram once gave Sarai to Pharaoh; Sarai now gives Hagar to Abram. This time, however, no deity intervenes; the arrangement is legal and proper.

But no happy solution results (16:4–6). Inevitably the women clash. The pregnant maid sees the lowering of hierarchical barriers, and the barren mistress resents loss of status. Reasserting power, Sarai afflicts (*ʿnh*) Hagar, who then flees to the wilderness. The blessed and exalted woman has become malicious and tyrannical. Her authority reaches into the wilderness. Finding Hagar by a spring of water, the messenger of Yhwh orders her not only to return to her mistress but also to "suffer affliction (^{c}nh) under her hand." The cruelty of Sarai continues, this time with heavenly sanction. Who will deliver Sarai from such dis-ease? Who will make possible healing reconciliation? Not Abraham, not her son, not the narrator, and not even God. To the contrary, the story countenances the division between the women.

As the narrative proceeds, God makes clear that only Sarai, no other woman, can bear the child of promise. She is destined for great things:

> And God said to Abraham:
>   "As for Sarai your wife
>   Call not her name^{a} Sarai^{b}
>   for Sarah$^{b'}$ (is) her name.$^{a'}$
> <u>I will bless her</u>
>   and also will give <u>from</u> her to you a son.
> <u>I will bless her</u>
>   and she will become nations;
>   royal people <u>from her</u> will be." (17:15–16)

Sarah's apotheosis is complete. If Hagar is woman in the gutter, Sarah is woman on the pedestal. Their positions illustrate well the strictures of patriarchy.

The exaltation of Sarah continues as Abraham responds to the divine words. Falling on his face and laughing,[29] he utters two speeches. The first, inward dialogue, poses through rhetorical questions an impossible situation:

> <u>Abraham . . . said</u> in his heart
>   "Shall a son be borne to one
>   who is a hundred years old?
>   Shall Sarah, the daughter of ninety years old
>   bear?" (17:17)

These words of Abraham specifically name Sarah. His second response, outward dialogue, pleads for the legitimacy of Ishmael, but it does not name Hagar:

> <u>And Abraham said</u> to the God,
>   "If only Ishmael might live in your presence!" (17:18)

Abraham's responses bring yet again divine sanction for Sarah as the sole designated mother of the chosen heir. A single speech makes three declarations (A, B, C, below). It begins by citing Sarah and Isaac (A). Conversely, it closes with Isaac and Sarah (C). Hers, then, is the first and last proper name. Between the two declarations occurs a promise of blessing for Ishmael, without reference to Hagar (B). Although central in the structure, the promise becomes peripheral to the story line. In other words, the beginning stress upon Sarah and Isaac and the ending stress upon Isaac and Sarah confine Ishmael. The extremities of the divine speech show in particular the special, exalted role of Sarah as mother.

>   God said,
> (A)   "No, but <u>Sarah</u>^{a} your wife will bear for you a son,
>   and you will call his name <u>Isaac</u>^{b}.

I will establish my covenant with him
    as an everlasting covenant
    for his descendants after him.
(B)   As for Ishmael, I have heard you.
    Surely I will bless him
        and I will make him fruitful
        and I will increase him more and more.
    Twelve princes he will bear
        and I will make him a great nation.
(C)   But my covenant I will establish with Isaac[b]
    whom Sarah[a] will bear to you by this time next year."

                    (17:19–21)

Yet another story ensures the status and destiny of Sarah (18:1–16). Disguised as three men, Yhwh visits Abraham by the oaks of Mamre. After receiving the hospitality of rest and food, the guests inquire about Sarah (18:9). Told that she is in the tent, the visitor (now singular) promises to return in the spring "when surely a son will be to Sarah your wife" (18:10). At this point the narrator intervenes to focus on Sarah. Four times her name appears in a report about her location and activity, her old age and infertility, and her immediate response to the promise.

Now-Sarah was listening at the entrance of the tent
    behind him.

Abraham and-Sarah (were) old, advanced in the days;
it was past to be to-Sarah (in the) manner of women.
So-laughed Sarah within herself. . . . (18:10b–12a)

Only after this narrated intervention does Sarah's direct response to the divine promise come:

After being worn out, (is there) to me pleasure—
    and my lord, (who) is old? (18:12b)

Yhwh replies, however, not to Sarah but to Abraham. Questions of reprimand precede a reiteration of the promise, with the name Sarah occurring at the beginning and end.

Why (is) this, Sarah laughed saying
    "Now shall I indeed bear when I am old?"
    Is anything too difficult for Yhwh?
    At the appointed time I will return to you in the spring
        and to Sarah (will be) a son. (18:13–14)

Sarah's laughter "within herself" (18:12) has been heard,[30] but out of fear she denies (*kḥs*) that it ever happened. "Not I-laughed." This time the divine reply comes directly to her. "No, for you-did-laugh." For the first and only time the deity speaks to Sarah. Yet not even this curt rebuke diminishes her exalted and unique status.

Elect among women, only Sarah can bear the legitimate male heir. And so, at long last, it comes to pass. "Yhwh visited Sarah . . . and did to Sarah as Yhwh had promised" (21:1). She bears a son to Abraham in his old age. Abraham names him Laughter (*Yiṣḥaq*) but Sarah interprets its meaning:

Laughter God has made <u>for-me</u> (*lî*).
All who hear will laugh <u>for-me</u> (*lî*) (21:6)

If Laughter (Isaac) is special to Abraham, how much more to Sarah! She claims the child for herself, "for-me." After all, he is her, not Abraham's, one and only son.

Ishmael, the other male child in the family, is thus a threat. So jealousy continues to breed rivalry between the two women: Sarah, wife of Abraham, and Hagar, wife of Abraham; Sarah, woman on the pedestal, and Hagar, woman in the gutter; Sarah, mother of Isaac, and Hagar, mother of Ishmael. Potential equality between sons counters actual inequality between their mothers. Power belongs to Sarah; powerlessness to Hagar. Sarah asserts authority against the other woman, as she did once before, and now against her child. Speaking to Abraham, she orders:

Cast out this slave woman and her son,
for the son of this slave woman
    will not inherit with my son,
                with Isaac. (21:10)

Language of contrast achieves several effects. First, the single phrase "her son" and the double phrase "with my son, with Isaac" show the lack of equality between the sons. Second, the name Isaac accords him dignity and power in contrast to the namelessness, and hence powerlessness, of both the slave woman and her son. Third, the combination "my son Isaac" bespeaks possessiveness, indeed attachment. It foreshadows language that in Genesis 22 applies to Abraham, rather than to Sarah. Yet in chapter 21 Abraham has no exclusive relationship with Isaac. He uses no speech of intimacy for either son. But the narrator and the deity attach him to Ishmael and to Hagar:

The matter was very distressing
    in the eyes of Abraham
    on account of his son.
But God said to Abraham,
    "Do not be distressed in your eyes
        on account of the lad
        and on account of your slave woman." (21:11–12a)

Possessive language, "his son," links Abraham and Ishmael, a paternal-filial connection that endures until Abraham's death (25:9).

Through direct and narrated discourse Genesis 21:1–11 delineates a decisive parental difference between Sarah and Abraham. Sarah speaks directly, using the vocabulary "my son Isaac." Her exclusive speech owns her one and only son. On the other hand, Abraham speaks not at all; he claims no father-son relationships. They appear only in the distancing of narration. The storyteller makes the claim for Abraham regarding both sons, "his son Isaac" (21:4,5) and "his son" Ishmael (21:11). Accordingly, unlike the bond between Sarah and Isaac, no unique tie exists here between Abraham and Isaac. Other texts support the observation. Before Genesis 22:7 Abraham never utters or implies the possessive "my son" for Isaac, though he does imply the epithet for Ishmael (17:18). Such witnesses, most especially chapter 21, dispute the father-son pairing of Genesis 22 to compel a closer look at Sarah's relationship to Isaac.

With single, unqualified attachment to "my son," Sarah prevails once more over against Abraham because God supports her.

> Everything that Sarah says to you, heed her voice;
> for in Isaac will be named to you descendants. (21:12)

Sarah, the chosen vessel of the legitimate heir, remains secure on the pedestal that patriarchy has built for her. To keep her there protects her from a test, but in doing so it exacerbates her tyranny, deprives her of freedom, and renders impossible reconciliation with Hagar.

If the phrase "my son Isaac" in 21:10 foreshadows the language of chapter 22, while reversing the parental figures, other associations similarly challenge the content.[31] In the wilderness with his mother Hagar, Ishmael comes close to death; a messenger of God intervenes to save him. On the mountain with his father Abraham, Isaac comes close to death; a messenger of God intervenes to save him. Thus are joined the two sons and the divine representatives. The presence of Hagar the mother and Abraham the father, however, skews the pairing. Chapter 21 shows that the proper match in parents are the mothers, Hagar and Sarah. This pairing argues correspondingly for the appearance of Sarah, not Abraham, in Genesis 22. As Hagar faced the imminent death of Ishmael, so Sarah ought to have faced the imminent death of Isaac. Explicit parallels between chapters 21 and 22 sustain the logic of the argument, and yet a bias for father-son bonding has defied the connection.

Another observation demonstrates the inappropriateness of Abraham as the parental figure for Genesis 22. Nowhere else in the entire narrative sequence does he appear as a man of attachment.[32] To the contrary. When Yhwh calls him, Abram obediently leaves his country, his clan, and his father's house to journey to an unknown land (12:1–4). Immediately after that commendable relinquishment comes an unflattering one: Abram passes his wife Sarai off as his sister (12:10–20). Later he even repeats this act of extraordinary detachment (20:1–18). In reference to the land, Abraham shows no possessiveness but instead allows Lot to choose (13:2–12). After warring with kings from the East and recovering all the goods and people captured, Abraham gives the king of Salem a tenth of everything, besides refusing to take anything not his own (14:1–24). Similar behavior appears in his less generous treatment of Hagar. On two occasions he gives power over her to Sarai and God (16:1–6 and 21:1–14). Hints of his involvement with Ishmael (17:18; 21:11) are negated when he sends the child away, along with Hagar. In another episode he gives gifts to Abimelech as they settle a dispute over wells (21:22–34). Be the incident an occasion for weal or woe, nowhere prior to Genesis 22 does Abraham emerge as a man of attachment. That is not his problem. How ill-fitted he is, then, for a narrative of testing and sacrifice.

Attachment is Sarah's problem. Nevertheless, Genesis 22 drops Sarah to insert Abraham. The switch defies the internal logic of the larger story. In view of the unique status of Sarah and her exclusive relationship to Isaac, she, not Abraham, ought to have been tested. The dynamic of the entire saga, from its genealogical preface on, requires that Sarah be featured in the climactic scene, that she learn the meaning of obedience to God, that she find liberation from possessiveness, that she free Isaac from maternal ties,[33] and that she emerge a solitary individual, nonattached, the model of faithfulness. In making Abraham the object of the divine test, the story violates its own rhythm and movement. Moreover, it fails to offer Sarah redemption and thereby perpetuates the conflict between her and Hagar. As long as Sarah is attached to Isaac (both child and symbol), so long Sarah afflicts Hagar.[34]

The text, however, permits the banished Hagar to forge for herself a future that God and Sarah have diminished. She chooses an Egyptian wife for her son and so guarantees the identity of her descendants (21:21; cf. 25:12–18). If it yield but small mercy, her act is nonetheless a sign of healing for this abused woman. By contrast, the biblical story allows no opportunity, however small, for Sarah to be healed. It attributes to her no action or word that might temper her affliction. Instead, it leaves her a jealous and selfish woman.

Patriarchy has denied Sarah her story, the opportunity for freedom and blessing. It has excluded her and glorified Abraham. And it has not stopped with these things. After securing the safety of Isaac, it has no more need for Sarah; so it moves to eliminate her. The process begins obliquely, yet with the telling phrase, "and it came to pass after these events" (22:20). As this phrase introduced the story of testing and sacrifice (22:1), so it returns to make a transition that continues the larger narrative.

Once again, continuation holds surprise. The narrative begets a genealogy (22:20–24). Its subject reverts to the family of Nahor, thereby recalling the genealogical preface to the entire saga (11:27–32). An unidentified speaker addresses only Abraham, who has just returned from the mount of sacrifice. Unlike the preface, this passage says nothing explicit about Sarah. Silence begins her removal. The words commence, "Behold Milcah also (*gam*) has borne children to your brother Nahor" (RSV). The particle "also" contrasts the two wives.[35] Though Sarah has borne only the singular child Isaac, Milcah has birthed eight sons. Bethuel, the last of them, holds special meaning because "Bethuel became the father of Rebekah" (22:23). Reference to this daughter forecasts a future for Isaac. The concluding item in the genealogy likewise implies contrast between women: "Moreover, his concubine, whose name was Reumah, bore Tebah, Gaham, Tahash, and Maacah" (22:24, RSV). Though Hagar, second wife of Abraham, bore the one son Ishmael, Nahor's concubine Reumah bore four sons. Yet the small family of Abraham and Sarah, excluding Hagar, and not the large family of Nahor and Milcah, including Reumah, carry the promise. The two families join later when the one and only child Isaac finds a wife in the daughter Rebekah (24:1–67).

If at the beginning of this entire saga barren Sarai threatened the demise of genealogy (11:30), at the end genealogy portends the demise of Sarah. Immediately after the report of 22:20–24, patriarchy dismisses Sarah. It has no further need of her, and so it writes a lean obituary (cf. 25:7–8).

> Sarah lived a hundred and twenty-seven years;
>   these were the years of the life of Sarah.
> And Sarah died at Kiriath-arba (that is, Hebron)
>   in the land of Canaan. . . . (23:1–2a, RSV)

The place of Sarah's death suggests another facet of her story. After the test, Abraham returns to dwell in Beersheba. But Sarah dies in Hebron. Thus the text reads as though husband and wife were never reunited in life. Indeed, "Abraham *went* to mourn for Sarah and to weep for her" (23:2b).

Sarah died alone. Then Abraham went to her. But immediately the story turns from Sarah to a long section in which Abraham bargains with the Hittites for burial ground (23:3–18). Only after some sixteen verses does Sarah re-enter the narrative. "After this, Abraham buried Sarah his wife in the cave of the field of Mach-pelah east of Mamre (that is, Hebron) in the land of Canaan" (23:19). Where she died, there was she buried. If early on patriarchy casts out the woman in the gutter (Hagar), the time comes when it also dismisses the woman on the pedestal (Sarah). Moreover, it allots Sarah no dying words. It leaves the reader to remember as her last words only the harsh imperative, "Cast out this slave woman with her son; for the son of this slave woman shall not be heir with my son Isaac" (21:10). This utterance haunts Sarah's portrait, crying out for release from possessiveness and attachment. And though the story for healing is at hand, it remains captive to a patriarchal agenda.

From exclusion to elimination, denial to death, the attachment of Genesis 22 to patriarchy has given us not the sacrifice of Isaac (for that we are grateful) but the sacrifice of Sarah (for that we mourn). By her absence from the narrative and her subsequent death, Sarah has been sacrificed by patriarchy to patriarchy. Thus this magnificent story of nonattachment stands in mortal danger of betraying itself. It fears not God but holds fast to an idol. If the story is to be redeemed, then the reader must restore Sarah to her rightful place. Such a hermeneutical move, wed to rhetorical analysis, would explode the entrenched bias to fulfill the internal logic of the story. And it would do even more: it would free divine revelation from patriarchy. Yet even there the matter does not end.

An Epilogue for Disorientation

We have presented two interpretations of Genesis 22. They share the theme of attachment, detachment, and nonattachment. They diverge in appropriating this theme to Isaac's parents. The patriarchal interpretation, given in the text, elects Abraham and so makes paternal bonding the idolatrous problem. The feminist interpretation, inspired by the text, chooses Sarah and so makes maternal bonding the idolatrous problem. An author's intentionality and a reader's response have thus yielded competing views. Although the two readings might coexist, however uneasily, becoming attached to either or both of them would violate this narrative of nonattachment.

To be faithful to the story no interpretation can become an idol. And so the essay concludes with a disorienting homily. After we perceive the sacrifice of Sarah and move to free the narrative from attachment to patriarchy, after and only after all these things, will we hear God testing us: "Take your interpretation of this story, your only interpretation, the one which you love, and sacrifice it on the mount of hermeneutics." If we withhold not our cherished reading from God, then we too will come down from the mountain nonattached. In such an event, we and the story will merge. Interpretation will become appropriation. Testing and attachment will disappear, and the worship of God will be all in all.

NOTES

1. This essay is an abridgment of a forthcoming study.

2. Bibliography on Genesis 22 is staggering. Claus Westermann lists numerous references from 1905 through 1978; see *Genesis 12–36, A Commentary* (Minneapolis: Augsburg Publishing

House, 1985), pp. 351–54. James L. Crenshaw adds to this list, including his own essay, "A Monstrous Test: Genesis 22," *A Whirlpool of Torment* (Philadelphia: Fortress Press, 1984), pp. 9–29. Surveys of the history of interpretation appear in two articles: S. Kreuzer, "Das Opfer des Vaters— die Gefährundung des Sohnes: Genesis 22," pp. 62–70, and F. Neubacher, "Isaaks Opferung in der griechishen Alten Kirche," pp. 72–76, both published in *Schaut Abraham an, euren Vater! Festschrift für Professor Dr. Georg Sauer zum 60 Geburtstag, Amt und Gemeinde* 27:7/8 (1986). For a study of the Akedah in art, see Jo Milgrom, *The Bilding of Isaac: The Akedah—A Primary Symbol in Jewish Thought and Art* (Berkeley: Bibal Press, 1988).

3. On rhetorical criticism, see the foundational document by James Muilenburg, "Form Criticism and Beyond," *JBL* 88 (1969): 1–18; for samplings of feminist hermeneutics, see *inter alia* Mary Ann Tolbert, ed., *The Bible and Feminist Hermeneutics,* Semeia 28 (Chico, Calif.: Scholars Press, 1983); Adela Yarbro Collins, ed., *Feminist Perspectives on Biblical Scholarship* (Chico, Calif.: Scholars Press, 1985); Letty M. Russell, ed., *Feminist Interpretation of the Bible* (Philadelphia: The Westminster Press, 1985).

4. For the classic literary analysis, see Erich Auerbach, "Odysseus' Scar," *Mimesis: The Representation of Reality in Western Literature* (Garden City, N.Y.: Doubleday, 1953). Most recently, cf. Francis Landy, "Narrative Techniques and Symbolic Transactions in the Akedah" and Jan P. Fokkelman, "'On the Mount of the Lord There Is Vision,' A Response to Francis Landy Concerning the Akedah," *Signs and Wonders,* ed. J. Cheryl Exum (The Society of Biblical Literature Semeia Studies, 1989), pp. 1–57.

5. All biblical citations refer to the book of Genesis, unless stated otherwise. Two translations of the Hebrew are used: mine and the Revised Standard Version. The former are left unmarked; the latter are designated RSV.

6. This literary reading follows the narrative in its final form rather than exploring the history of sources and traditions behind it. On that subject, see most recently Jean-L. Duhaime, "Le sacrifice d'Isaac (Gn 22, 1–19): l'heritage de Gunkel," *Science et Esprit* (1981): 139–56; Sean E. McEvenue, "The Elohist at Work," *Zeitschrift für die alttestamentliche Wissenschaft* 96 (1984): 315–32; Hans-Cristoph Schmitt, "Die Erzälung von de Versuch Abrahams Gen 22, 1–19* und das Problem einer Theologie der elohistichen Pentateuchtexts," *Biblische Notizen* 34 (1986): 82–109.

7. For the verb *nsh* with God as subject, cf. Exod. 15:25, 16:4, 20:20; Deut. 8:2,16; 13:3; 2 Chron. 32:31.

8. For an illuminating discussion of God as tester and provider (22:15), see Walter Brueggemann, *Genesis* (Atlanta: John Knox Press, 1982), pp. 188–94. Some commentators argue that the character of God (not just Abraham) is also tested here; see Kenneth R.R. Gros Louis, "Abraham: II," *Literary Interpretations of Biblical Narratives,* vol. 2, ed. Gros Louis with James S. Ackerman (Nashville: Abingdon, 1982), pp. 71–84 and Sidney Breitbart, "The Akedah—A Test of God," *Dor le Dor* 15 (1986/87): 19–28. An altogether different reading of the verb *nissāh* as "uplifted" (from *nēs*) is proposed by Hirsch Patcas, "Akedah, The Binding of Isaac," *Dor le Dor* 14 (1985/86): 112–14.

9. E.g., King James Version. For a grammatical discussion of *hinnēth,* see Thomas O. Lambdin, *Introduction to Biblical Hebrew* (New York: Charles Scribner's Sons, 1971), pp. 170–71; for a literary analysis, with reference to its use by a narrator, see Shimon Bar-Efrat, *Narrative Art in the Bible* (Sheffield: The Almond Press, 1989), pp. 35–36.

10. Among others who have made this point, see Gerhard von Rad, *Genesis* (Philadelphia: The Westminster Press, 1961), p. 239. For a discussion of links between Genesis 12 and 22, see Jonathan Magonet, "Abraham and God," *Judaism* 33 (1984): 160–70.

11. Such translations are designed to convey Hebrew vocabulary and syntax rather than felicitous English. Hyphens connecting words indicate a single word in Hebrew; they are used, however, only when deemed useful to the reader.

12. The phenomenon of repetition is important for understanding the structure, content, and meaning of Hebrew narratives. This phenomenon has numerous functions: to signal the boundaries and the connections of units, to aid memory, and to yield emphases. To indicate the presence of repetition in the relationships of words, phrases, clauses, and sentences, I employ a series of markers: e.g., <u>unbroken lines</u>, <u>broken lines</u>, and <u>dots</u>. These markers are arbitrarily chose but their use is purposeful and consistent.

13. Cf. von Rad, *Genesis,* p. 240.

14. Cf. the same reversal in 22:1.

15. The words, "took the knife," appear only twice in scripture, the other occurrence in Judges 19:29. On connections between these narratives, see Jeremiah Unterman, "The Literary Influence of 'The Binding of Isaac' (Genesis 22) on 'The Outrage at Gibeah' (Judges 19)," *Hebrew Annual Review* 4 (1980): 161–66.

16. The usual way of accounting for these two parts is to designate verses 15–19 a later addition. Westermann, e.g., writes that "one needs no deep insight to see the difference in style; vv. 15–18 are not narrative style" (*Genesis,* p. 363). True, but one does need deeper insight to discern the fit. The final form of the story may hold integrity. Cf. R.W.L. Moberly, "The Earliest Commentary on the Akedah," *Vetus Testamentum* 38 (1988): 302–23.

17. One usual way of explaining the unusual phrase "messenger of Yhwh" is to posit a redactor who altered the original text, "messenger of God." For an evaluation of this view, see Westermann, *Genesis,* p. 361. Rhetorically and theologically other interpretations prevail. Note the *inclusio* formed by the use of the Tetragrammaton at the beginning (22:11) and the end (22:14) of this unit. The inclusive emphasis underscores the character of the particular deity speaking to Abraham. Indeed, the switch from the generic Elohim (God), thus far used consistently in the story, to the divine name Yhwh highlights the self-revelation of the deity. If God is on trial also (cf. note 8), then Yhwh, the God of Abraham, discloses that this deity does not finally require child sacrifice.

18. On the deictic function of *ki,* see esp. James Muilenburg, "The Linguistic and Rhetorical Usages of the Particle *ki* in the Old Testament," *Hebrew Union College Annual* 32 (1961): 135–60; cf. Bar-Efrat, *Narrative Art in the Bible,* p. 30.

19. See Samuel Terrien, *The Elusive Presence* (San Francisco: Harper and Row, 1978), pp. 81–84.

20. This interpretation plays with three concepts: attachment, detachment, and nonattachment. The first two are interrelated, being positive and negative manifestations of an invalid mode-of-being in the world. This mode-of-being anchors existence in human relationships, rather than in God, with inevitable consequences of problems and sufferings. Nonattachment is a transcendent way of knowing and thinking. It moves human beings beyond interpersonal entrapments to a realization of the divine. Thus it offers a spiritual perspective that allows one to be in the world but not of it. In the language of Genesis 22, nonattachment is the fear of God. It frees human beings from one another so that they can be one with another. In addition to scriptural foundations, this interpretation builds on Zen Buddhism and Metapsychiatry. For further clarification, see Venerable Gyomay M. Kubose, "Non-attachment," *Zen Koans* (Chicago: Henry Regnery Company, 1973), pp. 65–126 and Thomas Hora, *Beyond the Dream* (Orange, Calif.: PAGL Press, 1986), *passim.*

21. Cf. 22:3, 6, 9–10.

22. On sacrificial substitutions as a way to divert violence, see Rene Girard, *Violence and the Sacred* (Baltimore: Johns Hopkins University Press, 1977), pp. 4–6.

23. On Genesis 22 as the ratification of an eternal covenant between God and Abraham, with a particular focus on vv. 15–18, see T. Desmond Alexander, "Genesis 22 and the Covenant of Circumcision," *Journal for the Study of the Old Testament* 25 (1983): 17–22.

24. A full examination of this structure and content awaits the forthcoming longer study. It includes a comparison of the promise made here to Genesis 12 and 15.

25. On the particle *ya'an*, see D.E. Gowan, "The Use of *ya'an* in Biblical Hebrew," *Vetus Testamentum* 21 (1971): 168–85.

26. For a different treatment of the absence of Isaac, see James Crenshaw, "Journey into Oblivion: A Structural Analysis of Gen. 22:1–9," *Soundings* 58 (1975): 243–56.

27. Despite the salutary warning by Carol Meyers about problems inherent in the word *patriarchy,* the term appears likely to remain. As shorthand, it designates male-centered and male-dominated cultures and texts with an implied critique of them. It names a pervasive social system. Meyers rightly pleads for an understanding of historical specificities in descriptions and evaluations of patriarchy. See Carol Meyers, *Discovering Eve: Ancient Israelite Women in Context* (New York: Oxford University Press, 1988), pp. 24–46.

28. See, e.g., Louis Ginzberg, *Legends of the Bible* (Philadelphia: Jewish Publication Society of America, 1968), pp. 128–38; also Shalom Spiegel, *The Last Trial* (New York: Pantheon Books, 1967). Cf. Yaakov Elbaum, "From Sermon to Story: The Transformation of the Akedah," *Prooftexts* 6 (1986): 97–116. On ancient interpretations, Jewish and Christian, see, *inter alia,* P.R. Davies and B.D. Chilton, "The Aqedah: A Revised Tradition History," *Catholic Biblical Quarterly* 40 (1978): 514–46; Sebastian Brock, "Genesis 22: Where Was Sarah?" *Expository Times* 96 (1984): 14–17; C.T.R. Hayward, "The Sacrifice of Isaac and Jewish Polemic Against Christianity," *Catholic Biblical Quarterly* 52 (1990): 293–306.

29. Note that the verb laugh (*shq*) forecasts the name of the son, Isaac (*yshq*).

30. Note the parallel to Abraham's laugh in 17:17 and the corresponding play on the name Isaac. Note also other similarities and contrasts between Abraham and Sarah: "Abraham said in his heart" (17:17a); "Sarah laughed within herself" (18:12a). Two rhetorical questions by Abraham, asked inwardly (17:17), are matched in part by Sarah's one question, perhaps also asked inwardly (18:12b); cf. Bar-Efrat, *Narrative Art in the Bible,* pp. 63f.

31. For comments on these two stories, chapters 21 and 22, from the perspective of the abandonment of children, see John Boswell, *The Kindness of Strangers* (New York: Pantheon Books, 1988), *passim* but esp. pp. 141, 144–45, 155.

32. The thesis of this paragraph emerged in a discussion with Professor Tikva Frymer-Kensky of the Reconstructionist Rabbinical College, Wyncote, Pennsylvania.

33. Genesis 24:67 suggests that the problem of mother-son bonding continued even beyond Sarah's death.

34. For a womanist perspective on the Hagar and Sarah stories, see Renita J. Weems, "A Mistress, a Maid, and No Mercy," *Just a Sister Away* (San Diego, Calif.: LuraMedia, 1988), pp. 1–19.

35. See Westermann, *Genesis 12–36,* pp. 366–67.

Sexual Politics
in the Hebrew Bible

Law and Philosophy
The Case of Sex in the Bible[1]

Tikva Frymer-Kensky

For the modern scholar, ancient law offers many challenges and types of inquiry. First and foremost, of course, it demands to be studied for itself, as a legal system of a society: How are problems adjudicated, what is to be done in the case of theft, what are the nature of property rights, and so forth? Second, it is a record of the socio-economic system of that society: What are the social classes, who holds the property and how, what are the economic concerns addressed by the laws? Third, it presents questions of intellectual history: Where did a given law come from, what is its relationship to other legal systems, what if any is the inner development within that society itself? And above all, it is an intellectual mirror of the philosophical principles of a given society. Through a culture's laws, we can see its values and some of its basic ideas about the world. Sometimes, our only access into the mind-set of a culture is through its laws. This is the case with sex in the Bible.

Sex is inherently problematic. At once cultural and physical, it defies categorization. In pagan religions there is a mystique, expressed through the sacred marriage ritual, in which sex has an important role in the bringing of fertility. The sacred marriage also gave rise to songs and poems that provided for the expression and celebration of sexual desire in a religious setting. Furthermore, the goddess of sexual attraction imparts a divine aspect to erotic impulse and a vocabulary to celebrate it and to mediate and diffuse the anxieties it may engender.

Sex and the Biblical God

But what about the Bible? Whatever may have been the case in empirical Israel, all the pagan sexual trappings disappear in the Hebrew Scriptures. The God of the Bible is male, which would make it difficult for him to represent the sex drive to a male. Even more, the God of Israel is only male by gender, not by sex. He is not at all phallic, and cannot represent male virility and sexual potency. Anthropomorphic biblical language

293

uses body imagery of the arm, right hand, back, face and mouth, but God is not imagined below the waist. In Moses's vision at Mount Sinai, God covered Moses with his hand until he had passed by, and Moses saw only his back (Exod 33:23). In Elijah's vision, he saw nothing, and experienced only a "small still voice" (1 Kgs 19:12). In Isaiah's vision (chapter 6), two seraphim hid God's (or the seraphim's) "feet" (normally taken as a euphemism), and in Ezekiel's vision (chapters 1–2), there is only fire below the loins. God is asexual, or transsexual, or metasexual (depending on how we view this phenomenon); but he is never sexed.

Nor does God behave in sexual ways. God is the "husband" of Israel in the powerful marital metaphor. But there are no physical descriptions: God does not kiss, embrace, fondle, or otherwise express physical affection for Israel. By contrast, in the erotic metaphor that describes the attachment of Israel to Lady Wisdom, there is no hesitation to use a physical image, "hug her to you and she will exalt you, she will bring you honor if you embrace her" (Prov 4:8). Wisdom is clearly a woman-figure, and can be metaphorically embraced as a woman. But God is not a sexual male, and so there can be no physicality.

God could not model sexuality, hence it could not be a part of the sacred order. In order to underscore this, God also does not grant sexuality, erotic attraction, or potency. These are taken as matter-of-fact components of the universe and are not singled out as part of God's beneficence.

There is a concern to separate the sexual and the sacred. Before the initial revelation of God at Mount Sinai, Moses commanded Israel to abstain from sexual activity for three days (Exod 19:15).[2] This temporal separation between the sexual and the sacred also underlies the story of David's request for food during his days of fleeing from King Saul, in which he assures Ahimelech that his men can eat hallowed bread because they have been away from women for three days (1 Sam 21:4–5).

The priests, guardians of Israel's ongoing contact with the Holy, were to be conscientious in preserving a separation between Israel's priestly functions and attributes and any kind of sexuality. They were not celibate, a totally foreign idea, but their sexual activity had to be a model of controlled proper behavior. The unatonable wrong of Eli's sons was sleeping with the women who came to worship; for this they lost forever their own and their family's right to be priests (1 Sam 2:22–25). The priest's family also had to be chaste. His wife had to be a virgin, for he was not allowed to marry a divorcee. His daughters had a particular charge to be chaste while under their father's jurisdiction: he could not deliver his daughter into prostitution, and, should a priest's daughter be improperly sexually active, she was considered to have profaned *her father* and was to be burned.

Any sexuality was to be kept so far from temple service that even the wages of a prostitute were not to be given to a temple as a gift.[3] All hints of sexuality were kept far away from cultic life and religious experience.

The separation of sexuality and cult is also embedded in the impurity provisions of the sacral laws. Israel's impurity rules were intended to keep intact the essential divisions of human existence: holy and profane, life and death. They conveyed no moral valuation, and even doing a virtuous and societally necessary act, like burying the dead, would result in entering the impure state. There was also no danger involved in such "impurity"; the impure individual was not expected to die or to become ill. Such impurities were characterized by two major features: the major impurities (which last a week) were contagious, in that all who come in contact with someone impure in this way will themselves become impure for a day. And all those who are impure are isolated ritually: they cannot come to the temple or participate in sacred rites for the duration of their impurity.[4] Under these regulations, any man who has had a sexual emission or anybody who has engaged in sexual intercourse must wash and will nevertheless be ritually impure until that evening (Lev 15:16–18). In this way, there was a marked temporal division between engaging in sexual activity and coming into the domain of the sacred.[5]

Control of Sexual Action by Law

Sexuality has been desacralized. It has not been demonized or condemned. On the contrary, it is not given sufficient status and importance to accord it a conscious valuation, even a negative one. It is talked about (or, most often, not talked about) as part of the social realm, as a question of societal regulation. The proper sphere for considering or mentioning sexuality was the law. The ideal state of existence envisioned by the Bible is marriage.[6] The monogamous nuclear family was established by God at the very beginning of human existence: "therefore a man leaves his father and mother and cleaves to his wife and they become one flesh" (Gen 2:24). Furthermore, "he who finds a wife, he finds a good thing and gets favor from the Lord" (Prov 18:22).[7] Within this marital structure, sexuality is not only permitted: it is encouraged. In God's description of life in the real world, he tells Eve, "your desire is for your husband, and he shall rule you" (Gen 3:16). Deuteronomy includes a provision for the exemption of a new bridegroom from campaigns for a year so that he may be free to cause his wife to rejoice (Deut 20:7, 24:5). The enjoyment of marriage is sexual as well as social:

> let your fountain be blessed;
> find joy in the wife of your youth—
> a loving doe, a graceful mountain goat,
> let her breasts satisfy you at all times;
> be infatuated with love of her always. (Prov 5:17–18)

And the wise man is encouraged to enjoy his marital sexuality.

Sexuality has a place in the social order in that it bonds and creates the family. The sex laws seek to control sexual behavior by delineating the proper parameters of sexual activity—those relationships and time in which it is permissible. Sexual behavior was not free. Despite the indubitable double standard in which adultery means sex with a married woman, men were also limited by the sex laws. In the case of homosexuality, men were more bound than women, since homosexuality was considered a major threat requiring the death penalty (whether real or threatened) and lesbian sex was not a matter of concern. The unequal definition of adultery results from the fact that for a man to sleep with a woman who belonged to some other household threatened the definition of "household" and "family"; for a married man to sleep with an unattached woman is not mentioned as an item of concern, and the very existence of prostitutes indicates that there were women with whom a man (married or unmarried) could have sexual experiences. This was not an unusual definition of adultery, and it has been suggested that this unevenness is the essence of male control over female sexuality, and that possibly it demonstrates a desire to be certain of paternity. Within Israel this treatment of adultery is not examined; it is part of Israel's inheritance from the ancient Near East and, like slavery and other elements of social structure, it is never questioned in the Bible.

The Pentateuchal laws also rule on sexual intercourse with a girl still living in her father's house, at which time she is expected to be chaste. According to Exod 22:15–16, if a man seduced an unbetrothed girl he had to marry her; he has engendered an obligation that he cannot refuse, and must, moreover, offer the customary brideprice. Her father had the option to refuse her to him, in which case the seducer must pay a full virgin's brideprice. The assumption in this rule is that the father has the full determination of his daughter's sexuality, a situation also assumed in the two horrible tales of the abuse of this right, Lot's offering of his daughters to the men of Sodom (Genesis 18–19) and the man of Gibeah's offering of his daughter and the Levite's concubine to the men of Gibeah (Judges 19). These men were attempting to cope with an emergency situation in which they felt their lives at risk, but the narrative considers them within their rights to offer their daughters, and Lot, in particular, is considered the one righteous man in Sodom.

The obligation a girl had to remain chaste while in her father's house is underscored in Deut 22:20ff., which prescribes that a bride whose new husband finds her not to be a virgin is to be stoned, because "she did a shameful thing in Israel, committing fornication while under her father's authority." There is good reason to suspect that this law was not expected to be followed. According to the procedure laid out in Deut 22:13–14, after the accusation, the case was brought before the elders at the gate, and the parents of the girl produced the sheet to prove that she was a virgin; once they did this, the man was flogged, fined, and lost his rights to divorce her in the future. Since the parents had plenty of time to find blood for the sheets, it is unlikely that a bridegroom would make such a charge; if he disliked the girl he could divorce her. If he nevertheless made such a charge, she and her family would have to be very ignorant not to fake the blood. But the law certainly lays down a theoretical principle very important to Israel, viz., that a girl was expected to be chaste while in her father's house. Stoning, moreover, is a very special penalty, reserved for those offenses which completely upset the hierarchical arrangements of the cosmos. In these cases, the entire community is threatened and endangered, and the entire community serves as the executioner.[8]

Stoning is also prescribed when a man comes upon a betrothed woman in town; in this case both are stoned; the girl because she did not cry for help (which would have been heard, since they were in town) and the man because he illicitly had sex with his neighbor's wife (Deut 22:23–24). The law assumes that the act was consensual: even though the word עִנָּה is often translated "rape," it rarely corresponds to forcible rape but rather implies the abusive treatment of someone else. In sexual contexts, it means illicit sex, sex with someone with whom one has no right to have sex.[9] The sense of the law about sex with a betrothed woman is that a girl, although still a virgin, is legally considered married to the man to whom she has been betrothed; hence the two are guilty of adultery and are deserving of death. Moreover, death by stoning is prescribed, whereas in regular adultery the penalty is death, but not by stoning. Sex with a betrothed girl is compound adultery: the rights of the future husband have been violated, and the girl has offended against her obligations to her father.[10]

There is a question as to who properly exercises control over sexuality. In Exodus, the father can refuse to grant his daughter to her seducer; and this kind of paternal control is also implied in Lot's offering his daughters and the man of Gibeah offering his. But Deuteronomy indicates that the father's rights were not all that absolute (at least by the time of Deuteronomy). In Deut 22:28–29, if a man grabs an unbetrothed girl and they are found, the man is to give the father 50 shekels, and he must marry her without the right to divorce her in the future. Unlike the comparable law in Exodus, there is not mention of the father's right to refuse to give his daughter to this marriage. The laws have superseded his discretion and now require what had once been the father's discretionary act.

Husbands also do not have limitless control over their wives' sexuality. According to Assyrian laws, a husband has a right to determine the penalty for his adulterous wife, or even to pardon her outright; his freedom is limited only by the fact that whatever he chooses to do to his wife, the same will be done to her adulterous partner. Israel also may have known of such husbandly determination, for the book of Proverbs, in warning the young man against adultery, warns him: "the fury of the husband will be passionate; he will show no pity on his day of vengeance. He will not have regard for any ransom; he will refuse your bribe, however great" (Prov 6:34–35). In the formal, scholastic formulation of the laws, however, the penalty for adultery is officially death, with no option of clemency.

Deuteronomy vests some of the control over these matters in the hands of the elders of Israel. It is their responsibility to uphold the social order and eliminate dangers to it. They try the recalcitrant son (21:18–21); they investigate the question of the bride's virginity (22:13–19); they oversee the release of a *levir* (25:7), and they perform the decapitated heifer ceremony (21:1–9).

But above all, the laws place the locus of control outside the discretion of individuals, by prescribing mandatory sentencing for certain offenses and leaving others for divine sanction. In the prohibited relationships of Leviticus 20, adultery, homosexuality, bestiality, and sex with step-mother, mother-in-law, and daughter-in-law are all to be punished by death; sex with a sister, sister-in-law, aunt, uncle's wife, and menstruant are also prohibited, but they are outside social sanctions and are to be punished by God.

The Bible defines the parameters of permissible sexuality by forbidding intolerable relationships. One may not have a sexual relationship that infringes on another family (adultery or sex with a girl still in her father's household), but within one's own family there are strong incest prohibitions, detailed in Leviticus 18 and 20, and Deuteronomy 27. One cannot have sex with father and mother, step-mother, paternal uncle[11] and his wife, and both maternal and paternal aunts.[12] In one's own generation, both sister and brother's wife are prohibited.[13] In the next generation, one's daughter-in-law and, we presume, one's daughter[14] are prohibited, as are one's children's daughters. Furthermore, once one marries, one's wife's lineage is off limits: mother-in-law, wife's sister (while wife is alive), wife's daughters and granddaughters.

These incest laws seem particularly complex, and it has been suggested that the laws sought to include all those women who might be found in the same household in an extended family. However, mothers-in-law would not have been expected in these households and the prohibitions on father's daughters are explicitly said to include those daughters born outside the household. Moreover, these laws took their final form when Israel already had nuclear households. The laws are defining and clarifying family lines.

There is a sense, expressed in Genesis, that the marital bond creates a family even though there are no blood ties, and so father's wife, father's brother's wife, and brother's wife are said to be prohibited because the "nakedness" (the conventional translation of Hebrew עֶרְוָה) of the woman is tantamount to the nakedness of her husband. So too, since one's wife is also bonded to him, her bloodlines (שְׁאֵר) are parallel to his own and thereby prohibited. Sex within the family would blur family lines and relations and cause a collapse of family relations, and sex with daughter-in-law is explicitly called תֶּבֶל "mixing," in Lev. 20:12.[15]

Sexuality as Danger to Boundaries

The power of sex to cross over the lines between households or blur distinctions between units of a family is an example of sex's power to dissolve categories. This is problematic on a national scale. This issue is clearly highlighted in Genesis 34, a chapter often called the "rape of Dinah," even though it is probably not about a forcible rape, and really is not a story about Dinah at all. Dinah had "gone out to see the daughters of the land."[16] Shechem saw her and lay with her, thus treating her improperly. In this way, he treated her as a whore (v 31), a woman whose consent is sufficient because her sexuality is not part of a family structure. Even though Dinah may have consented to the act, the fact that he had not spoken to her parents in advance constituted an impropriety. The integrity of the family has been threatened, and Dinah's own wishes are incidental. Shechem, who loved her, asked his father Hamor to acquire her for him as his wife. But there are implications to this, made explicit by Hamor, who not only tendered the offer, but extended it, saying to Jacob, "Intermarry with us; give your daughters to us and take our daughters for yourselves; you will dwell among us, and the land will be open before you" (34:9–10); he further says to his own fellow townsmen, "the men agree with us to dwell among us and be as one kindred," even intermingling "their cattle, substance and all their beasts." This intermixing was the great threat to Jacob's family. Even though the generation of Jacob's sons was the first to intermarry with the local inhabitants, they had to do so under controlled conditions in which they could remain a distinct unit. The free exercise of erotic love by Shechem threatened that type of control. There is, of course, also a concern that intermarriage with non-Israelite women would make it possible for them to influence their husbands to worship other gods (Deut 7:1–5), as reportedly happened to King Solomon. Ultimately, after the return from Babylon, when the community of Israel was small and in danger of being overwhelmed by the other people in the land, these dual concerns resulted in a ban on foreign wives during the time of Ezra.

The desire to maintain categories is also a cosmic issue. The Primeval History of Genesis, which underscores the basic features of human existence, is concerned to divide humanity from the divine realm, on the one hand, and the animal realm on the other. As humans become cultured creatures, they become more god-like, not resembling the great monotheist conception of God, but certainly like the divine beings to whom God speaks in Genesis 1–11, the בְּנֵי אֱלֹהִים. To preserve the difference between humans and divine, God takes steps to insure the ultimate mortality of humans. This difference is threatened when the בְּנֵי אֱלֹהִים find human women fair (they were, after all, created in the physical likeness of the divine beings) and begin to mate with them. To further reinforce the difference, God limited the human lifespan (Gen 6:1–4).

As a practical matter, one did not have to be overly concerned with human-divine matings. No divine beings were observed in the post-flood era seducing human women; presumably women were not successfully attributing unexpected babies to angelic intervention; and there is no record in the Bible of divine females coming to seduce the men of Israel, even in their sleep.

But the animal-human boundary was more problematic. The primeval history acknowledges a kinship between humans and animals: Genesis 1 understands God to have created the land animals on the same day as humans, and Genesis 2 records that the animals were first created as companions to Adam. After the flood, action was taken to establish a clear and hierarchical boundary between the human and animal world: humans could kill animals for food (sparing the blood), whereas no animal could kill a human without forfeiting its own life. In reality, this uncrossable boundary of human existence could be easily crossed by mating with animals. Such mating could threaten the very existence of humanity, for the blurring of borders would be a return to chaos.[17] Every legal collection strongly forbids bestiality (Exod 22:28; Lev 18:23; 20:15–16; Deut 17:21); Lev 18:23 explains that bestiality is תֶּבֶל "(improper) mixing."

The maintaining of categories is particularly important in the priestly writings, for one of the essential priestly functions was the maintenance of the categories of existence (pure and impure, holy and profane, permissible and impermissible foods, family lines, sacred time, sacred space). But preoccupation with neatness is not limited to Leviticus; Deuteronomy also manifests this concern, prohibiting even the wearing of linsey-woolsey cloth, which combines wool from animals and linen from plants (Deut 22:9–11, cf. Lev 19:19).

Deviations from these neat categories are dangerous, and Leviticus proscribes male homosexuality under penalty of death (Lev 20:13, cf. 18:22). This extreme aversion to homosexuality is not inherited from other Near Eastern laws,[18] and must make sense in the light of biblical thought. It does not really disturb family lines, but it does blur the distinction between male and female, and this cannot be tolerated in the biblical system. Anything that smacks of homosexual blurring is similarly prohibited, such as cross-dressing (Deut 22:5).[19]

It has long been noted that lesbianism is not mentioned. This is not because these Levitical laws concern only male behavior: bestiality is explicitly specified to include both male and female interaction with beasts. But lesbianism was probably considered a trivial matter: it involved only women, with no risk of pregnancy; and, most important, it did not result in true physical "union" (by the male entering the female).

Public Interest in Control of Sex

Issues such as adultery, incest, homosexuality, and bestiality are not simply the private concerns of families. Like murder, they are treated as a national issue for sexual abominations are thought to pollute the land. The very survival of Israel was at stake. Leviticus 18 relates that the inhabitants of the land before Israel indulged in the incestuous relations listed there, in bestiality and homosexuality and molech-worship, and that as a result the land became defiled and vomited out its inhabitants. Israel is warned against doing these same abominations: "Let not the land spew you out for defiling it, as it spewed out the nation that came before you" (Lev 18:28). Israel's right of occupation is contingent upon its care not to pollute the land with murder, illicit sex, and idolatry. The people must not only refrain from murder, they must not pollute the land by letting murderers go free or allowing accidental murderers to leave the city of refuge (Num 3.5:31–34) or by leaving the corpses of the executed unburied (Deut 21:22–23). So too, they must not only refrain from such illicit sex as adultery and incest, but must be careful to observe even such technical regulations as lot allowing a man to remarry his divorced and since remarried wife (Deut 24:1–3; Jer 3:1–4).

The danger to the nation that ensues from murder and adultery explains the mandatory death sentence; it also clarifies two very odd biblical rituals. In the ceremony of the decapitated heifer, when a corpse is found but no one can identify the murderer, the elders of the city nearest the corpse go to a wadi and decapitate a heifer, declaring their lack of culpability and seeking to avert the blood-pollution of the land (Deut 21:1–9, see also Patai and Zevit). The second ritual is the trial of the suspected adulteress (Num. 5:11–21; Frymer-Kensky 1984), which provides that whenever a husband suspects his wife he is to bring her to the temple, where she is to drink a potion made from holy water, dust from the floor of the sanctuary, and the dissolved curse words while answering "amen" to a priestly adjuration that should she be guilty the water will enter into her and cause her "belly to swell and her thigh to drop" (probably a prolapsed uterus). After this oath she returns to her husband. This ritual allowed a husband to resume marital relations after he suspected adultery. Otherwise, intercourse with a wife who had slept with another man could be expected to pollute the land in the same way as remarriage to a divorced wife who had been married in the interim.

Improper sexual activity had even greater danger than the threat to Israel's right to the land (which was certainly a serious consideration). The blurring of the categories of human existence through sexual activity was a danger to creation, for in biblical cosmology the universe is seen rather like a house of cards; if the lines are not kept neat, the whole edifice will collapse, "the foundations of the earth totter." Wrongful sexual activity can bring disaster to the world.

Conclusion

This is the great problematic of sex. The ideal of the bonded, monogamous nuclear family conveys a positive place for sexuality within the social order. But at the same time, the same sexual attraction which serves to reinforce society if it is controlled and confined within the marital system can destroy social order if allowed free rein. Sexuality itself is good, but the free exercise of sexuality is a prime example of wrongful activity. The exercise of free sexuality (particularly by the woman, who owes sexual exclusivity to the man) is the prime example of a lack of fidelity and a failure of allegiance. In time, all wrongful behavior was seen through the metaphor of sexual activity, with the result that in the prophets, particularly Hosea, Jeremiah, and Ezekiel, there is so much sexual imagery that it is hard to sort out what might be a literal depiction of too much sexual license from a metaphorical depiction of allegiance to foreign powers and other gods.

There is no coherent biblical treatment of sexuality. On the surface, sexuality is treated as a question of social control: who with whom, and when. There is only one explicit statement that sexuality is a cosmic force: "For love is fierce as death, passion is mighty as Sheol, its darts are darts of fire, a blazing flame; vast floods cannot quench love, nor rivers drown it" (Song of Songs 8:6–7). The stories of Pharaoh and Sarah, David and Bathsheba, and Amnon and Tamar show a sense that erotic attraction can cause men to abuse their superior position and strength.[20]

But all of this is inchoate and essentially inarticulate. There is no vocabulary in the Bible in which to discuss such matters, no divine image or symbolic system by which to mediate it. God does not model sex, is not the patron of sexual behavior, and is not even recorded as the guarantor of potency; and there is no other divine figure who can serve to control or mediate sex. Our only indication that the Bible considers sex as a volatile, creative, and potentially chaotic force is from the laws themselves. These laws of control reveal a sense that sexuality is not really matter-of-fact, that it is a two-edged sword: a force for bonding and a threat to the maintenance of boundaries. They cut through the silence on this topic, which we consider so important, but about which there is little explicit mention in the Bible. Through the laws we can find an inkling of biblical Israel's appreciation and anxiety about the topic of such vital concern.

The laws also reveal a great danger: when a society has such legitimate concerns about an important aspect of life, it needs a way to discuss and channel anxieties productively. This the Bible does not provide. We can see the concerns about sex expressed in the laws, but we cannot see how they were mediated, detoxified, expressed, and understood. The result is a core emptiness in the Bible's discussion of sex. This vacuum was possibly filled by folk traditions not recorded in the Bible. Ultimately, in Hellenistic times, it was displaced by the complex of anti-woman, anti-carnal ideas that had such a large impact on the development of Western religion and civilization.

NOTES

1. For previous studies see Cosby, Dubarle, Larue, and Perry. This essay is based on my book, *In the Wake of the Goddesses* (The Free Press: Macmillan, 1991).

2. The point of this command is to separate the sexual from the sacred experience. This purpose is often obscured by the unfortunate male-centered wording of the passage. God is reported as having commanded that the people wash and sanctify themselves and wash their clothes, making preparations for the third day (Exod 19:10–11). When Moses relayed this to the people, he added his own command, "do not approach your wives" (Exod 19:15). By this addition Moses explains how the people are to prepare for the third day, but he adds his own perspective, suddenly erasing half the people, addressing only the men. It is interesting that the Bible records this as Moses's invention rather than God's; it sheds new light on the Deuteronomic injunction to the people not to add to the laws.

3. On the basis of the interpretation of the term קְדֵשָׁה, "holy one," as a cult prostitute, scholars have long argued the existence of sacred prostitution in Israel, which the Bible was trying to stamp out. More recent work has indicated that there is absolutely no evidence that קְדֵשָׁה was a prostitute, nor that any sexual rites ever existed in ancient Israel. In any event, the wages not to be vowed to the temple are those of a זוֹנָה which everyone agrees is an ordinary prostitute-for-hire, not attached to the temple.

4. For a detailed discussion of these issues, see Frymer-Kensky (1983), Douglas. My analysis is somewhat different from that of Mary Douglas's classic study in that she does not distinguish between the "impurity" beliefs, which deal with a contagious state which is neither morally

deserved nor dangerous to the individual and Israel's separate set of dangerous pollutions, a non-contagious state caused by misdeeds which bring the perpetrator into the danger of divine sanction.

5. Menstrual taboos are also to some extent sexual taboos. In Israel, a woman was impure for seven days after the beginning of her menses. During this period, her impurity (as all impurity) was contagious, and could be contracted by anyone who touched her, or even sat in her seat. Intercourse with a menstruating woman was considered absolutely forbidden, and was sanctioned by the כרת penalty, which means the belief that one's lineage would be extirpated. The reminder in menstruation of a sexual dimension of existence would not by itself account for the seven-day duration of the impurity, however. Another element is at play, the blood and its association with death, for contact with death also results in a week-long impurity. It is noteworthy that only intercourse with a menstruant results both in temporary impurity and in the divine sanction of כרת.

6. That marriage was evaluated positively throughout the ancient Near East, see Lambert.

7. For Proverbs, see Snell. Snell notes the structural parallel to 8:33, in which Dame Wisdom says "he who finds me finds life and gets favor from the Lord."

8. On stoning, see Finkelstein. In addition to the two cases discussed here, stoning is used for the ox that gores a man to death (Exod 21:12–14), one who lures others into idolatry (Deut 13:7–8), the disobedient son (Deut 21:18–21), the practitioner of child sacrifice (Lev 20:3d), a sorcerer or necromancer (Lev 20:27), blasphemer (Lev 24:10–11), violator of the Sabbath (Num 15:32–35), and, by inference, the seditionist (1 Kings 21).

9. In the sexual uses of this root, there are instances where it means rape: in Judges 19–20, where the concubine in Gibeah was raped to death, and in the story of Amnon and Tamar, in which he is said to have overpowered her (2 Sam 13:12–13), and in Lamentations, in which the women of Zion are said to have been raped (Lam 5:11). But forcible rape is not always the issue. Some cases are ambiguous. In Deut 22:28–29, a man has grabbed an unbetrothed girl; he must marry her and not divorce her, because he has illicitly had sex with her. The same scenario is involved in the story of Dinah and Shechem (Genesis 34). There is no indication in the story that Shechem overpowered her. The issue is that she was not free to consent, and he should have approached her father first. Similarly, the man who sleeps with a menstruant (Ezek 22:10) or with his paternal sister (Ezek 22:11) is said to have "raped" her only in the sense of "statutory rape," i.e., that he had no right to have sex with her even if she consented. In Deut 21:10–13, the verb paradoxically seems to imply a failure to offer a sexual relationship. This is the case of a man who takes a captive woman as a wife. She must first spend a month in his house mourning her past; after which the man can have sex with her. If, however, he does not want her, he must emancipate rather than sell her, for he has "violated" her. He has put her in a position in which she expected to become his wife, and then has not carried through. The verb does not always have sexual connotations; in non-sexual contexts it means to treat harshly, exploitatively, and/or abusively. Sarah treated Hagar oppressively (Gen 16:6, 9); Laban warns Jacob not to treat his daughters badly (Gen 31:50). The most common subject is God, who is said to treat Israel badly (Deut 8:2, 3, 16; 2 Kgs 17:20; Isa 64:11; Nah 1:12), David and his seed (1 Kgs 11), the suffering servant (Isa 53:4), and individual sufferers (Pss 88:8, 89:23, 119:71, 75; Job 30:11). The most common victim is Israel, which is treated badly by God, by Egypt (Gen 15:13; Exod 1:11–13), and by enemies (2 Sam 7:10; Isa 60:14; Zeph 3:10; Ps 94:4; Lam 3:33).

10. In the case of actual rape, as when a man grabs the betrothed girl, the offense is capital, but only the man is culpable. Forcible rape is explicitly likened to murder, a realization that rape is a crime of aggression and violence rather than sex, and that the girl is a victim (Deut 22:25–27).

11. Occasionally in these laws, a male is mentioned, which seems to indicate that the law also considers women and their permissible relations, but does not consistently list all of a female ego's choices.

12. It is hard to know whether the omission of mother's brother means that mother's brother and his wife were permitted as being of a different family, or whether they would have been prohibited. A similar question arises with father's brother's children (first cousins) and with brother and sister's daughters. In this case it would seem that since father's brother is prohibited, brother's daughter must also be, even though it is not mentioned.

13. This was not always so in Israel. In Gen 20:16, Sarah and Abraham are described as having the same father by different mothers. A similar situation lies behind Tamar's entreaty to her would-be rapist paternal brother Amnon: "Speak unto the king, for he will not withhold me from thee" (2 Sam 13:13). This is not the only instance in which the patriarchal and Davidic narratives differ from later biblical law. Jacob is married to two sisters, which is not allowed in Leviticus. Jacob's and David's sons vie for inheritance position while, according to Deuteronomy, the first to be born is considered the first-born, whatever the wishes of the father.

14. The omission of daughter in the prohibited relations is another glaring omission. One might argue that since grandchildren are prohibited, children must also be, but one might equally argue that the idea of paterfamilias was still strong enough that the laws could not absolutely prohibit a father's access to his daughter. From the expectation of virginity in unmarried daughters, however, it is clear the father-daughter incest was neither expected nor encouraged.

15. It is also called זִמָּה in Lev 20:14, a term reserved in these laws for incest outside blood kin, applied to mother-in-law, wife's sister, wife's daughter and granddaughter.

16. Probably a snide remark on the order of, "she asked for it"

17. On the importance of categories in Israel, see Douglas, Frymer-Kensky 1983, and Finkelstein.

18. Though the Sumerian laws consider an accusation of catamy as parallel to an accusation that one's wife is fornicating.

19. Having eunuchs is not considered the same kind of blurring. A eunuch, like people with visible physical defects, could not serve in the temple But eunuchs were found in Israel, particularly in the royal court (2 Kgs 20:17–18; Isa 56:3–4; Jer 29:2, 34:19, 38:7, 41:16).

20. John van Seters believes this a particular motif in the Succession History and the Yahwist corpus. He also considers the concubine tales of Abner and Rizpah, and Adonijah and Abishag to be instances of this, but he does not sufficiently consider the political rather than sexual motivations of these acts. See further Blenkinsopp. I cannot agree that the emphasis is on love leading to death, though I agree with Van Seters that in none of these stories is the woman blameworthy.

References

Blenkinsopp, J.J.
1966 "Theme and Motif in the Succession History (2 Sam 11:2f.) and the Yahwist Corpust."
VTSup 15:44–57.

Cosby, Michael R.
1985 *Sex in the Bible*. Prentice Hall: Englewood Cliffs.

Douglas, Mary
1966 *Purity and Danger: Analysis of Concepts of Pollution and Taboo*. New York: Praeger.

Dubarle, A.M.
1967 *Amour et fecondité dans le bible*. Privat, Toulouse.

Finkelstein, J.J.
1981 *The Ox That Gored*. Transactions of the American Philosophical Society 71:26–29.

Frymer-Kensky, Tikva
1983   "Purity, Pollution and Purgation in Biblical Israel." Pp. 399–414 in *The Word of the Lord Shall Go Forth. Essays in Honor of David Noel Freedman*. Ed. Carol Meyers and M. O'Connor. Philadelphia: Free Press.
1984   "The Strange Case of the Suspected Sotah (Numbers v 11–31)." *VT* 34:11–26.

Lambert, W.G.
1963   "Celibacy in the World's Old Proverbs." *BASOR* 169:63–64.

Larue, Gerald
1983   *Sex and the Bible*. Prometheus: Buffalo.

Perry, Frank L.
1982   *Sex and the Bible*. Atlanta: Christian Education Research Institute.

Patai, Rafael
1939   "The ʿEgla ʿAnsfa or the Expiation of the Polluted Land." *JQR* 30:59–69.

Snell, Daniel C.
1987   "Notes on Love and Death in Proverbs." In *Love and Death in the Ancient Near East. Essays in Honor of Marvin H. Pope*. Ed. John Marks and Robert Good. Guilford, CT: Four Quarters Publishing Co.

Van Seters, John
1987   "Love and Death in the Court History of David." Pp. 121–24 in *Love and Death in the Ancient Near East. Essays in Honor of Marvin H. Pope*. Ed. John Marks and Robert Good. Guilford, CT: Four Quarters Publishing Co.

Zevi, Ziony
1976   "The ʿEgla Ritual of Deuteronomy 21:1–9." *JBL* 95:377–90.

Eroticism and Death in the Tale of Jael

SUSAN NIDITCH

Associations between eroticism and death and between sex and violence are old and intimate ones reverberating in the various cultural artifacts of Western and non-Western tradition, reflecting and, in turn, affecting the essential nature of human self-consciousness. Eroticism or the sex act itself may be equated with dying, as in Song of Songs 8:6,[1] or slaughter with sexuality, as in the battle imagery of the ancient Greeks explored brilliantly by Emily Vermeule.[2] Death itself may be imagined as a gay seducer, a male lover, as in the "harlequin" tradition explored psychoanalytically by David C. McClelland;[3] while other equally powerful traditions portray erotically charged and sexually potent goddesses as violent warriors who wade through the bodies of slain soldiers,[4] who wreak vengeance on the enemies of their beloved,[5] or who threaten the love objects themselves even while making offers of immortality and bliss.[6] Attraction and revulsion, longing and fear—images of love and death.

It is beyond the scope of this essay to explore the origins of this association. Freud's speculations on the forces of Eros and Thanatos, the loving, receiving and the aggressive, destructive sides of ourselves, remain relevant,[7] as do Jungian suggestions about competing sides of the unconscious. Erich Neumann, for example, suggests that the archetype of the mother has at a ground level two competing images of the feminine: the devouring, constricting womb who suffocates and kills, arresting development, and the nurturing, fertile, protecting originator and sustainer of life.[8] For Neumann these are the two sides of the unconscious, which is identified with the feminine. The conscious mind for him is to be identified with male symbolism in one Western version of the yin/yang.[9]

Closer to my own field, Delbert Hillers has been influenced by Neumann in his intriguing study of the bow of Aqhat.[10] The Canaanite tale tells of a king's longing for a son to be born to him. The gods finally answer Daniel's prayers, and the divine artisan Kothar gives the beautiful young man a fine bow and arrows as a gift. The bow—a magic, special weapon to be compared with Achilles' shield and the weapons prepared by

305

Kothar for Baal—is coveted by the goddess Anat, who has Aqhat slain when he refuses her offer of immortality for the bow.

Noting that the bow has explicitly sexual resonances elsewhere in ancient Near Eastern literature as a symbol of masculinity,[11] and drawing fine parallels with tales of Adonis, Attis, Gilgamesh, and other handsome manly lads who suffer at the hands of a goddess who holds or desires sexual power over them, Hillers suggests that Anat threatens Aqhat sexually. Aqhat's "bow" is his masculinity.[12] Influenced by Erich Neumann's studies of the Great Mother, Hillers writes that "the mythological theme springs from man's experience of woman as attractive, yet threatening to his sexuality and his life."[13] The end of the Aqhat tale, which exists only in fragmentary form, describes Paghat, Aqhat's sister, acting in the Anat role to Baal, dressing as a male warrior to avenge the death of her brother (CTA 19 iv 206). In another line (208) she appears to cover her armor and assumed maleness with the finery and make-up of an alluring woman presenting the intriguing liminal portrait of a woman dressed as a man dressed as a woman, a symbolization of other related aspects of her duality as seducer and killer, loving sister and merciless assassin. Hillers, again working from Neumann, suggests that Anat and Paghat are two models of womanhood, two archetypal levels of the feminine: the frightful killer-womb earth mother—the terrible aspect of archetypal feminine, a symbolization of the unconscious; and the loyal, loving sister—the anima, who occupies an archetypal level closer to the ego and the conscious mind. As articulated in Neumann's earlier work, the theory suggests that whereas the woman child identifies with her mother and the mother archetype, maturing to integrate the archetypal feminine within her, the male child never can become his mother and risks remaining in a love/fear relationship with all women; he is able to overcome his fear with the help of the solid and more fully positive image of the anima, the sister and/or wife.[14]

It might well be suggested that this theory of human development is based on outmoded notions of male and female psychology and child development. The relationship between the archetypal symbols explored by Neumann and actual human development is problematical. Neumann himself nuances his discussion of the relation of the archetypes to the psychology of real men and women in his later work, *The Great Mother*.[15] Here he more clearly emphasizes that the unconscious, reflected in a dual feminine archetype, is fundamental to the psyches of men and women; consciousness is male in the psyches of both genders. Neumann thus attempts more strongly to "depersonalize" his archetypes. The woman develops her "male" side too as she matures into consciousness. Of course such identifications between the unconscious and the feminine, and consciousness and the masculine, and suggestions that the female anima is not a star but a supporting actress in the drama of human development, make one, as a woman, wince. One senses that Neumann is ultimately concerned with men's development and cannot see women apart from their roles in men's lives, a theme to which we will return as we explore tales of Jael. Hillers himself might be faulted for too strongly dichotomizing the sister image from that of the devouring mother, and the terrible mother from the good mother. In *The Great Mother*, Neumann pays more attention to portrayals that share traits of various aspects of "the feminine," coming closer to describing what Lévi-Strauss would suggest is a mediating portrait, partaking of both sides of a dichotomy. Aqhat's loving sister is, after all, Yatpan's killer-seductress.[16] As Ronald Hendel notes, the tale of Aqhat contains many dynamics or dichotomies: male and female, hunter and hunted, appearance and disguise, sex and death.[17] It is against this interplay of themes that we must also appreciate the figure of Jael in Judges 4, 5 and more specifically the exquisite artistry of Judges 5:27.

Other scholars such as J. Glenn Taylor have drawn comparisons between Jael, assassin of Sisera, and ancient Near Eastern goddesses, in Taylor's case the Canaanite Athtart.[18] Jael, however, is not derivative or modeled after ancient Near Eastern goddesses, but like such figures is heroic and liminal, a warrior and seducer, alluring and dangerous, nurturing and bloodthirsty.

In his study of the prose account of Jael, Robert Alter beautifully traces nuances of mother, lover, and killer.[19] Jael offers to the vulnerable, fleeing Sisera food, choice food, protection, and warmth—a rug under which to hide and sleep. She comes to him secretly (*bl'ṭ*) (Judg. 4:21). The coming verb is often used in sexual entry contexts (see BDB *bw'*, "e"); the *l'ṭ* word evokes mystery, even romance. So Ruth comes to Boaz *blṭ* (Ruth 3:7). Jael comes to Sisera and kills. Alter is strangely anxious to contrast the portrait of Judges 4, rich in images of sex and death, with the poetic account of Judges 5 in which he sees the dominant image to be Jael as strong hammerer.[20] Themes of seductress are not for him found in Judges 5, and yet he does acknowledge sexual nuances of Sisera's position at death, describing the "image of the Canaanite general felled by the hand of a woman, lying shattered between her legs in a hideous parody of soldierly assault on the women of a defeated foe."[21] Jael is "standing over the body of Sisera, whose death throes between her legs—he's kneeling then prostrate—may be perhaps, an ironic glance at the time-honored martial custom of rape."[22]

Like Mordecai Levine some years before him, Alter notices the ironic connection between Sisera's position "between Jael's legs," the legs being a euphemism for sexual organs (so the afterbirth emerges), and his mother's hopes for women booty—called *raḥam raḥămātayim,* whose literal, root meaning is "womb."[23] Levine, somewhat less eloquently than Alter, sees in this "montage" the ironic juxtaposing of the warrior's loyal mother's thoughts and his assassin's actions, a veritable polemic against rape. The montage of mother and assassin contributes further to the counterpoint between beloved and assassin, genuine loyalty and false loyalty, feigned affection and nurturing care. Images of love and battle, of victor and vanquished, vie with one another creating tension, discomfort, and uncertainty. Who is the winner, who is the loser, and where is the reader's sympathy? Powerful emotions clash uncomfortably, creating exquisite uncertainty and tension. These themes and images are as strongly found in Judges 5 as in Judges 4. The same offer of best nourishment is coupled with an "aggressively phallic" assassination. The "driving through of the tent peg" into the ground at 4:21[24] is matched in 5:26 by the image of reaching for peg and hammer and "piercing his temple," *ḥlp* being a motion verb literally meaning "to pass through." The poetry is necessarily more telegraphic than prose, but the short-hand impressionistic imagery presents the same "myth" as in Judges 4. The impression, if anything, is more instantaneous than in the slower unrolling of the prose account. Themes of sex and violence, death and seduction are particularly strong in v. 27.

Alter's translation is by far the best and most sexually evocative of all I have seen, so much stronger than other recent examples.

Alter:

Between her legs he kneeled, fell, lay
between her legs he kneeled and fell
where he kneeled, he fell, destroyed[25]

Lindars:

He sank, he fell, he lay still at her feet;
at her feet he sank, he fell
where he sank, there he fell dead[26]

Lindars desexualizes the passage completely. So too Michael Coogan:

Between her feet he collapsed, he fell, he lay;
between her feet he collapsed, he fell
in the place he collapsed, there he fell in ruins[27]

Boling:

At her feet he slumped. He fell. He sprawled.
At her feet he slumped. He fell
At the place where he slumped, there he fell. Slain.[28]

Soggin:

Between her feet he sank, he fell, he lay;
there where he was struck, fallen, dead.[29]

Judges 5:27 evokes a powerful scene of eroticism and death. Its language is charged with sexuality, sexual submission intertwined, doubling with language of defeat and death, associations found elsewhere in Scripture, but nowhere as exquisitely or compactly.[30] My own translation and exegesis is as follows:

Between her legs he knelt, he fell, he lay
Between her legs he knelt, he fell
Where he knelt, there he fell, despoiled.

bên reglêhā, "Between Her Feet"

Translations "at her feet, between her feet" obscure the visceral sexual quality of the imagery. Like the hand, *yād*, the *raglayim*, "legs" or "feet," are used in Scripture as euphemisms for male or female organs. *Śaʿar hāraglāyim* in Isa. 7:20 refers to pubic hair. Urination is referred to as "pouring out his *raglāyw* (Judg. 3:24; 1 Sam. 24:3). As noted above, in a birthing context, the afterbirth comes out from between her "legs" (Deut. 28:57). The phrase "between her legs" can be erotic enough even without specific reference to private parts as in Ezekial 16:25, one of the classic passages in which the unfaithful Israel is described as a harlot: "and you parted your legs wide."

kāraʿ nāpal, "He Knelt, He Fell"

The kneeling word has connotations of defeat and death of one's enemies in Psalms 20:9 where it is paired with *nāpal* as in Judges 5:27.

They will kneel and fall
But we will rise and be restored.

It also is used in a visceral sexual context at Job 31:10 paired with another sexual image, which is not always recognized as such.

My wife will "grind" for another
Upon her will kneel others.

Some suggest that the wife's grinding or milling for others is a sign of her humiliation and servitude. Kittel's suggestion of "sensu obsceno" like that of the Rabbis (b.Soṭa 10a) and Marvin Pope[31] is more likely the case as confirmed by Isaiah 47:2.

Take millstones and grind flour
Remove your veil
Strip off (your) skirt
Reveal the thigh
Pass through rivers
Your nakedness will be revealed
Also will your shame be seen.

Babylon, the virgin, becoming the unhappy spoils of war, is to be sexually humiliated and abused. Thus kneeling and grinding create strongly sexual imagery in Job as kneeling between her legs in our Judges passage produces a synonymous image of eroticism and death. The image is further strengthened by the next verb in the chain of Judges 5:27 *nāpal*. Falling, a lowering of self, is the posture of petition and humility. So Haman who falls upon Esther's couch (Esth. 7:8), so the grateful Shunammite who falls at Elisha's feet (2 Kgs. 4:37) in obeisance. The falling word is also a popular one for death in battle or defeat (2 Sam. 1:4; 2 Sam. 1:25; 2 Sam. 2:23; Isa. 21:9).

At Judges 5:27 images of vulnerability, petition, and ignominious defeat in battle intertwine. Jael, the beautiful woman who lures the enemy with a fecund bowl of rich curds and gentle promises of comfort, is the warrior who fells the unsuspecting Sisera with a massive blow to the head. In sexual posture, in the posture of a would-be lover, a vulnerable petitioner, he falls.

šākab, "He Lay"

Images of sexuality, defeat, and death continue in the following verb of the chain *škb*, "to lie." Some references to lying are to legitimate sexual relations as in the conception of Solomon (2 Sam. 12:24) or in Micah 7:5. (You will not be able to trust even the one who lies in your bosom, your beloved.) See also Uriah's noble explanation to David as to why he does not wish to spend the night with his wife while his troops are in an open field on battle alert (2 Sam. 11:11). The vast majority of biblical uses of *škb* in a sexual context refer to illegitimate relations in rape, incest, ritual impurity, adultery, and so forth. It is not clear whether most biblical discussions of sex concentrate on problem situations—hence the negative associations of *škb*—or whether this particular term has special crass nuances. In any event, it appears in the contexts of rape and incest [Gen. 19:32, 34, 35 (Lot and his daughters); Gen. 34:2, 7 (the rape of Dinah); 2 Sam. 13:11, 14 (the rape of Tamar)]; of wife-stealing [Gen. 35:22 (Reuben's taking Bilhah); 2 Sam. 12:11

(the punishment of David that others will lie with his wives)]; of promiscuity [1 Sam. 2:22 (the activities of Samuel's sons)]; of seduction or adultery [Gen. 39:10, 12, 14 (Potiphar's wife)]; and a host of other forbidden sexual relationships [Lev. 20:11, 12, (father's wife and daughter-in-law); Lev. 20:13 (homosexuality); Lev. 15:24 and 20:18 (an unclean woman); Lev. 20:20 (aunt)].[32] Could these crass uses of *škb* color the scene in which Leah buys Jacob's conjugal services from Rachel for the price of some mandrakes (Gen. 30:15, 16)? Jacob is the hired lover, told with whom he will lie.

Like *nāpal*, the *škb* word also has significant associations with death and defeat. A mundane phrase for dying is to lie or sleep with one's ancestors (1 Kgs. 1:21, 2 Kgs. 14:22, etc.). The dead are those who sleep or lie in the grave (Ps. 88:6). Lying/sleeping/resting parallels are found in Job 3:13. See also Job 14:12. Battle death images employing *škb* apply to Meshech and Tubal (Ezek. 32:29) and Egypt (Ezek. 32:21). Via *škb* Judges 5:27 brings together the nuances of improper sexual intimacy, death, and the warrior's defeat.

šādûd, "Despoiled"

Finally we come to the word *šādûd*, "dealt violently with, despoiled, devastated." A common context of *šdd* words is the destruction of cities and of various enemies in war (e.g. Isa. 15:1, 23:1; Jer. 47:4). Jeremiah 4:30, however, provides a fascinating metaphor relevant to Judges 5:27.

> And you are despoiled[33]
> What are you doing in dressing in scarlet
> in decking yourself with golden ornaments
> in widening your eyes with make-up
> In vain you make yourself beautiful
> Your lovers despise you.
> They seek your life.

As in Hosea 2, Ezekiel 16, Jeremiah 2, and Isaiah 57 images of harlotry intertwine with images of the unfaithful people, whose lovers are really her enemies. Israel the people is devastated and destroyed by the allies she trusted; Israel the loose woman, still beautifying herself with flashy clothes, trinkets, and make-up, is sexually despoiled and ruined. The same double meaning attaches to Judges 5:27.

> Between her legs he knelt, he fell, he lay
> Between her legs he knelt, he fell
> Where he knelt, there he fell, despoiled.

The verse itself has the intoning repetitive quality of sacrificial or ritual death. The brief parallel phrases, the staccato verbs, the refrain, *kāraʿ/nāpal*, knelt/fell, build to the singly used passive participle despoiled/utterly destroyed.[34]

Double meanings of violent death and sexuality emerge in every line. He is at her feet in a pose of defeat and humiliation; he kneels between her legs in sexual pose. He falls and lies, a dead warrior assassinated by a warrior better than he; he is a supplicant and a would-be lover. This one verse holds an entire story. The final twist and nuance of the tale awaits the last line, which nevertheless retains the doubleness of meaning. He is despoiled/destroyed. The woman Jael becomes not the object of sexual advances, with the improper nuances of *škb,* and not the complacent responder to requests for mercy, but herself is the aggressor, the despoiler.

Eroticism and death especially in the context of battle is a theme explored by Emily Vermeule.[35] As in the "bow" material discussed by Hillers in which death is likened to emasculation and/or sexual humiliation, so here the defeated soldier is the woman, the one subdued, raped, and made love to.

> *Damazo* or *damnemi* have similar values, working in three related spheres of action: taming an animal, raping a woman, killing a man. In a duel, an isolated world inside the main battle, one soldier must be the female partner and go down, or be the animal knocked down.
>
> Homer's habit of playing on sex and war is not new with him, one imagines, but is common war talk and wartime humor.[36]

Vermeule points to "the ambiguity of slaughter and sex" as it appears in Greek battle painting of Amazons and Greek soldiers and notes that Homer has "a habit, at mocking moments, of treating enemies as lovers, fusing the effects of Eros and Thanatos."[37]

> The *oaristus* of war, the manipulated bodies, the lily-white fallen enemy stripped on the field with the spear lusting to taste him, the marriage with death, those "jeux meurtriers" which have struck some as a curious prelude to Alexandrian bad taste, seem rather very archaic and inevitable in war slang of all cultures.[38]

The Song of Deborah presents just such an epic battle context and, I suggest, the same juxtaposition of slaughter and sex. Here, however, the duelers are not two men, but a male warrior and a woman assassin disguised as a protector and ally, disguised as a "mere" woman. A man is not rendered womanish by another man, but is despoiled by a woman. He, in a pose to make love, is felled by her. And again as Neumann, Hillers, Hendel, and others' studies of portrayals of mythic warrior women suggest, such an ambivalent role of woman as potential nurturer become killer is not unique to this characterization of Jael. She participates in a broader archetype fusing in Freud's terms Eros and Thanatos. So Vermeule finds the same constellation of motifs in representations of the female man-eater, raptor sphinx that Alter finds in Jael, "a mother with her young? A lady with her love? A hungry predator."[39]

We conclude thus far then that language in Judges 5:27 is double, evoking simultaneously death and eroticism, that Jael's image in Judges 4 and 5 partakes of the same liminal cross-culturally evidenced archetype, and that the sexual subduing of the defeated male warrior, the play "on sex and slaughter," is typical of epic battle language, linked in the imagination of those who portray and create warrior figures, in the lore of warriors themselves. Does this understanding of the double imagery of the death of Sisera lead to a special view of Jael as a woman? What might it reveal about the author and audiences of the material? Might it contribute to feminist interpretation of Scripture or provide encouragement for feminist appropriators of biblical texts? Is the tale of Jael feminist literature in any sense? Why would this characterization of Jael appeal to an Israelite writer?[40]

M. Levine suggests that the writer is a woman, composing a polemic against rape.[41] It seems more likely that this archetype, like its specification in the Greek sphinx, manifests a man's fear of both death and his own sexuality, his insecurities, a male fantasy of

Eros become Thanatos. The woman not only rejects but slaughters her lover. Sisera comes to Jael as a vulnerable supplicant, not as a victorious rapist. Whatever the deep cultural and psychological roots of the image of the woman "raptor," the tale as told nevertheless has important resonances both for feminist appropriators and all marginals. A woman who is in some sense the permanent marginal in Israelite patriarchal culture becomes a lens through which to appreciate and sympathize with poorly armed Israelite peasant revolters who face well-armed Canaanite soldiers of the establishment. It is of importance that an Israelite author of an early period[42] imagines the "womanization" of the enemy to be accomplished by a woman assassin. The author identifies with her even while employing an archetype dripping with phantoms of male fears and insecurities. She is turned against the enemy, thereby doubly strengthening the self-image and confidence of the writer himself. What the author fears most he turns outward against his enemy. Jael has identification power for the early Israelite audience, for in a sense Israel is Jael; she becomes an archetype or symbol for the marginal's victory over the establishment.[43]

The sexual nuance of Jael's portrait, this aspect of her archetype, is also significant as specified in this Israelite tale, for as feminist scholars tell us sex is politics; sex is a visceral means of asserting power. Hence the origins of the image of the defeated warrior as a seduced or raped woman. Having a woman do the womanizing, the man despoiled just as he is in a position of sexual seducer himself, makes for an especially powerful portrait of the victor.

The figure of Jael provides, moreover, a fascinating challenge to some of the views of "the feminine" and female psychology one finds in authors such as Neumann and McClelland cited above, an alternate model to challenge an outmoded psychoanalytical cosmology. Jael is a symbolization of self-assertion, a force of change, one who breaks free heroically from oppressive and suppressive forces. She is thus not to be identified with Neumann's Jungian unconscious, a conservative force holding back however aggressively change and development—the power of the feminine in his terms—but with consciousness-development, ego, and change, the power of the masculine. She is moreover not the hero's helper but the hero herself.

A scholar and educator such as David McClelland helped to create in the 1950s and 1960s a worldview in suggesting, in his study of harlequin as lover/death, for example, that

> Whether in giving birth to a baby, nursing it, looking after a husband, or participating in the sexual act itself, a woman can be thought of as yielding or giving or surrendering herself in order to gain satisfaction.

Virtually suggesting that the unattached, "liberated" career woman risks schizophrenia, he writes:

> That is, the demon lover is in a sense the projection of her need to yield in order to fulfill herself. So he exerts a powerful attractive force. Yet at the same time he appears dangerous because he represents a sexuality that may be considered wrong or more seriously a surrender of consciousness or the self that may appear to threaten the central core of her being. In normal women the conflict is fairly readily resolved; they fall in love and learn more or less successfully how to fulfill themselves by only seeming to die in order to nurture and to create—less rather than more successfully in twentieth-century America where women too often try to pattern their lives after the male model which is quite different.[44]

One suspects that McClelland's treatment of harlequin symbolism evidences a man's effort to deal with some of his own ambivalences concerning women, his desire to appeal and to control. The woman is perceived as wishing, on some level, to be subdued and despoiled. The Jael tale read by modern women provides an alternate symbolism. One is not suggesting that women become men-slayers in some simple-minded reading, but rather that the tale is rich in images of directed action, self-assertion, and consciousness on the part of the underdog. The archetype expressing on many levels male anxieties can thus become a powerfully charged model for all marginals, in particular women.

NOTES

1. In his study of the Song of Songs, Marvin Pope suggests that love is associated with death in literature and ritual because people need to assert the power of love over death. I would suggest rather that a text such as Song 8:6 more literally asserts that on some level love is death and death love. Pope's analysis of images of love and death, while erudite and bibliographically extensive, reduces, rationalizes, and somehow misses the power of this metaphoric equation (*Song of Songs* [Garden City, New York: Doubleday, 1977], 228–29).

2. Emily Vermeule, *Aspects of Death in Early Greek Art and Poetry,* Sather Classical Lectures, vol. 46 (Berkeley: University of California, 1979), 101–2, 145 ff., 157–58, 163–64, 171–73.

3. David C. McClelland, *The Roots of Consciousness* (Princeton, N.J.: Van Nostrand, 1964), 182–216.

4. E.g. Anat. See the recent treatment of this scene from the tale of Baal and Anat (*CTA* 3.B.13–14) by Robert M. Good, "Metaphorical Gleanings from Ugarit," *JJS* 33 (1982):55–59.

5. E.g. Anat, Paghat. See Michael D. Coogan, *Stories From Ancient Canaan* (Philadelphia: Westminster, 1978), 46–47, 111–12.

6. E.g. Ishtar (*Gilgamesh Epic,* ANET³), 83–85; 505; Circe (*Odyssey*), 10:203 ff.

7. Sigmund Freud, *Civilization and Its Discontents,* ed. and trans. James Strachey (New York: W.W. Norton, 1962).

8. Erich Neumann, *The Great Mother: An Analysis of the Archetype,* trans. Ralph Manheim, Bollingen Series, vol. 47 (Princeton: Princeton University, 1964).

9. Jung himself writes as follows: "Just as every individual derives from masculine and feminine genes, and the sex is determined by the predominance of the corresponding genes, so in the psyche it is only the conscious mind, in a man, that has the masculine sign, while the unconscious is by nature feminine. The reverse is true in the case of a woman." *The Archetypes and the Collective Unconscious,* Bollingen Series, vol. 20 (New York: Pantheon, 1959), 175.

10. Delbert R. Hillers, "The Bow of Aqhat: The Meaning of a Mythological Theme," in *Orient and Occident; Essays Presented to Cyrus H. Gordon on the Occasion of his Sixty-fifth Birthday,* ed. Harry A. Hoffner, ADAT 22 (Neukirchen-Vluyn: Neukirchener, 1973), 71–80.

11. Hillers, "The Bow," 73–74.

12. Hillers, "The Bow," 73–78.

13. Hillers, "The Bow," 78.

14. On the anima-sister see Erich Neumann, *The Origins and History of Consciousness,* trans. R.F. Hull, Bollingen Series, vol. 42 (Princeton: Princeton University, 1954), 201–4.

15. Neumann, *Great Mother,* 148.

16. Neumann, *Great Mother,* 172, 194, 202–3.

17. Ronald Hendel, *The Epic of the Patriarch: The Jacob Cycle and the Narrative Traditions of Canaan and Israel,* HSM 42 (Atlanta: Scholars, 1987), 73.

18. J. Glenn Taylor, "The Song of Deborah and Two Canaanite Goddesses," *JSOT* 23 (1982):99–108.

19. Robert Alter, "From Line to Story in Biblical Verse," *Poetics Today* 4 (1983):615–37, 129–37; Robert Alter, *The Art of Biblical Poetry* (New York: Basic, 1985), 43–49.

20. Like Alter, Mieke Bal draws distinctions between portraits of Jael in Judges 4 and Judges 5. She argues that the prose account is "masculine" and authored by a man where the poetic account is "feminine" and, at least implicitly, authored by a woman, though the quality of the voice and not some specific identification of the author is her interest (Mieke Bal, *Murder and Difference: Gender, Genre, and Scholarship on Sisera's Death* [Bloomington: Indiana University, 1988]). Bal discusses the Jael tale again, presenting major threads of argument found in the book, in "Tricky Thematics," *Semeia* 42 (1988):133–55, 145—46.

21. Alter, "From Line to Story," 633.

22. Alter, "From Line to Story," 635.

23. Mordecai Levine, "The Polemic Against Rape in the Song of Deborah," *Beth Mikra* 25 (1979):83–84 (Hebrew).

24. Alter, "From Line to Story," 635.

25. Alter, "From Line to Story," 630.

26. Barnabas Lindars, "Deborah's Song: Women in the Old Testament," *Bulletin of the John Rylands University Library of Manchester* 65 (1983):158–75, 171.

27. Michael D. Coogan, "A Structural and Literary Analysis of the Song of Deborah," *CBQ* 40 (1978):146–66, 151.

28. Robert G. Boling, *Judges*, AB (Garden City, N.Y.: Doubleday, 1975), 104.

29. Alberto Soggin, *Judges*, OTL (Philadelphia: Westminster, 1981), 83.

30. Like the Rabbinic traditions he cites, Yair Zakovitch sagely recognizes the sexual nuances of language such as "between her legs," "lay," and "kneeled" but tends to overliteralize the scene in his exegesis, "Sisseras Tod," *ZAW* 93 (1981):364–74.

31. Pope, *Song*, 231.

32. In some instances in the Masoretic text, the object of *škb* has been vocalized to suggest a direct object of a transitive verb as in the English slang "to lay her." See Gen. 34:2; Lev. 15:24; 2 Sam. 13:14.

33. The word *šādûd* that I translate "despoiled" is not found in most of the Greek manuscript tradition. In the Greek or Septuagintal tradition, Jer. 4:30 begins "And you, what are you doing." *Šādûd*, a predicate adjective, is moreover in masculine form whereas the subject "you" is feminine. For these reasons, some modern commentators omit *šādûd*, suggesting that the word was not originally found in the Hebrew text of Jer. 4:30 [e.g. John Bright, *Jeremiah*, AB (Garden City, N.Y.: Doubleday), 31; William Holladay, *Jeremiah 1: A Commentary on the Book of the Prophet Jeremiah*, chaps. 1–25, Hermeneia (Philadelphia: Fortress, 1986), 144–45, who provides a most circuitous and speculative explanation for the word's presence in the Masoretic Hebrew text]. On the other hand, J.A. Thompson recently accepts the reading *sādûd*, translating "despoiled" [*The Book of Jeremiah* (Grand Rapids: Eerdmans, 1980), 231] and most older commentators also accept the Masoretic text translating *sādûd* with the wonderfully Victorian phrase "when thou art spoiled" or "spoiled one" thereby fully conveying the sexual nuance of the term. [See John Skinner, *Prophecy and Religion: Studies in the Life of Jeremiah* (Cambridge, England: Cambridge University, 1940), 37; S.R. Driver, *The Book of the Prophet Jeremiah* (New York: Charles Scribner's Sons, 1907), 26; A.W. Streane, *The Book of the Prophet Jeremiah, Together with Lamentations* (Cambridge, England: Cambridge University, 1805), 43]. This text-critical problem raises important and fundamental methodological questions. What constitutes an original text? Is it not equally worthwhile and more reasonable to discuss what constitutes a valid text? The Masoretic version of Jer. 4:30 makes excellent sense and contributes to the imagery of Israel the harlot. What of matters of prosody? Omitting *šādûd* allows one to divide the verse into three segments of equal length: And you, what are you doing/In dressing in scarlet/In decking yourself in

golden ornaments. On the other hand, my arrangement of the text allows for a prosodic structure whereby long and short lines alternate to create a limping, lament meter as the prophet mourns over the fallen people. This pattern continues in v. 31.

For these reasons, I accept the Masoretic reading. The lack of gender agreement may be explained by an author's veering between his female metaphor and male subject. As noted recently by Michael L. Barré, certain "inconsistencies in gender and even number are not uncommon in biblical Hebrew." Barré is particularly interested in references to geographic areas, treated as feminine in biblical Hebrew versus references to the people of that area, treated as masculine ["The Meaning of *lᵓ ᵓšybnw* in Amos 1:3–2:6," *JBL* 105 (1986):611–31, esp. 614 and 616].

34. For others' comments on the style of v. 27 see J. Blenkinsopp, "Ballad Style and Psalm Style in the Song of Deborah: A Discussion," *Bib* 42 (1961):61–76, esp. 74; Alan J. Hauser, "Judges 5: Parataxis in Hebrew Poetry," *JBL* 99 (1980):23–41, esp. 34–38.

35. Vermeule, *Aspects of Death* (cited in n. 2).

36. Vermeule, *Aspects of Death*, 101.

37. Vermeule, *Aspects of Death*, 102, 157.

38. Vermeule, *Aspects of Death*, 157.

39. Vermeule, *Aspects of Death*, 171.

40. For a presentation of material from Tamil folk tradition that makes for fascinating comparison with the biblical narrative explored here, see David D. Shulman, "Battle as Metaphor in Tamil Folk and Classical Traditions," in *Another Harmony,* eds. Stuart H. Blackburn and A.K. Ramanujan (Berkeley: University of California), 105–30. Shulman explores images of eroticism and death in battle in the *Cataka\d{n}\d{t}arāva\d{n}a\d{n} Katai* (see 122–23), noting that the "folk source," as opposed to the classical sources, "prefer(s) to identify violence with the woman, passivity with the male . . ." (120–21). He asks whether the violent portrait of the goddess Sītā "represent(s) a masculine fear of female sexuality" or "*female* fantasies of power . . ." (121).

41. Mordecai Levine, "A Polemic." In an interesting and methodologically fresh essay that probes the possibilities of reconstructing a history of Israelite women, Jo Ann Hackett describes Judges 5 as "a very female piece of literature." ["In the Days of Jael: Reclaiming the History of Women in Ancient Israel," in *Immaculate and Powerful: The Female in Sacred Image and Social Reality,* eds. C.W. Atkinson, C.H. Buchanan, and M.R. Miles, (Boston: Beacon, 1985), 15–38, esp. 32–33. Cf. Mieke Bal cited in n. 20 above.]

42. It is agreed among scholars that Judges 5 is an example of early Hebrew poetry dating to the twelfth or eleventh centuries B.C.E. I am in general agreement with Norman Gottwald's portrayal of this period as a time of revolt by rural "have-nots" against the urban upper classes, the "haves," in a Canaanite version of feudalism. For a full presentation of his view of early Israelite history see *The Tribes of Yahweh: A Sociology of the Religion of Liberated Israel 1250–1050 B.C.* (Maryknoll, N.Y.: Orbis, 1979).

43. Jo Ann Hackett's description of the period of the Judges as a time of "social dysfunction" ("In the Days," 25) and her examination of issues of status, power, and authority are relevant in this context (see "In the Days," 23–33).

44. McClelland, *The Roots of Consciousness,* 192.

Dealing/With/Women
Daughters in the Book of Judges

Mieke Bal

The Role of Critical Theory

The question of the relations between the Bible and critical theory is not one of application. Critical theory can be no more or no less meaningfully "applied" to the Bible than to any other ancient body of texts. But since theories are bodies of language of the same order as the text, I do not think there can be a question of application. At the most, theories can be brought into a dialogue with texts. In this sense, I would like to take the conjunction "and" in the theme of this volume on the Bible and critical theory, as I like to take the Hebrew conjunction "*waw*": at face value. I do not want to take it as a false coordination that conceals some other, "logical" relation, some subordination, on either side.

"And" stands for dialogue, for two equals speaking to each other, listening to each other, in an attempt to learn something from the encounter: to change. The success of the dialogue will be measured in this chapter in terms of relevance and of limits—and of the relevance of limits. The theory I will use, which is my own version of narratology,[1] will be brought to the text as a subtext, one that speaks with, or through, the biblical text, one that opens the text up, asks it questions. I will assess the relevance of this encounter against the theory's capacity to raise problems rather than solve them, to make it more interesting, make it speak more excitingly, than it used to do without the theory. It is to be challenged on its own terms. But the text, in response to that challenge, will challenge the theory, point out its limits, and force it to go beyond itself. As a result, the very dialogue between narrative theory and a body of biblical texts leads to a transgression of disciplinary boundaries. A fruitful encounter between critical theory and the Bible will end, I will argue, in an interdisciplinary venture. The only *critical* literary theory, then, criticizes itself, too. It must be an open, dialogic theory.

Killers and Victims

When I first read the book of Judges as a whole, I was surprised to see that the famous wicked woman, Delilah, had two colleagues in evil. Two other women tricked a male hero into a trap and killed him. In spite of her participation in the "right" cause, Yael, the murderess of Sisera, is generally criticized by commentators. She is blamed for breaking the sacred laws of hospitality and for the cruelty of her method of killing.[2] In fact, we need only to reverse the perspective and take the side of the Philistines to become aware of the close resemblance between the two murder stories. A third murderess is not so much blamed for her deed by commentaries, but fits the schema pretty well: the woman-with-the-millstone who, in 9:53, kills Abimelech. Although her deed is liberating, the victim himself thematizes the gender issue that underlies the event, and that is also elaborated in the prose version of Yael's act in chapter 4. It is shameful to be killed by a woman.

I had a hard time, as a feminist, defending these killers against attacks, and I agree that the impression of excessive violence in relation to gender is undeniably evoked by the book. I worked for quite some time on these female killers in the hope to understand better what issues underlie these stories.[3] It was only after concentrating on female violence that I became aware of another structure of violence in the same book. The impression of violence as a gender issue is at least as much caused by two other cases of violence: the sacrifice of Jephthah's daughter, and the rape, torture, and murder of an innocent "concubine" in Judges 19. At first sight, again, there is a contrast: the daughter of Jephthah, although killed, is a "pure" victim of a sacred murder. She is sacrificed to Yhwh. The "concubine" is, in the common view, a woman of lowly status, a status defined by her sexuality. Certainly not a virgin, she is killed in a way that repeats her degradation. Instead of being purified by fire and being devoted to the deity, she is debased, by men, raped to death. The horror of the two stories, the murder of two innocent women, match pretty well.

It was only after my attention—and my strong emotional response—had been drawn by these two stories, that I discovered a third case of a female victim. Just as the woman-with-the-millstone could only be inserted in the series of female killers after the establishment of the series—in other words, after we saw the similarities between the first two—similarly, this third victim almost escaped attention, and came to the fore once the similarities between the fate of the two other victims had been enhanced. Our third victim is Samson's bride, who was killed for the sake of male violence, too. Both third cases, almost hidden, will turn out to be in some sense the crucial ones, the ones that summarize the two others of the series. The narrative proximity between this victim and Delilah struck me as significant. Married, but not really, a virgin but not really, killed not by but with her father, she precedes the murderess who is not really the actual murderess of her victim, and who is, of the three killers, also the most clearly a lover of her victim—just as the bride is a lover of her indirect killer.

Three female killers, three female victims: a structure seems to emerge,[4] a structure that accounts for the excessively violent impression the book makes, a structure which I will replace for the coherence of history and theology that is usually the guideline for readings of the book as a whole. Indeed, although the difficulty of establishing a chronology of the book is acknowledged,[5] attempts continue to be made. The best analysis of the book that I know of, that of D.W. Gooding,[6] starts with a convincing refutation of the assumption that a dumb editor rather than a clever one composed the book; his own interpretation is as yet based on the assumption of the domination of the isotopies of war and theology. It will be my contention in this essay that in spite of the historical, political, and theological mainline of the book as a composition, there is an underlying interest that may have had at least some influence on the selection of the available material. I read the book for the counter-coherence of violence and gender. Given the restrictions of time and the work previously done, I will focus here on the victims, and try to return to the killers briefly at the end.[7]

Narrative theory will help raise the questions, enhance the problems. I enter the analysis with the key question of narrative theory: the question of the subject. The subject is involved in narrative at three levels: the subject of speech, the subject of vision, the subject of action. In other words, who speaks? who sees (I call it, technically, who focalizes)? who acts? I use these questions to overcome a naively realistic reading, in their capacity to account for narrative form. I also use them to overcome a fallaciously repetitive reading that would remain within the ideology of the text rather than criticize it. In other words, I will use them to try to overcome the paralyzing opposition, so common in biblical scholarship, between historical and literary approaches. The questions help to account not only for what happens in the stories but also for the responsibility for both events and their narrative rendering.

The Figuration of the Subject

The first surprise that the question of the subject has for us is the problem of anonymity. The three victims, as if by coincidence, have no names. No names; no narrative power. They are subjected to the power of, mostly named, men. The first act that awaits us, then, is to provide the victims with a name. A name that makes them into subjects, that makes them speakable. Naming the victims is an act of insubordination to the text. Is it a distortion? In fact, the problem of naming is a useful way to become aware of the need of readerly activity. But my goal is not to embellish the text; only to account for its effect. Therefore the names to be given have to be acceptable within the text, while also emancipating the reader—and the characters—from it. Jephthah's daughter is defined by her daughterhood. Her fate is a metonymic extension of her father. She will be given the name of *Bath*, which means "daughter" (*bat*). The "concubine" of chapter 19 is, as we shall see shortly, not a concubine in the now common sense. In order to grasp her status, we have to realize how her fate is connected to the house. Coming from Bethlehem, the house of bread, she is moved from house to house, thrown out of the house, and signified, in her utter victimhood, when she drags herself to the threshold of the very house she was kicked out of. What else can her name be but *Beth*, which alludes to "house" (*bayit*)? For Samson's bride, a character we will only meet briefly, the obvious name is *Kallah*. The word means "bride," but I wish it to be a pun on *kalah*, which means "consumption," "complete destruction." And indeed, the destruction of her is complete, both physical and symbolical. She is consumed by fire, and her remembrance is overshadowed by that of Delilah. The one who destroyed Samson's heroic strength is remembered, not the one who is its victim. Naming these women, then, is a first gesture to counter their oblivion. It is a first stage of their reinstatement into the history of gender relations as we try to reconstruct them. To rewrite these victims back into history is a way to correct the excessive and exclusive place the murderesses have been assigned in it.

It will not be possible to analyze the stories comprehensively. I will focus on an appropriate phenomenon which I call "narrative condensation," a term I will explain below. I will try to convince the reader of the following points. First, Bath and Beth are not only victims. They are also subjects, more fully than one would suspect, although within the limits of the patriarchal power that kills them. Second, their reputation is false and in itself evidence of a modern patriarchal ideology that repeats the repression the text stimulates. Third, the issues at stake in the stories concern primarily the power of the father. This has been repressed by the enhancement of the themes of obedience (Bath) and hospitality (Beth). These interpretations are quite common, and are both evidence of the "repetition-compulsion" that is in my view the basic strategy of ideological readings that my analysis argues against. These three points will be argued through the tiny textual details that exemplify the figure of condensation that is so appropriately iconic where the condensation, the being-one, of father and daughter is at stake.

Condensation is a figure of style and of thought that expresses two or more completely different ideas in a single expression. It is, of course, in the first place a figure in Freudian rhetoric. Freud claimed that condensation is used as a form of censorship. Those ideas that the subject cannot afford to acknowledge are repressed from consciousness and return in a defigured form. Condensation is one such form, displacement is another. *Narrative* condensation is the same figure, two or more ideas expressed in one expression, but then, narratively: in one narrative act. *The* narrative condensation is the one that conflates two different, often incompatible subject-positions. The following will illustrate this, thus demonstrating the critical power of narratology.[8]

Bath, Beth, and Virginity

How are Bath and Beth introduced? Bath is first represented, not only without a name, but conditionally, unknown, characterized only by the *firstness* that is so crucial to our idea of virginity: the first one to meet the hero after victory. She is the object of a vow. As a speech-act, the vow is a combination of trade and promise.[9] The promise concerns the future, the trade concerns a deal. The deal, here, exchanges Bath's life against a military victory which Jephthah feels unable to accomplish himself. He needs support from Yhwh. Yhwh, then, is the real victor. According to the tradition that we see at work, for example in Judges I, the victor is entitled to the chief's daughter as a bride. Just as Othniel, there, deserves Achsah, chief Caleb's daughter, Yhwh deserves Bath. The wording of the vow is quite similar in both cases and so is the situation: a difficult military situation that calls for the testing of the hero, the *gibbor*. Robert Alter would call it a type-scene.[10] The vow ends with a difference: Bath will not be given as a bride but as a burnt offering, not to a husband but to another, higher father (11:30–31).

Similarly, Beth is given away conditionally. The reversal of the situation only stresses the resemblance. The hero is in danger, but no military victory, only escape from danger is at stake. The same insecurity, however, highlights the same structure, shows the scene as a variant, by antithesis, of the type-scene whose structure is set in Judges 1. This woman is not given as a bride either, but as an object of sexual abuse. She is not given to the real victor, but to the strongest party. Strangely, the "concubine" is offered as a gift *together* with a virgin: "behold, my daughter, a virgin, and his concubine." Again, a woman is given away to insure safety, this time not of the army but of an individual man. And again, the status of that woman (virgin? concubine?) seems to be important. They are given as women, and for their specific womanhood.

What is virginity? In a well known, but not yet enough criticized essay, Freud in 1918 tried to explain the taboo of virginity. Why is it that "primitive people" shun defloration, while "civilized men" cherish it? In spite of Freud's attempt to establish a difference between the "savage" and his own kind, a difference that will then allow the similarity not to hurt too much, in both cases, and that is the important point, virginity, or rather, defloration, is an issue. Why, and how? Let us first turn to the status of these women, a "virgin" and a "concubine." The word usually translated as "virgin" (*betulah*) is used by Bath herself, not by Jephthah or by the narrator. The question "who speaks?" can be rephrased as "who speaks virginity?" and may be a crucial question. The narrator ends his presentation of the story with the words, "and she had known no man." Bath says something else. Her sentence is usually translated as "let me bewail my virginity" and is then interpreted as "bewail my childlessness, my futility." I am not so sure that this is the issue for Bath; this sounds like a male concern. In order to focus this problem clearly, we have to make a brief excursion into language problems. This is, then, the first limit narratology forces us to transgress.

In the Land of Wandering Rocks

The verb translated as "to bewail" has not, in Hebrew, a direct object. Hence we may as well give it an absolute meaning: to lament. The noun *betulah* is preceded by the same preposition as "mountains" in the same sentence: *ʿal*. The two segments *ʿal* the mountains, *ʿal* my *betulah*, although separated, may be considered as a broken parallelism.[11] This preposition is among the most variable in Hebrew. In one dictionary, one which is sometimes looked down upon but for which I shall argue later, it has at least twenty-eight meanings, one of which is to be a synonym of *ʾel*, for which the dictionary gives twelve meanings. It is clearly one of those words that shift with their context. With a spatial referent, it can mean upon, unto. The combination with the verb "let me go down upon" is odd. It seems quite plausible, given this uncertainty, and in accordance with one of its frequent uses to give it a meaning of confrontation and directionality: "towards" "in order to be confronted with." Towards the mountains, away from the father. If we wanted that feature of directionality to the other noun, as the Septuagint suggests we may,[12] interpreting it as temporal, it could mean, there, "towards my *betulah*," "until I will be confronted with it."

The noun *betulah* itself is subject to scrutiny for four reasons. It is often accompanied by the phrase: "she/who had not known man." In the episode of the bride-capture, at the end of the book, the description is even more explicit: "four hundred young girls, *betulah*, who had not known man by lying with him" (21:12). This is usually translated as "young virgins": the two nouns, *naʿarah* (young, unmarried girls) and *betulah* are then considered synonyms. If that were the case, the description would be four times repetitive; which seems excessive, even for the Hebrew Bible. The juxtaposition of these expressions makes me suspect they each add a feature to the described brides. A second reason to sense a different meaning in *betulah* is the quoted verse "my daughter, *betulah*, and his 'concubine.'" If being a virgin is a recommendation, then being a concubine is not; both women are, however, offered on an equal footing, as a gift valuable enough to compensate for the man. The third reason is that the narrator uses the description while Bath herself uses the noun. The fourth reason is now sufficiently strengthened: the absence of the accusative form and the use of the preposition-shifter, that takes the ideas of confrontation and directionality from its previous use.

These arguments all point at the same idea: that *betulah* refers, for Bath, to a state, a life-phase, that does not end, but towards which one goes, which one confronts. This points to a view, a vision, different from the one expressed by the narrator. If conceived this way, Bath's *direction* is what she is concerned with. "Leave me alone": she turns away from the father, and goes, in the direction of the mountains, the wilderness, and *betulah*, a phase. Her expression, then, is more independent from the narrator's than we are accustomed to assume possible, used as we are to a realistic, psychological narrative discourse. I contend that the biblical discourse, with its heterogenous background and composition, could very well accommodate what I like to call *wandering rocks*. Expressions, words, fragments of discourse that circulated within the culture even if they were, perhaps, no longer understood, resemble those glacial tilts that travelled with the ice and landed in an alien place where they were put to a use foreign to their origin. Yet, they remained undestructible. Just so, Bath's discourse, expressing a female conception of *betulah*, of the life-phase of ripeness, so thoroughly recuperated by the trade between men, yet still there, as a wandering rock, indestructible but used in an alien way.

It is well-known practice among many people, and our culture is no exception, to mark the transitions in the life of the individual by a ritual, a rite of passage.[13] Rites of coming-of-age, *bar-mitzvah*, first communion, are replaced, in secular culture, by graduation ceremonies. Among mothers and daughters, the first menstruation is often secretly celebrated. In many societies the rites of passage are very elaborate, and, as Victor Turner has pointed out in his structuralist interpretation of the rites,[14] the transition, a temporal moment, is often symbolized in a spatial form, by the wilderness where the initiate is kept in separation from the world of childhood, often for several months. In Bath's request, the latter aspect is present, as is the former.

Seen in the light of rites of passage, Bath's request receives an altogether different meaning. Coming out of the house of her father to celebrate the victor, her situation is similar to Achsah's. She can be expected to be given in marriage to the victor. This is how she obstinately, and justly, interprets her fate—as a wandering rock, out of place. She knows, then, that she has reached the age of transition. Taking leave from the father, she prepares for the next phase of her life, the *nubile* state, by organizing the rite of passage that belongs to it. The problem of her "not having known man," of her being due to the victor but whose identity is unclear, since the father failed as a *gibbor* and invoked divine rather than human help, is not her concern. The same event, then, receives a completely different, alien if not opposed meaning, according to the subject whose view is expressed. This is a first case of narrative condensation. The wandering rock of Bath's language, her almost formulaic speech, is not acknowledged as different any more, and readers take only the male view of virginity into account.

The concept of *betulah* comes to stand in a series of which *na'arah* is the preceding and *'almah* the following term: unmarried, marriageable, recently married. It will be shown to be a dangerous series: it indicates the phases of life wherein the ripeness of women becomes the bone of contention between men who struggle for her possession. I will turn to the concept of "concubine" shortly, but already we know that the "concubine" of chapter 19, Beth, is a recently married woman. The gift offered by the host in that story consists, then, of two women, both young, but of age: *sexually usable*.

Now we can see what comprises the narrative condensation. Bath speaks one language, the narrator another. Bath's is the language of the female subject who prepares for the future, for the next phase of her life. The narrator is concerned with virginity in the now common sense, which is not oriented towards the future but to the past, not a beginning but an end, not positive but negative. What can the importance be of this negative, male view of the woman in transition?

The Logic of Possession

In the already mentioned essay on the taboo of virginity, Freud, who is not only the justly praised discoverer of the importance of unconscious motivations in cultural behavior, but also the spokesman of contemporary male ideology, expresses the long-held view of virginity in the following words: "The demand that a girl shall not bring to her marriage with a particular man any memory of sexual relations with another is, indeed, nothing other than the logical continuation of the right to exclusive possession of a woman, which forms the essence of monogamy, the extension of this monopoly over the past."[15] The "logic" Freud expresses here, in the relation he establishes between sex and memory, is quite revealing. It is also "logically" problematic, and in that sense it comes close to a Freudian slip. The Hebrew language expresses the same idea in what we have always considered to be a euphemism: "to have known no man." I do not think it is a euphemism, an expression that softens the crudeness of its content. I think, to the contrary, that it is a specification that sharpens the content. What the expression conveys is, in the light of Freud's "logic," that from sexuality conceived as "sexual possession" there is no escape. The motivation for the concern with virginity is not so much, in Freud's view, the often-held idea that sexuality is defiling, hence that sex makes the woman less valuable because it pollutes her.

In a short paper, G.J. Wenham[16] argues that Mary Douglas's interpretation of defilement[17] is too narrowly symbolic. The loss of semen is a loss of life-liquid, and therefore takes a (less serious) place in the series of other losses of life-liquid, like blood in childbirth and menstruation. In this conception the defiling effect of sex pollutes the man in the first place. The woman, then, is defiled by contagion, I would say, metonymically. What makes the experience of sex devalue the woman is, rather than the bodily change, literally memory, that is knowledge, but knowledge of the past. This knowledge turns the woman into an *other*, an autonomous subject. It is that subjectivity that comes with sexual experience that apparently threatens the exclusivity of the possession. What matters *is* knowledge, what threatens purity is the contamination of the mind, what the male view of virginity is concerned with is basically the past, not the future. This is expressed in Hebrew in other words than the description of virginity. The Hebrew word for male is, significantly, *zakar*. Whether or not this is a homonym of different origin, the word does mean "to remember," and given the Hebrew use of the singular masculine as the root, "he will remember." To remember is a male prerogative, denied the women.

The male role in procreation is, indeed, something that has to be remembered, as opposed to the female role that is visible. Remembering is an urgent business, since paternity is never certain, while maternity is always sure. Expressions for sexuality and for maleness both enhance the importance of paternity. But, and this is the interesting detail that disturbs, this is a shift, a shift from husband to father. As Freud points out, the purpose of virginity is to make a new start, to bring no memory of any other man, including, we might now suggest, the father. This becomes particularly pointed since the recent discovery of widespread father-daughter rape as a modern patriarchal practice. It also helps us understand the reluctance of fathers to let their daughters go to another man—to give her away, as the jargon of marriage ceremonies has it. There is a condensation here; not a narrative one, although with narrative consequences, but a linguistic one, a condensation that conflates the position of father and husband, of possession in the present and possession in the past or, in yet another tune, of temporary possession and possession forever. Bath's sacrifice is a solution, be it a fatal one, to this dilemma: the father gives her away, but to a higher father, not to a man. And if Bath has been remembered as the virgin-daughter, it is because her view of what she is, her subjectivity, has been repressed in the subsequent readings of her story. Of the double view of *betulah,* the female view of her own life-phase has been repressed and only the negative concern with her possession has been preserved.

Beth's Marriage

The state of Beth is equally interesting. It is visible, even to an outsider, that her presentation is massively misunderstood. The sentence that introduces her is usually translated as, "a Levite from Ephraim took to him a concubine from Beth-lehem." Literally, however, it says, "he took to him a woman, a concubine from Bethlehem." As many scholars have pointed out, the order of the words "woman" and "concubine" seems odd. More "logical" would be, "he took to him a concubine, a woman from Beth-lehem," but we have learned to suspect logic. Another solution would be, "he took as his wife a concubine from Beth-lehem," but there is no indication that this is meant. In my view, these problems are caused by the anachronistic assumption that "concubine" means concubine. Again, it is the word that expresses the woman's status that is the trouble-maker. Note that two local indications, judged irrelevant by some scholars, are the figuration of an opposition that is also at play in the previous and the following chapters. The opposition can be interpreted right now through the meaning of the names: *Ephraim* is derived from a word meaning "pasture land" (Aramaic: ʾaphra) while *Beth-lehem* means "house-of-bread." I will come back to those meanings that will provide the background for the problematic statement about the woman.

The word translated as "concubine" is the central problem in this presentation of the woman. The "logic" of translation that chooses, first, the latinate word "concubine" and gives it the meaning that it literally has in Latin, bedmate, is anachronistic. It becomes circularly so when it is, next, assumed to refer to a lowly status. There is very little evidence for this connection. Phyllis Trible is among those who uncritically accept this meaning.[18] She makes great case of the lowly status of the woman on the basis of extremely thin evidence. This is an example of the way scholars sometimes tend to repeat each other, and of the dangerous consequences of this uncritical attitude. Trible, who works for a feminist hermeneutics, does the feminist cause a small favor by this acceptance.

Let us try to approach the word from the point of view of narratology, and keep in mind that this woman is the subject of an action described in verse 2. The opposition between the husband's pasture land and the house-of-bread of the father is the setting of the first part of the story. If we are faithful to the order of the words, and keep this opposition in mind, we must assume that the first description of Beth means something like, "he took to himself a wife, a (specification) from Beth-lehem." The specification can then be assumed to specify *what sort of wife* he took, and Beth-lehem apparently is relevant information there. In other words, he took a wife according to the tradition that was usual in Beth-lehem.

The dictionary gives several meanings of this non-Semitic noun, and suggests a connection with the Arabic word for "queen." Koehler and Baumgartner mention as a first, ancient meaning, "wife who, after marriage, remains with her father."[19] This form of marriage is known from nomadic societies. The husband, who had no stable place to live, wandered around with his flocks, and visited his wife at irregular intervals. As early as 1921 and 1931, Morgenstern examined quite a few cases of the type of marriage he calls *beena* marriage. Although the noun *pilegesh* seems to refer to a secondary wife (Gen. 22:24; 25:6), most of the occurrences make much more sense as cases of this type of marriage. I will contend in this article that the competition between this and the more usual type of marriage is the major anthropological issue in the book of Judges. This brings us, from narratology via philology, to anthropology as a discipline useful and necessary to understand these disturbing stories.

The term used by Morgenstern, *beena* marriage or *matriarchat,* suggests that the background of *pilegesh* is a matriarchal society. This is an interesting case of repression in anthropological discourse. Indeed, in many anthropological studies on kinship structure, matrilocal marriage is opposed to virilocal marriage, and matrilocal is easily confused with matriarchy. This is a false conflation. In other studies the marriage form at stake is called duo-local. In both cases, however, the husband is, again, conflated with the father. The woman is attributed much more power than she probably had, and many features of the stories remain unexplained. Morgenstern does not deal with Judges 19, which I consider the founding story for the transition that is at issue. In order for some clarity to emerge, we can call this marriage form *patrilocal* marriage, and oppose it, not to matrilocal but to virilocal marriage.

If we take it that *pilegesh,* in this probably very ancient story, refers to this type of wife, many elements found problematic by scholars suddenly fall into place. First, the introduction of Beth in verse 1: he took to him a wife, a patrilocal wife from Beth-lehem. The specification becomes meaningful: as a man from a pasture land, without stable dwelling, he took a wife firmly established in the house of her father. The rest of the story becomes, not only coherent, but extremely meaningful as an account of institutional transition.

The translation of verse 2 is even more problematic. Two translations compete: "she played the harlot against him"[20] and "she became angry with him." The first translation is derived from Hebrew texts, the second from the Greek translation. The difference involves Beth's position as either culprit or offended party, hence, her subject-position

on the level of action. Instead of being alarmed by this disagreement that entails ideological conclusions, Trible never questions the tendency of both translations. In the light
of the crucial importance of the meaning of the verb for the interpretation of the story,
I find it an almost comical problem. The same preposition whose flexibility was so helpful in Bath's story is the troublemaker here. It never occurs elsewhere with this verb,
zanah. Its spatial meaning was, in chapter 11, directional: towards. We get, then: she . . .
towards him, with a nuance of confrontation. Now the verb has to illuminate the problem. It is generally assumed to mean "to be unfaithful." Although it is often used in relation to sexual unfaithfulness, this is not always so. And although it usually refers to
women, it also refers to men (e.g. Num. 25:1). Koehler and Baumgartner, referring to
Winckler's *Geschichte Israels,* cite, as a first possible meaning, "means originally, that the
husband does not live in his wife's tribe." I confess I was flabbergasted by the coincidence; if there is an evolution, from the context of patrilocal marriage to regular prostitution, we glimpse an ideological evolution that affects the semantics of the word. The
meaning "to become angry" is given, in my dictionary, as derived from Akkadian while
the many other cases derive their meaning from the Aramaic. For the Akkadian, Judges
19 is the only case, and I feel justified to doubt this uniqueness. Comparative philology is
not meant to solve problems prematurely, nor should it be used to cover up interesting
possibilities.

Let us assume, for our story, the meaning "to be unfaithful," and given the coincidence between *pilegesh* and the ancient meaning of *zanah,* this unfaithfulness may have
to do with the transition from patrilocal to virilocal marriage. Narratology draws our
attention to Beth's status as the subject of the action of the verb. She is, then, unfaithful,
not *against* her husband, but *towards* him, in the directional, confrontational, and spatial
sense. She is unfaithful because she *goes to* her husband. This makes sense, too, in connection with the next statement, which has it that she leaves him, but after this "unfaithfulness." To whom is she unfaithful, then? To her father, who had the "right of exclusive
possession"? This woman acted as a relatively autonomous subject. She went to visit her
husband—whether or not on his instigation, that we cannot know. After the visit, she
went back to the father where she belonged, according to the institution of marriage that
binds her. The uncertainties in the translation and interpretation reflect the problematic,
uncertain situation Beth entered. As we will see, she will be crushed between the men
who compete for her exclusive possession. This is the narrative condensation *par excellence,* the one that conflates father and husband.

Beth's Father

This possibility explains an otherwise odd detail, frequently noticed but never satisfactorily dealt with. The most thorough analysis I know of is by Niditch, but she does
not manage to explain the story as a whole either, and especially not the details that concern me here.[21] When, later, the husband comes to the house of the father, the latter is
very happy to see his son-in-law and insists that the couple remain in the house-of-bread.
The reception he gives the husband does not seem plausible for the case of the lowly
woman, similar to a slave, bought from poor families, that the *Interpreter's Dictionary of
the Bible* presents as "concubine."[22] Why, many have asked, is he so happy to see the hus-

band of the either shamefully repudiated or infuriated daughter? And if so, why his insistence, why does he harass him to stay against his wish? My answer is simple: he is happy, because now, the husband is behaving according to the rules, because the threatened institution which guarantees his exclusive possession of the daughter, is back in order. Second, the reason that he insists is because he does not want the transgression to happen again. The rich reception in the house-of-bread displays his power, and indeed, the husband in turn, trying to compete with this powerful father, displays his own possessions. A third detail has a sad explanation as well. From the moment that the two men are together, Beth disappears from the story, only to reappear as the victim of the climax of violence of the book. The phrase "he went after her to her father's house to speak to her heart" is often mistakenly translated or interpreted as a sign of the husband's kindness. The heart, however, is the site of reason rather than of feelings, and the goal of the visit must be interpreted as persuasion, not conciliation. This is not a modern psychological novel.

Beth's marriage reflects the competition between patrilocal and virilocal marriage. This competition is more often at stake in the Hebrew Bible than is generally assumed. The wooing of Rebekah has virilocality as its condition, and Jacob had to integrate himself in a patrilocal environment for a long time, before he managed to emancipate himself from Lahan. Father and husband, in these cases, compete over the "memory" of the daughter. Within the preoccupation of biblical ideology, that competition concerns the question: Whose memory will she perpetuate, whose will her children be, which name will she serve? Not her own, in any case; of that, the writers who deprived Bath and Beth of a name have taken care. But they overlooked what female subjectivity can accomplish, even within the limits of the struggle between two forms of patriarchy.

It is time to introduce briefly a character who plays a role in Bath's story, and who is strikingly absent in Beth's, although not in its aftermath: Yhwh, the true hero, the "fiancé" of the chief's daughter. As the addressee of Jephthah's vow and the beneficiary of her sacrifice, he does not speak. Attempts to argue that his silence is evidence for his condemnation of the sacrifice do not seem convincing. If he does not speak for it, he does not speak against it either. In his alleged omniscience, he could have foreseen the outcome of the vow. If Jephthah accomplished the victory, it was, in the eyes of the *gibbor,* thanks to Yhwh's help. And, finally, while Yhwh knew how to prevent Isaac's sacrifice, he refrains from preventing Bath's. Yhwh is undeniably a father figure. Jephthah, we might conjecture, prefers to give up his daughter altogether rather than to give her to a man of the next generation. Giving her to the superfather, he keeps her at least at the "proper" side: the side of the fathers. The side of absolute property, of property with a *past*. The image of the deity that emerges from this story is that of a father figure who complies with the structure of power that trades daughters for military victory, who does nothing against this priority of business over life.

Now that we have become aware of this anthropological structure that figures these stories, it is easy to insert our third victim in this series. In fact, Kallah the bride exemplifies the issue. Her father almost gave her away to a husband, but he took her back, in order to give her to someone who would at least accept the rules of patrilocal marriage. This explains the strange fact that when Samson comes to visit her, she does live with her father but her father claims to have given her away already.[23]

Between Men

In Beth's case, the husband seems to end up winning: he manages to take Beth out of the house-of-bread, to the pasture land. But social changes produce dangerous situations, and the dangers in this case are very tough. In fact, the husband shows that he is not up to his newly acquired status. He is not able to see the daughter safely home. Hosted by another father, in other words, returning, out of weakness, to the father's house—again a house full of bread—he gives up his position. Beth is taken over by the father when the latter offers her, as well as his own nubile daughter, for sexual abuse. The gift has to be this double gift, not only in order to play the story off against Genesis 19 (Niditch calls it, ironically I would hope, more successful than the Lot story[24]), but mainly, in order to signify the gift as a fatherly act; the father gives daughters, his own and somebody else's alike. The inhabitants of the city are not satisfied with the women. They want the man. It is the man who has to be punished for subverting the institution. They want to teach him a lesson—about sex, knowledge, and possession; about sex *as* knowledge and possession.

This explains another strange detail. The men refuse to accept the two women from the hand of the father. When the husband throws his wife out, they do accept that gift. Why would they refuse two women, and accept one? Because they are concerned with a symbolic victory. The subversive husband has to be punished, either by being raped himself or by giving up his bone of contention. Taking the women from the father would obscure the issue. And if punishment is at stake, why does it have to take the form of rape? First, it seems naive to suppose that the entire male population of both Sodom and Gibeah is homosexual. As Niditch points out, in this culture homosexual rape is seen as a form of extreme humiliation: it is, in these stories, the destruction of the subject that the men want to perform, and is there a worse destruction possible than to treat a male as a female? But there is another, deeper motivation thinkable. In the eyes of the patrilocal ideology, the bond between father and daughter is the only "natural," acceptable one: possession with a past. To go away from the father, to be "unfaithful towards a man," is to go with any man; it is arbitrariness as opposed to naturalness. And from "any man" to "every man" is but one step, a step that even today is often made. A woman who divorces, or takes a lover, is often assumed to be public property, since, in the eyes of those who follow this "logic," she has shown herself by her act of autonomy to be "available." The punishment against this particular transgression, then, can be of only two kinds: either confinement, return to exclusive possession and the impossibility ever to enter the compromise situation of marriage (Bath); or gang-rape, public, mass abuse (Beth). Both punishments lead to the death of the female subject.

One question has to be answered still. Why does the father figure protect the husband? Why, in other words, this excessive hospitality? The father may compete with the husband; the very competition is a business between men. When it comes to a confrontation, the father will take the side of the other man, who may be of a different generation, but who still is of the same sex: the one that has interest in memory. Offering to give the daughters, Bath the Second and Beth, the father wins on both fronts: he protects the man, but he strips him of his otherness. Taking the patrilocal wife away from him, he turns him into a "normal" young man: he has submitted to the power of the father, yet he is a man, who may raise up seed for the father, a man with a future father-position.

The husband, in his turn, displays the cowardice that we know. His distorted report, later, shows that he is well aware of what he is doing. He has lost the struggle with the father, he must give up the woman, but at least he can confirm, in the very gesture of giving her up, his power over her. Power over the weaker compensates for the loss of power, for the humiliation that goes with submission. This we know to happen in other circumstances all the time. It explains why oppressed men oppress their women rather than fighting, with her, against the oppressing power. The gesture of throwing Beth out is thus a narrative condensation on the level of action: the act of submission and the act of exercising absolute power are conflated in one act. The gesture is of the same order as the one it inverts. Beth had been "unfaithful" against the father/towards him; he throws her back, towards the father's side, away from himself, submitting to the father, but, within the extreme violence that goes with revolutionary chaos, *over her dead body.*

The Daughters' Sacrifice

Three young, nubile women are sacrificed. Sacrificed: given up, in a symbolic gesture, to a higher power. Green defines sacrifice as "the voluntary or involuntary termination of human life in a ritualistic manner or for ritualistic purposes."[25] Turner stresses the symbolic aspect of sacrifice;[26] Girard its violence,[27] and Jay calls it "a remedy for having been born of woman."[28] All these theories of sacrifice fit our three women extremely well; none mentions them. That the "remedy" necessarily involves the "founding violence," hence, that Jay's and Girard's theories need each other, clarifies our three victims. Bath is burned to death, rather than given in marriage. Beth is momentarily taken away from the father, but given up, back, later. Kallah is burned to death *with* her father. The executioner of Bath is her father himself. Kallah is executed by a collective that represents the tribe of the father and the age-group, the generation of the husband. Beth is killed by . . . that is unclear.[29] She is offered by the father, actually given up by the husband, raped and tortured by the collective that punishes the intruder in the name of the father. But who kills her?

The initiative that Beth took to go and visit her husband in the beginning of the story is mirrored by her second "visit" at the end. She has been eliminated as a narrative subject, only to act again as what she then is: bereaved of all her "property," she can only fall down, but she does it at the threshold of the house, the house that is neither her father's nor her husband's, but that is owned by the father and inhabited by the husband. Is she dead, when she does not answer her husband's display of power when, refreshed by a good night's sleep, he *orders* her to stand up and come *home?* We do not know, and we are not supposed to know. Because this time, the executioner has to remain ambiguous. The husband does act as the sacrificial agent. Repeating his first gesture of violence, he now cuts her to pieces. This sacrificial gesture is equivalent in violence to the story as a whole. The gesture is symbolic. It turns Beth into a symbol. To speak with Shoshana Felman: Beth is *the scandal of the speaking body.* The gesture is also ambiguous. If Beth is still alive, the husband is her actual murderer. That cannot be, since the next chapter presents the war against the Benjaminites as a justified revenge on this intrusion of the purity laws. There is no way to redeem this man. But then, there is no way to redeem the following episode, the civil war, that ends in the enforcement of the new, virilocal marriage institution, upon the Benjaminites themselves.[30] A war that starts with an unacceptable sacrifice, that is led by Yahweh, and whose final scenes of bride-capture are often seen as a "merry end" of the book, in spite of the violence against women it entails. The three sacrifices, considered in this respect, are all three "improper." Bath is killed by someone who is not a priest. Samson transgressed the purity laws in his eating of the honey from a dead lion. Beth, the founding victim who undergoes all violence thinkable, is slaughtered by the hand of a priest who does wrong either way.

Counter-Rituals

If, in these stories, the men accomplish the ritual sacrifice of the women for whom there is no proper place in their competitive encounters, Beth and Bath, both within the limits of the subject-positions assigned to them, ritually counter the oblivion they are condemned to. Beth's gesture, her hand on the threshold, points in accusation to her murderer. She also claims entrance into the house. Whether or not she is already dead at the moment she is found there does not really matter. Her last act, as an already destroyed subject, is to claim her place in the house, to accuse the inhabitants of the house of their repudiation of her. What she points at is, ultimately, the house as the site of power and of male competition. The house is, to use a Freudian key term, *unheimlich:* a spooky place because it is familiar yet alien, dangerous in its very promise of safety.

Bath, who, condemned to death, has some more power to act out her subjectivity, initiates another ritual. Taking her companions with her to the initiation rite, towards the mountains, towards nubility, she becomes the occasion of a ritual of remembrance. It is, ironically, her, not her father that Israel, through the doing of her daughters, must remember. It seems typical, to me, that this apparently innocent passage is generally distorted and explained away as an etiological tale with no real ritual.[31] It is not a custom, as many translations have it, but a task, not to lament, but to sing or recount Bath-Jephthah.

And what about Kallah, the third nameless victim? At the time of her wedding, she was already crushed between the different male parties, her groom and her brothers. Rembrandt, who may very well be considered Holland's most interesting biblical scholar, painted the wedding scene on the model of Da Vinci's *Last Supper.* Isolated from the men around her, who are involved in their own deals, the woman sits in the middle, with a crowned head, in the position of Christ. This is not an ordinary typological interpretation. It is not Kallah who prefigures Christ, it is Christ who reminds us of Kallah, of her sacrifice, the desacralizing sacrifice of pure revenge. At the moment of her execution we see her neither act nor speak. How will *she* be revenged ?

This leads us back to the question of the beginning. The triangular situations in which the daughter is crushed to death between the men who strive for her possession display a spectacular absence. Where is Clytemnestra, as Marianne Hirsch in her paper on maternal anger rightly asked?[32] Where is Jephthah's daughter's mother? Where are the mothers who might have protected, or if they could not, have avenged their daughters' sacrifice? Absence can only signify negatively, thus promoting fantasy to take the place of the repressed. Reading a short article on child sacrifice I stumbled across a drawing which set my fantasy in motion.

It was a sketch of an Egyptian relief, found, like many similar ones, on Semitic territory.[33] What do we see? A tower, closely threatened by the enemy who is already busy climbing it. The situation is described in Judges 9:52. What does one do when the enemy is so close to the tower of defense? On the relief, the men stop fighting. They sacrifice to the god. They sacrifice, to be precise, children. Daughters. Between the men on the upper level, we see the women. They sit, and occupy an inferior position. According to Derchain, women, mothers, were not supposed to lament the sacrifice of their children.[34] Mothers, then, are utterly powerless, unable to protect their own flesh. Now, let this image trigger a story.

Try to imagine that at some point one of the mothers stands up. She pushes the men aside, with contempt for their inefficient strategy that kills their own memory rather than the enemy. Instead of looking up away from the battle, she looks down and faces it. At the moment that Abimelech approaches her tower too closely, she throws not a child but a millstone.[35] This, then, is the answer of the mother to the male way of dealing with daughters, wives, and warfare. The woman-with-the-millstone thus exemplifies the avenging mother that the Greek tradition stages in Clytemnestra. Her mighty body that is stronger than the *gibbor* who claims kinghood through his father, is represented in the tower that is its metaphor.

The figure of the avenging mother is, maybe, not absent from the book of Judges, but displaced. Displacement, the accompanying term for condensation, is the translation of the German *Entstellung*.[36] The word means both distortion and dislocation. The local dimension of the stories has already become obvious. The house as the site of the competition between men is the space where Bath meets her death sentence, Kallah her death, and Beth her expulsion, her death and her dismemberment. The mother, who "normally" lives inside that house, is pushed out of it, repressed. There is no place for her in the competition over the daughter. But the repressed returns, distorted, in the guise of the enemy Delilah, or the heroine Yael. Both women have maternal features and their actions in the encounter with the men are colored by nursing and mothering.[37] Dislocated, the mother returns, on the top of the tower of safety from which she had been expelled.

If we view the murderesses in the book as avenging mothers, the excess of violence attached to them becomes understandable. Since they avenge the excessive violence done to the daughters, their role has to be, in turn, displaced. But where repression covers oppression, violence cannot but increase.

Conclusion

I have tried to convince the reader of the interest of a narratological reading of the book of Judges, a reading that starts from the premise that the *subject* of narrative is a relevant category in that it responds to socially available subject-positions. In the course of the analysis, we have met with problems of language and philology. In their turn, those problems pointed at underlying, ancient struggles that disappear in translations that hastily try to solve problems instead of enhancing them and using them as heuristic tools. What we encountered was a social change of anthropological interest. The relation between social reality and narrative structure, then, turns out to be more complex than a naively realistic assumption would suggest.

If the book of Judges is historiographic, it is not only, not even predominantly, because it recounts wars and conquests. It is deeply historical in that it stages a social change of profound historical consequences. The change from one form of patriarchy to the next is the pre-text that needs to be remembered. It is in danger of oblivion when feminists and others tend to cover up historical change under the one term of patriarchy, and make it seem eternal, hence, unchangeable. It is only when the disciplines that study ancient texts are open to interdisciplinary collaboration—and biblical scholarship with its rich tradition could and should play a leading role in that endeavour—that the social function of narrative and the narrative function of social changes, the ideological function of ritual and ritual function of ideology, can be properly analyzed and understood. It is only on this condition that we can hope to undermine the language of power, and restore to the anonymous women the power over language.

Notes

This article is a condensed section of my book *Death and Dissymmetry: The Politics of Coherence in the Book of Judges* (University of Chicago Press, Chicago, 1988).

1. Mieke Bal, *Narratology: Introduction to the Theory of Narrative* (University of Toronto Press, Toronto, 1985).

2. See Alberto J. Soggin, *Judges: A Commentary* (SMC Press, London, 1981), and Robert Boling, *Judges: A New Translation with Introduction and Commentary* (Doubleday, Anchor Bible, Garden City, NY, 1975).

3. See Mieke Bal, *Murder and Difference: Gender, Genre and Scholarship on Sisera's Death* (Indiana University Press, Bloomington, 1988).

4. See Bal, *Death and Dissymmetry* for a full-length study of this structure.

5. See, for example, Boling, *Judges*.

6. D.W. Gooding, "The Composition of the Book of Judges," *Eretz-Israel*, 16 (1982), pp. 70–9.

7. Again, for a more detailed analysis, see Bal, *Death and Dissymmetry*.

8. For more about Freud's concept of condensation, see Sigmund Freud, *The Interpretation of Dreams* (first published in 1900), in *The Standard Edition of the Complete Psychological Works of Sigmund Freud* (24 vols.), ed. James Strachey (Hogarth, London, 1953), vol. 5, and Samuel Weber, *The Legend of Freud* (University of Minnesota Press, Minneapolis, 1982).

9. Austin's view of performativity is defended by Shoshana Felman, *Le Scandale du corps parlant. Don Juan avec Austin ou la séduction en deux langues* (Edition de Seuil, Paris, 1980). I use their concept rather than that redefined by others.

10. Robert Alter, *The Art of Biblical Narrative* (Basic Books, New York, 1981).

11. See James Kugel, *The Idea of Biblical Poetry* (Yale University Press, New Haven and London, 1981); Adele Berlin, *The Dynamics of Biblical Parallelism* (Indiana University Press, Bloomington, 1985); and Robert Alter, *The Art of Biblical Poetry* (Basic Books, New York, 1985).

12. K.H. Neukens, "Richter 11.37f: Rite de Passage und Übersetzungsprobleme," *Biblische Notizen*, 19 (1982), pp. 41–3.

13. Arnold van Gennep, *The Rites of Passage* (University of Chicago Press, Chicago, 1960).

14. Victor Turner, *The Forest of Symbols: Aspects of Ndembu Ritual* (Cornell University Press, Ithaca, 1967) and *The Ritual Process: Structure and Anti-structure* (Cornell University Press, Ithaca, 1968).

15. Freud, "The Taboo of Virginity," p. 193.

16. G.J. Wenham, "Why Does Sexual Intercourse Defile?" *Zeitschrift für die Alttestamentlische Wissenschaft*, 95 (1983), pp. 432–4.

17. Mary Douglas, *Purity and Danger* (Praeger, New York and Washington, 1966).

18. Phyllis Trible, *Texts of Terror: Literary-Feminist Reading of Biblical Narratives* (Fortress Press, Philadelphia, 1984).

19. L. Koehler and Walter Baumgartner, *Lexicon in Veteris Testamenti Libros* (Brill, Leiden, 1958).

20. A. Slotki, Commentary on Judges, in *Joshua and Judges: Hebrew Text and English Translation with Introduction and Commentary,* ed. A. Cohen (The Soncino Press, London, Jerusalem and New York, 1980), p. 279.

21. Susan Niditch, "The 'Sodomite' Theme in Judges 19–20: Family, Community and Social Disintegration," *Catholic Biblical Quarterly,* 1982, pp. 365–78.

22. O.J. Baab, "Concubine," *The Interpreter's Dictionary of the Bible* (Abingdon Press, Nashville, 1962), p. 666.

23. Julian Morgenstern, "Additional Notes on *Beena* Marriage (Matriarchat) in Ancient Israel," *Zeitschrift für Alttestamentliche Wissenschaft,* 49 (1931), pp. 46–58.

24. Niditch, "The 'Sodomite' Theme," p.376.

25. Alberto Ravinesh Whitney Green, *The Role of Human Sacrifice in the Ancient Near East* (Scholars Press, Missoula, Montana, 1975), p. 17.

26. Victor Turner, "Sacrifice as Quintessential Process: Prophylaxis or Abandonment?" *History of Religions,* 16 (1977), pp. 189–215.

27. René Girard, *La Violence et le sacré* (Grasset, Paris, 1972).

28. Nancy Jay, "Sacrifice as a Remedy for Having Been Born a Woman," in *Immaculate and Powerful: The Female in Sacred Image and Social Reality,* ed. Clarissa Atkinson, Constance H. Buchanan, and Margaret R. Miles (Beacon Press, Boston, 1985), pp. 283–309.

29. Robert Polzin, *Moses and the Deuteronomist* (Seabury Press, New York, 1980), pp. 200–2.

30. The relation between the story of Beth and the bride-captures, as the reversal and revenge of the imposition of one institution over the other, was established by Teresa Cooley, student in my seminar on Ideo-stories at the Harvard Divinity School.

31. See Slotki, in Cohen (ed.), *Joshua and Judges.*

32. Marianne Hirsch, "Clytemnestra's Children," lecture, Dartmouth College, Hanover, New Hampshire.

33. Ph. Derchain, "Les plus ancien témoignages de sacrifice d'enfants chez les sémites occidentaux," *Vetus Testsmentum,* 20 (1970), pp. 351–5.

34. *Ibid.,* and see Derchain's bibliography.

35. Mieke Bal, *Lethal Love: Reading Biblical Love-Stories, Differently* (Indiana University Press, Bloomington, 1987).

36. Weber, *The Legend of Freud.*

37. Bal, *Murder and Difference.*

Adultery in the House of David
The Metanarrative of Biblical Scholarship and the Narratives of the Bible

REGINA M. SCHWARTZ

I n our secular world we continue to authorize, albeit unconsciously, many biblical ideologies, granting the Bible the status not only of a spiritual guide but also a manual for politics. Furthermore, we often attach ideological formations to the Bible that are alien to it, ones that arose in its long and varied history of interpretation and that by association and confusion come to reap the same authority that we so reflexively attach to the Bible. I want to begin to disentangle that association, to separate the discipline of biblical studies from the Bible and then to proceed to offer a reading of biblical narratives that runs contrary to the assumptions that inform so much of biblical studies.[1] Biblical narratives make very different kinds of claims of legitimation from biblical scholarship (I use the phrase in a specialized sense here, restricting its application to the historical-critical scholarship forged in the atmosphere of German historicism). The ambition of "higher criticism" was to construct a metanarrative, a privileged metadiscourse capable of offering eventually the Truth about the history of the Bible's composition and hence necessarily about ancient Israelite history. Biblical narratives—and that plural contrasts with the singular metanarrative—make no such sweeping claim; their truths are multiple and conflicting, and they resist the consistency, continuity, and comprehensiveness that characterize metanarrative as surely as they resist being distilled into a single story. Ironic as it may sound, biblical narratives are far more compatible with the understanding of postmodernism distilled by Lyotard (xxiv) as "incredulity toward metanarratives" than they are with modern biblical scholarship. But upon reflection, there is little irony here, for the ancient narratives that arose in disparate social and historical circumstances are likely to exhibit the character of multiplicity, while modernism's biblical scholarship is bound to reflect the nineteenth century's passion for an authoritative metanarrative. If the biblical narratives cannot be accurately labeled "postmodern," it is only because they cannot exhibit incredulity toward metanarratives that await later periods to be imagined and still later ones to be critiqued. If we can sometimes discern the impulse toward metanarrative in the Bible—after all, this is a story that purports to span all of human history—it surfaces only to be stubbornly subverted by conflicting stor*ies*.

Biblical scholarship is preoccupied with history—not the same history that the Bible constructs, but a history that the Bible is expected to offer clues to—the political and religious history of the ancient Near East. I think it is crucial to make distinctions between those projects, that is, to make distinctions between the writing of history in the Bible and the writing of history in biblical scholarship, especially because they are so often, and so dangerously blurred. Dangerously, because the equation of the ideologies of biblical narratives with a positivist historian's understanding of "real events" turns what could be founding fictions of Western culture that are demanding critique, into "facts" that seem formidably unassailable. Dangerously, because the German historicism that gave birth to biblical scholarship is no "mere" positivism (as if there were such a thing); rather, every archeologist's spade and every linguist's verb ending is deeply inscribed with politics. Dangerously, because that very politics, once read into the Bible through the back door of something as seemingly innocent as "higher criticism," can even offer "evidence" for justifying the oppression of people. It is too late in the day, and our understanding of narrative is too advanced, to allow any pernicious notions of "biblical truth"—including those of "higher criticism"—to continue to stick. Here, I would like to separate the complex constructions of the nation in the David narratives from the national*ism* read into these narratives by biblical scholarship. I may as well confess at the outset that my own lenses have been tinted epistemologically by postmodern approaches to history rather than by the historicism that forged "higher criticism," and that they are tinted politically by a deep suspicion of exclusive national identities.

1. Biblical Scholarship

"Traditional history" as Foucault characterized it, "retracing the past as a patient and continuous development," strikes me as an apt description of the major pursuit in biblical studies for the past two centuries. The project that has dominated the field is the historical reconstruction of the biblical text; as one scholar prescribed in the nineteenth century, "the subject matter of biblical introduction is the history of the Bible."[2] This project is marked by its quest for origins—the origin of a given passage, the origin of a cultic practice, the original setting of the text—and by a deep commitment to charting development, whether the formation of the text (what is the extent of J and E and when did they come together?), the development of the ancient Israelite religion (what are the earliest signs of Yahwism?), or the development of political organizations in ancient Israel and surrounding nations (how did one institution, the tribal confederacy, become another, the monarchy?). Much biblical scholarship has been devoted to ascertaining sources—even though the Bible has unhelpfully obscured its sources (thank heavens Harold Bloom has clarified all that for us)—and many of the historical reconstructions of ancient Israel have been markedly teleological even though, as I have argued elsewhere (Schwartz, 1990), the Hebrew Bible depicts a history that stubbornly resists any notion of fulfillment or completion.[3]

These projects have their own history. In the nineteenth century, biblical scholarship saw itself as part of a larger Germanic historiographic tradition. This was not just a question of influence; "rather, the broader historiographic tradition shared the same methods, the same goals, the same prejudices . . . as biblical scholarship."[4] The chief assumptions were that history charts development, that its focus should be the development of the nation—the German nation in particular—and that the nation must be understood as an individual entity with its own unfolding spirit, its own internal laws of development. Organic metaphors predominate: the growth of an innate tendency, or a seed flowering into a nation. And according to such thinking, the nation's quest for power was virtually an ethical imperative, a natural flowering of the spirit. For Leopold von Ranke, "It must be the uppermost task of the state . . . to achieve the highest measure of independence and strength among the competing powers of the world, so that the state will be able to fully develop its innate tendencies" (Iggers: 9). Johann Gustav Droysen wrote of the idea of a "divine order," of "God's rule of the world" along with the insistence that that divine plan was working itself out in Prussia in particular. In his *History of Prussian Politics* (which he worked on for decades, leaving it unfinished at his death), Droysen tried to argue that ever since the fifteenth century, Prussian rulers (ever-conscious of Prussia's German mission) followed a consistent plan of action, a plan still unfolding in Germany (Iggers: 106). An emphasis on teleological development insistently marks his thought.

> The moral world, ceaselessly moved by *many ends,* and finally, . . . by the *supreme end,* is in a state of restless development and of internal elevation and growth. . . . With every advancing step in this *development* and *growth,* the historical understanding becomes wider and deeper. (Droysen: 15–16; my italics)

Droysen's philosophy of history is indebted to that of Wilhelm von Humboldt who in his famous essay "On the Task of the Historian" sounds at first surprisingly at odds with the prevailing notions of coherence and continuity. "What is apparent," he writes, "is scattered, disconnected, isolated" but then he explains that it is the historian's task to take what is "apparent" and show the hidden coherence: the historian "takes the scattered pieces he has gathered into himself and work[s] them into a whole."[5] Von Ranke also begins by talking about isolated events, but his interest soon turns to the notion of a cohesive hidden order informing seeming chaos. "Although [history] pursues the succession of events as sharply and accurately as possible, and attempts to give each of them its proper color and form . . . , still history goes beyond this labor and moves on to an investigation of origins, seeking to break through to the deepest and most secret motives of historical life." For Ranke, Humboldt, and Droysen, historiography unveils the inner logic in the randomness of events, and that logic is the course of national development.

As nationalism was the paramount concern in the founding fictions of German historicism, so the nation was also the preoccupation of one of the founding fictions—and I do use the term *fiction* here advisedly—of ancient Israel: the book of Samuel. It set the terms by which the institution of monarchy was to be understood and by which the nation of ancient Israel was defining itself. Knowing, as we do, that history was called upon to narrate the ideals of the German nation, its various "progresses," moral, military, political, religious, and that the story of ancient Israel, including commentary on Samuel, was written by historians who were also thinking about, even writing the story of Germany, it is no wonder that the two stories were often confused. All that development so faithfully outlined in the growth of the German nation was easily, all too easily, found in the growth of ancient Israel.

We can see this confusion at work in one of the most prominent biblical scholars of the late nineteenth century, Julius Wellhausen, when he writes in the introduction to his *Prolegomena to the History of Ancient Israel*, "It is necessary to trace the succession of the three elements [he is referring to the Jehovist, the Deuteronomic, and the Priestly] in detail, and at once to test and to fix each by reference to an independent standard, namely, the inner development of the history of Israel" (12). With this commitment to charting such "inner development," he cannot help but find it. The metaphors he uses to discuss his theory of the literary composition of the books of Judges, Samuel, and Kings are symptomatic:

> . . . we are not presented with tradition purely in its original condition; already it is overgrown with later accretions. Alongside of an older narrative a new one has sprung up, formerly independent, and intelligible in itself, though in many instances of course adapting itself to the former. More frequently the new forces have not caused the old root to send forth a new stock, or even so much as a complete branch; they have only nourished parasitic growths; the earlier narrative has become clothed with minor and dependent additions. To vary the metaphor, the whole area of tradition has finally been uniformly covered with an alluvial deposit by which the configuration of the surface has been determined. (Wellhausen: 228)

In this description of the text, he shifts from the metaphor of a plant with a new branch to a plant that has only parasitic growths, next it is overgrown with accretions, and then he dresses it (the plant wears "minor and dependent" clothes), only to proceed to drop the plant altogether to opt for geologic history; now the biblical text is comprised of layers of alluvial deposits, and presumably scholars can take out their spades and dig right through it. Whether as the growth of an organism or the accretion of geologic deposits, this is the picture of history that he quickly applies not only to the development of the text, but to its plot, that is, to the biblical narrative's own account of history. Deftly, almost without our noticing, the structure of the story of Germany becomes the structure of the story of Israel. According to Wellhausen, the history spanning Deuteronomy to 2 Kings offers "a connected view of large periods of time, a continuous survey of the connection and succession of race after race, the detailed particulars of the occurrences being disregarded; the historical factors with which the religious pragmatism here has to do are so uniform that the individual periods in reality need only to be filled up with the numbers of the years" (231).

When we read the secondary literature about David with German historicism in mind, we can detect signs of it virtually everywhere. Many biblical scholars' accounts, both of the development of the text and of the history of Israel, are informed by the same assumptions we detect in Wellhausen, for their story tells of the accretion of King David's power, alluvial deposit by alluvial deposit. Finding this presupposition of development in one too many places, I frankly began to be suspicious. If biblical scholars reconstructed the text that way because the whole discipline of textual studies was permeated by the assumptions of German historicism, so be it.[6] But find that development in the story of David, a story so marked by discontinuity and ideological conflict? How were biblical scholars going to reconcile the drive for finding continuity and development with this messy text? They found that continuity by fragmenting the text, by chopping it up into different documents, first into big pieces, then into smaller ones, and when they were finished, they had taken the amorphous, heterogeneous story we have been given and separated it into strands, each governed by—you guessed it—the criteria of development and continuity. Here is just one of the prominent source theories: a historian or historical school wrote a large strand of the story that bridges Judges to Kings according to a coherent principle—it was that Israel's fate was tied to the law in Deuteronomy (she is rewarded for obedience to that law and punished for disobedience). One version has it that it was written in exile, from the point of view of a hope for a nation of Israel that had failed, as an explanation of that failure.[7] Still, amid all of the stories describing the failures of Israel, there was also a recognizable drive to idealize David, and this contradiction—between the pessimism of the account and the optimism about David—is resolved by separating the documents. To be coherent, one document must espouse one ideology—say, that Israel is continually going astray from the law and must be punished for her sins—and the other document espouse another—say, that David is the ideal of kingship and kingship is the ideal for Israel.

To a surprising degree (surprising, because most of us assume that these decisions about sources were based only on linguistic data), the criterion of a consistent sympathy or ideology or the plot continuity of a narrative, whether pro- or anti-monarchy, pro- or anti-David, or pro- and anti-whomever or whatever the critic chooses to focus on, has been *determining* in separating strands of narrative and ascribing different authors. Sources have even been named for the character the author ostensibly sympathizes with—"the Saul source," "the Samuel source"—and when two basic sources did not resolve all the contradictions, more narrative strands had to be isolated to account for them, and when these were not named for a character, they were named for a continuous thread in the plot; hence, we have "the ark narrative," or "the rise of David narrative." Note how blithely the scholar who wrote the impressively learned Anchor Bible commentaries on 1 and 2 Samuel can take for granted in his introduction that *his* demand for coherence is also felt by his readers: "Numerous internal thematic tensions, duplications, and contradictions stand in the way of a straightforward reading of the story." What does he mean by a "straightforward" reading of the story? Whether he is suggesting that reading forward and reading straight means reading straight for the goal, reading teleologically, reading for development, or if he is defining "straightforward reading" in his sentence tautologically to mean the kind of reading we do when there are no "tensions, duplications or contradictions" (and I know of no such reading), he sets out to rectify the problem, rewriting the Bible into coherent stories, and the difficult one we have in our Bibles is either neglected, or worse still, it is "solved."

2. Biblical Stories

Writing on Nietzsche's *Genealogy of Morals*, Foucault distinguishes "effective history" from traditional history. If traditional history is devoted to searching out sources, establishing continuity, finding resemblances, and charting development, "effective history" turns to ruptures and discontinuities, to disrupting the fiction of the unity of the subject, and to breaking the commitment to seeking origins and ends.

> History becomes "effective" to the degree that it introduces discontinuity into our very being—as it divides our emotions, dramatizes our instincts, multiplies our body and sets it against itself. "Effective" history deprives the self of the reassuring stability of life and nature, and it will not permit itself to be transported by a voiceless obstinacy toward a millennial ending. It will uproot its traditional foundations and relentlessly disrupt its pretended continuity. This is because knowledge is not made for understanding; it is made for cutting. (154)

In complicated ways, the Hebrew Bible depicts history as a series of ruptures in which various identities are cut and re-cut, formed, broken, and reformed, rather than as a continuous process in which a stable entity called Israel develops. In Genesis 15, Abraham is told to cut three birds in half for a mysterious covenant ceremony in which fire passes between the pieces while the promise of a future nation is made to the patriarch. Does that cutting signify constituting Israel's identity or destroying it? Or both? Animals are not the only entities severed here; Abraham's descendents are to be separated from their home, "sojourners in a land not theirs," as part of the process of creating a new home, and yet, Yhwh will threaten that Israel's inheritance will be cut off. In another sense, Israel is already "cut off" in that it is separated from the other nations; that separation is defining, and it means that not Israel, but its enemies, have been "cut off" before it (2 Sam 7:9). Other forms of rupture characterize this history. In Israel's story, "cutting" is joined to an emphasis on "tearing away" and "breaking," and what is broken is not always Israel's enemies, nor, for that matter, is it always Israel. When he defeats the Philistines, David rejoices that Yhwh has "broken through" his enemies, comparing this bursting or breaking to the breaking of waters (2 Sam 5:20). The comparison of defeating enemies to breaking waters can be read as an allusion to the defeat of the Egyptian pursuers and the separation of waters at the exodus; again, Israel is formed by such breaking. But in another kind of internal rending, Israel is shattered. First, the kingdom is torn away from the king, a metaphor that is theatricalized in the story of King Saul tearing the cloak of the priest, Samuel, in a desperate attempt to hold on to his, and hence divine, favor: "As Samuel turned to go, Saul caught at the hem of his garment and it tore, and Samuel said to him 'Today Yahweh has torn the kingdom of Israel from you and given it to a neighbor of yours who is better than you'" (1 Sam 15:27–28). Later, the kingdom is torn away from King Solomon as it was torn from Saul (1 Kgs 11:11–13), but in this instance, we are told that it is not *all* torn away, for the sake of David. But if "for David's sake" here means not cutting off, elsewhere David is told that the sword will never be far from his house (2 Sam 12:10). I rapidly enumerate some of the ruptures in the story of Israel—ruptures that the language of cutting so overtly signals[8]—because they run counter to that strong drive in biblical scholarship to read that history as portraying development.

One version of "development" that has been ascertained frequently in the books of Samuel is the "rise of David," and with it, the corollary demise of King Saul; supposedly, Saul's paranoia, ineffectuality, and estrangement from Yhwh develop, and David's political astuteness, military success, and favor from Yhwh develop. But as more sensitive biblical scholars have noted, the depiction of Saul is more difficult than a progressive demise, and David is not always on the rise. In the very passage that asserts that David's power has been made secure by God—the Davidic covenant in which Nathan the Prophet delivers the oracle that David will have a secure dynasty, a permanent House—there is a curiously contradictory exchange. The setting: David has successfully taken over the house of Saul, he has been made king of both the north and the south and is at rest from his battles enjoying a brief period of peace, and he would like to build a house for God in Jerusalem, the city of David. The response comes from the Almighty: "*You* want to build *me* a house?" (the pronouns are emphatic). David is reminded that he is not God's patron; God is *his* patron. But then, after Yhwh corrects David on this score, clearly *limiting* the sphere of his influence, he proceeds to *expand* his power. It sounds as though David's ambition is simultaneously rebuked and rewarded. Here is the conflicting message: The Lord says, "Are you going to build me a house for me to live in: I haven't lived in a house from the day I brought up the Israelites until this very day! Instead I've gone about in a tent wherever I happened to go throughout Israel. Did I ever speak with one of the staff-bearers of Israel whom I appointed to shepherd my people Israel and say, 'Why haven't you built me a house of cedar?'" It continues, "I took you from the sheep pasture to be prince over my people Israel. I was with you wherever you went, clearing all your enemies from your path. And I shall make you a name like the names of the nobility in the land. I shall fix a place for my people Israel and plant it, so that it will remain where it is and never again be disturbed" (2 Sam 7:4–10). In this passage, God clearly suggests that the idea of a house, of permanence, of stability, is abhorrent, and yet he offers David a house as though it were desirable indeed; as the passage reads, the promise of a House is far from an unequivocally welcome one. We could probably wrench our imaginations into some resolution of this conflict—certainly many scholars have separated the account into independent strands so that there is no conflict left, but the price would be the elimination of one of the key conflicts in the Bible: the tension between, on the one hand, a nostalgia for an Israel that is not fixed and not "like the nations," nostalgia for a period of wandering dispossessed, for associating tent-dwelling with godliness and moral rectitude, and on the other hand, the longing for stability, for landed property, a standing army, a dynastic leadership, in short, for becoming a nation among the nations.[9]

Only four chapters later, someone other than Yhwh will also refuse an offer from David to take up residence in a house. Israel is at war when Bathsheba's husband, Uriah the Hittite, is called back from the front by the king in an effort to cover up his adultery with the now pregnant Bathsheba. But Uriah will not sleep with his own wife. He reminds the king of Israel that "the ark, and Israel, and Judah, abide in booths; and my lord Joab, and the servants of my lord, are camping on the face of the field; and I, shall I go into my house to eat and to drink, and to lie with my wife? As you live, and as your soul lives, I will not do this thing" (2 Sam 11:11). The passage casts a dark shadow back upon the earlier promise of a stable House. Everyone else has rallied to the field to meet the enemy—only David dwells in a house: "At the turn of the year, the time when kings go campaigning, David sent Joab and with him his own guards and the whole of Israel. They massacred the Ammonites and laid siege to Rabbah. David however remained in Jerusalem" (2 Sam 11:1). And it is while he stays in that house that he commits adultery and subsequently orders the murder of Uriah, thereby, among other things, undoing that promise of permanence and stability to his House:

> Next morning David wrote a letter to Joab and sent it by Uriah. In the letter he wrote, "Station Uriah in the thick of the fight and then fall back behind him so that he may be struck down and die." Joab, then besieging the town, posted Uriah in a place where he knew there were fierce fighters. The men of the town sallied out and

engaged Joab; the army suffered casualties, including some of David's bodyguard; and Uriah the Hittite was killed too. . . . When Uriah's wife heard that her husband Uriah was dead, she mourned for her husband. When the period of mourning was over, David sent to have her brought to his house; she became his wife and bore him a son. But what David had done displeased Yhwh. (2 Sam 11:14–27)

Henceforth, the nation is rent with civil strife, and the prophet who guaranteed that David's house would be forever secure now prophesies that the sword will never be far from David's House. It seems that a House is a bad idea after all. Conflicts like these are frequent because this text is not simply about the people, the nation, or its king *amassing* power, but because instead these narratives express ambivalence about power. Even as the story of Israel depicts an effort to become "like the nations," it depicts that very project as pernicious, for Israel depends for its identity on its distinctiveness, on being drawn "from the nations." These conflicting approaches to power are symptomatic of Israel's conflicting self-definitions: conflicting, because if the Bible is anything, it is the site of struggle, struggles that took place between widely different factions with different political and religious interests over hundreds of years.

For instance, the institution of monarchy itself is presented from wildly divergent points of view, often broadly drawn. How can the narrative depict the "development of the monarchy" when it is unsettled about what the nation is, let alone what monarchy is, and what it means for this entity called a nation to be ruled by that entity called "king"— let alone what kind of power these entities should or should not have. Rather than presupposing settled answers, these stories are intently interested in exploring such questions of definition. Is a king a tyrant who will enslave the people and seize their property, as the judge/prophet/priest Samuel (what is Samuel anyway?) warns them in his stirring testimonial against the abuses of kingship? If so, why does the same Samuel who delivers this scathing critique against monarchy anoint, not one king, but two?

He will take your sons and assign them to his chariot and cavalry, and they will run before his chariot. He will appoint for himself captains of thousands and captains of hundreds from them. They will do his plowing, harvesting, and grape-gathering and make his weapons and the equipment of his chariotry. Your daughters he will take as perfumers and cooks and bakers. Your best fields and vineyards and olive groves he will take and give to his servants. Your seed crops and vine crops he will tithe to make gifts to his officers and servants. Your best slaves, maidservants, and cattle, and your asses he will take and use for his own work; and your flocks too he will tithe. You yourselves will become his slaves. Then you will *cry out* because of the King you have chosen for yourselves. . . . (1 Sam 8:11–18, my emphasis)

The Israelites had "cried out" in Egypt, groaning under slavery to Pharaoh, and the promised land was promised as their hope of deliverance from such unbridled tyranny, certainly not as a reenactment of their enslavement. But, at the height of Israel's peace and prosperity, when the proverbial milk and honey were flowing, King Solomon married—could it be?—a daughter of Pharaoh. Shortly after his adultery, David himself had set a captured population to work as slaves, brickmaking to be precise, as the Israelites had in Egypt. Is this why Israel's liberator, Moses, is an Egyptian, to suggest that Israel is not simply delivered from Egypt, but fundamentally, delivered to Egypt? How could Israel become Egyptianized when from its inception it is the antithesis?

3. Sex and Power

On yet another level, the biblical story of the fortunes and misfortunes of King David's dynasty seems to have trouble keeping its agenda straight: if we thought it was preoccupied with the serious business of political and military history, the rise (or whatever that is) of monarchy (whatever it is), the narrative is interrupted by disturbing sex scenes like the story of David taking Bathsheba when he spots her bathing from his roof, or his son Amnon, overcome with passion, raping his half-sister, Tamar. Do the struggles for Israel's national definition have anything to do with these sexual scenes? The way in which these scenes are so carefully interwoven with political events would indicate that they must: the David-Bathsheba narrative is surrounded, before and after, by accounts of war with the Ammonite enemy. Immediately after describing the Israelite victory over them, the narrative turns to the rape of Tamar, which is followed by Absalom's murder of the rapist (his elder brother and the heir to the throne) and soon Absalom will try to usurp the throne and civil war will rend the nation. Simply put, Israel is threatened from without and from within and in the very midst are acts of adultery, rape, and incest. This is no accident: Israel's war with the sons of Ammon is a war of definition, the sexual violations are tests of definition, for in both, Israel's borders—who constitutes Israel and who does not—are at stake. Mieke Bal has already made it clear that the book of Judges, which is so explicitly about war and political intrigue, is also about sexual violence; she has even labeled that sexual violence a kind of counter-coherence.[10] These are not separate spheres, public and private, that have impact on one another—such a reading would say that the private acts of David have public consequences, that David is torn between private desires and public duties, that David's private affections get in the way of his public role (all of these arguments have been made)—instead, politics and sexuality are so deeply and complexly integrated as to be one, and it is anachronistic to even understand them as two different spheres of life (see Gunn, Gros Louis). The text itself claims their virtual synonymity when the prophet delivers the divine judgment on David's adultery with Bathsheba: "Thus says the Lord, 'Behold, I will raise up evil against you out of your own house; and I will take your wives before your eyes, and give them to your neighbor, and he shall lie with your wives in the sight of this sun. For you did it in secret; but I will do this thing before all Israel, and before the sun.'" That prediction is fulfilled when David's son Absalom sleeps with his father's concubines in a declaration of civil war; David's ostensibly private affair implicates the entire nation.

How can we account for the persistent figuring of national politics sexually, from the chastity of the "virgin queene" to the barbarians' "rape" of the countryside? Is it a vestige of dynastic monarchies that were in fact constructed upon exchanges of women, upon marriages that configured and reconfigured nations and empires? Or is the explanation more psychoanalytic, that we figure the body politic in the image of our sexuality and our larger institutions recapitulate our sexual dramas? Of the many kinds of explanation, certainly one is how women do figure in the econo-political system. There is no question that owning the sexual rights to a woman (or stealing them, as the case may be) confers power in patriarchy. As this is overtly the case for marriage to the king's daughter or sexual intercourse with the king's concubines, it is no less the case for non-royal sexual exchanges. Because, as Lévi-Strauss (1969) taught us, exchanging women establishes power relations between men, David's dominance over other men is signaled by both his military and his sexual conquests. Before David became king, he was a fugitive from the jealous King Saul and he turned for provisions to a man he had previously protected with his guerilla band, but the man denied David's power and refused to acknowledge his obligation to him, framing this refusal as a denial of David's very identity: "Who is David? Who is the son of Jesse? There are many servants nowadays who are breaking away from their masters. Shall I take my bread and my water and my meat that I have killed for my shearers, and give it to men who come from I do not know where?" In an unsubtle commentary on his poor judgment, the man is named Nabal or Fool. David decides to show him who he is by destroying Nabal and his entire household, but before he can, this test of David's identity, power, and right to the throne takes an interesting turn: the way the story unfolds, David does not kill Nabal (Nabal conveniently drops dead just to hear of David's threat to him); instead, David takes Nabal's wife. The power gain is presumably equivalent. The Fool's wife, Abigail, does acknowledge David and his power and colludes in her own exchange, engaging in a seduction that is entirely political, or should I say, politics is her seduction? "And when the Lord has done to my lord, according to all the good that he has spoken concerning you, and has appointed you prince over Israel, . . . and when the Lord has dealt well with my lord, then remember your handmaid" (1 Sam 25:30–31). David remembers right away and marries her.[11]

Later, when David takes another man's wife, Bathsheba, he does not need her. He is no fugitive, rather, he is at the height of his power, king of all he surveys, including Bathsheba. She is still the property of another man; in fact, two other men have rights to her before David, as the careful inclusion of her patronym (so rare for women in the Bible) "daughter of Eliam" reminds us. Her husband, Uriah the Hittite, is a loyal servant of the king, and moreover, a loyal servant of God—his name probably means "light of Yhwh," and we might well wonder what a Hittite, one of Israel's "others," is doing with such a name—let alone fighting Israel's holy war while King David lolls about at home during "the time when kings go to war." King David's taking of Bathsheba contrasts with the way David garnered power and women as a fugitive. In fact, the roles of Nabal and David have reversed: now, David is the Fool. The king is greedy as Nabal had been, and he denies his neighbor what is rightfully his, as Nabal had denied David provisions from his livestock and hospitality. When Nathan the prophet tells David a didactic parable about the rich man taking the poor man's only ewe-lamb, he drives home the point that the king's adultery is a violation of a property right: Bathsheba is compared to an animal, a favored animal, to be sure, one that is like a daughter (alluding to the Hebrew wordplay on Bathsheba's name, *bath*, "daughter"), and the only one the poor man has; but the polluting of his woman is analogous to the slaughter of his animal. If "the exchange of brides is merely the conclusion to an uninterrupted process of reciprocal gifts [from, say, wine to animals to women], which effects the transition from hostility to alliance, from anxiety to confidence, and from fear to friendship, . . . so the rules governing those exchanges—taboos on adultery and rape, determinations of brideprices and bride labor—are designed to maintain and protect that cooperation" (Lévi-Strauss: 68). But when women are stolen, rather than peaceably exchanged, the relational directions reverse, from friendship toward fear, from alliance toward hostility. In the Bathsheba story, the consequence of stealing another's wife is the murder of a loyal servant of the king; as we have seen, chaos ensues—"you have killed with the sword so the sword will never be far from your house"—and the death of a child born of such infraction is overdetermined. The biblical division of the universe into pure and impure further suggests that we understand adultery as adulteration. I quote Tony Tanner: "*Adulteration* implies pollution, contamination, a 'base admixture,' a wrong combination. . . . If society depends for its existence on certain rules governing what may be combined and what should be kept separate, then adultery, by bringing the wrong things together in the wrong places (or the wrong people in the wrong beds), offers an attack on those rules, revealing them to be arbitrary rather than absolute" (12–13, emphasis his). Adultery not only challenges the *rules* as arbitrary, it challenges the precarious identity of the societies that depend upon them for definition. According to Deuteronomy, the child of the adulterer cannot be admitted into "the Congregation of the Lord, even to the tenth generation" (Deut 23:3), that is, such a child is banned forever from the people of Israel. (The rabbis even relate the Hebrew term for illegitimate child, *mamzēr,* to the adjective, *zār,* "alien," "a stranger" [Levitsky: 6–12].) Vigorous laws on adultery are invoked to police Israel's borders because adultery clearly threatens the identity of Israel.

All of this anxiety about identity, political and sexual definition, has been succinctly summarized in that one biblical word: *nābāl.* It means not only fool, but also outcast, someone who has severed himself from society through a moral transgression, someone who has forfeited his place in society by violating taboos that define the social order. As a verb, it means to violate, and it is used especially to indicate sexual violations: the rape of Tamar, the rape of Dinah, the rape in Judges 19, adultery in Jeremiah 23, but it is also used, significantly, to indicate uttering false words, thereby disrupting the order of language. Its Akkadian stem was used to indicate breaking away (as a stone) or tearing away, and that ancient Akkadian sense of rupture is still attached to the Hebrew word used for an adulterer in ancient Israel, where sexual violation signals breaking away from, or rupturing, the norm. A variant of *nābāl* means corpse, and in ancient Israel, a corpse represents another rupture, this time not only from the social order, but from the order of life itself. Death represented the strongest degree of uncleanness, an "irreparable separation from God's life-giving power and from the center of life, the cult" (Roth: 401). And the outcast is not so very far from the corpse, for as a bearer of evil, the one cast out of society has not only no home, but "no name" (Job 30:8). The book of Job offers a Lear-like description of their pitiful undoing:

> They used to gnaw the roots of desert plants,
> and brambles from abandoned ruins;
> and plucked mallow, and brushwood leaves,
> making their meals off roots of broom.
> Outlawed from the society of men,
> who, as against thieves, raised hue and cry against them,
> they made their dwellings on ravines' steep sides,
> in caves or clefts in the rock.
> You could hear them wailing from the bushes,
> as they huddled together in the thistles.
> Their children are as worthless as they were,
> Nameless people, outcasts of society. (Job 30:3–8)

Who is a *nābāl* and who is not, what makes one cast-out and another not, is of course another way of asking who is an Israelite and who is not, what is Israel and what is not, for the outcasts define Israel's borders. While it is not made an explicit appellation in the Bathsheba episode, the term is most consistently used for an adulterer, and it *is* explicit in the episode that follows David's adultery, where his son Amnon rapes Tamar in an echo of David's forcible taking of Bathsheba. Retrospectively, what Tamar says of her rapist becomes an indictment of David: "this is not a thing men do in Israel." This is not a thing men do in Israel, but David *is* Israel. At his height, when the House of David is synonymous with the nation, David behaves like an outcast. But how can the House of David both define Israel and be cast out of Israel? What happens to the promise of a House that will be stable forever when its recipient is a *nābāl*, like the no-name homeless ones?

The meaning of *nābāl* deepens when we view David's act of adultery with Bathsheba not only in the light of the exchanges that characterize his other marriages, but in the light of the much larger issue of adultery that pervades the biblical text. Israel is continually whoring after other Gods, as the Bible pointedly puts it; the faithfulness or faithlessness of the people toward their God is always cast in sexual terms: "I am a jealous God, you will have none but me." It is a theology obsessed with the possibility and actuality of betrayal, with "going astray" as the term for both faithlessness and sexual transgression. Idolatry is repeatedly figured as sexual infidelity: "So shameless was her [Israel's] whoring that at last she polluted the country; she committed adultery with lumps of stone and pieces of wood" (Jer 3:9). It is in this context that the king of Israel goes astray. Even within the Bathsheba story itself, desire for God and human desire are homologized, for David's adultery is set in stark relief—not, as we would expect, to the fidelity of Bathsheba's husband to her, but to Uriah's faithfulness to God. Under the injunctions of holy war, to sleep with his own wife would be to be faithless to God; it is that fidelity, to his deity, that Uriah maintains despite the obvious attractiveness of his wife, despite his drunkenness, and it is that fidelity to his deity that he finally dies for. Meanwhile, David, so very careful about idolatry, has "gone astray" from God after all. I want to suggest that here the Bible offers us another key to the persistence of sexual metaphors for national identity. When biblical practices are called upon to describe national politics, they pass through a third term: transcendence. David commits adultery, but if David "goes astray" with other women so Israel goes astray when it worships other, foreign gods. Allegiance to Yhwh alone is meant to be constitutive of the nation. This metaphoric complex reaches a fevered pitch in the prophet Hosea, whom God tells to marry a harlot, because Israel has played the harlot with other gods, and to abandon her, as God will abandon Israel: "The Lord said to Hosea, 'Go, take to yourself a wife of harlotry, for the land commits great harlotry by forsaking the Lord'" (Hos 1:2).

In the act of adultery, David has violated a whole series of commandments: "You shall not kill; you shall not commit adultery; you shall not steal; you shall not bear false witness against your neighbor." And just before these laws regulating social order—the commandments about not killing, not having adultery, not taking what is your neighbor's—come the commandments about the exclusivity of desire for God. "You shall have no gods except me." A relation between the final five commands and the earlier ones that specify loyalty and gratitude and exclusivity of love toward God is thereby established. The logic could be paraphrased: you shall love only me, you shall not love your neighbor's God; translated to the social sphere, that means that you shall love only your wife, you shall not covet your neighbor's wife. Hence, in Yhwh's response to David's adultery with Bathsheba, it is not at all clear whom David has betrayed, her husband or God, for the infidelities are inseparable: "A sword will never be lacking in your house, because you treated *me* with contempt and took the wife of Uriah the Hittite to be your own wife" (my emphasis).

Both sexual fidelity and divine fidelity are preoccupations of a narrative that tends to construct identity as someone or some people *set apart,* with boundaries that could be mapped, ownership that could be titled. But if, as I have been arguing, the parameters of Israel's identity are very much at issue—which God is allowed and which is not, and which woman is allowed and which is not—then the identity of the nation and the people is not already mapped, but is in the process of being anxiously drawn and redrawn, and we must address the prior question: Is this people set apart, or is its hankering to "go astray" an effort to cross boundaries, or at least to blur them by being God's and being someone else's too? Which people are outside and which are inside the boundaries of the community of Israel? The biblical narrative's effort to construct Israel's past is no less than an effort to construct Israel, but it is not a construction in the sense of building a building, nor is it a "national spirit" unfolding, an institution growing, or an organic personality flowering. Instead, "Israel" is an inconsistent, fractured, complex, and multiple concept: a people who are bound by a law that they refuse to obey, a people who are defined by their nomadism but who are promised a land to settle and embark upon its conquest, a people who remember (or adopt) a shared history only to forget it constantly, a people who promise fidelity to their God only to go astray; and even these formulations are misleadingly stable, for each presupposes "a people" when defining them is very much a part of the task of this history. If this is a more palatable Bible than the one the heirs of German historicism give us—a Bible that admits that identity is a question not an answer, provisional not reified, and so cannot underwrite nationalism, imperialism, persecutions of the other, or any clear claims about who the other is—it is not an invitation to authorize this friendlier Bible. To seek biblical authority for the insight that history is ruptured and identity provisional is, as I've tried to show, to seek foundations in shifting sand. Adultery, rape, the people going astray: these violations are not just violations of commandments; they are violations of various identity-constructs of "Israel" and they become tests of definition in a text that is anxious about who this story is about, and whose story it is anyway. Perhaps it is the Book of K's, the work of some working-class Hittite androgyne.[12]

NOTES

1. This essay is drawn from my book on identity and the Bible. Early versions were delivered at a conference on theology and postmodernism at King's College, Cambridge University, in 1990, and at a conference on the Bible and Literary Criticism at Georgetown University in 1989. Subsequent versions were given at the Society of Biblical Literature and the University of California at Berkeley. I want to thank the members of those audiences for their helpful responses. An earlier published version appeared as Schwartz 1991.

2. Like any discipline, biblical scholarship is not monolithic. Recent interest in literary questions and the efforts of this journal [*Semeia*] have begun to make headway into the dominant methodology I characterize. For the David narratives, see esp. Gunn, who argues that the so-called succession narrative is not best described as history writing, Polzin, who is explicitly bracketing the concerns that preoccupy traditional biblical scholars (see esp. pp. 1–17), Sternberg, Fokkelman, Miscall, and Jobling.

Furthermore, not all traditional biblical scholars who are interested in sources depict a developmental vision of history for the Samuel narratives. Among the notable exceptions is Whybray, who points out that there are too many personal scenes for this narrative to be characterized as history; instead, he regards it as political propaganda. But his account of political propaganda is a far more coherent ideology than any I could detect, one that rivals those who see a developmental history in its vision of consistency: "Every incident in the story without exception is a necessary link in a chain of narrative which shows how, by the steady elimination of the alternative possibilities, it came about that it was Solomon who succeeded his father on the throne of Israel" (20–21).

3. Boorer's recently published brief survey of the major positions held by biblical scholars in this century shows how consistent their presuppositions are despite their different conclusions, for these theories take different stands on the same issue: the nature and extent of two layers of redacted material in the biblical text and how those two layers came together. (The two layers are the Dtr and the non-Dtr; Dtr means the Deuteronomic and/or Deuteronomistic, the distinction being part of the dispute about the "nature and extent of the sources.")

4. Oden: 6, cf. the whole of chapter 1. I am indebted to Oden's chapter for bringing the role of German historicism in biblical scholarship to the fore.

5. This does not necessarily mean the historian is an empiricist. Events are "only in part accessible to the senses. The rest has to be felt (*empfunden*), inferred (*geschlossen*), or divined (*errathen*)" (Humboldt: 4.35–36).

6. While my focus here is on the influence of German historicism on biblical study, classical philology had an equally formative role.

7. Noth: 80–431. This thesis of Martin Noth was considerably revised by Gerhard von Rad and Frank Cross who noted the positive elements in the Deuteronomistic history that conflicted with this sweeping principle. This critical history is summarized in McCarter: 4–8.

8. Mieke Bal has explored the provocative relation between speech acts, cutting, and violence against women in the book of Judges, esp. the sacrifice of Jephthah's daughter and the dismemberment of the concubine (1988: 129–68). Her critique of biblical scholarship surfaces throughout that study, but see especially pp. 9–39.

9. I hasten to add that this is not a deconstruction of the divine message that could characterize any and all utterance; this is an ideological conflict.

10. Bal 1988. See also the condensed version, 1990.

11. Sexual and political power are so completely fused again in the story of Saul's concubine that it is not quite right to claim that one is a metaphor for the other; they are not distinct enough to stand in for one another. Upon the death of Saul, his general, Abner, sleeps with one of the deceased king's concubines, Rizpah. When the king's son learns of it he is incensed; the act is clearly a sign of pretention to the throne, for the competition over who will succeed Saul—his son or his general—is fought out over sexual ownership of the concubine. The king's general does not like competition from the king's son: "Am I a dog's head? Here I am full of goodwill toward the House of Saul your father, and you find fault with me about a woman!" (2 Sam 3:8). That the degraded object, woman, could be the subject of such irony in the passage only shows how much importance men have vested in her for conferring power. Abner is sufficiently incensed over the contest about "the woman" to vow to betray Saul's son by joining the enemy David in a treaty. Needless to say, his betrayal is cast in the same terms—traffic in women—for the condition David sets to enter into any agreement with Abner ups the ante: David will take, not one of Saul's concubines, but Saul's daughter, Michal, thereby crushing all hopes for succession for both Abner and Saul's son.

12. I refer facetiously to Bloom's thesis that large portions of the Hebrew Bible were written by an aristocratic woman in the court of King Solomon.

REFERENCES

Bal, Mieke
1988   *Death and Dissymmetry: The Politics of Coherence in the Book of Judges.* Chicago: University of Chicago Press.
1990   "Dealing/With/Women." Pp. 16–139 in *The Book and the Text: The Bible and Literary Theory.* Ed. Regina Schwartz. Oxford: Blackwell.

Bloom, Harold
1990   *The Book of J.* New York: Grove-Weidenfeld.

Boorer, Suzanne
1989   "The Importance of a Diachronic Approach: The Case of Genesis-Kings." *CBQ* 51: 195–208.

Droysen, Johann Gustav
1897   *Outline of the Principles of History.* Introd. E. Benjamin Andrews. Boston: Ginn. (Partial translation of *Historik: Vorlesungen über Enzyklopädie und Methodologie der Geschichte;* see the 8th ed. [ed. R. Hubner], Munich: Oldernbourg, 1977.)

Fokkelman, J.P.
1981–   *Narrative Art and Poetry in the Books of Samuel.* 3 vols.
1986   Assen: Van Gorcum.

Foucault, Michel
1977   "Nietzsche, Genealogy, History." Pp. 139–64 in Michel Foucault, *Language, Counter-Memory, Practice: Selected Essays and Interviews.* Ed. D.F. Bouchard. Ithaca, NY: Cornell University Press.

Gros Louis, Kenneth R.R.
1977   "The Difficulty of Ruling Well: King David of Israel." *Semeia* 8:15–33.

Gunn, David
1978   *The Story of King David.* Sheffield: JSOT.

Humboldt, Wilhelm von
1903–1936   *Gesammelte Schriften.* Berlin: Behr.

Iggers, Georg
1983   *The German Conception of History.* Middletown, CN: Wesleyan University Press.

Jobling, David
1986   "Jonathan: A Structural Study in 1 Samuel." Pp. 12–30 in *The Sense of Biblical Narrative: Structural Studies in the Hebrew Bible.* Vol. I. 2nd ed. Sheffield: JSOT.

Lévi-Strauss, Claude
1969   *The Elementary Structures of Kinship.* Boston: Beacon. (Orig. 1949, *Les Structures élémentaires de la parenté.*)

Levitsky, Joseph
1989   "The Illegitimate Child in Jewish Law." *Dor le Dor: The Jewish Biblical Quarterly* 18:6–12.

Lyotard, Jean-François
1984   *The Postmodern Condition: A Report on Knowledge.* Minneapolis: University of Minnesota Press.

McCarter, P. Kyle, Jr.
1984   *II Samuel*. AB 9. Garden City, NY: Doubleday.

Miscall, Peter
1986   *I Samuel: A Literary Reading*. Bloomington: Indiana University Press.

Noth, Martin
1981   *The Deuteronomistic History*. Sheffield: JSOT.

Oden, Robert, Jr.
1987   *The Bible Without Theology*. New York: Harper and Row.

Polzin, Robert
1989   *Samuel and the Deuteronomist*. New York: Harper and Row.

Rosenblatt, Jason and Joseph Sitterson, eds.
1991   *"Not in Heaven": Coherence and Dissymmetry in Biblical Narrative*. Bloomington: Indiana
       University Press.

Roth, W.M.W.
1960   "NBL." *VT* 10:394–409.

Schwartz, Regina
1990   "Joseph's Bones and the Resurrection of the Text." Pp. 40–59 in *The Book and the Text:
       The Bible and Literary Theory*. Ed. Regina Schwartz. Oxford: Blackwell.
1991   "The Histories of David: Biblical Story and Biblical Scholarship." In *"Not In Heaven":
       Literary Readings of Biblical Texts*. Ed. Jason Rosenblatt and Joseph Sitterson. Blooming-
       ton: Indiana University Press.

Sternberg, Meir
1985   *The Poetics of Biblical Narrative*. Bloomington: Indiana University Press.

Tanner, Tony
1979   *Adultery in the Novel*. Baltimore: Johns Hopkins University Press.

Wellhausen, Julius
1957   *Prolegomena to the History of Ancient Israel*. Cleveland: Meridian.

Whybray, R.N.
1968   *The Succession Narrative*. SBT 2nd ser. 9. London: SCM.

Signs of the Flesh
Observations on Characterization in the Bible

ALICE BACH

> *What is character but the determination of*
> *incident? What is incident but the illustra-*
> *tion of character?*
>
> HENRY JAMES, *THE ART OF FICTION*

Every story needs a storyteller. Within the Bible, the importance of recognizing the biblical narrator as a figure telling a slanted story has been undervalued. Robert Alter has described the biblical narrator as "impassive and authoritative" (1989:176). While he acknowledges that ancient narratives may switch momentarily from the narrator's point of view to a character's angle of vision, he is content to describe pre-novelistic narrative as containing "a high degree of uniformity of perspective maintained by an authoritative overviewing narrator" (1989:176). Alter allows no room for an iconoclastic reader like Gayatri Spivak, who describes her task as "to read it and run with it and go somewhere else. To see where in that grid there are the spaces where, in fact, woman oozes away" (145).

I want to suggest a mode of reading in which one imagines the biblical narrator as a storyteller with whom the reader must contend, as s/he does with characters within the story. Instead of being seduced by the narrator's version, I am attracted to a strategy that allows the reader to step outside the reader's appointed place in order to defy the fixed gaze of the male narrator. I realize the difficulty in conferring upon the narrator, or indeed upon characters in the story, more "reality" or verisimilitude than the text itself would offer. I am not suggesting a "true" or historical identity for the narrator, but rather a fictive one based upon his agenda and upon his role as storyteller. If one challenges the notion of the omnipotent voice of the impassive narrator, the female characters will not be in so much danger of oozing away.

In my reading, the narrator shares with the characters a narrative life in the reader's consciousness. A tension is thus set up between the reader's desire to form narrative conclusions concerning characters and the narrator's attempts to control the reader's understanding of characters within the story. By fleshing out the narrator, we flush out his intentions. By refusing to award him the transparency he seeks as omniscient voice of truth, the reader will be aware of the narrator's motives, what he's up to in fashioning his story. Because the redactors have spliced the biblical narrator's voice with that of the author and of God himself, one task of a literary critic who is suspicious of the narrator's identity as the authoritative voice of truth is to separate the role of the narrator as self-interested agent from the narrator as the teller of the tale. To make the narrator visible, and thus his agenda more identifiable to the reader, one needs to regard his version of the story as a self-conscious telling of the tale, intended to convince us that he has provided the true account of what happened.

One way to figure out the narrator is to shift our readerly identity from that of ideal reader, an individual who would believe, understand, and appreciate every word and device of the text, to that of suspicious narratee. In using the term *narratee*, I invoke Gerald Prince's concept of narratee-character as the fictive one addressed by the narrator. The signals that he sends out within the text to the narratee are then read by the reader to smoke him out. Prince argues, I think persuasively, that interpreting the signals sent to this narratee-character, a construct created by the author, allows one to categorize the narration *according to the type of narratee to whom it is addressed* (15). Even if the narratee is not explicitly addressed, as he is not in the majority of biblical narratives, when the narrator lavishes his opinions upon him, the narratee "becomes as clearly defined as any character" (Prince: 18). Thus, constructing a narratee within the biblical text is a technique that may help the biblical critic figure out the narrator's game since the narratee "constitutes a relay between narrator and reader, he helps to establish the narrative framework, and he serves to characterize the narrator" (Prince: 23).

A second strategy of reading characters, connected to the first, is to retrieve or reconstruct characters from the structuralist wasteland in which they are mere actants of the plot. By looking at sights not within the narrator's gaze, for instance, a reader may be able to "see" characters who are not primary agents of the plot. Literary techniques suggested by Seymour Chatman and Baruch Hochman focus the delineation of character within the insight of the reader rather than within the fixed gaze of the narrator. Shifting the gaze from the narrator's eye to the reader's "I" is especially important for feminist readers since the elements of structural analysis applied to character often deflate female biblical characters, who are not usually the focal point of narration.

Sighting the Biblical Narrator

Only recently has biblical criticism moved past the positivistic New Critical arena in which one assumes that there is *one* correct interpretation of story and characters that can be adduced from a *proper* analysis of form. Among the most totalizing of the presuppositions that underlie such a formalist reading of the text is that language has a stabilizing force, that it means what it says and says what it means. The New Critic looks for a balanced order, and not surprisingly, finds one. In contrast, Bakhtin finds limitless textual diversity, although arguably because he is looking for diversity rather than singularity.

Language for Bakhtin at any given moment of its historical existence is heteroglot from top to bottom: "it represents the co-existence of socioideological contradictions between the past and present, between different epochs of the past, between different socioideological groups in the present, between tendencies, schools, circles and so forth, all given a bodily form" (291). As Ilona Pardes's eloquent study suggests, the Bible is just such a text of many tongues.

In a view related to the formalist ignoring of the effect of a reader on the text, many interpreters have continued to ignore the effect of a female reader upon the text. As I shall argue in this paper, too often biblical critics have been ideal readers, allied with the patriarchal narrator, and have not recognized that he was telling it slant. This kind of reader makes the desired audience stance explicit; he is the audience presupposed by the narrative itself. A bumptious narratee, on the other hand, will challenge the privileged role of the narrator and recast him as the fictive henchman of the author.

In traditional biblical interpretation, critics have commonly figured the narrator as omniscient and entwined with the divine voice without questioning his reliability as a narrator. Indeed, the biblical narrator has a privileged position within the text, possessing the ability to move outside time and space. Since there is no textual distinction between the implied author and the public narrator, readers have equated the two voices, while considering themselves part of a universal audience. As Bakhtin has indicated, authorial discourse is "directed toward its own straightforward referential meaning," and authorial narrators possess a stronger voice than that of characters who are contained within the events of the story (187). Clearly, the biblical narrator, not being content merely to tell his tale, has made himself such a significant literary presence.

Meir Sternberg has described the biblical narrator's function with great economy:

> the narrator enjoys free movement in time (among narrative past, present and future) and in space (enabling him to follow secret conversations, shuttle between simultaneous happenings or between heaven and earth). These two establish an unlimited range of information to draw upon or, from the reader's side, a supernatural principle of coherence and intelligibility. (Sternberg: 84)

When the authorial voice is equated with that of the deity, as it is in the biblical narratives, the plot thickens. I am assuming that the narrator is male, like the community (ideal reader) he represents. Harold Bloom has hypothesized a female author for the J material in the Torah. Since I understand the narrator to be a figure in the text, one whose authority is never questioned within the text, and I recognize the control the patriarchal society exerted upon women, I find it hard to imagine a female in antiquity who would be credited with omniscience. I am surprised that Bloom did not use the occasion of his female designation to confront the politics of reading, exploring the convention generally assumed "that the voice of authority is male, albeit a comprehensive male voice in which sexual distinctiveness is to some extent neutralized" (Culler: 205). It seems that Culler has identified a more provocative question concerning the ways in which readers construct the identity of the narrator.[1]

The omniscient biblical narrator has a task of the utmost significance: he is the prophet of prophets. His most privileged job is to relate the word of the Lord, thus proving that the narrator's authority is secondary only to that of the deity, to whom he is scribe. The ultimate evidence of his omniscience is that he is privy to God's "feelings."

His audience believes his explanations, that waters flooded the earth because the Lord repented of making human beings and "it grieved God in his heart" (Gen 6:6), and that Saul lost his kingship because God repented making Saul king (1 Sam 15:11). There is no episode in which the narrator's voice represents or supports a point of view different from that of the Bible's central ideology. In fact, the choice of omniscient narrator strengthens the biblical view of an omnipotent deity and "serves the purpose of staging and glorifying an omniscient God" (Sternberg: 87).[2] Gérard Genette has described this narratorial function as providing the foundation of verisimilitude. When the narrator engages in extra-presentational acts—"judgments, generalizations about the world, directly addressed to the narratee" (Lanser, 1992:16)—he renders the textual events (as well as characters' behaviors) more plausible (Lanser, 1992:17).

Sternberg does not resist the narrator's version, but rather describes how the text functions to preserve the only "correct" account by silencing "alien and erroneous viewpoints (not excluding criticisms of God or appeals to idols)." These voices that are not compatible with the norms of the implied author occur on the surface of the text, or on the level of story, but the narrator discredits these errant discourses, silences them. Sternberg claims that to allow a dissonant voice even a momentary breath of life would make the narrator "a maker rather than a shaper of plot" (128). By viewing the narrator as teller of the tale rather than the creator of the tale, Sternberg fuses the identity of the fictive narrator with the "real" author and thus avoids the morass of untangling sighs and whispers of voices other than the narrator/author. He cannot allow the narrator to become one of several possible narratorial voices directed to the narratee, because that would sever the indivisible authoritative troika: deity, author, narrator. The voice of the narrator is the "voice of the one and indivisible truth" (128).

This statement of Sternberg's furnishes an important clue about his strategy of reading. By privileging or foregrounding rhetorical or structuralist techniques—e.g. persuasion, sound patterns, syntactical structures, narrative or thematic structures, repetitions, and motifs—and thrusting into the background the question of reading, as Sternberg does, one ignores many questions of interpretation.[3] Sternberg sees no ambiguities related to the identity or loyalties of the narrator, and certainly no possibilities of multiple or indeterminate readings engendered by the reader's suspicions of the narrator's version, because Sternberg endorses the ideology of the biblical narratives, seeing the rhetorical conventions as expressions of ideology and, quite properly from his perspective, a unified biblical theology controlling the forms and structures within the text. Sternberg calls this the "ideology of narration" (84–128).[4]

It would seem, as Freud suggested in *Moses and Monotheism*, that the establishment of patriarchal power is linked to the preference for an invisible God. In the biblical text the everywhere present and nowhere visible narrator relates the story of the omnipotent God of the Patriarchs. Freud's argument that the replacement of a matriarchal social order with a patriarchal one is an advance of intellect over "lower psychical activity" raises a question of whether the promotion of the invisible over the visible is not a consequence of the establishment of paternal authority, a consequence of the fact that the paternal relation is invisible. A similar process can be observed in traditional interpretations of biblical texts, whenever the role of the author and narrator are conceived as paternal. When the allegiance of the reader rests with this paternal pair, to whose credit everything in the text accrues, the reader has been unsuitably engaged: in other words, a simple case of literary seduction.

Like Sternberg, Alter is eager to please the father narrator and allows only for an ideal reader, one who believes that the events portrayed are "true." His observation that the role of the narrator helps the biblical authors express God's will to the community reveals his interpretive alliance with the author, projecting a straight line from author to narrator to reader.[5] Put another way, Alter does not leave room for a fictive or implied narratee except for the complicit one who accepts the convention that the omniscient voice serves the pivotal function of reporting "God's assessments and intentions, or even what He says to Himself" (157). One technique for adjusting the tension between narrator and narratee is to posit that the narratee occupies a position similar to that of a fictive character and thus is "immanent to the text" (Leitch: 254). Imagining various types of narratees gives us a glimpse at the cards the narrator is holding. The portrait of the fumbling pharaoh in the account of the plagues in Exodus tells us that the narrator expected an anti-pharaonic attitude in his narratees.

Although the narrator doesn't like to cast his shadow across the biblical narratives, one instance of his performing as a character is to be found in the book of Deuteronomy, when he assumes the persona of Moses preaching directly to the community of Israel. The narratee, therefore, also materializes as the audience listening to Moses on the plains of Moab. Usually, however, the narratee maintains a more elusive presence. Although authors usually try to create the illusion that the gap between the narrator and the reader is narrow, the narrative audience is firmly planted within the elements of the fiction. Thus an irritable or suspicious narratee could question the story told through the narrator's fixed gaze and surreptitiously glance around the fictive landscape to pick up clues about the story ignored by the narrator. In the biblical narrative, irritable voices, like Miriam questioning Moses's power as sole prophet of Israel, are quickly silenced. Their cause must be taken up by an equally suspicious or irritable reader.

One interpretive strategy that can undermine the authority of this fictive narrator, and give us a clue about assumptions the author has made about the reader, is to pose the question, "What sort of reader would I have to pretend to be—what would I have to know and believe—if I wanted to take this work as real?" (Rabinowitz: 96). The answer to that question for critics of the Bible has usually been a "faithful reader." But what of the critic who refuses that role? S/he sets up a tension between author and audience, delineating a gulf between the narrative audience and the authorial audience. To read with suspicion, I construct just such a restive audience, very far from the ideal one projected by biblical critics who imagine only an audience harmonious with the agenda of the implied author.

Of course such a description of a fictive audience presupposes an acceptance on the part of that audience of the text as fiction, making the double-level aesthetic of true/not true possible. For some interpreters of biblical texts, it is not within the scope of their inquiry to imagine a fictive biblical text, an implied reader or audience, and an unreliable narrator. Alter and Sternberg, then, have acknowledged that the biblical author has designed his work rhetorically for a specific hypothetical audience, but neither critic addresses the question of a narrative audience or an implied narrator at variance with the author. In order to peel the ideology of the text away from the story, a necessary task for the feminist critic, the hypothesis of a volatile narrative audience is helpful.[6]

An ideal reader himself, Alter does not question the biblical convention of describing God's intentions with precision. Alter's view of the narrator does, nonetheless, offer a valuable observation in comparing the anonymity of the narrator to the more histori-cally designed "characters" who interpret and mediate God's will to the reader, the bibli-cal prophets. The lack of information about the personal history of the narrator "assumes for the scope of his narrative a godlike comprehensiveness of knowledge that can encom-pass even God Himself" (Alter, 1981:157). I would add to Alter's theory that the more invisible the narrator, the less likely he is to raise the hackles of dissident readers. The more blurred the portrait of the narrator, the easier it is for the reader to "forget" the narrator's alliances. Faithful readers share the narrator's theological code, male readers the gender code, and those whose political stripe matches that of the narrator the politi-cal code. Suspicions arise when the reader does not share the social, political, and gender codes of the narrator. The more codes one does not share with the narrator, the more incongruent the reading (Bal, 1988a:5). Thus, the narrator, like the characters in the text, will come to exist as a figure possessing various attitudes in the consciousness of the reader.

Theorists focusing upon modern literature have been concerned with questions of how the reader "sees" what the narrator describes. A literary convention that acknowl-edges the voice of the narrator as separate from the story being narrated is referred to as framing. Genette attempted to fine-tune the concept of point of view or narratorial voice by distinguishing "focalization," or the consciousness that absorbs a narrative (the reader), from "voice," the discourse that tells the narrative (the narrator).[7] As Bal points out in her counterargument to Genette, to identify narrative point of view one must make a distinction between the vision through which the elements are presented and the identity of the voice that is narrating that vision. To put it succinctly, one must distin-guish between "the one who sees and the one who speaks" (Bal, 1985:101). Bal awards different status to the one who sees and the one who narrates (Bal, 1985:110–114). When the reader's squint reveals something other than what the biblical narrator expresses, the reader can conclude only that the narrator is not omniscient. The story that he tells can thus be read as a version or modified retelling of an autonomous story, rather than the story. Literary readings of this two-tiered model point directly to a narra-torial perspective that is limited, not omniscient. As Bal has demonstrated, the technique of focalization can re-view female biblical characters, while at the same time making the reader conscious of the narrator's role in shaping a version of the autonomous story (Bal, 1988 a & b). As I shall argue below, the narratorial focalization of Bathsheba has been central to traditional interpretations of the encounter between David and her.

Characters Seen

In biblical texts, a crucial ambiguity for the feminist reader revolves around the nar-rator's providing one version of how female characters behave within the situations in which they have been placed and another *imagined* version that might be provided by the female figure—if one could reconstruct her story. A continuing concern of mine has been to find a method for retrieving the female character who may have been flattened or suppressed by the weight of the story that is not hers. A necessary first step is to abandon the Proppian idea that the characters are of no interest in themselves, but rather are agents of the plot, secondary elements necessary to the enactment of the story. In a male-driven plot, the functions of female agents are going to be limited. In the process of constructing character out of the text, the reader reads her own experience into the text, giving expression to what Pardes calls "the counter female voices which attempt to put forth other truths" (4).

One way to shake off the strictures of the structuralists and to identify these counter voices is to propose that character can exist in our consciousness as an element independent of the story in which the character was originally discovered. In reading, as in life, a sequence of events can lend itself to various interpretations depending upon the perspective or context in which the observer places the material. The literary work is more than a detailing of events. In the sphere of the reader's mind, character does not have to be reduced to minimal functions. Hochman, in his persuasive study of the dynamic "existence" of characters, argues that "a work of literature is an entity made up of things not there, a conjuring of absent nonexistent parts" (33). Thus, we do not respond passively to characters as they have been presented within the story, but rather we respond actively to them or even appropriate them (Harvey: 54, 73, 111). When we respond to the narrator in a negative way and reject his codes, we may reject his story. At the same time, one of the characters from that story may live on in the reader's mind. The details of Miriam's outrage at Moses that result in her being isolated from the community for seven days may blur, the reader may reject the alliance between God and prophet that results in punishment of Miriam, but the figure of Miriam, contentious in speech and vulnerable in illness, can live on in the reader's consciousness.

Chatman has observed that the experience of reading often involves the retention of our image of a character, not only apart from events but also long after we have forgotten the events of the story (118–119). The reader will then create a "paradigm of traits." From the collection of gestures, actions, thoughts, including what the narrator and other characters (both reliable and unreliable) report about the character, the reader transforms this paradigm of traits into a character. This process, described by Chatman as one of accretion of such elements as scene, setting, and character within the reader's mind, results in the character taking on an existence independent of the original story. This notion is helpful in moving away from the theory of characterization formulated by Forster and still common among biblical literary critics, which refers to round and flat characters, who derive their dimension and shape from the narrator's version of the story.

Using these strategies, I would like to try to retrieve Bathsheba from the end-of-the-road category of nonperson. Adele Berlin separates the figure of Bathsheba, as an object of adultery in 2 Samuel 11–12, from the active mother Bathsheba attempting to secure the throne for Solomon, her son, in 1 Kings 1–2. While Berlin uses the flattening structuralist term "actant" for the earlier portrait, she uses categories more akin to the paradigm of traits model suggested by Chatman for Bathsheba the Queen Mother, "with feelings and reactions developed beyond the needs of the plot" (Chatman: 30). I intend to collect the shards of Bathsheba's story from the narrator's ongoing tale of David, with the intention of giving Bathsheba a subjectivity apart from her role in the story of David.

The reader first sees Bathsheba when the narrator and David see her—from the monarch's rooftop, bathing. The scene invites the reader to assume the voyeuristic perspective of a spectator squinting at a keyhole. Let us assume for the moment that Bathsheba is unaware of our gaze. Within a few verses we are introduced to this female character through a list of intimate statements about her body. The reader is privileged to observe signs of the flesh through the narrator's gaze: 1. the woman is bathing (v. 2);

2. the woman is beautiful; 3. the woman is having sex with the king. She is identified for us in a traditional way: she is the daughter of Eliam and the wife of Uriah the Hittite. Then we are sent more sexual signals: 4. she has just been purified from her menstrual period and is presumably at the fertile time in her cycle; 5. she has conceived and is pregnant.

Her only direct speech describes her function in the story, "I am pregnant" (2 Sam 11:5; NRSV, here and throughout). The narration does not provide any details of her state of mind. Not even "I am pregnant with your child." We are not told if this turn of events in her life has thrown her into a panic. She is not given the pious extended speech patterns of Abigail, another of David's wives. Nor does she possess the acid tongue of Michal, who has chastised David a few chapters earlier for getting physical in the sight of Israel. By withholding from the reader Bathsheba's reactions to the sexual demands of the king or to her own act of adultery, the narrator has eliminated a direct route of sympathy between the reader and the female character.

Akin to the much-repeated question posed by Sternberg: "What did Uriah know and when did he know it?" at least one female reader has been drawn to reverse the question: What did Bathsheba know and when did she know it? Undoubtedly she was the first to know that she was pregnant by the king. But after she informs David of this messy development, she disappears inside her house. Not until the narrator has reported the incidents surrounding Uriah's death does he bring her out again to be glimpsed by the reader. The spectator will be disappointed if he expects another erotic fantasy. The scene has darkened. The woman is mourning for her husband. Paralleling the first scene, the monarch sends for her, brings the woman to his house, only this time it is a one-way trip. The narrator chooses two phrases that remind us of her function: she becomes his wife, and she bears him a son (2 Sam 11:27). This time there is no ogling of her naked beauty; no more is she the delicious fantasy figure, appearing wordlessly in bed while her husband is out of town. We can not look at her anymore, for she is the king's wife. In her proper role as royal mother, we will meet her again.

The question for me, if not for Sternberg, is how did Bathsheba feel about being brought to live permanently with the man who had seized her without a word? Figuring Bathsheba as an openly constructed character, borrowing Chatman's term, allows the reader the freedom to move beyond the printed page, to view characters as independently memorable (118). Following Chapman's suggestion that the audience reconstructs characters from evidence "either implicit or announced in an original construction," I want to imagine Bathsheba as an open-ended character by treating her "as an autonomous being, not merely as a plot function" (119). Wondering about her story prompts questions. Perhaps in lamenting for her husband, she is lamenting her own helplessness. She had no power to resist the king's sexual demands. Has she connected her carrying of David's child with Uriah's death? Is what the narrator calls mourning for her husband, perhaps lamenting for her own female destiny?

We are never told how Bathsheba feels about David. The story supplies no direct details about Bathsheba's reactions to her suddenly altered status as wife to the king of Israel and Judah. By comparing her story with that of the other narratively important wives of David, Michal and Abigail, we can excavate embedded signals that add to the laconically narrated portrait of Bathsheba.

While David sees Bathsheba first,[8] Michal is the one who gazes at David. The power of the male gaze shows us what is lacking in Michal's gaze. Men's desire naturally carries power with it. David's gaze carries the force of action and of possession, both lacking in the female gaze. The first item of information the narrator tells us about Michal is that she loved David (1 Sam 18:20). Her strong love causes her to rescue her outlaw husband from the deadly intentions of her father the king. But her gaze is not powerful enough to possess him sexually. The only time the reader catches David in bed with Michal, it is a stone image, an idol (1 Sam 19:16), not David in the flesh. The real David has escaped Michal and her bed. Michal does not possess the object of her gaze; David does. Before they have exchanged a word, David has pulled Bathsheba into his bed. Their exchange is sexual, not verbal.

In contrast, there are *no* signs of flesh in the connection between David and Michal when she helps him elude Saul. No terms of endearment are exchanged; Michal could have been a loyal ally or soldier in her only direct speech to David, "If you do not save your life tonight, tomorrow you will be killed" (1 Sam 19:11). Even in this critical moment in which she chooses her husband over her father, there is no sign of intimacy between Michal and David. Even though she has owned the gaze of beloved, she could not dominate him.

Michal reappears in David's story after David has become king. The narrator reports that the king has taken "more concubines and wives, more sons and daughters were born to David" (2 Sam 5:13–16). The narrator gives a sharp signal of David's sexuality through his report of the names of eleven children who were born to the king in Jerusalem. None of them are children of Michal; her bed and her womb have remained empty. She is absent from the story until she catches sight of her husband "leaping and dancing before the Ark" (2 Sam 6:16). She is at the window, separated from the sexual heat of her husband. She can merely observe her husband leaping and dancilg, verb forms that evoke David's sexuality. The reader observeq Michal framed, enclosed, at the window observing David in a moment of physical abandon. Once again she is distanced from the flesh. From the window she cannot touch him or participate in the joyous frenzy. She is above it all. As her speech reminds us, David is a king without clothes, "*uncovering* himself today before the eyes of his servants' maids, as any vulgar fellow might shamelessly *uncover* himself" (2 Sam 6:20). Michal is a trenchant observer, but no longer one with a gaze of desire. Her no longer beloved David has been uncovering himself before concubines and wives for quite some time, as the report of the eleven named and other unnamed offspring confirms. She has observed the sign of his flesh, but she has not been a player.

In his rejoinder to the wife in the window, David makes clear that God has chosen him above the house of Saul, something Michal knows only too well. And he assures her that he will be even more contemptible in future days, which foreshadows his rapacious activity with Bathsheba a few chapters later. But just as David can risk leaping before the sacred altar of God, so he can leap with another man's wife and survive God's displeasure. Indeed he will even survive my readerly displeasure.

The narrator remarks tersely at the close of the narration called by Kyle McCarter "The Bathsheba Affair": "The thing that David had done displeased the Lord" (2 Sam 11:27b). Once again by reporting divine displeasure, the narrator reminds the reader of his privileged position, adding a frame of verisimilitude to his story. A narrator who knows the mind of God certainly must have got his story straight. The tantalizing ambiguity of the thing that David did, the sin he committed, remains to tease the reader. Is it his murder of Uriah? His taking of another man's dearest possession? Is there a chance that the sin (for both narrator and God) is that of seizing Bathsheba, first temporarily, then permanently? The answer to this questiol gives a clue about the loyalties of the reader. Sternberg refers several times to "Bathsheba's infidelity," ironically permitting her a moment of subjectivity that is also a characterization of blame. Sternberg reads the bedding of Bathsheba in another place as "the love affair between David and Bathsheba" (202). Whether this phrase is a courtly euphemism or blind sentimentality, the suggestion of rape as the sin David has committed would unquestionably make this reader uncomfortable. It even makes me uncomfortable. Suggesting such a violent filling of the gaps has been instructive. It has shown me that the analysis of a male fantasy of sexual primacy does not result in a reinvented text of female potency. No wonder Bathsheba grieves.

Bathsheba Heard

During her first scene in the so-called court history, Bathsheba is not a player. By the time her son Solomon has become an adult contender for the throne, however, she is ready. No longer the nubile bather, seen but not heard, she returns, empowered by what? Years of life at court? A slightly curdled mother's milk? Like Rebekah she angles for the prize for her son, unlike Rebekah she does not have to scheme alone. Nathan, the prophet who guided David, helps Bathsheba achieve the monarchy for Solomon.

The narrator picks up his tale with some information that evokes the earlier story of David and Bathsheba. David is cold and needs someone to warm his (c)old body. This time the narrator does not invite the reader to peep at the young woman. Abishag the Shunammite is brought to the king. He himself does not choose her or send for her. Like Bathsheba she is described as very beautiful. Abishag, however, is not the object of David's gaze or ours. She will attend David's body as nurse, not as lover. Abishag performs a traditional, and safe, feminine role, while the young Bathsheba, the object of male desire, had been a potential threat. In the narrator's tale of Abishag being brought to David, there is no hint of the eager sexual energy ignited when David saw Bathsheba. David's erotic energy typified by his seizure of Bathsheba in the early years of his reign has vanished. The king now requires a woman in his bed, explicitly not as a sexual companion. Might the omnipotent narrator be sneering at the king's lost potency?

Shooting Bathsheba

In conclusion I'd like to rerun the tale of David and Bathsheba one final time, casting the narrator as filmmaker. The most direct signal that the narrator is engaged in the eroticization of woman can be seen by the way he controls and limits what we see. The narrator performs the function of a camera, slowing panning over the female body. The first frame reveals the length of her entire naked body at her bath, and then a tight shot directs our gaze to a more intimate record, as the narrator discusses the woman's fertility cycle. She is primed to become pregnant. The narrator's report that David lies with her seems redundant. The taking of the woman is his erotic fantasy.

The woman's identity is not important. Learning that she is the wife of Uriah does not alter David's desire. The narrator shows his hand in these first few frames by emphasizing male ownership of the woman's body's fertility and its interiority; at the same time he shows her vulnerability since her body is not inviolable. The scene has been constructed for a male spectator. The woman has been completely objectified. The male figure commands the scene; he articulates the look and creates the action.

Signs of male domination remind us that the film story has been constructed by men for male spectators. While female spectators may be part of the audience, as Kaplan argues in *Women and Film,* they must either identify with the woman as object or they must appropriate the male gaze. When Bathsheba announces that she has conceived, David does not respond to her, but sends for Joab, his trusted intermediary, and Uriah, the man he has wronged. In a narration that reveals nothing of the woman's response to the king, her silence reinforces the power relationship between the king and a woman brought to his bed. A male viewer might well share the narrator's voyeuristic pleasure in this scene, picturing the woman as enigma, as other, viewed as outside of male language in which deals are cut.

To cut the deal for Solomon to become David's successor, Bathsheba needs words. No longer the eroticized object of male sexual desire, she now plays the game like the loquacious Abigail, who convinced David to change his plans with honeyed words. Bathsheba in her plea to the king sounds much like Abigail, docile, compliant. The sexual Bathsheba has been replaced by a safer queen. Speaking in the familiar cadences of a deferential wife, she is no longer dangerous. Like Michal who saved David from Saul, Abigail who saved him from bloodguilt, Bathsheba now plays an acceptable social role. She saves David from appointing the wrong son king.

But let us consider this final scene as a cinematic midrash employing elements of the earlier films/readings. Remember Bathsheba, the nubile young woman, rosy in her bath? Now she is seen as clothed, driving, ambitious, just like the men surrounding her. The camera eye records Nathan writing Bathsheba's dialogue with the king, signaling that her ambition is not to be feared. As she delivers Nathan's speech, the audience is assured that Bathsheba is supported by the divine prophet. Bathsheba goes to David, who is seen being tended by Abishag, an asexual object. "What do you desire?" asks the king, an ironic twist evoking and recalling his sexual desire that is now dead. Bathsheba is all business, reminding the king that he had promised to make Solomon his heir. Like Abigail before her, Bathsheba uses a verbal strategy of flattery and humility to get David to change his mind at a crucial moment in Israel's history. Like Abigail, Bathsheba is the subject of this scene, reminding the failing king that it is within his power to alter the events of state and halt the power grab of Adonijah. "But you, my lord the king— the eyes of all Israel are on you to tell them who shall sit on the throne of my lord the king after him" (1 Kgs 1:20).

Another ironic signal in this scene of reversals. If all eyes had been upon Bathsheba bathing in the earlier scene, now all eyes are upon David faltering on the throne.

To give the necessary authority to the woman's request, Nathan backs up Bathsheba's story, another reversal from an earlier scene: the angry Nathan who had prophesied the death of the nameless infant son, the sexual connection between David and Bathsheba (2 Sam 12:1–15), now speaks out in favor of Solomon, the second son of the pair. David then recalls a vow made in an earlier scene:

As the Lord lives, who has saved my life from every adversity, as I swore to you by the Lord, the God of Israel, "Your son Solomon shall succeed me as king, and he shall sit on my throne in my place," so will I do this day. (1 Kgs 1:29–30)

But had he made such a vow to Bathsheba? Nathan's mention of the vow to Bathsheba (v. 13) is ambiguous. Is this a strategy to convince the muddled monarch that such a vow had been made? There is no textual mention of such a vow. One would also assume that if Bathsheba had been given assurance of her son's ascendancy to the throne, she would not have needed Nathan to encourage her to remind the king of his promise. While the origin of the promise from David to Bathsheba concerning Solomon is draped in obscurity, what is clear is that Bathsheba has been vindicated in the best tradition of patriarchal culture. She has become the triumphant mother, whose son triumphs over the sons of David's other wives. Finally Bathsheba is seen as the mother working to achieve for her son what God intends for him to have. Thus, she has been transformed from sexual object to Queen Mother. Finally, Bathsheba has been cast in the familiar role of good mother, working to protect and extend the tradition. In this final scene she is heard and not seen.

Conclusion

Although authors usually try to create the illusion that the gap between the narrator and the reader is narrow, the narrative audience is firmly planted within the elements of this fiction. We have followed the narrator's gaze, blinked when he blinked, turned a blind eye when he wanted acts concealed. I hope I have suggested possibilities for eye-opening readings in which an irritable or suspicious narratee can question the story told through the narrator's fixed gaze and can surreptitiously glance around the fictive landscape to pick up clues about the story that didn't tempt the narrator. In the instance of Bathsheba we can refuse to stand watch with the narrator and David on the rooftop. As feminist readers we can read it, avert our gaze, and go somewhere else. When faced with an authoritative overviewing narrator, we can cast a cold eye.

NOTES

1. Lanser, expanding upon her observation that narrators as people all have gender, argues that in authored texts the reader assumes that the "presence of a female name on the title page signals female narrative voice in the absence of markings to the contrary" (Lanser, 1981:166). While Lanser has offered an observation that critics have overlooked in plotting the conventions of reading, she is dealing with authored texts. Further work needs to be done on the assumptions made about narratorial identity in anonymous and multiauthored texts.

2. Sternberg points to an important difference between the compositional nature of Homeric or Near Eastern texts and biblical composition that reflects a crucial difference in their epistemology and theology. In the Bible, according to Sternberg, the regulating principle is "the interplay between the truth and the whole truth" (89).

3. For a thorough examination of the elements of essential conflict in viewpoint between reader-response critics and structural critics, see Suleiman: 3–5.

4. To smooth out the wrinkles in quirky characters, who sometimes do not reflect the divine message, Sternberg eliminates incongruities by arguing that the recipient of the divine point of view is the narrator and not the other characters (85–87).

5. Alter is certainly not alone in combining the narrative and authorial audiences. Even so august a charter of readers' maps as Iser does not acknowledge a duality in the reader until the final chapter of *The Implied Reader*. Prince's distinction between real readers, virtual readers, ideal readers, and narratees leads to a more subtle analysis of readerly roles. See Gibson: 265–269 for an early acknowledgment of the problem of the identities of the reader.

6. This hypothesis would be a parallel to the hypothesis of a female reader reading male-authored texts suggested by Elaine Showalter in her pivotal article, "Feminist Criticism in the Wilderness." Showalter contends that the *hypothesis* of a female reader changes our understanding or vision of a text. In other words, shifting the gaze of the reader/viewer creates another story.

7. See Genette, especially chapters related to *mode* and *voix*.

8. In a private conversation, Professor Jack Sasson suggested to me that Bathsheba may have engineered the initial meeting with David, since she was bathing in the evening, a time marked by a distinct chill in the Jerusalem air. I tried to construct a reading in which a sly Bathsheba had noticed the monarch pacing his rooftop in the early evening and decided to make herself the object of his gaze. Neither surprised nor rendered helpless by David's rapacious actions, in this reading Bathsheba is actually the puppeteer pulling David's strings. Such a reading would support the idea that the pregnancy was a plot twist intended by Bathsheba, who schemed to become the mother of the future king. My continued resistance to such a reading has further underscored to me the strength of Chatman's argument, that the reader formulates hypotheses about characters based upon the reader's own gaze (116–26). Thus, Sasson's speculations and my own reflect the suggestion that there is a literary process in which character is openly constructed, a process that combines the investment of emotion and interest on the part of the reader with the poetics of character.

REFERENCES

Alter, Robert
1981   *The Art of Biblical Narrative*. New York: Basic.
1989   *The Pleasures of Reading*. New York: Simon & Schuster.

Bach, Alice
1990   "The Pleasures of Her Text." Pp. 25–44 in *The Pleasures of Her Text*. Ed. Alice Bach. Philadelphia: Trinity Press International.

Bakhtin, Mikhail
1984   *Problems of Doestoevsky's Poetics*. Ed. and trans. Caryl Emerson. Minneapolis: University of Minnesota Press.

Bal, Mieke
1985   *Narratology: Introduction to the Theory of Narrative*. Toronto: University of Toronto Press.
1988a   *Murder and Difference: Gender, Genre, and Scholarship on Sisera's Death*. Trans. Matthew Gumpert. Bloomington: Indiana University Press.
1988b   *Death and Dissymmetry: The Politics of Coherence in the Book of Judges*. Chicago: University of Chicago Press.
1991   *Reading "Rembrandt": Beyond the Word-Image Opposition*. Cambridge: Cambridge University Press.

Berlin, Adele
1983   *Poetics and Interpretation of Biblical Narrative*. Sheffield: Almond.

Bloom, Harold
1990   *The Book of J*. Trans. from Hebrew by David Rosenberg. Interpreted by Harold Bloom. New York: Grove & Weidenfeld.

Chatman, Seymour
1978   *Story and Discourse.* Ithaca: Cornell University Press.

Cixous, Hélène
1974   "The Character of Character." *New Literary History* 5:384–400.

Cohn, Dorrit
1978   *Transparent Minds.* Princeton: Princeton University Press.

Culler, Jonathan
1988   *Framing the Sign: Criticism and Its Institutions.* Norman: University of Oklahoma Press.

Forster, E.M.
1927   *Aspects of the Novel.* New York: Harcourt, Brace.

Freud, Sigmund
1939   *Moses and Monotheism.* Trans. James Strachey. London: Hogarth.

Genette, Gérard
1972   *Figures III.* Paris: Editions du Seuil.

Gibson, Walker
1950   "Authors, Speakers, Readers, and Mock Readers." *College English* 11 (Feb):265–69.

Harvey, W. John
1965   *Character and the Novel.* Ithaca: Cornell University Press.

Hochman, Baruch
1985   *Character in Literature.* Ithaca: Cornell University Press.

Iser, Wolfgang
1974   *The Implied Reader.* Baltimore: Johns Hopkins University Press.

Kaplan, E. Ann
1983   *Women and Film.* New York: Routledge, Chapman, and Hall.

Lanser, Susan Sniader
1981   *The Narrative Act: Points of View in Prose Fiction.* Ithaca: Cornell University Press.
1992   *Fiction of Authority: Women Writers and Narrative Voice.* Ithaca: Cornell University Press.

Leitch, Vincent
1988   *American Literary Criticism from the Thirties to the Eighties.* New York: Columbia University Press.

McCarter, Kyle
1980   *I Samuel. A new translation with introduction, notes and commentary.* AB. Garden City: Doubleday.

Pardes, Ilana
1992   *Countertraditions in the Bible: A Feminist Approach.* Cambridge: Harvard University Press.

Prince, Gerald
1980   "Introduction to the Study of the Narratee." Pp. 7–25 in *Reader-Response Criticism.* Ed. Jane Tompkins. Baltimore: Johns Hopkins University Press.

Rabinowitz, Peter
1987   *Before Reading: Narrative Conventions and the Politics of Interpretation.* Ithaca: Cornell University Press.

Showalter, Elaine
1985   "Feminist Criticism in the Wilderness." Pp. 243–270 in *The New Criticism: Essays on Women, Literature, and Theory.* New York: Pantheon.

Spivak, Gayatri Chakravorty, with Elaine Rooney
1989   "In a Word, *Interview." differences* 2:124–56.

Sternberg, Meir
1985   *The Poetics of Biblical Narrative.* Bloomington: Indiana University Press.

Suleiman, Susan R., ed.
1980   *The Reader in the Text: Essays on Audience and Interpretation.* Princeton: Princeton University Press.

Sacrifice and Salvation
Otherness and Domestication in the Book of Judith[1]

AMY-JILL LEVINE

Exegetical studies of the text of Judith have tried to keep pace with its peripatetic heroine. At first, like Judith on her roof, they were located in the relatively rarified atmosphere of historical investigation. Then, just as Judith summoned the Bethulian leaders, so convincing works have called upon predominant forms of literary analysis. And, like Judith trodding that dangerous path to the foreign camp, recent examinations have made forays into the alien territories of feminism, psychoanalysis, and folklore studies. Regardless of the approach, however, Judith the character is usually identified as a representation of or as a metaphor for the community of faith. Although her name, widowhood, chastity, beauty, and righteousness suggest the traditional representation of Israel, the text's association of these traits with an independent woman and with sexuality subverts the metaphoric connection between character and androcentrically determined community. This paper explores how Judith the Jew/ess (*Ioudith*) both sustains and threatens corporate determination as well as how that threat is averted through her reinscription into Israelite society.

All women are other, as de Beauvoir declares: woman "is defined and differentiated with reference to man and not he with reference to her . . . He is the Subject, he is the Absolute—she is the Other."[2] But this generic otherness itself neither problematizes Judith's potential to represent Israel nor threatens Israelite society. The community is traditionally represented by female figures ranging from the virgin (2 Kgs 19:21; Isa 37:22; Lam 1:15; 2:13; Jer 14:17) to the bride (Jer 2:2–3; Hos 2:15b) to the whore (Hosea 1–4; Ezekiel 16) to the widow (Lam 1:1; Isa 54:4–8). Rather, Judith's being a woman who nonetheless speaks and acts in the world of Israelite patriarchy creates the crisis. At the beginning of the book, when she is apart, ascetic, and asocial, Judith is merely a curiosity with metaphoric potential. Present in the public sphere, sexually active, and socially involved, she endangers hierarchical oppositions of gender, race, and class, muddles conventional gender characteristics and dismantles their claims to universality, and so threatens the status quo.[3] Judith relativizes the normative cultural constructions of the community. Her ultimate return to the private sphere and consequent reinscription into androcentric Israel both alleviate the crisis precipitated by her actions and discourse and reinforce the norms they reveal. Yet because her return is incomplete, the threat of the other remains.

Judith appears at first to be a classic metaphor both for the nation and for all women. Not only does her name mean "the Jewess," but also she "is a widow, for the Jewish nation is living at the time of grave danger and affliction, like a forlorn widow."[4] Judith is the text's only named woman character and thus the only woman recognized by its male-defined world.[5] Further, because her name is a generic, its applicability can easily be extended beyond the individual. The women of Bethulia are all like Judith in that each is a "Jewess." Through her name, Judith is associated with gentile women as well. Judith the daughter of Merari evokes and rehabilitates Judith the daughter of Beeri, the Hittite wife of Esau who "made life bitter for Isaac and Rebecca" (Gen 26:35).[6] But this metaphoric identification of Judith with the Jewish community as well as beyond to gentile women breaks down. Judith the woman can only incompletely represent Israel. The community is historically active; women per se are not. Judith is thus both part of and apart from her people.

Metaphoric connections between the heroine and the community extend beyond Judith's name to gender-determined categories. Yet gender alone does not define their common characteristic. Israel's traditional representations as virgin, continent bride, adulterous whore, and celibate widow also share a sexual thematic. Faithful Israel is sexually controlled; her faithless antitype is sexually loose. Consequently, the chaste widow Judith—like the virgin Dinah (Jdt 9:9–10)—represents the holy community. Yet the connection between widow and virgin is severed as Judith's rhetoric unties the lines identifying her with both Israel and other women. The initial prayer in chap. 9 identifies the rape-victim Dinah by a generic term; she is called simply a "virgin" (. . . *parthenou*, 9:2). But unlike "Judith," this generic does not function as a proper name. Dinah has been robbed of her personhood. Further, Judith equates Dinah's rape with the siege of Bethulia, and the association is reinforced by the resonance between the name of the town and the Hebrew for "virgin," *btwlh*.[7] Judith, however, assumes the man's role of protector-avenger associated with her ancestor (cf. 9:2, . . . *tou patros mou symeon*). Indeed, like Simeon she expresses no sympathy for the Shechemite women.[8] That the deity "gave their wives for a prey and their daughters to captivity" (9:4) Judith interprets as a sign of divine justice. Mention of these victims occurs in the context of social egalitarianism—the deity "strikes slaves as well as princes" (9:3) and is called the "god of the lowly, helper of the oppressed, upholder of the weak, protector of the forlorn, savior of those without hope" (9:11)—but Judith herself does not recognize gentiles as in need of protection. Were Judith fully to embody Israel, then the traditional representation of the deity as the (male) savior of the female-figured community would be challenged. Were all women to be like Judith, not only Holofernes would lose his head. Were Judith to represent gentile women, then the paradigmatic identification of Israel as chosen from among the nations would be compromised. Such separation of Judith from corporate Israel, from Jewish women, and from gentiles preserves the text's patriarchal ethos.

While Judith's widowhood conforms to the traditional representation of Israel as a woman in mourning and while both she and Bethulia are draped in sackcloth, Judith's particular representation—her status, rhetoric, wealth, beauty, and even her genealogy—aborts the metaphor.[9] This widow is hardly the forlorn female in need of male protection. Given the negative associations of her husband's name, Manasseh, his absence is almost welcome; he shares the name of the king held responsible for the Babylonian exile (2 Kgs 21:12–15; 23:26–27; 24:3–4). Moreover, the circumstances of his death, heatstroke while watching the binding of barley sheaves, graphically anticipate the decapitation of Holofernes. The phallic imagery of the bound sheaves prefigures the general's dismembered head; both symbolize castration.[10] The psychosexual suggestiveness of this imagery is complemented by barley meal's ritual function; it is the offering required of a man who suspects his wife of infidelity even "though she has not defiled herself" (Num 5:15). Linguistic parallels make the ties between Manasseh and Holofernes even more pronounced. While the general is decapitated by Judith, Manasseh is cut down when the burning fever attacks his head (*kai ho kausōn ēlthen epi tēn kephalēn autou*). Each man takes to his bed (*kai epesen epi tēn klinēn autou* [8:3] *kai Olophernēs propeptōkōs epi tēn klinēn autou* [13:2]), and each dies. Manasseh's absence is necessitated by the demands of Israelite patriarchy: Judith's actions would have subjected him, had he been alive, to sexual disgrace.[11] Only Holofernes realizes the danger of humiliation: "It will be a disgrace if we let such a woman go without enjoying her company, for if we do not embrace her she will laugh at us" (Jdt 12:12). By her sexually charged presence, the widow Judith therefore threatens the masculine ethos of the Assyrian army.

The specified length of Judith's mourning has been claimed "to heighten the picture of her loyalty and devotion" to her dead husband,[12] but the reference to "three years and four months" or forty months (8:4) is overdetermined. The length of her mourning and the meaning of her widowhood extend beyond concern for the absent spouse. First, the period recapitulates the forty years Israel spent in the wilderness. From the time of the Passover/the barley harvest, Judith undergoes a period of testing and purification. But this analogy does not require her to mourn for Manasseh any more than the generation in the wilderness needed to mourn for Egypt. Second, the three years and four months structurally parallel the thirty-four days of the siege (7:20). Third, the detailed description of Judith's mourning stresses her otherness. Upon her husband's death, Judith removed herself from Bethulian society and specifically, from men.

Judith had to be a widow—that is, sexually experienced but unattached—in order for her to carry out her plan. And she had to stay a widow. Upon completing the festivities in Jerusalem, she "went to Bethulia, and remained on her estate . . . Many desired to marry her, but she remained a widow" (16:21–22). Remarriage for levirate purposes would create a new lineage and consequently challenge the power structure of Bethulian society. Further, as a widow safely returned to her proper place, the private sphere, Judith preserves her identification with Israel: no longer active, she no longer subverts the metaphor. A utilitarian reading would even claim that Judith remains a widow both because she had nothing to gain by marriage and because no man was worthy of her. Only the text's females act in a fully efficacious manner;[13] only Judith displays well-directed initiative; only her maid competently follows instructions. The men are weak, stupid, or impaired: Manasseh dies ignominiously; Holofernes is inept; Bagoas is a eunuch; Achior faints at the sight of Holofernes's head. Uzziah, who shares Judith's ethnicity and elevated social status and who, because he is descended from Simeon, might even be able to claim levirate privileges, is the biggest disappointment. Judith must correct his naive theology, and she stands firm while he wavers in his faith (cf. 7:30–31).[14] The only fit male companion for Judith is the deity, and it is with him she communes in prayer on her roof. Yet given the lack of his direct presence in the text, this relationship is a bit one-sided. Indeed, Coote has argued that Judith "represents a kind of reversal of the type of rescue pattern underlying the exodus story, in which a male hero (the Lord) rescues a female figure (Israel) from captivity."[15] Rather than conform to the traditional image of widow, Judith's representation follows both divine and male paradigms.

Like her name, gender, and widowhood, Judith's genealogy betrays her metaphoric function. This list is not an invention designed to mock the elaborate pedigrees fabricated by post-exilic aristocrats (so Bruns), nor is its purpose primarily to indicate Judith's Samaritan origins (so Steinmann).[16] On the one hand, the genealogy anchors Judith to Israelite history. The reference in 8:1 to "Israel" reinforces the symbolic value of Judith's own name. Further, as the connection to Israel (=Jacob) signals Judith's talents for deception and for crossing boundaries, so names like Gideon, Elijah, Nathaneal, Joseph, and Merari portend her abilities to function in such roles as judge, prophet, ambassador, and priest. She supersedes her genealogy and so her generation's representative of "Israel." On the other hand, because neither the Israel of 8:1 nor any of the others listed in her family tree has made his mark in history—they, unlike Judith, have not lived up to their names—the inscription of each in history is due entirely to her. She is the one who also reinscribes the branch of her family that had been written out (Jdt 9:2; cf. Gen 49:7 as well as the silence in Jdt 8:1–2): the line of Simeon. Thus while Judith's genealogy situates her within the historical community and makes her its representative, it is Judith herself who confers value, meaning, and legitimacy to those whom she represents. The relationship between the representation (i.e., Judith) and the represented (i.e., her historical community) which undergirds any metaphoric identification is consequently rendered problematic.

In terms of her relationship to the present generation of Bethulians, Judith is marked as other by her wealth, beauty, and religiosity. Rich, gorgeous, pious, as well as independent, Judith is particularly distinguished from others of her sex. The women in Bethulia are weak from thirst, robbed of their voice by their husbands (cf. 4:12), and controlled by the town leaders (7:32b). Even Judith's maid lacks her freedom. These distinctions are first established through a geographical notice with attendant value hierarchies. Judith is defined spatially as superior to the rest of Bethulia: the "women and young men" are associated first with the "streets of the city and . . . the passages through the gate" (7:22); she is on her roof (8:5). They are unsheltered and in need of protection; she is in a tent and is, additionally, either unaware of or unconcerned with the danger below: she distributes neither her wealth nor her water. Instead, her wealth allows her to enhance her beauty and so further distinguish herself: she has water for bathing while the people are fainting from thirst (7:22). The text then dwells on the material goods available for her adornment: "She bathed her body with water and anointed herself with precious ointment . . . and put on a tiara, and arrayed herself in her gayest apparel . . . and put on her anklets and bracelets and rings and her earrings and all her ornaments . . ." (10:3b–4). Originally she was "beautiful in appearance, and had a very lovely face" (8:7); now she rivals Helen of Troy. Chabris and Charmis notice "how her face was altered" (10:7), and to the men in the Assyrian camp she was "marvelously beautiful" (10:14). Even Judith herself acknowledges the striking "beauty of her counte-nance" (16:7). The enemy soldiers "marveled at her beauty, and admired the Israelites, judging them by her . . ." (10:19). Although they mistakenly perceive Judith as repre-senting her contemporaries—only Judith possesses such striking beauty—the soldiers' judgment supports Judith's identification as a traditional metaphor of Israel.

Judith's piety also supports her metaphoric identification with Israel even as it sev-ers her connection to the Bethulian population (8:5–6, 28–29, 31; 9:1–14; 10:2, 8; etc.). No fanatical ascetic, the truly observant widow demonstrates her faith both by fast-ing and by eating at appropriate occasions (a trait that will serve her well in Holofernes's camp). This religiosity is distinguished from the bad theology and related practices of the Bethulian leaders. The men return to their posts (8:36), but Judith engages in devo-tional activities "at the very time when that evening's incense was being offered in the house of God in Jerusalem" (9:1). As a woman, she is technically marginal to the opera-tion of the official cult. But on her roof, she can participate in devotions without endan-gering the status quo. Close to the deity in spirit and in physical location, she is removed from the people both religiously and spatially. The summary verse of her introduction (8:7–8) confirms her various unique attributes and retains the emphasis on her piety. While her beauty plus the "gold and silver, and men and women slaves, and cattle, and fields" left to her by her husband would be sufficient to distinguish her from other Bethulains: "no one spoke ill of her because (*hoti*) she feared God exceedingly" (8:8).

When the woman of whom the community spoke chooses herself to speak to them, she unleashes otherness into the public sphere. By sending her *female* slave out of the female-defined household into the male-dominated public sphere, Judith weakens the gender divisions defining Israelite society; by conveying Judith's summons to the town leaders, the female *slave* inverts social hierarchies. These inversions continue throughout Judith's contact with men in positions of power. By accepting Judith's theological pro-gram, the Bethulian leaders both reinforce her metaphoric potential to represent the faithful community and acknowledge her potentially subversive voice. When they endeavor to redirect her discourse toward piety (8:31), she makes public her intent to act; they are reduced to accepting her words (8:33–34; 10:9). And those words subvert the metaphoric understanding of language in the public sphere—the sharing of a com-mon code—just as her actions subvert her metaphoric identification with Israel. For example, Judith promises "to be a thing which will go down through all generations of our descendants" (8:32), but her "thing" (*pragma*) is a sign lacking any definitive refer-ent. In the Assyrian camp, Judith continues to transgress linguistic expectations. Her use of *double entendres* (e.g., the double referents to "lord" [*kyrios*] 11:5, 6, 11; 12:14) fur-thers her subversive intent.

Exploitation of conventional expectations is indicated by more than Judith's rhet-oric. According to Alan Dundes, when Judith removes "the garments of widowhood and mourning (10:3) to wear attractive alluring garb [she] appears to move metaphorically from death to life."[17] Yet this is one more metaphor Judith undercuts, for the "life" into which she moves is of a very peculiar sort. The private widow becomes a public woman; she undergoes a total inversion from ascetic chastity to (the guilt of) lavish promiscuity. Nor does she simply enter the life of the community either through association with her neighbors or through levirate marriage; rather, she leaves town. Finally, she moves not directly from death to life but rather from death of one sort, that of the widow separated from her besieged and dying society, to death of another, that of the assassin active among a doomed population. The Assyrian camp is a realm of the dead: characterized by killing and populated by the castrated Bagoas, the beguiled, the besotted, and the beheaded. That Holofernes's "god" is the "historically dead" Nebuchadnezzar and that the army represents the "historically conquered" Assyrian empire further denies the gentiles any association with life. Only when Judith returns to her people and celebrates with them in Jerusalem does she both create and enter the realm of life. But at that moment, tainted by death as well as confirmed as a dangerous other active in the public sphere, she threatens the structure of the very life she engenders and upholds.

Upon her return, the seeds of Judith's threat begin to flower in Israel. By her actions and by her presence, she offers those previously marginal to or excluded from the power base—Jewish women, Achior the gentile, the maidservant—roles in society and cult. The conditions under which gender-determined, ethnic, and class-based integration occur, however, differ according to the text's treatment of women, proselytes, and slaves. Before Judith entered the Israelite public sphere, the Jewish women were separated from their husbands and from the place of action by their leaders' command (7:32). In 15:12–13, "all the women of Israel" (*pasa gynē Israēl*) gather to see her and bless her; some even dance in her honor. In turn, she distributes branches (*thyrsa*) to her companions.[18] These women, who then "crowned themselves with olive wreaths," reveal their transformation into active agents. Last, Judith leads "all the women" (*pasōn tōn gynaikōn*) while "every man" (*pas anēr Israēl*) followed them. Thus the female population of Israel, like the sword-brandishing (13:6–8) and head-bearing (13:15) Judith, become both graphically and by their actions phallic women.[19] Such inversions of male-female leadership patterns are permitted if not necessitated by the extraordinary circumstances of Judith's deed and Israel's rescue. However, they cannot be allowed to continue unchecked. Only by remaining unique and apart can Judith be tolerated, domesticated, and even treasured by Israelite society. The women consequently must return to their home and their husbands.

Just as Judith transforms the social roles of the Israelite women, so she transforms the life of the gentile Achior. Like Rahab before him and like Judith herself, Achior's name and reputation remain alive among the people (14:10). However, because Achior is male, this new social and religious position can be marked on his flesh as well as in his new community. The gentile man's incorporation into Israel is the inverse of the Jewish woman's position in the Assyrian camp.[20] Achior becomes a Jew first by sharing a meal with the leaders of Bethulia and second, primarily, through his circumcision. Judith too is physically altered (10:7) in preparation for incorporation into the alien community, but her mark of difference is not permanent: the makeup is washed off each night. Similarly, Judith refrains from becoming "like the daughters of the Assyrians" (12:13) by refusing Holofernes's food. Finally, Achior's incorporation into the Jewish community is confirmed by his singular movement. Unlike Judith, who moves back and forth from populated areas to liminal sites, Achior moves only to Israel. While Judith thus is figured as other to both Jew and gentile, Achior the convert mediates between the two.

Although gender-determined and ethnic integration occur during the course of the narrative, incorporation of Judith's servant does not. On the one hand, she appears to be Judith's double: linguistically, *habra* is related to *habras*—"graceful, beautiful"—which could serve as Judith's other name. Similarly, Judith adopts for herself in 11:5–6 titles of subservience—slave (*doulē*) and handmaiden (*paidiskē* [which can connote "prostitute"])—used elsewhere for her maid (*paidiskē* in 10:10, *doulē* in 12:15; 13:3). Yet, on the other, the patriarchal culture can deal with only one woman who speaks and acts; another such exceptional individual would too severely compromise the status quo. Thus, until Judith's death, her "favorite slave" must remain silent and in service.

The relationship between Judith and her maid is ironically paralleled by that of Holofernes and his eunuch. In Jdt 12:11, Bagoas is described as in charge of Holofernes's personal affairs; we have already been told that the maid oversees Judith's estate. Further, Bagoas summons Judith just as the maid summoned the leaders of Bethulia. In 13:3, both maid and eunuch receive the same instructions. But the parallelism is dramatically incomplete. Bagoas is the only named character in the text who is not somehow brought into Judith's community Incorporation is accomplished if the act of severing or sacrifice—of the past, of the gentile community, of one's foreskin—is brought about by the Jews themselves and serves the needs of their community. The form of incorporation in turn supports the text's concern with gender roles. Circumcision and that for which it substitutes, castration, both call attention to sexual difference rather than to undifferentiated integration. This difference is necessary for social organization and so for preservation of the status quo, as the removal of Judith from the public sphere and the return of the Bethulian population to their normative lives indicate. Achior, who as circumcised accepts sexual difference, fits into the community. So does Holofernes, once he is dead, since his (symbolic) castration would otherwise deny that difference. The eunuch, who as castrated but alive problematizes sexual difference, does not fit into the community.

Because she muddles sexual difference through her inversion of gender roles, Judith cannot as easily as Bagoas be erased from the story. She must somehow be domesticated, and this is done in part through representations of the other which evoke Judith yet which lack her subversive force. Achior's conversion, the presence of Holofernes's head, the maid's freedom, and, especially, the stories people tell about the pious widow all substitute for Judith.[21] They serve to maintain her presence in the public sphere while concurrently displacing her threat. The future is thereby protected. To preserve the status quo and to restore the sexual difference that determines it, Judith's actions must also be rendered kosher. Her concluding psalm reinforces traditional gender roles first by stressing the irregularity of conquest by the "hand of a female" (*thēleia*)[22] and second by giving full glory to the deity. Next, Judith submits to priestly ministrations (16:18); at this time, she also gives up the evidence of her time in the Assyrian camp: "Judith also dedicated to God all the vessels of Holofernes, which the people had given her; and the canopy which she took for herself from his bedchamber she gave as a votive offering to the Lord" (16:19). This celebration in Jerusalem (16:18–20) reappropriates the sacrifice in 13:6–9. The initial ritualized killing, which included the purification and festive garbing of the celebrant, her sexual abstinence, the painless slitting of the victim's throat (he being "overcome with wine" [13:2]), the aid of the assistant in disposing of the parts, the retention of a portion of the sacrifice for the community, and the efficacy that such an offering brings to Israel as a whole is given its full value only when the account—and the vessels, the canopy, and the general's head—become part of the communal celebration.

Moreover, the sacrifice in Judith 16 makes proper the parodic event in 13: Judith's victim is an inappropriate offering; she is not a priest, and the killing required two strokes. The heroine's direct links to the divine, coupled with her temple-oriented piety. suggest she plays the man's role of priest as well as of warrior. But, because such subversion of gender roles threatens Israelite society, her sacrificial and military actions must be constrained and contained.[23] Through the rewriting of her sacrifice as well as the sacrifice of the tokens of her deed, her transgressions are expiated.

Then, Judith herself must leave the public sphere, and life must return to normalcy. No longer the united "people" (cf. *ho laos* in 16:20) comprised of men and women, now "each man (*hekatos*) returned home to his own inheritance, and Judith went to Bethulia and remained on her estate" (16:21). The women, so prominent during the celebration, are completely erased. The inversion of gender roles is ended, and the status quo is reinforced. But even in her return, Judith resists complete domestication. Because she is not described as reentering the lifestyle described in 8:4–6[24]—she returns to her estate (16:21), but no mention is made of her earlier ascetic religiosity—she becomes other to her past. Her activities in the public sphere have thus not only changed the fate of the Bethulian population, they have changed Judith herself. On her estate but not on her roof, and in touch with the local population (as one might conclude from the mention of the repeated proposals), Judith is not comparably closer to the Bethulian society she already once disrupted. Like Holofernes, the only way Judith will no longer directly threaten ordered (i.e., gender-determined) Israelite society is through sacrifice, severing, and death.

Judith's distribution of property, her death, and her burial may be seen as inverse images of Achior's circumcision and Holofernes's decapitation. Complete incorporation requires a sacrifice with attendant communal benefits, and Judith in death conforms to this textual rubric. Because she is not male, she can neither lose her foreskin nor, given the metaphoric connection between decapitation and circumcision, her head. Judith has only two possessions which could be sacrificed: her property and her life. Given the threat even her reputation poses to the community, it is not inappropriate that she surrender everything. Consequently, "she set her maid free. Before she died she distributed her property" (16:23, 24). Then, Judith's only remaining public appearance is her burial; not surprisingly, 16:23 explicitly notes that "they buried her in the cave of her husband, Manasseh." In death, she is made to conform to her traditional role as wife.

All that remains of the intrusion of Judith's otherness into the public realm is her "fame" (16:23). That is, her deed becomes incorporated into public memory and public discourse, and it is thereby controlled. Yet each time her story is told, this woman who represented the community as well as exceeded that representation, will both reinforce and challenge Bethulia's—and the reader's—gender-determined ideology.

NOTES

1. A revised version of "Character Construction and Community Formation in the Book of Judith," SBLSP (ed. David J. Lull; Atlanta: Scholars Press, 1989) 561–69. I am grateful to Laura Lomas, Laura Augustine, Emily Stevens, and especially, Jay Geller, for their numerous insightful criticisms and suggestions on earlier drafts, and to George Nickelsburg, Richard Pervo, and David Halperin for their helpful comments on the seminar paper.

2. Simone de Beauvoir, *The Second Sex* (New York: Bantam, 1961) xvi.

3. Jonathan Z. Smith, "What A Difference A Difference Makes," *"To See Ourselves as Others See Us": Christians, Jews and "Others" in Late Antiquity* (ed. J. Neusner and E.S. Frerichs; Chico, CA: Scholars Press, 1985) 36: "The 'other' emerges only as a theoretical issue when it is perceived as challenging a complex and intact world view." At this point, the different becomes both alien and dangerous. Cf. James G. Williams, *Women Recounted, Narrative Thinking and the God of Israel* (Sheffield: Almond, 1982) 78: Judith "captivates Holofernes and the Assyrians in a fashion reminiscent of the wisdom tradition's warnings against . . . the 'alien woman' (Prov 6.24–25; Sir 9.8–9; 25.21)." While Smith notes that "Difference most frequently entails a hierarchy of prestige and a concomitant political ranking of superordinate and subordinate" (4–5), he does not classify women among his proximate others. Feminist criticism, which posits gender as a prime matter of inquiry, suggests that by her very difference, woman challenges traditional methodological and epistemological perspectives. See, among others, Elaine Showalter, "The Feminist Critical Revolution," *The New Feminist Criticism* (ed. E. Showalter; New York: Pantheon, 1985) 3–10; Gayle Greene and Coppélia Kahn, "Feminist scholarship and the social construction of woman," *Making a Difference, Feminist Literary Criticism* (ed. G. Greene and Coppélia Kahn; London and New York: Methuen, 1985) 1–36.

4. L. Alonso-Schökel, "Judith," *HBC* 810; cf. his "Narrative Structures in the Book of Judith," *Protocol Series of the Colloquies of the Center for Hermeneutical Studies in Hellenistic and Modern Culture* 11 (ed. W. Wuellner; 1975) 14–15: "As a widow, [Judith] can represent the Jewish people in her affliction"; "as a weak woman lacking the support of her husband, she can show and reveal better the force of God (9:10–11; 13:14–15; 16:6)." Cf. even Luther's comment that "Judith is the Jewish people, represented as a chaste and holy widow" (cited by, *inter-alia*, T. Craven, "Artistry and Faith in the Book of Judith," *Semeia* 8 [1977] 77). On the connection of Israel/the Jewish nation and Judith see also Craven, *Artistry and Faith in the Book of Judith* (Chico, CA: Scholars Press, 1983) 85; D.R. Dumm, "Judith," *JBC* 626. On the name's allegorical potential see Williams, *Women*, 76, representing literary-critical reading; M.P. Coote, "Comment on 'Narrative Structures in the Book of Judith,'" *Colloquies*, 21–22, on the significance of the name for the female warrior; and C. Moore, *Judith* (AB 40; Garden City, NY: Doubleday, 1985) 179.

5. Jdt 8:1 breaks the pattern of the first seven chapters, in which a plethora of male names and so individual male subjects appear. Alonso-Schökel sees the break caused by the genealogy in terms of plot rather than gender: it interrupts the campaigns of Holofernes and Nebuchadnezzar ("Narrative Structures," 4).

6. Noted by E. Bjorkan, "Subversion in Judith: A Literary-Critical Analysis" (Senior Thesis, Swarthmore College, 1987) 53. One should add to Bjorkan's work the further connection between the two women: neither has children.

7. *Inter alia*, Alonso-Schökel, "Judith," 806, and his less sanguine comments in "Narrative Structures," 18–19.

8. Cf. the possible contrast to Dinah, who "went out to visit the women of the land" (Gen 34:1).

9. Ironically, the Mishnah's description of widows fits Judith better than the literary metaphor. On the autonomous widow, see the excellent discussion by Judith Romney Wegner in *Chattel or Person? The Status of Women in the Mishnah* (New York and Oxford: Oxford University Press, 1988) esp. 138–43.

10. On the relationship between decapitation and castration see Alan Dundes, "Comment on 'Narrative Structures in the book of Judith,'" *Colloquies*, 28–29. The tie between decapitation and genital mutilation adds another dimension to the well-known trope connecting Holofernes with Shechem, and Judith with Dinah/Simeon.

11. See W. Shumaker, "Critique of Luis Alonso-Schökel on *Judith*," *Colloquies*, 32.

12. M.S. Enslin, *The Book of Judith* (Jewish Apocryphal Literature 8; Leiden: Brill, 1972) 111.

13. Commenting on 15:11, Craven (*Artistry,* 104 n. 73) observes: "The text reads *ten hemionon,* 'mule' in the singular . . . Could it be that Judith's female donkey, like Judith herself, can do what it usually takes a team to do?"

14. Cf. Toni Craven, "Redeeming Lies in the Book of Judith," paper presented to the Pseudepigrapha Section, AAR/SBL Annual Meeting, Anaheim, 1989.

15. "Comment," *Colloquies* 21. Such a reversal endangers both the tradition and the status quo.

16. J.E. Bruns, "The Genealogy of Judith," *CBQ* 18 (1956) 19; M. Steinmann, *Lecture de Judith* (Paris: J. Gabalda: 1953) 72.

17. "Comment on 'Narrative Structures,'" *Colloquies* 28.

18. The combination of the *thyrsa* with the decapitated head and the women's celebration is strongly reminiscent of the *Bacchae,* another story in which gender-roles are muddled and in which an "other" is both dangerous and desirable.

19. J. LaPlanche and J.-B. Pontalis, *The Language of Psychoanalysis* (New York: Norton, 1973), define the phallic woman as one "endowed, in phantasy, with a phallus." In one such phantasy, she is "represented . . . as having an external phallus or phallic attribute" (311). The identification is often applied to threatening women manifesting "allegedly masculine character-traits" (312).

20. For a discussion of the parallels between Judith and Achior, see Adolfo D. Roitman's essay, "Achior in the Book of Judith: His Role and Significance," in *No One Speaks Ill of Her: Essays on Judith,* ed. James C. Vanderkorn (Atlanta, GA: Scholars Press, 1992).

21. Cf. Coote, "Comment," *Colloquies* 26: "It is often patriarchal societies, where male and female roles are sharply distinguished and women have a passive role, that in fantasy produce myths of a female savior." In fantasy, the danger woman poses to the status quo is limited. Woman does in myth what she cannot do in the real world.

22. On the use of "female" rather than "woman" (*gynē*) cf. 9:10, 13:15, 16:5; Craven, *Artistry,* 91 and n. 40; and esp. P.W. Skehan, "The Hand of Judith," *CBQ* 25 (1963) 94–109.

23. Judith's appropriation of Holofernes's sword is to be equated not only with her assumption of male markers but also with castration. Castration is suggested also by Judith's comparison in 16:7 to figures who castrate their fathers: the young men, the sons of the Titans, and the giants in 16:7. Judith, like Medusa the archetypal phallic woman, castrates with "the beauty of her countenance" (16:7e). Consequently, she must be disarmed, and her disarming presence must be removed from the public sphere.

24. As observed by Roitman, "Achior in the Book of Judith."

Judith, Holding the Tale of Herodotus

Mark Stephen Caponigro

Is the Book of Judith in part modeled on Herodotus's account of the Persian invasions of Greece in the fifth century B.C.E.? Was the author of Judith acquainted with the *Histories*? The idea is by no means a new one; and most students of Judith seem not to find it very interesting.[1] But if it should ever come to be seen as not only interesting but even probably correct, it would alter our appreciation of Judith, its author, and its genre. No less important, it would offer another curious detail to complicate further our already very complicated ideas about Hellenistic Jewish culture.

What follows is an attempt to argue that the author of Judith (henceforth to be called "the Auctrix") did indeed have some acquaintance with the *Histories* of Herodotus, and borrowed from them something of their narrative structure, as well as certain specific narrative elements, for use in her own post-biblical, fictional history/hagiography.[2] The argument is based on the observation that several places in the Septuagint text of Judith, in themselves difficult to understand, become much more explicable when they are recognized to be less than perfectly coherent adaptations of Herodotean material to a new and different story.

It should be established at once that similarities between Judith and Herodotus, no matter how close or how numerous, are in themselves useless for the purpose of this argument. If a feature in Judith reminds us of something in Herodotus, but on the other hand can be thought reasonably to have an independent, non-Herodotean origin, then it does not help us at all in affirming a Judith/Herodotus connection.

So for example, the basic international predicaments in Judith and Herodotus are strikingly similar: The ruler of a mighty empire in the East, a monarch of overweening and tyrannical complexion, sends a great and terrible host against some smaller states to the West, to punish them for somehow offending him; the invading force is frightfully destructive: some of the Westerners are overrun; others capitulate, which the reader is urged to consider shameful; but still others, the heroes, resist, and are able first to embarrass the invader, and at last to defeat him decisively; the victory is attributed in large measure to the rare or even super-human virtues of the defenders, especially those of a few remarkable individuals who emerge to lead the defense, and also in part to divine assistance. But none of this is useful. This outline of an invasion story, common to Judith and Herodotus, looks long and complex enough nearly to force the conclusion that the later writer got it from the earlier. In fact, however, every item in the outline can be found as well in biblical literature and the history of Israel. No Judith/Herodotus connection can be persuasively affirmed on this basis.

Then there is this: In both narratives the leader of the invading army receives a warning that points out how difficult it will be to defeat the defenders holding out against him, on account of some terrific virtue that they have; he does not heed the warning, and in the ensuing conflict the terrific virtue of the defenders is made manifest. Xerxes, the second of Herodotus's royal invaders, in fact has two such counselors: his uncle Artabanus, who praises the Athenians and preaches about divine justice that strikes down the lofty (*Hist.* vii.10) at the outset of the campaign; and Demaratus, the deposed king of Sparta, who answers Xerxes's questions about the likelihood of Greek resistance by warning him not to attack the Spartans at Thermopylae (vii.101–104). In Judith the discouraging counselor is Achior (5:5–21). Both he and Artabanus receive angry replies to their words, and both suffer as a result a kind of banishment, more brutal in the case of Achior. By contrast, Demaratus's no less discouraging advice provokes laughter in the king. Momigliano, however, was especially impressed by how Demaratus's analysis of Spartan military prowess, directly dependent on the Spartans' obedience to *nomos,* "Law," resembles what Achior says about the Israelites, declaring them invincible provided they avoid sinning against their God (5:17, 20–21).

But this gets us nowhere. Achior in fact says nothing specifically about Torah, even when he is talking about the Exodus and Sinai. And more generally, his message is quite at home in biblical literature, sounding something very like the Deuteronomic theory of Israelite history. Also he himself, saying what he does at this point in the story, plays a role like that of the Gentile prophet Balaam (cf. Numbers 22–24, especially the angry reaction of Balak at 24:10–11; and the use of the verb *prophesy* in Jdt 6:2). Once again what seemed like solid evidence for Herodotean influence on Judith turns out to be problematic.

There are however other places in Judith that are clearly reminiscent of Herodotean material, and, besides, have no apparent origin in biblical literature or Israelite history. Moreover they are not in themselves very easy to understand; they show the signs of strain and forcing, the introduction of something alien into a place where it does not belong and was not meant to be.

The first of these places is at Jdt 2:7, a detail in Nebuchadnezzar's orders to Holofernes: "And you will proclaim to them to have earth and water prepared." The Persian practice of demanding earth and water from foreign states as a sign of their submission to the Persian king is well known from Herodotus (vi.48; vi.94; vii.131ff). Where did the Auctrix learn of it? From Herodotus? Or from some other, non-Herodotean, quite possibly even non-Hellenic channel of information about Persian matters?

Before we answer, we should make a couple of observations. First, there is nothing in Judith that explains the point of preparing earth and water; there is nothing in the immediate context, and there are no other references to Nebuchadnezzar's demand elsewhere in the book. Apparently the Auctrix considered a demand for earth and water appropriate to the kind of speech Nebuchadnezzar is making, and not needing to be explained. How did the Auctrix's contemporary readers understand Nebuchadnezzar's demand? How would we understand it, if the relevant passages in Herodotus were not extant and we knew nothing of the Persian practice? As a metaphorical expression equivalent to a demand for the absolute surrender of all territory? Perhaps; but the purpose of the campaign is not really to conquer territory.

On the other hand, having Herodotus helps us only so far. Nebuchadnezzar's demand is in fact quite different from anything put on the lips of Darius or Xerxes. Herodotus makes a clear distinction: those states that indicate their submission by offering the earth and water will not be punished by the Persian king; those that do not submit, will be punished. Both invading kings seem to take the distinction seriously. Darius is glad to have an excuse to conquer the Greek cities that do not submit (vi.94); and Xerxes, who sent heralds after earth and water to many places in Greece (vii.131–132), makes a point of not sending any to Athens and Sparta, in part because the Athenians and Spartans mistreated the heralds of Darius (vii.133), but also no doubt because he wants to remain free to crush them. It is quite contrary to this pattern, then, and pointless too as a result, that Nebuchadnezzar demands earth and water from states that he intends to punish all the same.

Also, in Herodotus the protocol is simple and straightforward: heralds are sent out to the state in question in advance of the king's army, make the demand, and return with or without the tokens of submission. (In Judith something like this may in fact be intended in Nebuchadnezzar's original message to the West during his campaign against the Medes. Otherwise the adjective "empty-handed," which is how his ambassadors are said to return to him in 1:11, is purely metaphorical.) But in Nebuchadnezzar's speech, the procedure becomes rather more complicated. Holofernes is charged to order the Westerners to "have earth and water prepared"—whatever that may mean; it does not sound quite the same as giving earth and water to a herald, nor is Holofernes expected to carry it back to Nebuchadnezzar if it is offered. Then, in 2:10–11, Nebuchadnezzar distinguishes between those who surrender to Holofernes, and those who do not. Holofernes is to punish the latter harshly; the former he is to keep under guard until Nebuchadnezzar himself comes to punish them (cf. also 2:7b: "for I will go out in my wrath against them"). The purpose of the double punishment is less than clear. Holofernes seems to be given two quite separate, hardly compatible roles: one, that of the Herodotean earth-and-water herald, sent out in advance of a king who is sure to follow and take action upon the basis of the herald's report; the other, that of the agent chosen to go forth and himself carry out the will of the king, the king staying at home. (Hence also the difficulty of translating *proerchesthai* in 2:19. Is it "to go forth from," as translated above, or is it "to proceed ahead of"?)

We are left with two alternatives. 1. The Auctrix got the earth and water for 2:7 from a non-Herodotean source. In that case we must admit the possibility that the demand for earth and water was used in Persian diplomacy—and why now Persian?, why limit ourselves to that?—in ways quite unlike what Herodotus told us; and we must accept the coincidence that a narrative detail reminding us very strongly of something in

Herodotus, but not in fact coming from there, should have dropped into a narrative that also happens to remind us of Herodotus. 2. The Auctrix got it from Herodotus. And in that case we have to cope with the curious differences discussed above.

But in fact this alternative is the easier. What seems to have happened is that the Auctrix, loosely following the outline of Herodotus's invasion narratives, wanted to include a reference to that element in the story which vividly recalls both the Western heroes' bold defiance and the Eastern despot's vengeful wrath. Is the incoherence of the introduced element a result of ineptitude or of art? Let us say, of art. The style of the Auctrix is learned and allusive, and also what we might call impressionistic, achieving its effect by a non-literal, history-resistant, even incoherent deployment of allusions. Well known examples are the startling association of names in 1:1, and the impossible chronology of 4:3. The names and historical events that appear in Judith do not signify themselves; rather, they signify what they felt like in the stories where the Auctrix first found them. She made from them her vocabulary, with which to tell a new story having nothing necessarily to do with the history or histories she had read. So one vocabulum in her lexicon is the demand for earth and water—by the way we observe that her sources and her allusions are not all biblical; with that she hoped to add the wrath of Darius and Xerxes, setting their faces against Greece, to her portrait of Nebuchadnezzar.

We seem to find another example of this stylistic feature at 2:1–3. The palace conference of the king with his servants and nobles do not recall any obvious biblical precedent. Moreover, it is not consistent with the characterization of the utterly autocratic and resolute Nebuchadnezzar established in chap. 1 (cf. especially 1:12). If 2:1–4a has been lost in a lacuna, it is doubtful that an editor would have supplied anything like it.

Again it is a question of Xerxizing the portrait of Nebuchadnezzar, in preparation for the subsequent Xerxish invasion. The relevant passage in Herodotus is vii.5–11. It begins with a speech by Mardonius urging Xerxes to invade Greece, and culminates in the conference of Persian nobles whose support for the campaign Xerxes seeks to elicit. A brief analysis will show how much this passage has in common with Jdt 2:1–3.

Neither an easy verse to understand nor to translate, Jdt 2:1–3 means literally something like this: "And in the eighteenth year, on the twenty-second day of the first month, there was talk, in the house of Nebuchadnezzar the king of the Assyrians, of punishing all the earth, as he had spoken."[3] There are at least two problems of interpretation here. First, the palace discourse seems not to come from the mouth of Nebuchadnezzar, but rather to be made by another, or by others, for his benefit; and that is inconsistent, as we observed, with what was established in the previous chapter, that the intention to punish the West was originally and particularly Nebuchadnezzar's, and was solemnly resolved upon (1:12). The narrative problem of how to bridge the gap between the victory celebration of 1:16 and the commission of Holofernes in 2:4–13 we might expect to have been solved by saying simply that the king remembered his oath and called up his general. Instead we get this curious indirect expression, which sounds almost as though the king needs to be reminded of his earlier resolve, or egged on to carry it out.

Secondly, just how is the "talk" related to Nebuchadnezzar's conference in 2:2–3? Some translators take "talk" to mean "deliberation" or "discussion," and treat it as a summary anticipation of the conference. But then the *kai* at the beginning of 2:2, which we would usually expect to set off a new and separate item, must be somehow overlooked, as though we had the license to consider it a not really meaningful Semitic particle placed there to help along the narrative flow.

Both these difficulties are clarified by recognizing that the Auctrix has inserted here a much compressed adaptation of the Herodotean passage mentioned above, vii.5–11. That passage too falls into two parts. The first, 5–7, tells of how Xerxes, originally not disposed to undertake a campaign against Greece, is persuaded to do so by Mardonius in the first place, then by some medizing Greek aristocrats. This is the model for Jdt 2:1. The second, 8–11, relates a different event, Xerxes's conference with the assembled Persian nobles. First he himself speaks, presenting his plan to invade and conquer Greece, and justifying it in large measure by recalling the wrongs committed by the Athenians for which they need to be punished. Then Mardonius responds, speaking in favor of the plan, and finally Artabanus, speaking against it, to the kings' displeasure, to which we referred above in a different context. Xerxes's convocation of the nobles and his speech to them form together the model for Jdt 2:2; Mardonius's speech is the model for 2:3. (The Auctrix chose not to use the speech of Artabanus here, but kept it in reserve. In fact she did use it later as one of the models for Achior's speech, though we were not ready to assert that when discussing the Achior passage above.)

It should be observed that in her adaptation of vii.5–7, the Auctrix kept her inconsistency minimal. The strangely impersonal expression, "there was talk of punishing as he had spoken," is in fact not really inconsistent with what we learned of Nebuchadnezzar's manner of expression, as well as of the unchallenged location of all authority in his person, chap. 1. On the other hand, it falls short of actually saying that he needs to be persuaded to carry out the very course of action that he resolved upon earlier, throwing rather a mist of obscurity around a palace loudly resounding with grave international threats.[4] As for Xerxes's conference, Herodotus is very interested, here as elsewhere, in presenting the delicacy of the Persian monarchy's relations with an uncertainly loyal, easily disaffected nobility. That is not the interest of the Auctrix at all, whose Nebuchadnezzar seems to be able to count on perfect submissiveness at home. So Nebuchadnezzar's conference in 2:2–3 is not intended as a test of loyalty. And if those of us who are disposed to ask such questions ask the question, Just why then does Nebuchadnezzar bother summoning his nobles?, the simple answer comes back, Because that is what Xerxes did, and Nebuchadnezzar is supposed to look, at least a little, like Xerxes.

Finally there is the problem of Bethulia. At Jdt 3:9–10 Holofernes reaches Esdraelon and encamps apparently not far to the west of Scythopolis. The reaction of Judea is given in the following chapter: it is assumed that Holofernes intends to make for Jerusalem and destroy the Temple, even as he has destroyed so many other shrines of subject-peoples; the inhabitants of the northern hill country prepare apparently for siege; and Joakim the high priest instructs the inhabitants of Bethulia and Betomesthaim, the latter or both of which seem to be somewhere to the south or southwest of Esdraelon and to the north or northeast of Dothan, to take control of the ascents into the hill country, "because through them was the way leading to Judea, and it would be easy to check the advancing enemy, the path of advance being narrow, enough for a maximum of two men" (4:7). The issue will show that it is precisely by Bethulia that Holofernes wants to pass.

The problem of Bethulia is really twofold. First, if it is the prime intention of Holofernes at this point in his campaign to take Jerusalem—that is not made explicit, but the assumption of the Judeans at 4:1–3 is never doubted, and Judith later will impress Holofernes with her promise to lead him to Jerusalem, at 11:19—, then why does he not choose the much easier way to get there, from Scythopolis south along the west bank of the Jordan to the vicinity of Jericho, and only then westward into hill country, and a much shorter stretch of it too, until he reaches the capital? Not only does this impractical strategy strike us as being the most unlikely brainchild of any prudent commander; but also there seems to be no precedent for it either in the Bible or in the history of Israel. All invaders entering the Jordan valley from the north and heading for Jerusalem, from Sennacherib to the Seleucids, seem to have been able to get there without encountering major military obstacles. Or do we know of any of them being held up in the hills south of Esdraelon? In the second century B.C.E. it certainly was not true that Syrian invaders could find access to the Judean heartland only by way of the northern hill country, when Judas Maccabeus and his successors had to fight battles to the west and to the south of Jerusalem, and in its very vicinity.

The second part of the problem is: What specifically are the defensive tactics that the people of Bethulia are supposed to take up in order to control their narrow mountain pass? This is most unclear. We do not find a Hellenistic phalanx of hoplites blocking the pass, nor do hilltop guerrillas send missiles down upon the Assyrians as they attempt to defile. So are the Bethulians obeying the command of Joakim, or not? They are, but with gestures that must strike us as rather feckless: what seem to be some sort of earthworks they throw across the passes, they strew stumbling blocks in the plains, and they get ready to hunker down behind the new walls of their mountain fastnesses (5:1). It is little wonder that the job of laying siege to Bethulia should turn out to be so easy (7:1–18). What is more of a wonder is that Holofernes does not just turn his back on Bethulians, once he has chased them inside their walls, and head toward Jerusalem.

To make sense of this we need to remember a few of the things that the Auctrix is interested in. She is interested in locating her heroine at some distance from Jerusalem, independent of the Temple (cf. 9:1b—a rival cult?) and beyond the manipulation of the hierarchy, but at the same time responsible for the deliverance of Jerusalem; she is interested in presenting Judith as the only effectual defender of Bethulia; she is interested in the story of Dinah and Shechem, and in vindicating the vengeance of Simeon (9:2–4); she is interested, says Toni Craven, in mountains and hilltops.[5] And beyond all these interests of hers, she is absolutely required by the story she is telling to bring up the curtain on two scenes, the only two which are strictly necessary: the besieged town, being the home of the heroine; and the camp of the besiegers, in particular the tent of the villainous enemy general.

The location of Bethulia satisfies some of these interests: it is distant from Jerusalem; it is with but a slight strain in the neighborhood of Shechem; and it is in the hill country. But now the Auctrix faces the problem of having to keep Holofernes pinned at that location long enough for Judith to have time to get at him. There is no good strategic reason, as we have seen, for his hanging around there; the Bible is no help in offering any, nor is the history of Israel.

Her solution, of course, is to borrow Thermopylae from Herodotus (for the disposition of the pass, see vii.176; for the battle, vii.201–233). By suggesting that Holofernes's path to Jerusalem is like Xerxes's path to Athens and the other Greek cities by way of Thermopylae, that is, by suggesting that Holofernes wants to capture Jerusalem, that his only way of getting there is through the narrow passes in the hill country south of Esdraelon, and that it is very easy to block his progress through those passes, all of which the Auctrix accomplishes by 4:7: she is able to establish that Holofernes has no choice but to confront Bethulia, that he will not be able to leave that region until he has decisively defeated the Bethulians, and that Judith's offer to betray her countrymen and guide him through Judea to Jerusalem at 11:19 will appear to him very attractive.

Having established all that, she is in no way compelled to prove it, her style being what it is. The Thermopylae parallel is at once dropped. There are no Israelite hoplites at Bethulia; only one person in Bethulia is allowed to be heroic, and that is Judith. And since the story of Judith is necessarily the story of a siege, the Israelites of Bethulia shift their priorities from defending the mountain passes to defending the wall of their town, so smoothly that we hardly notice passing by the end of chap. 7 into a strange new narrative predicament.

Can we detect a Herodotean presence farther on in Judith? Probably not. But it is worth noting that the heroine has something in common not only with Ephialtes, the Greek traitor at Thermopylae, but also with the false traitor Themistocles, the Athenian leader who promises the Persians that he will surrender the Athenian fleet to them, and so lures their own ships into a risky position, resulting in their terrific defeat, at Salamis. Moreover both Themistocles and Judith are first introduced in their respective stories as correct and encouraging interpreters of divine will to a dismayed group of their fellow citizens (for Themistocles and the oracle, see vii.143–144; for Salamis, viii.40–95). It is not impossible, then, that Themistocles may have served as a model for Judith. But that would be a rather more abstract kind of borrowing than how we saw the Auctrix used Book vii of Herodotus, and so probably requires a different argument in its defense. It is just as likely that we find in this a sign of a literary taste for the Greek historiographical style, especially the Herodotean style, serving as a model for prose fiction, a taste that would include the liar/hero, like Themistocles and like Judith, in its stock of admirable characters. On a different note, but which is no doubt a sign of the same thing, we recall that Herodotus locates a great deal of important history in bedrooms; and so there is no need to be surprised that Holofernes should meet with catastrophe in his bedroom.[6]

In conclusion, it is hoped that this examination has made a Judith/Herodotus connection seem much more credible than it seemed in the past. The method it is based on has sought out problem spots in the first half of Judith that are more or less solved or explicated when they are considered to be adaptations of Herodotean material. But once the connection is established on the basis of these few spots, it is possible to re-read Judith with a new appreciation of how well the Auctrix understood Herodotus's narrative art, and how wisely she adapted it to her own ends. For example, the war between Nebuchadnezzar and Arphaxad in chap. 1 is a brilliant adaptation for her short story form of what Herodotus accomplishes in a much more leisurely way, the magnification of the Eastern empire's might through a description of its earlier triumphs. And the character of Achior shows another aspect of the Auctrix's genius: learned in biblical literature and acquainted as well with Greek historiography, she is able to combine elements from both traditions into an interesting and effective new creation.

We may as well admit at once, that when we say the Auctrix was acquainted with Greek historiography, we may be talking only about Herodotus, but we may also mean something more. Once it is allowed that the Auctrix knew Herodotus, it must also be allowed that she is likely to have known other Greek authors as well. Is there evidence in Judith of any non-Herodotean Greek source? Probably there is, for those with eyes to see it. Moses Hadas, for one, detected the close resemblance between the story of the besieged Bethulians, lacking water, agreeing to surrender if no relief comes by the fifth day (7:30–31), and at last saved by divine intercession at the hand of Judith, and a story told in the Chronicle of Lindos about a siege of that city by the Persians, its lack of water, and its deliverance from having to surrender at the end of a five-day truce by a great rainfall sent by Zeus, with whom their patroness Athena had interceded; the goddess then unnerved the Persian commander by a personal epiphany. If that is another Greek story that the Auctrix liked and appropriated—and of course she would be interested in stories about sieges—, we must once again applaud her genius in adapting something so foreign to an impeccably Jewish setting.

And given her talent for compressing and adapting a story that interests her, is it impossible to discover beneath Jdt 1:13–15 a version of the final defeat and death of Darius III? Alexander defeated Darius in 330 B.C.E. at Gaugamela, near ancient Nineveh; Darius withdrew to Ecbatana, hoping to gather fresh support; Alexander took first Babylon, then Susa, then Persepolis, burning the palace there (cf. 1:14), then at last turned north against Ecbatana and Darius; Darius fled toward Ragae, then beyond it toward Hyrcania; Alexander pursued, and just as he reached Darius, the Persian king was fatally wounded by his own people (Arrian, *An.* iii.19–21). Aside from the necessary difference of names, only the last detail is remarkably different from the account in Judith of the death of Arphaxad. And that is just the sort of thing that the Auctrix would have altered: Nebuchadnezzar, himself plunging the fatal pikes into his foe, comes across as altogether more terrible than poor Alexander, gazing ruefully on the corpse of Darius.

Let us close with two questions touching on larger issues in Judith studies, which other students of Judith and of contemporary Jewish literature will be able to answer better than the present writer.

1. Can we be certain that the Septuagint text of Judith represents an original version of the story of Judith ancestral to all others? This student of Judith is doubtful. As was said above in another context, the story of Judith is the story of a siege; and so in principle we should grant priority to a tradition, perhaps found in one or more of the midrashim, that restricts itself to the context of a siege, presenting it with greatest simplicity and directness; other matters, like Jerusalem vs. Bethulia as the original besieged site, for the moment can be left aside. As for the Septuagint Judith, it has been observed here that one of the principal narrative techniques of the Auctrix is to borrow narrative elements from other sources and adapt them to her own text, but in a way that allows a certain incoherence to remain; but this is especially true of the first half of the book, i.e. chaps. 1 to 7. It was also observed that the invasion story and the siege story do not stand in a quite logical relation to one another. It might be possible to conclude that the story of Judith that begins in chap. 8 is not original with the Auctrix; rather, that she only worked it up in accord with her own interests, fashioning for it a seven-chapter prologue.

2. Is it possible that in the second or first centuries B.C.E. an author writing in Hebrew and learned in biblical literature also knew Greek and was acquainted with any of the Greek classics? There seems to be a pattern of attributing a Greek literary education only to those Jewish writers who wrote Greek of a good quality, not to those who wrote it more colloquially or barbarically, and *a fortiori* not to those who wrote in a

Semitic language. So what happens to the pattern if the Auctrix turns out to have known Herodotus? Would it be preferable to conclude that not only did the Auctrix know Greek, but the original language of Judith is Greek, only cleverly disguised to look like a translation from Hebrew? Or, on the other hand, would we like it more if the Auctrix were thought to be ignorant of Greek, and to have picked up these stories out of Herodotus, the Chronicle of Lindos, etc., from some purely oral story-telling source that passed along the gems of Greek historiography to barbarian nations? Can a place be found for a Jewish writer who could read Greek—and Ionic at that—and yet preferred to write in Hebrew?

Notes

1. See Moses Hadas, *Hellenistic Culture: Fusion and Diffusion* (New York and London: W.W. Norton & Company, 1959) 165–169, and Arnaldo Momigliano, "Biblical Studies and Classical Studies: Simple Reflections about Historical Method," *BA* 45 (1982) 227–228, for favorable presentations of the idea. The relevant section of Momigliano's article is printed by Carey A. Moore, interested but not committed, in his commentary on Judith: *Judith* (AB 40; Garden City, NY: Doubleday, 1985) 154–155.

2. This paper is a newer, neater version, I hope also an improved one, of a paper read at the 1988 Annual Meeting of the Society of Biblical Literature, in Chicago. I am grateful to all who offered comments and encouragement, and especially to William Adler, Shaye Cohen, Louis Feldman, and Richard Pervo.

3. The words translated by "there was talk . . . of punishing" are *egeneto logos . . . ekdikēsai*. This is not impeccable classical syntax; as a result, the notoriously slippery noun *logos*, the meaning of which a "good" author would have fixed by clearer syntax and context, is hard to interpret. "There was talk of punishing" might be supposed to mean more fully, "There was deliberation taken with a view to punishing," or even, "A speech was made, proposing the punishment of." Nor is that all. It is possible that *egeneto logos ekdikēsai* might be meant to translate a Hebrew original something like this: *wayhî dābār linqōm*. In late biblical texts, *dābār* followed by an infinitive can mean a decree or official command to do something (cf. 2 Chr 30:5; a less clear example is at Dan 9:25, where *dābār* is probably a prophetic word rather than a decree). So the difficult words in Jdt 2:1 could perhaps be translated, "There was issued a decree ordering the punishment of." That is indeed more vivid than the Greek; it sounds biblical enough, and accords with how *logos* is used elsewhere in Judith, for example at 2:3. But whether it gives a quite satisfactory sense is uncertain, seeing that it is not obvious how to relate a decree in 2:1 to the campaign conference of 2:2–3, or to the instructions to Holofernes, 2:4–13; to say nothing of the most basic question, To whom might such a decree be addressed?

4. Another possible Herodotean model for this verse, one that would keep the palace discourse more appropriate to the monarch's fiery personality, is at v. 105: after the destructive Athenian adventure at Sardis, Darius is said not only to have prayed for divine assistance in punishing the Athenians, of whom he seems not to have heard before, but also to have ordered a slave to remind him of them daily just before dinner; we are told again about this slave at vi.94.

5. Toni Craven, *Artistry and Faith in the Book of Judith* (SBLDS 70; Chico: Scholars Press, 1983) 79–80.

6. In her review of Richard I. Pervo's *Profit with Delight: The Literary Genre of the Acts of the Apostles,* in *JAAR* 58 (1990) 307–310, Marion L. Soards argues that a text like Acts can be more conveniently compared, with respect to genre, to ancient historiography than to the ancient novel, which is Pervo's direction; and that insofar as the narrative of Acts is entertaining, it functions precisely as an ancient history ought to function, Herodotus leading the way in this regard.

That is a valuable and important observation. We may wish to follow it up by asking more generally why ancient historiography seems to have been so useful a discovery for the biblical tradition.
This observer's guess is that the value of historiography for Jews and Christians, who applied it for
the most part to one or another kind of hagiography, lay in its balance of a conservative, ancestor-
regarding, community-regarding concern for truth—historiography claiming basically to tell the
truth—, especially the truths traditionally valued by the community, against the more free and personal celebration of individual experience. One of the wonderful effects of Judith is to assure the
Jewish reader of the value of her Jewish identity even while she is amazed, and amused, by the
bizarre and inimitable sanctity of the heroine. That Judith was received as genuine history already
in the time of Clement of Rome is testimony to its success in remaining faithful to the community
and its truths.

Feminist Identities in Biblical Interpretation

Our own lives are shaped by struggles between our various identities—race, class, gender, sexual orientation, age are the ones that come immediately to mind—we have to be flexible in our readings. More than just the feminism that looks at gender in readings, this new wave of feminism acknowledges struggles between various feminisms as well as by the cultural backlash against feminism. Many of the articles in the second bibliography, "Feminist, Womanist, and Mujerista Theologies" (p. 533) demonstrate the intersection of race with gender. One can add to these multiple axes of identity, other types of oppressions, such as class, age, colonialism, sexual orientation. However, it is important to note that this new wave of feminism presents and highlights contradictions among feminist readers, rather than defining all feminists as one harmonized group.

As more scholars and readers join the "feminist project," the question of the identity of the reader/interpreter will assume a larger place within interpretation. I have included three articles that reflect types of this new wave of doing feminism. To provide the reader with clues to the biases of the interpreter, this new wave of feminist interpreters of the Bible and those like Plaskow and of the broader field of theology have attempted to bridge the opposition between so-called objective criticism and the identity of the interpreter. In breaking away from male-centered readings, feminists now acknowledge other differences, e.g., race, class, age, geographical location. In the academic world of the Bible and theology one's own religious identity becomes central too. We can see the importance of this location in Plaskow's article, one that foregrounds the interpreter's Jewishness when reading and surviving in a Christian-dominated discipline. To read the Roundtable discussion of women with disabilities is to understand the daily assumption of "abled" readers of a text. Another example of challenging the position of the dominant culture in academics is my own article, "With a Song in Her Heart: Listening for Scholars Listening for Miriam." Written in a prose style that is more "colorful," or "informal" than the standard scholarly genre, this piece suggests a bridge between academic writing and journalistic prose. In each of these three pieces, the voice of the author insists on its own life within the interpretation.

Rereading the Body Politic
Women and Violence in Judges 21

ALICE BACH

> *Every woman adores a Fascist,*
> *The boot in the face, the brute*
> *Brute heart of a brute like you.*
>
> SYLVIA PLATH, "DADDY"

Rape is a weapon.[1] Rape is a weapon to reassert the power of a man over an enemy. Rape is used to create fear in women. Across time, legend and history have mythified not the strong woman who defends herself successfully against bodily assault, but the beautiful frail woman who dies while protecting her "innocence." Victory through physical triumph is a male prerogative incompatible with femininity. Rape is a subject that has been exposed by feminist criticism in one literature after another. We have come to understand that rape is not so much a sexual crime as it is a means of physical, mental, and spiritual domination. So powerful is the impulse for feminists to identify rape, even within literary texts, that feminist literary critics have inscribed what Adrienne Rich has called, "more than a chapter in cultural history," but rather "an act of survival" (90) in the process of analyzing rape narratives.

J. Cheryl Exum challenges the biblical authors with her suggestion of female figures being raped by the pen—if not the penis (1993: 171–202). While this suggestion may seem to exist totally within the realm of metaphor, it is more than a tour de force. Because reading is such an intimate experience, its form of violation is almost as frightening as a physical experience. The importance of Exum's oppositional reading is that it asserted her right to read representations of violation critically, skeptically; to refuse to remain the victim of the narrative force of the biblical narrator. If women can march through city streets to "take back the night," then feminist critics can also "take back the texts," or at least recognize what is at stake in the process of representing rape and the act of reading violence.

One way to reclaim my power as a reader, to take back the text, is to follow a synchronic strategy of reading. Synchronic approaches give the reader a great deal of latitude in making connections between texts. Central to such a semiotic theory is that the connections in the text have been made in the unconscious mind, as in my own recent connections between the accounts of ethnic genocide in Rwanda and in Bosnia and the so-called "carrying off" of the women of Shiloh in Judges 21. My decision to employ a synchronic reading, then, stems from my desire to examine two related subjects: first, I shall look at biblical texts in which women are sexually threatened or raped, and second, I shall compare the violation of one woman in Judges 19–20 with the narrative that follows it, in which an entire group of women are victimized. Just as Freud rendered iconic dreams readable through language, so a synchronic critic sees signifying force in the gaps, margins, echoes, digressions, and ambiguities of a text. The silence about the women of Shiloh, both in the biblical narrative and in the interpretations of this text, is as loud as the silence of the women themselves, given no voice or no subjectivity in the narrative. In these current days of sexual atrocities toward women of genocidal proportion, I have explored their biblical story expressly to end the silence of victimized women in Judges 21.

To analyze the structure of associations that produce a new reading of the collective rape of the women of Shiloh in Judges 21, I shall build upon other recent literary readings by women (Mieke Bal, J. Cheryl Exum, Alice Keefe, Susan Niditch 1982) of the unnamed woman raped in Judges 19.[2] The tragedy and violence of women's sexual experience had not been explored in depth until the moments of outrage expressed in Phyllis Trible's *Texts of Terror* and in subsequent writings of Bal, Exum, and others. Bal emphasized that the agents of the *pilegesh*'s death are as unclear as is the moment of her death. The act keeps being displaced from one man to the next. The contamination by collective guilt is obviously problematic to all readers. Bal focuses her gaze upon the body of the woman, the body that is "subsequently used as language by the very man who exposes her to the violence when he sends her flesh off as a message" (Bal 1988a:3).

Another kind of message is sent by the sexual violence committed by the Israelites in order to get wives for the men of the tribe of Benjamin. Judges 21 depicts two kinds of rape: the sexual rape of women of Shiloh and by extension, the economic rape of their fathers and brothers, who are by ancient standards the offended parties. There is collective violation in both acts. While an event of rape is not acknowledged openly in Judges 21, it is encoded within the ambiguity, the indirections of the text. The result is to naturalize the rape. By reading against the grain of the writer's intention to narrate the carrying off of women as wives for the men of Benjamin as necessary and natural, one sees how the biblical authors, men who possessed both benevolence and reason, could inscribe a rationale for oppression, violation, and exploitation within the very discourse of the biblical text.

In my reading of Judges 21, I inhabit the border life of the text. I shall make use of the friction between the narrative in chs. 19–20 and the one in ch. 21, not privileging one over the other. My initial move is to scrutinize the cultural ideology that supports rape as a stock narrative device for disorder in the biblical narrative. Literary critics from various fields are currently engaged in a polemic over the function and meaning of rape in its textual representation.[3] I share a belief with many cultural critics that readers, like texts (and for that matter characters within texts), are always sites where pluralities intersect. So that the friction between the biblical concept of rape, or more usually "not-rape," and our own intense feelings of abhorrence at the violation of the female body provide a major site for my reading. Reading Judges 19–21 as a single narrative unit allows me to follow the progression of violence from the representation of one violated female figure (*pilegesh*) to the representation of a violated tribe of females (daughters of Shiloh), thus raising the spectre of the tribes of Israel as guilty of a brutal male assault, an act of genocide.[4] My final strategy is to reread Judges 21 through the lens of the rape camps recently uncovered in Bosnia. And to fill the female silence in the one text with the witness from the other.

Writing the Body Politic on Women's Bodies

Depicting, narrating, or representing rape certainly does not constitute an unambiguous gesture of endorsement. The consciousness of what constitutes rape is very different now from what it has been in earlier times. One advantage of a synchronic analysis is that the reader can move forward or backward through time. Michel Foucault is correct that "the lateral connections across different forms of knowledge and from one focus of politicization to another [makes it possible] to rearticulate categories which were previously kept separate" (Foucault 1980: 127). Thus, a synchronic reading cognizant of cultural theory needs to inhabit both the insular territory of the biblical world and other cultural arenas where the practice of sexual violence has been represented, such as the genocide in Bosnia. This essay hopes to map the comings and goings between these sites.

When a woman is raped in the Hebrew Bible, who has lost respect, who is the offended party? The biblical narrator does not raise a literary eyebrow at either the Levite in Judges 19 or Lot in Genesis 19 for using women's bodies as shields to defend themselves against sexual violence. Nor does the Bible characterize as rape "carrying off" women to become the wives of the remaining men of an offending tribe in Judges 21. So the Foucauldian story of rape as evidence of ubiquitous domination is suppressed. The threat of homosexual rape is averted in Genesis 19, but sexual violence toward the *pilegesh* in Judges 19 is *doubly* suppressed; its homosexual element is disavowed by the Levite in his retelling of the story, and the corpse of the *pilegesh* is defiled by the Levite himself after her ravaged body has been returned to him.

A standard cultural myth is that rape is an unavoidable consequence of war. Looking solely at modern times, we remember that rape was a weapon of revenge as the Russian army marched to Berlin in World War II. Rape flourishes in warfare irrespective of nationality or geographic location. "Rape got out of hand," writes Susan Brownmiller, "when the Pakistani Army battled Bangladesh. Rape reared its head as a way to relieve boredom as American GI's searched and destroyed in the highlands of Vietnam" (32). Of course, in modern times rape is outlawed as a criminal act under the international rules of war. Rape is punishable by death or imprisonment under Article 120 of the American Uniform Code of Military Justice. Yet rape persists as a common act of war.

Since the focus of this article is the interweaving of modern gynocidal activities of war with narratives of rape and one of gynocide, let us look at the mirror story of a gang of men in Genesis 19 and Judges 19. When one reads each of these stories as a linear narrative, emphasizing its beginning, middle, and end, one concludes that such a narratologic strategy is far from innocent. Viewed schematically, the beginning of the story focuses the reader upon the details it offers and suggests that other details or reality are insignificant (e.g., the reactions of Lot's daughters to the pounding on the door or to their father's magnanimous offer); the events of the beginning of the story lead to the middle and set up a causal inevitability (the threatened Levite thrusting the *pilegesh* out-side the door); and finally, the story's end appears as the unique result of all that has come before. Most important in this seemingly logical progression of a linear narrative is that it creates a sense of order, as though the conclusion (i.e., the rape and torture of the *pilegesh*) is the only possible outcome. Unless the reader listens for the woman's story muffled in the gaps and silences of the male narrative, the reader becomes a voyeur, com-plicit with the orderly retelling of the story. While listening to the silence is one effective narratological strategy for moving outside the power of the text, the reader can also examine narrative elements that aid the storyteller in the representation of rape.[5]

One narrative element provides a first clue: night, לילה the dark time of abandon. The two parallel stories of men threatening men occur at night: the men of Sodom call out to Loy, "Where are the men who came to you *tonight*?" (Gen. 19:5). The Ben-jaminites also come knocking at night. They "know" the woman all through the night, a continuous connection of nighttime horror, when men turn into ogres. As Bal so memo-rably characterizes this scene: "she dies several times, or rather, she never stops dying" (Bal 1988a: 2). But the classification of even this rape, which seems so explicitly violation to a modern reader, is not clearly rape in the context of ancient law. Remember, the Levite *gave* the woman over to the mob. Compare another night scene earlier in the book of Judges: a Gazite mob lay in wait all through the night for Samson at the city gate, but they do not try to kill him עד־אור הבקר, until the coming of the dawn. The difference between the two situations is two-fold: first, the Gazites' plan to capture Sam-son fails, and second, they evidence no sexual designs upon Samson. The male victim is also the male hero. He survives, indeed, he triumphs.

Night is not always a sign in biblical texts for dangerous, loathsome acts. Night is figured as the time for important dreams, from the wrestling of Jacob with the angel to the apocalyptic dreams of Zechariah: ראיתי הלילה והנה־איש רכב על־סוס אדם (In the night I saw a man riding on a red horse; Zech. 1:8). The medium at Endor has her visions at night. But the dreams of Zechariah and the woman at Endor are embedded with symbols of death. Usually it is the horrors of battle that occur in the light of day. Needless to say, these are usually victories for Israel, not negatively signed acts. The tak-ing of the young women of Shiloh in Judges 21 occurs in the daylight. Thus, one has the first indication of difference between the individual occurrences involving Lot and the Levite from the unified act of the Benjaminites taking wives from the virgins of Jabesh-Gilead and of Shiloh. Getting wives for Benjamin is a victory for Israel: not against a for-eign enemy, but a triumph that reunites the tribes, the men of Israel.

It is crucial to ask of a historical period whose literature is given over to the cove-nant between its members and God, how rape can function as a stock device and what is the relation this genre bears to gender. While several female characters are raped in bibli-cal narrative—Dinah, David's daughter Tamar, the unnamed *pilegesh*—the rape least dwelled upon narratively by recent interpreters is the national rape of the daughters of Shiloh, initiated by the tribes of Israel. The text does not even name the action rape. It is figured as a political necessity, not a sexual crime. Indeed, the elders have created a problem for themselves through an ill-conceived vow: לנשים ואנחנו נאנחנו נשבענו ביהוה לבלתי תת־להם מבנותינו לנשים מה־נעשה להם לנותרים (What shall we do for wives for those who are left, *since we have sworn by the Lord* that we will not give them any of our daughters as wives?; Judg. 21:7). To understand the cleverness of this surface-seeming foolish vow, one must look at the double misreading of the Levite, who both covers up sexual violence (to himself) and uncovers it (to the *pilegesh*). It is up to the reader to recover the reading that denigrates women. Through a rereading of ancient narratives about male brutality toward women, I believe it is possible to envision rape as more than a symptom of war or even evidence of its violent excess.

Ovid's *Metamorphoses* offers an example of another ancient Mediterranean text built upon the representation of sexual violence. The Latin text retells the rape or attempted rape of many individual mythic women, among them Daphne, Europa, Syrinx, Arethusa, Thetis, Galatea, Pomona, Persephone, and Callisto. Unlike the narrator/storyteller of the biblical rape events, Ovid's narrator systematically focuses on the victim's pain, horror, humiliation, and grief. Ovid highlights the cruelty of sexual violation, showing the part of violence and degradation as clearly as the erotic element. Leo Curran observes that rape is sometimes used by Ovid as a strategy to remind the reader that "whatever else is going on in the foreground, rape is always present or potential in the background" (1978: 217). I would counter Curran's support of Ovid's depiction of rape with the caution that the goddesses and mortal women who were victims of these rapes rarely suffered serious consequences beyond getting pregnant and bearing a child— serving to move the story line forward. Lest the reader be left with the idea of great sensitivity to rape in ancient classical myths, it is important to note that Ovid also wrote in his version of the rape of the Sabine women, "Grant me such wage and I'll enlist today," adding a flippant but not unheard-of note to his other descriptions of rape in ancient Rome.

In contrast to the use of rape as a metaphor for social dissolution or for male warrior codes, the Greek mythic texts often use rape as a device to portray the enormous sexual prowess of the gods. Even when Semele is immolated after being penetrated by Zeus's lightning bolt, the mortal woman's pain and fear are not part of the story. The male-focused story continues as does the life of her unborn fetus, Dionysus, who is brought to term in his father's thigh. The immolation is blamed on the jealousy of Hera; the nurturing and birthing of Dionysus is attributed to Zeus. Hera herself had an ingenious way of annually recovering her virginity by bathing in a sacred river.

In medieval French romances, rape is not presented as the malevolent act pictured by Ovid, but rather is mystified and romanticized. Rape is viewed as a permissible act of manhood, woman as warrior's booty. Chrétien de Troyes, for example, systematically shifts away from the literal representation of the female experience of violence toward the moral, erotic, and symbolic meaning rape holds for male characters. While Chrétien admittedly tends to rosy up rape in the *Chevalier de Lion*, he embeds the legal codification of rape evidence: the woman fought back, she tried as hard as she could to get away, she resisted—such are the proofs required of a woman prosecuting a man in medieval rape trials (Gravdal 1991: 42ff).

Returning to the biblical stories of rape or attempted rape, let us see if any of these proofs are evidenced. Annette Kolodny describes a critical position that corresponds to mine in comparing rape narratives in the Hebrew Bible. "The power relations inscribed in the form of conventions within our literary inheritance . . . reify the encodings of those same power relations in the culture at large" (Kolodny 1980: 97). Women do not fight back, they do not try to get away, indeed the women's struggles and pain are not narrated. Women, even the violated ones, are as silent, compliant, as uninvolved as the narrator understands them to be. For in biblical law, rape is a crime against the father or husband of the woman. A woman has no right to initiate a trial. While Dinah's brothers exact retribution from Shechem and Absalom from Amnon, there is no articulated remorse on the part of biblical rapists. There is only one woman who screams "rape," and retells her story quite volubly and graphically to her husband and to her servants. One remembers from Genesis 39, through the narrative of the wife of Potiphar accusing Joseph of raping her, that a woman in the Bible is supposed to be hysterical and outraged at rape. While the Egyptian woman behaves in the accepted manner, it is all a sham, her hysterics histrionics, as the audience knows full well that the woman is lying about rape. And we remember her as the narrator wants us to, a seductive woman asking for sex.

Writing Hatred upon the Body Politic

As I have noted, what I am referring to as rape in Judges 21 is not referred to as such in the Hebrew narrative. Instead of creating disorder in the biblical narrative as similar acts have in Latin or medieval narratives, these biblical instances of sexual violence are misread by interpreters as political exigencies. Finding enough virgins to wive the men of Benjamin is a political problem that men need to solve. Jabesh-Gilead has been defeated in battle, so carrying off their daughters requires no justification.[6] The arena of war (whether it be holy war or civil war) provides men with the perfect psychological backdrop to give vent to their contempt for women. Whether narrative rape or actual gynocidal violence, rape in war is a familiar act with a familiar excuse.

If this argument seems too harsh, look at the narrative, the male explanation for male action. The only narrational concern at the outcome of the Shiloh incident is that the act of taking these girls must not be misunderstood by the males of the clan. So the elders instructed the Benjaminites, saying, "Go and *lie in wait* in the vineyards" (לכו וארבתם בכרמים), "and watch; when the young women of Shiloh come out to dance in the dances, then *come out* of the vineyards and each of you *carry off* a wife for himself from the young women of Shiloh, and go to the land of Benjamin" (מבנות שילו והלכתם ארץ בנימ ויצאתם מן־המרמים וחטפתם לכם איש אשתו; Judg. 21:21). The verbs חסף (ambush) and ב (carry off) are violent physical actions that contrast sharply with the whirling of the women's celebratory dance. The verb ארב embodies both physical harm and action against an enemy; it is used to describe the Philistines lying in wait to ambush Samson, ויסבו ויאאדבר־לו כל־הלילה בשער העיר (Judg. 16:2). The narrator relates that Joshua must ambush Ai and its king as he did at Jericho (when Joshua and all Israel saw that the ambush had taken the city; Josh. 8:21). Both these uses of ערב differ from its use in Judges 21 in that ambushing a national enemy is the context in the Samson and Joshua texts. It is the women of Shiloh who are to be ambushed in Judges 21. This ambushing of women goes back to the model of the heroic rape, where the desire for women and violence to women go hand in hand.

The only other biblical use of the verb ָ is found in Psalm 10:9, לחטוף עני יחטף עני במשכו ברשתו יאדב במסתר כאדיה בסכה יאדב (they lurk in secret like a lion in its covert; they lurk that they may carry off the poor). In Psalm 10 חסף is also used in combination with ארב. Both scenes evoke images of violence performed by a powerful party onto a poor or helpless one. In the Psalm, God is expected to intercede against the jackals terrorizing the poor. Presumably the women of Shiloh have no need of rescue; they have the Benjaminites as husbands.

It is a struggle to sympathize with the men of Israel even if their confederation is endangered. For the men of Israel in Judges 21 are never the ones who are in danger. Indeed, wiving the Benjaminites is a problem on account of another of those foolish male vows that results in women being sacrificed to protect male honor. As the Israelites conceive their plan, "if their fathers or their brothers come to complain to us, we will say to them, 'Be generous and allow us to have them; because we did not capture in battle a wife for each man. But neither did you incur guilt by giving your daughters to them'" (Judg. 21:22). The traditional understanding is that the Israelites had to be united as twelve tribes, to keep their covenant with God. Since they had vowed not to give Benjamin their daughters as wives, how could they then ensure that the tribe would survive? After annexing the virgins of Jabesh-Gilead there is still a shortfall. To tidy up the mess, the men devise a plan to wive the girls of Shiloh. Dancing perhaps the same ritual as the friends of the daughter of Jephthah, who had suffered mortally from a father's foolish vow, now the girls of Shiloh are to be sacrificed, not killed, but taken as wives. Taken *as wives*—the escape clause that naturalizes the violent action and even lets their fathers off the hook, since they had not offered them as wives to the offensive (but still "men of Israel") Benjaminites. Once again, women have been the victims in a male shell game of sexual violence.

What might be interpreted by a modern reader as the nefarious plundering of the females ripening in the vineyards at Shiloh is obliquely connected by the biblical narrator to each man doing what was right in his own eyes. Perhaps the repetition of this phrase is meant as a promonarchic statement studded with sarcasm. Perhaps the phrase is a clear-eyed assessment of the importance of inter-tribal loyalties with a wink at sexual politics. At best, the reader is nudged toward an interpretation unfriendly to the tribes' resolution of their problem. But can a feminist critic let the biblical narrator soothe the reader as easily as he plans to soothe the fathers and brothers of the maidens of Shiloh? The well-known call to arms of Hélène Cixous reminds me of our obligation as readers: "Language conceals an invincible adversary because it is the language of men and their grammar. We must not leave them a single place that's any more theirs alone than we are." From a feminist viewpoint, the biblical understanding of rape and its punishment serves to show an asymmetrical relationship between women and men, coding sexual violence in ways that make it culturally acceptable. A second hint that the foolish vow resulting in the carrying off of the Shiloh women may not have been so foolish. The narrative raises the question of rape or seizing of women as an expected outgrowth of war. Triumph over women by rape is also a way to measure victory, "part of a soldier's proof of masculinity and success, a tangible reward for services rendered" (Brownmiller 1976: 33). The neat resolution of the entire story reading Judges 19–21 also helps to bury deep within the literary unconscious the memory of homosexual attack.

One more category of rape augments my intertextual reading of Judges 21. In the minds of the male formulators of the story and their ideal audience, the horror of homosexual rape is far greater than that of a male violating a female. Substituting the violence done to himself with violence to the *pilegesh* explains the Levite's rage. Unharmed himself, he retains honor and standing within the community, enough to be able to incite the other tribes to violence against Benjamin. Unsanctioned male sexual appetite can ignite the proper rage of all Israel and does result in the vow to cut off the tribe of Benjamin, that is, to ensure that Benjamin loses his power among the tribes. But had the Levite himself been the victim of rape, the shame and humiliation would have been too great for him to have related his story publicly as he does in Judges 20. Further, it would have been unthinkable to readmit Benjamin as a tribe had its crime been a taboo that smashed sexual boundaries instead of merely stretching them.

The key semes that generate this reading are those of substitution, of offering the woman in place of the male in both Genesis 19 and in Judges 19, of offering the Levite's version of the story in Judges 20 in place of the one the reader has just witnessed—when bedeviled men press hard against him. Their nefarious act is stopped by the angels. Divine intercession restores Lot to the proper side of the door and rescues him at the last moment from narrative destruction. The divine narrator sends a strong symbolic message by blinding the men who would look and lust after what is forbidden to them (Gen. 19:11). Nowhere in this Genesis text is a female substituted for a male. It takes divine intervention to halt homosexual intercourse. God responds furiously by destroying the Sodomites who would break through that door, that taboo, that binds men in community in the Hebrew Bible.[7]

What is the situation in Judges 19? The Levite and his host were enjoying themselves much as the Levite had recently enjoyed himself with the father of his *pilegesh*. The men of the city, a perverse lot, surrounded the house, and pounded on the door: ויאמרו אל־האיש בעל הבית הזקן לאמר הוצא את־האיש אשר־בא אל־ביתך ונדענו ("They said to the old man, the master of the house, 'Bring out the man who came into your house, so that we may have intercourse with him'"). The Levite made no move. The Ephraimite went outside, as had Lot, to try to deal with the men: האיש בעל הבית ויאמר אלהם ויצא אליהם.

הזשת אל־אחי: אל־תרעו נא אחרי אשר־בא האיש הזה אל־ביתי אל־תעשו את־הונבלה ("No, my brothers, do not act so wickedly," pleads the Ephraimite, "since this man is my guest do not do this vile thing"; Judg. 19:22–23). The repetition is intentional; the one text recalls the other. Men threaten other men by pounding on the door. The door that leads to death is the boundary, the shield. In this account the Levite never risks death going outside the door, but rather, the Levite seizes his *pilegesh,* and "pushes her outside" to the waiting mob on the other side. Can we consider the Benjaminites' act rape if the Levite handed her over to them?

In his version of the story that he tells in Judges 20, the Levite states that the men of the mob intended to kill him. So he gave them the *pilegesh*. But there is a piece missing: there is a lack of logic that is unquestioned by the other men, the narrator, or most interpreters. Why was the mob satisfied by the offer of the *pilegesh*? In Genesis 19, the mirror of the story, the mob rejected the offer of the daughters. It took divine intercession to protect Lot from homosexual rape. Divine intervention was not afforded the Levite.[8] Perhaps that explains the Levite's murderous rage. Could the rape of one woman initiate total tribal warfare in Israel (Keefe)? Is the ensuing battle an uniterated *herem* as Niditch suggests (1993: 69–71)?[9] Perhaps the Levite knew the confederation could not cut off Benjamin as easily as he could cut up the *pilegesh*. Perhaps the Judges' version of the story has been inverted to protect the men of Israel from the specter of sodomy.

Are there any further textual clues about denying homosexual rape? Back to the *pilegesh*. In the morning, she is unable to return to the "safe" site even after the Levite opens the door. The Levite shows no emotion at seeing her collapsed form on the threshold. He also appears to think she is alive. Why else would he command her to get up? Thus, the violated woman, perhaps by this time a corpse, *nebelah*/(n(a)b(e)l),[10] surely a disgrace, a *nabalah*/(n(a)b(a)l) has never returned inside, to the place of safety, of life, where the Levite and Ephraimite have remained all through the night. Unlike Lot, the *pilegesh* has no divine messenger to bring her back to the safe side of the door. One reading of the fate of the *pilegesh,* then, is that she has been broken so that the final boundary, the door, could hold firm and protect the Levite against shame and death. She has collapsed on the death side of the door. Another possibility is that her body was the boundary that stopped the mob from committing rape—that is, rape of the Levite. Another woman found on the wrong side of the door is Tamar. After raping her, Amnon called to his servants, "Put this woman out of my presence, and bolt the door after her" (2 Sam. 13:18). The door becomes the marker between security and danger, honor and shame, life and death.

In a lucid synchronic reading that links Genesis 19 and Judges 19–20, Niditch observes that a homosexual rape would have been worse than the rape of the *pilegesh,* in the eyes of Israel, and ethically indefensible (1982). Niditch does not, however, address the absence of anger or moral outrage on the part of the narrator. Nor does she explain the rage of the Levite in the following chapter of Judges. Perhaps the biblical narrator has slammed the door on sodomy so effectively that no reader, even a modern one, dares to press up against that door. Like Lot and the Levite, who are exonerated for offering women as substitutions, the reader is exonerated for not wondering if perhaps the Levite had not been the victim after all. But the misreading demands the answers to two crucial questions: Why else the Levite's extraordinary rage? Why else the cutting up of the sacrificial victim?[11] One must account for the Levite transforming the Benjaminites' threat to sodomize him into a desire to kill him. The shame and horror of sodomy were equivalent to death. Unruly unlawful male sexuality according to the tale as used in Genesis does result in the death of the Sodomites. But the Levite has eluded death. He escapes punishment over her dead body. The Levite further vilifies the dead female body by using it to incite his countrymen. Choosing to misread the sign of her body, the men exact revenge on Benjamin. But then, in order to assuage the guilt and anger against their brothers, they amplify the violence done to one woman by violating many women. Each act of violence is justified by hiding the truth behind the door, throwing out lies to distract the spectators. Men's misreadings result in the mistreatment of women. The substitution of women for men occurs in both the story of Judges 19 and in the revenge taken in Judges 21. Gender inversion of the tale becomes the Levite's security.

While the violations of individual women in Genesis 19 and Judges 19–20 have become the subject of earnest debate in the feminist community, the carrying off of the women of Shiloh has been met with near silence. The representation of violence and pain of rape have been lost in a welter of interpretations that talk about reuniting the tribes of Israel, fighting a holy war in YHWH's name, assuring the continuation of the tribe of Benjamin. Male and female commentators alike seem to identify deeply with the portrait of female victimization expressed in the narratives of violence to one woman, but silence greets the genocidal brutalization of the women of Shiloh.

Breaking the Silence of the Women of Shiloh

Feminist criticism combines the personal and the political and insists on a kind of self-consciousness that is explicit about the origins of one's projects and the position from which one speaks. Undermining the traditional academic boundaries between professional and subjective is an example of the interaction between personal and political. I suspect that it would be impossible for any woman to write about rape without becoming emotionally involved in the work.[12]

Because the biblical text remains silent about the young women of Shiloh, I shall describe some of the documented atrocities from the recent gynocidal actions in Bosnia. The parallel seems strong, for the recent atrocities were committed during an ethno-religious civil war, a war in which men's violence was inscribed upon women's bodies. In both situations there is the strong patriarchal association of the female body with territory, so that raping one and conquering the other come metaphorically to the same thing. For those readers clinging to the "marriage" element of the Judges 21 text, let me add that what Beverly Allen calls "enforced pregnancy" (1996: 87) was also practiced by the Christian Serbs against Muslim women. The following testimony was offered by a survivor of the Susica camp in eastern Bosnia. The witness was testifying about several young women who had been selected (for enforced pregnancy):

> They started selecting young women. The first was only 14, the second could have been 16 or 17 . . . I knew them all, they were from Vlasenica . . . Then they started yelling, "We want the muslims to see what our seed is." The women were never seen again . . . We know that Dragan Nikolic knows about it very well. That's what he did . . . He told us himself: "I am the commander of the camp. I'm your God and you have no other God but me." (Sells 1996: 21)

What I would like to suggest is that after reading rape accounts such as the one quoted above from the recent genocide in Bosnia, the reader will fill the gaps and silences in Judges 21 with the cries of the victims of ethnic/religious rape of massive proportions. As I have argued elsewhere (1997) we do not read in a linear fashion. Regardless of the order of one's reading, what is immediately apparent is that female readers will feel an emotional connection between the plight of the Muslim women of Bosnia and the virgins of Shiloh—if readers allow themselves to dwell upon that sliver of biblical narrative. I do not mean to imply that men will not feel horror at these atrocities, but I have searched all the traditional accounts of holy war in Israel, of war suborned by YHWH, of war won by YHWH, and nowhere is there a mention of the carrying off of the women of Shiloh as rape, or even a hint that such a deed might have been divinely sanctioned but *against their will*. Much like violence portrayed in cartoons, the carrying off of the dancing maidens is accomplished without pain, without struggle, without resistance. If the narrative were focalized even for a moment through the eyes of the victims, one would be required to appropriate the female body as a sign of the violator's power. But the women remain as passive signifiers; the biblical storyteller is not interested in representing their experience. Thus, the reader must inhabit the gap, the silence, and through the power of imagination break the silence of the women of Shiloh. To leave them in silence is gynocide.

Notes

1. I would like to thank Melissa Wilcox for superb research assistance and insightful conversation during the writing of this article.

2. I have resisted supplying a name for the *pilegesh*, as Bal and Exum have done. Bal (1988b) calls her Beth; Exum (1993), Bath-sheber. Her anonimity creates a problem for the reader trying to identify her in a retelling of the narrative. This very difficulty underscores the gap or silence created by the biblical storyteller. By referring to her as *pilegesh*, I hope to maintain the narrational vagueness and lack of subjectivity that anonymity of a character presents in a story.

3. There is a growing scholarly literature on rape, reflecting the consciousness of real-life rape as well as literary and metaphoric rape. See especially Brownmiller's classic, *Against our Will: Men, Women, and Rape;* Roland Barthes, "Striptease," in *Mythologies* (trans. Annette Lavers; New York: Hill and Wang, 1972), pp. 84–87. For literary rape, see discussion in Bal (1988a & b); Exum (1993); Teresa de Lauretis, "The Violence of Rhetoric: Considerations on Representation and Gender," in *Technologies of Gender* (Bloomington: Indiana University Press, 1987); Muriel Dimen, "Power, Sexuality, and Intimacy," in Alison Jagger and Susan Bordo (eds.), *Gender/Body/Knowledge* (New Brunswick: Rutgers University Press, 1989); Trudier Harris, *Exorcising Blackness: Historical and Literary Lynching and Burning Rituals* (Bloomington: Indiana University Press, 1984).

4. To the reader who thinks the term gynocide is an overreading, an exaggeration, of the act of "carrying off" the young women of Shiloh, I can say only that we shall never know how the women characters in the text perceived their predicament. The silence of the women in the text will be filled by each reader.

5. Another subtle reference to rape comes from the mother of Sisera (Judg. 5:30) standing at the window, waiting for her son, triumphant in war. She waits for him to bring her "spoil of dyed stuffs embroidered, two pieces of dyed work embroidered for my neck as spoil." And without a shiver, she wonders about her son and the other victors, "Are they not finding and dividing the spoil?—A girl or two for every man; spoil of dyed stuffs for Sisera?" The irony of the text as traditionally interpreted comes from the fact that Sisera is dead, not that a woman is serenely imagining the rape of other women.

6. The classical interpretation understands the carrying off of the women of Shiloh as part of a "holy war," sanctioned by YHWH and a reflection of the tribal confederation. The amphictyony theory has been discredited by most scholars. However, much of this scholarship has remained unchallenged in relation to the narratives in Judges 21, being part of a holy war, and thus inevitable and justifiable. See von Rad's foundational study of holy war in which he argues that an amphictyony-type confederation of the Israelite tribes is both political and cultic (*Der heilige Krieg im alten Israel* [Zurich: Zwingli, 1951]). Smend's study modifies von Rad's theory, assuming that the amphictyony before Samuel was solely cultic and neither political nor military (*Yahweh War and Tribal Confederation* [Nashville: Abingdon Press, 1970]). For a review of the many views of holy war in the ancient Near East, see Moishe Weinfeld, "Divine Intervention in War in Ancient Israel and in the Ancient Near East" (*History, Historiography, and Interpretation* in H. Tadmore and M. Weinfeld [eds.]; [Jerusalem: Magnes Press, 1983]). Niditch questions the amphictyony theory but settles for half a cake, reading Judges 19–21 as "the acting out of this sort of justified holy war situation in a symbolically charged, rich narrative medium" (1982: 375). A concise review of the scholarly chain of argument appears in Ben Ollenburger's introduction to the English translation of von Rad's *Holy War in Ancient Israel* (Grand Rapids: Eerdmans, 1991), pp. 1–34.

7. I would like to call attention to Wilson's reading from a queer perspective in *Our Tribe: Queer Folks, God, Jesus, and the Bible* (San Francisco: HarperSanFrancisco, 1995). She emphasizes that the sin of Sodom is not that of homosexual threat, but rather that of ethnic and sexual violence (168–69). Her suggestion that the "same-sex male-appearing angels" at the door in Genesis

19 are gay, and thus, are the potential victims of the story, is an intriguing example of gap-filling with one's ideological position.

8. One has the same narratological pattern in parallel stories in Genesis 22, where divine intervention halts child sacrifice of a male child and Judges 11–12, where there is no divine intervention to rescue a female child.

9. I do not claim to reflect the narrator's understanding of "tribe," nor his view of the situation between the tribe of Benjamin and the other tribes. Niditch notes that the *herem* is considered as appropriate form of aggression only against outsiders. "When the ban is used as a technique to keep ingroup miscreants in line by a nervous and insecure leadership with the power to enforce its will," it becomes divisive (1993: 70). Clearly this is the situation in Judges 21. Niditch shares my puzzlement over the designation of tribe in this context, and the situation of exogamous marriage, neither of which has much historical evidence. I suggest that the story does not function historically, but rather serves to suppress the homosexuality in Judges 19 as well as the violent rape in Judges 21.

10. The noun *nebalah,* defined in BDB as disgraceful folly, "to do a thing disgraceful according to Israel's standards," is used in conjunction with all the biblical rape narratives; in Judg. 19:24 the term may refer to the threat of homosexual rape; in Judg. 20:6 the term clearly refers to the gang rape of the *pilegesh;* in Gen. 34:7 to the rape of Dinah. For further discussion of the term *nebalah,* see Keefe (1993: 82).

11. Many scholars have noted the similarity between the cutting up of the *pilegesh* and Saul's cutting up of the yoke of oxen in 1 Sam. 11:5–7. In both narratives the pieces are sent to the tribes of Israel to incite them to battle. Niditch (1982: 371) sees the dismembered body as a part of the division of the body politic. Reading through the gender code, Exum argues that "by leaving her husband the woman makes a gesture of sexual autonomy, so threatening to patriarchal ideology that it requires her to be punished sexually in the most extreme form" (1993: 181).

12. For riveting descriptions of the scenes of horror in the Bosnia rape camps, see, *I remember = Sjecam Se: Writings by Bosnian Women Refugees,* edited by Radmilla Manojlovic Zarkovic, with Fran Peavey (San Francisco: Aunt Lute Books, 1996). Note: The memoirs appear in the original Serbo-Croatian, along with English, Spanish, and Italian. Also Hukanovic Rezak, *The Tenth Circle of Hell: A Memoir of Life In the Death Camps of Bosnia,* trans. Colleen London and Midhat Ridjanovic, ed. Ammiel Alcalay (New York: Basic Books 1996). I recommend these works with the warning provided by Beverly Allen. "A repetitive serial form may easily hook even a reader disgusted by the events the text relates into wondering at least what comes next. This scene was so horrible, can the next one possibly be worse? And so the reader may keep turning the pages, caught in spite of her or his revulsion in the formal pleasure of repetitive linear narrative" (1996: 32). As I have noted above, this sort of narrative risks placing the reader in the position of voyeur.

REFERENCES

Allen, Beverly
1996   *Rape Warfare: The Hidden Genocide in Bosnia-Herzegovina and Croatia.* Minneapolis: University of Minnesota Press.

Bach, Alice
1997   *Women, Seduction and Betrayal in Biblical Narrative.* Cambridge: Cambridge University Press.

Bal, Mieke
1988a   "Speech Acts and Body Language in Judges." Pp. 1–32 in Elaine Scarry (ed.), *Literature and the Body: Essays on Populations and Persons.* Baltimore: Johns Hopkins University Press.
1988b   *Death and Dissymetry.* Chicago: University of Chicago Press.

Brownmiller, Susan
1976   *Against Our Will: Men, Women, and Rape.* New York: Simon & Schuster.

Curran, Leo
1978   "Rape and Rape Victims in the Metamorphosis," *Arethusa* 2: 213–41.

Exum, J. Cheryl
1990   "Murder They Wrote." In Alice Bach (ed.), *Pleasures of Her Text.* Philadelphia: Trinity Press International.
1993   *Fragmented Women: Feminist (Sub)versions of Biblical Narratives.* Valley Forge, PA: Trinity Press International/Sheffield: Sheffield Academic Press.

Foucault, Michel
1980   *Power/Knowledge: Selected Interviews and Other Writings, 1972–1977.* Ed. and trans. Colin Gordon. New York: Pantheon Books.

Gravdal, Kathryn
1991   *Ravishing Maidens: Writing Rape in Medieval French Literature and Law.* Philadelphia: University of Pennsylvania Press.

Griffin, Susan
1981   *Pornography and Silence: Culture's Revenge Against Nature.* New York: Harper & Row.
1986   *Rape, The Politics of Consciousness.* San Francisco: Harper & Row.

Keefe, Alice
1993   "Rapes of Women/Wars of Men." *Semeia* 61: 79–97.

Kolodny, Annette
1980   "Dancing in the Minefields: Some Observations on the Theory, Practice, and Politics of A Feminist Literary Criticism." Reprinted, pp. 96–113 in R. Warhol and D. Herndl (eds.), *Feminisms: An Anthology of Literary Theory and Criticism.* New Brunswick: Rutgers University Press, 1993.

Niditch, Susan
1982   "The 'Sodomite' Theme in Judges 19–20: Family, Community, and Social Integration." *CBQ* 44: 365–78.
1993   *War in the Hebrew Bible: A Study in the Ethics of Violence.* Oxford: Oxford University Press.

Rich, Adrienne
1972   "When We Dead Awaken: Writing as Revision." Reprinted in Barbara Charlesworth Gelpi and Albert Gelpi (eds.), *Adrienne Rich's Poetry.* New York: Norton and Co., 1975.

Scarry, Elaine
1985   *The Body in Pain: The Making and Unmaking of the World.* Oxford: Oxford University Press.

Searles, Patricia, and Ronald J. Berger, eds.
1995   *Rape and Society: Readings on the Problem of Sexual Assault.* Boulder: Westview Press.

Sells, Michael
1996   *The Bridge Betrayed: Religion and Genocide in Bosnia.* Berkeley: University of California Press.

Trible, Phyllis
1984   *Texts of Terror: Literary-Feminist Readings of Biblical Narratives.* Philadelphia: Fortress Press.

Transforming the Nature of Community
Toward a Feminist People of Israel

JUDITH PLASKOW

A post-patriarchal Judaism begins with the insistence that women as well as men comprise Jewish humanity. Confronted with a religious system that projects women as "other," Jewish feminists assert that Jewish women's experience is an integral part of Jewish experience and that women with men make up Jewish community. No account of Judaism is complete unless it considers fully and seriously the experience of women, and no Jewish community is fully Jewish unless women play an equal role in shaping and defining it.

This principle, simple as it seems, necessitates far-reaching changes in Jewish self-understanding. Since the Jewish textual tradition treats men as normative Jews, Jewish history must be rewritten to include the history of women. The boundaries of Jewish memory must be altered and expanded to incorporate women's experience and teachings. Jewish law must be reargued and reconstructed as the presence of women as lawmakers makes certain new norms imperative and certain old ones unthinkable. New Jewish liturgy must mark important turning points in women's lives and reflect the contours of women's spiritualities. The very concept of God must be rethought, and new symbols for God created.

Since to consider the totality of these changes would require a book rather than a single chapter (see Plaskow 1990), in this article I will limit myself to the implications of the assumption of women's full humanity for the concept of Israel. Defining Israel as the Jewish community and the Jewish people, I will explore the nature of an Israel that takes women's experience seriously. Feminists have argued that women have been marginalized within the community of Israel and excluded from some of the central experiences of Jewish religious life (Koltun; Heschel). What have been the sources and costs of women's marginalization, and what would constitute rectification? What resources for change lie within Jewish self-understanding, and in what ways does Judaism need to be transformed? These questions are at once practical and theological. The issue of Israel is an issue concerning Jewish communal form and practice, the embodied shape and nature of Jewish life. One cannot hope to create a feminist Jewish people, however, without also considering certain theological questions—the significance and spiritual dimensions of community, the conceptualization of difference in Jewish life, and the key concept of chosenness.

The Communal Nature of Personhood

Any understanding of Israel must begin with the recognition that Israel is a community, a people, not a collection of individual selves. The conviction that personhood is shaped, nourished, and sustained in community is a central assumption that Judaism and feminism share. To the Jew, the feminist, the Jewish feminist, the individual is not an isolated unit who attains humanity through independence from others or who must contract for social relations. Rather, to be a person is to find oneself from the beginning in community—or, as is often the case in the modern world, in multiple communities (Waskow, 124). To develop as a person is to acquire a sense of self in relation to others and to appropriate critically a series of communal heritages.

For feminists, insistence on the communal character of human selfhood is articulated over against the individualism of the dominant strand in Western culture and represents the intersection of a number of streams of experience and analysis. The consciousness-raising groups of the 1960s that marked the beginning of the second wave of feminism provided important evidence of the communal nature of human life. Examining our experience in the consciousness-raising context, women were able to piece together the processes of socialization and learning that shape the female role. We were able to see that our self-understandings, our life choices, our expectations of ourselves as women were not the products simply of our own growth and development but of powerful social forces that had molded us from birth. Moreover, at the same time we came to see the communal origins of the constraints on our lives, we also experienced community as the source of our liberation. Coming to a clear understanding of gender as socially constructed, we experienced a new opening of self, a sense of freedom to be and become our own persons rather than to live out prescriptive social roles. But this new sense of autonomous selfhood, like the traditional female self, came and could have come only with others. It was only as we sat and spoke together, as many women told of feelings and troubles that each had seen as her own, that "hearing drew forth . . . speech," and we were able to experience and understand the connections between what had been laid out for us and our own choices (Morton, 29; Plaskow 1979, 198–209). We apprehended selfhood not as something brought ready-made to community but as both shaped by community and enlarged by common commitment and struggle.

This direct and powerful experience of the connection between self and community has been supplemented by trenchant analytical critiques of liberal individualism as a basis for feminist theory. In *The Radical Future of Liberal Feminism,* Zillah Eisenstein argues that there is a fundamental contradiction between the liberal view of persons as isolated and self-created and feminist insistence on the social nature of women's oppression. Insofar as mainstream American feminism unconsciously adopts the dominant cultural assumption that individuals can freely and independently form their own lives, it cannot explain the oppression of women as a class or the role of social and political institutions in protecting patriarchal power relations. Only a theory that understands "sex-class oppression" and that "recognizes the importance of the individual within the social collectivity" can generate a politics that will liberate women (Eisenstein, chaps. 1, 8).

Feminist experience of communal personhood and feminist political and philosophical analyses of social selfhood cohere with women's historical experience of embeddedness in and responsibility for relation. As an extensive literature on women and relation attests, women generally have been denied the luxury of believing in the separate individual ego; we have been forced to know ourselves as dependent and depended on by others (Gilligan; Chodorow; Keller; Heyward). While much of the literature of relation is based on white middle-class women's experience, the testimony of minority women only expands and deepens this insistence on connection. For many minority women the sense of group solidarity in oppression has been a basic reality of existence (hooks 1984). Under the conditions of patriarchy, women's experience of relation has been distorted by sex, race, and class oppression, and women have been kept from self-determination within the web of connection. But this cannot negate the fact that women's relegation to the sphere of relation has kept women alive to a basic dimension of human experience that feminism affirms even as it seeks to transform the material character of human relations.

The knowledge that human beings are located in community is, of course, not limited to women. Shared by many cultures, it is central to both Jewish theology and the Jewish social experience. If to be a woman is to absorb and wrestle with a cultural understanding of femaleness, so to be a Jew is to absorb the history of the Jewish people. Jewish memory is communal memory and centers on community even as it forms and is formed by community. The covenantal history that begins in the Bible with Abraham, Isaac, and Jacob finds its fulfillment only at Sinai, when the whole congregation answers together, "All that the Lord has spoken we will do" (Ex 19:8). Though the Israelites are designated a people even in Egypt (Ex 1:9), it is only when they receive life and teachings as a community at Sinai that their prior history becomes important to remember. If you obey my covenant, God tells them, "you shall be to me a kingdom of priests and a holy nation" (Ex 19:6); at the moment of establishing the covenant, its corporate nature is affirmed (Gendler, 83; Buber, 138). From Sinai on, the Jewish relationship to God is mediated through this community. The Jew stands before God not as an individual but as a member of a people.

The theological significance of community in Judaism finds expression in religious, social, and national life. While the observant Jew is expected to pray three times daily whether alone or with others, there is a definite bias on behalf of public prayer. Maintaining a daily *minyan* (quorum for prayer) is regarded as an important function of the synagogue. Certain key prayers simply cannot be said unless there are ten men (sic) present, and the divine presence is said to rest in a unique way on the congregation. According to Rabbi Johanan, "When God comes to a synagogue and does not find a *minyan* there, [God] is angry, as it is written, 'Why, when I came, was there no one? When I called was there no one to answer?' (Is 50:2)" (*Encyclopedia Judaica*, "Minyan"; Katz, 176–77). It seems that once God establishes a covenant with the people as a whole, God is fully present only with and among the community. The individual who prays privately loses an important dimension of worship, and God hardly recognizes the people unless they are together.

Beyond the requirements of prayer, the sociological exigencies of Jewish existence also made for community. In some areas of the diaspora anti-Semitic legislation compelled Jews to live in certain districts, but even in areas where ghettos were not mandated by law, the Jews' relation to the larger political order was mediated through the Jewish community. Local communities (*kehillot*) operated semi-autonomously both in relation to each other and the wider Gentile culture, offering their members a range of services that today would be provided by a combination of charitable, religious, and state institutions (*Encyclopedia Judaica*, "Community"; Katz). Just as the Jew's relationship to God is mediated through membership in the Jewish people, so the Jew's relationship to society was mediated through the *kehillah*, which, in addition to providing for individual and communal needs, levied the taxes to be paid to the government and generally managed relations with the non-Jewish world.

Women in the Jewish Community

The similarities between feminist and Jewish understandings of the relation between self and community are substantial and genuine, and I have addressed the theme of community in Judaism without irony. Yet from a feminist perspective the Jewish emphasis on community is deeply ambiguous and ironic, for it coexists with the subordination of women within Jewish communal life. Affirming community, Judaism affirms a male community in which the place of women is an open and puzzling question. At times it seems as if women are simply not part of Israel at all; more usually, women's presence in the community is assumed, but assumed as clearly peripheral.

When, for example, God enters into a covenant with Abraham and says to him, "This is my covenant, which you shall keep, between me and you and your descendants after you: Every male among you shall be circumcised" (Gn 17:10), women can hear this only as establishing our marginality. Even if circumcision is not itself the covenant but only the sign of the covenant, what role can women have in the covenant community when the primary symbol of the covenant pertains only to men? This important passage seems to presuppose a religious community composed of males only, an impression reinforced by other texts. The covenant at Sinai is spoken in male pronouns, for example, and its content assumes male hearers (Bird, 49–50). But the very same sources that can be taken to indicate the exclusion of women from Israel are often contradictory or equivocal. The appearance and disappearance of women in many biblical narratives and the legal regulation of women's sexuality and status where unique biology or some anomaly demand it, make clear that, while women are hardly equal in the Israelite community, they are also not simply absent.

The place of women in the community of Israel can be illuminated most fully by Simone de Beauvoir's notion of woman as "other." In her classic work *The Second Sex*, de Beauvoir argues that men have established an absolute human type—the male—against which women are measured as "other." Women cannot simply be excluded from community, for the relationship between men and women is not like other relationships between oppressor and oppressed. Men and women are parts of a totality in which, biologically speaking, both sides are necessary. Without women, it is impossible for any community to continue. Yet as far as normative Jewish texts are concerned, women do not define the values that make the community distinctive or that warrant its perpetuation. Women are not the subjects and molders of their own experiences but the objects of male purposes, designs, and desires (de Beauvoir, xv, xix, xvi). Thus women *are* part of the covenant community, but precisely in a submerged and non-normative way.

It is not simply narrative sources that reveal the place of women in the Jewish community, moreover, but also *halakhah* (Jewish law). *Halakhah* seeks to regulate communal behavior and make communal ideals concrete. In the case of women, legal exemption from public prayer and Torah study and legal subordination within the patriarchal family together carve out a restricted communal role. As Moshe Meiselman suggests (Meiselman, 14), the proper sphere of women is captured by Psalm 45:14, "The entire glory of the daughter of the king lies on the inside." The rabbis saw in this passage confirmation of the supposedly private nature of women's role and enforced this view through *halakhic* rulings. Since in many periods of Jewish history women helped earn the family livelihood, the Jewish division of male and female roles does not correspond exactly to the public/private distinction in our modern sense. What is written into law, however, is male control of public religious values and the male definition of women in terms of female biology.

Jewish feminists have often, and with reason, seen the restricted role of women in the Jewish community as a justice issue. The fact that we have been excluded from the public religious forum and socialized to a limited set of family roles has kept women from fully developing as persons and has deprived the Jewish community of the energy and talents of half its members. *Halakhah* has cordoned off from women just those avenues of religious expression the tradition values most highly. Torah study, Torah reading, leadership of the congregation, daily participation in public prayer are important vehicles of religious experience that women either have not been encouraged to develop or have been altogether denied.

Yet once we see the importance of community in the Jewish experience, we must add to all this another dimension of loss that women suffer. Over and above the value of participation in any particular religious activity is the spiritual aspect of community itself. It is not just that community is the space within which one fulfills a range of religious duties and reaps a range of spiritual rewards, but that community is the primary vehicle and place of religious experience. Thus, God did not enter into the covenant at Sinai because it was easiest to speak to the people when they were gathered together. God's speech established them as a community, and it was as a community that they heard the voice of God. If women are submerged in the Jewish covenant community, then we are excluded from the center of Jewish religious experience. There is no Jewish way to go off into the desert and have an independent relationship to God. Relationship to God is experienced and mediated precisely through the community that maintains women's marginality.

No panegyric on the virtues of private spirituality can disguise the fact that the nature of religious experience in Judaism is fundamentally communal or that the historical importance of public worship has a spiritual grounding. The divine presence rests in community in a uniquely powerful way.

But this means that the exclusion of women from full membership in the Jewish community is *in itself* apart from exclusion from this or that religious obligation, exclusion of women from a profound and central dimension of Jewish spiritual life. Women's otherness is not just a matter of social and religious marginality but of spiritual deprivation.

Toward a Redefinition of Israel

Ending this social and spiritual marginality requires a far-reaching transformation of Jewish life. To recreate Israel from a feminist perspective, we must incorporate women's experience into the understanding and practice of the Jewish people so that women's contributions to Jewish community are not driven underground, thwarted, or distorted, and men's are not given more weight and status than they ought to enjoy. Until that happens, both our concept of Israel and the dynamics of Jewish life will remain thoroughly misshapen by sexism.

As Jewish feminists seek equality in a tradition that takes seriously the importance of community in human life, we must not neglect the centrality of community by repeating in relation to Judaism the liberal feminist mistake of seeing women as individuals who happen to be discriminated against in the Jewish system. Insofar as we fight for equality assuming as given the Judaism in which we are to be equal, we run the risk of gaining access to a community that structures its central ideas and institutions around male norms, but without changing the character of those ideas or institutions. Women in Judaism—like women in any patriarchal culture—are rendered invisible *as a class*; we are seen as "other" *as a class*; we are deprived of agency *as a class*. Until we understand and change the ways in which Judaism as a system supports the subordination of Jewish women as a sub-community within the Jewish people, genuine equality of women and men is impossible.

The real challenge of feminism to Judaism emerges, not when women as individual Jews demand equal participation in the male tradition, but when women demand equality *as Jewish women,* as the class that has up until now been seen as "other." To phrase the feminist challenge to Judaism in an other than liberal way, we might say that the central issue in the feminist redefinition of Israel is the place of difference in community. Judaism can absorb many women rabbis, teachers, and communal leaders; it can ignore or reinterpret certain laws to allow women to participate fully in a *minyan;* it can make adjustments around the edges; it can live with the ensuing contradictions and tensions without fundamentally altering its self-understanding. But when women, with our own history and spirituality and attitudes and experiences, demand equality in a community that will allow itself to be changed by our differences, when we ask that our memories become part of Jewish memory and our presence change the present, then we make a demand that is radical and transforming. Then we begin the arduous experiment of trying to create a Jewish community in which difference is neither hierarchalized nor tolerated but truly honored. Then we begin to struggle for the only equality that is genuine.

The Issue of Difference in Community

Since the insistence that women be accepted in Judaism as women may seem neither new nor radical, it is important to define where its challenge lies. It is not the recognition of difference that is in itself difficult. Judaism has always recognized—indeed insisted on—the differences between women and men. But it is of the essence of these differences as traditionally understood that they have been stratified and defined from the perspective of the dominant group. What is new about Jewish feminism is that *women* are claiming the right to define and assess our differences, that we are revaluing and renaming what has been used to oppress us. The fact that this undertaking on the part of Jewish feminists is analogous to struggles both of minority feminists and of Jews in the modern West brings into focus the enormous obstacles to creating communities rich in diversity and accountable to different perspectives. Examining some of the connections between the feminist, Jewish, and Jewish feminist situations may help clarify what is at stake in redefining Israel as a community that honors difference.

The feminist context is in some ways the most instructive for understanding the problem of difference in community because contemporary feminism has had a strong ideological commitment to including all women. The consciousness-raising groups of the 1960s tried to free themselves from the structures of domination in the wider society in order to provide spaces where every woman could be heard. Commitment to the bonds of sisterhood in the face of the pervasive nature of sexism was supposedly rooted in affirmation of all women's experience and each woman's struggle. As minority women increasingly have made clear, however, feminist theory and priorities often have ignored the multiple communities that shape women's lives. Assuming that male/female difference is the oldest and only important social difference, white middle-class feminists many times have constructed accounts of women's experience that falsely universalize a particular cultural and class perspective (Moraga and Anzaldua; hooks 1981 and 1984; Hull, Scott, and Smith; Spelman 1988). The identification of "woman" with white middle-class—often Gentile—women is a continuing problem in feminist writing. It is illustrated by the persistence of anti-Semitic stereotypes in feminist literature, the additive analyses of sexism and racism that ignore the reality of many women's lives, and the exclusionary phrase "women and blacks" that appears and reappears in feminist writing (Spelman, 1982, 42–46). The message such work communicates to minority women—Jewish women as well as women of color, although in different ways—is that if we want to be part of the "women's" movement, we should bring ourselves as women in the abstract (i.e. women of the dominant group), leaving aside the particular women we happen to be (Spelman 1988).

Commitment to feminism does not, then, automatically entail willingness to relinquish race, class, and religious privilege—or even to acknowledge they exist. While, in part, the persistence of race and class prejudice within the women's movement can be attributed to a liberal ideology that disguises the real power relations within society, fear of difference is itself a factor that continues to divide women from each other. Once we acknowledge the diversity and multiplicity of women's loyalties, what guarantee is there that we will find a common ground? Moreover, Audre Lorde suggests that when women have been educated in a society that sees all difference in terms of inferiority and superiority, "the recognition of any difference must be fraught with guilt" (Lorde, 118). Concerned that—as has so often happened in the past—recognizing difference will lead to inequality, feminists repeatedly have adopted the strategy of pretending that differences among women do not exist. But, of course, denying differences does not abolish them; it simply allows traditional forms of domination to continue unacknowledged. Moreover, avoiding differences prevents women from mining the knowledge and power that are rooted in our racial, ethnic, and religious particularity and from using "difference as a springboard for creative change" (Lorde, 115).

If feminism claims to respect difference and yet at the same time denies it, the modern West's offer of civil rights to the Jews was never premised on the acceptance of difference, even as a theoretical possibility. Jewish emancipation—the grant of full citizenship and legal equality—was based on the expectation that "in the absence of persecution and enforced segregation, Jews and Judaism would assimilate to the prevailing social and cultural norms of the environment" (Hyman, 165). The dominant groups in various European nations explicitly claimed the right to define the reality to which Jews would accommodate themselves. Jews were granted free access to the wider culture, but only at the cost of the communal autonomy that had characterized Jewish life for centuries and that had provided Jews with community, identity, and a set of common beliefs and values. In the words of a liberal deputy to the French national assembly, "One must refuse everything to the Jews as a nation but one must give them everything as individuals" (Hertzberg, 360). Relinquishing all Jewish particularity, Jews were to become German or Briton or French people of the Jewish religion, a religion that would now stress universal values and give up its peculiar and discriminatory forms. Insofar as Jews insisted on continuing to define their identity in ethnic as well as religious terms, they were regarded as reneging on a clear bargain and as occasioning the discrimination that legal emancipation did not eradicate. As *The Christian Century* asked rhetorically in a 1930s editorial, "Can democracy suffer a hereditary minority to perpetuate itself as a permanent minority, with its own distinctive culture sanctioned by its own distinctive cult form?" (cited in Eisen, 34). The writer is unable to imagine a democracy in which citizens share certain common values, yet also maintain allegiance to traditional sub-communities.

In the early period of emancipation Jews embraced the benefits of citizenship, accepting—sometimes willingly, sometimes out of necessity—the implicit or explicit conditions that went along. Two hundred years later, however, the communal and individual costs of emancipation are very clear assimilation, fragmentation, loss of self-determination, loss of common identity and purpose. In traditional society Jews may have been outsiders, but they had an important defense against indifference or hatred; their own communal self-understanding radically contradicted the world outside. In the modern world Jews have more deeply internalized society's expectations and values, becoming divided from the Jew within the self. Social contempt for Jewish particularity finds its echo in Jewish contempt for Jewish noses, Jewish hair, Jewish assertiveness, Jewish mothers, Jewish history, Jewish religious life. Jews unable to affirm our own Jewishness or even to understand its meaning have little energy or creativity to bring to our Jewish communities.

The long struggle by Jews in the modern era to "prove the religious, intellectual, and social viability of Judaism within an open . . . society" (Hyman, 170)—and the struggle of contemporary minority feminists to address differences within the feminist community—makes *The Christian Century*'s question anything but rhetorical. Why is it unthinkable for minority communities to perpetuate themselves within a democracy—or within a movement? Is communal identity and cohesion really at odds with participation in a wider society? Given that in the modern world most individuals belong to more than one community, that communal loyalties diverge and overlap, is it not possible to affirm a common commitment to a national or feminist identity without denying other aspects of the self? Is it not possible that the interaction of distinctive sub-communities could enrich a total community? And given the tremendous costs of self-division, is it not in the interests of the state or the women's movement to allow individuals their communal roots? Is not the dream of many Jews in the modern world—acceptance by the broader culture in and through our particularity and not despite it—a worthy starting point for reconceptualizing community?

And what then of Jewish feminists? Jews among feminists, feminists among Jews, Jewish feminists have experienced the burden of difference in all the various communities to which we belong. The distrust of difference that has characterized feminism in relation to minority women and modern nationalist movements in relation to Jews is equally present in the Jewish community. Indeed, non-Orthodox Judaism places women in the same position in the Jewish community that Jews have found ourselves in relation to the modern state. The bargain is less obvious because the character of Jewish women's bonds and culture is less obvious, being part of the great silence that shrouds women's experience. But insofar as women have distinctive rituals, a history, literature, modes of connection that grow out of centuries of sex-role segregation, these are to be abandoned for the privilege of participating in a dominant male culture that does not recognize anything of value in what will now be lost (Prell, 585). Moreover, since Jewish women, like Jews in modern society, are expected to internalize the values of the dominant group, we are also to forget our own history and forget even that it has been forgotten. Lacking a community of Jewish women to counter the perceptions of a male-defined Jewish culture—or a WASP-defined feminist one—our heritage of power as Jewish women is translated into anxiety lest we be dominating Jewish mothers, lest we be perceived as "taking over," or lest there be a "princess" lurking in our souls. The "other's other," we take in both the images of Jews and specifically Jewish women in the wider society, and also the projections of Jewish men.

Clearly the liberal notion of equality cannot provide an adequate theoretical basis for transforming Israel on feminist terms. Yet the gains of liberalism must not be repudiated in moving beyond it, any more than the costs of emancipation mean it should be revoked. Historically, liberalism made possible the recognition of Jews and women as human beings, an achievement that is the indispensable prerequisite of our true equality. But once we realize that recognizing others as individuals is fully compatible with fostering the power and self-understanding of dominant groups, it becomes necessary to move to an understanding of community that incorporates the accomplishments of liberalism and at the same time responds to its flaws. Jewish feminists want from the Jewish and feminist communities what women of color want from the feminist community, what self-affirming Jews want from the wider culture: equality in our particularity, acknowledgment of the many communities that shape our lives, acknowledgment of our complex history and experience, and attention to that history and experience in the formulation of cultural or religious norms and values.

Chosenness, Hierarchy, and Difference

It is not sufficient, however, simply to call the Jewish community to an acceptance of difference. To understand more fully those aspects of Judaism that thwart Jewish acceptance of diversity, we must examine further those ideas that have contributed to Judaism's long history of conceptualizing difference in terms of hierarchical separations. Suspicion and ranking of difference have been aspects of Judaism from its beginnings. Thinking of itself as a "kingdom of priests and a holy nation," the Jewish people understood its own holiness partly in contradistinction to the beliefs and behavior of surrounding nations. Serving the Lord meant shunning and destroying foreign gods and morality, thus refusing the "snare" of a different religious system (Ex 23:23–33). Paralleling external differentiation were a host of internal separations that set apart distinct and unequal objects, states, and modes of being. On a religious level, to be a holy people was both to be different from one's neighbors and to distinguish between and differently honor pure and impure; Sabbath and week; kosher and non-kosher; Cohen, Levi, and Israel (grades of priests and ordinary Jews); and male and female. On a social level the "otherness" of women was the first and most persistent among many inequalities that have marked Jewish life. Differences in wealth, learning, and observance; differences in cultural background and customs; differences in religious affiliation and understanding have all provided occasions for certain groups of Jews to define themselves as superior to different and non-normative "others." The distinction between men and women was never a unique hierarchy but emerged as part of a system in which many people and aspects of existence were defined in terms of superiority and inferiority (Setel 1986; Falk).

This hierarchical understanding of difference is perhaps the most significant barrier to the feminist reconceptualization of Jewish community. Jewish feminists cannot transform the place of women's difference within the people of Israel without addressing the larger system of separations in which it is embedded. In the context of the reconceptualization of Israel it is the notion of chosenness that is the chief expression of hierarchical distinction and therefore the most important focus for discussion. As a central category for Jewish self-understanding that is emblematic of other gradations, chosenness provides a warrant and a model for ranked differentiations within the community and between Israel and others. If Jewish feminism is to articulate a model of community in which difference is acknowledged without being expressed in hierarchical distinctions, it will have to engage the traditional Jewish understanding of difference by rejecting the idea of chosenness without at the same time denying the distinctiveness of Israel as a religious community.

Chosenness is a complex and evolving idea in Judaism that is by no means always associated with claims to superiority. While there is a strand in Jewish thinking that attributes chosenness to special qualities in the Jews and that argues for Jewish hereditary spiritual uniqueness and supremacy, by and large Israel's election is viewed not as a matter of merit or attributes but of responsibilities and duties. When the notion of chosenness first appears in the Bible simultaneously with the establishment of Israel as a covenant community, there is no apparent motive for Israel's special status but God's steadfast love and (itself unexplained) earlier promise to the 4 patriarchs (Dt 7:7–8). Israel's standing as God's "own possession among all peoples" (Ex 19:5–6; Dt 7:6) is linked to acceptance and observance of the covenant; this constitutes its specialness in its own eyes and in the eyes of others (Dt 4:5–7). When Deutero-Isaiah shifts emphasis from election of Israel as holy community to election of Israel as servant to the world, he still gives no reason for God's selection. This prophet of exile calls Israel "a light to the nations" and interprets its suffering as a sign of chosenness and future redemption (Is 49:6; 53), but election is marked by suffering, not by exaltation (Eisen, 16–18; *Encyclopedia Judaica*, "Chosen People"; *Encyclopedia of Religion*, "Election"; Atlan, 56–57).

If ascription of supernatural sanctity to Israel is the exception rather than the rule, however, this eliminates only some of the troubling aspects of the notion of chosenness.

When election is understood as obligation or taken for granted as the foundation of the *halakhic* life, the privileged nature of Israel's relationship to God remains even while explicit claims to superiority are absent (Atlan, 56). After all, the traditional male Jew who each morning blesses God for not making him a woman is said to be giving thanks for the special burden and responsibility of *halakhic* observance rather than deliberately vaunting his prerogatives. But however humbly he accepts his legal burden, his prayer nonetheless presupposes that women are exempt from *halakhic* responsibility, that the other side of his privilege is their exclusion. This same dichotomy applies to the gift of chosenness, which is similarly acknowledged in the morning blessings. The Jew is grateful to be a Jew because the burden of Jewishness is a boon and privilege others do not share. As the daily liturgy makes amply clear, the lot of the Jews is singular; their special destiny is God's unique choice, not one path among many. Whether this destiny is characterized in terms of the *noblesse oblige* of witness and service or straightforward claims to metaphysical superiority, it still constitutes a hierarchical differentiation.

To express the import of election in relation to the issue of difference, chosenness says that the Jewish difference is different from other people's difference; that Jews are different differently from the way in which other groups are different from one another. Jewish difference is not one among many, the uniqueness of a people as all peoples are unique, having their own history and task. Jewish difference is a matter of God's decision, God's mysterious and singular choice bestowing upon the Jews an unparalleled spiritual destiny. This difference is a hierarchical difference, a statement of privilege—even if burdensome and unmerited privilege—in relation to those who are not chosen.

Feminists troubled by this hierarchical understanding of the relation between Jews and others are hardly alone in our concern. Since emancipation, the concept of chosenness has been as much a source of embarrassment to Jews as of sustenance. Its exclusivity has seemed to many Jews to be in conflict with the desire for civic equality; its assumption of a special destiny to be in tension with the simple humanity of the Jew that was the premise of emancipation. In the last two hundred years the concept of chosenness has been almost endlessly refashioned as Jewish thinkers have tried to find ways to discard and retain it at the same time. Chosenness has been reinterpreted in terms of mission to the nations and universal ethics; the notion of Jewish superiority has been roundly rejected; the boundaries between God's choosing and Jewish God-consciousness have been thoroughly confused (Eisen, 1–22). Yet with the exception of the Reconstructionists' explicit repudiation of election, few of these reinterpretations have eliminated the stubborn implication of privilege the concept of chosenness entails.

In this situation feminist criticism of chosenness may seem simply to add one more small voice to what is already a surfeit of inconclusive discussion. Yet if feminists share many of the concerns of other critics, we also have a distinctive perspective to bring to the conversation. While most reinterpretations of election have focused on the relation of Jews to the wider society—seeking to reconcile chosenness with equality and participation in a pluralistic culture—feminism calls attention to the function of chosenness in relation to Jewish self-conception and the internal dynamics of the community. Feminist objections to the idea of chosenness center not just on its entanglement with external hierarchical differentiations but with internal hierarchies as well.

Chosenness is not just a statement about Jewish relations with other peoples but a focus for Jewish self-understanding. If Jews are set apart from others through a unique call to God's service, this call must first express itself in Jewish communal life. The holiness that leads to external differentiation is lived out through observing the internal separations that mark a holy community. Since chief among these many separations is the differentiation between male and female, chosenness becomes linked to the subordination of women and other groups in the rhythms of Jewish existence. It is not that one can draw a direct line from the idea of chosenness to the creation of "others" within the Jewish community or that the former provides an explicit model for the latter. But both are part of a cluster of important ideas that make graded differentiation a central model for understanding difference, and the two are also linked to each other both historically and psychologically.

It is worthy of note, for example, that in the same period in which Deutero-Isaiah elaborated the notion of chosenness, placing its significance in a world-historic context, there emerged for the first time persistent use of female sexuality as a symbol of evil. In an earlier period, when election was understood primarily in terms of Israel's observance of the commandments, women's sexuality was strictly controlled within the patriarchal family but was not seen as negative in and of itself (Setel 1985, 86, 88–90). This means that as the experience of exile gave rise to a new and more elevated interpretation of chosenness, the status of women diminished. The precise connection between these ideas is difficult to establish, but their historical correlation speaks to the real association between different types of hierarchical thinking. Moreover, the fact that both ideas emerge in relation to the exile suggests that the process of distinguishing between normative and non-normative Jews may be linked to the notion of chosenness through the dynamics of Jewish suffering.

The concept of chosenness has been an important solace to Jews in the face of anti-Jewish oppression, and it was often articulated more strongly where suffering was more severe. Emphasis on the unique destiny of the Jewish people and on the differences between Jew and Gentile would have provided an important counterbalance to the painful messages of the world and helped make Jewish misery intelligible and bearable. The self-concept that emerged as a compensation for suffering and outward rejection, however, was exaggeratedly elevated. As such, it was necessarily in tension both with the constant realities of life in a hostile culture and with the truth of human imperfection. Though nothing in their lives would have made this realization easy, Jews were not really so different from their neighbors, except that the complex of forces that made for their oppression also kept them from acting out their sense of superiority and/or rage. In this situation in which an enlarged self-concept was challenged by daily experience, someone had to bear the weight of "otherness" reflected in the mirror of the Gentile world, and also the pain and anger, lusts and temptations that Jewish flesh is heir to. Although there were many groups within the Jewish community, which in different periods carried part of this burden, the Jewish woman was always a safe recipient of Jewish male projection. Marginalized in the wider society as well as Jewish culture, she represented both the "otherness" the male Jew rejected for himself and the qualities that could not be acknowledged in a chosen people. A member of the elect, she was nonetheless the underside of that election (Breitman 1987, 1988). It is thus no coincidence that a new notion of chosenness and a new image of women entered the world together, for one demanded the other as its psychological complement and completion.

A dynamic in which an over-elevated self-understanding must be balanced by the creation of "others" within the elect community points the way to change, however, through its own reversal. If the notion of the Jews as the chosen people seems to require the subordination of women, the withdrawal of projection from women is the correlate of a measured and clear-eyed understanding of the self. The male Jew's acknowledgment of his own simple humanity is integrally related to the recognition of Jewish women as normative Jewish human beings, just as the acceptance of women as human fosters the recognition of all Jews' simple humanity. The rejection of chosenness and the rejection of women's "otherness" are interconnected pieces of the wider project of finding ways to conceptualize and live with difference that are not based on projection and graded separations.

If feminists reject the concept of election, however, what remains of the distinctiveness of Israel and its relationship to the choosing God? Modern Jewish thinkers have hesitated to give up the idea of chosenness because they have been afraid that, with it, they would surrender the rationale for Jewish existence. But chosenness is necessary to justify Jewish life only on a view that does not take seriously the communal nature of human existence. If human beings are isolated individuals who must be persuaded to link ourselves with others, then Jewish commitment, like any form of communal engagement, requires argument and warrant. If, however, community is constitutive of personhood, then it needs no supernatural vocation to connect the Jew with Jewish living. Jewishness is a rich and distinctive way of being human, of linking oneself with God and with other persons, of finding a pattern within which to live that gives life depth and meaning. That is enough reason to be a Jew.

To argue for the self-justifying nature of Jewish life is not to reduce Judaism to a sense of group belonging or to define Israel without reference to God. The Jewish people came into being as a result of and in response to profound religious experiences, and it has been the purpose of its long history to ever more deeply comprehend and live out the relationship to God that drew it from its first hour. While the notion of a supernatural deity who singles out a particular people is part of the dualistic, hierarchical understanding of reality that the feminist must repudiate, to reject this idea of God is not to reject the God who is met in community and wrestled with in history. Nor is it to deny that loyalty to God has been at the center of Jewish identity and an important part of what makes that identity distinctive.

Indeed, the purpose of a feminist critique of chosenness and redefinition of Israel is not to truncate Jewish spirituality but to liberate it from its connection with hierarchical dualisms. So long as the Jewish people holds onto a self-understanding that perpetuates graded distinctions within the community, Jewish spirituality will be defined by and limited to a small proportion of Jews. Women will be excluded from the relationship with God that comes through full participation in community. The history of their experience and understanding of God will be excluded from Jewish memory. Only a Jewish community that permits and desires its members to be present in their particularity and totality can know in its fullness the relationship to God that it claims as its center.

What must replace chosenness, then, as the model for Jewish self-understanding is the far less dramatic *distinctness*. The Jewish community and the sub-communities within it, like all human communities, are distinct and distinctive. Jewish experience has been variously shaped by gender, by place of dispersion, by language, by history, by interaction with other cultures. Just as the total Jewish experience is always located within a wider world, so the experiences of Jewish subgroups have taken place in some relation to a larger Jewish life and self-understanding. The term *distinctness* suggests, however, that the relation between these various communities—Jewish to non-Jewish, Jewish to Jewish—should be understood not in terms of hierarchical differentiation but in terms of part and whole.

The use of a part/whole model for understanding difference has a number of implications. First of all, it points to the greater unity to which different groups belong, making it possible to acknowledge the uniqueness of each group as part of a wider association of self-differentiated communities (Falk, 122). Jewish women are part of the larger Jewish community as Jews are part of a larger heterogeneous culture. The parts are distinct. They have their own history and experience, and depending on their character, their own institutions, religion, practices, and beliefs. The content of this distinctness creates an internal sense of group identity and community and also allows the group to distinguish itself from others. Without this distinctiveness—were such a "without" even imaginable—we would lack the richness and diversity, the color and the passion, the insights and the wisdom that make up human history and culture. But while distinction is necessary, inevitable, a cause for celebration, the boundaries of distinction need not be rigidly guarded by graded separations. Boundaries can also be places where people can touch. Awareness of the wider communities to which any community belongs fosters an appreciation of distinctness that need not be rooted in hierarchy or in projection onto others of rejected aspects of the self.

Second, if the different groups and subgroups that make up a community or nation are parts of a greater whole, there is no whole without all the pieces. Though Jewish history frequently has been abstracted from its varied surroundings and studied as an independent subject—and though the histories of other peoples often make scant reference to the Jews—Jewish history is part of the history of the peoples and cultures among whom the Jews have lived. Thus, for example, unless European history includes the experience of Jews, it is not truly European history but rather the history of the dominant Christian cultures within Europe. Similarly, unless Jewish history and community include the history and experience of women, it is not truly Jewish history or Jewish community but male Jewish history and community. Such exclusion is destructive not only to the groups ignored but also to the rich tapestry of Jewish life that grows in distinctness and beauty with the distinctness and beauty of its various portions.

Third, what is true of communities is also true of selves. Where the boundaries between communities are marked by hierarchical separations, normative humanity is defined without reference to groups that are less valued. Thus Europeanness is defined without reference to Jews, Jewishness without reference to Jewish women. But the further effect of this separative understanding of community is that individuals within subordinate groups repress those aspects of themselves that are despised in the culture. Jews do not bring the special contributions of Jewishness to bear on wider social issues. Jewish women, as we gain equal access to Jewish communal life, deny our own experience for normative male practice and discourse. Those whose differences might have enriched and challenged the greater communal life learn to forget or keep hidden pieces of themselves.

We are brought back to the spiritual injury that such forgetting entails, and to the potential for liberation in a different model of community. To be wholly present in our lives in all our power is to touch the greater power of being that is the final unity within which all particulars dwell. To deny our complex particularity, as individuals or communities, is to diminish our connection to the God known in and through the experience of community. The community or self that spends its energy repressing parts of its totality truncates its creative power and cuts itself off from its full possibilities (Ackelsberg, March 1983, October 1983). A Jewish community that defines itself by walling itself off from others without and within marshals strength at its boundaries to the detriment of the center. It nourishes selves that must deny parts of themselves and thus cannot bring their uniqueness to the enrichment of a common life. To create Jewish communities that value particularity is to create places where Jews in their complex wholeness can bring their full power to the upbuilding of Jewish community and the other communities in which Jews dwell. It is in the distinctiveness that opens itself to difference that we find the God of Israel and of each and every people.

REFERENCES

Ackelsberg, Martha. "Personal Identities and Collective Visions: Reflections on Being a Jew and a Feminist." Unpublished lecture, Smith College, March 8, 1983.

———. "Towards a Feminist Judaism." Unpublished lecture delivered at the Jewish Women's Conference: Challenge and Change, October 1983.

Atlan, Henri. "Chosen People." In *Contemporary Jewish Religious Thought: Original Essays on Critical Concepts, Movements and Beliefs.* Ed. Arthur A. Cohen and Paul Mendes-Flohr. New York: Charles Scribner's Sons, 1987.

Bird, Phyllis. "Images of Women in the Old Testament." In *Religion and Sexism: Images of Women in the Jewish and Christian Traditions.* Ed. Rosemary Ruether. New York: Simon and Schuster, 1974.

Breitman, Barbara. "Psychopathology of Jewish Men." *Letter to Tikkun* 2 (1987).

———. "Lifting Up the Shadow of Anti-Semitism." In *A Mensch Among Men: Explorations in Jewish Masculinity.* Ed. Harry Brod. Freedom, California: Crossing Press, 1988.

Buber, Martin. *Israel and the World: Essays in a Time of Crisis.* New York: Schocken Books, 1963.

Chodorow, Nancy. *The Reproduction of Mothering: Psychoanalysis and the Sociology of Gender.* Berkeley and Los Angeles: University of California Press, 1978.

De Beauvoir, Simone. *The Second Sex.* Trans. H.M. Parshley. New York: Bantam Books, 1961.

Eisen, Arnold. *The Chosen People in America: A Study in Jewish Religious Ideology.* Bloomington: Indiana University Press, 1983.

Eisenstein, Zillah. *The Radical Future of Liberal Feminism.* New York: Longman, 1981.

Falk, Marcia. Response to "Feminist Reflections on Separation and Unity in Jewish Theology." *Journal of Feminist Studies in Religion* 2 (Spring 1986).

Gendler, Everett E. "Community." In *Contemporary Jewish Religious Thought: Original Essays on Critical Concepts, Movements and Beliefs.* Ed. Arthur A. Cohen and Paul Mendes-Flohr. New York: Charles Scribner's Sons, 1987. See also Atlan, 81–86.

Gilligan, Carol. *In a Different Voice: Psychological Theory and Women's Development.* Cambridge: Harvard University Press, 1982.

Hertzberg, Arthur. *The French Enlightenment and the Jews: The Origins of Modern Anti-Semitism.* New York: Schocken Books, 1968.

Heschel, Susannah, ed. *On Being a Jewish Feminist: A Reader.* New York: Schocken Books, 1983.

Heyward, Carter. *The Redemption of God: A Theology of Mutual Relation.* Washington, D.C.: University Press of America, 1982.

hooks, bell. *Ain't I a Woman: Black Women and Feminism*. Boston: South End Press, 1981.

———. *Feminist Theory: From Margin to Center*. Boston: South End Press, 1984.

Hull, Gloria, Patricia Bell Scott, and Barbara Smith. *All the Women Are White, All the Blacks Are Men, But Some of Us Are Brave*. Old Westbury, New York: The Feminist Press, 1982.

Hyman, Paula. "Emancipation." In *Contemporary Jewish Religious Thought: Original Essays on Critical Concepts, Movements and Beliefs*. Ed. Arthur A. Cohen and Paul Mendes-Flohr. New York: Charles Scribner's Sons, 1987. See also Gendler, 165–70.

Katz, Jacob. *Tradition and Crisis: Jewish Society at the End of the Middle Ages*. New York: The Free Press of Glencoe, 1961.

Keller, Catherine. *From a Broken Web: Separation, Sexism and Self*. Boston: Beacon Press, 1986.

Koltun, Elizabeth. *The Jewish Woman: New Perspectives*. New York: Schocken Books, 1976.

Lorde, Audre. *Sister Outsider*. Trumansburg, New York: The Crossing Press, 1984.

Meiselman, Moshe. *Jewish Woman in Jewish Law*. New York: KTAV and Yeshiva University Press, 1978.

Moraga, Chérrie, and Gloria Anzaldua. *This Bridge Called My Back: Writings By Radical Women of Color*. Watertown, Massachusetts: Persephone Press, 1981.

Morton, Nelle. *The Journey Is Home*. Boston: Beacon Press, 1985.

Plaskow, Judith. "The Coming of Lilith: Toward a Feminist Theology." In *Womanspirit Rising: A Feminist Reader in Religion*. Ed. Carol P. Christ and Judith Plaskow. San Francisco: Harper and Row, 1979.

———. *Standing Again at Sinai: Rethinking Judaism from a Feminist Perspective*. San Francisco: Harper and Row, 1990.

Prell, Riv-Ellen. "The Vision of Woman in Classical Reform Judaism." *Journal of the American Academy of Religion* 50 (December 1982): 575–89.

Setel, Drorah. "Prophets and Pornography: Female Sexual Imagery in Hosea." In *Feminist Interpretation of the Bible*. Ed. Letty M. Russell. Philadelphia: The Westminster Press, 1985.

———. "Feminist Reflections on Separation and Unity in Jewish Theology." *Journal of Feminist Studies in Religion* 2 (Spring 1986): 113–18.

Spelman, Elizabeth V. "Theories of Race and Gender: The Erasure of Black Women." *Quest: A Feminist Quarterly* 5 (1982): 36–62.

———. *Inessential Woman: Problems of Exclusion in Feminist Theory*. Boston: Beacon Press, 1988.

Waskow, Arthur. *Rainbow Sign: The Shape of Hope*. Unpublished manuscript, 1987.

With a Song in Her Heart
Listening to Scholars Listening for Miriam

ALICE BACH

Miriam figures prominently in a 1994 collection of essays entitled *A Feminist Companion to Exodus-Deuteronomy*. Three of the articles about Miriam in the collection are concerned with establishing the relation of her song to the song attributed to her brother Moses (Exod. 15.1–18). Is Miriam's song (Exod. 15.19–21) a female echo to the song of Moses?[1] Or is Miriam's finale, as Trible argues in her essay for the collection, all that remains of her story after the patriarchal redactors have inserted their man Moses into the text? Janzen, in his piece, also wants to find a priority of the Miriamic version, but argues differently from Trible to reach a similar conclusion. Beginning with the assumption that the Song of Moses is "an elaborate answer to the Song of Miriam and the women," van Dijk-Hemmes reviews much of the literature in which Miriam's song is understood to be the initial version. These articles are attuned to the best historical and redactional theories associated with contemporary biblical scholarship and engage the gendered concerns of their authors. All three scholars have the same agenda: "to seek Miriam buried under the work of patriarchal storytellers."[2] Trible similarly refers to Miriam's fragmented story as "buried within Scripture," and understands her own task to be "unearthing the fragments, assembling them, pondering the gaps and constructing a text." The figure of the narrator/redactor as constructed by these biblical scholars holds all the cards. The implicit assumption that redactors in their eagerness to suppress the story of Miriam carelessly overlooked a few signs of the powerful female prophet presents difficulties for me.

To focus the concern on the priority of Miriam's narrative reflects the contemporary interpreters' desire to return some importance to the female literary figure. However, by concentrating upon the ancient redactors, whose political and theological programs are well known, one ignores the narrative as it appears in final form. Further, one creates another story, one in which the battle is between a female-authored/performed Song of the Sea and the redactors who have set about to drown it in the shifting undercurrents of patriarchy. This analytic strategy, founded on the binary oppositions so dear to the hearts of structuralist interpreters, is an accepted way to argue for a suppressed story beneath the one that presents ideological difficulties for the reader. As such I do not intend to disable or discredit the scholars who employ such a method. Nor do I imply that my reading should displace the earlier ones upon which mine draws. What I want to suggest is that we cannot simply replace an old authority with a new authority, but that new alignments need to be made across borders, types, and scholarly disciplines. Instead of a song that is attributed either to Moses or to Miriam, I hear one that is contrapuntal. Hearing a song of lament in these scholarly arguments, a song that mourns the diminished voice of the female prophet Miriam, I want to understand that melody and how it results in a new song of Miriam. Then, I would like to suggest a hybrid strategy, heterogeneous and unmonolithic, that interweaves the textual analyses of Trible, van Dijk-Hemmes, and Janzen, with the cultural perspective of Meyers and the midrashic portrait presented by Graetz, together with a midrash of my own.

The articles about Miriam in *A Feminist Companion to Exodus-Deuteronomy* attest to the fact that the story of Exodus 15 has not eradicated Miriam. Clearly, Miriam could have disappeared with a stroke of the scribal stylus, but Exodus 15 reflects not annihilation, but an answer to the question of who has won the battle of narrative voice. At least for a time. Clearly, the main battle in the Exodus story is a national one, not a gendered one. In my reading, the story in the first half of the book focuses on the struggle of a subjugated people to overthrow their oppressors; the book of Exodus in its final form reflects the effort of a people to write their own history and establish their identity. The difficulty for contemporary readers, as evidenced by our three textual scholars, is that they are looking for signs of another struggle, the contested and gendered position of the primary leader in the celebration of Israel's victory at the Sea.

Who holds the power to narrate is in my view what is truly at issue in the three articles concerned with the narrative qualities of the biblical text. Since scholarly interpreters have consistently awarded this power within the Exodus text to the figure of the redactor, for the moment I shall center the power to narrate within the redactor. If he holds the power to narrate, he also has the power to block other narratives from forming or emerging. He can erase the memory of versions that have predated his own. To maintain the scholarly position that a suppressed text lies beneath the redacted one requires some skill at re-visioning. And, I would add, a willingness to examine the question of who holds the power in the text. The reader simultaneously must fix one eye on each of these two texts while fighting to keep in view a third narrative, the scholarly reconstruction that will reflect power for its ideological Position.

Trible refers to her theological program as "an enterprise [that] welcomes all lovers of Scripture who seek to redeem life from patriarchal death."[3] A brief analysis of this description is remarkable for its clues to the interpretation that follows. Lovers of Scripture, I would imagine, are those people who read the Scripture sympathetically, with an eye to preserving it. But is that Trible's enterprise? I think her statement quoted above needs emendation. She is a lover of her *interpretation* of Scripture. What she understands to be the diminution of Miriam in the redacted text has stirred Trible to shine a light on the Scripture, to bring Miriam out of the shadows. The interpreter states that her reading is life-giving; the patriarchal one is death dealing. Perhaps I am begging the question, but Trible's claim that her enterprise restores life to Scripture seems too positivistic a statement to leave unexamined. If her reading restores life, then those who prefer the traditional interpretation in which Moses is the leader of the Song have chosen to embrace death. Neither interpretation can make universal claims for the correct meaning of the biblical text. Trible's unexpressed agenda is as clear to me as that of the redactors who consigned women to the dusty creases of the Bible. While Trible's analysis of the biblical discourse presents a stirring picture of the female prophet, it is, in my opinion, a new mosaic of Miriam, not one that was waiting to be uncovered. Although arguing from the settled position of "us" reading "them," Trible's provocative reading can be seen as more fluid than its overt intention. Resisting Trible's fixed position of reading, another interpreter can use Trible's literary mosaic of Miriam as a midrashic compilation, understanding that it is as ignited by ideological considerations as any rabbinic midrash.

Van Dijk-Hemmes negotiates between the shoals of Trible and Janzen, turning their questions of priority and dependence into a statement about the authenticity of the Sea narrative. After presenting M. Brenner's argument that Miriam's song is actually a Levitical composition of the Second Temple Period that reflects an earlier tradition, rather than the early composition desired by Trible and Janzen, van Dijk-Hemmes concludes from a reading of the Sea narrative that Miriam is the founder of a women's literary song tradition. I would agree with van Dijk-Hemmes's suggestion that these various textual considerations of Exodus 15 are "based upon an inadequate reading convention."[4] It seems to me that the inclusion of Meyers's and Graetz's articles in this collection points toward a possible interpretative strategy that challenges the convention of reading through one method or discipline. Borrowing from Bal's idea of reading through transdisciplinary codes, demonstrated in *Murder and Difference*,[5] allows new alignments that avoid reading from univocal perspectives.

Accepting that Miriam is at the very least within the tradition of women producing celebratory ritual songs brings us to questions about the position of female musicians during the early Iron Age in Israel. Such questions are examined by Carol Meyers in her article "Miriam the Musician." Working from a feminist perspective, Meyers combines archaeologic, ethnomusicologic, and anthropologic insights to view the gendered roles related not only to the musicians but also to the instruments they play. Meyers's article is a splendid example of the benefit of moving outside the borders of biblical studies, refusing the structures of time and location, to enrich one's cultural perspective. One of her conclusions is that there existed during the early Iron Age a women's performance genre of drum-dance-song within a variety of Near Eastern and Mediterranean locations. Most noteworthy for me is Meyers's application of Rosaldo's research on the status of women within groups, suggesting that the women of Israel singing at the Sea, under the leadership of Miriam, would have been connected as a community of female performers, and as such accorded a high measure of status.

The image of women being connected in musical communities allows room for a midrashic method of reading, a sort of literary nomadism that wanders outside the borders of nation and time and imagines Miriam and the female drum-dance-singers of Israel dreaming of their own liberation while performing for the people of Israel at their defining moment at the Sea. If one looks at the musical artifacts described in Exod. 15.20 as part of a gender code, the song that Miriam sings can be understood as a triumphant voice celebrating female emancipation.

Following Meyers's adaptation of anthropologic methods to biblical concerns, let us try on briefly the ethnographic strategy of what James Clifford and George Marcus have termed *writing culture*. In the text of Exodus 15 the elements of warfare—the horses, the riders, their armor and their shields, the chariots—point toward a male culture. If as Meyers argues, there were communities of female performers, might they not have been rejoicing in the destruction of the dominant male culture, exemplified by and encoded within the language of warfare?

A classical echo of a lyric that appeals to the elements of women's culture over militaristic ideals is attributed to Sappho:

> Some say the cavalry corps
> some infantry, some again
> will maintain that the swift oars
> of our fleet are the finest
> sight on dark earth; but I say
> that whatever one loves, is.[6]

There is general agreement among contemporary classical scholars that Sappho was a choral personality, a leader of a community of women that excluded men from its number and performed music together on the island of Lesbos in the seventh century. There is not agreement on the nature of this ancient community, whether it was a *paideia,* a community in which young women were educated, or a *thiasos,* a community of a cultic nature, most probably connected to the cult of Aphrodite.[7] According to Bowra, the members of Sappho's *thiasos*

> were bound to each other and to their leader by ties of great strength and intimacy, and Maximus of Tyre was not far wrong when he compared the relations between Sappho and her pupils with those between Socrates and his disciples. But while Socrates held his young men together by his personal influence and the glamour he gave to the quest for truth, Sappho was bound to her maidens by ties which were at least half religious.[8]

Positing the existence of the classical *thiasos* parallels Meyers's idea of the powerful connections among women drum-dance–singers of ancient Israel, celebrating the festival commemorating the Exodus. Bowra argued that the women's *thiasos* associated with the cult of Aphrodite composed the music that was essential to the cultic ceremonies, and "in song her [Aphrodite's] devotees were trained by Sappho."[9] There may have been other *thiasoi,* companies of young women musicians who performed at Mitylene, controlled by female rivals of Sappho, Gorgo, and Andromeda. For the purposes of this discussion the distinction between secular and sacred etiology of Sappho's community is not important. The comparison that interests me is between Sapphic communities and the drum-dance musicians of ancient Israel. Both choral groups provide evidence from the ancient Mediterranean world of communities of women performing lyrics of their own composition, lyrics that embed codes of women's culture. Whether the community was cultically based or secularly constructed, "these compositions presuppose or represent an interaction, offstage, as it were, with a choral aggregate."[10] The view that women's language slips through the dominant language of the lyric or song, as is so clear in the Sapphic lyric quoted above, is as compelling in my opinion as the view in the articles under consideration which imagine Miriam's song being deflected or silenced by biblical redactors.

Meyers pushes her anthropologic argument further, claiming that a group of female performers could exert a transformative influence over their audience "not only because of the social function of the performance but also by virtue of the intrinsic appeal of expressive events."[11] This argument, connected to Meyers's central argument in *Discovering Eve* that women enjoyed considerable status and social power during the premonarchic period, supports the views of Trible and Janzen that once upon a time Miriam was a powerful figure in Israel. Such claims of social power for the women of premonarchic Israel, Miriam among them, seem to me to be overstated on behalf of feminist values. I do not want this statement to be misunderstood. I am not in any way advocating a retreat from feminist analyses or theories. Certainly recent changes in the field of biblical studies have stimulated the kinds of interpretations and research about women in Israel that are found in this volume. Choice of method does in some ways predetermine the range of results, as can be seen by the articles that use source theory to unearth a text behind the final one. My own reading reveals my interests in comparing the differences between the literary figures as created by the biblical authors and the world of women, private, away from the gaze of men. From this perspective the fragment of Miriam's song (Exod. 15.19–21) reflects allusions to that private female reality in which women's culture develops.

Ironically, the position of women as marginal, the starting point of recent scholarly research, has been relocated as feminist criticism has gained acceptance in academic circles. Whatever one's particular term(s) of definition, it seems indisputable that feminist critics are more central, gaining in power and acceptance. As feminist biblical investigations are discussed and reflected upon, they are becoming normative, as in Janzen's building upon both Trible's and Burns's feminist literary analysis of Exodus 15. What needs to be remembered, I think, is that this change in perspective has more to do with the political location of the interpreters than with uncovering some historic, suppressed truth about ancient Israel woven into the fabric of the biblical narrative. As Emory Elliott has observed, "the historian is not a truthteller, but a storyteller . . . and a nation's official history is ultimately more than a story about which there is widespread agreement."[12]

Naomi Graetz does not remain within the literary borders of the Bible, but rather she looks at the extended midrashic expansions of the biblical narrative as providing an integral piece of Israel's epic history. Examining various rabbinic midrashim, both ancient and modern, Graetz concludes that contemporary rabbinic midrashim are no more sympathetic to Miriam, or to a woman's perspective, than classical ones. Graetz recognizes the confining nature of reading through the *peshat* of the text, but she does not acknowledge that one person's *peshat* is another's *derash,* that while the authors of rabbinic midrash make claims for providing the plain or self-evident meaning of a text, in actuality all reading is interpretative and reflects the ideology of the reader. She rightly shines a light on the problem of Jewish feminists trapped between the desire to remain within their religious interpretative tradition and the frustration with the rabbinic blindness toward women's concerns. Her conclusion that "there is no monopoly on interpretations" seems indisputable. But the article itself suffers from a timidity at confronting the rabbinic interpretations as patriarchal products. Even though she does a fine job of pointing out the weaknesses of the rabbinic interpretations for feminist readers, Graetz allows these rabbinic interpretations to dominate the focus of the Miriamic retellings she presents. She is caught in the desire to maintain a unifying vision of a Jewish identity rather than to allow Miriam's song to be heard as one of discord.

In conclusion, I would like to accept Graetz's challenge that "we start imaginatively re-engaging with our sacred texts, by writing midrash." Midrashic storytelling, revisioning the biblical narrative from one's own perspective, points toward a contrapuntal, nomadic style of reading. Such a reading eludes the borders of accepting reading conventions and certainly makes no claims for historical truth. My midrashic model wanders between dual horizons, synchronically from within various locations within the biblical narrative and midrashically from an interpreter's filling of narrative gaps.

Miriam's Song

The battle had roared around them.

Pressing close to Miriam at the shore of the Sea were the women of Israel. As dawn broke across the seamless sea, they had turned from the signs of death floating toward them. As the tide washed onto the land, shields and broken weapons cluttered the beach. A few young men picked among the tangled metal, shouting with triumph when they found the empty helmet of an Egyptian soldier.

"YHWH has indeed answered our prayers. The Egyptians have sunk like lead into the sea. We have been delivered." Moses and Aaron had gathered the men to pray on an outcropping of rocks not far from where the women stood together. "Who is like you, O Lord, among the gods of the heavens?"

"YHWH has brought us a miracle," Zipporah said, and adjusted her veil over her sea-damp hair.

Not a single Israelite had been lost when the walls of water collapsed over the pursuing Egyptian army. Miriam bent to dip her fingers into the pooled water gently lapping at her feet. She let the water fall in rivulets over her upturned soil-smeared face. The rage had gone out of the water. The fear had gone out of the bodies of the men standing at the shoreline. Backs that had been stooped from years of work had become straight with pride. YHWH had indeed performed a miracle. In the name of Israel. The sea had been stopped. In the name of YHWH the sea had been split. Now in the name of the Song the Sea stroked the shore.

Miriam picked up her circular drum and struck it with the flat of her hand. "The rulers of Canaan shall melt away. Their weapons shall melt with them. YHWH will plant us, his people, on the mountain of God." Timbrels shook in the hands of the dancing women. Miriam struck the drum with the palm of her right hand. "Sing to the Lord," she cried. "YHWH has triumphed gloriously."

Other women reached for their lyres and drums and began to sing softly. "We shall sing to the Lord," they repeated, taking comfort in the familiar words, "YHWH has triumphed gloriously."

Small children sat on the shore and listened to the songs of their mothers and sisters. It had happened just as Moses had promised them. The Pharaoh had been swallowed by the sea; his angry soldiers would never threaten the Israelites again.

"Will there be a day when we sit and spin our thread in the sunlight without remembering the shields of our enemy, lying useless and unclaimed upon the shore?" a young woman wondered.

Zipporah cradled her lyre. "The strength of YHWH is more than the strength of chariot and lyre. YHWH will let the earth bring forth plants of all kinds." She touched the hair of her son sitting nearby. "Instead of war, we shall have music to fill our days."

The men raised their arms in honor of YHWH. "The earth has swallowed our enemies. Even now Moab trembles and the clans of Edom dread the Lord God of Israel. Glory to YHWH, the great Warrior."

Miriam shook her head at the women, who let their instruments fall silent. "Do not become downcast. God will give us wings of doves. We shall fly over the wars of men. We shall fly with the power of YHWH high above this sea of death."

Believing her words, the music began again.

Sing to the Lord,
for YHWH has triumphed gloriously.
Horses and riders YHWH has cast into the sea.

When the celebrations and prayers had ended, the people began their journey to Canaan. Miriam walked before the people with Moses and Aaron. They talked about living in the sight of YHWH when they got to the land of Canaan. A land of milk and honey. "Your music shall end our days of work and bring joy to our nights," Moses told her.

But as the months passed, Moses spent more of his time in the company of the elders and Miriam found herself walking behind the men, in her old familiar place with the women, telling stories to the children, wondering when the journey would end. The people began to murmur, to fear that God might drown them in a sea of dusty earth, that their days were no better now than they had been in Egypt.

As they waited for the sign from God that their journey was nearing its end, they scanned the sky for signs from YHWH. The cloudless sky reminded the travelers of their dependence on YHWH, for wisdom, for direction, for the precious water of life. Not the foaming swirls of water YHWH had sent to swallow their enemies, but gentle water, a gift from YHWH to bathe their salt-creased faces and soothe their parched throats.

The women told stories to their children as they bathed their small bodies. "Feel this cool water, sweet water drawn from the well which follows the people of Israel wherever we go; the well is named for the leader of the Song, for our prophet Miriam."

Their number was smaller. God had been angered at the greed of the people and had sent a plague to kill the teasing taste of meat within them. From the cloudless sky had rained down quail to drown the people in their own desires. While the people gathered in small groups, whispering in fear and praying that YHWH would forgive their dreams of meat, Miriam approached her brother Moses. "We must be strong so that the people can continue the journey. They have lost heart. They have become frightened as they were before God tossed the horse and the chariot into the sea. Even Zipporah has said that the song has dried up in her heart."

"I cannot care for this people all alone," Moses cried out.

"I can raise my voice to the Lord as well as you. With singing to remind the people that God has sent to the bottom of the sea weapons and oppressions."

"God will allow us to triumph over all our enemies," Moses reminded her. "With horse and chariot we shall triumph gloriously. The men of Israel shall return the Philistines into the sea."

Miriam laughed. "Has the Lord YHWH indeed spoken only through Moses, my brother?"

Suddenly God appeared in a pillar of cloud. "I have spoken to Miriam in dreams. But to Moses, and only to Moses, do I speak without words."

"Praise to YHWH the warrior who wins all our battles," cried Moses, falling on the ground before God.

Miriam spoke no words. Could YHWH allow the sword to silence the timbrel?

Miriam looked back toward camp, where the people waited for her. Enfolded in a disease that could be cured only by the touch of YHWH, she waited. She could hear the women singing, tuneless melodies that reminded her of childhood and the closeness of her mother. Day and night their music wound around her, as though to fill her time of punishment with the power of songs. Wordless, the sweet melodies soothed her like the soft breath of women, reminding her of their joy at the Sea. Their dream was fading like the timbrels, now silent.

With tears in her eyes, she sang softly,

Sing to the Lord, for He has triumphed
A Horse, a rider, He once hurled into the sea.

NOTES

1. A. Brenner, *The Israelite Woman: Social Role and Literary Type in Biblical Narrative* (Sheffield: The Biblical Seminar, 2; Sheffield: JSOT Press, 1985), p.52.

2. J.G. Janzen, "Song of Moses, Song of Miriam: Who is Seconding Whom?" in *A Feminist Companion to Exodus-Deuteronomy*, ed. Athalya Brenner (Sheffield: Sheffield Academic Press, 1994), p. 197.

3. P. Trible, "Bringing Miriam out of the Shadows," in *A Feminist Companion to Exodus-Deuteronomy*, p. 166.

4. F. van Dijk-Hemmes, "Some Recent Views on the Presentation of the Song of Miriam," in *A Feminist Companion to Exodus-Deuteronomy*, p. 206.

5. M. Bal, *Murder and Difference: Gender, Genre, and Scholarship on Sisera's Death* (trans. M. Gumpert; Bloomington: Indiana University Press, 1988).

6. M. Barnard, *Sappho: A New Translation* (Berkeley: University of California Press, 1958), p. 41.

7. For an argument against the religious nature or cultic association of the women within Sappho's institution, see D.L. Page, *Sappho and Alcaeus* (London: Oxford University Press, 1955). For an elegant analysis of Sappho's poetry that examines traces of Sappho's consciousness in the face of masculine norms of behavior, see J. Winkler, "Double Consciousness in Sappho's Lyrics," in *Constraints of Desire: The Anthropology of Sex and Gender in Ancient Greece* (London: Routledge, 1990), pp. 162–87.

8. C.M. Bowra, *Greek Lyric Poetry* (London: Oxford University Press, 1936), pp. 187–88.

9. Bowra, *Greek Lyric Poetry*, p. 189.

10. G. Nagy, *Pindar's Homer: The Lyric Possession of the Epic Past* (Baldmore: John's Hopkins University Press, 1990), pp. 370–71.

11. C. Meyers, "Miriam the Musician," in *A Feminist Companion to Exodus-Deuteronomy*, p. 228.

12. E. Elliott (ed.), *Columbia Literary History of the United States* (New York: Columbia University Press, 1988), "Introduction," p. xvii.

Roundtable Discussion
Women with Disabilities—
A Challenge to Feminist Theology

ELLY ELSHOUT, FACILITATOR

I initiated this roundtable in order to define the experiences of women with disabilities as an important *locus theologicus* within feminist theology and the *ekklesia gynaikon*.[1] My intent is to enrich the plurality and complexity of these two conversations. I also offer this study as both a lifeline and theoretical tool for women with disabilities, so that they may more readily participate in these conversations.

I begin with my own story as a woman with disabilities. A year ago I attended my niece's confirmation. I watched the ceremonies from my wheelchair. I don't remember much, because after the ceremonies were finished, the bishop suddenly came up to me, and before I realized what was happening, he made the sign of the cross on my forehead and then strode out of the church. I was bewildered. And for a long time afterward, I troubled myself with thoughts of how I could have prevented this experience.

This incident is stamped indelibly on my memory as the "clerical assault." I felt victimized—a man had touched me against my wishes and had assaulted my bodily integrity. And as a woman with disabilities, I was made to play the role of a child who is present only to show off the prestige and power of a dignitary. This church had attacked my self-respect. Feelings of humiliation, anger, and self-accusation, as well as jealousy of other women (without disabilities) filled my heart. I became acutely aware of the double jeopardy of my position as a woman and a woman with disabilities. Moreover, I came to reflect upon the differences of power between women and the fact that the experiences of women with disabilities go unnoticed due to the "blind spots" of both the feminist movement and feminist theology.

Emancipation for Women with Disabilities?

The majority of women with disabilities are involved in the emancipation movement of people with disabilities. Nevertheless, as is the case in all arenas of society, the interests of women with disabilities are treated as inferior to those of men with disabilities.

Nasa Begum highlights the obstacles peculiar to women with disabilities as they struggle to live independently and enjoy sexual relationships.[2] The development of a positive self-image and the ability to enter and enjoy sexual relationships is already complicated for persons with disabilities because one's body plays such an important role in self-image and sexuality. Men with disabilities are often privileged with more education than women with disabilities and therefore, they are able to draw upon more resources in the development of self, as well as in employment and personal or sexual relationships. Men with disabilities are also more likely to find a caregiver than are women with disabilities. (The caregiver is usually a woman—this perpetuates the social ideal of the selfless female caregiving for men.) Moreover, women with disabilities are more vulnerable to sexual abuse.

Women with disabilities experience exclusion in both the politics of disability rights and in the feminist movement. In the latter instance, various feminist strategies contradict the needs and interests of women with disabilities. The feminist strategy of complete separation from patriarchal society ignores the fact that women with disabilities experience constant and concrete barriers such as physical inaccessibility. Their situation could often be described as one of complete separation. It is not clear, then, what this feminist strategy has to offer women with disabilities. Feminists who criticize the traditional sex roles of wife and mother are not sensitive to the fact that women with disabilities are taught from a very early age that they are not fit to be lover or wife, let alone mother. Women with disabilities are taught that they are asexual. Surely this is as oppressive as heterosexism. The feminist movement is also not sufficiently conscious of its own "ableism." The feminist movement enables, empowers, and strengthens women. Thus, many "fit women" will not easily admit that women with disabilities embody all that they don't want to be. As a result, the patriarchal way of judging a person on how good-looking, healthy, or productive he or she is, is perpetuated by feminists. Women, in this way, continue to victimize each other.

This victimization is insidious. Before we can work together to overcome it, we must first understand how patriarchy defines and excludes the disabled person. To facilitate this understanding, I have interpreted Mary Daly's seven characteristics of the "Sado-ritual Syndrome" in terms of the position of persons with disabilities.[3] Daly's analysis is quite helpful since it provides feminists with the tools to look critically at their own participation in patriarchal oppression.

Obsession with Purity. According to Daly, this obsession consists of the efforts of men to make women invisible and incapable of acting. They are declared unfit to play a part in the society of men. Within patriarchy women are unclean and contagious; they must be eliminated. All health services in this country regard people with disabilities in the same way. People with disabilities are made invisible; they are placed in institutions and locked out of society by the inaccessibility of public places, homes, and places of employment.

Erasure of Responsibility. Health services for people with disabilities are administered by large systems or bureaucracies. Accountability is diffused throughout the bureaucracy; providers and administrators can hide behind these structures. Moreover, people with disabilities are usually at the mercy of such bureaucracies. People with disabilities may not have either the physical ability or the physical access to take charge of their treatment.

Inherent Tendency to Spread. Health service bureaucracies continue to grow as scientists define more and more "defects." As more and more persons view themselves as increasingly "defective" the demand for treatment and therapy also increases.

Women as Token Torturers. Persons with disabilities are enticed to overcome all obstacles—to become able. Seduced by the culture of ableism, they continue to push the limits of their disabilities. As a result, persons with disabilities may never learn to accept themselves or they may do harm to themselves in the process of becoming "successful." As a woman who lives independently and has earned an advanced academic degree, I continue to push myself, though sometimes I should know better than to be co-opted by the culture of ableism.

Fixation upon Details. Medical science and health services focus on diseased organs, parts, and limbs. The human body is never considered as a whole. This fixation is carried over into bureaucratic practice as well. One's needs must be itemized and broken down on an endless series of medical forms. Requests for special equipment and facilities are so complicated that one can receive a pair of crutches, though her request for a wheelchair is long overdue.

Acceptable and Normative. In our society it is quite acceptable to consider people with disabilities unwanted. This is evident in the proliferation of tests to determine whether a fetus is disabled. If a test is positive, many persons will terminate their pregnancies.

Legitimation by "Objective" Scholarship. The development and proliferation of reproductive technology bears the stamp of medical progress. Yet it perpetuates the biases of ableism and serves the interests of the state to decrease its expenditures on behalf of people with disabilities.

Daly's analysis readily prompts persons with disabilities to self-consciousness and critique. Persons with disabilities could also follow the logic of Daly's argument and declare the inevitability of society's hostility toward them. Some persons with disabilities have followed a path analogous to Daly's. They argue that the standards of the not-disabled society are intolerable. (I agree with them on this point.) They have set up a counterculture in which the dominant principles of health, productivity, and beauty are criticized. They use the label "disabled persons" as a nickname for themselves.[4]

Both Daly and the counterculture of disabled persons, however, concentrate on "victim-thinking." As a result, they accept their status of invisibility within patriarchy. I agree with Elisabeth Schüssler Fiorenza that it is imperative that we retrieve and display the other side of oppression, namely resistance, power, struggle, and strength. Yet, as I described earlier, women with disabilities may not find solidarity in feminism.

Solidarity amid Difference

Mary Hunt has developed very workable concepts such as "likely" and "unlikely" coalitions of "justice-seeking" friends.[5] These concepts refer to the problems and triumphs of coalition-formation across different social, racial, class, and sexual orientations. These differences are manifested as differences of power. It is essential that we come to terms with these differences in power as well as the difference in power which exists between women with disabilities and women without disabilities. Unless we come to terms with this power differential, women with disabilities and women without disabilities will remain an "unlikely coalition."

A way to deal with this difference between women with and without disabilities is through compromise. I believe compromise is essential to coalition-building. Compromise requires that both parties give up something. This process requires intense discussions. Thus, differences are analyzed and remain visible. Compromise prevents us from erasing differences and assuming complete harmonization. The process of compromise acknowledges that both sides have a position and that both have strengths as well as something particular to offer the coalition.

The strategy of finding compromise is one with which women with disabilities are quite familiar. Indeed, searching for compromises is a strategy that might have been written for women with disabilities. Women with disabilities functioning depends upon our ability to *reach a compromise* with our bodies, which so often let us down. This is not an admission of weakness, but a hopeful activity. In this activity of compromise, we create new relationships with ourselves, others, and the spaces that surround us, and, in turn, gather new sources of strength and pleasure in our bodies.[6]

Ethics of solidarity in the *ekklesia gynaikon* must be reshaped, according to Schüssler Fiorenza, in an "open bounded space."[7] In this space, women with disabilities offer a real challenge where it is taken for granted that one is healthy and has a job and a partner. They also challenge people who speak about the right to health instead of the right to health care. Women with disabilities also provide a new and critical perspective in issues of reproductive technology, eugenics, and the dilemmas of caregiving and career. In this open bounded space, we need the courage to have the conversations that involve conflicting interests and values that surround differences in abilities. We will find common ground and differences in the fears and disappointments we experience when handicapped children are born; the conflicts of having both a career and children; the challenges and triumphs of living with disabilities; the reproductive pressures that medical technology places on women, etc.

This conversation needs to take place in social-political terms. Most likely it will engender a new and critical feminist anthropology. Such an anthropology will not only take gender into account, but will also consider sickness, disabilities, and age as powerful shapers of self and society.[8]

Conclusion

To conclude this roundtable initiative, I introduce the disabled body as a new metaphor for the discussions of feminist theology and the *ekklesia gynaikon*. This metaphor is a feminist critical assumption of Paul's ecclesiological metaphor of the body of Christ in Corinthians 11–12. This metaphor signaled Paul's attempt to harmonize the differences among the people of the early Christian church. The metaphor of the disabled body, however, represents the social reality of the differences and conflicts of women's experiences. The disabled body is acquainted with pain and disappointment. New relationships, new wholeness can be forged only in difference and conflict. In proclaiming "I am a theologian and moreover I am a woman with disabilities," I put forth a new challenge for feminist theologians.

ELLY ELSHOUT

NOTES

1. Women with disabilities includes women with serious and/or chronic, though not necessarily visible, health problems.

2. Nasa Begum, "Disabled Women and the Feminist Agenda," *Feminist Review* 40 (Spring 1992).

3. Mary Daly, *GYN/ECOLOGY: The Metaethics of Radical Feminism* (Boston: Beacon Press, 1978).

4. Simon van der Veen, "Integratie, het evangelie voor gehandicapten?" *Maandblad Geestelijke Volksgezondheid* 12 (1981): 1047–54.

5. Mary Hunt, *Fierce Tenderness: A Feminist Theology of Friendship* (New York: Crossroad, 1991).

6. Gon Buurman, *Aan hartstocht geen gebrek, handicap, erotiek en lichaamsbeleving; met tekst van Karin Spaink* (Amsterdam, 1991).

7. Elisabeth Schüssler Fiorenza, "Ethiek en politiek van bevrijding" in *Over hoeren, taarten en vrouwen die voorbijgaan,* ed. Hedwig Meyer-Wilmes and Lieve Troch (Kampen, 1992), 13–47.

8. See Valerie C. Saiving, "Our Bodies/Our Selves: Reflections on Sickness, Aging, and Death," *Journal of Feminist Studies in Religion* 4, no. 2 (1988).

Dorothee Wilhelm

About the Hostile Land in Me

I am a pioneer. I cannot plan the ways I walk. I am always striking against symbolic and material frontiers that determine my living area. My bodily condition is not planned. While English speakers argue about the term *dis-ability* as *non-ability,* I refer to my bodily situation as "differently abled." Differences between human abilities are not planned. Yet those who are considered different from some arbitrary norm are actually threatened by nonexistence. First, they are marginalized or erased by a social system of symbols that reinforce the normative, the ideal. There are no suitable and affirmative body concepts for differently abled persons. Second, differently abled persons are threatened by nonexistence via material conditions, including inaccessible buildings, modes of transportation, etc. This threat of nonexistence or erasure can also be quite literal—as was the case with Nazi Germany's policy of destroying the disabled, whose lives were considered less than worthy. The threat of nonexistence continues in Germany in the two ways I have just described. Differently abled persons are again the victims of attacks. Differently abled persons are reminded again and again of how "inconvenient" we are.

"Blind Spots"

I agree completely with Dr. Elly Elshout that the oppressive features of the traditional roles assigned to women figure differently for women, depending upon the status of one's abilities. In what follows, I first emphasize the importance of her call for making the experiences of women with disabilities an important *locus theologicus* within feminist theology and the *ekklesia gynaikon* via my own experiences as a differently abled woman. Second, I develop a starting point for a life together—a commitment to liberation, wherein no woman is liberated until all women are liberated.

A good deal of theological speech is about "man." This speech has been justly criticized by feminist theologians as androcentric: "Man" literally and culturally refers to men. The talk of theology has generally focused on the experiences of men (who are also the intended audience), which are taken as normative. Any talk of, or talk directed to, women's existence and experience are added as an excursus or special case. The emerging speech, which focuses on "woman" or "women" in general, that is, the language of feminists, repeats this two-tiered construction in an analogous way. Such talk often pictures women as a homogeneous group (much like man really signaled white men). Hence, it denies the differences between women and installs a special group of women as "normal." Such normalization renders invisible those who deviate from this homogeneous group (white, able-bodied, elite women). This language does not reflect the experiences of differently abled women. Hence, the "blind spots" of the feminist movement and theology vis-à-vis women who do not fit the norm, of which Elshout speaks. Replacing the word "man" with "differently abled women" is not convenient.

"Job-Sharing"

This construction has two sides: First there is the group of so-called normal men and women who exert power of definition on all others. As a result all others are located through their relationship to this group. This is related to how I understand patriarchy, following Elisabeth Schüssler Fiorenza's definition of patriarchy as "a socio-cultural system in which a few men have power over other men, women, children, slaves, and colonized people."[1] Patriarchy is a structural and symbolic order of domination, in which persons are measured according to the measure of young, not differently abled white, Christian, heterosexual males. All other groups are extensions of the traditional household, in which the father, as head of the family, was/is the point of reference for all members of the house, from "his" wife to "his" dog.

The other side of this construction is the job-sharing between normals and deviants in the interest of normals. This "job-sharing" delegates to black men and women, white women, Jews, differently abled people, etc., all those features which white men wish to deny about themselves. Judith Plaskow aptly describes this "Throughout the history of Western thought, women, Blacks, and other oppressed groups have had attributed to them as their nature human traits which men could or would not acknowledge in themselves. Sexuality, bodiliness, dependence, moral and intellectual failure were all peculiarities which belonged to everyone except ruling class males."[2] In grouping white women, black women and men, Jews, colonized, and differently abled people together, I do not deny the differences of their experiences. Yet, we are also joined together as "deviants" in a fundamental sense because we fail to meet the norms of patriarchy. Still, our deviations from this measure vary, and therefore, we are placed in various relationships of oppression vis-à-vis each other.

In my everyday life as a differently abled woman my "patriarchal assignment" as a "dis-abled" woman casts me as the embodiment of sadness and suffering. If I am able to manage my "condition" then I am allowed to be admired. The following example illustrates my point. A year ago I went to the hospital to be examined. The competent doctor, who had examined me once before, did not recognize me. After looking at my chart he remarked: "Sure, you're that real pitiable person!" I answered: "If you're as well as I am, you're real fine." He responded: "It's good when you can take it like you do—you deal with your handicap in an admirable way." I replied: "You cannot imagine how I live.

I reject that I'm the one whose job it is to represent or overcome sadness, and your job in life is anything you would like it to be. You're only occupied with your fantasies." He looked at me as though I had spoken in a different language.

In this situation I was first made a thing, because I could be identified only by my hospital papers. I was made a thing once more, because the doctor fixed me with his fantasies and fears, which he believed to be validated by his empathetically imagining what it must be like to be me. In my exertion to avert the gaze of the ten eyes of the hospital personnel who were present, and who had decided to identify their fears with me, I could feel the meaning of "power of definition." Their gaze reflected the power of definition of the institution "hospital." That institution establishes the measure of "normal" bodies, which is, in turn, legitimated and reinforced by societal ideals and images.

Marking Off

As Elly Elshout indicates, the feminist movement also engages in the destructive habit of *marking off*. Marking off occurs when groups carelessly articulate their strengths or identities in terms that disparage groups who bear undesirable traits. A group marks off who it is by aligning itself against what it is not. Feminists want to be fit, whole, independent, and in control of their bodies. These are aspects that are largely denied to differently abled women. Feminists wish to be what differently abled women are not. Thus, we not only bear the weight of their fears, but we also cannot be feminists given their definition.

Kneeling and Standing Upright

Johann Baptist Metz declared "Who can't stand upright, can't really kneel." I understand Metz's phrase to mean that only the person who possesses a free and unbroken attitude can express by her or his body the humility with which she or he accepts herself/himself as a part of creation. But Metz's language presents problems.

The forced kneeling of a slave (or any other person on the lower levels of patriarchy) who is not allowed to stand upright indicates the troubled order of creation, in which men rule over other men, women, children, slaves, nations, etc. Kneeling ambiguously figures both humility and humiliation. Metz's picture, however, also recalls the "uprightness" which figures superiority: autonomy, enlightenment, adultness, being-of-age. Uprightness is also the image which readily distinguishes us from the stooped four-legged animals. Human superiority dramatically emerged when we got off our hands and feet. The kneeling to which the political theology of Metz refers, is one which can only follow the prior act of standing upright. Only the person who stands as a "subject in front of God"[3] can then display humility before God. Those whose location is one of subjection must first become subjects (who stand upright) before they can humble this same subjectivity before God.

Bad luck for me. My visions of liberation need other body pictures. Kneeling and standing upright is difficult for me. I do not wish, however, to abolish the speech of "standing upright," but to call attention to its limited reach. It is not suitable for expressing a hope for all. If I want to figure in this hope, I have to sign in alternative theological body-concepts which apply to my situation. This signing requires a creative action of many people, however, if it is to become a *locus theologicus* within the *ekklesia gynaikon*.

Don't Make Any Images

In order to complement Elshout's looking for solidarity amid difference I suggest a feminist-liberation-theological retrieval of the Decalogue's prohibition of images as a possible way out of the "job-sharing" dilemma. "Don't make any images" means "You should not try to get power over your co-creatures. They are all creatures of God. Do not make them into lifeless images which fit into your catalogue of undesirable traits. Do not destroy their possibilities of living differently. Respect all persons. Every one of them is holy in a special way."

"Don't make any pictures" also has a personal meaning: When you see me—differently abled, young, white, and female (or if I were black, old, and male)—don't believe you know anything about me. I own all information about me, and no one is allowed to take definition-power over my life or appropriate me, or make me a thing. Without a reciprocal, respectful coming together, we will remain invisible to each other. Your images of normalcy or of my suffering actually cloud your vision. What you see when you meet me are *your fears, your hurts*.

We are all broken in some fashion. Let us meditate on our brokenness rather than making it a characteristic only of the so-called disabled. Step back from your daily consciousness and try to see how fragile you are as a not yet differently abled person and how much you need your co-creatures, how dependent you actually are. I have to do this all the time—since I always have to negotiate the "hostile land" in and around me. My soul has been colonized by images that promise happiness, love, and the possibilities of forming the world—if one is young, beautiful, not differently abled, white, rich, that is, just "normal." Let's not colonize each other. Let's try to make no more images in respect of creation.

NOTES

1. Elisabeth Schüssler Fiorenza, *In Memory of Her,* German trans. *Zu ihrem Gedächtnis: Eine feministisch-theologische Rekonstruktion der christlichen Urspünge,* trans. Christine Schaumberger (Gütersloh: Chr. Kaiser, 1988), 62.

2. Judith Plaskow, "Blaming the Jews for the Birth of Patriarchy," *Nice Jewish Girls: A Lesbian Anthology,* ed. Evelyn Torton Beck (Boston: Beacon Press, 1989), 301.

3. Johann Baptist Metz, *Glaube in Geschichte und Gesellschaft: Studien zu einer praktischen Fundamentaltheologie* (Mainz: Grunëwald-Verlag, 1984), 4.

Carole R. Fontaine

The challenges to feminist theology raised in Prof. Elshout's article, "Women with Disabilities," are ones that are immediately recognizable to any woman who finds herself physically or emotionally "challenged," as our society has euphemistically chosen to refer to our situation. As a person who has struggled with chronic illness lasting over a decade, I responded immediately to the issues in this roundtable. The daily battles that confront a differently abled person in our society are often so overwhelming and oppressive that their absence from most discussions of the condition of women presents itself to us as yet another disability in talking with others engaged in the feminist enterprise. Whether it is the unquestioning retrieval of the body as the major source of identity and fulfillment, or the barely concealed irritation that so often infuses interactions of the normal with those who have special needs, the function of this lacuna in feminist thought is the continuation of the invisibility of disabled women. How are we supposed to enter into conversations about valuing the body and trusting one s intuitions, dearly held points of feminist doctrine, when giving that status to the body in our own lives can often annihilate the self-esteem we have so carefully built up in opposition to a world that judges us primarily by what we can produce? If we are cynical about the liberation projects going on all around us, if we shake our heads in private over the pitying comments of our sisters about our status as nonmothers—as though essentialist arguments about fulfillment through motherhood are divine givens, if we have grown tired of waiting in a world of heavy doors, obstructed ramps, and able-bodied persons double-parked in our parking spaces, we have reason.

Anyone with disabilities could easily relate stories like Elshout's tale of clerical abuse. My own situation is one of intermittent difficulties; good days can be very good and bad days can send me to an emergency room. I do not always look visibly different, and this carries its own set of problems, that of invisible disabilities. "You look fine," said an airline steward as I attempted to preboard a flight, having forgotten my cane. "So does Magic Johnson," I replied, "but that doesn't mean much, does it?" In a world that measures by externals, meting out what little care may be found on the basis of who looks the worst, persons with invisible disabilities wage a constant fight to be acknowledged as less than they appear to be—an ironic war in which to be a tired and desperate foot soldier.

One of the places in which I have experienced the most potent examples of exclusion is the world of the church. The physical organization of most sanctuaries is a nightmare of pain: hard edges, no handholds, inadequate heat, and seating that must surely be unpleasant even for normals. The stares of those around me when I do not stand or sing (singing is a biomechanically sophisticated act that most take for granted, but which some persons with head injury may not) are enough to insure that whatever may be going on, I am viewed as a less than full participant.

It seems to me that the physical organization of churches only reflects that institution's deep ambivalence about the presence of the sick and disabled in its midst. Though supposedly mandated to act as sanctuary and healing presence to such persons, in fact we are a deep embarrassment to the institution's ideology of healing. How dare we not get well! Haven't we heard that God has come with healing in his wings? Is our faith defective, perhaps, that we so stubbornly resist owning the full promise of healing? Perhaps we have sinned? Have we failed to repent with a contrite heart? Whatever the secret explanations the Church gives for our presence, we know by its fruits of exclusion that we continue to be a presence of dubious value. I wept when I first attended a baseball game at Boston's Fenway Park and saw the special rows reserved for wheelchairs, as well as the other fine attempts to make us welcome. Were they there only because it was expected that men would be viewing the game, and they had a right to be participating fans? (There were women seated there, too.) Regardless of the reason, I remember reflecting on the fact that our bodies were made more welcome at a secular sporting event than in the very places where we are taught to seek healing of spirit and flesh.

At least some of the theological ambivalence about those with disabilities may be located in the tradition's source documents, the Bible. Surveying both Testaments synchronically, we come away with a comprehensive view of the way the societies producing those documents understood disability. While it is probably the case that views of illness and disability changed over time, especially during times of contact with foreign cultures, some of which had concepts of medicine in the late period, there is an underlying unity in the way the Bible views persons so afflicted.

Illness and Disability as Undesirable Conditions

In a medically naive society, one based on agricultural production, those who cannot participate fully are naturally seen as existing in a more precarious, and less desirable state. While this often leads to injunctions to treat the disabled with special care (Lev 19:14; Deut 27:18), the overall view of the disabled is that, as less than whole, they are more at risk (Deut 28:29; Isa 59:10; Matt 15:14; Luke 6:39; 2 Pet 1:9; Rev 3:17). When the literary trope of "blindness" or "lameness" appears, it is usually negative in meaning (Prov 25:19; 26:7; Isa 29:9; 43:8; 56:10; Matt 23:16–19; 23:24–26; John 9:40, 41). Thus, when true believers are told to mutilate themselves—become disabled—if necessary in order to enter the Kingdom, the society's extreme repulsion and amazement at such a suggestion serves to highlight the seriousness of the demands being made (Matt 18:8; Mark 9:45). The notion of casting away one's hand or foot underscores the importance of the requirement for ethical purity over that of "physical" purity. When the disabled are made the special objects of divine care (Jer 31:8; Micah 4:6–7; Zeph 3:19; Luke 14:13), this emphasizes the remarkable compassion of the one doing the good deed, not the deserving nature or dignity of the recipient (see below).

Special Origin of Disabilities

While there is some recognition that disabilities may result from accidents (Mephibosheth in 2 Sam 4:4) or be classified as "birth defects" (John 9:1–3; Acts 14:8), the Bible is clear that, by and large, the meaning of the disability has something to do with the deity or malicious subdeities. This is by no means a new concept invented by Israel or the New Testament; it is present in some of the earliest myths from Mesopotamia.[1] It is Yahweh who creates the disabled (Exod 4:11) and who can reverse the disabilities (Ps 146:8). Sometimes the motive for such actions is punishment for sins (Zeph 3:19). In later times, malicious spirits, subdeities, are explicitly named as responsible for the brokenness (Matt 12:22; Luke 7:21; Acts 8:7). Whatever the reason for the disability, its "otherworldly" origin sets its bearer apart, marked as specially cursed, protected, or objectified for the sake of divine healing action. Persons bearing such marks of "otherness" may expect to be treated differently by the normal members of the group.

Disability and Illness as Forms of Impurity

As Prof. Elshout rightly suggests, based on Daly's analysis of the "Sado-ritual Syndrome," concepts of purity are at work in society's view of the disabled. Those who view us fear becoming what we are; we are a sign in their midst of how fragile and precarious bodily purity really is. Nowhere is this better exemplified than in Levitical passages about access to the sacred precincts:

> And the LORD said to Moses, "Say to Aaron, None of your descendants throughout their generations who has a blemish may approach to offer the bread of his God. For no one who has a blemish shall draw near, a man blind or lame, or one who has a

mutilated face or a limb too long, or a man who has an injured foot or an injured hand, or a hunchback, or a dwarf, or a man with a defect in his sight or an itching disease or scabs or crushed testicles; no man of the descendants of Aaron the priest who has a blemish shall come near to offer the Lord's offerings by fire; since he has a blemish, he shall not come near to offer the bread of his God. He may eat the bread of his God, both of the most holy and of the holy things, but he shall not come near the veil or approach the altar, because he has a blemish, that he may not profane my sanctuaries; for I am the LORD who sanctify them." (RSV; Lev 21:16–22)

This passage refers, of course, to disabled men; women, as nonmen, are disabled by nature in this kind of thinking. While disabilities in men cannot totally eradicate their rights as males, these rights are severely curtailed, at least in matters of holiness. This may be the reason that Zephaniah speaks of God removing the "shame" of the disabled and the outcast. In the paradigm of male honor and shame, being less than fully male is certain cause for self-loathing. That the unacceptability of the disabled before God finds its way into proverbial form in 2 Samuel 5:8, regardless of its sarcastic, or metaphorical application to the Jebusites in that text, is significant, because proverbs express the unexamined folk-ideas of a group, ideas that are felt to be so universally true they no longer require examination or explanation.[2]

The Disabled as Objects of Divine Action

The dignity of the disabled and their status as potentially valued members of their societies is directly challenged by the Bible's continuous portrayal of them as objects of divine action. When they are being healed (Isa 29:18; 35:5–6; 42:16, 18; Matt 9:27–38; 12:22; 15:30–31; 21:14; Mark 8:22–23; Luke 4:18; 7:21–22; 13:11, etc.), they serve as marvelous plot-devices that show off the power of God or the Anointed One. In effect, they form part of the group of God's "special interests" in the New Testament: like Romans, tax-collectors, and women, they show how remarkable is Jesus's broad-based concern and willingness to interact with society's "throwaways." The disciples' questions to Jesus about the man born blind are illustrative, as is the Messiah's answer, "Rabbi, who sinned, this man or his parents, that he was born blind?" Jesus answered, "It was not that this man sinned, or his parents, but that the works of God might be made manifest in him" (John 9:2–3). In this divine contract between Creator and creature, apparently creatures may be afflicted, willy-nilly, in order to pump up the deity's resume as healer.

While no one could argue about the desirability of such healing extended to all who suffer, the relentless characterization of the disabled as objectified beneficiaries of divine healing robs them of their true status as courageous, coping, creative persons—persons who are valued just as they are. As objects of healing, the disabled also experience a negative valuation when the healing does not materialize: Job's wretched plight serves as a sign to his friends that he must be a very great sinner indeed, or why would he be so afflicted? For those whose physical conditions are not likely to improve, the questions of faith and personal meaning raised by the Bible's continued stress on the disabled/ill person as one in the state of awaiting divine healing can demoralize and disempower rather than providing a means for continued growth.[3]

In summation, the Bible's representation of the sick and disabled reflects the social world out of which it came, a world in which survival depended on individual health or group care for its more disadvantaged members. Concepts of purity, divine origin of disability, and objectification for theological and literary purposes all work together to paint a negative picture of the possibilities and powers of the disabled. At least one of the challenges faced by such persons is overcoming the burden of this characterization. It is no wonder that churches respond so slowly and ineptly to the special needs of this community, for they are themselves handicapped by their theological legacy. Nowhere is this more potently visible than in the Bible's view of those who are other than physically whole, and feminists who locate themselves within traditions for which the Bible is still normative need to be aware of the content and impact of its outlook on this topic.

Toward a Feminist Re-reading of the Bible for Disabled Women

As is often the case when direct appropriation is not possible for the critical feminist, situating the voice of the marginalized as *central* rather than peripheral can produce a dramatic rereading of biblical materials. The New Testament's emphasis on spirit over flesh is usually detrimental when applied to women, since they are viewed primarily as "fleshmakers," ones who induce men to fleshy thoughts which often produce actions issuing in the production of yet more flesh creatures, babies. For disabled women, however, the New Testament's preference for "spirit" as the defining construct of human anthropology actually *works*. We know better than to identify fully with bodies that are so patently unable to give shape and structure to the yearnings of our spirits. We *know* we are more than the flesh that sometimes seems much more like a trap that ensnares us than the medium that allows us to manifest our inner thoughts. Cast off an offending member to achieve a greater good? No problem: these are the kind of compromises that make up our daily struggle, and the Bible—unlike most of the medical profession—understands that we are more than the physical body, more than our disabilities and limitations.

Similarly, the Bible's view of the disabled as candidates for divine healing can also cut across the medical profession's too easy dismissal of possibilities and hope for those in our circumstances. The orthopedic specialist who told me to accustom myself to debilitating pain and that I would never walk without a cane again could not imagine that I would ever hike to inaccessible waterfalls or lead dance workshops—but I do. New studies in psychoneuroimmunology (PNI) are confirming that the spiritual practices of many religions offer a real advantage in the management of health problems.[4] Attitude and image can create miracles where Western medicine can only shake its collective head. Certainly we must be on guard against purity fetishes, objectification, and negative evaluations should "healing" not be complete or even visible, but the Bible's claim that faith makes a difference ought to be heard and celebrated. The healing stories of the New Testament emphasize over and over again that the faith of the one healed is as much a part of the healing action as the divine compassion that is extended (Matt 9:22; Mark 5:34; 10:52; Luke 8:48; 17:19; 18:42; Acts 14:9), thus mitigating somewhat the overall objectification and passivity in the characterization of the disabled or chronically ill. While it is important to us to be seen, heard, included, and valued as we are in our brokenness, we must not accept the narrowed choices and silence that society prefers for us. The Bible, in suggesting that our attitudes and expectations shape our experience and ability to receive healing, gives us back the power to imagine ourselves differently and to craft a reality that more accurately reflects our talents as survivors.

NOTES

1. See the myth of Enki and Ninmah, in Thorkild Jacobsen, *The Treasures of Darkness: A History of Mesopotamian Religion* (New Haven: Yale University Press, 1976), 113–14.

2. See discussion in my *Traditional Sayings in the Old Testament: A Contextual Study,* Bible and Literature 5 (Sheffield, U.K.: Almond Press, 1982), 28–53.

3. The Book of Job is of particular help in such cases, since it makes clear that affliction is not a product of sin, or lack of faith, and that howling one's angry questions at heaven is a more wholesome, faithful response than exonerating the deity with lies.

4. See, for example, Jeanne Achterberg, *Imagery in Healing: Shamanism and Modern Medicine* (Boston: New Science Library. 1985), as well as works by Deepak Chopra and others engaging in the exploration of "Body/Mind" medicine.

Nancy L. Eiesland

Feminist theology, with its limits and edges, includes some people and excludes others. Dr. Elly Elshout makes clear that within feminist social and religious movements women with disabilities have often been excluded. Though we have sometimes been denied physical access and social support within feminist circles, we have, nevertheless, internalized many feminist ideas and strategies and used them in service of our own emancipation. Many women with disabilities are now outsiders within.[1]

Not long ago I gave a guest lecture in a feminist ethics course at a mainline seminary in the United States. The participants in the class were enthusiastic about understanding the social and ethical issues raised by women with disabilities, until I noted that many people with disabilities were critical of the antidisability bias present in some feminist pro-choice arguments. A student asked, "Wouldn't you agree that it is a woman's right to decide whether she wants to have a disabled child?" This woman's question highlighted the tense conversations that must take place about the conflicting interests and values that surround "abilities." The consideration of reproductive technology and selective abortion, in particular, is just one area in which the exclusion of women with disabilities has resulted in the destructive perpetuation of antidisability bias within feminist circles.

Exposing this bias and understanding our position as women in a male-dominated society and as disabled in a society dominated by able-bodies is fundamental to feminist scholarship. Despite recent contributions to the field by Susan Wendell and Barbara Hillyer, we still do not have a sufficient understanding of a feminist theory of disability.[2] These theoretical efforts must be joined by feminist biblical scholars, theologians, and philosophers. Religion has played a large part both in buttressing the stigmatization, exclusion, and elimination of people with disabilities and in providing the vision and commitment for radical change toward a better society. We must discover this history of oppression and create and reclaim our stories of resistance and survival.

As Elshout notes, the emancipatory efforts of some, mostly Western, women with disabilities have been consolidated in the international social movement of people with disabilities.[3] One significant contribution of this movement has been to define people with disabilities as a minority group whose minority status results not from any shared physical or cultural characteristics but rather from being singled out by others in the society in which we live for different and unequal treatment. Perceiving people with disabilities as members of a minority group rather than as victims of a private physical, mental, or emotional tragedy provides the framework for understanding how such factors as negative stereotypes, prejudicial attitudes, and environmental segregation affect the lives of people with disabilities.

Despite the many advances made by and within the disability rights movement, here, too, gender bias exists. The women with disabilities who join efforts in the disability rights movement find their concerns dismissed as private matters, not worthy of lobbying efforts. Furthermore, the majority of women with disabilities are not involved in the emancipation movement of people with disabilities. In fact, most women with disabilities are impoverished women of color whose homes and bodies have been wracked by war, poverty, and malnutrition. The politics of disability are intimately connected to the politics of gender and justice.

Recognition of the minority group status of people with disabilities is vital for coalition-building. First, women with disabilities must build coalitions with other women with disabilities whose disability, race, ethnicity, culture, sexual orientation, class, or nationality differ from their own. Holding our bodies together in the midst of such diversity necessitates that we address our internal differences, exploring the potential sources of wisdom, excitement, conflict, and oppression they disclose. In speaking of faith for a better world we may find an appreciation of our common interests and our uncommon experiences.

Women with disabilities must also, as Elshout counsels, engage able-bodied feminists, especially within women-church. Women with disabilities enable the feminist community to rethink the meaning of difference in its midst. Our presence reminds everyone that the boundaries of group difference are ambiguous and shifting, without clear borders. Individuals who are currently able-bodied have a greater than 50 percent chance of becoming physically disabled, either temporarily or permanently. Ours is the only minority you can join involuntarily, without warning, at any time. For many temporarily able bodies, our bodies in trouble predict their future and urge them to confront these radical transformations.

Women with disabilities have learned that compromising with our bodies and with others who care is a slow, painful process in which our legitimate needs sometimes press hard against real limits. Holding our temporarily able and disabled bodies together reveals that we are collectively "a body in trouble." Essayist Nancy Mairs used the term to identify her struggle to comprehend her own body. She wrote, "Now I am who I will be. A body in trouble. I've spent all these years trying alternately to repudiate and to control my wayward body, to transcend it one way or another, but MS [multiple sclerosis] rams me right back down into it. . . . Rescue from the body is merely another word for death."[4]

I appreciate Elshout's metaphor of the disabled body for the conversations and practices that characterize feminist theology and women-church and believe that it accurately depicts the social reality of women's struggle for justice. Yet I have come to think of feminist theology and women-church as the accomplishments of "a body in trouble." To me, this metaphor also identifies the reality of women-church and feminist theology as a communion of struggle. This struggle takes place on many levels. It is a struggle against self-annihilation—the denial of our real bodies. The fear and loathing that society teaches women to have of our own bodies is a continual threat to our well-being and spiritual wholeness. We also struggle for full participation and inclusion of all women, recognizing that our bonds of understanding are tenuous and our aversion to difference is ever present. Finally, it is the struggle against injustice and oppression that makes all vulnerable to the erasure of our bodies.

The "body in trouble" depicts not victim-thinking, but a liberatory realism that is necessary for survival in difficult times and adverse circumstances. Each morning as I rouse myself I realize again that I am a body in trouble. Most days, this realization doesn't keep me from doing what needs to be done; rather it holds me to my limits. It keeps me in my body. So, too, recognition of women-church and our conversations about feminist theology as the accomplishments of a body in trouble help us to know that we can do what needs to be done and that it will not be easy.

As Elshout makes clear, the experience and knowledge of women with disabilities make vital contributions to feminist religious studies, theology, and women-church. Among these contributions is the identification of women with disabilities as part of a distinct and fluid minority group and new metaphors for conceiving our ever-evolving body. She has constructively joined what must continue as women with disabilities and able-bodied women work out our compromises.

NOTES

1. The situation of women with disabilities is similar to what Patricia Hill Collins identifies as the "outsider-within" status of African-American women. Patricia Hill Collins, *Black Feminist Thought: Knowledge, Consciousness, and the Politics of Empowerment* (New York: Routledge, 1991), 11–13.

2. Susan Wendell, "Toward a Feminist Theory of Disability," *Hypatia* 4, no. 2 (Summer 1989): 104–124; Barbara Hillyer, *Feminism and Disability* (Norman: University of Oklahoma Press, 1993).

3. Diane Driedger, *The Last Civil Rights Movement: Disabled Peoples' International* (New York: St. Martin's Press, 1989).

4. Nancy Mairs, *Remembering the Bone House: An Erotics of Place and Space* (New York: Harper and Row, 1989), 234–35. Other works by Mairs include *Plaintext: Deciphering a Woman's Life* (Tucson: University of Arizona Press, 1986); *Carnal Acts* (New York: HarperCollins, 1990); *Ordinary Time: Cycles in Marriage, Faith and Renewal* (Boston: Beacon Press, 1993).

Valerie C. Stiteler

I respect the author of this roundtable discussion for her willingness to honor the presence of women with disabilities within the feminist movement by insisting that our experiences with patriarchy be incorporated into the emerging feminist disciplines. Women with disabilities are still in the early stages of developing a methodology which enhances expression of our experiences and expresses the uniqueness of our embodiment.

The issues she raises are varied and complex. Before I begin my response, I want to say first that I consider myself to be a woman with a disability. This is both a personal and political statement. There are hundreds of thousands of people in the United States who have a medically or socially defined "disability," but only a fraction of these people describe themselves as being "disabled."

Thirty years ago, I was diagnosed with retinitis pigmentosa. My diagnosis defined me medically as being visually impaired. As I grew in my selfhood and empowerment, I went from being a visually impaired woman, to a blind woman, to a woman with a disability. Defining myself as "visually impaired" implied I was somehow "defective." Claiming myself as a woman with a disability, however, acknowledges my personal commitment to the joyousness of my blindness and my willingness to join others who want to work toward gaining the civil and social freedoms to which all disabled people are entitled.

As a self-identified woman with a disability, I, too, have had mixed reactions from my feminist sisters to my presence within the feminist community. Often I have been welcomed warmly and efforts have been made to respond to my requests for support. Many times women would openly engage me in conversation about how we could be together as a community where all of us—able-bodied and disabled—could share equally. Unfortunately, this warm response to me has been more the exception than the rule.

My presence at feminist gatherings has more often seemed to spark feelings of fear, anger, and guilt among many of my sisters. My requests for support in order to participate fully in groups set off chain reactions ranging from women assuming a caregiver role (resulting in my being infantilized), to open and hostile rejection.

I left these gatherings confused and angry. I felt violated. I was treated with less respect than I am by purveyors of patriarchy. I could not understand why my sisters who value inclusion and believe in honoring every woman's gifts would reject me so completely. I join the author in wondering why these reactions of able-bodied sisters to disabled sisters is so prevalent in the feminist community.

I begin my response by uplifting my disabled sister's truth. Elshout's story is echoed by many other women with disabilities both inside and outside the feminist movement. She charges the feminist movement with "ableism," which is in some way fostered as "the feminist movement enables, empowers, and strengthens women." She continues: "Thus, many 'fit women' will not easily admit that women with disabilities embody all that they don't want to be. As a result, the patriarchal way of judging a person for how good-looking, healthy or productive he or she is, is perpetuated by feminists." I agree that ableism exists in the feminist movement and Elshout's remarks provide us with the clues as to why. Feminist theologies of embodiment can generate negative attitudes towards disability. Theological discourse reclaiming female spirituality and power allows women to view disability as a return to female disempowerment and self-hatred.

Furthermore, patriarchal norms of bodily perfection and independence generate false expectations of achievement forcing disabled women to attempt to "overcome" their disabilities so to appear as "normal" as possible.[1] Constant attempts to achieve this mask of normality only lead to the isolation of the disabled woman and erosion of her selfhood.

Woman as Image of Disability and Agent of Sin

Many feminist theologies of embodiment based in the Jewish and Christian scriptures provide superb methods for reinterpreting the creation story depicting woman as the agent of sin resulting in the fall of humankind. The transformation of the iconic image of womanhood as sinful, weak, and dependent has been hard won in feminist theology. Unfortunately, many of the traditional images of the sinful woman are still ascribed to women with disabilities. Add to these images the Levitical view of disability as confirmation of sin and a pattern emerges of disabled woman as sinner.

Most feminist theologies of embodiment addressing the Genesis story focus on the woman's actions in relation to eating from the tree of knowledge. I contend that in order to understand the full import of the role of Eve as icon for sinful woman it is necessary to begin not with her supposed temptation of man but with her creation. In Genesis 2:21ff., God put man into a deep sleep and removed one of his ribs for use in the creation of woman. In effect, in order to create woman, God disabled man (a perfect creation). Woman was created in brokenness and disunity. The creation of woman is our first scriptural image of disability. If it can be argued from this interpretation of Genesis 2, that woman's essential nature is "disabling," then perhaps here is where the scriptural tradition of disability as evidence of sin really began. In any case, I believe this iconic image of womanhood as essentially disabled has affected many women's awareness of their embodiment.

Feminist women strive to cast away the oppression assigned to us by the patriarchal influences within the Jewish and Christian traditions. We renounce the view of ourselves as the agents of sin. We embrace our power, strength, independence, and beauty. The feminist movement did not adopt patriarchal attitudes toward the human body so much as it created theologies of embodiment rejecting anything representing our oppression by patriarchy or interfering with the pursuit of wholeness. Since women with disabilities do not embody the feminist notion of wholeness, this leads us to reject our disabilities as integral aspects of our embodiment.

The consistent emphasis on wholeness in feminist theologies of embodiment lends credence to my thesis. An examination of feminist writings, particularly liturgical texts, will bear this out.

The Influence of Patriarchy on Feminist Attitudes toward Disability

Patriarchal social constructs of womanhood and disability further complicate the relationships in feminist communities between able-bodied and disabled women. The patriarchal definitions of disability devalue women with disabilities to social roles as receivers of charity dependent on the good will of the dominant, able-bodied culture. Assigning able-bodied women roles of caregiver creates co-dependence between the two groups leading to the disempowerment of both parties.

This is a subtle form of patriarchal manipulation that heightens the oppression of all women. Disabled women are convinced their disabilities interfere with their capacity to achieve independence unless they image able-bodiment so well that they mimic normalcy; many, therefore, accept roles as disempowered victims. Able-bodied women are forced into the patriarchally defined role of caregiver usually reserved for the rearing of children or caring for the sick. The juxtaposition of these roles creates the potential for miscommunication and hostility between able-bodied and disabled women in the feminist movement. The impress of these patriarchal roles also creates arenas for unequal power structures to develop within feminist communities when women with disabilities are present.

Patriarchy has been very successful at using medically and socially defined disabilities to undermine the cohesiveness of the feminist movement. Using disability to thwart women's understanding of embodiment is particularly shrewd. Since not all physical or social limitations are regarded by patriarchy to be disabilities, attending to what patriarchy defines as disabling will be important to the feminist dialogue on embodiment.

A New Metaphor for Feminist Theology

At the conclusion of her statement, Elly Elshout presents us with the image of the disabled body as a new metaphor for feminist theology. "This metaphor is a feminist critical assumption of Paul's ecclesiological metaphor of the body of Christ in Corinthians 11–12. This metaphor signaled Paul's attempt to harmonize the differences among the peoples of the early Christian church. The metaphor of the disabled body, however, represents the social reality of the differences and conflicts of women's experiences. The disabled body is acquainted with pain and disappointment. New relationships, new wholeness can be forged only in difference and conflict." I am very impressed with the disabled body as a new metaphor for developing feminist critical method. I would like to hear more about why Elshout feels the disabled body is a feminist critical assumption of Paul's use of the image of the body of Christ. I agree that the disabled body is a valuable metaphor for feminist theology, but I do not think the Pauline metaphors of the body are useful for developing a methodology that addresses the experience of women with disabilities. We know Paul had some kind of disability, but there is little to indicate his relationship to it. Images of the body occurring in 1 Corinthians 11–12 are unifying models of bodily wholeness. Is this what is meant by the feminist critical assumption?

I am also concerned about Elshout's remarks about the disabled body as the image for the social reality of the differences and conflicts of women's experience. I am distressed by her comment that the disabled body is acquainted with pain and disappointment. Her remark seems to negate the possibility of joy and cooperation I feel is inherent in this image.

A Metaphor for Ongoing Creation

I would begin the conversation about the use of the disabled body as a metaphor for feminist theology by returning to Genesis 2:21ff. I would reexamine the passages referring to the removal of man's rib as an act of ongoing creation. God formed man and then continued man's creation by changing his body. The removal of the rib—an image of disability—resulted in the creation of woman. Add to this the remark man makes in Genesis 2:24 where he affirms the goodness of woman and acknowledges her role as his partner.

I would then examine other direct scriptural references to disability for their application to women with disabilities from a feminist perspective. For instance, we can learn from the exchange between God and Moses in Exodus 4:10–16. When Moses refused to accept God's invitation to lead the Israelites out of Egypt because of his speech impediment, God not only asserted that Moses's speech patterns were essential for persuading the people to leave Egypt; God also proclaimed that human disabilities are part of the Divine plan for beloved Creation.[2] God's promise to use Moses's disability to save the Israelites ignites images of the power and beauty of our disabilities. The Exodus passage continues with God prompting Aaron to provide support for Moses as he communicated God's message to the people. Here is a helpful model of cooperation with which to begin our dialogue between able-bodied and disabled feminists.

I regard the Gospels to be more authoritative than the Pauline epistles. I would continue exploration of the disabled body by critically examining the parables involving people with disabilities. Instead of focusing on Jesus's actions in a particular passage, I would experiment with uplifting the disabled person's actions as revelatory. I suggest doing a Bible study on the woman with the issue of blood (Mark 5:21–43). I would begin the Bible study by establishing that the woman's issue of blood was a disability and then discuss how she used her disability to gain access to Jesus and to her own healing.[3]

Having considered the woman's use of her disability as positive and as source of her salvation, we may find other passages in which we can begin to reinterpret some of the disability images found in the Scriptures. Many of the images in the Bible are negative, but some of the passages about disabled and sick people have been inappropriately interpreted because of the social stigma surrounding disabilities.

The disabled body is a powerful image. It has the potential to help us move out of the confining images of bodily perfection and unity inherent in patriarchal religious doctrines by representing us with a new image of a disabled God. It can provide us with the foundation for a relational model of cooperation based in the ongoing renewal of beloved Creation. Valuing the disabled body presents opportunities for feminists to reexamine their beliefs about their own embodiment by learning how disabilities provide positive aspects to our embodiment.

Principles for Emancipation

Truth telling is the first principle of emancipation for women with disabilities. I offer you only my own truth with this response. I feel each woman's disabilities enhance her embodiment differently. Some of our disabilities are results of medical conditions, some are not. Some of us require the support of others to live well, some do not. I regard my blindness as an aspect of my unique embodiment. My truth wells up from my own embodied experiences. Communicating our truth requires each woman naming for herself what her experience of disability is and how she chooses to relate to it.

By encouraging each woman to name the experience of disability for herself, both women who identify themselves as being disabled and women who identify themselves as being able-bodied can begin to apprehend and explore their beliefs about disability. We may discover we have negative attitudes toward certain aspects of female embodiment. We also may learn that disability is only a systemic metaphor created by patriarchy to deter us from deeper explorations of self.

The second principle of emancipation is "embracing" our disabilities.[4] Embracing our disabilities means accepting them as part of our uniqueness; acknowledging them as a source of our embodied power and allowing a sense of holiness to flow through our disabilities. Honoring them for their contribution to our lives will help dispel the stigma generated by patriarchy.

The third principle of emancipation is becoming aware that our embodiment extends beyond our own individual bodies and entwines with all of Creation. Our bodies, like our lives, are constantly renewing. Our connection with all creation allows us to come together as sisters in cooperative support, guiding and refreshing one another.

Women with disabilities offer the feminist movement the encouragement to expand and deepen our embodiment. We are unique, blessed, and powerful. This is the revelation and the mystery of the disabled body!

NOTES

1. Valerie C. Stiteler, "A Disabled Woman's Journey to Empowerment," *Bay Lines* (Journal of the Bay State Council of the Blind, Boston, Mass.) (October 1993): 4.

2. Valerie C. Stiteler, "Gathering Together: Forming Faith Communities among Persons with Disabilities," *Disability Issues* (Journal of the Information Center for Persons with Disabilities, Boston, Mass.) 8 (July 1993).

3. Valerie C. Stiteler, "Singing without a Voice: Using Disability Images in the Language of Public Worship," *Liturgical Ministry* 4 (November 1992).

4. Valerie C. Stiteler, "A Disabled Woman's Journey," 6.

Adele B. McCollum

Considering how common illness is, how tremendous the spiritual change that it brings, how astonishing, when the lights of health go down, the undiscovered countries that are then disclosed, what wastes and deserts of the soul . . . how we go down into the pit of death and feel the waters of annihilation close above our heads and wake thinking to find ourselves in the presence of the angels and the harpers. . . . it becomes strange indeed that illness has not taken its place with love and battle and jealousy among the prime themes of literature.[1]

Unlike literature, religion has not entirely omitted discussion of disease or disability. The literature of most religions addresses disability, healing, and the causes thereof. However, what religions have said about disability is often troubling, and, as a functional metaphor, disability has been explored only marginally in the study of women and religions. This is quite likely due at least in part to the actual marginalization of those with disabilities in both the literatures and communities of religions. A cursory examination of religious literature indicates that not only has there been marginalization, but where there is discussion it has been judgmental and pejorative and has often masqueraded under the guise of compassion.

I absorbed some of these attitudes toward body and ability from my folk culture. My maternal grandmother, who lived with us, had a quaint manner of keeping us on the track she thought was proper. If I dressed up and presented myself for approval she said, "Handsome is as handsome does." If she saw me sitting still she would say, "Idle hands are the devil's workshop," and likely as not hand me a bucket of peas to shell. When I accomplished a new physical skill and wanted to demonstrate, she said, "Pride goeth before a fall." Needless to say the message was that we should work and do actively but not be too uppity about it because it was no more than was expected anyway. Disability, in her scheme of things, meant one could not do, and according to her interpretation of Calvinist Providence this calamity was probably deserved punishment. If not deserved it was still God foreseen (*pro,* forward, + *vidēre,* to see) and therefore, was presented as coming from God for some reason. Either the person deserved it as punishment, it was an example with a lesson, could be avoided by overcoming laziness or, transcended by hard work and deliberate effort.

During summers I was sent to the country cousins to avoid polio epidemics in the city. My paternal grandmother and aunts cared for me and they, very unlike my maternal grandmother, were old-school Irish Catholic. From them I heard that if I was good I would not get polio. Good meant I should say my prayers, not steal pennies, do as I was told, and go to church. I don't recall ever having any chores to do because work was God's punishment. While the penalty for stealing pennies was severe (kneeling with arms outstretched cruciform for what seemed like hours), compassion for the elderly and disabled seemed to abound.

"Mrs. C has the rheumatism again."

"Poor soul. She's going to go straight to heaven, the way she's suffered."

"Aunt F's palsy is worsening."

"Poor dear, God's sure got something special in mind for her."

"Fr. B called. Wants us to pray for D. His unit got blown up in Italy someplace and his leg is gone."

"Better have a Mass said and send a cake 'round to the family."

If I were to summarize the remnants of this mixed background, I would say I was taught that health is both earned and deserved. It can be taken away by God if you are naughty. If you work hard and do as you're supposed to do you will avoid sickness and disability or at least overcome them, just as being good allows us to overcome death. Those "afflicted" are probably lazy, secretly sinful, or being used by God to educate the rest of the world. Since we don't know which it is, we should pray so God will fix it. I distinctly remember going with my grandmother to take a cake to Mrs. C and asking as we walked, "If she was bad and God is punishing her why are we giving her cake?"

This conflicting message of condemnation, compassion, and incipient Pelagianism strikes me now as an issue both of religion and social class. We were expected to adopt some combination of paternalism and judgment toward those with disabilities. When my brother and his wife had a child born with disabilities there was a good bit of murmuring on both sides of the family. Some said this was a "special child" while others self-righteously reported that there was "nothing like that" on our side of the family so it had to come from the in-laws. In the long run all agreed that it was the responsibility of the victim to improve with effort.

No combination of these Calvinist, Thomist, Pelagian perspectives on disability inherited from personal religious history seems to apply to my present situation. God does not have something special in mind for me; I am not suffering vicariously to be like Jesus or to spring souls from purgatory; I have sinned both less and more than some acquaintances; I am not here to be the embodiment of evil, justice, mercy, or transcendence; and I am not here so others can learn patience, compassion, charity, to overcome adversity, or learn to be grateful for what they have.

Proffered secular explanations fail also. I am not lazy, in need of attention, did not bring it on myself, choose to be sick, acquire it because I did not want to get married, I do not like being dependent or anything of this sort. Welcome to the world of immune deficiency. Scientific explanations for it: toxic waste, global warming, ultraviolet exposure, biological mutations, genetic loading, seem to have little effect on daily reality. So what does it all mean?

Twelve theological dictionaries and etymological sources yield: **transcendent:** The primacy of the spiritual over the material and empirical; surpassing the ordinary as in Deity.

The roots of such attitudes have far-reaching tendrils in Western scholarship as well as in folk culture. Woolf identifies a source in literature:

> Literature does its best to maintain that its concern is with the mind; that the body is a
> sheet of plain glass through which the soul looks straight and clear, and, save for one
> or two passions such as desire and greed, is null, and negligible and non-existent. On
> the contrary, the very opposite is true. All day, all night the body intervenes; blunts or
> sharpens, colours or discolours, . . . The creature within can only gaze through the
> pane . . . ; it cannot separate off from the body like the sheath of a knife or the pod of
> a pea for a single instant.; it must go through the whole unending procession of
> changes, . . . until there comes the inevitable catastrophe; the body smashes itself to
> smithereens, and the soul (it is said) escapes.[2]

This passage enunciates established ideas toward the body which in turn affect attitudes
toward and treatment of people associated with body, especially women, and women
with disabilities.

Other theological roots can be gleaned:[3]

> We can learn something of man's soul . . . in contrast to the lower animals . . . he is
> not pinned down to merely material objects; he can rise above everything in the visi-
> ble world, and pass into a higher region. (p. 49)

> Man's soul . . . being fitted by its nature for the contemplation of immaterial things . . .
> must be immaterial and spiritual; or, more plainly, it must be a spirit. (p. 49)

> Some power within us raises the data supplied by the senses to a higher plane—a plane
> which the senses of themselves could never have reached. (p. 51)

> The Soul is Immortal . . . the destruction of the body does not involve the destruc-
> tion of the soul; it is immaterial. (p. 57)

> The justice of God demands that there should be a future state in which [this]
> inequality is redressed. (p. 58)

The lesson is evident. The body is lower but we are instructed to go higher. What is
good (soul) is immaterial. The body is destroyed but not the soul. Bodily senses cannot
conduct us to the higher plane, in fact they are an obstruction on the way.

Jonathan Edwards is no more benign. All afflictions are intended to reprimand and
improve.

> *Resolved*, after afflictions, to enquire, What I am the better for them; What good I
> have got by them; and, What I might have got by them.[4]

As told to me, the cause of blindness, the withered hand, lameness, and plague was
sin, the source of punishment, which in turn was an example of God's justice. The con-
tinuance of disability came from lack of faith in God's healing power; an appropriate
response to it was a penitential attitude, willingness to learn and become better, perseverance, and forbearance. The only way to salvation was to transcend the physical.

From Socrates's desire to escape the body, many Gnostic assertions of matter as
trap for the soul, traditional Roman Catholic and Puritan teachings, until more modern
examples of Christian Science and Evangelical Healers the message is consistent. Body is
less valuable than soul or spirit, those with flawed bodies are sinful, cursed, or pitiable
moral examples.

The lessons absorbed were plain. Transcend sin, work hard, and, always, improve yourself spiritually by suffering. The body is temporary and is not your godlike portion. The senses need redemption, and affliction is one way of redeeming them. Follow the rules and none of this will happen to you. And by all means don't get bogged down in the flesh.

None of this made much sense to me until 1970 when the movement of women awakened some of us. It is no accident that it is women theologians and religionists attempting to redeem body and its differences as a focus of debate. First, women are disproportionately maligned, decentered, and impaired by anti-body philosophies of Cartesian schizophrenia. Second, it is a source of conflict for a feminist theorist to overlook multiple realities. Feminist/womanist integrity demands that the different realities of women with disabilities be recognized. Third, like the physically challenged, feminists can look neither backward nor forward to fixed points on the philosophical horizon.[5] Honest theory cannot speak from any Archimedean point that ignores the changeabilities of nature, body, matter with which women continue to be so closely associated.

Each of these three thought impediments: disdain for body, scorn of different realities, and insistence on fixed realities, ambushes the work of women with disabilities who may be trying to relocate theory in concrete physical experience.

Transcendence has traditionally pointed in the direction of the mind or the soul, leaving the body behind on its own, invisible, transformed, celestialized, resurrected, or restored. This is especially conflicting for women who have been most connected to nature, matter, mater. If salvation has to do with transcendence and transcendence has to do with surmounting barriers, one of the immovable barriers for women has been the body. Time and again, women have been admonished to become as men in order to be saved. In other words, women must somehow transcend their own corporeal and carnal natures. In such theory all women are disabled males.

Is the woman with disabilities twice disabled in terms of salvation? Or perhaps, because women are by nature disabled, women with physical differences are less disabled. Perhaps the disability renders her asexual and consequently less female and carnal than her sisters. If so, perhaps she can be engaged as a model of transcendence since her "natural" disability of womanhood is somehow canceled or overcome. Shouldn't this then give women with disabilities both a spiritual and epistemic advantage? But that's another essay.

Let me examine briefly what the paradox of transcendence and immanence might mean when generated from body, change, and deterioration. When theologians speak of transcending body they do not mean what I mean. Overcoming barriers and locating freedom in physical restrictions constitute my idea of transcendence. In other words, it is body which provides the location and possibility for transcendence. Any idea that salvation, transcendence, rapture, or anything else will occur without the body is an absurdity without ground. If the bumper sticker "In case of rapture this car will be unmanned," were true we would not allow such Christians to have driver's licenses. When I say that transcendence depends on the immanence of the body I am not, in Hegelian fashion, claiming that the master depends on the slave. I am instead positing body as the origin of constructed reality. And if reality begins with body, it cannot be transcended without dissociating from reality. If first order creation is not by breath, words, or ex nihilo alone but is constructed through bodily perceptions, that world, that reality, is contingent on body for its existence. In addition to returning creation to body where it belonged pre-patriarchy, this assertion also lays claim to the idea that outside the body there is no salvation.[6]

For some of us with disabilities constructed reality looks like this: concern is not limited to mind, or even to mind before body. The soul may see through a transparent body but no such thing exists for women, even less so for women with extra physical challenges.

Let me be specific about my own. Body is ever present though changeable and unpredictable. I don't call myself disabled because it is clear that I am able and capable. Handicapped does not apply either because I am not the "cap in hand" beggar which was the source of that word; nor do I play any sport well enough to earn a handicap. I am often, as my grandmother used to say, "crippled up." However, I prefer being physically challenged. It describes more precisely than any of the other terms in use, how life presents itself to me and how I address life. I also think of my body as the great betrayer. Today it jogs or at least walks briskly. Tomorrow it may gasp for air. Today I pace before the class; tomorrow I teach from a wheelchair. Today my fingers type flawlessly. Tomorrow they are red, swollen, painful, and can't even open the medicine that brings relief. I can no longer depend on health and energy on a continuum.

Notions of fixed reality, permanent ideas or identities, unchanging gods, predictable archetypes or patterns find no match in my present experience. While I hardly think of physical challenges as postmodern, they provide concrete experience of living without certainty, with nothing given or absolute, with no trail more defined than another. This creates a challenge to traditional ideas of transcendence which rely on positing nonmaterial a priori/a posteriori beginnings and endings. Only when health and strength seem certain and normative are attitudes and theories of redemptive or provident suffering possible. When we were children we could actually seek suffering for its benefits to the soul, vowing to let the dentist drill our teeth without novocaine and "offer it up" for any one of several suffering relatives in purgatory. We were invincible children; there were immutable universals.

It is these suppositions based on fixed norms next to which all else is mutant, variant, or deviant which lead people to voice amazement that those of us with chronic disease or physical challenge act very much as they do. Notions of the body as impediment to the good and the real blind us to the value of body as locus of enlightenment.

A colleague just yesterday provided an anecdote. Her sister was graduating and it was announced that the class valedictorian was someone with lupus. The sister went on to exclaim how truly amazing it was that someone with lupus could also be first in the class. My colleague, well schooled in multiple realities, answered immediately, "Have I got a friend who would repudiate that!" The sister's reaction is all too familiar and strikes me as similar to the amazement of men when they actually found a woman capable of making a mark in history.

If the presupposition is that the subject is less capable, inferior, weak, or impaired, and yet she continues to function at the level of the strong, somehow she must be unreal, above human status, a special being. To say otherwise is to cast doubt on one's own ability and worth. I prefer to argue that it is *because of* rather than in spite of difference that someone achieves. Physical challenge is an additional qualification which provides an advantageous standpoint or insight not available to others.

Zen-like I want to say that a broken teacup is not a flawed example of a teacup but a perfect example of a broken teacup. Enlightenment and transcendence won't come from a glued teacup becoming the standard teacup. They are already there. Transcendence is not gained by avoiding or overcoming body because body is the prism of creation.

NOTES

1. Virginia Woolf, "On Being Ill," in *The Moment and Other Essays* (1947; reprinted in Collected Essays, 4 vols., New York: Harcourt, Brace, World, 1966), 4:193.

2. Woolf, 194.

3. The Most Reverend M. Sheehan, *Apologetics and Catholic Doctrine: A Course of Religious Instruction for Schools and Colleges,* 4th ed (Dublin: M.H. Gill and Son, 1959), page references given in text.

4. Jonathan Edwards, "Resolutions," No. 67, Aug 17, 1723, in *The Works of President Edwards,* ed. Sereno B. Dwight, 10 vols. (New York: S. Converse, 1829–30), 1:73.

5. "A life-sentence can be pronounced in many ways; and there are as many ways of meeting it. What is common to all who have received it—the consumptive, the paralyzed, the deaf, the blind—is the absence of a fixed point on the mind's horizon." Marchesa Iris Origo, Introduction to *A Measure of Love* (London: Cape Publishers, 1957).

6. Some may find this suspiciously close to the Mormon assertion that body is a necessary acquisition on the path of salvation. It is related, although I do not regard human embodiment as a step in a hierarchy of bodies. Again, this is another essay.

Margaret Moers Wenig

[EDITORS' NOTE: What follows is a sermon that was originally delivered at Hebrew Union College–Jewish Institute of Religion.]

When Moses addressed the Israelites gathered on the shore of the Jordan, poised to enter the land of Canaan, he made sure they understood that the Covenant was made with all of them,

Atem nitzavim hayom kulchem

You stand this day *all* of you, before Adonai your God
the heads of your tribes, your elders and officers
every one in Israel, men, women and children.
and the strangers in your camp
from the one who chops your wood to the one who draws your water,
to enter into the sworn covenant
which Adonai your God makes with you this day.[1]

Like Moses, we in the Reform movement try to include in our covenantal community as many as wish to join. We welcome those who were born Jews and those who chose to be Jews and even those who are not Jews at all. Some congregations reach out to Russian Jews, and some are beginning to reach out to lesbian and gay Jews. But 17 percent of the Jewish people still could not enter the doors or participate in worship in most of our synagogues.[2]

Velo itchem levadchem anochi koreit et habrit hazot v'et haalah hazot. Ki et asher yeshno po imanu omed hayom lifney Adonai eloheinu. V'ey asher eynenu po imanu hayom.

I make this covenant . . . not with you alone but with those who are standing here with us this day . . . and with those who are not with us here this day.[3]

Yet the covenant was made with them as well. They are people with disabilities.

A person with disabilities now has a civil right to access. The Americans with Disabilities Act requires renovated or newly constructed restaurants, hotels, theaters, doctors' offices, pharmacies, retail stores, museums, libraries, parks, and schools to be accessible. Religious institutions, however, are exempt from the public accommodations aspect of the law. Why? Though 90 percent of religious organizations supported the ADA and requested no religious exemption, a few right-wing religious groups got to the White House and protested that such legislation would be an infringement of their constitutional rights. So, for political reasons, all religious institutions are exempt.[4] How ironic, then, that a restaurant cannot legally keep people with disabilities out but a church or synagogue can.

The Torah, however, anticipated the ADA by a few thousand years: *"Lo t'kalel cheresh v'lifney iver to titeyn michsohl"* (You shall not insult the deaf or place a stumbling block before the blind).[5] And so, despite their civil exemption, some synagogues have begun to remove physical barriers. In one major city, people who use a wheelchair could enter one quarter of the Reform synagogues; many offer Braille prayerbooks; and one can accommodate people who are deaf. With money we can remove physical barriers, but attitudinal barriers are more difficult to overcome.

Attitudinal Barrier No. 1

Some people imagine that people with disabilities don't live in our community, so we don't need to make our synagogue accessible to them.

Most congregations have older members with disabilities whose existence the newer lay leaders learn of only when their names are added to the Kaddish list. Most congregations have children with disabilities whom parents rarely mention and never bring to services.

If we live and work and pray in places that are inaccessible to people with disabilities, we will believe that such people don't exist . . . until we visit Berkeley, California, for example, where people in wheelchairs are everywhere. Where do they come from? They come from their homes in which they would remain confined were it not for accessible streets and shops.

If we live and work and pray in places that are inaccessible to people with disabilities, we will continue to believe that they don't exist . . . until we attend a performance of the National Theater for the Deaf, for example, and see hundreds of people signing to each other, and we realize that American Sign Language is not just for the rare child who requires an interpreter but is the living language of an entire community of people, including many Jews.

People with disabilities will remain invisible to us as long as our congregations are inaccessible to them. It's not simply that they don't speak our language, it's that we don't use theirs either.

Attitudinal Barrier No. 2

Some people come to synagogue to escape life's problems. They don't want to be reminded of the vulnerability of being human. They don't want to be around people who are disabled.

The fear of wasting a congregation's limited resources to reach out to people with disabilities who will never come is a pretext. Deeper is the fear that they will come, and in droves; and then what able-bodied person would want to belong to such a synagogue? One rabbi, who has a successful program of outreach, reported that "the initial reaction of the congregation, was negative." When he invited people with disabilities to a service accessible to them, able-bodied members saw the wheelchairs, walkers, and white canes and thought it was a healing service.[6] Some people fear catching what people with disabilities have.

Attitudinal Barrier No. 3

Some people believe that people with disabilities are limited emotionally and intellectually. If they can't be articulate in our language, they can't be worth talking to.

Jewish law long disqualified the *cheresh* (deaf person) from status as a full adult Jew. He could not make contracts, buy and sell property, count in a minyan, or affect a marriage or divorce. He was never considered a bar mitzvah no matter what his age . . . until 150 years ago when R. Abraham Samuel Benjamin Sofer visited the Vienna Institute for the Deaf and Dumb and observed the accomplishments of its pupils. Last year a thirteen-year-old Philadelphia boy, Eugene Chernyakhovsky, celebrated becoming a bar mitzvah. Eugene can't walk, talk, or use his hands because of cerebral palsy, but with his feet he operates a joy stick and a pedal mounted on his wheel chair and enters commands into a computer which activates a voice synthesizer. Eugene begged his atheist Soviet immigrant parents to provide him with a Jewish education. Said his mother, at the celebration of his bar mitzvah, at which Eugene led the service, read Torah, and gave a speech, "Eugene has brought religion into our lives."[7]

Jews with disabilities engaged in Jewish learning! And teaching? This year a rabbinical seminary for the deaf opened in cooperation with the Reconstructionist Rabbinical College.

Attitudinal Barrier No. 4

Our pity and our paternalism.

Cartoonist John Callahan was featured in the *New York Times Magazine* section this summer.[8] He is a C5–6 quadriplegic with no control of his lower body and only minimal control of his upper body. He can, however, hold a pen. He rails against the pitying patronizing attitude many people have toward people with disabilities. He also rails against the romanticization of people with disabilities by people without them. In his cartoons he portrays people with disabilities with brutal honesty and laughs at them—or more accurately with them. "Yes," he writes, "quads wish they were paras, paras wish they were able bodied, and the able bodied wish they were Jane Fonda."

One cartoon shows a sheriff in pursuit of an outlaw. When the sheriff comes across an abandoned wheelchair in the desert he points to it and says to his men, "Don't worry, he won't get far on foot." Another cartoon shows a man without arms asking for a drink at a bar. The bartender refuses, saying, "I'm sorry Sam, I can't serve you a drink because you can't hold your liquor." Those of us who have not lost our hearing, our sight, or our mobility, might feel inhibited from laughing at those who have. But if we could laugh with them, we might understand that in that laughter lies a measure of acceptance we need to reach. Callahan says he would like to get married and have children. "I think it would be fun to hear the whir of little wheels around the house."

When I was pregnant for the first time I had a series of nightmares in which I gave birth to a "deformed" baby. Each time I awoke crying. Then one night, somewhere around the sixth month, I had a dream in which I had to have an emergency c-section and once again an "imperfect" child emerged from inside me. Everyone in the delivery room gasped with shock and disgust. But in this dream, the baby reached out her arms for me, as if to say "Well, I love you." The deformed child we fear bearing is ourselves. It is our own fear of being different and isolated, of being dependent or abandoned. It is our fear of being able to love or be loved less, accomplish less, or be worth less than other people. You see, we need to learn not only about ramps and sign language. We need to learn, really learn one of the mysteries of Creation:

> *Vayomer Elohim, "Naaseh adam b'tzalmeynu, kidmuteynu."*
> *Vayivra Elohim et haadam b'tzalmo b'tzelem Elohim bara oto.*

God created us in the divine image.[9]

When we pray that God not be deaf to our pleas, we mean that God not ignore our pleas. But when a theologian who is deaf speaks of God as deaf, she doesn't mean that God ignores her pain, she means that God understands it. Yes God understands her and God speaks her language.[10] In a religious school class, a teacher tried to reassure a student who was deaf by explaining, "In the world to come, you will be able to hear." "No," protested the child, "in the world to come, God will sign."

In the world to come God will sign.

And in this world? Perhaps our synagogues could purchase a few Braille copies of *Gates of Prayer*.[11] Perhaps our synagogues could train an in-house sign language interpreter or hire one as needed. Perhaps rabbis could circulate copies of their sermons for people who cannot hear them, and tapes of the newsletter for those who cannot read it. Perhaps we could invest in assistive listening devices and the lighting helpful to those who read lips. Perhaps we could build ramps and widen bathroom doors. Perhaps the Union of American Hebrew Congregations[12] could even help poor congregations pay for renovations or equipment that would make them accessible to their older members who built and sustained those synagogues but now cannot use them. And perhaps a child who is deaf could learn from a rabbi who is deaf and even aspire to become one. Perhaps we all can learn from people with disabilities. (Can you imagine how we at the New York School[13] would be changed by a single classmate, student, or teacher who is deaf?)

Perhaps, when our synagogues are accessible and people with disabilities do pray with us, then we will use liturgies sensitive to them. We may not be able to "imagine a world without color" but some of our congregants inhabit just such a world. We may not be able to "imagine a world without sound" but some of our congregants inhabit just such a world.[14] I love the *Gates of Prayer* and *Gates of Repentance* and am very fond of some of the men who helped compose them, but not everyone in our congregations can say, "I have been created with eyes, the blessing of sight, to see the world's beauty and holiness," or "with ears to hear sacred words, to hear the sounds of wisdom, beauty and love." We have not all "been given legs to walk in God's path" or "been blessed with the ability to regenerate life."[15]

Perhaps we should not say "We have walked sightless among miracles,"[16] "been blind to our authentic selves,"[17] or "deaf to God's voice," or "deaf to the cries of the oppressed." And for *"al titalam mit'chinateynu,"* surely we can do better than "do not be deaf to our plea."[18]

Could we raise these issues in our congregations? I think we could. I think we may. I think we just may. Because we do believe that the Covenant was made with every one of us here today and with those not here today. We will do it for people we do not yet know. We will do it for people in our own families or circles of friends who do now or may someday have disabilities. And we will do it for ourselves, our own vulnerable selves, created every one of us in the image of God.

NOTES

I was challenged to give this sermon by the witness and writing of Professor Christine Smith and Rev. Valerie Stiteler.

1. Deut. 29:9–11.
2. Bruce Black, "Jews with Disabilities," *Reform Judaism* (Fall 1992): 4.
3. Deut. 29:13–14.
4. This account was provided by Chai Feldblum, one of the authors of the ADA.
5. Lev. 19:14.
6. "Rabbi Jim Kaufman of Temple Beth Hillel recalls that it took quite a while before his congregants were able to view people with disabilities as human beings. 'The initial reaction of the congregation was negative,' he says. 'They were disabled phobic. Congregants came to the sanctuary to get away from life's problems, and it looked like I was conducting a healing service." Black, "Jews with Disabilities," 6.
7. Joyce Vottima Hellberg, "Making His Jewish Voice Heard," *Philadelphia Inquirer,* 4 May 1992.
8. June 7, 1992.
9. Gen. 1:27, as translated in the *Gates of Repentance: The New Union Prayerbook for the Days of Awe* (New York: Central Conference of American Rabbis, 1978), 197.
10. The Rev. Kathy Black (who is not deaf but has worked in deaf ministry) wrote an article, "Is God Deaf?" which prompted the Rev. Christine Smith to write, "One of the challenges of the disabilities community will surely be to suggest that God is paralyzed, blind or deaf." Smith, "Revelation Confronts Denial—Handicappism," in *Preaching as Weeping, Confession and Resistance: Radical Responses to Radical Evil* (Louisville: Westminster/John Knox Press, 1992), 45.
11. *Gates of Prayer: The New Union Prayerbook* is the Reform movement's prayer book. (New York: Central Conference of American Rabbis, 1975).
12. The national synagogue body of the Reform movement.
13. Of Hebrew Union College—Jewish Institute of Religion, one of the four campuses of the seminary of the Reform movement.
14. One of the Evening or Morning services in the Reform movement's prayer book contains a litany:

> Can we imagine a world without color, a world without the grace of blue,
>   the life of green?
> We give thanks for eyes that see, for the sublime gift of beauty. . . .

Can we imagine a world without sound, never knowing the joy of song?
We give thanks for words that speak to the mind, for hymns of joy
and songs of sorrow, and for souls that know how to listen. . . .

(Gates of Prayer, 93)

15. *Gates of Repentance,* 378–79.
16. *Gates of Prayer,* 170.
17. *Gates of Prayer,* 256.
18. *Gates of Repentance,* 269.

A Case History
Numbers 5:11–31

Introduction to A Case History

In this section of the Reader we shall look at the text of the Sotah, the biblical prescription for a woman who may have committed adultery. One uses the conditional *may* because if there had been witnesses to the act of adultery, both the adulteress woman and her adulteress partner would have been put to death, according to the laws in Deuteronomy. "If a man is caught lying with the wife of another man, both of them shall die, the man who lay with the woman as well as the woman" (Deut. 22:22).

The case of the Sotah discussed in the Book of Numbers (5:11–31) occurs when a man suspects his wife of committing adultery. The man makes formal accusation to the priest and the community, and the guilty or possibly guilty woman is brought to the Temple, where she is made to drink a potion concocted by the priest. This potion will destroy her, or her ability to bear children, depending on one's interpretation, if she is guilty. If she is innocent of the charge of adultery, she will be able to bear her husband's children.

The Sotah is unique in biblical law: it is the only trial by ordeal; it is the only occasion in which a person can be accused of a capital crime without two witnesses. The half-disrobed woman with disheveled hair, appearing as though she had been caught in an intimate act, is not even permitted to utter the self-incriminatory oath: the ritual oath is recited by the priest. Only the potion itself is put in the mouth of the woman.

> Then the priest shall make her take an oath, saying, "If no man has lain with you, if you have not turned aside to uncleanness while under your husband's authority, be immune to this water of bitterness that brings the curse. But if you have gone astray while under your husband's authority, if you have defiled yourself and some man other than your husband has had intercourse with you, let the priest make the woman take the oath of the curse and say to the woman—"the Lord make you an execration and an oath among your people, when the Lord makes your uterus drop, your womb discharge; now may this water that brings the curse enter your bowels and make your womb discharge, your uterus drop!" And the woman shall say, "Amen. Amen." (Num. 5:20–22)

She is forced to swallow what she knows. In my view, then, the Sotah is a unique vehicle for envisioning what is denied, repressed, and silenced in ancient Israelite culture. However, this is only my view or interpretation of the Sotah. The other articles in this section focus on social, legal, and ritual aspects of the Sotah. I have called the section A Case History because each of these articles reads the same seventeen verses—yet each reads the selection differently. By reading all of the articles, you will be able to discern what one gains from a feminist reading and what one might be losing. Of course, none of the articles is "right" or "true." Each one bears a portion of truth, and read together they will give the reader a much more complex and nuanced view of the ritual of Sotah than any of them read singularly.

The Strange Case of the Suspected Sotah (Numbers V 11–31)

Tikva Frymer-Kensky

The trial of the suspected adulteress in Num. v 11–31 is highly unusual within the corpus of Israelite Law. Like the case of the decapitated heifer (Deut. xxi 1–9), it is one of the few instances in which we have a detailed description of a ritual to be performed in answer to a crisis in the legal system: in the case of the decapitated heifer, the problem of an unsolved murder; in that of the Sotah, the issue of a suspected adulteress. The two crimes involved here—murder and adultery—are crucially dangerous to the fabric of Israelite society and are therefore punishable by death. In both circumstances—the discovery of a murdered body and the suspicions of a husband—it is impossible to "solve" the case by normal legal means, for in one case (the heifer) there is knowledge of a crime (murder) but no suspect, and in the other (the Sotah) there is a suspect (the wife) but no knowledge whether a crime has been committed. Since the issues of murder and adultery are too serious to be allowed to pass unpunished, special quasi-legal procedures or rituals are prescribed to resolve the situation by religious means. In the case of the decapitated heifer, the goal of the ritual is to forestall bloodguilt upon the people; in the case of the Sotah, to punish adultery. In both instances, the ritual procedures are described in detail. The passage about the Sotah in Num. v 11–31 is found in a group of Priestly rituals. It is essentially a descriptive ritual instruction whose concern is to prescribe the circumstances of the trial and to describe the acts to be performed in the ritual and the words of the curse with which the woman is to be adjured.

The inherent interest of such an extraordinary trial has led to considerable discussion of the passage in Num. v 11–31. Despite such attention, however, the passage has not been fully understood, and questions remain about the nature of the trial and the ultimate punishment of the woman. Part of the difficulty lies in the difficult language of

463

the passage, which contains technical terms that are otherwise unknown;[1] even the key term used for the drinking potion, *mê hammārîm hamĕʾārărîm*, is not completely understood.[2] The problems of the text are compounded by the involuted structure which makes the passage appear repetitious and disjunctive. A realization of the primarily ritual nature of the passage, however, clarifies the structure and provides insights into the nature of the trial and its result.

The repetitions and disjunctions (e.g. at *v.* 21) led scholars of the critical school to divide the chapter into (at least) two original sources,[3] attributed by some to originally distinct rituals.[4] However, whatever literary prehistory the text may have had, it now has a unified structure and should be treated as a coherent whole. The recent studies of this text by Michael Fishbane,[5] Herbert Chanan Brichto,[6] and Jacob Milgrom[7] have therefore taken a holistic approach to the passage. Such an approach is in accord with recent developments in biblical textual study which emphasize the appreciation of the composition and literary structure of individual passages and whole books.[8] This literary approach to the biblical text has revealed certain techniques such as subscripts,[9] repetitive resumptions and *inclusios*,[10] and inversions (see Talmon [n. 8, 1975], pp. 358–78), which are used in the composition of biblical passages, and in their editorial redaction and amalgamation into larger units. It is now clear that repetition, in particular, is not necessarily a sign of either multiple origins or bad style, but a classic biblical technique used variously to unify compositions with complex structure, to resume narrative after a long hiatus (as, e.g., Ex. xl 34–38 is taken up at Num. ix 15 f.), and to resume narrative after short digressions.

The discovery of the literary use of repetition illuminates the structure of Num. v 11–31, which can be considered a paradigmatic case of the use of *inclusio*-repetition to unify a passage with a complex structure. Since the passage is a descriptive-prescriptive narrative, it is necessarily complex. Events are given in basically chronological order, and the main focus of the passage is on the principal characters of the action, the priest and the woman. The purpose of the passage, however, is to inform the priest exactly what to do in the circumstances described in the introduction. All the details of the action must therefore be given, including the preparation of the potion to be drunk and of the woman's offering, and the exact words of the priest. The passage describes (prescribes) how the meal-offering is brought by the husband (*v.* 15), held by the woman during the adjuration (*v.* 18), and offered by the priest (*v.* 25); how the potion is prepared by the priest by putting dust from the floor of the tabernacle into an earthenware bowl full of holy water (*v.* 17), is held in the priest's hand during the adjuration (*v.* 18), has the curse dissolved in it (*v.* 23), and is given to the woman to drink (*vv.* 24–27); how the woman is brought by her husband (*v.* 15), is stood before the Lord (*vv.* 16, 18), holds the meal-offering in her hand (*v.* 18), is adjured by the priest (*vv.* 19–21), says "Amen, amen" (*v.* 22), has the meal-offering taken from her hand (*v.* 25), and is given the potion to drink by the priest (*vv.* 24–27). In order to include all these detailed elements while maintaining the form of a simple narrative and without taking the "spotlight" away from the principal actors, the text relies on a carefully organized structure based on a systematic use of *inclusio*-repetition.

The text begins with an introduction which states the circumstances under which the ritual may be used. It describes the events of the ritual and concludes the descriptive prescription of the ritual with a recapitulation of the circumstances under which it may be used. A statement about the post-ritual resolution of the case is appended: after the trial, if the woman is innocent, the husband is to be free from any penalties for false accusation, and if she is guilty, she is to bear her punishment (see below). The structure of the passage can be represented schematically:

A. *Introduction:* the circumstances under which the ritual is to be performed (*vv.* 12–14).
B. *Action*
   I. *Initiation* by the husband: bringing the woman and the offering (*v.* 15).
   II. *Preparation* by the priest: preparation of the woman and potion (*vv.* 16–18).
   III. *Adjuration* by the priest with the woman's acceptance (*vv.* 19–23).
   IV. *Execution* by the priest: making the offering, having the woman drink (*vv.* 24–28).
C. *Recapitulation:* circumstances under which the ritual is to be performed (*vv.* 29–30).
D. *Addendum-Resolution:* post-ritual resolution (*v.* 31).

Each stage of the action is complex, detailing the treatment not only of the woman, but of the potion and the meal-offering. It is for this reason that in each section of the action (B) the key word that describes the action is repeated twice. In *v.* 15, the repetition of *hby*ᵓ "(the man) brings," could be explained by the fact that the man brings both the woman and the offering; the repetition of the verb emphasizes that he must bring the offering in order to bring the woman. In the other three sections, the repeated verbs have the same referents: the priest stands the woman before the Lord, *hᶜmyd* (*vv.* 16, 18); the priest adjures the woman, *hšbyᶜ* (*vv.* 19, 21); and the priest has the woman drink, *hšqh* (*vv.* 24, 27).

These three repetitions are the main reason for the extensive source-criticism of this passage. However, they are not accidents of literary history, nor do they indicate that the actions were actually performed twice. In each case the key word introduces the section and marks its prime act. It in effect serves as a heading or *incipit* of that section. Since there is more than one act in each stage of the ritual, and since the passage must detail all the actions to be performed, each section of the passage must include all the acts to be performed at that point. Each action section, therefore, first indicates the prime act of each stage and then describes the coordinate act to be performed at that stage: the preparation of the potion, the recitation of the promise of acquittal for the innocent, or the performance of the meal-offering. After the description of the relevant co-ordinate act, each section then returns to the prime act of each stage of the ritual, giving it a fuller exposition. It marks its return to the prime act by the *inclusio* device of repeating the passage with which the section opened. A diagrammatic representation of the last three sections of the action passage would thus be:

Preparation		
The priest stands the woman before the Lord	—————— prepares the potion ——————	The priest stands the woman before the Lord
Adjuration		
The priest adjures the woman	_____ promises acquittal _____ for innocence	The priest adjures the woman

Execution

The priest has the woman drink	————— makes an offering —————	The priest has the woman drink

The main action of each stage of the ritual is mentioned first, in a sense "headlining" the purpose of each stage of the procedure. In practice, however, it seems that the co-ordinate act preceded the main event. This is explicitly stated in the execution section, in which the co-ordinate act (the offering of the meal-offering) must be performed before the actual drinking (*v.* 26). This is an important point, because it emphasizes that without the meal-offering there is no efficacy in the drinking of the potion. Similarly, in the adjuration section the woman is promised an acquittal if she is innocent, and this promise is given before the priest performs the actual adjuration itself. The situation is not as clear in the preparation section, and we do not know whether the co-ordinate act—the preparation of the potion—is simultaneous with or antecedent to the main action (the stationing of the woman), i.e. whether the potion is prepared before the woman is stood before the Lord or while she is standing there. Because of the pattern of the text in the other sections, it seems probable that the potion is prepared before the woman is stood before the Lord, although the psychological effect would be greater if the woman could see the potion being prepared. In any event, the text achieves its object by its elaborate use of headline-*inclusio:* it provides the priest with the detailed information that he needs to perform this ritual while it focuses on its more important elements.

The "envelope" structure of the action section (B) of the text is mirrored in the passage as a whole. The ritual action is set off by a frame that consists of an introduction (A) and a recapitulation (C). The recapitulation, which is in the form of a Torah-subscript (cf. Fishbane [see n. 5]), and the introduction form an *inclusio*-like set. Together they constitute what might be considered the "law" itself, i.e., the circumstances under which the ritual is to be performed. As might be expected, the recapitulation is more laconic. It sets out two circumstances, divided by an *ʾô*, if a woman strays and is defiled, or if the husband becomes jealous. The more exact definition of the circumstances is given in the introduction, *vv.* 12–14. This also has an involuted structure and uses *inclusio*-repetition to demarcate the conditions discussed. The complex structure of the introduction leads to an apparent incongruity between *vv.* 12–13, in which it seems that the woman has been defiled, and *v.* 14, in which the question of defilement has been left open. This led scholars to assume that there were originally two introductions that had been juxtaposed (cf. Stade [see n. 3], pp. 166–75), or to treat *vv.* 12–13 as a general statement rather than as the actual protasis of the law (see Brichto [n. 6], p. 57). As in the rest of the passage, however, the repetitions in the introduction are purposeful. There are two circumstances envisioned: a case when a man's suspicions are aroused after his wife has strayed (*vv.* 12b–14a = 29b), and a case in which a man is suspicious even though his wife has not strayed (*vv.* 14b = 30a). As in the subscript, the latter case is set off by an *ʾô* in *v.* 14b:[11]

12b   Should a man's wife stray and commit an offense against him
        and a man lie with her carnally,
13   and it was hidden from her husband and done clandestinely,
        and she was defiled,

> and there were no witnesses against her,
> and she was not caught (*in flagrante*)
> 14   and a "jealous" mood comes over him (the husband)
> and he is "jealous" of his wife—and she was defiled;
> Or if a "jealous" mood comes over him (a husband) and he is "jealous" of his wife—
> though she was not defiled:

The key issue in the introduction, as in the procedure, is the woman's defilement. It is raised in *vv.* 12b–13a, when the text states that the woman has strayed and lain with a man in secret and been defiled. There they follow additional qualifiers (that there were no witnesses against her and she was not caught) and the statement that the husband got jealous, before the text repeats the statement that she was defiled and then gives the alternative possibility that the husband became jealous without her having been defiled. This repetition of "and she was defiled" in *v.* 14a, with the new information encased by it, may either be a later expansion (marked off with a repetitive resumption) or an original clarification in an *inclusio*. The recapitulation in *vv.* 29–30 exactly parallels the introduction: the first circumstance is that the woman has been defiled, and the second that she has not. The motivating cause of the trial is the husband's suspicious "jealousy" and, continues the appended resolution (*v.* 31), this suspicious jealousy is the prerogative of husbands. The man can accuse his wife with impunity, knowing that even if she is acquitted by the trial, he will not be charged with false accusation. The emphasis on defilement, moreover, may indicate that a husband not only could bring his wife for this test if he suspected her, but that he may have been obligated to do so. We know that a man could not remarry his divorced wife if she had slept with someone else in the meantime, for this would be considered a polluting act (Deut. xxiv 1–4); it is possible that sexual union with a defiled wife would also have been thought to pollute the land. A suspicious husband might therefore have been obligated to bring his wife to the test in order to avoid such defilement.

Results of the Trial

The possible results of the trial are indicated by two different phrases. If the woman is innocent, she is expected to bear seed, *wnzr'h zr'*; if she is guilty, "her belly will swell and her thigh will fall," *wěṣābětâ biṭnāh wěnāpělâ yěrēkāh*. The "bearing of seed" indicates that the fertility of the woman is at stake; the most probable explanation of the guilty woman's punishment is that she suffers a prolapsed uterus. There is no reason to suppose that the woman was pregnant at the time of the trial:[12] pregnancy is not mentioned, and *nzr'h zr'* is a term for conception rather than delivery.[13] Conception is the reward for innocence, either in the sense that the woman is capable of bearing seed (unlike the guilty woman, see G.R. Driver, *Syria* 33 [1956], p. 76) or that she is being rewarded for her innocence (Gray, *Numbers,* p. 48). We cannot discard the further possibility that the waters themselves, coming from the sacred realm (holy water, with dust from the tabernacle floor) and bearing the name of God, were believed to function as an impregnating force, and that the woman was believed to become pregnant as a direct result of this trial.[14]

The results of guilt also involve fertility. There have been numerous attempts to explain the difficult terms *wĕṣābĕtâ biṭnāh wĕnāpĕlâ yĕrēkāh*.[15] Since *yārēk* is well attested as a term for the male genitalia, particularly in the forms *yṣᵓy yrk* "those who come out of the thigh," i.e. the descendants (Gen. xlvi 26; Ex. i 5; Judg. viii 30; cf. probably Gen. xxiv 2), it seems likely that *yrk* here refers to the female genitalia. The "falling" of the genitalia is obviously a sexual disfunction. The phrase may be independent, indicating some form of sterility. It may also belong with *ṣābĕtâ biṭnāh,* together designating a particular reproductive failure, probably a prolapsed uterus.

The common translation of *ṣābĕtâ biṭnāh* as "her belly swells" is based on the ancient versions (e.g. LXX's use of forms of πρήθω). A verb *ṣābâ* "to swell" is not otherwise known in biblical Hebrew or the cognate languages. A swelling belly, moreover, seems to be a description of pregnancy rather than of unfortunate events. This prompted Driver to suggest (*Syria* 33, p. 75) that the verb is related to Syriac *ṣbāᵓ* "was dry and hot," which is applied mostly to wood and trees. According to Driver, the allusion is to the ancient belief (attested in Hippocrates and Galen) that women whose uteruses are too dry and hot cannot conceive. This etymology, however, does not explain the translation "swell" in the versions. Furthermore, it seems more likely that *ṣbāᵓ* "to be dry" has a Hebrew cognate *ṣiyyâ* "parched land," it is difficult to account for the variation in the roots. Another suggestion for *wĕṣābĕtâ biṭnāh* might be offered. There is an Akkadian root *ṣabû/ṣapû* "to soak, flood" which is used in Old Babylonian letters in the sense of saturating the soil. The verb also appears in a medical text (R. Labat, *Traité akkadien de diagnostics et pronostics médicaux* 1 [Paris and Leiden, 1951], p. 124, line 20): *šumma ŠÀ.MEŠ-šu iṣṣanabū šinātišu tabāka la ilî* "if his intestines flood but he cannot urinate." According to W.G. Lambert (*Babylonian Wisdom Literature* [Oxford, 1960], p. 332 note to 1.28), this root is unrelated to *ṣbᶜ,* "to dye" (Arabic, Hebrew, and Aramaic), but may be a cognate of Syriac *ṣapî,* "to purge." If Lambert is right,[16] *wĕṣābĕtâ* in our passage may be related to a root *ṣby* "to flood." The woman's uterus is to be "flooded" directly by the curse-bearing waters. This would certainly make the woman unable to conceive. The distention caused by such flooding would account for the translation in the ancient versions, "her belly swells."

The most probable explanation for the phrase *wĕṣābĕtâ biṭnāh wĕnāpĕlâ yĕrēkāh* is that the woman suffers the collapse of the sexual organs known as a prolapsed uterus. In this condition, which may occur after multiple pregnancies, the pelvic floor (weakened by the pregnancies) collapses, and the uterus literally falls down. It may lodge in the vagina, or it may actually fall out of the body through the vagina. If it does so, it becomes edematous and swells up like a balloon. Conception becomes impossible, and the woman's procreative life has effectively ended (unless, in our own time, she has corrective surgery). Today, women do exercises to maintain the strength of the pelvic floor. Furthermore, they do not normally have as many pregnancies as women in the past could expect to have. As a result, the prolapsed uterus today generally afflicts older women, although cases of women in their forties are not unheard of. In ancient times, when women had more pregnancies and no knowledge of preventive exercise, the condition may have afflicted much younger women. However, it was certainly not a normal event, and would have been considered a great calamity. In the case of the errant wife, the potion that she drinks would be considered (through the agency of God) to enter her innards and cause this condition, possibly by "flooding" (if the root is cognate with *ṣabû*) the uterus and thereby distending it. Since the prolapsed uterus is visibly and palpably swollen with fluids once it leaves the body, it would have been natural to assume that all prolapsed uteruses were swollen, whether or not they fell out of the body. The phrase *wĕnāpĕlâ yĕrēkāh* could also be an allusion to this "fall" of the uterus, with *yārēk* a synonym for *beṭen*. *Yārēk* might also refer to the genitalia, in which case the "falling" might be the sagging of the cervix or of the external genitals under pressure from the collapsed uterus.

There remains the question of the timing of the results. If the guilty woman was to suffer the collapse of her reproductive system, was this expected to happen as she stood before the Lord? Even if the anticipated result was abortion (which does not seem likely), was she expected to abort immediately? This is not an idle line of inquiry, for it is the key to the essential nature of the legal procedure. If the woman is expected to suffer the consequences immediately, then any women who did not would be immediately exonerated, regardless of what might happen later. Indeed, if she could be proved guilty by immediate results (as would happen in an ordeal), then we would expect the court to punish her immediately with the penalty appropriate for adultery, which is death. Immediate results, however, are not indicated by the text. In the first place, the innocent woman is not only expected to be immune from any immediate catastrophe (*v.* 19), but is also expected to conceive (*v.* 28). Moreover, our passage, which so meticulously details the procedure to be followed from the time that the husband initiates the action, ends with the drinking of the potion. If a result were expected immediately, we would expect this descriptive-prescriptive ritual text to continue with the priest's obligation to lead the woman, if guilty, down from the altar and deliver her to the people or to their leaders. We might even expect the text to provide a ritual appropriate for the acquitted woman's readmission to the community, perhaps a washing and changing of clothes (cf., e.g. Lev. xvii 15), perhaps a rebinding of the hair, and possibly a statement that she is impure until the evening. However, the text says nothing of the sort, but rather ends the procedure with the drinking itself. The text clearly signals the end of the ritual by the Torah-subscript which recapitulates the circumstances under which the procedure should be used.

The ritual trial of the Sotah ended with the drinking of the potion. Nothing further was done, and we can assume that the woman went home to await the results at some future time. The text ensures that society will take no further action by affixing an addendum resolution that provides the appropriate legal outcome of the case. If the woman should prove to be innocent—by becoming pregnant at some time in the future—her husband is nevertheless "free from guilt" and cannot be held liable for false accusation. If, on the other hand, the woman is in fact guilty, *tiśśā' 'et'ăwônāh*, "she will bear her punishment." This is not a vague statement that she should be punished appropriately, and it does not mean (as has been assumed) that she should be killed, which is the prescribed penalty for adultery. On the contrary, as W. Zimmerli has shown (*ZAW* 66 [1954], pp. 8–,11), *nś' 'wn* in the Priestly writings means in effect that there is to be no human penalty; punishment is to be expected from God. Thus one who breaks a negative commandment unwittingly must "bear his penalty" unless he brings an atoning sacrifice (Lev. v 17); the sacrificial atonement clearly indicates that the punishment expected was to come from God. Such divine sanction was expected to punish someone who ate a *šĕlāmîm* offering on the third day (Lev. vii 18, xix 8), whoever did not wash after eating the flesh of animals who have been killed by other animals or who have died of illness (Lev. xvii 16), and whoever did not offer the Passover sacrifice (Num. ix 13, *ht'w yś'*).

The idea of "leaving the punishment to God" is not confined to sacrificial contexts. Divine sanction is invoked on a man who has intercourse with his aunt (Lev. xx 19) or his sister (Lev. xx 17); in the case of the sister the sanction is further specified as *kārēt,* a penalty almost certain to be from God and probably involving extirpation.[17] The unspecified sanctions implied by the phrase *nśɔ ɔwn* are also expected for the "prophet" who makes inquiries for an idolater and for his enquirer (Ezek. xiv 10), and for the idolatrous Levites and temple servitors (Ezek. xliv 10, 12). Similarly, when the wilderness generation is punished by God with one year's wandering for each day that the envoys toured the land, this punishment is expressed as *tśɔw ɔt ɔwntykm,* "you shall bear your punishment" (Num. xiv 34).

The closest parallels to the significance of *tśɔ ɔt ɔwnh* in our text are Num. xxx 16 and Lev. v 1. In Num. xxx 16 a woman has sworn a vow in which she has obligated herself to do something and has bound herself to the obligation (tacit or explicit, depending on the language of the vow); should she not fulfill her vow, certain unpleasant results would devolve upon her. If her husband has heard her vow and does not cancel her fulfillment of it immediately, but cancels it later, then these consequences, which would normally apply to her (*ɔwnh* "her 'punishment'") will descend on him, *wnśɔ ɔt ɔwnh,* "he will bear her punishment." In Lev. v 1 an imprecation calling for witnesses (presumably to a crime) has been pronounced respecting the entire community. If a witness has heard this imprecation and does not come forward to testify, then the consequences (sanctions) of the adjuration will fall upon him, *wnśɔ ɔwnw.* In these two examples, the term *ɔwn,* which can refer to the entire guilt-penalty complex, clearly refers to the consequences or sanctions that were invoked in the vow or adjuration. When these sanctions are put into play, the individual must "bear" (*nśɔ*) the results. In certain circumstances an individual can be immune from these sanctions (*ɔlh*[18]); this is expressed by the term *nqh.* Num. v 39 uses this classic oath terminology. The innocent woman is promised immunity from the sanctions (*v.* 28, *wnqth*); the sanctions are spelled out as *wĕṣābĕtâ biṭnāh wĕnāpĕlâ yĕrēkāh,* and the guilty woman is expected to bear these consequences, *tśɔ ɔt ɔwnh* (*v.* 39).

The Nature of the Trial

Num. v 11–31 is essentially a descriptive text that describes (and at the same time prescribes) a unique religio-legal procedure. In this procedure a woman who has been accused of adultery by her own husband drinks a sacred potion while she accepts an adjuration that the potion will cause grievous injury to her reproductive system if she drinks it while guilty. The procedure ends with the drinking of the potion. After the woman drinks, she presumably returns to her home and husband on the assumption that she would not have dared to drink the potion if she had been guilty, but would rather have confessed instead. Final proof of the woman's innocence would be pregnancy; final proof of her guilt would be the "belly-swelling and thigh-falling" which possibly describe the prolapsed uterus.

It should be obvious that to call this procedure a "trial by ordeal" is unwarranted and misleading. Judicial ordeals are distinguished by two important and interrelated aspects: the god's decision is manifested immediately, and the result of the trial is not in itself the penalty for the offense. To use modern terminology, the god is the "jury" that gives a "verdict" of guilt or innocence during the ordeal, and the judges then impose a "sentence" in accord with this "verdict." In the trial of the Sotah, on the other hand, the society has relinquished its control over the woman to God, who will indicate his judgment by punishing her if she is guilty. Not only does God decide whether she is guilty, but even the right of punishment is removed from society and placed in the hands of God. The ritual of the Sotah most closely resembles the classic purgatory oath, in which the individual swearing the oath puts himself under divine jurisdiction, expecting to be punished by God if the oath-taker is guilty. Num. v 11–31 describes a legal "curse" which functions as an oath once the woman has accepted the conditions of the curse by answering "Amen, amen." Conflation with trials by ordeal has resulted in unnecessary confusion about the mechanism and result of the Sotah procedure. The only feature of this procedure that is similar to ordeal trials is the drinking of a potion, which in form looks like the potion-ordeal known from Africa. Drinking of potions, however, is also known to accompany such oaths as the drinking of Maat among the Nuer. Purgatory oaths may consist of words alone; the words may also be accompanied by ritual, symbolic, or "magical" actions which effectuate the oath. The drinking of a mystical potion actuates the words of the oath, for the potion is expected to punish the guilty party. The use of such an oath as a means of resolving the societal problem posed by suspicion of adultery is a uniquely Israelite institution.[19] It is therefore presented in the Bible as a special "supernatural" procedure granted to Israel as a divine ritual instruction (Torah).

Additional Note on the Meaning of *mĕʾārărîm* and *mārîm*

The term used for the trial waters has been the subject of extensive investigation. The meaning of *mĕʾārărîm* is beyond dispute. The waters are perceived as doing the "cursing" themselves, i.e., if the woman is guilty the waters will carry out the spell (E.A. Speiser, "Angelic 'Curse' in the Old Testament," *JAOS* 80 [1960], pp. 198–200, followed by Brichto [see n. 18], p. 112, and [n. 6], p. 58). The problems lie with the phrase *mê hammārîm*. Despite the translation in the Targum and Vulgate, the term cannot mean "bitter waters." Dust and ink cannot turn water bitter or alkaline. There is also no death in the passage to suggest "bitterness of death" (as Noth, *Numeri*, p. 47, Eng. tr: pp. 50–1). Even Gray's suggestion (p. 52) that *mr* means "having an injurious effect" (cf. Jer. ii 19 and iv 18) runs foul of the grammar of *mê hammārîm*, which cannot be translated as noun-plus-adjective. There have been several suggestions to take *mārîm* from other roots. Sasson's suggestion of *mrr* "to bless" (based on Ugaritic) would yield the merismus "waters that bless and waters that curse," therefore waters of judgment; it would not explain the phrase *ûbāʾû bāh hammayim hamĕʾārărîm lĭmārîm* of vv. 24 and 27 (see J.M. Sasson, "Numbers 5 and the 'Waters of Judgment,'" *Biblische Zeitschrift*, N.F. 16 [1972], pp. 249–51). Snaith's suggestion of *mārar* from Arabic *marra* "pass by" and *marmara* "cause to flow" would mean waters of abortion, but the trial is not restricted to pregnant women ([see n. 12], p. 202).

The two most interesting explanations of *mê hammārîm* have related the word to the function played by the waters in this trial, a focus supported by the LXX translation τοῦ ἐλεγμοῦ "(waters) of disputation." G.R. Driver suggested the root *mry* (*mrh*), "to rebel," which would yield a noun *māreh* "disputed, doubtful matter," with an abstract plural *mārim,* "contention, dispute, doubt" ("Two problems in the Old Testament examined in the light of Assyriology," *Syria* 33 [1956], pp. 73–4). This suggestion alleviates the grammatical difficulties, and accords well with the Greek translation; it has therefore been adopted by the *NEB.* However, the verb *mrh* in Hebrew refers to "disobedience, rebellion" rather than to "doubt" or "contention"; Driver derives the latter connotations from Arabic *marā* III "to dispute," *miryatu(n)* "doubt," and *mariyatu(n)* "doubtful matter." A meaning "waters of rebellion" simply does not fit the context. The most attractive suggestion is that of Brichto, who derives the word from *yrh,* Hipʿil, "to teach" (Brichto [see n. 6], p. 59, n. 1). The formation is like *maddāʿ* "knowledge," here in an abstract plural. *Mê hammārim* would thus mean "waters of instruction, waters of revelation"; the term would thus refer to their function in the trial. The phrase in *vv.* 18, 19 and 24 would mean "the 'spell-effecting' revelation-waters," and the difficult clause of *vv.* 24 and 28 would mean that the spell-effecting waters would enter the woman to effect the revelation of guilt or innocence.

Notes

1. Such terms as *mnḥt qnʿt,* "meal-offering of jealousies," *mnḥt zkrwn,* "meal-offering of remembrance," and *mzkrt ʿwn,* "evocation of wrong-doing" (all in *v.* 15) are restricted to this passage.

2. See the additional note at the end of the article.

3. On the question of sources see B. Stade, "Beiträge zur Pentateuchkritik," *ZAW* 15 (1895), pp. 157–8; G.B. Cray, *A Critical and Exegetical Commentary on Numbers* (Edinburgh, 1903), p. 49 (who sums up the previous work), and R. Press, "Das Ordal im alten Israel," *ZAW* 51 (1925), pp. 122–6. J. Morgenstern, "Trial by Ordeal Among the Semites and in Ancient Israel," *Hebrew Union College Jubilee Volume* (Cincinnati, 1925), pp. 128–9, denies the relevance of all previous attempts to distinguish the sources and includes a chart of all previous attempts to divide the chapter into its strands.

4. e.g. M. Noth, *Das vierte Buch Mose, Numeri* (Göttingen, 1966), p. 46; Eng. Tr. *Numbers* (London, 1968), p. 49, would see originally separate types of divine judgment in a) the effect of the holy water, b) the curse-oath, and c) the acts of writing words in the book and consuming the book. M. Weinfield suggests that "the strand prescribing the writing of the curse shows signs of more advanced religious conceptions" in that in it the water induces the curse, whereas in the earlier "strand" God is responsible. ("Ordeal of Jealousy," *Encyclopaedia Judaica* 12 [Jerusalem, 1971], cols. 1449–50.)

5. "Accusations of Adultery: A Study of Law and Scribal Practice in Numbers 5:11–31," *HUCA* 45 (1974), pp. 25–45.

6. "The Case of the *Śōṭā* and a Reconsideration of Biblical Law," *HUCA* 46 (1975), pp. 55–70.

7. "The Case of the Suspected Adulteress, Numbers 5:11–31: Redaction and Meaning," a paper read to the Society of Biblical Literature in New York in 1979, and later published in *The Creation of Sacred Literature,* ed. R.F. Friedman (Berkeley, 1981).

8. The number of studies using this approach to the text is too great to enumerate. For earlier studies, see C. Kuhl, "Die Wiederaufnahme—ein literarkritisches Prinzip?" *ZAW* 64 (1952) pp. 1–11, Meir Weiss, "Die Methode der 'Total-Interpretation,'" *SVT* 22 (1972), pp. 88–112. And more recently, S. Talmon–M. Fishbane, "Aspects of the Literary Structure of the Book of Ezekiel," *Tarbiz* 42 (1972/4), pp. 27–41 (Hebrew) and S. Talmon, "The Textual Study of the Bible, A New Outlook," in F.M. Cross and S. Talmon (ed.), *Qumran and the History of The Biblical Text* (Cambridge Mass., 1975), pp. 321–400.

9. Fishbane, see n. 5, and "Biblical Colophons, Textual Criticism and Legal Analogies," *CBQ* 42 (1980), pp. 438–9.

10. The two terms refer to the same phenomenon: repetitive resumption is a term usually applied to an editorial device; *inclusio,* a more general term, is also applied to author practice. For repetitive resumption see Kuhl (n. 8). The term "repetitive resumption" was originated by H.M. Wiener, *The Composition of Judges II 11 to I Kings II 46* (Leipzig, 1929), but I have not been able to get this book. For the many *inclusios* in the Psalms, see M. Dahood, Psalms I–III (Garden City, New York, 1965–70), index s.v. *inclusio.*

11. The relationship between the introduction and recapitulation was recognized by Fishbane (see n. 5), who pointed out that Num. v 29–30 are a resumptive-*torah*-subscript to *vv.* 12–14, and therefore should be understood as parallel to it. He correctly concluded that since there are clearly two cases in *vv.* 29–30, divided by an *ʾô,* so too *vv.* 12–14 must represent two separate cases. However, Fishbane erroneously took the new case to begin with the *waw* in *v.* 14a. He drew a misleading comparison to two of the Laws of Hammurabi, *LH* 132 (public suspicion) and *LH* 131 (accusation by husband) and therefore understood the two cases of Num. v 12–14 to be 1) and allegation of conjugal infidelity based in suspicion alone (*v.* 14) and 2) an allegation apparently unsubstantiated by probable cause, but in which there was public suspicion. According to Fishbane (p. 37) the purpose of the "draught-ordeal" was to establish *de jure* that which was known *de facto.* However, there is no hint in *vv.* 12–13 that the public was involved in any way or that the woman had been the subject of gossip or scandal; it is simply stated that a woman has strayed. The two possible circumstances envisioned by the introduction and recapitulation are not the two that Fishbane delineates. The husband's jealousy alone initiates the Israelite procedure, and the law is parallel only to *LH* 131. The two circumstances envisioned are the guilt-defilement of the woman or her lack of defilement.

12. As H.W. Robinson, oral communication reported in Gray, p. 48, N.H. Snaith, *Leviticus and Numbers* (London, 1967), p. 203, and W. McKane, "Poison, Trial by Ordeal and the Cup of Wrath," *VT* 30 (1980), p. 474.

13. The only occurrence of the verb which might have the sense of "delivery" is Lev. xii 2, possibly meaning "if a woman delivers and gives birth to a boy," although here too the meaning "conceives" is possible. In this verse, a sense of "deliver" might be implied by the use of the *Hiph ʿil (tzryʿ),* i.e. "she gives forth seed." The verb *nzrʿh,* "be sown with seed," could have no connotation of "delivery." The idea of being "implanted" belongs to the whole complex of metaphors in which a woman is seen as a field and the earth is seen as Mother Earth. For a study of the biblical use of these images see my article "The Planting of Man," in the anniversary volume for Marvin Pope.

14. There is no explicit statement about "divine conception" in the Old Testament. It appears, however, in post-biblical literature: in Philo, in possible Jewish legends about the birth of Moses, and in Christian literature. It is possible that this idea, which is known from other Near Eastern religions, was not considered impossible in Israel, and that a reflection of this idea is seen in the "conception" of the innocent woman. For a study of the post-biblical materials, see Allan Kensky, "The Strange Midrash on the Birth of Moses," a paper presented to the Society for Biblical Literature in 1981.

15. These terms have been understood in various ways. The Mishnah understood them to he symbolic: since the woman began to sin with her thigh and continued with her womb, the penalty begins with the thigh and then extends to the womb, though the rest of the body does not escape injury (M. Sotah I 7). Josephus took the two phrases together to describe dropsy (*Ant.* II xi 6). Brichto takes the two to indicate pseudo-cyesis or hysterical pregnancy (see n. 6, p. 66), and Sasson suggests that the "thigh" indicates the genitals and that the penalty is thrombophlebitis, which can cause swelling around the vulva and belly, sometimes accompanied by edema in the legs (*BZ,* N.F. 16 [1972], p. 250, n. 15). H.W. Robinson and G.R. Driver both take *wěnāpělâ* to indi-

cate abortion: Robinson concludes that the woman was pregnant at the time of the trial and that even though her belly swells with pregnancy, she will abort *(apud* Gray, p. 48). Driver sees alternative results: if the woman is pregnant, she will abort; if she is not, her womb will get hot and dry (*wĕsābĕtâ biṭnāh*) and she will not be able to conceive. The term *nēpel* refers to abortion in Ps. lviii 9; Job iii 16, and Eccles. vi 3. However, the term is applied to the foetus itself: it is the foetus that "falls (out)," rather than the "thigh." Since, moreover, there is no reason to suppose that the woman was pregnant at the time of trial, it is unlikely that the "thigh falling" refers to abortion.

16. One should note that the *CAD* disagrees with Lambert and relates the Akkadian verb *ṣabû* to the root meaning "color," Hebrew *ṣbʿ* (*CAD* Ṣ, s.v. *ṣabû*).

17. Donald Wold, "The Kareth Penalty in P: Rationale and Cases," *SBL Seminar Papers* 1 (1979), pp. 1–45.

18. For *ʾlh* as "sanctions" see Brichto, *The Problem of "Curse" in the Hebrew Bible* (Philadelphia, 1963), pp. 22–76.

19. Both the form and the function of this ritual are paralleled by Near Eastern materials, but the combination of form and function is not found outside Israel. The function is that of the Laws of Hammurabi 131, in which a woman who has been accused of adultery by her husband swears an oath to her innocence. As in Num. v, this is enough: the Laws envision an ordeal only in cases of public scandal. The form of the trial in Num. v bears some resemblance to the drinking of a potion in an incomplete text from Mari (*ARM* X:9), in which several minor deities appear to take an oath before Ea, promise fealty to the city of Mari and its ruler, and drink a potion of water mixed with dust and "cornerstone" of the gate of Mari. As in Num. v, the dust carries some of the numenous power of the place and the drinkers understand that the power of the oath will bring punishment to whoever swears falsely. The Mari drinking, however, is not part of a legal trial.

The Case of the Suspected Adulteress, Numbers 5:11–31

Redaction and Meaning

JACOB MILGROM

Modern critics uniformly regard the text of the law of the suspected adulteress (Num 5:11–31) as a conflation of at least two sources. Two procedures are employed to test the suspect, an oath and an ordeal (16–24, 27–28), with a sacrifice perhaps constituting a third test (15, 25–26). Moreover, repetitions abound (16b = 8a; 19a = 21a; 21b = 22a; 24a = 26b = 27a; 12b–14 = 29f.)[1] Notwithstanding this evidence for multiple sources, it is to the merit of two scholars, M. Fishbane and H.C. Brichto, that they see this text as a logical and unified composition.[2] It is submitted that their conception of the text is correct, with the exception of two additions, verses 21 and 31, which, however, provide the key to unlock the redaction and meaning of the text.

The Suspected Adultress, Num 5:12–31

A. *The Case, 12–14*
    1. outside suspicion, 12–13
    2. husband's suspicion, 14

  B. *Preparation of the Ritual-Ordeal, 15–18*
    1. *minḥāh,* 15
    2. water, 17
    3. woman, 18 (16)

  C. *The Oath-Imprecation, 19–24*
    1. oral adjuration, 19–22
    [interpolation, 21]
    2. written adjuration dissolved and to be imbibed, 23–24

B′. *Execution of the Ritual-Ordeal,* 25–28
   1. *minḥāh,* 25–26a
   2. water, 26b
   3. woman, effect on, 27–28

A′. *The Case,* 29–30 (resumptive subscript framed by inverse inclusion)
   1. outside suspicion, 29
   2. husband's suspicion, 30
   [postscript, 31]

The unity of the text is projected into clear relief by its structure. As can be seen by the diagram, it consists of five sections arranged in introverted (chiastic) order. The facts of the case begin and end the text (12–14, A; 29–30, A′) and contain the following common elements: *tiśṭeh ʾiššāh* (29, 12), *niṭmᵊʾāh* (29, 12, 13, 14), *taʿabōr ʿālā(y)w rûaḥ qinᵊʾāh* (30, 14) and *qinnēʾ +et ʾištô* (30, 14). Though the closing statement (A′) is only a summary of the case, it nevertheless articulates all its essential elements: the wife's straying and defilement and the husband's suspicions. The exact nature of the charges levied against the accused are not easily decipherable and their elucidation is not really germane to this paper. Tentatively, the hypothesis of M. Fishbane[3] will be accepted—that in view of a similar case in Codex Hammurabi, two situations are predicated: the woman has aroused suspicion in the community (12b–13, 29; cf. CH 132) or the suspicion has originated with her husband (14, 34; cf. CH 131). Bifurcation along these lines is clearly evident in the closing statement, A′, but the initial *waw* of verse 14 in the opening formulation A will have to be rendered as "or."

The introverted structure of this text is projected in the clearest relief by comparing the preparation and execution sections of the ritual-ordeal (15–18, B; 25–28, B′). First, these sections contain common expressions: *minḥat qᵊnāʾōt* (25, 15, 18), *ʾazkārātāh/mazkeret/zikkārōn* (26, 15, 18), *wᵊlāqaḥ hakkōhēn* (25, 17), *lipnê YHWH* (25, 16, 18), and *wᵊhiqrîb ʾōtāh* (25, 16). Second, the structure of the components of each section is identical: *minḥāh*-water-woman. The recognition of this similar substructure clarifies two ostensible anomalies. First, the text ostensibly states that the woman was placed before the altar (16) before the preparation of the water (17). However, by using a repetitive resumption (18a), the author thereby indicates that the waters were prepared by the priest prior to the placement of the woman before the altar. The structure indicates the same sequence both in the preparation and in the execution: the woman's role follows that of the water. Second, the purpose of verses 27–28 is now seen in proper perspective. These verses are not just an editorial summation or a "prognosis,"[4] but again, in keeping with structural symmetry, they provide a kinetic counterpart to the static picture of verse 18. Both passages find the woman standing before the altar. In verse 18 she holds the *minḥāh* in her hands; in verses 27–28 the waters are working their effect within her.

Sections B and B′ reveal another inverse symmetry, not in language but in procedure, as illustrated in the diagram on the following page.[5]

The *minḥāh* offering brought by the woman or, rather, by the husband on her behalf (15) is of the cheapest edible grain, barley (cf. 2 Kgs 7:1), and it is deprived of the otherwise two essential elements of the *minḥāh*, the oil and frankincense (Lev ch. 2). During the oath it remains in the hands of the woman; thereafter, in a dedicatory rite it is

THE RITUAL-ORDEAL

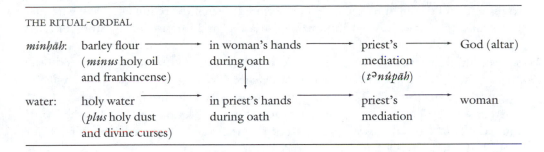

transferred by the priest to the altar, i.e., to the realm of God. The ordeal water undergoes a procedure symmetrically opposite to the *minḥāh*. It originates in God's realm, the sanctuary layer, from which the priest draws forth the water. In contrast to the two elements *withdrawn* from the woman's *minḥāh*, two elements are *added* to the water to increase its sanctity and, hence, its efficacy—i.e., the dust from the sanctuary floor and the written oath containing the divine name. During the recitation of the adjuration, this water is in the priest's hands while the woman holds the *minḥāh* in her hands. The priest then transfers the woman's *minḥāh* to the sacred realm of the altar and transfers the sacred water to the profane realm of the woman's body. Thus the introversion is symmetrically balanced: the priest is the medium by which both the woman's profane offering is dedicated to the Lord and the divinely empowered water enters her profane body.

The middle section (19–24, C), the oath, is the pivot of the entire structure and, hence, its most important section. Its verbal elements tie it to all the other sections. Thus, it twice repeats the following elements from A, and in chiastic order: *šākab ʾiš ʾōtāk, śāṭît, tumʾʾāh* (19–20, 12–13), and from B it repeats *mê hammārîm hamʾʾārʾrîm* (19, 24, 18). From B′ it borrows *hammayim hamʾʾārʾrîm lʾmārîm* (27, 24), *wʾṣābʾtāh biṭnāh wʾnāplāh yʾrēkāh* (27, 21, 22), *ʾālāh bʾqereb ʿammāh* (27, 21), *wʾniqqʾtāh* (28, 19), *wʾniṭmʾʾāh* (27, 28, 19, 20), and from A′ *tiśṭeh taḥat ʾîšāh* and *niṭmʾʾāh* (29, 19, 20). The conditions of the curse are stated in negative form before the positive (19, 20), but in their recapitulation they appear in reverse order (27, 28).

Section C exhibits inner cohesion through the use of introverted or chiastic phraseology. Thus the element of *šākab* in the adjuration begins the negative statement of the oath and ends its positive restatement (19–20). The oath-curse, *šʾbuʿāh-ʾālāh*, mentioned twice in 21, is also introverted. Moreover, the compound expression for the ordeal water, "spell-inducing *mārîm* water" (19, 24), is not only introverted (in the last verse in which it occurs, 24) but is also broken into single components, "spell-inducing water" (22) and "*mārîm* water" (23). Thus every possible permutation of this compound is accounted for.

Yet it is patently clear that section C is inflated because of the intrusion of verse 21. Not only is the notice that the priest adjures the woman repeated here (19aα, 21aα) but also the content of the adjuration (21b, 22a). Thus, the beginning and end of the oath are not clearly demarcated in the text, the result being that both the Mishnah (Sot 2:3) and Philo (Laws 3:60) acknowledge differences of opinion concerning its exact wording. Nevertheless, there can be little doubt that originally 22 followed 20, for then the adjuration reads smoothly and lucidly: ". . . If a man other than your husband has had carnal relations with you may this water that induces the spell enter your body causing the belly to distend and the thigh to sag. . . ." Furthermore, even if the redundancies of 21 could be justified there is no way of harmonizing the jarring and abrasive juxtaposition of 22 to 21, which would imply that first her physical condition will make her a byword and then she will drink the water. However, it is clear that the sagging thigh and distended belly are not the cause but the effect of the water. Hence instead of the sequential verb *ûbāʾû*, "May [this water] enter" (22), one would have expected the infinitive construct *bᵊbôʾ*, "As [this water] enters," the same construction as the previous *bᵊtēt*, "As [the Lord] causes" (21).[6] However, *ûbāʾû* follows both logically and grammatically after 20, for then the prescribed ordeal is a consequence of the accusation.

Fortunately, the reason for the interpolation of 21 is not difficult to discern. Without it, the adjuration contains no mention of the name of God, and the formula gives the impression that the powers of the curse inhere in the water. It was therefore essential to add 21 to the adjuration in order to emphasize that the imprecation derives its force not from the water but from the Lord. It may therefore be conjectured that originally the present formula (minus 21) was an ancient Near Eastern incantation for an ordeal employing magical water which did not invoke the name of any deity.[7] It may have been incorporated into the Israelite cult at local high places or shrines and converted into an oath by having the suspected adulteress respond "amen" (22b). The priestly legislator, however, found the formula unacceptable, since it ostensibly attributed the effect of the oath to the water itself. Since the formula was already accepted and in widespread use he would have incurred too much resistance had he attempted to alter its wording. Instead he followed the simple and more acceptable expedient by adding a statement affirming that the efficacy of the oath was due to the God of Israel (21b). And to forestall the protest that no change in the text was necessary, since an oath implied the invocation of the Deity, he also added a new thought, namely, that the convicted adulteress would become a byword among her people (21a; cf. Jer 29:22).

The wording of these two clauses that now comprise the text of the oath in 21 was made to fit artistically and coherently with the rest of the oath formula. Thus the Lord will *yittēn* (21), make her a byword in response to *her (way)yittēn*, allowing a man other than her husband to have carnal relations with her (20b). Also, the effect of the imprecation (21b) is given in the reverse order of 22a, the thigh preceding the belly, again providing a chiastic balance. Another chiasm was produced within 21 with the words "oath," *šᵊbûʿāh*, and "imprecation," *ʾālᵊh*. Finally, the repetition of the instruction to the priest (21a) was added, underscoring the fervent insistence of the legislator that this next element be added to the imprecation. Of course, it is this repetition which fully exposes the interpolation, but it is even more tellingly betrayed, as already indicated, by the discrepancy in the order of events: the effect ostensibly anticipates the cause, i.e., first we are informed that she will become a byword (21b) and only afterward that her condition will be caused by the water (22a).

Nonetheless, there can be no doubt that the interpolation of 21 took place during the early formation of the text and not during its final stages—this for the compelling reason that the clause stating that the guilty woman will become an object of derision (21a) is also present in the execution section (27b). Indeed, the presence of the byword in the execution passage (B´) presumes that it was already an element of the adjuration (C).

There is a second interpolation in the text that needs to be explained: the postscript of 31. That it is a postscript and is not an organic part of the text is clear from the structure of the final section (29–30, A′). The section is encased by an inverted inclusion *zōʾt tôrat . . . hattôrāh hazzōʾt* (cf. also 6:21). Thus, in thought and in form, the law of the suspected adulteress is finished and sealed by this concluding inclusion. What, then, is the purpose of the postscript of verse 31? First, let us understand its meaning. The first half, *wᵊniqqāh hāʾiš mēʿāwōn*, "the husband shall be free from punishment," is clearly addressed to the husband, it is to assure him that he has nothing to lose by bringing his wife to the ordeal. His suspicions will either be proven or laid to rest, and in the latter case a harmonious relationship may be restored. The second half of the verse, *wᵊhāʾiššāh hahiwʾ tiśśāʾ ʾet ʿawōnāh*, "that woman shall suffer her punishment," would seem to be addressed to the suspected adulteress. Understood this way, however, this addendum is a pointless redundancy.[8] However, one should not forget that the idiom *nāśāʾ ʿāwōn* implies that she is punished through divine agency (e.g., Lev 5:1, 17; 7:18, 17:16; 19:8; 20:17, 19; Num 9:13 [with the synonym *ḥēṭʾ*]; 14:34; 30:16.[9] Thus, this clause is not addressed to the woman but to her husband and community; it reminds them that if the adulteress is convicted by the ordeal, her punishment rests not with them but solely with God. And this brings us to the very heart of the matter concerning the purpose of this ritual and its place within biblical jurisprudence. It confronts us with the glaring paradox postulated by this ritual: the adulteress, proven guilty by the ordeal, namely, by God Himself, is not punished with death! True, her punishment is just, "poetically" just. She who opened herself to illicit seed is doomed to be permanently sterile. Yet the gnawing question still remains: having been proven guilty of adultery, why is she not summarily put to death?

The magnitude of this question reaches its full limits when Israel's law of adultery is compared with that of its neighbors. Ancient Near Eastern law—except for the Bible—allows the husband to mitigate or even waive the death penalty against the adulterer.[10] In Israel, however, the death sentence may not be commuted. All biblical sources agree that the prohibition against adultery was incorporated into the national covenant at Sinai to which every Israelite swore allegiance (Exod 24:1–8; Deut 5:24–26) and all subsequent generations were bound (Deut 29:9–14). Indeed, when both Hosea and Jeremiah score Israel for violating the Sinaitic covenant they specify the sin of adultery (e.g., Hos 4:2; Jer 7:9). The testimony of Jeremiah is particularly striking, since he expressly pinpoints adultery as the cause of Israel's national doom (Jer 5:7–9; 7:9–15; 29:23a). Thus in Israel the inclusion of adultery in the Sinaitic covenant guaranteed legal consequences. Adultery had to be punished with death, else God would destroy the malefactors and, indeed, the entire community which had allowed it to go unpunished. Why, then, is the adulteress convicted by the ordeal, i.e., by God Himself, permitted to escape death?

The key to the answer, I submit, lies in the fact that the guilty woman was *unapprehended by man.* That this element is the most significant in her case is shown by the fact that it is cited four times in her indictment, each in a different manner: (1) *wᵊneʿlam mēʿēynê ʾišāh,* "unbeknown to her husband"; (2) *wᵊnistᵊrāh,* "she keeps secret" (or "it was done clandestinely"); (3) *wᵊhiʾ lōʾ nitpāśāh,* "without being apprehended"; (4) *wᵊʿēd ʾên bāh,* "and there is no witness against her" (v 13). These clear redundancies, among others, lead one critic to assert that their purpose is "to give weight to what might (and all too correctly!) be seen as a transparent charade . . . to protect the woman as wife in the disadvantaged position determined for her by the mores of ancient Israel's society."[11] This stylistic inflation, however, may have been deliberately written with a judicial purpose in mind: to emphasize the cardinal principle that the unapprehended criminal is not subject to the jurisdiction of the human court. Since the adulteress has not been apprehended—as the text repeats with staccato emphasis—then the community and, especially, the overwrought husband may not give way to their passions to lynch her. Indeed, even if proven guilty by the ordeal, they may not put her to death. God has provided that the punishment be built into the ordeal and there is no need for human mediation. Unapprehended adultery, a sin against man (the husband) and God, remains punishable only by God, and that punishment is inherent in the ordeal.

Supportive evidence may also be adduced from the absence of the technical verb for committing adultery, *nā'ap,* which is found in the Decalogue (Exod 20:15; Deut 5:17) and the Priestly Code itself (e.g., Lev 20:10, four times in this one verse!). Thus, though the legislator expressed the woman's infidelity in four different ways, it may be no accident that he refrained from using the legal term *nā'ap,* for he wished to disassociate this woman's fate from the death penalty imposed for adultery. The glaring omission of the term *nā'ap* is, then, but another indication that her punishment lies outside the human court.

There is yet another consideration which buttresses this conclusion. It has been shown in cross-cultural studies that societies will resort to ordeals when the people at large suspect an individual of committing an infraction which endangers the whole community. In such a situation a quick and decisive verdict is necessary. The prolonged procedures of judicial investigation or the awaiting of divine retribution in the case of a false oath cannot be tolerated.[12] But what danger does the suspected adulteress pose to her community that would mandate an immediate decision by God? Surely it cannot be that she violated one of the commandments of the Decalogue. If so, the ordeal would have been instituted for other suspected covenantal infractions, e.g., idolatry, Sabbath violation, thievery. However, the fact remains that the ordeal is prescribed for the suspected adulteress and for no other case! The reason, then, must be sought in the dreaded consequences which the priestly law wishes to forestall at all costs: that she be lynched by mob rule or its legal equivalent, a kangaroo court.

A word needs to be said concerning the penalty itself. Whereas man has no choice but to put the apprehended adulteress to death, God metes out a more precise retribution. It is called the measure-for-measure principle, poetic justice, custom-made for each criminal in order to make the punishment precisely fit the crime. For example, Jacob, who deceived Esau with a goatskin garment (Gen 27:16), is himself deceived by a similar garment (Gen 37:31–35). God's sentence that Israel must wander forty years in the wilderness is retribution for the forty days the spies spent in the Holy Land gathering their demoralizing data (Num 14:33f.: see also Ezek 4:4–6). So the adulteress who acquiesced to receive forbidden seed is doomed to sterility for the rest of her life.[13] The ordeal clearly presumes belief in its efficacy, to wit: the guilty woman would be so fearful of its consequences that she would rather confess than subject herself to its dreaded consequences. Thus at an attested river ordeal in Mari, one of the litigant's representatives drowns in the "River-god." He then requests that the lives of his three remaining representatives be spared the ordeal and he will renounce his claim.[14]

Finally, that the suspected adulteress is not put to death either by man or God provides the necessary clue to explain how an ordeal with its inherent magical and pagan elements was allowed to enter the legislation of the Torah, or to answer the paradox as it was phrased by Nachmanides (*ad loc.*): this is the only case in biblical law where the outcome depends on a miracle. The answer, I submit, is inherent in the ordeal: it provides the priestly legislator with an accepted practice by which he can remove the jurisdiction and punishment of the unapprehended adulteress from human hands and thereby guarantee that she will not be put to death.

This, then, is the meaning of the subscript, verse 31. It encourages the suspicious husband to bring his wife to the ordeal by promising him complete exoneration if his suspicions are proven unfounded, and it also reminds him and the rest of his community *wᵊhāʾiššāh hāhiwʾ tiśśaʾ ʾet ʿăwōnāh,* that since the woman's alleged crime was unapprehended by man, she is removed from the jurisdiction of man.

If this subscript is a gloss, as the structure of the text has indicated, it is a correct one. Its author has understood the thrust of this law and its place in biblical jurisprudence, and by inserting it he has made sure that we will understand it too.

In sum, the biblical law of the suspected adulteress provides a unique example of how the priestly legislators made use of a pagan ordeal in order to protect a suspected but unproven adulteress from the vengeance of an irate husband or community by mandating that God will decide her case.

NOTES

1. E.g., G.B. Gray, *Numbers* (I.C.C., 1903), pp. 43–49; Baentsch, *Exodus, Leviticus and Numeri* (*HKAT,* 1903), pp. 363–64.

2. M. Fishbane. "Accusations of Adultery: A Study of Law and Scribal Practice in Numbers 5:11–31," *HUCA* 45 (1974): 25–45; H.C. Brichto. "The Case of the Sota and a Reconsideration of Biblical Law," *HUCA* 46 (1975): 55–70.

3. "Accusations," pp. 35–38.

4. *Ibid.*

5. This Lévi-Straussian model was suggested to me by Shalom Feldblum in a graduate seminar given at the Hebrew University.

6. Ezek 5:15b–16 affords an exact analogy when the announcement of the punishment in the infinitive *baʿăśôtî* and *bᵊsallᵊḥî* is also written *after* the identical effect, i.e., Israel becoming a byword (15a).

7. E.g., E. Reiner, *Šurpu, AFO,* Beiheft II (Graz, 1968), cols. III, IX.

8. The rabbis take advantage of the ambiguity for their ethical purposes: "only if the husband is himself clear of sin will his wife suffer her punishment," i.e.. the ordeal will only work in the case of an impure wife of a pure husband (Sifre, Numbers, 21). It was probably this rabbinic teaching that prompted Jesus to decide in the case of an apprehended adulteress: "he that is without sin among you, let him be the first to cast a stone at her" (John 8:2ff.). She indeed was released, not because Jesus's appeal touched the assembly's conscience but because he cited the law: cf. D. Daube, "Biblical Landmarks in the Struggle for Women's Rights," *The Judicial Review* 23 (1978): 177–97.

9. Cf. W. Zimmerli, "Die Eigenart der prophetischen Rede des Ezechiel," *ZAW* 66 (1954): 1–26.

10. E.g., CH 129; MAL 14–16; LH 192f.: cf. Pritchard, *Ancient Near Eastern Texts* (Princeton, 1950), pp. 171, 181, 196.

11. Brichto, "The Sota."

12. Cf. T. Frymer, "Studies in Trial by River Ordeal" (diss. Yale, 1976), pp. 1–59.

13. The rabbis reveal ingenuity in discovering other instances of measure-for-measure punishment in her case: cf. Num R. 9:24: Tosef Sot 3:1–19.

14. Cf. G. Dossin, "L'ordalie à Mari," *Comptes rendus de l'Académie des Inscriptions et Belle-Lettres* (1958): 387–92.

Numbers 5 and the "Waters of Judgment"

JACK SASSON

Numbers 5:11–31 contains what has been regarded as either an "ordeal of jealousy" or a "rite to establish a child's paternity."[1] The narrative has usually been assigned to P, but, in view of comparative Near Eastern data dealing with ordeals, it certainly reflects a tradition deeply imbedded in the past.[2] It concerns a husband seized by a fit of jealousy who, lacking the proper number of witnesses [cf. Deut. 19:15; Numb. 35:30], brings his wife to the temple and forces her to undergo a divinely controlled trial.[3] Preparation for the ritual begins with the husband providing a meal-offering, an act, perhaps, designed to involve him in the proceedings.[4] A priest, perhaps equivalent to the *manzaduḫlu* of the Nuzi ordeals,[5] accompanies the wife before YHWH.[6] Dust[7] from the tabernacle's floor is then added to the sacred waters[8] of an earthen vessel. The priest loosens the woman's hair,[9] and places the meal offering between her hands. In his hands, the priest carries a liquid, *mēy hammārîm ha-meʾārarîm*.

This phrase, *mēy hammārîm ha-meʾārarîm*, has been rendered something like the following: "the waters of bitterness that causes the curse [JPS]"; "the water of bitterness that induce the spell [*The Torah*]"[10]; "the water of bitterness that brings the curse [RSV]"; and, with characteristic bravura, "the water of contention which brings out the truth [NEB]." In view of verse 28, however, it seems unlikely that misfortune was the only effect of the ordeal. On the contrary, the woman who successfully weathered her husband's charges was expected to conceive: certainly a sign of blessing to a Near Eastern wife. Additionally one fails to see why a bit of dust should embitter the waters.[11] It is unlikely that the addition of ink (verse 23) could have rendered the waters toxic. Although Israel as well as Egypt produced a potentially harmful ink (*Megillah* 1.2), Mishnaic rabbis insisted (*Ṣotah* 2.4) that the mix be manufactured out of a compound of soot, *gum arabia,* and water.[12]

Driver connects *mārîm* with Hebrew *mārāh,* "to be rebellious," and produces a translation that is reflected in the NEB passage quoted above.[13] But it would probably be more fruitful to relate *mārîm* to Ugaritic *mrr* which, in many passages parallels *brk* "to bless." As one example, 2 Aqht. 1:35–37 is offered: *"Ybrk/[dni]l mt rpi. ymr. gzr/[mt h]rnmy,* He blesses Daniel, Man of *Rpi,* blesses the hero, man of *Hrnmy."* Other Ugaritic instances can be gathered from Gordon's UT, #1659. For these reasons, the phrase *mēy hammārîm ha-meʾārarîm* should be considered as a *merismus,* consisting of "waters that bless" and "waters that curse," hence "waters of judgment."

An interesting example of this double-edged function of a potion, that of punishing the sexually guilty while blessing the innocent, is related in Pausanias VII:25:13. The Greek traveler comes to Aegae, a city on the Crathis river in Achaion, and speaks of an Earth priestess who drank bull's blood before she entered the cave to prophesy. Unchaste, the priestess could expect instant death. If "virtuous" ("before her election [she] must not have had intercourse with more than one man"), she will be inspired. Pausanias himself thinks this practice to be an ordeal, while Pliny (Nat. Hist. 28:147), who reports the same event, does not.[14]

The remaining description of the ordeal sheds further light on the juridical quality of the potion. The accused receives instruction from the priest, is given an oath, and accepts its consequences by stating: Amen. The oath was worded as follows: "May YHWH give you among your people, as a curse and an imprecation in giving you a 'thigh that falls' and a 'belly which swells.'[15] May these *'waters that curse'* sink into your innards in order to 'swell the belly and drop your thigh.'" Note that in this verse (22) only this primitive quality of the "waters of judgment" is mentioned in an oath that carries threats of dire consequences.

Once the oath, with its emphasis on the "waters which curse," was written on a parchment, its potency was transferred by dissolving the ink into the liquid. Again, note how the balance is restored, so to speak, when the priest "blots [the ink] into the 'waters that bless.'" This choice of words cannot be accidental.

With these powerful elements effectively counter-balanced, the priest gives the woman to drink from the "waters of judgment" with the result that the "'waters that curse' entered her (in order) to bring blessing." This is, admittedly, an unsatisfactory translation of *ûbāʾû bāh hammayim ha-meʾārarîm lemārîm* (v. 24). But if credence is given to this rendering it would imply the ritual aims, primarily, to judge on the innocence—not the guilt—of an accused, and, in so doing, clear her of wrongdoings. In other words, the judged is presumed innocent and is given, through imbibing the drink, the opportunity to vindicate herself.

The woman's meal-offering is then taken by the priest, waved before YHWH, and partially burnt on the altar. Additional draughts are then taken before signs of the lady's guilt or innocence begin to appear.[16] In the case of the former, the expected unwelcome symptoms become evidence. Otherwise, the ordeal ends happily with the blameless wife cleared and rendered able to conceive.

NOTES

1. *A. Phillips,* Ancient Israel's Criminal Law, 1970, pp. 147 and 118ff.

2. The earliest attestation of river ordeal dates to the time, or slightly later of Entemena of Lagash (*ca.* 2460 B.C.) cf., now, *D.O. Edzard,* Sumerische Rechtsurkunden des III. Jahrtausends . . . (Abh. Bayer. Akad. d. Wiss., Phil.-Hist. Kl. NF 67), 1968, No. 98, 99 (pp. 153–160). For the Akkadian evidence, see *Driver* and *Miles,* The Assyrian Laws, pp. 86–118, The

Babylonian Laws, 1, pp. 63–65. Most recently, *G. Cardascia* contributed a good study on this topic to the *W. Eilers Festschrift* (1967), 19–37.

3. Much interesting and valuable material is contained in the Mishnah especially *sub. Ṣotah* 1–6; 9:9. In this paper the translation of *H. Danby* (Oxford, 1933) has been used.

4. It is unclear whether the woman walks into the temple with the offering in hand or the husband presents it to God before submitting it to his wife (v.18). For the problem, cf. *Gray,* Numbers, p. 50. At any rate, the offering is called *minḥat zikkārôn, mazkeret ʿāwôn,* "a meal-offering of remembrance, recording wrongdoing" [NEB: "grain-offering of protestation conveying an imputation of fault"]. See the remarks of *Ṣotah* 2:1: "[The husband] brought the meal-offering in an Egyptian basket and put it in her hands so as to tire her."

5. *Von Soden,* Akkad. Handwörterbuch, 605. Among the early Arabs, a similar role was played by the *Kāhīn,* cf. *J. Morgenstern,* HUC Jubilee Volume (1875–1925), pp. 116–117.

6. *Ṣotah* 1:5 specifies: "They take her to the Eastern gate which is over against the entrance of the Nicanor gate. . . ."

7. *G.R. Driver's* comments on this passage in Syria, 33 (1956), pp. 73–76 do not seem applicable. He quotes a Hittite text (ZA, 45 [1939], 200–201), in which a sick man is given a potion containing "clay from the archive room." Although water ordeal was known to the Hittites (cf. *Laroche* apud *Cardascia,* op. cit., 203 on KUB XII:3: iii:29ff and KBo VIII:42v.9), Driver's example is clearly a "medical" formula.

His other example, drawn from *Ebeling's* article in Orientalia, 22 (1953), 359–361, belongs to the genre of counter-spells against witches. Perhaps more to the point are the oath-releasing ceremonies mentioning water, *Reiner* Šurpu III:31 (cf. also III:21, 62).

8. Drawn from the "Sea of Bronze"? 1K.7:23–26. This, of course, does not go counter to 2 Chr. 4:6; Ex. 30:18–31. In an unpublished Mari text translated by *Dossin* in La Divination en Mesopotamie Ancienne (1966), p. 79 (partial transliteration in *Finet,* Annales du Centre d'Étude des Religions, Université Libre de Bruxelles, 3 [1969?], 125–126), a palace functionary is said to have offered one ox and six sheep to Dagan. Upon completion of this act, a *muḫḫum-priest* rises and presents Dagan's request for *me-e za-ku-tim.* Since *zukkūm,* in Mari at least, seems to mean "to test for (cultic) purity," it is possible to suggest that the *me-e za-ku-tim,* not unlike the *mayim qedōšim* of Numb. 5:16 was designed to insure a certain degree of cleanliness on the part of the drinker.

9. A symbol of guilelessness? (cf. *J. Morgenstern,* Rites of Birth . . . Among the Semites, (1966), pp. 100, 233[86]. To contrast the priest's hair (Lev. 21:10; 10:6)? (cf. *Ṣotah* 3.8).

A curious New Testament incident is reported in Luke 7:36–50. A woman of easy virtue [sic] approaches Christ while banqueting. She untangles her hair [implied] and wipes Jesus's feet which had been moistened by her tears. Her sins were instantly forgiven (cf. John 12:1–2; Mark 14:3–9; Matt. 26:6–13). On the basis of Numbers 5:11ff, is it possible that Luke was offering evidence to strengthen Christ's claim as ultimate judge?

10. See also *E. Speiser,* Oriental and Biblical Studies, p. 108.

11. Noted also by *G.R. Driver,* Syria, 33 (1956), p. 73.

12. See also *Lucas, Harris,* Ancient-Egyptian Materials and Industry[4], pp. 362–363.

13. *Syria,* 33 (1956), p. 73.

14. See further the discussion of *J. Frazer* in his commentary on Pausanias's *Description of Greece,* V (1898), pp. 175–176.

15. No one can claim a universally accepted diagnosis on the basis of the scriptural indications. See *Gray,* Numbers, 53–54. Some render "miscarriage," understanding "thigh" as a euphemism for "genitals" (NEB; *Driver,* Syria 33 [1956], pp. 73ff). Others accept Josephus's (Ant. III:xi:6) suggestion that the descriptions fits the symptoms of dropsy (edema). In this, they might be supported by Akkadian texts which speak of this disease as one sent to perjurers by Ea (cf. CAD A/1, 144).

One may be forgiven for introducing yet another suggestion which has been reached through conversations with neighborly medical practitioners. Should "thigh" be taken as a euphemism for "genitals," the biblical description fits a varicosic disorder known as thrombophlebitis. The causes of this disease are many; often a sharp blow either on the body or on the psyche may produce blood clots that lead to complications. But especially during pregnancy, the unlucky sufferer would find swelling around the vulva and belly, sometimes even accompanied by edema in the legs. In acute cases, thrombophlebitis can lead to death. Consult *R.C. Benson,* Handbook of Obstetrics and Gynecology (1964), pp. 92–93

16. *Ṣotah* 3.4 wonders about the lapse in time before the ordeal took effect.

Accusations of Adultery
A Study of Law and Scribal Practice in Numbers 5:11–31[*]

MICHAEL FISHBANE

I
n biblical law, the institution of marriage was protected by a categorical prohibition of adultery (Exod. 20:14; Deut. 5:17). However, we must turn to the various legal compilations in the Hebrew Bible for further insight into the jurisprudence of this apodictic censure.[1] The collation of laws known as the Holiness Code (Lev. 17–26) is very strict as regards family purity. We are here interested in the catalogue of injunctions on sex and marriage as recorded in Lev. 20:10–21. Lev. 20:10 states the following case against adultery:

> If a man commits adultery with a married woman, committing adultery with his kinsman's wife, both the adulterer and adultress shall be killed.[2]

But despite its explicit formulation, this statute does not explicate the circumstances under which such a law could be enforced. The requisite details are clearly stated in Deut. 22:22. This case is also included within a corpus of laws on sex and marriage (Deut. 22:13–29). It promulgates the law for adultery whensoever the perpetrators of said act are caught *in flagrante delicto*. As formulated, the crime is both a public and witnessed event. Laws addressed to the same social situation, with similar terminology, are known from cuneiform law from diverse periods and locales.[3] Deut. 22:22 states:

> If a man is caught having intercourse with a married woman, both that man—who had intercourse with the woman—and that woman shall die. You must destroy evil from Israel.[4]

The inclusion of this statute within a series of sex laws suggests an interesting comparison with Babylonian law.[5] Deut. 22:22 is followed (vv. 23–27) by cases of intercourse between a man and a woman who are betrothed. Correspondingly, the case of adultery in the Laws of Hammurapi (LH 129), in which the perpetrators of the act are caught *in flagrante*, is followed (LH 130) by a case involving intercourse between a betrothed couple. LH 131–132 continue this catalogue of sex laws with cases involving unsubstantiated accusations of adultery. Now in view of the foregoing correspondences between LH 129–130 and Deut. 22:22–27, we would have expected laws similar to those which appear in LH 131–132 to have their reflex in the Deuteronomic corpus. However, such biblical cases as deal with unsubstantiated accusations of adultery appear in Num. 5:11–31. They have been included in the corpus of ritual praxes found between Lev. 1:1 and the benediction in Num. 6:22–27. This collection is formally set off from surrounding context by the following *inclusio:*[6]

> Exod. 40:33b   *wayʹkal Mōšeh ʹet hammˁlāʹkāh*
>   "And Moses completed the work" (sc. of the tabernacle)
> Num. 7:1a   *wayʹhî bˁyôm kallôt Mōšeh lˁhāqîm ʹet hammiškān*
>   "And when Moses completed the erection of the tabernacle"

The incorporation of Num. 5:11–31 within this diverse priestly corpus is apparently motivated by the fact that the ordeal which accompanies accusations of adultery is performed by a priest (v. 15), in the tabernacle (v. 17), together with various ritual offerings (vv. 15, 18, 25, 26). Nevertheless, the relationship of Num. 5:11–31 to the laws in Deut. 22:22–27 and LH 129–132 is a matter of interest, and will occupy our attention in a latter stage of the discussion.

     I. Num. 5:11–31 is a valuable document among the ritual and legal prescriptions of the Hebrew Bible. Its value derives from the fact that it has preserved both the praxes and oaths of the ordeal imposed on a woman accused of adultery. This combination of sacred act and sacred word is common among the recovered rituals of the ancient Near East;[7] but there are regrettably few examples in the Hebrew Bible. Num. 5:11–31 is a notable exception; so is Deut. 21:1–9, which prescribes the praxis and oath of absolution in cases of unaccountable homicide.[8] Otherwise, the *verba sacra* which accompanied ritual praxis have not been preserved. This situation is presumably due to the type and nature of the received texts themselves. Nevertheless, commentators of the stature of Y. Kaufmann have concluded that the priestly praxes within the biblical cult were conducted in silence.[9] This position is not without methodological difficulties. It presupposes that the received descriptions exhaust the scenario of a ritual. Were the Psalms totally divorced from cultic events in ancient Israel, in contrast to the rituals of Mesopotamia and the Second Temple? Texts like Num. 10:35–36 or I Chron. 15:26–16:36 suggest otherwise. It is, further, hard to imagine that the ritual described in Lev. 16 was without an accompanying prayer—especially in the light of v. 21 and Mišnah Yoma 4:1–2.[10] Finally, Kaufmann has unduly complicated his own case insofar as he classified all verbal-complements to ritual praxis as "magical," and understood magic in a pejorative sense. At all events, a text like Num. 5:11–31 warrants a more cautious judgment relative to the conjunction of *hieros logos* and ritual praxis in the Israelite cult.

     But despite this exemplary preservation of cultic procedure, numerous difficulties obscure the exegesis of Num. 5:11–31. Confusions as to the correct sequence of the ordeal already beset early Rabbinic sources.[11] In addition, generations of commentators have attempted to elucidate the laws, rituals, and the redactional processes preserved in this text. The central concern of our study will be to further clarify the various aspects of Num. 5:11–31. In the process of our analysis, we intend to formulate a new methodological approach, one which will utilize a number of hitherto unnoticed legal and structural analogues within both the Hebrew Bible and cuneiform texts. As background for our analysis of Num. 5:11–31, a brief resume of the present state of scholarship is necessary.

II. The text of Num. 5:11–31 has been subjected to critical analysis by such scholars as Stade,[12] Carpenter,[13] Baentsch,[14] and Press.[15] Numerous difficulties have been discussed. In their various analyses, they stressed repetitions of discrete actions (as the approach before YHWH, vv. 16, 18; the oath, vv. 19, 21; the draught, vv. 24, 26–27; and the meal offering, vv. 15, 18) and/or variations in technical terminology (as the meal offering, vv. 15, 18; and *ʾazkārāh*-offering, vv. 15, 18). Starting primarily from his assumption of "two parallel introductions" (vv. 12–13, 29–30). Stade divided the "zusammengesetzten Character der Eiferopferthora" into two distinct sources.[16] G.B. Gray summarized the assured results of exegesis on Num. 5:11–31 for his generation. He noted that "the text has either been interpolated and otherwise modified, or it rests on a compilation from two parallel but distinct *tôrôth*."[17] Accordingly, such recent commentators as North have concluded that the present text reflects a harmonized redaction—both with respect to the quantity of documentary sources and the degree to which the ordeal is magical or not.[18] At this point, however, we must turn to another putative contradiction which has been generally accepted.

Stade spoke of the lack of harmony between vv. 12–13 and v. 14. Verses 12–13 state decisively that the woman is guilty, whereas v. 14 leaves the case open. This judgment supplemented his above-noted contention regarding two introductions, and was a key factor in his division of the text into two sources. Their introductions are: A. vv. 12–13, and B. vv. 14, 29–30. Verse 30, which replicates v. 14, reflects the original elements of source B. It was presumably transferred to its present position by a later redactor, and supplemented with an independent introduction (v. 29).[19] The absence of any introduction at v. 14 left this vestige of source B without "motivation"—and "contradictory" vis-à-vis source A.

But while Stade has insightfully observed a relationship between vv. 12–13 and vv. 14, 29–30, he has confused an explanation of the origin of the "contradiction" between vv. 12–13 and v. 14 with an explanation as such. More must be said. The relationship between the prologue and epilogue of Num. 5:11–31 needs to be thoroughly reconsidered. The reconstruction of documentary sources established by Stade, and followed *mutatis mutandis* by many scholars,[20] led to a complete dissection of the text. Exegesis was strained to account for the present redaction of Num. 5:11–31. More fundamentally, such analysis ignored those stylistic and form-critical elements which are of decisive importance for the exegesis of prescriptive texts in the priestly corpus. It is to a reassessment of this text, and its reinterpretation on the basis of both inner biblical and ancient Near Eastern evidence that we must now turn. The stylistics of the legal formulation in Num. 5:11–31 requires attention first. Such an analysis will clarify the particular conjunction of the laws involved, and will prepare the way for their later interpretation.

III. Biblical legal terminology had two means of introducing the protasis of casuistical case law: a) *ʾîš ʾîš kî/ʾādām kî*, "If a man . . ." and b) *ʾîš ʾîš ʾăšēr*, "A man who. . . ." Each formula is characteristically followed by a verb.[21] Their Akkadian interdialectal forms are *šumma awīlum* and *awīlum ša*, respectively.[22] The first of these biblical formulations, *ʾiš ʾiš kî*, occurs in Num. 5:12. Its purpose is to introduce the case and prescribe its adjudication. Further, in biblical legal expression, subordinate and contrastive cases are conventionally introduced by the particle *ʾim*.[23] The translation of this technical term is "or"/"if." However, what is of specific importance for our stylistic analysis is the fact that subordinate cases can also be introduced by the particle *waw*. This feature has the same meaning as *ʾim* and occurs frequently in biblical law, as may be noted by such sequences as: Lev. 15:2, 19; 17:8, 10, 13; 18:6, 18 ff.; 20:2, 4, 9ff.; 24:15ff.; Num. 5:6; 8; 6:2, 9; 9:10, 13.[24] This stylistic observation bears decisively on our analysis of Num. 5:11–31. We suggest that the occurrence of the legal particle *w(aw)* at v. 14 explains the conjunction of vv. 12–14 as two separate but related laws. Verses 12–13, introduced by the protasis *ʾiš ʾiš kî*, construe a law distinct from, but formally related to, the case presented in v. 14. So interpreted, the conjunction of these verses reflects a convention of casuistical legal formulation, not two redacted sources.

We are now in a position to carry our analysis of the formulary of this text a step further. To do so, an additional stylistic convention must be observed. S. Talmon has studied the "Synonymous Readings in the Textual Traditions of the Old Testament."[25] The investigation focused on the substitution of words and phrases used synonymously and interchangeably with each other in two parallel passages—either within the MT alone, or within the MT and the Dead Sea Scrolls. Talmon dealt with nouns and verbs; we wish to supplement his analysis with respect to particles. It will be noted from the examples cited below that the particles *w(aw)* and *ʾô* are used either synonymously in the same case (example a), or interchangeably in parallel passages (example b).

(a) Num. 9:9–14 states the law that a second (v. 10) "Paschal offering to YHWH is enjoined if a man or his posterity is either defiled by a corpse *or (ʾô)* on a long journey." There is no other mitigating circumstance, as v. 13 makes clear: "but if that man is either pure *or (waw)* not on a journey, and refrains from the paschal offering—such a man will be cut off from his kin."

(b) Lev. 20:27 formulates a polemic against divination by the medium of a "ghost *or (ʾô)* familiar spirit." In the parallel passage, Deut. 18:11, the particle used is *waw*.

Just as our recognition of the formulaic sequence *ʾiš ʾiš kî/w(aw)* elucidated the bipartite structure of the laws in vv. 12–14, so the recognition that the particles *ʾô* and *w(aw)* are interchangeable clarifies the sequence *ʾăšer/ʾô* in vv. 29–30. Consequently, vv. 29–30 emerge as two separate but related laws. These cases are precisely symmetrical in structure and terminology to the two cases which appear in vv. 12–14. Moreover, both formulations are followed by a description of the ordeal; vv. 15–28 in the one case, vv. 30a–31 in the other. But despite the symmetry of structure and content, the formulation which appears in vv. 29–31 is unquestionably more terse. From a formal point of view it would appear that vv. 29–30 recapitulate the opening cases by means of a topical summation of their constitutive elements. This interpretation of the relationship between vv. 29–30 and vv. 12–14 puts the entire unit of Num. 5:11–31 in a new light. With it we come to the core of the form-critical issue, one which opens up a wider field of vision for Num. 5:11–31 in particular, and prescriptive rituals generally. We choose to recognize in the topical resumption found in vv. 29–31 a biblical analogue to the scribal phenomenon of a concluding subscript. This feature has long been known to cuneiform scholars, but its significance for the clarification of structural issues in biblical literature has not been explored. An explication of the subscript, and its bearing on Num. 5:11–31, must now be considered.

IV. A. Rainey classified Lev. 6:1–7:38 as a prescriptive ritual text which gives an Administrative order of rituals, in contrast to the Didactic order in Lev. 1:1–5:26.[26] He correctly noted that each sacrificial ritual is defined as a *Tôrāh,* or "instruction." Thus each new prescription (Lev. 6:2, 7, 18; and 7:2, 11) is introduced with the formula: "This is the *tôrāh* of the . . . (sacrifice)." This series of prescriptive rituals is followed by a separate document, the initiation of the Aaronids (Lev. 8–9). B. Levine has interpreted it as a narrative descriptive ritual,[27] But what is significant for the present discussion is that the preceding series of sacrificial prescriptions in Lev. 6–7 concludes (v. 37) with a *resumptive subscript* of all the *tôrôt* detailed. This summation opens with the formula "This is the *tôrāh* as regards the . . . (sacrifices)," and recapitulates the topics of the preceding rituals.

Subscripts which recapitulate the constitutive contents of an "instruction" frequently appear in the prescriptive ritual texts of the Hebrew Bible. The formulation of these summations have a standard introit: "This is the *tôrāh* of . . ." For the sake of clarity and brevity we shall limit our discussion of this phenomenon to the prescriptive rituals in Lev. 11–15.

Lev. 11 distinguishes permissible from forbidden foods in accordance with its taxonomy of the species, and concludes in vv. 46–47 with a topical summation of its contents. Lev. 12 enumerates the varying periods of post partum pollution following male (vv. 1–4) or female (v. 5) births. As with cases of impurity generally, reunion with the community was preceded by a sacrifice. Such is prescribed in vv. 6–7a. The subscript follows in v. 7b together with an amelioration of the prescribed sacrifice whensoever it would exceed the woman's financial means (v. 8). Lev. 13 follows and deals with diagnostic techniques and rituals concerned with various skin blemishes and their miasmic properties. This extensive document concludes at v. 59 with a topical resumption of the categories discussed. As in cases of impurity, Lev. 13 is followed by a prescription of rituals which precede reunion with the community. In this particular case (14:2–20), the prescription begins (v. 2) with the *tôrāh*-formula (cf. Chs. 6–7) and is followed by an amelioration of the sacrificial obligation whensoever it would exceed the individual's financial means (vv. 21–31). The resumptive subscript in v. 32 refers to the recuperative stage only. A new stage is operative from Lev. 14:34; these laws of blemishes and miasma are formulated for conditions which would obtain in the Land of Canaan. This entire text concludes with a resumptive subscript in vv. 54–57. The *inclusio* of the formula in vv. 54a and 57b recalls the formulation in Num. 8:84a and 89b which also brackets a concluding summation. And finally, Lev. 15 follows with prescriptions concerning polluting discharges; including running sores on the male member (vv. 2–15), emission of semen (vv. 16–18), and menstrual or other flows (vv. 19–26). The subscript appears in vv. 32–33.

It will be noted that in all cases from Lev. 11–15, a resumptive subscript follows the prescriptive ritual. Each resumption is brief and summary; only the constitutive topics are noted. Even in those cases where a *tôrāh*-formula introduces a prescription (Lev. 6–7;

14:2), the text is also concluded by a topical resumption (cf. Lev. 7:37; 14:32). This internal similarity of Lev. 11–15 is all the more striking insofar as it is formally distinguished from the surrounding context by an *inclusio;* whereby Lev. 16:1 (cf. the distinct opening in 16:2) recapitulates the death of the two sons of Aaron mentioned in Lev. 10:1–2. Thus both as regards the literary inclusion which envelopes it, and the formulaic summations which constitute its parts, we are led to the conclusion that Lev. 11–15 reflects residual archival techniques, and is a Levitical "series" on the subject of purity and danger.[28]

To make the form-critical argument more salient we shall adduce analogous archival techniques from Akkadian prescriptive incantation-prayers and rituals. Thus, each text of the *šu.ila*-series of incantation-prayers characteristically begins with the formula *šiptu.* The text itself is formally separated from a title or topic line which opens with the formula *inim.inim.ma,* and is set off from the foregoing prayer by a transverse line.[29] Similar form and terminology can be found *inter alia* in other prescriptive incantations and rituals, e.g., in a series of texts against underworld demons,[30] in the *Maqlû*-series[31] and in the *Lamaštu*-series.[32] Precisely this phenomenon of resumptive summary is what is found among the incantations in the Ritual Tablets which accompanied the Assyrian Dream Book.[33]

Numerous additional examples might be cited from inventories, consignments, scholarly lists, and the like. We shall present here several additional cases particularly because of their Western provenience:

(a) The *Doppelurkunde* is the phenomenon of encasing a tablet in a clay envelope, sealed and inscribed with a summary of its contents.[34] L. Fischer long ago observed that an analogue to this feature may be found in the sealing techniques of the Aramaic papyri of Elephantine.[35] He further compared contemporary Egyptian and Greek phenomena; the later Rabbinic *geṭ m^equśśar* (now attested in the Naḥal Ḥever materials);[36] and Jer. 32:6–15, which refers to a real estate contract *ḥātûm w^egālûy,* "sealed and open" (cf. Isa. 29:11f; Neh. 6:5).[37]

(b) Y. Muffs has elucidated the relationship between the Aramaic summaries found on Neo-Assyrian cuneiform receipts and records and the summaries and formulary which appear in the Elephantine papyri.[38]

(c) B. Levine has shown that Ugaritic inventories and consignments have archival total-lines similar to those found in Sumerian and Akkadian texts. We may add that such totals often appear as topical summations on the sides of these tablets—obviously to expedite filing and cataloguing. He noted various biblical examples of total-lines as well.[39]

V. On the basis of the form-critical considerations just discussed, it is obvious that the cases cited in Num. 5:29–30 are a resumptive *tôrāh*-subscript to the cases presented in vv. 12–14. Thus v. 29 is a topical resumption of vv. 12–13, and v. 30a resumes the case in v. 14. Moreover just as the ritual-ordeal in vv. 15–28 is the resultative apodosis of vv. 12–14, v. 30b is a topical excerpt of vv. 16b and 18a. As we noted above the case of the unchaste woman (v. 29) is distinguished from the case involving a "fit of jealousy" (v. 30a) by the particle *ʾô.* According to the subscript, then, there is a *clear* bifurcation of two mutually exclusive but related laws. Both cases involve an allegation of unchastity, are without witnesses, and involve the honor of the husband.

In sum, Num. 5:11–31 fits precisely into the form-critical-structure adduced. Instead of two separate sources, with component addition and redactional harmonizations, two distinct cases emerge; to wit:

> 1) An allegation (vv. 12–13) of conjugal infidelity, apparently substantiated by probable cause, common knowledge, or *prima facie* evidence—but wherein the wife has neither been seen nor caught *in flagrante delicto* by her husband or witnesses; and
> 2) An allegation (v. 14) of conjugal infidelity based on suspicion, pure and simple. There is no reasonable justification for the allegation.

In both cases the allegation is adjudicated under the *tôrat haqqᵉnāʾōt;* although only the second refers to this term in its formulation. Some clarification of this terminology is thus in order.

A first step in this regard is to realize that "jealous" meant something different to the translators of King James than to us. A look at *A New English Dictionary* (1901) makes it clear that the inclusive sense of this term was one of attentive, zealous concern for (personal) prerogative or possessions. It is precisely within this definition that the semantic range of biblical uses can be understood. Space does not allow a complete classification, although the following broad categories for the stem *qnᵓ* can be made: a) as relates to divine indignation and attention to personal honor or uniqueness (e.g. Exod. 20:5; 34:24; Deut. 32:21f.; Ezek. 39:25); possessions or prerogatives (e.g., Num. 25:11; Isa. 42:13; Ezek. 16:42; Zech. 8:2); b) as regards human indignation and attention to divine honor or prerogatives (e.g., Num. 25:11, 13; I Kings 19:10, 14); or personal honor and interests (e.g., Gen. 30:1; 37:11; Num. 5:11 *bis;* II Sam. 21:2). By extension, this concern may involve or include fury, anger, and passion (e.g., Ps. 37:1; Prov. 3:31; Eccles. 9:6). This semantic range of this term is illuminated by the Akkadian interdialectal correspondent: *naʾādu,* whose meanings include "attention," "scrupulous concern," and "zeal."[40] Thus *nādu* is used to express human attention to the will and prerogatives of a God.[41] Thus, it is frequently used in royal inscriptions to characterize the zeal of a ruler[42] for his protective deities, as in:

> *rēʾu kēnu nādu ᵈenlil ᵈmarduk*
> A righteous shepherd, zealous for Enlil and Marduk.

We suggest, therefore, that *tôrat haqqᵉnāʾōt* means "the jurisprudence regarding (personal) zeal (or attention to honor)," and *rúᵃh haqqinnᵓāh* means "a fit of suspicious (zealous) indignation," or the like.

VI. In the preceding sections we attempted to establish the juridical bifurcation of the laws in Num. 5:12–14, 29–30 on the basis of stylistic and structural criteria from biblical and ancient Near Eastern literatures. An analysis of the contents of these cases followed. We may now expand our discussion on this issue, and turn to cuneiform law—a sphere which left its clear impress on biblical legal formulation and convention.

In the opening section we noted the similarity between LH 129–30 and Deut. 22:22–27 as regards both content and arrangement. We further observed that LH 131–32 continue the case arrangement with laws dealing with allegations of adultery. In contrast, the related biblical laws do not appear with Deut. 22:22–27, but in Num.

5:11–31.[43] Recognition of the juridical similarity between LH 131–132 and Num. 5:11–31 can now serve as the basis for the further clarification of the biblical cases. Not only are the contents of these laws similar, but references to an oath and an ordeal further accentuate their affinity. LH 132 states:

> If a finger has been pointed at a man's wife because of another man, but she has not been caught lying with that other man, she shall leap into the River for the sake of her husband.

The public aspect of this accusation is to be contrasted with the private aspect in LH 131:

> If a man's wife was accused by her husband, but she was not caught while lying with another man, she shall make an oath by the god and return home.

What is of importance here is the similarity in form and content between LH 131–132 and Num. 5:12–14, 29–30. In LH 132, a public accusation has been made. The woman has not been caught *in flagrante delicto,* and there are no witnesses. Driver and Miles comment: "How the evidence is produced is hard to say, but the fact is probably known in the district."[44] Apparently the husband is not part of the accusation, or at least it doesn't originate with him. The intent of the water ordeal is ambiguous. It seems that its purpose is to establish *de jure* that which is "known" *de facto.* The motivation, "for the sake of her husband," presumably arises from his zealous concern for both her adjudication and his public exoneration. Similarly, in Num. 5:12–13, a public accusation has been made. The fact is "known," although the means for this knowledge can only be presumed. The woman has not been caught *in flagrante delicto,* there are no witnesses, and the husband is not originally involved. Here, too, the intent of the draught-ordeal is ambiguous. It seems that its purpose is to establish *de jure* that which is "known" *de facto.* The motivation whereby the husband goes to trial is explained by the inclusive rubric: *tôrat haqqᵉnā'ōt,* viz. his zealous concern for both his wife's adjudication and his own exoneration (cf. v. 31).

A similar homology of legal content extends to LH 131 and Num. 5:14. In LH 131 there is a private accusation, based on a husband's suspicions of his wife's conjugal infidelity. The husband is directly involved, but grounds for the allegation are not stated. The praxis is an oath-ordeal. Similarly, Num. 5:14 is a private accusation based on a husband's suspicion of his wife's infidelity. Here, too, the husband is directly involved, but the grounds for the allegation are not stated. An oath and draught-ordeal are prescribed. As in the first case, the aggrieved husband brings his wife to trial and is directly involved in the proceedings. It would seem, then, that in biblical law—whether the allegation is based on public hearsay or private suspicion—it is the responsibility of the husband to present the arraignment and seek umbrage.

In the foregoing analysis we attempted to establish that the two mutually exclusive but related laws in LH 131–132 have the same juridical bifurcation argued for Num. 5:12–14. No final proof suggests itself, but the similarity in form, content, and case arrangement is most compelling. Nevertheless, a complexity remains: Are the separate praxes of oath and water-ordeal in LH 131–132 conflated into a composite ritual in Num. 5:11–31? We think not. Evidence from cuneiform sources suggests a different solution, and runs counter to the assumption of "various" praxes preserved in the text.[45]

Any elucidation of this problem must consider the following evidence: In the ancient Near East water-ordeals were frequently preceded by oaths. Two types have survived. In the one type, exemplified in cases from Elam,[46] the water-ordeal is employed to resolve a deadlock arising out of conflicting testimonies (much as the *niš ilim*-ordeal at Nuzi was executed when and after court evidence conflicted);[47] in the other, both the oath and the water-ordeal are two aspects of one praxis. Thus, in a middle Assyrian text, an individual who is to undergo the water-ordeal swears to his innocence and invokes the gods to vindicate him.[48] Such an oath as is embedded in this incantation-prayer might well have accompanied a case like LH 132, but is absent owing to the nature of the received legal source.

Even more illuminating with respect to the praxes in Num. 5:11–31 is another cuneiform text from the middle Assyrian period which combines both oath and draught-ordeal. The fragment (VAT 9962) is presented as published by Ebeling[49] with our translation:

1. . . . . *aḫ-ḫi-ri ki (?)-ma (?) siparri*
2. [*ḫi*]-*pí* . . *tu* . . . *te pâni-šu i-za-zu marê (meš) ta-me-tu*
3. [*ḫi*]-*pí i-ḫab-bu-ú i-šat-tu-ú i-tam-mú-u i-za-ku-ú*
4. [*ḫi*]-*pí* NIGIN (= *napḫar?*) *aḫ-tu-bu áš-ta-ti at-ta-me a-zu-ku*

. . . . as copper
(Broken) . . . before him stand the litigants
(Broken) . . . they will draw (water), drink, swear and be pure
(Broken) Everything (?); I have drawn (water), drunk, sworn and am pure.

What is noteworthy for our purposes is that the draught-ordeal is accompanied by an oath and an asseveration of innocence. The sequence of verbs: *šatû*, "drink"; *tamû*, "swear": *zakû*, "be pure/innocent," are precisely the interdialectal correspondences to the verbs used in Num. 5:11–31; *viz. šty*, "drink"; *šbʿ*, "swear"; *nqy* and *ṭhr*, "be pure/innocent." The content and terminology of the ordeal in Num, 5:11–31 is clarified by this cuneiform document,[50] as is its combination of oath and ordeal. When we add to this evidence the legal formulary of the casuistical framework, the archival subscript, and the interlocking concatenation of laws in LH 129–32 and Deut. 22:22–27 + Num. 5:11–31 respectively, the cumulative threads of our analysis are firmly brought together.

VII. Our discussion of the cases of witnessed (Lev. 20:10; Deut. 22:22) and unwitnessed adultery (Num. 5:11–31) utilized legal sources exclusively. It remains to consider the thematic reflection of these laws in the non-legal portions of the Bible[51]— both because it preserves aspects of the laws not otherwise attested, and because of the insight it provides concerning the concrete theology of ancient Israel.[52] In this legal motif, the separate aspects of the above cases, and their symbols, are not altogether distinguished. In the divine or prophetic accusations of covenantal infidelity, Israel is caught *in flagrante delicto,* so to speak; divine suspicion, or zeal, is not without foundation. Consequently, we shall note that traces of the draught-ordeal appear in various forms in this motif. On the one hand, it appears in cases of witnessed adultery; a combination originally illogical and juridically unnecessary. On the other hand, this vestige of the ordeal splits off from its judicial function in cases of alleged adultery, and becomes a symbol of the fact of divine judgment. In such cases, however, the original setting of the draught-ordeal is not altogether obscured.[53]

The motif of a faithless Israel who whores after false gods, and confuses Baʿal with

YHWH, is retrojected in the period of the desert wanderings—where it assumes a paradigmatic form. Num. 25:1–15 describes the scandalous episode of the sins with Baᶜal Peᶜôr. This theological motif of infidelity and divine anger is highlighted through the figure of Phineas the priest. Witnessing the fornication of an Israelite and a Moabitess in the course of their worship of Baᶜal, he drew his lance and stabbed them *in flagrante*. Phineas was rewarded for this display of indignant zeal (stem: *qnʾ*) on YHWH's behalf (cf. v. 11).

Aspects of this legal motif are more fully developed in prophetic literature. Hos. 142 dramatizes Israel's infidelity to YHWH, and attraction to Baᶜal (2:10, 15, 18–19), through a symbolism wherein the prophet marries a whore (1:2; cf. 3:1, an adulteress). By means of this image, YHWH arraigns Israel (stem: *ryb*, 2:4) for adultery (stem: *nʾp*, 2:4); uses the formula of divorce (1:6, 9; 2:4); and threatens to strip (stem: *pšṭ*) and kill her (2:5).[54] In short, Israel has abandoned her first husband (2:9), the love of her youth (stem: *nᶜr*, 2:17). YHWH was Israel's *baᶜal*-husband (2:18), but she proved unfaithful, and was caught *in flagrante* with her lovers. But YHWH will have compassion (stem: *rḥm*, 2:25) on Israel and will renew his covenantal love (2:18–25). The use of the marriage formula (2:25), which reverses the divorce, accentuates the covenant renewal here, and illuminates the theological undertone inherent in the use of this "Sinaitic" formula in Lev. 26:12.[55]

Jeremiah (2–3) also arraigns Judah (stem: *ryb*, 2:9, 29) for her false alliances (2:18, 36) and prostitution to false gods (2:23–26). To accentuate this infidelity, the marriage formula is mockingly used (2:27). YHWH is infuriated, for Israel was his bride from her youth (stem: *nᶜr*, 2:2). Judah is compared to her sister Israel (3:6–10). Just as the latter was adulterous (stem: *nʾp*, 3:8) and divorced by YHWH, so will this be the fate of adulterous Judah. Israel abandoned her first (cf. 3:1) *baᶜal*-husband (cf. 3:14), and was caught *in flagrante* with her lovers. But YHWH will have compassion on Israel (stem: *rḥm*, cf., 31:13) and will renew his covenantal love (3:11–25). The use of the marriage formula (3:5, 19; cf. 31:32) underscores the legal background of the arraignment and covenant renewal.

Similarly, in a series of disconnected pronouncements, Deutero-Isaiah uses the imagery of conjugal infidelity to objectify Israel's relationship with YHWH. Israel adulterated (stem: *nʾp*, 57:3) her covenant with YHWH (57:3–14) and was divorced (50:1). She was his bride from her youth (stem: *nᶜr*, 54:6), but abandoned (54:6) her first *baᶜal*-husband (54:5). But YHWH will have compassion (stem: *rḥm*, 54:7–8) on his abandoned bride and will renew his marriage with her (62:4–5). These various elements gain additional significance in the light of the pericope which appears in 51:17–23. Here YHWH refers to himself as the prosecutor of Jerusalem (stem: *ryb*, 51:22) who takes away the "cup of poison" which he had formerly given his people to drink. This specific conjunction of arraignment and draught, in the context of adultery, divorce, and marriage, suggests that the cup-figure is related to the ordeal in Num. 5:11–31. The original tool of the ordeal is here symbolic of judgment and exile. YHWH has indignantly charged Israel with adultery. The use of the draught as part of this legal motif gives it additional force. These disjoined images from the law of witnessed and unwitnessed adultery coalesce in the Book of Ezekiel, and certify, retroactively, the coherence and interpretation of the motif in Deutero-Isaiah.

In Ezek. 16, God informs (stem: *ydᶜ*, 16:2; cf. Jer. 2:19) Jerusalem of her crime.

Described is how YHWH pledged his troth to Israel (16:8), and married her in her youth (stem: *nˤr*, 16:22, 43). But Israel committed adultery with foreign countries and gods (16:25–34). She was caught *in flagrante* by YHWH who, in his indignant zeal (stem: *qnʾ*, 16:38), charged her with the laws of adultery and bloodshed (*mišpˈṭê nōʾăpōt wᵉšōpᵉkōt dām*, 16:38). The punishment of Jerusalem is that she will be stripped (stem: *pšṭ*, 16:39) and stabbed (16:40–41). By her excess, she has out-whored her sisters (16:46–58). But YHWH will recall (stem: *zkr*) the betrothal of her youth (stem: *nˤr*, 16:59–63; cf. Jer. 2:2) and will renew his covenant with Israel.

This entire motif is taken up again in Ezek. 23 and further developed. The entire unit is preceded by the formal charge (stem: *ydˤ*, 22:2) that among the sins in which Jerusalem has been caught is that of adultery (22:11). This motif is developed in Ezek. 23 through the imagery of the whoring sisters (Samaria and Jerusalem, Ezek. 23:2, 4) in two separate units, vv. 2–27 and 37–49. In the first unit, the harlotry of the sisters, to foreign countries and gods, is a betrayal of the marriage of their youth (stem: *nˤr*, 23:8, 19, 20). Jerusalem (23:22–27) is as guilty as her sister. YHWH has caught her *in flagrante,* and indicts her because of his indignant zeal (stem: *qnʾ*, 23:25). Jerusalem will be mutilated, stabbed (23:25), and stripped (stem: *pšṭ*, 23:26). In the second unit of the framework (23:36–49), the sisters are again accused of adultery (stem: *nʾp*, 23:37, 43, 45) and indicted by the law of adultery (*mišpaṭ nōʾăpōt*, 23:45). Caught in the act, they will be stoned and stabbed (23:47).[56]

Enclosed between these condemnations are two additional units, vv. 28–31 and 32–34. They are followed by a conclusion, v. 35, which is similar in content to the conclusions of each of the units of the framework, vv. 27 and 48–49. In these middle sections, Jerusalem is given the "cup" of her sister to drink. Once again the draught is used as a symbol of judgment, and not as an aspect of an ordeal. Its connection with the legal background of adultery clarifies its force in this context, and illuminates those cases like Deutero-Isaiah where it occurs among separate oracles. Finally, it is noteworthy that the symbolic use of the cup-figure in other prophetic arraignments (e.g., Jer. 25:15; 49:12; 50:22) employs the same key stems as appear in Num. 5:11–31.

The extension of the legal *topos* in Num. 5:11–31 as a motif for God's relationship to Israel is typologically similar to the extension of other socially based *topoi,* such as Suzereign-Vassal, Master-Slave, or Father-Son, together with their specific legal and/or familial terminologies. The socio-cultural matrix out of which such an image could arise is reflected in Hosea's condemnation of the syncretism with the Canaanite Baˤal-cult. In his polemic, Hosea acknowledges the popular syncretism of Baˤal as Lord and Husband with YHWH, insofar as he specifically rejects it in 2:18–19; as do Jeremiah (3:14; 31:31), and Isaiah (54:1; 62:4–5). It would thus seem that this *topos* has its background in Canaanite mythology, which dramatizes the relationship between Baˤal and his consort ˤAttart. In the Bible, continuation of this syncretism is evident in the paranomastic use of these terms to express fertility (e.g., *baˤaltî* in Jer. 3:14; Isa. 54:5, and *ˤaštᵉrôt* in Deut. 7:13; 28:4, 18, 51), and in the specific references to the continuous worship of ˤAttart as *mᵉleket haššamayîm* in Jer. 7:18; 44:17–19, 25.[57] It seems that, on the residual folk level, at least, many believed that YHWH had a consort, and worshipped him as a Baˤal.[58] The prophets inverted this mythologem to their own ends: Israel was condemned as the harlot of Baˤal, having abandoned her covenant vows to be a faithful wife.

VIII. In conclusion, we may note the reflex of the law of adultery in Prov. 6:20–35. This entire unit is, we believe, an inner-biblical midrash on the Decalogue. Occasionally, citations from the Decalogue accompany prophetic accusations (Jer. 7:9; Hos. 4:2). What makes this case significant is that the various prohibitions are presented in the light of a general warning against adultery—or, more specifically, in the light of the seduction of false wisdom. This particular theme is dominant in Prov. 5 and 7 as well. Together with 6:20–35, these passages are in direct contrast with divine wisdom, Prov. 8–9.[59]

The unit opens with a stereotypic injunction to the "son" to heed the words of his father and mother, and to bind them close. These teachings will protect and accompany him when he goes on the way, when he lies down, and when he arises (6:20–22). Strikingly, it is elsewhere (Deut. 6:6–8) reemphasized that it is a father's duty to teach his son "these words" when he goes on the way, when he lies down, and when he arises. An Israelite should bind them close to him always. It would appear that these are the words of the Decalogue previously stated.

Among the words of the Decalogue, in addition to respect for parents, are the injunctions against adultery, theft, and covetousness (Deut. 5:17–18). These transgressions follow in Prov. 6:25–35 with respect to the seductive wiles of the whore of wisdom. The adept of wisdom is counseled not to covet her beauty (6:25). Contact with her is adulterating. She is like a kinsman's wife: whosoever has intercourse with her will not be exonerated (stem: nqy, 6:29). Just as a thief is prosecuted for his crime (6:30–31), so is an adulterer (nōʾēp ʾiššāh) doomed (6:32). Indeed, the indignant zeal (stem: qnʾ) of an aggrieved husband (6:34) is difficult to assuage (6:35).

Thus, with this midrash on adultery, we return to the Decalogue with whose apodictic censure of conjugal infidelity our study opened. In the process of unraveling the various technical threads which sealed the meaning of the laws of witnessed and unwitnessed adultery, we encountered a widespread motif used to dramatize the relationship of God and Israel. As a legal *topos,* it proved a rich source for "instruction from the priest, counsel from the sage, and divine word from the prophet" (Jer. 18:18).

NOTES

*I wish to thank Profs. Baruch Levine, Nahum Sarna, and Shemaryahu Talmon for their helpful criticisms and suggestions. Final responsibility is, of course, mine.

1. The collection of laws known as the Covenant Code, Exod. 21–23, contains a short unit on sex and marriage (22:15–16, 18). No law of adultery is mentioned.

2. The protasis to the law contains two parallel clauses asyndetically juxtaposed. This is very similar to cases which are conflations from more than one textual tradition, cf. S. Talmon, "Double Readings in the Massoretic Text," *Textus* I (1960), pp. 144–85. Additionally, we may note that the penalty is recorded in the singular, although the subject is in the plural. This irregularity most likely is due to the fact that the penalty clause is a frozen technical term.

3. Cf. the Laws of Eshnuna 28, the Laws of Hammurapi (LH) 129, and text IM 28051 according to the re-interpretation of S. Greengus in "A Textbook Case of Adultery in Ancient Mesopotamia," *HUCA* 40–41 (1969–70), pp. 33–44. Laws and rights of the enraged husband vary.

4. The Hebrew stem *mṣʾ* must be rendered "caught," as has been convincingly established by S. Iwry, "והנמצא A Striking Variant Reading in IQIsᵃ," *Textus* 5 (1966), pp. 33–43. Iwry also showed that in related cuneiform laws the corresponding term is ṣabātu, "to catch." The stem *mṣʾ*

is the legal "catch-world" of the entire corpus of sex laws in Deut. 22:13ᵃ29; cf. 22:14, 17, 20, 22, 23, 25, 27, 28.

5. The questions of comparison and origin in cuneiform and biblical laws considered separately and together are difficult but important. See the remarks of A. Goetze, "Mesopotamian Laws and the Historian," *JAOS* 69 (1949), pp. 115–20. We shall return to this question in Section V below.

6. This use of the *inclusio* is similar to the repetitive resumption first studied by C. Kuhl, "Die 'Wiederaufnahme'—ein literarisches Prinzip?" *ZAW* 64 (1952), pp. 1–11. This phenomenon, with other features of this paper, forms the basis of a comprehensive analysis of structural techniques in the Bible by S. Talmon and this writer.

7. The Mesopotamian material is plentiful. Representative is E. Ebeling, *Die Akkadische Gebetsserie "Handerhebung"* (=HH), Deutsche Akademie d. Wissenschaften, 20 (Berlin, 1953) where the incantation-prayer, or *šiptu*, is separated by a transverse line from the ritual found at its conclusion. The ritual prescription opens with "Its ritual," written *kikiṭṭušu* (e.g. 15:26) or *epuštušu* (e.g. 19:13; 65:27). The bifurcation: *šiptu-epuš annam* is frequent in L. King, *Babyl. Sorcery and Magic*. On a wider level, special Ritual Tablets were added to such incantation series as e.g., *Maqlû* (see G. Meier, *Die Beschwoerungssammlung Maqlu, Archiv fuer Orientforschung* Beiheft, 2, 1937), or *Šurpu* (see E. Reiner, *Šurpu AFO* Beiheft, 11, 1958). A.L. Oppenheim has produced a Ritual Tablet for the Assyrian Dream Book (see "The Interp. of Dreams . . ." *Proceedings of the American Philosophical Society,* 46, 1955); cf. his "Analysis of an Assyrian Ritual (KAR 139)," *H R* 5 (1966), pp. 250–326, where both praxis and incantation are explicitly prescribed.

8. This text, its Near Eastern background and its theological refocusing, has been well-studied by A. Roifer, "The Breaking of the Heifer's Neck," *Tarbiz* 31 (1961), pp. 119–43 (Hebrew). Deut. 26 offers another example of this combination of act and word.

9. *The Religion of Israel,* ed. M. Greenberg (Chicago, 1960), pp. 303f; *Toledoth Ha-Emunah Ha-Yisra'elith,* V, 476–78 (Hebrew).

10. Lev. 16 has been studied in the light of Assyrian ritual analogues by B. Levine, "Kippurim," *Erez-Israel* 9 (1969), pp. 88–95 (Hebrew).

11. Cf. Mishnah Soṭa 3:2.

12. "Beitraege zur Pentateuchkritik," sec. 3, "Die Eiferopferthora," *ZAW* 15 (1895), pp. 166–75.

13. *The Composition of the Hexateuch,* J. Carpenter and J. Harford-Battersby, 1902, p. 191.

14. *Exodus, Leviticus und Numeri, HKAT,* 1903, 363f. Also in 1903, Holzinger, *Numeri*. Reflecting this literary analysis with a broader panorama, J. Morgenstern, "Trial by Ordeal among the Semites," *HUC Jubilee Volume,* 1925. Other comparative data has been collected by: Hempel, s.v. "Ordal," *Religion in Geschichte und Gegenwart²*; ibid., s.v. "Gottesurteil" in *Reallexion der Vorgeschichte,* T.H. Gaster, *Myth, Legend and Custom in the Old Testament* (N.Y:, 1970), pp. 280–300.

15. "Das Ordal im alten Israel," *ZAW* 51 n.f. 10 (1933), pp. 121–40, 227–55.

16. Stade (*supra,* n. 12), p. 167.

17. *Numbers,* ICC (Edinburgh, 1903), p. 49.

18. See *Numbers, Old Testament Library* (London, 1968), p. 49.

19. Stade (*supra,* n. 12), pp. 167–168, 172.

20. See e.g. R. Rendtorff, *Die Gesetze in der Priesterschrift* (Göttingen, 1963), pp. 62–63.

21. But the verb can precede the noun as in Exod. 21:2. On the functional analogy of the temporal sequences of the verbs in casuistical formulations see S. Paul, *Studies in the Book of the Covenant in the Light of Cuneiform and Biblical Law, VTS* 18 (Leiden, 1970), p. 117, n. 1.

22. See the discussion in Paul (*supra,* n. 21), Appendix II.

23. Subordinate clauses in Akkadian are introduced by *kī*; cf. W. von Soden *Grundriss d. akk. Grammatik* (Rome, 1952), p. 215.

24. It should be noted that *waw* functions as contrastive in such disjunctive legal series as Ezek. 44:22 and Hag. 2:12. Similarly, such a reading is suggested for the oaths in Judg. 11:31, as already noted by the medieval exegete R. Kimḥi.

25. As cited, *Scripta Hierosolymitana* 8 (1961), pp. 335–83.

26. "The Order of Sacrifices in Old Testament Ritual Texts," *Biblica* 51 (1970), pp. 307–18.

27. "The Descriptive Tabernacle Texts of the Pentateuch," *JAOS* 85 (1965), pp. 307–18.

28. See *supra*, n. 6.

29. E. Ebeling, HH. The type is *šiptu* + incantation-prayer + *enimnim-ma* + title (and sometimes ritual). On this feature, see the remarks by A. Falkenstein in his comprehensive study *Die Haupttypen der Sumerische Beschwoerungen, Leipziger Semitische Studien* (=LSS) n.f. 1, 1931, pp. 4–7; and taken up by W. Kunstman in his specific typological study of this series *Die Babylonische Gebetsbeschwoerung*, LSS, n.f. II, 1932, esp. pp. 3–6.

30. E. Ebeling, *Tod und Leben Nach den Vorstellungen der Babylonier* (Berlin, 1931), texts collected on pp. 146–50. The form: *šiptu* + incantation-prayer + *enimnim-ma* + title. Here the beginning is broken. But these incantations were surely prescriptive, as similar incantations against *eṭimmu*-demons in E, and introduce the incantations beginning with *šiptu* with this long introit: *šumma amēlu eṭimmu iṣbat-su-ma ina zumri-šú,* "If an underworld demon has (become) fastened to the man's body . . ."

31. G. Meier, *op. cit.* Note the frequent structure of *én* + incantation-prayer + *inim. nim-ma* + general title in Sumerian, as II: 1–18; 19–75. That the titles in lines 18 and 75 serve for the preceding incantation respectively is clear when it is noted that in the Ritual Tablet, these texts are referred to (IX:28; 29) by their incipits in Akkadian and are followed by reference to the same ritual which followed the Sumerian phrase in the text itself.

32. D. Myhrman, "Die Labartu-Texte," *Zeitschrift fuer Assyriologie* 16 (1902), pp. 141–200 follows a typology similar to that in notes 29–31, above.

33. See the edition of A. L. Oppenheim, *supra*, n. 7, pp. 300–4. The structure is *én* + incantation-prayer + *inim. nim-ma* + general title summation; cf. KAR 252, Il:19–23, 253; III:4–17, 20–38, 47–51, 52–58.

34. This has been studied by various legal historians; see, most recently E. Koffmahn, *Die Doppelurkunde aus der Wueste Juda* (Leiden, 1968).

35. "Die Urkunden in Jer. 32:11–14 nach den Ausgrabungen und dem Talmud," *ZAW* 30 (1910), pp. 136–42.

36. See Y. Yadin, "Camp IV—The Cave of Letters," *Bulletin of the Israel Exploration Society* 26 (1962), esp. p. 214, n. 10 (Hebrew).

37. On this last, see the remarks of H. Gevaryahu, "Various Observations on Scribes and Books in the Biblical Period," *Beth Miqra* 43 (1970), pp. 368–74 (Hebrew).

38. See his important discussion in *Studies in the Aramaic Papyri from Elephantine* (Leiden, 1969), pp. 189–190 where the origins of the Elephantine formulary are established. Muffs also noted the NeoAssyrian Aramaic docket summaries in L. Delaporte, *Épigraphes arameens* (1912), pp. 32, 38, and those which are found at Elephantine (cf. A. Cowley, *Aramaic Papyri of the Fifth Century,* 1921), and include deeds of removal (6:22), to a house (8:35), of money (10:23), of resignment of a slave (28:17). Such summaries are also found in the Arsham archive from Elephantine published by G.R. Driver, *Aramaic Documents* (Oxford, 1957). It would seem, then, that biblical literature has transformed a purely notational or archival practice onto a literary level.

39. See his discussion (*supra*, n. 27), and references.

40. This differs slightly from von Soden, *AHwB,* 8, 693, s.v.

41. See Lambert, *Babylonian Wisdom Literature* (Oxford, 1960), pp. 86, 264; or *HH* 102, 20, *inter alia.*

42. See the texts collected s.v. *naʾādu* and *rēʾu* in M.-J. Seux, *Épithètes Royales Akkadiennes et Sumériennes* (Paris, 1967).

43. Note the remark of T. Meek in *ANET*, p. 171, n. 103 ad LH 132: "cf. Num. 5:11–31." Our discussion will be limited to LH. It should be noted that unsubstantiated allegations of adultery are well-known in cuneiform law, e.g. U. 7739 Par 10, ii, 3–12 in J.J. Finkelstein, "Sex Offenses in Sumerian Laws," *JAOS* 86 (1966), pp. 369–70; Middle Assyrian Laws 17. All cases differ in detail and punishment.

44. *The Babylonian Laws*, I (Oxford, 1952), p. 284.

45. Other magical aspects of the praxis are suggested from various cuneiform analogues: (a) The text, v. 18, states: *pāraʿ* in connection with letting loose the woman's hair. A parallel can be found in W. von Soden, "Eine altassyrische Beschwoerung gegen die Daemon Lamastu," *Orientalia* 25 (1956), pp. 141–48, Rev. 16: *pè-ra-sà wa-ša-re-at* (cf. *ibid.*, *Revue Assyriologique*, 18, p. 166, Rev. 15); (b) For the case of "dust mixed together with sacred water," see E. Ebeling, "Besch. gegen d. Feind u. d. Boesen Blick," *Archiv Orientalni* 17 (1949), pp. 191–95 (for a praxis using "dust from the library," see G. Meier, *Zeitschrift fuer Assyriologie* 45 [1939], pp. 200–1); (c) In an incantation praxis Ea tells Marduk to use a "pure draught" to counter a charm, see Ebeling, *Orientalia* 22 (1953), pp. 358–61; (d) References to a *kilkillu*-vessel which contained water used in an oath praxis may be found in R. Harris, review of J.J. Finkelstein, *Cuneiform Texts in the Brit. Mus.*, pt. 48 (London, 1968), in *Jour. of the Econ- and Soc. Hist. of the Orient* 13 (1970), pp. 315–16; (e) The ritual of waving seems to be a magico-ritual praxis, cf. II Kings 5:11 and the myth of Telepinus in Gaster, *Thespis²*, p. 310. The biblical form *hēnĭp*, there and in Num. 5:25 (cf. Isa. 30:28) has its interdialectal form in Ug. *šnpt*, see D. Hillers, *BASOR* 198 (1970), p. 42.

46. V. Scheil, *Mémoirs de la mission archéologique de Perse*, XXII (Paris, 1930), p. 162.

47. Cf. *inter alia*, E. Speiser "Nuzi Marginalia," Or 24 (1956), pp. 15–23; E. Drafkorn, "Ilani Elohim," *JBL* 76 (1957), pp. 216–24

48. E. Ebeling, *Tod u. Leben*, pp. 96–99 (=VAT 9962, No. 134, rev. 5–9).

49. *Supra*, n. 48, p. 95 II. 1–4.

50. The sequence in vv. 24–27 remains a notorious crux, if the commentaries are any witness. The issue was first debated in rabbinic courts, see Mishnah Sota 3:2. The problem may possibly be resolved by regarding v. 27a as a repetitive resumption of the text in v. 24—thereby bracketing this supplementary or clarificatory insert. On this principle, see Kuhl (*supra*, n. 6). Philological problems remain as well. On attempts to analyze the *mārim*-waters. see G. R. Driver, "Two Problems in the OT Examined in the light of Assyriology," sec. II, *Syria* 33 (1956), pp. 73–77; and J. Sasson, "Numbers 5 and the 'Waters of Judgment,'" *Biblische Zeitschrift* 16 (1972), pp. 249–51.

51. An early tradition, continued by many moderns, already connected the praxis in Exod. 32:20 with Num. 5; see *Liber Antiquitarum Biblicarum*, XII, 7 (ed. G. Kisch, Notre Dame, 1946, p. 148), *Targ. Yerushalmi, Midrash Haggadol* (ed. M. Margolioth, Jerusalem, 1956, p. 690), *TJ Aboda Zara*, ch. 3, Halakha 3, and the commentaries of Rashi, Rashbam, and Ibn Ezra. The reasoning of Ibn Ezra was: "For otherwise how did the Levites know who the idolators were?" Deut. 9:21 is of no help here. The dissenting opinion states (e.g., W. Beyerlin, *Origins and History of the Oldest Sinai Traditions*, Oxford, 1965, pp. 131–32 and nn. 553–54; p. 559) that the issue is not one of guilt but one of a praxis intended to dispose of the numinous powers of the idol.

52. The ensuing discussion is necessarily brief. A seminal methodological study of one particular motif can be found in Sh. Talmon, "The 'Desert Motif' . . . ," *Biblical Motifs*, Brandeis Texts and Studies, III (Cambridge, 1966), pp. 131–63.

53. The connection between the cup-figure and Num. 5 was already made by Press (*supra*, n. 15). However, his failure to connect it with an integrated series of verbs left his remarks both unmotivated and somewhat schematic. For other attempts to explain the cup, see H. Gressman, *Sellin Festschrift* (Leipzig, 1927), and U. Casutto, *Orientalia* 7 (1938), p. 283.

54. For illuminating parallels in cuneiform and Aramaic materials with Hosea and other prophets who share this legal motif, cf. C. Kuhl, "Neue Dokumente zum Verstaendnis von Hos

2:4–15," *ZAW* 52 (1934), pp. 102–09, and C.H. Gordon, "Hos. 2:4–5 in the Light of New Semitic Inscriptions," *ibid.*, 54 (1936), pp. 277–80; 55 (1937), p. 176.

55. The use of marriage and divorce formulae for illuminating Lev. 26 was first made by Y. Muffs, "Studies in Biblical Law, IV" (The Antiquity of P), *Lectures at the Jewish Theological Seminary*, 1965.

56. The form of death was not indicated in the legal compilations. It is also difficult to reconstruct the punishment on the basis of the motif. It seems that in case of adultery the husband divorced the woman, and she was stripped and stabbed. In some cases it seems that she was stoned and had her ears cut (cf. Ezek. 23:25, 47). Was all this part of one punishment? What about the reference to the removal of her breast in Ezek. 23:34, or the brand of harlotry mentioned in Jer. 3:3? What was, in fact, burned is also not clear from the various vestiges of the law in this motif.

57. The problem of identity is complex. Ishtar's epithet: *šarrat šamē*, "Queen of Heaven," is the interdialectal equivalent of Jer. 7:18; 44:17–19, 25 (K). The G in 44 agrees with the MT as against the G and T in 7:18. Presumably, these last versions preserved the early association of this goddess with the evening star. Do Jer. *loc. cit.* and the 5th c. Egyptian Aramaic text recording *mlkt šmyn* (cf. D.W. Thomas, *PEQ*, 82 [1950], pp. 13–14) reflect ʿAttart? Assyrian influences on Egypt and Judea, and the MT use of ʿaštōrôt suggest this. Yet ʿAnat, also a consort of Baʿal, was called *baʿlatu šamêm(e) rāmêm(i)*, "Mistress of the High Heavens" (see Ch. Virolleaud, *Comptes Rendus de l'Académie des Inscriptions et Belles-Lettres*, 1962, p. 109); and in her aspect as Carthaginian *Tenit* was called Juno Caelestis by the Romans. To increase complexity, ʿAnat and ʿAttart (and ʿAṭirtu) were identified in the late Ramesside period (see J. Edwards, *JNES* 14 [1955], pp. 49–51). At all events, M. Dahood's suggestion (*Revista Biblica* 8 [1960], pp. 166–68), that the goddess is Šapaš, seems unlikely.

58. This syncretism continued in various forms, cf. Zeph. 1:4–5, a contemporary of Jeremiah, and Isa. 65:3. It may be noted that the verbal stem *zny*, "to whore," appears frequently to dramatize Israel's infidelity to Yahweh; especially in the motifs studied in section VII. G. Cohen has suggested that Exod. 13:14–15 hints at the marital relationship between Yahweh and Israel— since this text uses the stems *zny* and *qnʾ* in a covenantal context. See G. Cohen, "The Song of Songs and the Jewish Religious Mentality," in *The Samuel Friedland Lectures* (New York, 1966), p. 7. For an alternative proposal for the origin of this imagery, see the suggestive remarks by A. Fitzgerald, "The Mythological Background for the Presentation of Jerusalem as a Queen and False Worship As Adultery in the OT," *CBQ* 34 (1972), 403–16.

59. The background of adultery, but not the Decalogue-midrash, has been noted in the recent commentaries on the Book of Proverbs, cf. B. Gemsen, *Sprüche Solomos*, *HAT* 16 (Tübingen, 1963), pp. 35–52; A. Barucq, *Le Livre des Proverbs* (Paris, 1964), pp. 70–100; R.B.Y. Scott, *Proverbs and Ecclesiastes, Anchor Bible* (New York, 1965), pp. 53–77. The presentation of adultery and punishment in Prov. 6, in contrast to Ezekiel 16 and 23, for example, has raised some legal-historical questions; see M. Weinfeld "On the Conception of Law within Israel and without," *Beth Miqra* 17 (1964), esp. p. 63 (Hebrew), and cf. S. Loewenstamm, "Laws of Adultery and Murder in the Bible," *ibid.*, 18 (1964), pp. 77f.

Good to the Last Drop
*Viewing the Sotah (Numbers 5.11–31) as the Glass Half Empty and Wondering How to View It Half Full**

> *R. Joshua b. Karhah said: Only two entered the*
> *bed and seven left it. Cain and his twin sister,*
> *Abel and his twin-sisters. "And she [Eve] said:*
> *I have gotten a man . . ." R. Isaac said: When*
> *a woman sees that she has a child she exclaims,*
> *"Behold, my husband is now in my possession."*
>
> BERESHIT RABBAH 22.2

> *It is important for us to guard and keep our bod-*
> *ies and at the same time make them emerge from*
> *silence and subjugation. Historically, we are the*
> *guardians of the flesh; we do not have to abandon*
> *that guardianship, but to identify it as ours by*
> *inviting men not to make us "their bodies," guar-*
> *antors of their bodies. Their libido often needs*
> *some wife-mother to look after their bodies. It is in*
> *that sense that they need a woman-wife* [femme]
> *at home, even if they do have mistresses elsewhere.*
>
> LUCE IRIGARAY,
> "THE BODILY ENCOUNTER
> WITH THE MOTHER"

The most tempting aspect of producing feminist readings of biblical texts is to implicate readers in the act of resisting a stable set of attitudes about male representations of women as constructed in the literature of ancient Israel. The strategy I am adopting comes from one of the generals of the French Resistance: Jacques Derrida. His model of reading is undergirded by a desire to resist two complementary beliefs about texts: (1) a text has identifiable borders or limits; (2) a text exists within a stable system of reference to other texts of "information" (its context) that can be represented, for example, by appending scholarly notes.[1] Much biblical critical theory has remained tightly locked within the borders of texts that are determined by constructions of provenance, dating, and canon, and any other limits that scholars have assigned to the work.[2] Limits are considered here as "everything that was to be set up in opposition to writing (speech, life, the world, the real, history, and what not, every field of reference—to body, mind, conscious or unconscious, politics, economics, and so forth)" (Derrida 1979: 257). By selecting a pre-text[3] or source whose central concern is the control of women's sexuality, Num. 5.11–31, the ritual of the Sotah, I intend to focus the reader's attention upon traditional readings that have preserved patriarchal values while containing woman as the object of male anxieties. The Sotah narrative invites a departure from traditional interpretations, which figure the woman as social and material reproducer of children.

The challenge here is to stir up a new brew, where men's attempts to control women's bodies are reread as male vulnerability—the fear of woman engorging male power through her enveloping sexuality. The mysterious water that the woman is forced to drink is contained within a vessel handed to her by the priest. This ritual vessel is metonymic for the womb containing semen, for a sexually pure wife guarantees her husband a womb vessel filled solely with his seed. This ritual is necessary because the purity of the womb vessel is in doubt. Similarly, on a literary level, readings have been contained within institutional "vessels," or canons, immobilizing feminist readers as surely as the liquid in the Sotah vessel maintains the wife under the husband's control.

Encamped outside traditional textual borderlines, I have escaped the boundaries of Num. 5.11–31 and its mishnaic expansion, Tractate Sotah, into modern commentaries, creating a narrative of Sotah, a text that permits a husband to accuse his wife of adultery, without having the two witnesses traditional in Israelite law in cases of capital crimes. My text presents additional characters: ancient sages, who made no pretense of covering up their desire to inflict pain upon errant women, assuming the guilt of the woman brought before the priest, and recent interpreters of the ritual, who share an agenda of normalizing the text. My Sotah text reflects a Derridean concern with the relation between texts once their borders have been blurred. A borderline perspective allows the reader to pose questions that historical investigations have not asked about the impact of these texts upon a woman reader.[4]

To blur borders further, to demonstrate how one part of a text may be relevant to others, I have added con-texts of biblical sexual politics: Genesis 39, a narrative in which a woman attempts to initiate sexual activity with the male hero; Proverbs 5 and 7, texts of warning in which an ʾishshah zarah stands poised to seduce the male reader; and Deut. 22.13–30, in which laws governing sexual activity reflect male attempts to control female sexuality. To these con-texts of women's improper behavior, the Sotah ritual stands as an antidote.

Feminist biblical scholars in the past two decades have used literary strategies of reading to point out that women are defined in relation to their family roles: they are daughters, wives, and mothers.[5] Although literary feminists studying the ancient world have struggled with the difficulties of reading male-authored texts, which do not provide access to women's inner thoughts, or tell us much about their daily lives, most of the readings have not attempted to break out of the institutional containers, which view biblical texts as discrete measured works without a context.[6] By stressing the borderless nature of texts, I hope to dissolve barriers that have prevented readings that extend beyond the verses of a biblical passage. In spite of my desire to dissolve borders, I do not claim to recover women's lived reality in my reading. While the account of the Sotah may not add material details about women's lives in ancient Israel, I think it reveals a lot about what women had to put up with. Political theorist Susan Okin provides a set of questions that are tied to such a concern. Her sharp distinction in looking at the ways men and women have habitually been defined by social and political philosophers will be useful in my analysis of the Sotah narrative. She writes: "Philosophers who, in laying the foundation for their political theories, have asked, '*What are men like?* What is man's potential?' have frequently in turning to the female sex, asked '*What are women for?*'" (Okin 1979: 10, italics mine).

The problem of how a reader survives the ritual of Sotah, when she cannot swallow the implicit threats to women stirred up in the ritual, can be solved by posing Okin's political question, *What are men like?*, as a psychoanalytic one. This strategy is particularly well suited to biblical texts, since they are male-authored, and thus contain the symptomatic utterances of the author/narrator. From a psychoanalytic perspective, the text operates as a pair of male doubles: the male narrator and the ideal reader, who is also male. Thus, while the woman is the object of the text of Numbers 5, she is excluded from the male dialogue. The reader is allied with the male author/narrator by ignoring the sexual desire of the female character and by joining the author in a critique of her sexual behavior. As I found in my reading of modern interpreters, the gender of the reader does not determine the reading. Frymer-Kensky, for example, like her male counterparts, is not concerned with forming an alliance with the female character in the text. Trying to imagine a female reader contending with male subjectivity, a critic reading with a feminist-psychoanalytic strategy can subvert a text's desire so as to hear what it does not wish to say. "Son and father agree to write the mother out of the text, for to desire her is not to have the phallus. They conspire both to rid the text of her and to entrap her in it; she is immured" (Segal: 169). Reading the text against its demand, however, *reading as a woman*, allows the subversion of male doubling and allows the figured woman in the text to communicate with a feminist reader. Reading through the sexual codes, a feminist reader charts the literary coercion traditional institutions have used to define the female as other.

Sotah with a Twist

The Sotah is unique in biblical law: it is the only trial by ordeal; it is the only occasion on which a person can be accused of a capital crime without two witnesses. The half-disrobed woman with disheveled hair, appearing as though she has been caught in an intimate act, is not even permitted to utter the self-incriminatory oath: the ritual oath is put in the mouth of the priest. Only the potion is put in the mouth of the woman. She is forced to swallow what she knows. In my view, then, the Sotah is a unique vehicle for envisioning what is denied, repressed, and silenced in ancient Israelite culture.

The Sotah is not unique in making a woman's fate be determined by men. It is not unique among biblical descriptions of ritual in its textual ambiguities that make it difficult to determine what actually occurred. Interpretations of the Sotah are not unique in having focused upon elements of historicity in the text: Is the ritual indeed a trial by ordeal? What are the components of the drink? What occurs physiologically to the woman after swallowing the brew? Does she die? Does she become sterile? Is the Sotah a divine forerunner of RU 486, a chemically induced abortion? Num. 5.11–31 is not the only text that interpreters have failed to read as a political text expressing the fears of its male authors toward woman and their colonization of the female body. Symbolically, the woman becomes the currency of the exchange between males. This transaction bears similarities to the Deuteronomic laws concerning undesirable sexual acts. Under the dictates of a phallic economy the father or husband can demand reparation for the damaging of the woman's body. Female sexuality uncontained deflates the phallic economy in which all gains accrue to the master (Benstock 1991: 95).

In the ancient Near East, whose cultures demonstrated a flourishing phallic economy, a man could buy his way out of an adulterous situation by compensating the husband and accepting a discounted wife. Unlike its neighbors, Israel had no provision for a husband to mitigate the death penalty for a wife and her partner convicted of adultery.[7] The fact that the crime of adultery was incorporated into the Sinaitic covenant guaranteed its fateful consequences. "Unless it [adultery] was punished with death," Milgrom argues, "God would destroy the malefactors and indeed the entire community that had allowed it to go unpunished" (1990: 349).

But what if the duplicitous wife is not caught?

Because the concern with ensuring paternity was so strong in Israel, a ritual was devised to further protect the husband from the possibility of a "wandering wife," and its attendant loss of prestige. The Sotah ritual described in Num. 5.11–31 is constructed around suspicion of adultery, rather than proof of the crime in which two witnesses were required in order to pass sentence of death. The horror of trial by ordeal applied to the woman accused indicates the social view of adultery. Further, it reflects the patriarchal attempt to assure a husband that his honor could be restored if he had so much as a suspicion that his wife had been fooling around. Female erotic desire, then, was understood as erratic, a threat to the social order. By drowning such desire, the traditional order was assured of continuing dominance over women's bodies.

Fateful In/fidelities

As I have stated, the ordeal of Sotah described in Num. 5.11–31 is unique in the Bible, but there are other biblical texts that reflect male anxiety about female sexuality. Genesis 39 evinces the dangers of rampant female sexuality, and, in Proverbs 5 and 7, the ʾishshah zarah is the paradigm for the woman who uses her sexuality to ensnare men. I shall use these two texts as examples of male-authored warnings about women's sexuality, warnings that are textual defenses of the trial by ordeal. Both the Egyptian woman and the ʾishshah zarah are examples of woman's sexuality out of control. The Sotah stands as an antidote.

Numbers 5.3 permits a suspicious husband to accuse his wife of adultery without fear of punishment. The figure of the lascivious wife in Genesis 39 supports a husband's suspicion of adultery. Potiphar is told by his wife that his servant has attempted to rape her. A measure of uncertainty salted with suspicion must exist in Potiphar's mind, since he throws Joseph into prison rather than ordering him killed. Both the Sotah and Genesis 39 indicate the presence of a smoking gun, but no body. In each case suspicion of women's sexual impurity results in loss of honor for the husband. Since the sexual activity described by the wife of Potiphar has not been witnessed by any other character—in other words, she has not been caught *in flagrante delicto*—her situation bears certain similarities to that of the woman accused in Numbers 5. Genesis 39, however, presents witnesses who have heard about the sexual invitation and its rejection. Joseph knows a story different from the one told by his mistress; he remains silent. The narrator and reader know that no sexual crime has been committed. Thus they convict the woman for letting her sexual desire flame out of control. If, however, the reader chooses to place the woman in the subject position, and to question the anxiety of the male narrator and of the character Joseph, she can produce a reading that transforms the female character from the mute figure silenced under the terms of phallocentric discourse. This act of reading is what French feminists have termed "producing an alternative female imaginary" (Irigaray: 197). As I have argued elsewhere, reading to recover the suppressed story of the wife of Potiphar can result in a story of fatal attraction, female obsession with the male love object (1993).

In Numbers 5, like Genesis 39, no crime at all need be committed. The vivid images in the husband's imagination are all that is necessary to bring his wife to the tabernacle to drink the bitter water. On the basis of suspicion of her activities, the Israelite husband could bring his wife before the priest, who would administer the *me hammarim*, "bitter water,"[8] to determine her guilt or innocence. As in rituals of this sort, the punishment was incorporated within the act (or ordeal) itself. An innocent woman survived drinking the potion; a guilty one suffered some sort of punishment related to her sexuality. Interpretations of exactly what the woman's punishment was have varied widely from the time of the Tannaim to the present day.

In Genesis 39 the wife's sexual fantasy condemns her to narrative humiliation; in Numbers 5 the husband's sexual fantasy condemns his wife to drink the bitter water and be publicly humiliated. Even if the woman is found to be innocent and survives the ordeal (both the biblical text and its expansions emphasize the possibility of the woman's guilt, as I argue below), she has been shamed in front of the community. The priest, the male mediator figure representing her husband's rights, unbinds her hair, an act that evokes a picture of female sexuality unbound: the loosed hair of the loose woman. Holding her husband's jealousy offering in her hands, the woman stands submissively while the priest acts as her mouthpiece, reciting her self-condemning oath. Having been revealed in the presence of the community, even an innocent wife will have difficulty regaining status and respect, since the husband's suspicion has been transmitted to the community. Verse 31 attempts to stabilize the husband's position. He is exonerated regardless of her guilt or innocence. The very ambiguity of the wife's position—did she or didn't she?—separates her from the usual position of the wife-woman, who receives her social identity from her husband.

The husband free from blame differs from the case of the newly married man who falsely accuses his bride of sexual impurity.[9] Deuteronomic law states that if the father can present proof of his daughter's virginity, the husband receives a dual punishment: he must pay reparations to her father (100 shekels of silver) and he may not divorce his wife, who has been slandered/degraded (Deut. 22.19). If, however, the father cannot produce the evidence to clear his daughter, she is assumed to be impure and is stoned to death in front of her father's door. The execution carried out at the father's door provides a vital clue to the integral connection in both cases between the father and the husband: if the girl is guilty, the father has either knowingly or not offered for sale to the husband damaged goods. In the case of the girl's innocence, the husband must pay damages to the father, whose good name has been damaged. Thus the law reflects the men as subjects of the concern and the woman as the object of male ownership.

Only another man can verify the husband's accusation. In the Sotah ritual, the priest functions as intermediary, acting on the husband's suspicion. According to traditional interpretations, the father God enters the bitter waters to determine the woman's guilt or innocence. The physical evidence confirming her innocence is a clean functional womb revealed to the community of witnesses after the deity's "inspection." In the Deuteronomic law, the father produces the bloody evidence of his daughter's sexual purity, again assuring a clean functional womb. As in the case of the Sotah, the woman's version of her own story is not considered. Thus, even when a husband can be punished for falsely accusing his wife of sexual impurity (Deut. 22.19), she is not to be believed. The law reflects the concerns of the phallic economy: it protects her father if she is innocent; it protects her husband if she is guilty.

The textual emphasis on the woman's secrecy in Num. 5.13 undergirds the author's concern with the difficulty of discerning female sexual purity. Four times within the indictment, the "fact" of the woman's secrecy is repeated: "without the knowledge of her husband," "she keeps secret," "without being forced," "and there was no witness against her" (v. 13). Like a too-rapid heartbeat, the repetition is a telling clue about the power of male fears and fantasies about women's secrets. It is not surprising that the patriarchal society has fashioned a law that protects men's suspicion of women and their dark secrets.

Tractate *Sotah* in the Mishnah elaborates the biblical case law in Num. 5.11–31. The sages describe even more pain and suffering in store for the bad wife. It is worth looking in some detail both at the passage in Numbers and at the Mishnah's interpretation of it in order to understand the fierce reaction in biblical as well as postbiblical Israel to the act of adultery as a crime both against the husband and against the larger community. According to Jewish law, a wife faced a punishment of death if she willingly had sexual relations (*wayyitten ʾish bak ʾet-shekobto*, Num. 5.20) with a man other than her husband (*shakab ʾotak*, Num. 5.19; *shikbah ʾimmi* is the invitation of the wife of Potiphar to Joseph in Gen. 39.7). If there is no witness to the act ("none of the men of the house was in the house," Gen. 39.11), it is assumed the woman was not taken by force, but was a willing participant. Deut. 22.23 states that a woman who is taken in the city and does not cry out for help is equally guilty with the man who lay with her (*shakab ʾimmah*). Hittite law even more sharply defines the woman's culpability: "[I]f [a man] seizes her in (her) house, it is the woman's crime and the woman shall be killed" (§197; *ANET*, 196). Clearly there was an ancient connection between the territory of the woman (inside her house or the city) and her ability to control any situation occurring within "her" borders. If, however, the act occurs in the countryside, the Deuteronomic lawgivers understood the crime differently. Away from the structured life of the town, the woman's (assumed) screams would not have been heard. She is exonerated, but the man is put to death, his crime equated with the act of someone who attacks and murders his neighbor (Deut. 22.27). One can infer from this crime against a woman's sexual purity, a capital crime, as is murder, that a sexually ravaged woman had no more future than a dead woman. Thus, a woman who participated voluntarily in her own defilement (allowing another man access to her husband's private place) would invoke the same death penalty: the swallowing of the bitter Sotah.

After the husband has accused his wife of adultery, he is enjoined to bring her to the priest for the trial by ordeal, after bringing to the tabernacle a cereal offering for his own "jealousy." Later sages indicate that the *torat sotah* is in effect even if the lover or the husband is a castrate. Thus, even if her unfaithfulness could not have resulted in progeny and even if the husband could not have been concerned about the paternity of his subsequent children, she would still be required to drink.[10] For some of the rabbis, then, the protection of paternity becomes secondary to the protection of male honor and integrity of the household. This reading of *torat sotah* would indicate the male desire to compensate a castrated husband by assuring him the same rights in respect to his wife as a potent man. Its inclusion in *Sidrah Naso* implies that no man may threaten the position of the husband, even a man without procreative organs. What a vivid illustration of the woman as mode of exchange in the phallic economy!

The root *sth* is used in Numbers 5 to describe the activity of the adulterous woman as a "turning aside" from the marriage path. In three of the four examples (vv. 19, 20, 29) the verb is used in connection with the wife "turning aside from under her husband's control"; extramarital sexual relations for a wife are understood as her breaking out of her proper place (*tahat ʾishek* "underneath your husband," *ʾishah*, "her husband," in v. 29). Some standard translations do not acknowledge the vivid verbal portrait of sexual activity that is suggested by the Hebrew: RSV reads "under your husband's authority"; JPS reads "while married to your husband." Neither allows for a possible sexual allusion.

In addition to its use in Numbers 5, the root *sth* is found in only one other biblical book, Proverbs, where the young man is warned to "turn aside" from the way of evil men (4.15) and not to allow his heart "to turn aside to the path" of the seductive woman (7.25) since her house is the way to Sheol, going down to the house of death (7.27).[11] Indeed, the victim is compared with an ox headed for the slaughterhouse, a deer bounding toward a noose, a bird winging into a snare (7.22–23). Extending the text's animal metaphors produces a reading in which the young man with the eager innocence of an animal rushes exuberantly toward a predetermined death. Female sexuality is a trap baited by a predatory female hunter. If the youthful male reader of Proverbs stumbles on the paths of wicked men (*reshaʾim*), there is no indication that he will end up in the dire shape predicted if he sets his foot on the path of the *ʾishshah zarah*. The connection of turning aside (*sth*) for sexual purposes with punishment occurs only in the instance of misreading the scented trap of the *ʾishshah zarah*.

In spite of the conventional interpretation in English of *ʾishshah zarah* as a foreign woman, the Hebrew word *zarah*, meaning "strange," does not necessarily equate such "foreignness" with ethnicity. The word can imply otherness, as reflected in the woman who is depicted by the RSV as a "loose woman" or "adventuress." Her otherness is understood in contradistinction to the good woman, *ʾeshet hayil*, who is not described in terms of her sexuality. Thus, *ʾishshah zarah* is foreign to goodness, to wisdom. Scholars continue to dispute whether she is actually a foreigner or, as I suspect, a woman whose explicit sexuality made her a social outcast and therefore an outsider.[12] In each case, nevertheless, the turning aside is clearly on to the path of illicit sexual relations since the verbal root is *sth* rather than *swr*. The far more common root meaning "turn aside," *swr,* is not always understood in an explicitly sexual manner even when used in connection with women, e.g., by the author of Proverbs of the beautiful woman "turning aside (*sarat*) from the paths of discretion" (11.22). One assumes that these are improper paths, but the text does not indicate that they are necessarily sexual ones.

In the Proverbs account, the *ʾishshah zarah* is firmly rooted on the evil path, indeed her house leads to Sheol. There is no warning for a female reader not to stray into these paths; rather the warning is presented to her potential male victim. It is the vulnerable young male, a nameless parallel to the chaste hero Joseph, who must be warned against "turning aside," or turning *toward* the *ʾishshah zarah,* a parallel to the character of the Egyptian wife. The roles of the two women in Proverbs, the *ʾeshet hayil* and the *ʾishshah zarah,* are fixed; the author of Proverbs expects no textual engagement between a wife-woman and her sexual twin. He is not concerned with exploring possible shadings in either woman's character. Nor is he worried about stones in the paths of young women, causing them to stumble. It is male readers (the sons) to whom the author (the father) addresses his collection of maxims and warnings. Once again the woman is the object of male anxiety: subduing her sexuality is the key to his safety.

In the prohibition in Numbers 5, God instructs Moses (v. 11) to present the case of a woman who is suspected of wandering (*tisteh,* v. 12) from the authority of her husband. Thus the crime and its ritual punishment are seen to be devised by the deity, not by the community. If there is a warning to the woman, it is in the description of her startling punishment: "when the LORD makes your thigh fall away and your body swell" (RSV). The Hebrew text is more vivid than the English translation: literally, "when God causes your thigh (*yarek*) to droop and your womb (*bitnek*) to swell" (v. 21). These terms are suggestive of the sexual act. The word *yarek* is a commonly understood euphemism for sexual organs (e.g. Gen. 24.2, 9; 46.26; 47.29; Exod. 1.5; Judg. 8.30). In these other biblical usages, the word refers to the male "seat of procreative power," according to BDB, although in Num. 5.21, 22, 27, BDB considers *yrk* as parallel to *btn*. The word *beten* is often understood to refer to the womb (e.g. Gen. 25.23, 24; 38.27; Hos. 12.4; Job 10.19; 31.15; Qoh. 11.5; Ps. 139.13). The parallelism (*yarek // beten*) in vv. 21, 22, 27 suggests strongly that *yrk* does not mean "thigh" but "reproductive organs" (as against BDB) and thus emphasizes the wife's role as bearer of the husband's legitimate heirs. It is her place of procreation (*yarek // beten*) that has been violated, and thus will be deformed or destroyed by the priestly potion, a magical brew of holy water and the dust from the floor of the tabernacle (v. 17). If these terms tell us what women are for, they also make it clear what women are not for. The male fantasy imagines the woman as possessing the *yarek,* the seat of procreative power, and thus threatening to "reverse the body symbolism on which the father's authority is established" (Newsom: 153). A similar version of this pervasive fantasy occurs in the Proverbs description of the *ʾishshah zarah* as "sharp as a two-edged sword" (5.4).

Unbinding the woman's hair, and placing the husband's jealousy offering (*minhat qenaʾot,* v. 15)[13] into her hands, the priest functions as proxy of the offended male, the husband, and of the deity whom the woman's sexuality has taunted. Yet, as the male unbinding another man's woman, he is also the mirror of the lover, touching the forbidden woman. The *minhat qena'ot* held in the wife's hands symbolizes her potential danger, as the one holding and possibly controlling his sexuality. It can also echo the secret lover, whom she held instead of her husband, the sex that resulted in jealousy. Then the priest pronounces the terms of the trial by ordeal, the no-win situation for the woman. In my opinion a strong subtexual suggestion of sexual language exists in the Hebrew text. I provide below an interpretation that intentionally teases out these nuances.

> If no man has *profaned your body,*
> if you have not *turned aside to uncleanness*
> while *you should have remained underneath your husband,*
> be free from this *bitter water that brings forth the agony.* (v.19)

> But if *you have turned toward your lover,*
> though under your husband's power,
> if *some man other than your husband*
> *has placed his seed inside your house,*
> *then let the water that brings this curse*
> *pass into your bowels*
> *and make your womb swell*
> *and your thigh fall open.* (vv. 20, 22)

The most remarkable aspect of the priest's speech, as I have interpreted it, is the extent of "guilty" language, shown here in italics. The emphasis is placed on the woman's sexual acts and the agony that results from her turning aside from her husband. If she is innocent, none of these wrenching pains will occur. But as they are all detailed, her possible purity is drowned, or at least diluted, by the volume of curse that issues from the priest's mouth. Thus, the stream of language acts to accuse and punish as much as the priestly potion streaming into the woman. If the woman is innocent, the water will pass through her, and she will continue to function as a wife, to produce her husband's children (v. 28).[14] A sympathetic interpretation states that if the husband is innocent, the wife will be tested by the bitter water; if the husband has accused his wife wrongly, the wife will not be harmed (Phillips 1981). By picturing so vividly the woman having had sex with a man other than her husband, the text makes it difficult to remember that she might be innocent and not have to undergo the punishment that is described in such detail. By having these words pronounced about her, the woman is verbally punished even if the bitter water does not punish her physically. There is no incantation mentioned that will give equal time to her innocence. A reading that assigns guilt to the husband's accusation would switch the focus of the text from his fears, simultaneously switching power to the wife. The dominance of the husband over his wife is reflected, then, in the text's emphasis on her guilt. The husband's honor is further restored by his dominance over the shadow of the unknown lover, whose intimacy with the wife has been both recalled and repudiated by the priest. If the woman has committed the acts of which she has been accused, then YHWH's judgment shall transform the water:

> the water that causes the agony shall stream into [enter] her
> and shall cause her bitter pain
> and her belly/womb shall swell
> and her thigh/womb shall sag. (v. 27)

Instead of her lover's semen entering her, it is the water of judgment that streams into the woman. The poison will cause her belly/womb to swell with pain and in torment her sexual organs will collapse.[15] A most arresting allusion to the sexual act gone wrong. The string of verbs in vv. 20–21—*'et-yerekek nophelet ve'et-bitnek tsavah*, "your thigh/sexual organs shall *sag/fall away* and your womb *swell/distend*"—echoed in v. 27, focuses attention upon the sexual act. Thus, a connection is made between the husband's loss of prestige through his wife's adulterous act and the loss of erection. The wife's sagging (and therefore empty) womb becomes a symbol of measure for measure punishment meted out for the husband's loss of prestige. Through the punishment that drains her of sexuality and power, he regains his authority.

What Are Men Like?

Many rabbinic sages assume that the result of the woman's drinking the bitter water is death. *Bemidbar Rabbah* records an *aggadah* (Naso 9) that illustrates the magical or divine nature of the bitter water, which can discern the difference between a good woman and an evil one. Two married sisters look very much alike but live in different towns. The one who lives in Jerusalem is "clean." The other is "defiled," and goes to her good sister and pleads with her to take her place in the ritual of the bitter water. The good sister agrees, drinks the water, and is unharmed. Returning home, her sister, who has played the harlot, comes out to embrace her. As they kiss, "the harlot smelled the bitter water and instantly died." While the story supports the view that a clean woman will be untouched by the water, as she has been untouched by a man other than her husband, it also makes clear that death caused by the bitter water is the just punishment for an adulterous woman.

There are no recorded cases of the administration of the *torat sotah*, although the *aggadah* quoted above gives the rabbinic view of unavoidable death to the guilty woman—even if she has not actually swallowed the potion. Proximity to the judgmental drink is sufficient to cause punishment. There are no *aggadoth* that record a happy ending for the innocent woman. Jewish tradition maintains that Rabbi Johanan ben Zakkai, shortly after the destruction of the Second Temple, abolished the ordeal, because he felt that divorce was sufficient to separate the husband from his possibly adulterous wife (*m. Soṭah* 9.9). The Tosefta (*Soṭah* 14.2) offers a less romantic explanation. "The ritual of bitter waters is performed only in cases of suspected [unprovable, without witnesses] adultery, but now there are many who fornicate in public (with witnesses)." In any case, the fact that the sages may have rejected the ordeal *in principle*, Romney-Wegner observes, does not allow us to assume that "it constitutes a rejection of the double standard that assigned women far less sexual freedom than men" (Romney-Wegner 1988: 54).

In the Mishnah's elaboration of the law of the *sotah*, the sages separate the wife's sexuality into two parts. "By paying bride-price the husband acquired both the sole right to intercourse with her and (still more important to the sages) the sole right to utilize her reproductive function" (Romney-Wegner 1988: 52–53). This second aspect of the husband's property rights is emphasized in the Mishnah tractate *Soṭah*, chs. 1–6: A wife who is sterile, past menopause, or for any other reason unable to bear children, does not have to drink the priestly potion. But if the husband divorces such a wife on his suspicion of her sexual impurity, Rabbi Meir says she does not receive her *kethubah*, "marriage settlement." Rabbi Eliezer, who clearly knows what women are for, adds that the husband is justified in marrying another woman and having children with her (*Soṭah* 4.3). Thus, even being suspected of sexual impropriety has its price.

If the wife is unable to bear children, the threat to the husband is more symbolic than real. A Talmudic passage links the Soṭah with the instance of Maacah, the mother of Asa the king, who is punished with the loss of her status as queen because she has made an "abominable image." Rabbi Judah defines *miphlezeth,* the "abominable image," as an object which "intensifies licentiousness (*maphli lezanutha*), as R. Joseph taught: It was a kind of phallus with which she had daily contact" (*Avodah Zara* 44a). Touching the phallus, like touching the golden calf, puts the woman in contact with the locus of male power. While Queen Maacah's crime involved holding a symbolic phallus, anxiety was also raised at the possibility of the woman touching a penis. Deuteronomy presents the case of a woman whose husband is wrangling with an opponent in the marketplace; the wife goes to his aid. In trying to defend her husband, she touches the crotch of the other man, an offense that shames her husband, but, more alarming, brings her into contact with the male organ. A woman seizing a man's genitals will have her hand cut off (Deut. 25.12).

The sages linger over the image of the adulterous woman, the woman who has enticed the wrong man:

> If she were clothed in white garments, he [the priest] covered her in black ones. If she had upon her ornaments of gold, necklaces, earrings, and rings on her fingers, they take them from her in order to disgrace her; and after that he brings an Egyptian rope[16] and ties it above her breasts. Everyone who wants to behold her comes to gaze at her. (*m. Soṭah* 1.6)

After undressing her in the text, the ancient rabbis embellish the violent destruction of the woman alluded to in the biblical account:

> Hardly has she finished drinking before her face turns yellow and her eyes bulge and her veins swell, and they say, "Take her away! take her away! that the Temple Court be not made unclean." (*m. Soṭah* 1.7)

A later rabbinic description is even more graphic:

> She painted her eyes for his sake, and so her eyes bulge. She braided her hair for his sake, and so the priest dishevels her hair. She beckoned to him with her fingers and so her fingernails fall off. She put on a fine girdle for his sake, and so the priest brings a common rope and ties it above her breasts. She extended her thigh to him and therefore her thigh falls away. She received him upon her womb, and therefore her belly swells. She fed him with the finest dainties; her offering is therefore the food of cattle. She gave him to drink choice wine in elegant flagons, therefore the priest gives her to drink the water of bitterness in a piece of earthenware. (*Bemidbar Rabbah* 9.24)

In the rabbinic view, the punishment is not extraordinary. The principle of measure for measure that opens *Soṭah 7, bammidah sh'adam 'oded bah moddin,* states that the punishment fits the crime: since she "adorned herself for transgression," God undressed her:

with her thigh (*hayarek*) did she first transgress,
and then with the belly (*beten*),
therefore shall the thigh be stricken first

and then the belly
and the rest of the body shall not escape. (*m. Soṭah* 1.7)

The sages then provide other examples of measure for measure: Samson, who looked at women with lust in his eyes, has his eyes gouged out by Philistines; Absalom was vain about his hair so he was suspended by his glorious hair. Absalom (again) had copulated with the ten secondary wives (*pilagshim*) of his father; thus, ten javelins are thrust into him. Clearly there is intentional sexual imagery in these biblical examples cited as parallels to the ritual of the *Soṭah*. For the ancient rabbis, measure for measure acted as a control against sexual transgressions, by men or women. An adulterous person lost whatever merit she or he may have achieved throughout the rest of their life. Rabbi Judah haNasi ruled that merit held in suspense the immediate effects of the bitter water, but the "woman would not bear children or continue in comeliness, but *she will waste away by degrees and in the end will die the self-same death*" (*Soṭah* 3.5). Thus, ancient readers probably believed that if a woman drank the ritual water she would not survive.

The Glass Half Empty

Modern interpreters seem intent on mopping up the bitter waters and downplaying their deleterious effects on the suspected wife. In doing so, however, they do not recognize their own interest in normalizing the Sotah as a Jewish ritual. Their cool medical explanations of a prolapsed uterus or false pregnancy stand in stark contrast to the hot fantasies of the ancients. One reading suggests that among the horrible physical effects that take place upon drinking the bitter water for the adulterous wife who has conceived through that union, the fetus will be aborted. If, on the other hand, the woman is innocent and has conceived with her husband, she will "retain the seed" (v. 28) and bear her husband's child (Romney-Wegner 1988: 52).

After referring to Numbers 5 as "a harrowing ordeal" (55), Brichto argues that the dangers in trial by ordeal are physical, and "the danger in the potion is hypothetical—and at that, explicitly nonexistent if the woman is innocent" (56). Frymer-Kensky rejects the category of trial by ordeal as "unwarranted and misleading." She prefers to consider the Sotah as an example of the classic purgatory oath. Milgrom wavers, claiming that the genius of the Sotah ritual is that it removes the ability to punish from human hands and gives it into the divine realm, which would indicate trial by ordeal. In his Numbers commentary, he refers to the ritual as "the ordeal." Nonetheless, because Milgrom does not understand the resulting punishment of the woman as death, but merely sterility, he views the ritual of Sotah as lacking the critical element of a classic trial by ordeal: death of the guilty person. In contrast, Fishbane assumes its status as trial by ordeal. He offers a form-critical analysis of similarities between the "draught-ordeal" ritual described in Numbers 5 and the Babylonian parallel of a case of suspected adultery in *Code of Hammurabi* 131–32. What all these analyses overlook is that the ritual of Sotah is initiated by the husband's suspicion of his wife's adulterous activity. The biblical text echoes the fear of female secrecy four times in one verse: "it is hidden from the eyes of her husband, she is undetected, since she was not caught, and there is no witness against her" (v. 13). This fear of what another man might be doing inside his wife's house (or body) results in a protection of that house by the husband through the ritual of Sotah.

These historical critics are concerned with the extent of the woman's physical punishment—is it miscarriage, sterility, or death?—and whether the trial was actually carried out. What I find of central interest in Numbers 5 is not its degree of historicity, but rather what its existence tells us about men's fear of women's sexuality. As I have shown, concern with sexual politics allows the reader to see what is at stake in patriarchal guarding and regarding the female body. The existence of the Sotah within the biblical corpus functions as a means of social control over wives who might ignite their husband's anger. The ritual shames her, even if she is found innocent. Accepting the text's construction of a situation in which the husband and community must be able to determine a woman's sexual purity, the contemporary scholars under review here have produced a unified picture of woman as threat to her husband's status. Remaining within the framework of belief that accepts suspicions about women's sexual lives, their techniques do not disrupt the fixed binary oppositions that categorize sexuality and gender.

Milgrom argues that the trial actually protects the woman from the "lynch-mob mentality" of the angered community (1990: 348–50). Because the ritual has been assigned to the priest, and thus, the opportunity of dealing with the errant wife has been removed from the hysterical mob, an innocent woman would be protected from the wrath of her accusers. Brichto goes even further in transmuting the ordeal into a balm by asserting that the Sotah protects "the woman as wife in the disadvantaged position determined for her by the mores of ancient Israel's society." While the argument may seem attractive to those concerned with preserving the woman's life, it does not seem to have been one professed by ancient interpreters. Each time they refer to the woman put to the ordeal of bitter waters, they describe calamitous physical results. While they linger textually over the destruction of the guilty woman's body, they create no such parallel about the preservation of the innocent woman's body. While the interpreter as observer can gaze at a guilty woman's body, it would be a crime against the husband to gaze at an innocent wife's body. Describing her physically would be equivalent to undressing her. The guilty woman has already been observed in her nakedness, her husband already shamed.

That one could in theory assume an ordeal that at the least causes sterility as a way of protecting the woman is difficult to support. A sterile woman in a culture in which women function as childbearers does not have a salutary future. Protection seems to be constructed for the husband, who, even upon his narrowest suspicion of his wife's infidelity, can force her to submit to this ordeal. The text even provides for the safety of the suspicious husband in the event that the wife is proved innocent. He is completely exonerated even if his suspicions are proved false (v. 31).

Fishbane has delineated a complex and elegant inner-biblical exegesis that connects the prophetic use of the unfaithful wife motif (as illustrated by Hos. 1–2; Isa. 50.1; 51.17–23; 57.3–14; Ezek. 16; 23) as a metaphor for Israel's infidelity to YHWH with the divine judgment exercised in the ordeal in Numbers 5 (Fishbane 1974: 40–45). Certainly connecting the motif of an adulterous woman's betraying her husband with the people Israel's betrayal of YHWH is a striking example of the vitality of midrashic technique at work. What is troublesome is that Fishbane, like the early midrashists, assumes the guilt of the woman in Numbers 5. Reading with the ideology of the text, he raises no suspicions about the possible motives of the accuser.

In overlooking the indeterminate nature of the crime as presented in the Sotah,

Fishbane produces a new text, one in which the woman is known to be guilty of the crime. In the prophetic view, Israel's harlotry is overt; the people have been plainly worshiping other gods. It would seem that the legal texts upon which the prophets are playing would be those that refer to such a *witnessed* offense of adultery (Exod. 20.14; Lev. 20.10; Deut. 22.22), not to the *suspected* adultery in Numbers 5.

A narrative text that contains motifs of both the trial by ordeal ritual and of Israel as harlot is Exod. 32.19–20, where Moses (acting as priest) makes a potion from the golden calf that the people of Israel are required to drink. While this text has been connected since Talmudic times with the Sotah ritual (*Avodah Zarah* 44a), there are two noteworthy differences. In the Exodus text, after drinking, all the guilty people of Israel are struck down by a divine plague. Their communal act is met with communal punishment, whereas the Sotah sets the isolated woman apart from the community. Most important, Moses has seen their act of infidelity. "When he approached the camp and saw the calf and the dancing, Moses' anger burned hot . . ." (v. 19). The priest in the Numbers ritual, on the other hand, has no proof of the woman's guilt at the time he makes her swallow the drink. Moses plays the role of the priest mixing up the deadly brew, although his actions at the outskirts of the camp appear to be impulsive, stemming from his fury at the people's disloyalty to YHWH. He is not carrying out part of a formal ritual. In the Exodus text YHWH claims the dual role of shamed husband and divine vindicator. Both biblical recipes contain divine ingredients. Moses's brew contains the powdered remains of other gods, and the Sotah is made viable by the presence of YHWH.

The "when" and "how long" of the ritual and its resultant punishment concerns Frymer-Kensky. She envisions the woman going home "to await the results at some future time" (1984: 22), yet the text does not imply any passage of time from the point of swallowing the potion to its devastating effect. While Frymer-Kensky's reading provides the woman an element of privacy—the woman would suffer her punishment at home—such a thoughtful emphasis on privacy directly counters the publicness of the ritual undergone upon the altar of the tabernacle. As I understand the measure-for-measure principle upon which this text is based, at best the woman would be rendered sexually dysfunctional for her sexual philandering. A parallel element requires a public punishment for a public sexual display. Since the wife did not remain at home alone, she will be publicly punished. Since the wrong man saw her body, everyone will see her sexually humiliated.

Brichto and Milgrom consider the effect of the bitter water upon the guilty woman to be more sinister, and more permanent, than abortion: sterilization. While I am more persuaded by an interpretation that embraces long-term effects than by one that supposes spontaneous abortion, I am skeptical that a husband would deprive himself of a fecund wife on the basis of his suspicions. In its favor, a barren or menopausal wife was exempt from the ordeal—which leads one to conclude that the potion had to affect the woman's ability to bear children. In this light Milgrom's "cleansing of the womb" theory, which would return to the husband a wife able to conceive, has merit. The ordeal shares with many ancient laws involving women the overriding concern with protecting paternity, assuring the husband that any child born to his wife is his.

Another element of the readings of these scholars (Fishbane, Brichto, Frymer-Kensky, Milgrom) that I find curious is that none of them is struck by the fact that the woman is condemned to undergo the ordeal on the basis of her husband's suspicion, not on proof. And that if the woman was proved guilty, as reflected by some womb-shaking punishment, they do not imagine that death would be the result. Cases of "proved" adultery were treated as capital crimes; it would seem that the swollen womb and sagging thigh would be all the evidence one would need that the woman was guilty. Indeed the proof would be of divine origin, since the magical (or divine) nature of the potion is that once inside the woman it discerns the purity or defilement of her body.

Milgrom argues that God has taken the punishment out of the hands of the outraged community, and thus the husband and community are forbidden to cause the death of the woman. YHWH has punished her through sterilization (1990: 349). If one accepts Milgrom's softer interpretation, the punishment remains in patriarchal hands: the deity avenges the crime against the husband. The woman is deprived of speech and action. *What is the woman for* in Milgrom's interpretation? She is the vessel through which the male-concocted brew flows. If she is a proper vessel, the liquid fills her like semen. She will bear the children of her husband. If she is an improper vessel, the liquid redefines her. She will no longer bear children.

Each of these modern interpretations remains within the borders of the biblical ritual. While the analyses describe or reflect the husband's existing suspicion of his wife, they all serve to augment the sense of suspicion about women that is produced by the biblical text. The concentration on suspicion of the woman also leaves unexamined the biblical constraint upon a wife not to behave in a suspicious manner, not to arouse her husband's anxieties. What I find missing in the recent analyses is any acknowledgment of the consequence to the woman of shaking up the sexual/gender system. At the same time there is no attempt to challenge, or even comment upon, the institutional structure of patriarchy that used the ritual of Sotah to put a woman in her place.

The Glass Half Full

From the sampling of midrashic texts imagining the fate of the wandering wife, it seems clear that the ancient rabbis were not embarrassed about creating violent sexual images of punishment for the wife who might have double-crossed her husband. In their attempt to limit the negative impact of the Sotah text, modern interpreters generally ignore the violent language in these texts. The readings of Milgrom and Brichto defend the practice of the ritual of Sotah as a strong means of protection of the woman against her irate husband. But the possibility of vengeance as the husband's motive is ignored, as are the images of shrinking genitalia and distended womb. Such considerations would provide the reader with an alternative possibility to the woman's guilt.

As more scholars apply feminist theories to the Sotah, the presumption that the male point of view is universal or normative will be dissolved. The scant or perfunctory examination of women's responses to this corrosive text is an example of how much work needs to be done in the area of feminist analysis of biblical texts. Romney-Wegner, for instance, has added to the literature of the Sotah by producing such a critical analysis of the text as legal document. She notes two prongs of discrimination reflected by the ritual of the Sotah: (1) there is no corresponding ritual for an errant husband, since adultery is defined as a crime committed by a wife against her husband, not a husband against his own wife. (2) The Sotah is the only case in either the Bible or the Mishnah that circumvents the normal rules of evidence, in which two witnesses are necessary in capital cases; the result is a double standard of due process. The wife's personal rights are diluted by the husband's property rights.

Romney-Wegner's insights are important to a feminist analysis of ancient legal texts that kept women contained. Since her interests are legal and not literary, however, the powerful language of the text, and the rabbinic fantasies that expand upon it, are out of her purview. She does not wonder about the effect upon the image of women when a society creates its only trial by ordeal in order to punish their improper sexual behavior. Clearly the integration of research on women from many different fields is needed to circumvent the borders of our particular disciplines. Each analysis of the Sotah will present a partial picture until we use an interdisciplinary analysis that encompasses many partial views.

The crucial element of the Sotah text, regardless of whether one wishes the accused woman to suffer a horrible death or merely to sip a noxious cocktail, is that it reflects the potency of male imaginings. As surely as the innocent bird eagerly wings toward the tempting snare, the husband imagines his wife as luscious Eve, the source of trouble and the root of desire. A tamed Eve pleases men, a wild one frightens them, but in neither aspect does she serve the needs of women. The Sotah both reflects and supports the patriarchal social system that cannot accept the woman without seeking to offset the threat that she represents, a threat of dissolution, anarchy, and antisocial disorder.

NOTES

* I am grateful to my colleagues, Arnold Eisen and Howard Eilberg-Schwartz in the Department of Religious Studies at Stanford, for reading successive drafts and encouraging me toward writing the article I wanted to write. A.J. Levine of Swarthmore College offered much food for thought and diet soda.

1. Kamuf's introduction (1991: 255) to Derrida's article, "Living On: Border Lines," which I have quoted here, serves as a description of biblical institutional resistance to deconstructive thinking. Derrida's article invites readings that overflow the possibilities of borders and of complete reference. Thus, I follow the leader in resisting biblical critics' concern with staying within contextual limits, canonical, linguistic, temporal.

2. For an article that suggests one way in which indeterminate readings of the deconstructive kind may be applied to biblical texts, see Greenstein 1989.

3. I adopt this term from Bal, who suggests that a text's "double meaning keeps reminding us of the active work on preceding texts, rather than the obedient repetition of them" (1991: 430). This article owes much to the genie-like character that drives the work of Bal, who refuses to be content inside the container of biblical literary convention.

4. Perhaps it would be helpful to remind the reader that my reading is not intended to replace or dominate earlier interpretations. Rather I pose different questions. The case is analogous to a gendered reading of *Cinderella*. In analyzing the folktale, tradition critics would focus upon the ritual of the prince placing the glass slipper upon the woman's foot (is the slipper always glass? is the incantation formulaic?); archaeologists might provide the shape of the slipper and suggest it wasn't glass but linen; philologists will attempt to provide a link between the ancient word *xxx*, "pumpkin" and its etymological cognate, *yyy*, resulting in the modern word *coach*. These scholarly investigations have no impact upon the forceful moral codes that keep women waiting for the prince. *Cinderella* has been all too clear to women. In fact, the straight line from women's obedience to the salvific arrival of the prince was not broken until questions were raised about the ideological biases of the storytellers and their interpreters.

5. Some of the most subtle and helpful of these works have been produced by Bird, Exum, Fuchs, Meyers.

6. I suggest to the reader two notable exceptions to encased readings. Bal's biblical studies (1985, 1987, 1988a, 1988b) illustrate the benefits of transdisciplinary readings of codes in order to break disciplinary borders. *Reading Rembrandt* (Bal 1992) is a startling performance in which a literary critic reads visual works and shows how they both fill the gaps of the literary texts they augment and produce further questions about those texts. Exum (1992) examines the traditional views of Greek tragedy and suggests untraditional ways in which biblical texts can be read as tragic without being dependent upon the classical model.

7. Hammurabi §129; Middle Assyrian Laws §§14–16; Hittite Laws §§192–93; *ANET* 171, 181, 196.

8. Scholars have debated the meaning of this difficult term. Sasson has suggested that *mrr* is connected to the Ugaritic root, "to bless," with a resulting merismus, "waters that bless and waters that curse." Also imbuing the term with powers of judgment, Brichto argues that one cannot derive *marim* from the verb *mrr*, to be bitter. He supports his suspicion with the contention that neither the dirt from the tabernacle floor nor a few drops of ink could account for bitterness. He has provided an intriguing suggestion that one read the term *marim* (as derived from the verb *yrh* "to teach") *mei hammarrim* as a construct with a hiphil plural of abstraction, understood as "spell-inducing water" (59). In addition, a reading that understands *me hammarim* as spell-inducing waters that would "teach" the guilt or innocence of the woman is compelling.

9. Phillips argues, I think convincingly, that the question in this case is not paternity so much as the husband's eagerness to recover the *mohar*, "bride price" (1981: 13).

10. *Bemidbar Rabbah* 9.17. *Sidrah Naso*, where this interpretation appears, is thought by some scholars to be based upon the ancient Tanhuma, which frequently preserves original readings not found in Buber's edition. See the introduction to *Bemidbar Rabbah* (trans. J.J. Slotki; London: Soncino Press, 3rd edn, 1983).

11. Fishbane (1974: 44) reads the connection between the motif of female seduction and Prov. 6.20–35 as an inner-biblical midrash on the Decalogue. According to Fishbane, "what makes this case significant is that the various prohibitions are presented in the light of a general warning against adultery—or, more specifically, in the light of the seduction of false wisdom in contrast with divine wisdom, Prov. 8–9." Thus, the tension is between the adulterous woman and the good woman.

12. Bird (1974: 87 n. 44) designates *ᵓishshah zarah* as the "other" woman, contrasting her with the wife. De Vaux (1965: 36) considers the term to contain nothing more loaded than "the wife of another man." For further discussion, see Camp 1985; Humbert 1937; McKane 1970: 285, 287; Snijders 1954: 103–104.

13. The connection between the offering of jealousy (*qnᵓ*), which becomes the *torat haqenaᵓot* in Num. 5.29, and the husband's sole and complete rights to his wife, is emphasized through a linguistic play. The husband has a legal right to protect jealously (*qnᵓ*) his acquired property (*qny*).

14. *Bemidbar Rabbah* assures the woman that if she is pure, the water will not affect her, "for this water is only like dry poison placed upon healthy flesh and cannot hurt it" (9.33). Characterizing the water as poison certainly makes clear its deleterious effect upon the one who must swallow it.

15. Frymer-Kensky supplies a medical explanation for the result of the flooding of the woman's sexual organs. According to her interpretation, the woman suffers the "collapse of the sexual organs known as a prolapsed uterus . . . Conception becomes impossible, and the woman's procreative life has effectively ended (unless, in our own time, she has corrective surgery)" (1984: 20–21). What I find most interesting about this description is its offering of analgesia for what the

text describes as "bitter pain." Put another way, the interpreter seems intent on slowing the pulse of the passage, rendering it safe for a modern reader.

16. The text reads *hevel mitsra'*, literally "rope made from rushes," which was a contemptuous name for a slave (who had presumably been forced to make the rope in Egypt) and was considered a badge of shame. One is tempted to connect this mention of shameful rope with the Egyptian courtier's wife who shamed her husband with her adulterous longings. A rabbinic play on *hbl* is tempting since the noun also means "birth pangs."

REFERENCES

Bach, Alice
1993   "Breaking Free of the Biblical Frame-Up: Uncovering the Woman in Genesis 39," in *A Feminist Companion to Genesis* (ed. Athalya Brenner; The Feminist Companion to the Bible, 2; Sheffield: Sheffield Academic Press): 318–42.

Bal, Mieke
1985   *Narratology: Introduction to the Theory of Narrative* (Toronto: University of Toronto Press).
1987   *Lethal Love: Feminist Literary Readings of Biblical Love Stories* (Bloomington: Indiana University Press).
1988a   *Murder and Difference: Gender, Genre, and Scholarship on Sisera's Death* (trans. Matthew Gumpert; Bloomington: Indiana University Press).
1988b   *Death and Dissymmetry: The Politics of Coherence in the Book of Judges* (Chicago: University of Chicago Press).
1992   *Reading Rembrandt: Beyond the Word-Image Opposition* (Cambridge: Cambridge University Press).

Benstock, Shari
1991   *Textualizing the Feminine: On the Limits of Genre* (Norman: University of Oklahoma Press).

Bird, Phyllis
1974   "Images of Women in the Old Testament," in *Religion and Sexism* (ed. R.R. Ruether; New York: Simon & Schuster): 41–88.
1989a   "The Harlot as Heroine: Narrative Art and Social Presupposition in Three Old Testament Texts," *Semeia* 46: 119–39.
1989b   "Women's Religion in Ancient Israel," in *Women's Earliest Records: From Ancient Egypt and Western Asia* (ed. Barbara S. Lesko; BJS; Atlanta: Scholars Press): 283–98.

Brichto, H.C.
1975   "The Case of the *Sota* and a Reconsideration of Biblical Law," *HUCA* 46: 55–70.

Camp, Claudia
1985   *Wisdom and the Feminine in the Book of Proverbs* (Sheffield: Almond Press).

Derrida, Jacques
1979   "Living On: Borderlines" (trans. James Hulbert), in *Deconstruction and Criticism* (ed. Harold Bloom *et al.*; New York: Seabury Press).

Exum, J. Cheryl
1985   "'Mother in Israel': A Familiar Figure Reconsidered," in *Femininist Interpretation of the Bible* (ed. Letty M. Russell; Philadelphia: Westminster Press): 73–85.

1992   *Tragedy and Biblical Narrative: Arrows of the Almighty* (Cambridge: Cambridge University Press).

Fishbane, Michael
1974   "Accusations of Adultery: A Study of Law and Scribal Practice in Numbers 5.11–31," *HUCA* 45: 25–45.

Frymer-Kensky, Tikva
1984   "The Strange Case of the Suspected Sotah (Numbers v 11–31)," *VT* 34: 11–26.

Fuchs, Esther
1987   "Structure and Patriarchal Functions in the Biblical Betrothal Type Scene: Some Preliminary Notes," *Journal of Feminist Studies in Religion* 3: 7–13.
1988   "For I Have the Way of Women: Deception, Gender and Ideology in Biblical Narrative," *Semeia* 42: 68–83.

Gallop, Jane
1990   "Why Does Freud Giggle When the Women Leave the Room?" in *Psychoanalysis and . . .* (ed. R. Feldstein and H. Sussman; New York: Routledge): 49–54.

Greenstein, Edward L.
1989   "Deconstruction and Biblical Narrative," *Prooftexts* 9: 43–71.

Humbert, Paul
1937   "La femme étrangère du livre des Proverbes," *Revue des études sémitiques* 6: 40–64.

Irigaray, Luce
1985   *This Sex Which Is Not One* (trans. Catherine Porter; Ithaca: Cornell University Press).
1991   "The Bodily Encounter with the Mother," in *The Irigaray Reader* (ed. Margaret Whitford; Oxford: Basil Blackwell): 34–46.

Jackson, B.S.
1975   "Reflections on Biblical Criminal Law," in his *Essays in Jewish and Comparative Legal History* (Studies in Judaism in Late Antiquity, 10; Leiden: Brill): 25–63.

Jacobus, Mary
1982   "Is There a Woman in This Text?" *New Literary History* 14: 117–41.

Kamuf, Peggy (ed.)
1991   *A Derrida Reader: Between the Blinds* (New York: Columbia University Press).

McKane, William
1970   *Proverbs* (OTL; Philadelphia: Westminster Press).

McKeating, Henry
1979   "Sanctions against Adultery in Ancient Israelite Society, with Some Reflections on Methodology in the Study of Old Testament Ethics," *JSOT* 11: 57–72.

Milgrom, Jacob
1981   "The Case of the Suspected Adulteress, Numbers 5.11–31: Redaction and Meaning," in *The Creation of Sacred Literature* (ed. Richard F. Friedman; Berkeley: University of California Press): 69–75.
1990   *Numbers* (The JPS Torah Commentary; Philadelphia: Jewish Publication Society of America).

Neufeld, E.
1944   *Ancient Hebrew Marriage Laws* (London).

Newsom, Carol A.
1989   "Woman and the Discourse of Patriarchal Wisdom: A Study of Proverbs 1–9," in *Gender and Difference in Ancient Israel* (ed. Peggy L. Day; Minneapolis: Fortress Press): 142–60.

Okin, Susan Moller
1979   *Women in Western Political Thought* (Princeton: Princeton University Press).

Phillips, Antony
1973   "Some Aspects of Family Law in Pre-Exilic Israel," *VT* 23: 349–61.
1981   "Another Look at Adultery," *JSOT* 20: 3–25.

Romney-Wegner, Judith
1988   *Chattel or Person? The Status of Women in the Mishnah* (New York: Oxford University Press).

Sasson, Jack
1972   "Numbers 5 and the Waters of Judgment," *BZ* 16: 249–51.

Slotki, Judah J. (trans.)
1983   *Bemidbar Rabbah* (London: Soncino Press, 3rd edn.).

Snijders, L.A.
1954   "The Meaning of *zar* in the Old Testament," *OTS* 10: 97–105.

Vaux, Roland de
1965   *Ancient Israel: Its Life and Institutions* (New York: McGraw-Hill).

Feminist Bibliography: Bible

ED. NOTE: This bibliography has been divided into two parts for the ease of readers who may be particularly interested in studies focused on works on feminist readings of the Hebrew Bible, and articles that deal more generally with the joint perspectives on race and gender in Jewish and Christian religion, esp. Asian, womanist, and *mujerista* theologies.

Feminist Interpretations of the Hebrew Bible

Alonso-Schekel, L.
1975. "Narrative Structures in the Book of Judith." *The Center for Hermeneutical Studies in Hellenistic and Modern Culture*. Berkeley, CA: Center for Hermeneutical Studies in Hellenistic and Modern Culture, *Colloquy* 11:1–20.

Bach, Alice.
1998. "Reading the Body Politic: Women, Violence and Judges 21." *Biblical Interpretation* 3:2–19.
1998. "Whatever Happened to Dionysus?" In *Biblical into Cultural Studies*. Ed. J. Cheryl Exum and Stephen Moore. Sheffield: Sheffield Academic Press, forthcoming.
1998. "Whitewashing Athena: Bernal, the Bible, and the Critics." *JSOT* 77:3–19.
1997. *Women, Seduction, and Betrayal in Biblical Narrative*. Cambridge: Cambridge University Press.
1997. "Directing Salomé's Dance of Death." *Semeia* 74:103–126.
1997. "Throw Them to the Lions, Sire: The Bible as Cultural Artifact in American Film." *Semeia* 74:1–12.
1996. "Tracing Eve's Journey from Eden to MTV." *Biblical Media in Translation*. American Bible Society Paulist Press.
1995. "Mirror, Mirror in the Text: Reflections on Reading and Rereading." Pp. 80–86. In *A Feminist Companion to Esther, Judith and Susanna*. Ed. Athalya Brenner. Sheffield: Sheffield Academic Press.
1993. "Breaking Free of the Biblical Frame-Up: Uncovering the Woman in Genesis 39." Pp. 318–342. In *A Feminist Companion to the Genesis*. Ed. Athalya Brenner. Sheffield: Sheffield Academic Press.

1993. "Good to the Last Drop: Viewing the Sotah (Numbers 5:11–31) as the Glass Half Empty and Wondering How to View it Half Full." In *The New Literary Criticism and the Hebrew Bible*. Ed. J. Cheryl Exum and David J.A. Clines, Sheffield: JSOT Press.

1993. "Reading Allowed: Feminist Biblical Criticism Approaching the Millenium." *Currents in Biblical Research* 1,1:215–235.

1993. "Signs of the Flesh: Characterization in Biblical Narratives." *Semeia* 63.

1990. "Mieke Bal and the Method Which is Not One." *Union Seminary Quarterly Review*, 44, 3/4:333–341.

1990. "The Pleasure of Her Text." Pp. 25–44. In *The Pleasure of Her Text: Feminist Readings of Biblical and Historical Texts*. Ed. Alice Bach. Philadelphia: Trinity Press International.

Bal, Mieke.

1996. *Double Exposures: The Subject of Cultural Analysis*. With Edwin Janssen, *Das Gesicht an der Wand*. New York: Routledge.

1994. "Head Hunting: 'Judith' on the Cutting Edge of Knowledge." *JSOT* 63:3–34.

1994. *On Meaning-Making: Essays in Semiotics*. Sonoma: Polebridge Press.

1993. "A Body of Writing: Judges 19." In *A Feminist Companion to Judges*. Ed. Athalya Brenner Sheffield: Sheffield Academic Press.

1991. "Lots of Writing." *Semeia* 54:77–102.

1991. *On Story-Telling: Essays in Narratology*. Ed. David Jobling. Sonoma: Polebridge Press,

1991. *Reading "Rembrandt": Beyond the Word-Image Opposition*. The Northrop Frye Lectures in Literary Theory. Cambridge; New York: Cambridge University Press.

1990. "Dealing/With/Women: Daughters in the Book of Judges." Pp. 16–39. In *The Book and the Text: The Bible and Literary Theory*. Ed. Regina M. Schwartz. Cambridge: Blackwell Press.

1989. "Reading as Empowerment: The Bible from a Feminist Perspective." In *Approaches to Teaching the Hebrew Bible as Literature in Translation*. Ed. Barry N. Olshen and Yael S. Feldman. New York: Modern Language Association of America.

1988. *Murder and Difference: Gender, Genre, and Scholarship on Sisera's Death*. Trans. Matthew Gumpert. Bloomington: Indiana University Press.

1988. "Tricky Thematics." *Semeia* 42:133–155.

1987. *Lethal Love*. Bloomington: Indiana University Press.

———— and Inge E. Boer. Eds.

1994. *The Point of Theory: Practices of Cultural Analysis*. New York: Continuum.

Bar-Efrat, Shimon.

1989. "The Narrative of Amnon and Tamar." Pp. 239–282. In *Narrative Art in the Bible. Bible and Literature* 17. Sheffield: Almond Press.

Berlin, Adele.

1982. "Characterization in Biblical Narrative: David's Wives." *JSOT* 23:69–85.

Bird, Phyllis.

1991. "Israelite Religion and the Faith of Israel's Daughters." Pp. 97–108. In *The Bible and the Politics of Exegesis*. Ed. David Jobling, Peggy Day, and Gerald Sheppard. Cleveland: Pilgrim Press.

1991. "Women's Religion in Ancient Israel." Pp. 283–298. In *Women's Earliest Records: From Ancient Israel and Western Asia*. Ed. Barbara S. Lesko. Brown Judaic Studies. Atlanta: Scholars Press.

1989. "The Harlot as Heroine: Narrative Art and Social Presupposition in Three Old Testament Texts." *Semeia* 46:119–139.

1989. "To Play the Harlot: An Inquiry into an Old Testament Metaphor." In *Gender and Difference in Ancient Israel.* Ed. Peggy Day. Minneapolis: Fortress Press.

1981. "'Male and Female He Created Them': Gen 1:27b in the Context of the Priestly Account of Creation." *Harvard Theological Review* 74:129–159.

1974. "Images of Women in the Old Testament." In *Religion and Sexism.* Ed. R.R. Ruether. New York: Simon and Schuster.

Bloom, Harold.

1990. "The Representation of Yaweh" and "The Psychology of Yahweh." Pp. 279–306. In *The Book of J.* Ed. David Rosenberg and Harold Bloom. New York: Grove Weidenfeld.

1986. "From J to K, or the Uncanniness of the Yahwist." In *The Bible and the Narrative Tradition.* Ed. Frank McConnell. Oxford: Oxford University Press.

Brenner, Athalya.

1997. *The Intercourse of Knowledge: On Gendering Desire and "Sexuality" in the Hebrew Bible.* Biblical Interpretation Series 26. Leiden: E.J. Brill.

1996 "Porno Prophetics Revisited: Some Additional Reflections." *JSOT* 70:63–86.

1994. "An Afterword: The Decalogue—Am I an Addressee?" In *A Feminist Companion to Exodus-Deuteronomy.* Ed. Athalya Brenner. Sheffield: Sheffield Academic Press.

1994. "Who's Afraid of Feminist Criticism? Who's Afraid of Biblical Humour? The Case of the Obtuse Foreign Ruler in the Hebrew Bible." *JSOT* 63:38–55.

1994. "Who's Afraid of Feminist Criticism?" *JSOT* 63:35–37.

1993. *On Gendering Texts.* Leiden: E.J. Brill.

1985. *The Israelite Woman: Social Role and Literary Type in Biblical Narrative.* Sheffield: JSOT Press.

Brenner, Athalya. Ed.

1996. *A Feminist Companion to the Hebrew Bible in the New Testament.* The Feminist Companion to the Bible 10. Sheffield: Sheffield Academic Press.

1995. *A Feminist Companion to Wisdom Literature.* The Feminist Companion to the Bible 9. Sheffield: Sheffield Academic Press.

1995. *A Feminist Companion to the Latter Prophets.* The Feminist Companion to the Bible 8. Sheffield: Sheffield Academic Press.

1995. *A Feminist Companion to Esther, Judith and Susanna.* The Feminist Companion to the Bible 7. Sheffield: Sheffield Academic Press.

1994. *A Feminist Companion to Exodus–Deuteronomy.* The Feminist Companion to the Bible 6. Sheffield: Sheffield Academic Press.

1994. *A Feminist Companion to Samuel and Kings.* The Feminist Companion to the Bible 5; Sheffield: Sheffield Academic Press.

1993. *A Feminist Companion to Judges.* The Feminist Companion to the Bible 4. Sheffield: Sheffield Academic Press.

1993. *A Feminist Companion to Ruth.* The Feminist Companion to the Bible 3. Sheffield: Sheffield Academic Press.

1993. *A Feminist Companion to the Genesis.* The Feminist Companion to the Bible 2. Sheffield: Sheffield Academic Press.

1993. *A Feminist Companion to the Song of Songs.* The Feminist Companion to the Bible 1. Sheffield: Sheffield Academic Press.

Brichto, H.C.
1975. "The Case of the *Sota* and a Reconsideration of Biblical Law." *HUCA* 46:55–70.

Bronner, Leila.
1994. *From Eve to Esther: Rabbinic Reconstructions of Biblical Women.* Louisville: Westminster/ John Knox Press,
1991. "Biblical Prophetesses Through Rabbinic Lenses." *Judaism* 40.2:171–183.

Brooten, Bernadette J.
1996. *Love between Women: Early Christian Responses to Female Homoeroticism.* Chicago: University of Chicago Press.
1982. *Women Leaders in the Ancient Synagogue: Inscriptional Evidence and Background Issues.* Chico: Scholars Press.

Burns, Rita.
1987. *Has the Lord Indeed Spoken Only Through Moses? A Study of the Biblical Portrait of Miriam.* Atlanta: Scholars Press.

Bynum, Caroline Walker.
1991. *Fragmentation and Redemption: Essays on Gender and the Human Body in Medieval Religion.* New York: Zone Books.

Callaway, Mary.
1986. *Sing, O Barren One: A Study in Comparative Midrash.* Vol. 91. *SBL Dissertation Series.* Atlanta: Scholars Press.

Camp, Claudia.
1991. "What's So Strange About the Strange Women?" Pp. 17–32. In *The Bible and the Politics of Exegesis.* Ed. David Jobling, Peggy Day, and Gerald Sheppard. Cleveland: Pilgrim Press.
1988. "Wise and Strange: An Interpretation of the Female Imagery in the Proverbs in Light of Trickster Mythology." *Semeia* 42:14–36.
1985. *Wisdom and the Feminine in the Book of Proverbs.* Decatur, GA: Scholars Press.
1981. "The Wise Woman of 2 Samuel: A Role Model for Women in Early Israel." *Catholic Biblical Quarterly* 43:14–29.

Castelli, Elizabeth.
1986. "Virginity and Its Meaning for Women's Sexuality in Early Christianity." *Journal of Feminist Studies in Religion* 2:61–88.

Cixous, Hélène.
1993. "Bathsheba or the Interior Bible." *New Literary History* 24.4:820–836.

Clines, David J.A.
1990. "What Does Eve Do to Help? and Other Irredeemably Androcentric Orientations in Genesis 1–3." Pp. 25–48. In *What Does Eve Do to Help? and Other Readerly Questions to the Old Testament.* Sheffield: JSOT Press.

——— and Tamara C. Eskenazi.
1991. *Telling Queen Michal's Story: An Experiment in Comparative Interpretation.* Sheffield: JSOT Press.

Collins, Adela Y.
1985. *Feminist Perspectives on Biblical Scholarship. Biblical Scholarship in North America,* Vol. 10. Chico: Scholars Press.

Craven, Toni.

1983.   *Artistry and Faith in the Book of Judith. SBL Dissertation Series.* Atlanta: Scholars Press.

Darr, Katheryn Pfisterer.

1991.   "More than the Stars of the Heavens: Critical, Rabbinical, and Feminist Perspectives on Sarah," and "More Than a Possession: Critical, Rabbinical, and Feminist Perspectives on Hagar." Pp. 85–131 and 132–163. In *Far More Precious Than Jewels.* Louisville: Westminster/John Knox.

Day, Peggy.

1992.   "Anat: Ugarit's Mistress of Animals." *Journal of Near Eastern Studies* 51:181–190.

1991.   "Why is Anat a Warrior and Hunter?" Pp. 141–146. In *The Bible and the Politics of Exegesis.* Ed. David Jobling, Peggy Day, and Gerald Sheppard. Cleveland: Pilgrim Press.

1989.   *Gender and Difference in Ancient Israel.* Minneapolis: Fortress Press.

1987.   "Abishai the Satan in 2 Samuel 19:17–24." *Catholic Bible Quarterly* 49:543–547.

Dijk-Hemmes, Fokkelien van.

1989.   "Tamar and the Limits of Patriarchy: Between Rape and Seduction (2 Samuel 13 and Genesis 38)." In *Anti-Convenant: Counter-Reading Women's Lives in the Hebrew Bible.* Ed. Mieke Bal. Sheffield: Almond Press.

Exum, J. Cheryl.

1996.   *Plotted, Shot, and Painted.* Sheffield: Sheffield Academic Press.

1993.   *Fragmented Women.* Sheffield: JSOT Press.

1990.   "The Centre Cannot Hold: Thematic and Texual Instabilities in Judges." *Catholic Bible Quarterly* 52:410–431.

1990.   "Murder They Wrote: Ideology and the Manipulation of Female Presence in Biblical Narrative." Pp. 45–67. In *The Pleasure of Her Text.* Ed. Alice Bach. Philadelphia: Trinity Press International.

1989.   "The Tragic Vision and Biblical Narrative: The Case of Jephthah." Pp. 59–83. In *Signs and Wonders: Biblical Texts in Literary Focus.* Ed. J. Cheryl Exum. Atlanta: Scholars Press.

1985.   "'Mother in Israel': A Familiar Figure Reconsidered." Pp. 73–85. In *Feminist Interpretation of the Bible.* Ed. Letty M. Russell. Philadelphia: Westminster.

———— and David J.A. Clines. Eds.

1993.   *The New Literary Criticism and the Hebrew Bible.* JSOT Supplement Series. Sheffield: JSOT Press.

———— and Johanna Bos. Eds.

1988.   "Reasoning With the Foxes: Female Wit in a World of Male Power." *Semeia* 42.

Fewell, Danna Nolan. Ed.

1992.   *Reading Between Texts: Intertexuality and the Hebrew Bible.* Louisville: Westminster/John Knox.

———— and David M. Gunn.

1991.   "Tipping the Balance: Sternberg's Reader and the Rape of Dinah." *Journal of Biblical Literature* 110:193–211.

1990.   "Controlling Perspectives: Women, Men, and the Authority of Violence in Judges 4 and 5." *Journal of the American Academy of Religion* 58:101–123.

1989.   "Boaz, Pillar of Society: Measures of Worth in the Book of Ruth." *JSOT* 45:45–59.

1989.   "Is Coxon a Scold? On Responding to the Book of Ruth." *JSOT* 45:39–43.

1988.   "A Son is Born to Naomi!: Literary Allusions and Interpretations in the Book of Ruth." *JSOT* 40:99–108.

Fiorenza, Elisabeth Schüssler.

1994. *Searching the Scriptures,* Vol. 2, *A Feminist Commentary.* New York: Crossroad.

1993. *Searching the Scriptures,* Vol. 1, *A Feminist Introduction.* New York: Crossroad.

1992. *But SHE Said: Feminist Practices of Biblical Interpretation.* Boston: Beacon Press.

1992. "Feminist/Womanist Hermeneutics," *Anchor Bible Dictionary,* Vol. 2, Pp. 784–791.

1989. "Biblical Interpretation and Critical Commitment." *Studia Theologica* 43:5–18.

1989. "The Politics of Otherness: Biblical Interpretation as a Critic." In *The Future of Liberation Theology.* Ed. Marc Ellis and Otto Maduro. Maryknoll: Orbis Books.

1988. "The Ethics of Biblical Interpretation: Decentering Biblical Scholarship." *Journal of Biblical Literature* 107:3–17.

1985. "Remembering the Past in Creating the Future: Historical-Critical Scholarship and Feminist Biblical Interpretation." *Feminist Perspectives on Biblical Scholarship.* Ed. Adela Y. Collins. Chico: Scholars Press.

1983. *In Memory of Her: A Feminist Theological Reconstruction of Christian Origins.* New York: Crossroad.

Fishbane, Michael.

1974. "Accusations of Adultery: A Study of Law and Scribal Practice in Numbers 5:11–31." *HUCA* 45:25–45.

Fontaine, Carole R.

1989. "A Heifer From Thy Stable: On Goddesses and the Status of Women in the Ancient Near East." *Union Seminary Quarterly Review* 43:67–91.

1988. "The Deceptive Goddess in Ancient Near Eastern Myth: Inanna and Inaras." *Semeia* 42:84–102.

Frymer-Kensky, Tikva.

1991. *In the Wake of the Goddess.* New York and London: Oxford University Press.

1984. "The Strange Case of the Suspected Sotah (Numbers V 11–31)." *Vetus Testamentum* 34:11–26.

1983. "Pollution, Purification, and Purgation in Biblical Israel." Pp. 399–414. In *Word of the Lord Shall Go Forth: Essays in Honor of David Noel Freedman.* Ed. Carol Meyers and Michael O'Connor. Winona Lake: Eisenbrauns.

1981. "Patriarchal Family Relationships and Near Eastern Law." *Biblical Archaeologist* (Fall): 209–214.

Fuchs, Esther.

1988. "For I Have the Way of Women: Deception, Gender, and Ideology in Biblical Narrative." *Semeia* 42:68–83.

1985. "The Literary Characterization of Mothers and Sexual Politics in the Hebrew Bible." In *Feminist Perspectives on Biblical Scholarship.* Ed. Adela Y. Collins. Chico: Scholars Press.

1985. "Who is Hiding the Truth? Deceptive Women and Biblical Androcentrism." In *Feminist Perspectives on Biblical Scholarship.* Ed. Adela Y. Collins. Chico: Scholars Press.

1982. "Status and Role of Female Heroines in the Biblical Narrative." *Mankind Quarterly* 23:149–160.

Furman, Nelly.

1989. "His Story versus Her Story: Male Genealogy and Female Strategy in the Jacob Cycle." *Semeia* 46:141–149.

Gevaryhu, H.

1989. "Deborah, the Wife of Lapidot." *Jewish Biblical Quarterly* 18:135–140.

Gottwald, Norman K.
1994. "Social Class as an Analytic and Hermeneutical Category in Biblical Studies." *Journal of Biblical Literature* 112:3–22.

Graetz, Naomi.
1991. "Miriam: Guilty or Not Guilty." *Judaism* 40.2:184–192.

Greenstein, Edward L.
1989. "Deconstruction and Biblical Narrative." *Prooftexts* 9:43–71.

Gunn, David M.
1989. "In Security: The David of Biblical Narrative." Pp. 133–151. In *Signs and Wonders: Biblical Texts in Literary Focus*. Ed. J. Cheryl Exum. Society of Biblical Literature. *Semeia Studies*. Atlanta: Scholars Press.

——— and Danna Nolan Fewell.
1993. *Narrative in the Hebrew Bible*. Oxford: Oxford University Press.

Hackett, Jo Ann.
1987. "Women's Studies and the Hebrew Bible." In *The Future of Biblical Studies: The Hebrew Scriptures*. Ed. David N. Friedman and Alan Williamson. Atlanta: Scholars Press.

Hyman, Naomi M. Ed.
1997. *Biblical Women in the Midrash: A Sourcebook*. Northvale: Jason Aronson.

Jeansonne, Sharon Pace.
1990. *The Women of Genesis: From Sarah to Potiphar's Wife*. Minneapolis: Fortress Press.

King, Karen L. Ed.
1988. *Images of the Feminine in Gnosticism: Studies in Antiquity and Christianity*. Philadelphia: Fortress Press.

Kraemer, Ross S.
1992. *Her Share of the Blessings: Women's Religions among Pagans, Jews, and Christians in the Greco-Roman World*. New York and London: Oxford University Press.
1988. *Maenads, Martyrs, Matrons, Monastics: A Sourcebook on Women's Religions in the Greco-Roman World*. Philadelphia: Fortress Press.
1983. "Women in the Religions of the Graeco-Roman World." *Religious Studies Review* 9:127–139.

Kristeva, Julia.
1989. "Semiotics of Biblical Abomination." Pp. 90–112. In *Powers of Horror: An Essay on Abjection*. Trans. Leon S. Roudiez. New York: Columbia University Press.

LaCocque, André.
1990. *The Feminine Unconventional: Four Subversive Figures in Israel's Tradition*. Minneapolis: Fortress Press.

Landy, Francis.
1983. "Two Versions of Paradise." Pp. 183–265. In *Paradoxes of Paradise: Identity and Difference in the Songs of Songs*. Bible & Literature Series. Sheffield: Almond Press.

Lanser, Susan.
1988. "Feminist Criticism in the Garden: Inferring Genesis 2–3." *Semeia* 41:67–84.

Levine, Amy Jill.

1992. "Diaspora as Metaphor: Bodies and Boundaries in the Book of Tobit." In *Diaspora Jews and Judaism.* Ed. J. Andrew Overman and Robert S. MacLennan. Atlanta: Scholars Press.

1992. "Sacrifice and Salvation: Otherness and Domestication in the Book of Judith." Pp. 17–30. In *"No One Spoke Ill of Her": Essays on Judith.* Ed. James C. VanderKam. Early Judaism and Its Literature, Vol. 2. Atlanta: Scholars Press.

Meyers, Carol.

1993. "Returning Home: Ruth 1.8 and the Gendering of the Book of Ruth." Pp. 85–114. In *A Feminist Companion to Ruth.* Ed. Athalya Brenner. Sheffield: Sheffield Academic Press.

1991. "To Her Mother's House: Considering a Counterpoint to the Israelite *Bet'ab.*" In *The Bible and the Politics of Exegesis.* Ed. David Jobling, Peggy Day, and Gerald Sheppard. Cleveland: Pilgrim Press.

1989. "Women and the Domestic Economy of Early Israel." Pp. 265–278. In *Women's Earliest Records: From Ancient Egypt and Western Asia.* Ed. Barbara S. Lesko. Brown Judaic Studies. Atlanta: Scholars Press.

1988. *Discovering Eve: Ancient Israelite Women in Context.* New York: Oxford University Press.

1973. "The Roots of Restriction: Women in Early Israel." *Biblical Archaeologist* 41:91–103.

Milgrom, Jacob.

1981. "The Case of the Suspected Adultress, Numbers 5:22–31: Redaction and Meaning." Pp. 69–75. In *The Creation of Sacred Literature.* Ed. Richard F. Friedman. Berkeley: University of California Press.

Milne, Pamela J.

1992. "Feminist Impressions of the Bible: Then and Now." *Bible Review* 8.5:38–43, 52–55.

1989. "The Patriarchal Stamp of Scripture: The Implications of Structural Analyses for Feminist Hermeneutics." *Journal for Feminist Studies in Religion* 5:17–34.

Moore, Stephen D.

1996. *God's Gym: Divine Male Bodies of the Bible.* New York: Routledge.

Newsom, Carol A.

1989. "Woman and the Discourse of Patriarchal Wisdom: A Study of Proverbs 1–9." Pp. 142–160. In *Gender and Difference in Ancient Israel.* Ed. Peggy Day. Minneapolis: Fortress Press.

——— and Sharon H. Ringe. Eds.
The Women's Bible Commentary. Louisville: Westminster/John Knox.

Nicol, George G., Revd.

1988. "Bathsheba, a Clever Woman?" *The Expository Times* 99:360–363.

Niditch, Susan.

1989. "Eroticism and Death in the Tale of Jael." Pp. 43–57. In *Gender and Difference in Ancient Israel.* Ed. Peggy Day. Minneapolis: Fortress Press.

1987. *Underdogs and Tricksters: A Prelude to Biblical Folklore.* New York and San Francisco: Harper & Row.

O'Brien, Julia M.

1996. "Judah as Wife and Husband: Deconstructing Gender in Malachi." *Journal of Biblical Literature* 115:241–250.

Ochshorn, Judith.
1981. *The Female Experience and the Nature of the Divine.* Bloomington: Indiana University Press.

Ostriker, Alicia.
1994. *The Nakedness of the Father: Biblical Visions and Revisions.* New Brunswick: Rutgers University Press.
1993. *Feminist Revision and the Bible.* Oxford: Blackwell Press.

Pagels, Elaine.
1995. *The Origin of Satan.* New York: Random House.
1987. *Adam, Eve, and the Serpent.* New York: Random House.

Pardes, Ilana.
1992. *Countertraditions in the Bible.* Cambridge, MA: Harvard University Press.

Rashkow, Illona N.
1990. "The Rape of Dinah." Pp. 75–96. In *Upon Dark Places: Anti Semitism and Sexism in English Renaissance Biblical Translation.* Bible & Literature Series 28. Sheffield: Almond Press.

Romney-Wegner, Judith.
1988. *Chattel or Person? The Status of Women in the Mishnah.* New York: Oxford University Press.

Russell, Letty M. Ed.
1985. *Feminist Interpretation of the Bible.* Philadelphia: Westminster.

Sackenfeld, Kathy D.
1985. "Feminist Uses of Biblical Materials." In *Feminist Interpretation of the Bible.* Ed. Letty M. Russell. Philadelphia: Westminster Press.

Sasson, Jack.
1972. "Numbers 5 and the Waters of Judgment." *Biblische Zeitschrift* 16:249–251.

Schwartz, Regina.
1997. *The Curse of Cain: The Violent Legacy of Monotheism.* Chicago: University of Chicago Press.

Schwartz, Regina, Ed.
1990. *The Book and the text: The Bible and Literary Theory.* Cambridge, MA; Oxford, UK: Blackwell.

Shields, Mary E.
1995. "Circumcision of the Prostitute: Gender, Sexuality and the Call to Repentance in Jer. 3.1–4.4." *Biblical Interpretation* 3:61–74.
1993. "Subverting a Man of God, Elevating a Woman: Role and Power Reversals in 2 Kings 4." *JSOT.*

Steinberg, Naomi.
1993. *Kinship and Marriage in Genesis: A Household Economics Approach.* Minneapolis: Fortress Press.
1988. "Israelite Tricksters, Their Analogs and Cross-Cultural Study." *Semeia* 42:41–60.

Tapp, Anne Michele.
1989. "An Ideology of Expendablity: Virgin Daughter Sacrifice in Genesis 19.1–11, Judges 11.30–39 and 19.22–26." In *Anti-Convenant: Counter-Reading Women's Lives in the Hebrew Bible.* Ed. Mieke Bal. Sheffield: Almond Press.

Trible, Phyllis.

1994. *Rhetorical Criticism: Context, Method, and the Book of Jonah.* Minneapolis: Fortress Press.

1991. "Genesis 22: The Sacrifice of Sarah." Pp. 170–191. In *"Not In Heaven": Coherence and Complexity in Biblical Narrative.* Ed. Jason Rosenblatt and Joseph Sitterson. Indiana Studies in Biblical Literature. Bloomington: Indiana University Press.

1990. "The Pilgrim Bible on a Feminist Journey." *Princeton Seminary Bulletin* 11:232–239.

1989. "Bringing Miriam Out of the Shadows." *Bible Review* 5:14–25, 34.

1985. "Huldah's Holy Writ: On Women and Biblical Authority." *Touchstone* 3:6–13.

1984. *Texts of Terror: Literary-Feminist Readings of Biblical Narratives.* Philadelphia: Fortress Press.

1982. "The Effect of Women's Studies on Biblical Studies." *JSOT* 22:3–4.

1981. "A Meditation in Mourning: The Sacrifice of the Daughter of Jepthah." *Union Seminary Quarterly Review* 36:59–73.

1978. *God and the Rhetoric of Sexuality.* Philadelphia: Fortress Press.

1976. "Two Women a Man's World: A Reading of the Book of Ruth." *Soundings* 59:251–279.

1973. "Depatriarchalizing in Biblical Interpretation." *Journal of the American Academy of Religion* 41:30–48.

Weems, Renita J.

1992. "The Hebrew Women Are Not Like the Egyptian Women: The Ideology of Race, Gender and Sexual Reproduction in Exodus 1." *Semeia* 59:25–34.

1988. "A Mistress, a Maid, and No Mercy." Pp. 1–21. In *Just a Sister Away: A Womanist Vision of Women's Relationships in the Bible.* San Diego: LauraMedia.

Wenham, G.J.

1972. "*Betulah: A Girl of Marriageable Age.*" *Vetus Testamentum* 22:326–48.

Yee, Gale A.

1993. "By the Hand of a Woman: The Metaphor of the Woman Warrior in Judith." *Semeia* 61:99–132.

1992. "The Theology of Creation in Proverbs 8:22–31." In *Creation in the Biblical Traditions.* Ed. Richard Clifford and John Collins. Washington, DC: Catholic Biblical Association of America.

1989. "I Have Perfumed My Bed With Myrrh: The Foreign Woman." *JSOT* 43:53–68.

1988. "Fraught With Background: Literary Ambiguity in 2 Samuel 11." *Interpretation* 42:240–253.

Feminist, Womanist, and Mujerista Theologies

ED. NOTE: Please note that this bibliography is to be consulted in conjunction with the larger "Feminist Bibliography: Bible." Citations for some scholars appear in both places.

Albrecht, Gloria H. 1995. *The Character of Our Communities*. Nashville: Abingdon Press.

Baskin, Judith R. 1994. *Women of the Word: Jewish Women and Jewish Writing*. Detroit: Wayne State University Press.

Birnbaum, Lucia Chiavola. 1993. *Black Madonnas*. Boston: Northeastern University Press.

Brock, Rita Nakashima. 1988. *Journeys by Heart*. New York: Crossroad.

—— and Susan Brooks Thistlethwaite. 1996. *Casting Stones: Prostitution and Liberation in Asia and the United States*. Minneapolis: Fortress Press.

Broner, E.M. 1994. *Mornings and Mourning: A Kaddish Journal*. San Francisco: HarperSanFrancisco.

Cantor, Aviva. 1995. *Jewish Women/Jewish Men: The Legacy of Patriarchy in Jewish Life*. San Francisco: HarperSanFrancisco.

Cannon, Katie G. 1995. *Katie's Canon: Womanism and the Soul of the Black Community*. New York: Continuum.

Carr, Anne E. and Elisabeth Schüssler Fiorenza. 1989. *Motherhood, Experience, Institution, Theology*. Edinburgh: T. & T. Clark.

Case-Winters, Anna. 1990. *God's Power*. Louisville: Westminster: J. Knox.

Chung, Hyun Kyung. 1990. *Struggle to be the Sun Again: Introducing Asian Women's Theology*. Maryknoll: Orbis Books.

Clark, Elizabeth A. and Herbert Richardson. Eds. 1996. *Women and Religion: The Original Sourcebook of Women in Christian Thought*. New expanded edition. San Francisco: HarperSanFrancisco.

Cutter, William and Yaffa Weisman. Eds. 1996. *And We Were All There: A Feminist Passover Haggadah*. Los Angeles: American Jewish Congress Feminist Center.

Davidman, Lynn and Shelly Tenebaum. Eds. 1994. Feminist Perspectives on Jewish Studies. New Haven: Yale University Press.

533

Eilberg-Schwartz, Howard. 1994. *God's Phallus and Other Problems for Men and Monotheism.* Boston: Beacon Press.

1992. Ed. *People of the Body: Jews and Judaism from an Embodied Perspective.* Albany: State University of New York Press.

Fiorenza, Elisabeth Schüssler. Ed. 1996. *The Power of Naming: A Concilium Reader in Feminist Liberation Theology.* Maryknoll: Orbis Books; London: SCM.

1994. *Jesus, Miriam's Child, Sophia's Prophet: Critical Issues in Feminist Christology.* New York: Continuum.

1993. *Searching the Scriptures,* Vol. 1, *A Feminist Introduction.* New York: Crossroad.

1989. "In Search of Women's Heritage." In *Weaving the Visions.* Ed. Judith Plaskow and Carol P. Christ. San Francisco: Harper & Row.

1988. "Waiting at the Table." In *Diakonia: A Church for Others.* Ed. Norbert Greinacher and Norbert Mette. Edinburgh: T. & T. Clark.

1984. *Bread not Stone: The Challenge of Feminist Biblical Interpretation.* Boston: Beacon Press.

Fischer, Irmtraud. 1994. *Die Erzeltern Israels.* Berlin: de Gruyter.

Fishman, Sylvia Barack. 1993. *A Breath of Life: Feminism in the American Jewish Community.* New York: Free Press; Toronto: Maxwell Macmillan.

Gebara, Ivone. 1989. *Mary, Mother of God, Mother of the Poor.* Maryknoll: Orbis Books.

Gilson, Anne Bathurst. 1995. *Eros Breaking Free.* Cleveland: Pilgrim Press.

Gossen, Gary H. and Miguel Leon-Portilla. Eds. 1993. *South and Meso-American Native Spirituality: From the Cult of the Feathered Serpent to the Theology of Liberation.* New York: Crossroad.

Gottlieb, Lynn. 1995. *She Who Dwells Within: A Feminist Vision of a Renewed Judaism.* San Francisco: HarperSanFrancisco.

Grant, Jacquelyn. 1989. *White Women's Christ and Black Women's Jesus.* Atlanta: Scholars Press.

Hauke, Manfred. 1995. *God or Goddess?: Feminist Theology—What Is It? Where Does It Lead?* Trans. David Kipp. San Francisco: Ignatius.

Heschel, Susannah. 1995. *On Being a Jewish Feminist.* With Introductions and a New Preface. New York: Schocken Books.

Heyward, Carter. 1995. *Staying Power.* Cleveland: Pilgrim Press.

1989. *Speaking of Christ.* New York: Pilgrim Press.

1987. *Revolutionary Forgiveness.* Maryknoll: Orbis Books.

Hunt, Mary E. 1991. *Fierce Tenderness.* New York: Crossroad.

Isasi-Diaz, Ada Maria. 1996. *Mujerista Theology: A Theology for the Twenty-First Century.* Maryknoll: Orbis Books.

1993. *En la lucha.* Minneapolis: Fortress Press.

——— and Yolanda Tarango. 1988. *Hispanic Women Prophetic Voice in the Church: Toward a Hispanic Women's Liberation Theology = Mujer Hispana voz profetica en la iglesia: hacia una teologia de liberacion de la mujer Hispana.* San Francisco: HarperSanFrancisco.

Isherwood, Lisa. 1994. *Introducing Feminist Theology.* Sheffield: Sheffield Academic Press.

Johnson, Elizabeth A. 1995. *In the Embrace of God.* Maryknoll, NY: Orbis Books.

1992. *She Who Is.* New York: Crossroad.

King, Ursula. Ed. 1994. *Feminist Theology from the Third World: A Reader.* Maryknoll: Orbis Books.

LaCugna, Catherine Mowry. 1993. *Freeing Theology. The Essentials of Theology in Feminist Perspective.* San Francisco: HarperSanFrancisco.

Lee, Hwain Chang. 1994. *Confucius, Christ, and Co-Partnership: Competing Liturgies for the Soul of Korean-American Women.* Lanham: University Press of America.

Long, Grace D. Cumming. 1993. *Passion and Reason.* Louisville: Westminster/John Knox.

Maitland, Sara. 1995. *A Big-Enough God*. New York: Henry Holt.

Miller-McLemore, Bonnie J. 1994. *Also a Mother*. Nashville: Abingdon Press.

Mohin, Lillian. Ed. 1996. *An Intimacy of Equals: Lesbian Feminist Ethics*. London: Onlywomen.

Moltmann-Wendel, Elisabeth. 1995. *I Am My Body: A Theology of Embodiment*. Trans. John Bowden. New York: Continuum.

Moody, Linda A. 1996. *Women Encounter God: Theology across the Boundaries of Difference*. Maryknoll: Orbis Books.

Morales-Gudmundsson, Lourdes E. Ed. 1995. *Women and the Church: The Feminine Perspective*. Berrien Springs: Andrews University Press.

Morrison, Melanie. 1995. *The Grace of Coming Home*. Cleveland: Pilgrim Press.

Oduyoye, Mercy Amba. *Daughters of Anowa: African Women and Patriarchy*. Maryknoll: Orbis Books.

Plaskow, Judith. 1990. *Standing again at Sinai: Judaism from a Feminist Perspective*. New York: Harper & Row.

——— and Carol P. Christ. Eds. 1989. *Weaving the Visions*. San Francisco: Harper & Row.

——— and Carol P. Christ. Eds. 1979. *Womanspirit Rising*. San Francisco: Harper & Row.

Procter-Smith, Marjorie and Janet R. Walton. Eds. 1993. *Women At Worship: Interpretations of North American Diversity*. Louisville: Westminster/John Knox.

Purvis, Sally B. 1993. *The Power of the Cross*. Nashville: Abingdon Press.

1993. *Transfigurations*. Minneapolis: Fortress Press.

Rae, Eleanor. 1994. *Women, the Earth, the Divine*. Maryknoll: Orbis Books.

Raphael, Melissa. 1996. *Thealogy and Embodiment: The Post-Patriarchal Reconstruction of Female Sacrality*. Sheffield: Sheffield Academic Press.

Rodriguez, Jeanette. 1994. *Our Lady of Guadalupe*. Austin: University of Texas Press.

Ruether, Rosemary Radford. 1989. *The Wrath of Jonah: The Crisis of Religious Nationalism in the Israeli-Palestinian Conflict*. San Francisco: Harper & Row.

1987. *Contemporary Roman Catholicism: Crises and Challenges*. Kansas City: Sheed & Ward.

1985. *Womanguides*. Boston: Beacon Press.

1983. *Sexism and God-Talk*. Boston: Beacon Press.

——— and Marc H. Ellis. 1990. *Beyond Occupation: American Jewish, Christian, and Palestinian Voices for Peace*. Boston: Beacon Press.

——— and Rosemary Skinner Keller. Eds. 1995. *In Our Own Voices: Four Centuries of American Women's Religions*. San Francisco: HarperSanFrancisco.

———, Naim S. Ateek, and Marc H. Ellis. Eds. 1992. *Faith and the Intifada: Palestinian Christian Voices*. Maryknoll: Orbis Books.

Russell, Letty M. 1993. *Church in the Round: Feminist Interpretation of the Church*. Louisville: Westminster/John Knox.

1988. Ed. *Inheriting Our Mothers' Gardens: Feminist Theology in Third World Perspective*. Philadelphia: Westminster.

1987. *Household of Freedom: Authority in Feminist Theology*. Philadelphia: Westminster.

1985. Ed. *Feminist Interpretation of the Bible*. Philadelphia: Westminster.

——— and J. Shannon Clarkson. Eds. 1996. *Dictionary of Feminist Theologies*. Louisville: Westminster/John Knox.

Schaupp, Joan. 1995. *Elohim: A Search for a Symbol of Human Fulfillment*. San Francisco: International Scholars Publications.

Schottroff, Luise. 1995. *Lydia's Impatient Sisters: A Feminist Social History of Early Christianity*. Louisville: Westminster/John Knox.

Stevens, Maryanne. Ed. 1993. *Reconstructing the Christ Symbol: Essays in Feminist Christology*. New York: Paulist Press.

Thistlethwaite, Susan Brooks. 1989. *Sex, Race, and God*. New York: Crossroad.

Townes, Emilie M. 1995. *In a Blaze of Glory: Womanist Spirituality as Social Witness*. Nashville: Abingdon Press.

1993. *Womanist Justice, Womanist Hope*. Atlanta: Scholars Press.

1992. Ed. *A Troubling in My Soul: Womanist Perspectives on Evil and Suffering*. Maryknoll: Orbis Books.

Webster, Alison R. 1995. *Found Wanting*. London: Cassell.

Welch, Sharon D. 1990. *A Feminist Ethic of Risk*. Minneapolis: Fortress Press.

1985. *Communities of Resistance and Solidarity*. Maryknoll: Orbis Books.

Williams, Delores S. 1993. *Sisters in the Wilderness*. Maryknoll: Orbis Books.

Young, Pamela Dickey. 1995. *Christ in a Post-Christian World: How Can We Believe in Jesus Christ When Those around Us Believe Differently—or Not At All?* Minneapolis: Fortress Press.

Permissions Acknowledgments

PHYLLIS BIRD, "The Place of Women in the Israelite Cultus." Reprinted from *Ancient Israelite Religion*, edited by Patrick Miller, Pam Hanson, and S. Dean McBride (1991), pp. 397–419. Copyright © 1987 Fortress Press. Used by permission of Augsburg Fortress. SUSAN ACKERMAN, "'And the Women Knead Dough': The Worship of the Queen of Heaven in Sixth-Century Judah." Reprinted from *Gender and Difference in Ancient Israel*, edited by Peggy Day (1989), pp. 109–124. Copyright © 1989 Fortress Press. Used by permission of Augsburg Fortress. CAROL MEYERS, "Women and the Domestic Economy of Early Israel." Reprinted from *Women's Earliest Records*, edited by Barbara Lesko (1989), pp. 265–277. Reprinted by permission of the Scholars Press. ESTHER FUCHS, "Structure and Patriarchal Functions in the Biblical Betrothal Type-Scene: Some Preliminary Notes." Reprinted from the *Journal of Feminist Studies in Religion* 4 (Spring 1988), pp. 7–13. Reprinted by permission of the Scholars Press. HOWARD EILBERG-SCHWARTZ, "The Problem of the Body for the People of the Book." Reprinted from the *Journal of the History of Sexuality*, 2: 1 (1991), pp. 1–24, where it originally appeared as "People of the Body: The Problem of the Body for the People of the Book." Reprinted by permission of the University of Chicago Press. ESTHER FUCHS, "Status and Role of Female Heroines in the Biblical Narrative." Reprinted from *Mankind Quarterly* 23 (1982), pp. 149–160. Reprinted by permission of the Council for Social and Economic Studies. CAROL A. NEWSOM, "Woman and the Discourse of Patriarchal Wisdom: A Study of Proverbs 1–9." Reprinted from *Gender and Difference in Ancient Israel*, edited by Peggy Day (1989), pp. 142–160. Copyright © Fortress Press. Used by permission of Augsburg Fortress. PHYLLIS BIRD, "The Harlot as Heroine: Narrative Art and Social Presupposition in Three Old Testament Texts." Reprinted from *Semeia* 46 (1989), pp. 119–139. Reprinted by permission of the Scholars Press. NELLY FURMAN, "His Story Versus Her Story: Male Genealogy and Female Strategy in the Jacob Cycle." Reprinted from *Semeia* 54 (1991), pp. 35–55. Reprinted by permission of the Scholars Press. ESTHER FUCHS, "The Literary Characterization of Mothers and Sexual Politics in the Hebrew Bible." Reprinted from *Semeia* 46 (1989), pp. 151–166. Reprinted by permission of the Scholars Press.

J. CHERYL EXUM, "Who's Afraid of 'the Endangered Ancestress'?" Reprinted from *The New Literary Criticism and the Hebrew Bible,* edited by J. Cheryl Exum and David J.A. Clines (1993), pp. 90–113. Reprinted by permission of the Sheffield Academic Press. CAROLE R. FONTAINE, "A Heifer from Thy Stable: On Goddesses and the Status of Women in the Ancient Near East." Reprinted from *The Pleasure of Her Text,* edited by Alice Bach (1990), pp. 69–95. Reprinted by permission of the Trinity Press International. SUSAN ACKERMAN, "The Queen Mother and the Cult in Ancient Israel." Reprinted from the *Journal of Biblical Literature* 112:3 (1993), pp. 385–401. Reprinted by permission of the Scholars Press. CLAUDIA V. CAMP, "The Wise Women of 2 Samuel: A Role Model for Women in Early Israel?" Reprinted from the *Catholic Bible Quarterly* 42 (January 1981), pp. 14–29. Reprinted by permission of the Catholic Biblical Association of America. EDWARD L. GREENSTEIN, "Reading Strategies and the Stories of Ruth" is published here for the first time, courtesy of the author. DANNA NOLAN FEWELL AND DAVID M. GUNN, "'A Son is Born to Naomi!': Literary Allusions and Interpretations in the Book of Ruth." Reprinted from the *Journal for the Study of the Old Testament* 40 (1988), pp. 99–108. Reprinted by permission of the Sheffield Academic Press. REUVEN KIMELMAN, "The Seduction of Eve and the Exegetical Politics of Gender." Reprinted from *Biblical Interpretation* 3 (1995), pp. 1–39. Reprinted by permission of E.J. Brill Publishers. PHYLLIS TRIBLE, "Genesis 22: The Sacrifice of Sarah." Reprinted from *"Not in Heaven": Coherence and Complexity in Biblical Narrative,* edited by Jason Rosenblatt and Joseph Sitterson (1991), pp. 170–191. Reprinted by permission of the Indiana University Press. TIKVA FRYMER-KENSKY, "Law and Philosophy: The Case of Sex in the Bible." Reprinted from *Semeia* 45 (1989), pp. 141–149. Reprinted by permission of the Scholars Press. SUSAN NID-ITCH, "Eroticism and Death in the Tale of Jael." Reprinted from *Gender and Difference in Ancient Israel,* edited by Peggy Day (1989), pp. 43–57. Copyright © 1989 Fortress Press. Reprinted by permission of Augsburg Fortress. MIEKE BAL, "Dealing/With/Women: Daughters in the Book of Judges." Reprinted from *The Book and the Text: The Bible and Literary Theory,* edited by Regina Schwartz (1990), pp. 16–39. Reprinted by permission of Blackwell Press and the editor. REGINA M. SCHWARTZ, "Adultery in the House of David: The Metanarrative of Biblical Scholarship and the Narratives of the Bible." Reprinted from *Semeia* 54 (1991), pp. 35–55. Reprinted by permission of the Scholars Press. ALICE BACH, "Signs of the Flesh: Observations on Characterization in the Bible." Reprinted from *Semeia* 63 (1993), pp. 61–70. Reprinted by permission of the Scholars Press. AMY-JILL LEVINE, "Sacrifice and Salvation: Otherness and Domestication in the Book of Judith." Reprinted from *No One Spoke Ill of Her: Essays on Judith,* edited by James C. Vanderkam (1992), pp. 17–30. Reprinted by permission of the Scholars Press. MARK STEPHEN CAPONIGRO, "Judith, Holding the Tale of Herodotus." Reprinted from *No One Spoke Ill of Her: Essays on Judith,* edited by James C. Vanderkam (1992), pp. 47–58. Reprinted by permission of the Scholars Press. ALICE BACH, "Rereading the Body Politic: Women and Violence in Judges 21." Reprinted from Biblical Interpretation 5:3 (1997), pp. 1–19. Reprinted by permission of E.J. Brill. JUDITH PLASKOW, "Transforming the Nature of Community: Toward a Feminist People of Israel." Reprinted from *Standing Again at Sinai* by Judith Plaskow (1990), pp. 15–34. Copyright © Judith Plaskow. Reprinted by permission of Harper-Collins Publishers, Inc. ALICE BACH, "With a Song in Her Heart: Listening to Scholars

Listening for Miriam." Reprinted from *A Feminist Companion to Exodus-Deuteronomy,* edited by Athalya Brenner (1994), pp. 243–255. Reprinted by permission of the Sheffield Academic Press. ELLY ELSHOUT, Roundtable Discussion: "Women with Disabilities—A Challenge to Feminist Theology." Reprinted from the *Journal of Feminist Studies in Religion* 10 (1994), pp. 99–134. Reprinted by permission of the Scholars Press. TIKVA FRYMER-KENSKY, "The Strange Case of the Suspected Sotah (Numbers V 11–31)." Reprinted from *Vetus Testamentum* 34 (1984), pp. 11–26. Reprinted by permission of E.J. Brill Publishers. JACOB MILGROM, "The Case of the Suspected Adultress, Numbers 5:11–31: Redaction and Meaning." Reprinted from *The Creation of Sacred Literature,* edited by Richard P. Friedman (1981), pp. 69–75. Reprinted by permission of the Regents of the University of California. JACK SASSON, "Numbers 5 and the 'Waters of Judgment.'" Reprinted from *Biblische Zeitschrift* 16 (1972), pp. 249–251. Reprinted by permission of Verlag Ferdinand Schoeningh GmbH. MICHAEL FISH-BANE, "Accusations of Adultery: A Study of Law and Scribal Practice in Numbers 5:11–31." Reprinted from the *Hebrew Union College Annual* 45 (1974), pp. 25–45. Reprinted by permission of the Jewish Institute of Religion. ALICE BACH, "Good to the Last Drop: Viewing the Sotah (Numbers 5.11–31) as the Glass Half Empty and Wondering How to View It Half Full." Reprinted from *The New Literary Criticism and the Hebrew Bible,* edited by J. Cheryl Exum and David J.A. Clines (1993), pp. 26–54. Reprinted by permission of the Sheffield Academic Press.